MUD, MUSCLE, AND MIRACLES

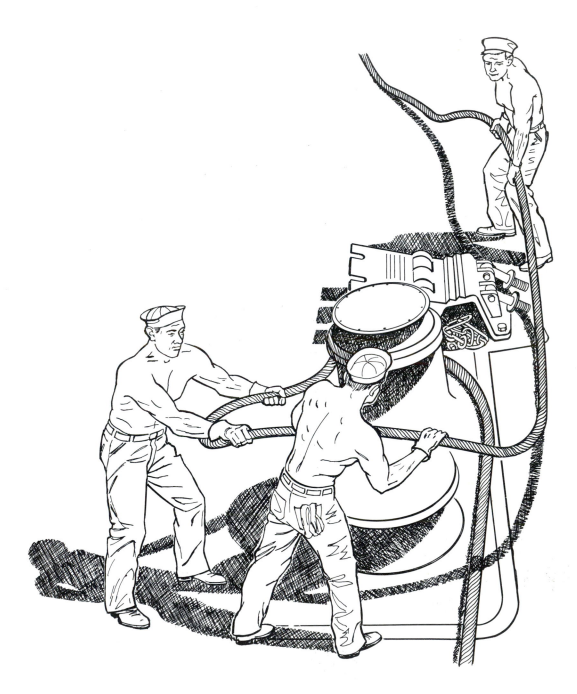

BITTS AND ROUND TURNS

MUD, MUSCLE, AND MIRACLES

Marine Salvage in the United States Navy

Captain C.A. Bartholomew, USN

A joint publication
of the
Naval Historical Center and Naval Sea Systems Command

Department of the Navy
Washington, D.C.
1990

Library of Congress Cataloging-in-Publication Data

Bartholomew, C. A., 1940–
    Mud, muscle, and miracles : marine salvage in the United States Navy
/ C.A. Bartholomew.
      p. cm.
    Includes bibliographical references.
    1. Salvage—United States—History. 2. United States. Navy—
History. 3. United States. Navy—Search and rescue operations—
History. I. Title.
VK1491.B37 1990   359.4'6–dc20   89–29806
ISBN 0–945274–03–3

Printed in the United States of America

BOOK EDITOR

SSR, Incorporated
Shirley Sirota Rosenberg, Paula Kaufmann, Werner Janney, Stan
Baer, George T. Winn, *editorial staff*; Ronna Hammer, *designer*; Philip
Colprit, *illustrator*.

For sale by the Superintendent of Documents, U.S. Government Printing Office
Washington, DC 20402

MARINE SALVAGE—*A science of vague assumptions based on debatable figures taken from inconclusive experiments and performed with instruments of problematic accuracy by persons of doubtful reliability and questionable mentality.*

Contents

CONTENTS

Tables

Illustrations

CONTENTS

PHOTOGRAPHS

CONTENTS

DIAGRAMS

MAPS

This fine record of our Navy's exploits in rescue, salvage, and emergency repair drives home the point, in page after page, of just how unforgiving the sea can be. Written in plain language and derived in great measure from accounts by the men who have done the deeds themselves, it is moreover a story of exceptional determination and professionalism. How heartening for both mariners and the public-at-large to know, even if only in the back of their minds, that such talent is standing by, ready to help, when trouble is at hand and whether this nation is at peace or at war. (And it has been my experience that trouble is seldom far away.)

Indeed, this candid record of both the successes and failures of U.S. Navy salvage at sea reinforces the time-honored, mariner's axiom that constant vigilance is the price of safe navigation.

—ADMIRAL WILLIAM J. CROWE, JR., USN (RETIRED)
Former Chairman, Joint Chiefs of Staff

Foreword

ADMIRAL I.C. KIDD, JR., USN (RETIRED)

The history of salvage in general, and of divers in particular, probably goes back to well before Noah's voyage in his ark. For those early times, of course, the records are less than complete. Nevertheless, the need for appropriate methods of salvage, diving, recovery, and repair was manifest even then. In fact we hear much talk today about the lessons learned from salvage history. But have we really learned? Has remedial action been taken? Are we adequately postured? Unfortunately, in most instances, the answer is a resounding, No.

Noah's shipmates and the salvors of the time established quite well that when the wreck is big enough and too far from saltwater to even consider refloating, we should leave it right where it is, build over it on occasion, and strip and scavenge as needed. (Robinson Crusoe used this option to advantage.) Where beautification is a factor, we can cut away and haul off what is unsightly, leaving to the sea the final task of shielding from inquisitive eyes the evidence of human failure to tame the awesome might of the oceans.

Until recently the salvor's environment was unparalleled in danger. Then space exploration captured our curiosity and imagination. It has been fascinating to watch space engineers and astronauts turn to salvors for counsel on how to cope with disaster in the vast expanses of the unknown. For although the speeds are somewhat higher, the distances a bit greater, and tolerance for reaction times much reduced in the new ocean of space, the basics of physics, the pressures, and the dependence on the ingenuity of the "man on the scene" remain unchanged. Space explorers have even borrowed the suits of salvors as models. Thus it will be no surprise at all to have the follow-on volumes of this book, which chronicles the human reach into uncharted regions, include the efforts and exploits of our salvors in space.

And why shouldn't the Navy take the lead and vigorously assist the National Aeronautics and Space Administration as it tailors its requirements for the years ahead? From their experiences over the centuries, salvors may well envy the weightlessness enjoyed by these new "space divers." But with it all there is still the penalty of inertia. One salvage old-timer, for example, recently cautioned NASA to fight to save the space tug that was part of its plan to build a space station. And while they were about it, he warned, it would be best to add another and buy two. Salvors have certainly learned the hard way on far too many occasions that only one tug is often useless.

Salvors have always been a small community of specialists, elite in their competence but often dependent on commercial augmentation. Only recently has the burden of fast reaction gradually shifted from commercial talents to purely naval assets and personnel. This transition, of course, has been due largely to the phenomenal growth in international naval dependence on surface ships and submarines of ever-increasing complexity and combat potential. It is not surprising that as more and more lives are placed at ever-increasing levels of risk in peacetime operations, we have seen a parallel increase worldwide in national demands for appropriate attention to the safety and well-being of salvors. I believe dependence on Navy salvors will continue to grow inexorably due to, among other factors, such increasing public demand for prompt information and the ever-present interest and curiosity tied to the welfare of survivors.

Where did an accident or casualty occur? Why did it happen? Am I in danger? To what extent is the environment endangered? Indeed, such international public pressures promise to drive a growth in the numbers, competence, and education of both salvors and divers to a far greater degree than did such purely national and professional motivators of the past as saving lives and learning how to avoid repetition of disasters. Writing off a job such as the 1923 *Honda Point* disaster as "too hard," or simply letting wrecks sit as monuments to inadequacies, are cavalier attitudes no longer available to any nation.

In an attempt to get this message across to decisionmakers, we beat our individual and collective heads against the bulkheads of budget restrictions. But it is often to little or no avail, for no one likes bad news. It is very easy with a wave of the hand to declaim: "This could never happen to us, to one of our ships, or to our Navy. And besides, it's too expensive to maintain a capability we will probably never need. We will gamble, save the money, and hope it doesn't come to pass on our watch." This is a mind-set I have found in the four corners of the world. In fact it is quite normal and predictable. We all face the same dilemma each time an insurance premium stares us in the face. The insurance industry has compiled a sobering record of the numbers of people who have dropped expensive premiums, only to find the coverage needed ten days later. But by then, it is too late. We can expect to see the same thought processes relative to salvage.

When the mess to be cleared away is large enough, we have long relied upon international efforts and cooperation. This situation is likely to continue, with organizations such as the United Nations playing ever larger roles. Every day the risk of international disaster grows. Too many parallels for comfort can be drawn from the furor generated by Chernobyl. The plugging of Panama, Suez, Kiel, and the St. Lawrence come to mind as possibilities, not to mention the specter of a nuclear accident, however small, in some congested harbor. It is a foregone conclusion that our U.S. Navy salvors and divers will be among the first called. Our Supervisor of Salvage has his work cut out for him in terms of developing plans that are monumental in scope and unimaginable to minds unaware of the staggering complexities of salvage work.

As a small group of experts in a large Navy, salvors have depended—too often without realizing it—on attention, interest, and support from unlikely quarters of the compass. Often this has been in the person of an individual who, frequently by pure chance, has adopted the salvage community and undertaken to block for it in budget battles, ship and equipment acquisitions, promotion opportunities, and other arenas. When S–51 was lost off Block Island in 1925, we acquired such a supporter in the person of then-Captain Ernest J. King who commanded the Submarine Base at New London. As on-scene commander, he met and came to admire men like Commander Edward Ellsberg and Chief Edward Eddy. He never lost sight of the breed, and in later years would ask, "How goes it with the divers?" It hurt Navy salvage not one bit to have this great gladiator move up to become Commander-in-Chief of the U.S. Navy. That interest alone kept alive an awareness of the importance of salvors throughout the entire Navy. Just how many tinkerers or budget-cutters King kept in line by making it clear he had his eye on them, we shall never know.

Admiral Ben Morrell, who founded the SeaBees, and Admiral Chester Nimitz after him, took a similar personal interest that generated the same atmosphere of awareness and respect. In the early sixties divers again enjoyed a steadying hand from the Chief of Naval Operations himself, Admiral David L. McDonald. Like a bolt out of the blue, he stepped into a particularly tough budget battle with the Secretary of Defense on the subject of heavy lift ships. The day had been long; to help pay for the Vietnam War, the OSD-directed cuts had been savage. The CNO sat quietly and with the great dignity that was his style. During a momentary lull, he said, "And I have an addition to add at this point—two heavy lift ships to be bought from Britain—originally acquired from Germany."

The looks around the room were what you might expect: incredulous. Any addition at this point in the budget cycle was unheard of. Yet this great man had the professional wisdom, vision, and knowledge of the needs of salvors to step in at a critical juncture. The two lift ships had just become available and would otherwise be scrapped. Instead, McDonald put them in our national salvage savings account! The rest is history.

Such unexpected support has often been our salvation, but it is spotty and too frequently a matter of chance. Navy salvage needs to institutionalize support at the top for the small but critical group of dedicated men and women whose importance is generally lost sight of until they are urgently needed. *Thresher* always comes to mind as a classic example of the frantic flaps surrounding disasters. In that instance, when *Thresher* was lost in 1963, the *Trieste* was available, but she was on the wrong coast. We had not thought through how to move her quickly. The salvage effort was stymied by the limiting overhead heights of both railroad tunnels and highway overpasses—handicaps not routinely uppermost in salvors' minds.

The conclusion here is that instead of relying on chance, the salvage community needs to recruit on a continuing basis the interest and support of senior people. Although perhaps not experienced salvors and divers themselves, these people, like Admiral King, may have been exposed at close range to the near miracles that can be accomplished when the Navy's and nation's reputations are on the line. The Navy salvage organization might consider carefully selecting and adopting such "sea daddys" and keeping them aware of how much they are needed. To me, this need seems far too important to be left to chance.

In the area of career opportunities and development, there is also much work to be done. I do not believe we have yet hoisted aboard the drastic changes that science has cranked into the salvor equation. Available depths and available devices have created a need for much more education for salvors and divers.

A roster of the academic credentials held by today's heroes in general is sobering. Where is the Navy's parallel program of early, graduate education for selected salvors and divers in all aspects of the sea?

And how hard are we looking for recruits? There appears to be no bar to having the salvage community recruit from the Naval Post Graduate School and throughout academia. Likely candidates are those who have selected a related field of graduate education, but who may have absolutely no idea how they are going to use such an education. Why not inspire them with a desire to be part of a historically elite group whose accomplishments are written every day. In my view we sorely need a long line of those waiting to join the club. Many who would do well, enlisted personnel and officers alike, simply do not know what awaits them.

Unsung and often inadequately rewarded, the salvor and diver have always been to me the absolute epitome of all that is fine among mariners.

This was also the view of my father, himself a diver. "From them," he said, "you can count upon the unvarnished truth. There is no margin for error in their profession. Mutual dependence is a total commitment. Seek them out. Listen carefully. Take their advice. It will always be the very best available. I know of no other body of men whose priorities are in such perfect order." Pretty strong words for a youngster of but a few years. But today I can report without reservation that my father's words were the best pieces of advice ever passed along to a son.

Some forty-five years later the Navy faced one of its more mortifying moments when a major design problem was impacting an entire class of naval combatants. A complex technical decision had to be made and made quickly. In my position as Chief of Naval Materiel, I turned by choice and force of professional habit to Admiral Monroe Hart, the Navy's senior diver, and made him chairman of the investigating board. Although the inquiry was not in his specialty, "Roe" Hart fell back on his diver's instincts of improvisation and determination, along with his gift of inspirational leadership. The decision was correct and prompt. Once again a Navy diver had "salvaged" the Navy and its reputation from the brink of grave difficulty.

I have a long list of such heroes. Names like Bill Searle, Gene Mitchell, Huntly Boyd, and Colin Jones are but the more recent of those whose selfless professionalism have made our Navy look so well and have added pages of lustre to our great nation. Here again, then-Lieutenant Commander Bart Bartholomew saved both Navy and nation from the trauma of losing our newest and best of a brand-new-class *Spruance* as it rested precariously on a listing, broken, and sinking floating drydock off Pascagoula, Mississippi. Not an inspirational sight.

Indeed, reading between the lines and looking at the photographs that accompany *Mud, Muscle, and Miracles,* even the uninitiated can envision the terror of unknown dangers, the frustration of repeated failures, and the tears of satisfaction as tremors of movement are felt for the first time or a particularly reluctant prize breaks the water's surface. As for the professionals who have been there and done it themselves, the book makes those stark records come alive even more. The heroes and heroics that fill every page are a muster of a special breed.

Everyone even remotely connected to Navy salvage owes Captain Bart Bartholomew, a hero of mine for many years and the current Supervisor of Salvage, a special debt of gratitude for parenting this splendid effort to get the essential details down on paper before any more years slip by. The pages read like a quartermaster's notebook kept by a seasoned professional, from whose crisp unadorned sentences might later flow an embellished version of a particular period or incident.

From the days of harbor clearance at Casablanca in 1942 to the refloating of the battleship *Pennsylvania* after she was hit by a kamikaze in Buckner Bay at the bitter end of the war, through another thirty-five years of active duty, this antique has remained grateful for the inspiration that salvors and divers have given me when I most needed it. I am deeply honored to have known them and to have shared a cup of coffee with them in their mess.

Preface

Webster defines salvage as "the act of rescuing a ship and its cargo." This definition, which connotes the saving of property, is the basis of the commercial marine salvage industry. For the naval salvor, however, the definition is much broader. It includes not only the rescue of ships and their cargoes but also the location of objects lost in the sea and the clearance of sunken vessels and other obstacles from navigable waterways and marine installations in the general pursuit of policy and objectives.

This chronicle traces the evolution of U.S. Navy salvage forces and of salvage operations within the Navy. Salvage operations, and indeed Navy salvage as a whole, cannot be looked at as a series of independent, random incidents. Like the Navy itself, salvage operations are part of a constantly changing continuum affected by changes in technology, national policy, budgets, and other influences inside and outside the Navy. Only by viewing salvage operations in this way can we understand the evolution of salvage within the Navy, the value of Navy salvage to the nation, and the place of salvage operations in the maritime activity of the world.

Salvage is not for every one. It is hard work—dirty, dangerous, and demanding. The jobs look easier than they are. The risks are high, the problems severe and unique, and the line between success and failure thin.

Salvage is also tremendously exciting and satisfying. The thrill of a salvor when a stranded ship refloats or a sunken wreck rises has few parallels. On the other hand, the defeats are devastating. Because salvage is the kind of work it is, it attracts people who invariably have tremendous abilities and confidence, with egos to match. It also requires mature individuals willing to take extraordinary risks but with the judgment not to take unnecessary ones, and who are able to submerge their egos so they can function as members of a team.

The United States Navy has developed and maintains a salvage capability because salvage has military purposes. It is cheaper and quicker to recover and repair a battle-damaged ship than it is to build a new one and train a new crew. When cleared of obstructions, ports and harbors whose facilities have been systematically blocked and destroyed by a retreating enemy, can be used for logistic support of friendly forces. Objects recovered from the ocean depths may be returned to service or analyzed to determine why they failed so the cause of failure may be corrected.

Mud, Muscle, and Miracles is neither a technical history nor a detailed account of the salvage work undertaken by the U.S. Navy. Rather, it is intended to add to the general knowledge of the sea and to document one portion of the history of the U.S. Navy. It explains how salvage and the Navy salvage organization have developed and contributed to the overall objectives of the Navy and the nation. The specific salvage operations described illustrate unique aspects of naval salvage, particular problems or techniques, and trends or progress. The omission of a particular salvage operation in no way denigrates the importance of that operation. There is simply not enough room here to review all Navy salvage operations.

Just as no major salvage job is accomplished by one person, this book is also the work of many people working together to record the toil of a small but important part of the U.S. Navy. Three are foremost: Commander Bill Milwee, USN (Retired), Lieutenant Commander Jim Bladh, USN (Retired), and Vice Admiral Dave Johnson, USN (Retired). These three provided much of the detailed research, helped structure the book, advised on its direction, and kept it moving toward completion.

Special mention must also fall to Mr. Alex Rynecki and Ms. Helen Sliteri who, in response to tasking from my predecessors, compiled a preliminary salvage history that served as a starting point for this document.

Throughout this project, the staff of the Naval Historical Center gave valuable assistance in planning, reviewing, editing, and printing the history. I especially thank Dr. Dean C. Allard, Director of Naval History; Dr. Ronald H. Spector, the former Director of Naval History; and Ms. Sandra Doyle, Contemporary History Editor. Their professional help fine-tuned this publication and helped bring the project to fruition.

Many others, in and outside the Navy, helped by reviewing draft chapters, providing supplemental information, contributing family photographs and records, and making other important contributions. The assistance of those listed below, as well as others not named, is gratefully acknowledged.

Lieutenant Commander John W. Ackerman, USN (Retired)
Master Chief Petty Officer W.F. Aichele, USN (Retired)

Mrs. Nan C. Alpaugh
Commander Bruce C. Banks, USN (Retired)
Mr. Peter S. Barracca
Ms. Helen Bebout
Captain J. Huntly Boyd, USN (Retired)
Captain James J. Coleman, USN (Retired)
Lieutenant Commander Lebbeus Curtis VII, USN
Commander Billie L. Delanoy, USN (Retired)
Judge Rosemary Denson
Commander Anton Drabik, USNR (Retired)
Mr. David W. Genereaux
Captain James W. Greely, USNR (Retired)
Captain David Hancox
Rear Admiral C. Monroe Hart, USN (Retired)
Mr. Robert R. Helen
Captain Colin M. Jones, USN (Retired)
Captain William N. Klorig, USN (Retired)
Lieutenant Commander Robert E. Kutzleb, USN (Retired)
Captain Charles S. Maclin, USN (Retired)
Commander Joseph F. Madeo, USN (Retired)
Captain Walter L. Marshall, USN (Retired)
Captain Bruce B. McCloskey, USNR (Retired)
Ms. Wanda L. Milwee
Captain Eugene B. Mitchell, USN (Retired)
Captain Robert B. Moss, USNR (Retired)
Lieutenant Commander John C. Naquin, USN (Retired)
Captain John B. Orem, USN (Retired)
Mr. Harold Price
Mr. Neil R. Price
Captain Willard F. Searle, Jr., USN (Retired)
Commander Robert K. Thurman, USN (Retired)
Mr. Jerry D. Totten
Captain John Ulrich, USN (Retired)
Mr. Peter Williams

The team that produced this chronicle has an interest in the technical and academic aspects of salvage that long predates their qualifying as Navy salvage officers. That interest led to their reading everything they could find on the subject and collecting small, specialized libraries. Thus when this history was being planned, it seemed logical to go to the sources well known to all active in the field, and to supplement these readings with the thousands of salvage reports that the Navy had stowed away in some room.

How grossly we underestimated the task! The modest body of well-known literature does not begin to cover the broad scope of Navy salvage. More significantly, it focuses on the "how" of individual salvage jobs, not on the "why" of the development of salvage in the Navy. Furthermore, the room we had envisioned as filled with salvage reports does not exist. Over the years the Navy's occasional, well-intentioned purges of files and attempts to reduce paper have resulted in the destruction of many, many salvage reports.

In retrospect, however, one of the biggest boons to this book was the inadequacy of existing literature and the nonexistence of that room. Had those simple sources filled the bill, much information may never have surfaced. Fortunately, salvors are pack rats, and many of the reports on their way to the scrap heaps have wound up in the hands of salvors who thought the documents might be of some future value. Through the generosity of many of these salvors and their families, these records, personal recollections, and photographs were made available to us and proved invaluable in putting together this history and ensuring its accuracy. (Few records and no personal recollections were accepted without independent corroboration.)

Photographs used throughout the text come from the excellent collections at the Naval Historical Center, National Archives, U.S. Naval Institute, the large but generally uncataloged collection of the Supervisor of Salvage, and the private collections of salvors. Many of the more unusual photographs and most of those depicting the salvors came from the private collections.

The tenacity, ingenuity, and vision of Navy salvors past and present has provided the sum and substance of information on these pages. To these courageous men I humbly dedicate this volume.

WORKING DIVER

CHAPTER ONE

The Early Days

Marine salvage, as old as seagoing, is a unique part of the maritime world. Around it has grown a specialized technology, a tough-minded international industry, a broadly based naval community, and a unique body of law. Naval salvage is similar in technology to its commercial counterpart, but it is undertaken for far different reasons than is the business of saving property for financial gain. The Navy has a salvage organization and conducts salvage operations because they advance the objectives of the Navy and the nation.

Retrieval of things lost in or threatened by the sea serves many purposes: the return of ships to service, the recovery of valuable property, the collection of data for analysis of failures, and the removal of threats to the environment. Returning ships to service and recovering cargoes takes on special significance in wartime, when conservation of resources is of utmost importance.

In peacetime, salvage operations not only recover ships and material but also contribute to the Navy's mission of showing the flag, both at home and abroad. Domestically, the operations are excellent opportunities to show the public the Navy at work solving real problems and contributing to the public good. Internationally, and consistent with the Navy's function as an instrument of public policy, salvage operations can be undertaken for political gain. Politically beneficial salvage operations include removal of a stranded naval vessel from the coast of another country, removal of a wreck in a foreign harbor, clearance of an international waterway, or operations on a foreign-flag merchant ship when no other salvors are available.

Naval salvage operations fall into four general categories: (1) afloat and stranding salvage, (2) harbor clearance, (3) submarine salvage, and (4) deep-ocean operations. The problems and techniques of each category are unique, but all combine seamanship and engineering—complementary disciplines that must be balanced in the proportions required by the particular task.

In the first three types of salvage, people—with their skill, imagination, ingenuity, perseverance, and plain guts—are the dominant and controlling factor. In deep-ocean operations, technology dominates, but the same human qualities are required in equally large measure.

Afloat salvage is assistance provided to ships that are afire, flooding, battle damaged, or victims of other misfortunes at sea. This kind of salvage can be conducted by any type of ship, but serious cases usually require the services of specially configured salvage ships or rescue tugs with trained personnel. In wartime, when naval operations in the combat zone are intense and damage to ships frequent, afloat salvage is constant. Many jobs are small and warrant no more than a line or two in a ship's log. However, the cumulative effect of such jobs mounts.

Stranding salvage is the refloating of grounded ships to restrict damage to the ship or the environment, return a valuable ship to service, or save cargo. Ships aground on beaches and reefs are in a dangerous situation. In conditions they were not designed to withstand, they are exposed to structural loadings that can cause their destruction. Wind and sea combine to make the position of the ship progressively more dangerous and the salvage harder. Stranding salvage is always difficult, dangerous, and urgent. It requires unusual seamanship of a high standard, imaginative engineering, and salvage ships or tugs with heavy, specialized ground tackle to pull the grounded ship into deep water. Close relatives, afloat and stranding salvage are primarily the province of the seaman, but the application of engineering principles is mandatory and the services of a salvage engineer invaluable. When they occur in a harbor, afloat and stranding salvage may be called harbor salvage.

Harbor clearance, the removal of sunken ships or other obstacles from harbors or navigable waterways to restore the waterway to use, is a varied and challenging segment of naval salvage. The tools and equipment, as well as the variety of conditions and problems faced by the salvor in harbor clearance, are quite different from afloat and stranding salvage, and almost infinite. The greatest difference lies in the reason for the work. Military action, accident, or natural disaster may block a waterway. Harbor clearance is undertaken to remove the wrecks; returning them to service is of lower priority. Harbor clearance is primarily an engineering effort. The engineer is dominant though the seaman has a vital role as well.

The peculiarly naval task of *submarine salvage* places special requirements on both seamen and engineers. The problem of submarine salvage was of great concern when submarines were in their infancy and losses were relatively frequent at depths where salvage was practical with simple resources. Because of the techniques used and the organizations developed, the salvage of some of these submarines forms an important part

2

of the story of Navy salvage. More recently, deep-diving nuclear submarines lost at great depths have made salvage of entire hulls impractical. Complex search operations have been staged to locate these hulls and discover the cause of their loss. Submarine losses attract such widespread international attention that the military and political benefits of a salvage or search operation may outweigh the costs of developing and implementing complex and expensive technology. As long as submarines are operated, the Navy must remain alert to the possibility that these complex warships may have to be salvaged from the ordinary hazards of the sea or from the sea bottom at great depths.

In *deep-ocean operations*, objects are located, investigated, and recovered from the ocean floor, sometimes at great depths. It is in these operations that the relative roles of engineers and seamen are most nearly balanced. This kind of work in the deep ocean requires engineering at least as sophisticated as that involved in going into space. The application of ocean technology demands outstanding knowledge of the sea and its environmental conditions, and the ability to use this knowledge. Thus, in deep ocean operations, as in all branches of salvage, the seaman and the engineer must work together; neither can do the job alone.

A salvage job is the sum of the abilities and strengths of a coordinated team in which each member supports the others. A salvor must be able to function both independently and as a team member. Success in salvage, whether a small operation or a large-scale national effort, results from a proper balance of four elements: (1) trained and experienced individuals, (2) well-designed and soundly built ships, (3) the right equipment, and (4) an umbrella of operational concepts and doctrine for employment of the first three elements. While the balance will shift with the type of work, none can stand without the others. Similarly, the resources of the nation, the Navy, and industry must work together to provide the United States with salvage services that will adequately protect its coasts and resources in peacetime and expand to meet national objectives in an emergency.

From a technical viewpoint, naval and commercial salvors do the same things. The similarity has influenced the development of both naval operations and the commercial salvage industry. Indeed, before worldwide operations required a large naval logistics force with a specialized salvage organization, naval salvage was often done by contract.

Until World War I there was no permanent salvage organization in the U.S. Navy. Teams were assembled by the Navy for specific jobs and disbanded when the work was complete. Even in World War I, when Navy salvage units were first established, the bulk of the salvage work was done by commercial salvors hired to supplement the naval effort and to provide salvage services outside the combat zone. Again in World War II, the marine salvage industry, designated as the Naval Salvage Service, formed a vital part of the total salvage organization and made it possible for uniformed naval salvors to be employed in direct support of combat forces.

The value of the marine salvage industry and of the naval salvage contractor, in particular, to the Navy and U.S. maritime operations was recognized by the passage of enabling legislation that became known as the Salvage Facilities Act (Public Law 80–513). In 1948 Congress authorized the Secretary of the Navy, inter alia, to "provide salvage services by contract or otherwise for public and private vessels upon such terms as he determines to be in the best interests of the United States."[1] Reflecting the lessons of the war, the act laid the legislative foundation for the long and valuable relationship between the Navy and the marine salvage industry that continues to benefit both. Contractors provide an important augmentation of naval salvage forces and give the Navy a greater capability than would be economical to maintain in peacetime. American salvage companies extend the salvage capability of the Navy and provide an option for accomplishing work when fleet units cannot or should not be used. Overseas contractors give the Navy the means to respond to salvage emergencies in areas where fleet forces may not be available. Navy contracts, in turn, provide a de facto subsidy to the American salvage industry, thus ensuring that a strong industry is available upon which mobilization can be based.

In the Navy there are three distinct levels of salvage activity. The first level is the management of salvage—the administration, training, budgeting, development, acquisition, and, most important, planning that makes possible an organization capable of conducting operations. This management of the salvage organization and the planning for the future, rather than the more glamorous operations themselves, properly occupies most of the time of senior salvors. Without continuous, intense management effort before and during a specific operation, there would be no successful salvage. The senior salvors engaged in this management must have a thorough grounding in the nuts, bolts, and sweat of salvage operations.

At the second level are the so-called routine salvage operations. These minor salvage operations, each posing its own unique challenge, may mean only a few hours underway for a salvage ship or a few days of diving and rigging for a small team. In wartime this activity is continuous; in peacetime nearly so. These small salvage operations, each important and with the value of the whole being greater than the sum of its parts, make up the bulk of the work of salvors. It is from these routine operations that most lessons are learned and most technical development takes place.

---

[1] 10 USC 7361(a).

4

The final level of activity occurs when there are major operations. Major operations in peace and war may be likened to the huge freak waves that appear irregularly at sea, dramatically change the pattern of activity, and are gone. Their effect is greater than their frequency warrants. A salvage organization must be prepared for the tremendous changes that major operations bring. The managerial difficulty lies in being prepared for the challenges of these events without maintaining an organization that is too large and overequipped to carry on its day-to-day business economically. The Navy has addressed this problem in a number of ways. The occasional major salvage operation, for example, receives much attention at all levels and may help to accelerate changes in doctrines, procedures, and acquisition plans.

Except in the U.S. Navy, salvage has been taught exclusively in the dear school of experience. The system developed in the Navy for training salvage officers and salvage mechanics has no equivalent. Navy salvors are thoroughly trained in the theory and practice of salvage before they ever participate in a salvage operation. The training is academically and physically tough, for it is far better to weed out those who are unsuitable at the training stage than during a critical operation.

Formal technical and operational training in salvage provides basic understanding and skills in a few weeks rather than through a long apprenticeship. As World War II and Vietnam proved, rapid training is especially useful in times of national emergency when many salvors are needed quickly. In peacetime this training supplies the Naval Reserve officers and others who form a large portion of the complement of salvage ships and units and augment the cadre of regulars. These trained and experienced reserves, after they complete their short active service, are building blocks for emergencies. Because naval and commercial salvage use similar technology and techniques, many Navy salvors move easily into commercial salvage, thus further improving cooperation between the U.S. Navy and the American salvage industry.

In the days when wooden sailing ships formed the naval fleets of the world, warships could be kept at sea with no support as long as their crews could stand it. They never ran out of fuel because they used none. Repairs could be undertaken by the crews in any sheltered bay. Paradoxically, the application of technology, metal construction, and steam propulsion to warships in the nineteenth century limited warships' range and mobility. They became dependent on supplies of fuel and on repair bases capable of keeping the hulls sound and the machinery turning. Logistics took on a new meaning for navies. In the U.S. Navy it led to forces that grew from the Fleet Train of the Spanish-American War to the Base Force that followed World War I, the huge Service Forces of World War II, and the Mobile Logistic Support Force of the 1970s and 1980s.

The same technology that limited the range and mobility of warships and led to the development of logistics forces made organized salvage possible. When a wooden ship ran ashore, the crew could sometimes free it by judicious use of ground tackle and muscle, but often there was little to be done other than rescue the crew and save the cargo, a situation that gave rise to the cottage industry known as "wrecking" practiced by coastal inhabitants. The ship that sank was usually lost as there was seldom the means to raise it. With the application of steam power to tugs, it became practical to provide assistance to ships stranded on a lee shore. Powered tugs were able to maneuver in the face of the wind and sea rather than be driven by them. During these early years of stranding salvage the basic techniques—laying heavy ground tackle to seaward and pulling against it with purchases to move the grounded ship into deep water— were developed. The contemporaneous development of power machinery, compressors, pumps, and the like combined with the growing human ability to work underwater to make it possible to refloat wrecked vessels that could previously only be left to the sea.

In the midnineteenth century the United States had a prosperous and growing shipping industry, but there was a dark side to it. In 1860, for example, thirty-five American ships with a value of $1.5 million were wrecked each month with an annual loss of life estimated at 1,500. Professional salvors who understood and could apply the seamanship and engineering skills of salvage were few; the field was dominated by self-appointed amateurs who often did more harm than good. The situation was intolerable for the insurance underwriters because losses caused premiums to escalate. On 11 May 1860 the Board of Marine Underwriters of New York City met in special session and called upon Captain Israel J. Merritt of Long Island, New York, to put marine salvage on a businesslike basis. Captain Merritt, with a Gloucester mackerel schooner and $8,000 worth of salvage equipment, formed the Coast Wrecking Company. The foundation was laid for the American salvage industry that the Navy was to use so effectively in the future.

Early Navy Salvage

Salvage capability in the Navy developed, as did the modern Navy, in the last quarter of the nineteenth century. There were no formal salvage forces; the Navy relied on temporarily formed organizations. The divers, whose primary jobs were ship maintenance and torpedo recovery, were trained at a school set up in Newport, Rhode Island, in 1882 under the direction of Chief Gunner's Mate Jacob Anderson. Salvage, which often required underwater work, was a natural extension for these divers.

The records of the Bureau of Construction and Repair for the early years of the twentieth century show numerous Navy salvage operations. These included the pumping, patching, and raising of the 204-foot gunboat *Machais* (PG 5), sunk during a storm at Pensacola, Florida, in 1907, and the salvage of three Spanish gunboats, *Isla de Luzon*, *Isla de Cuba*, and *Don Juan d'Austria*. The latter were salvaged after being sunk or scuttled at the Battle of Manila Bay and later served in the U.S. Navy under their original names. No doubt many jobs went unrecorded or records have been lost.

One of the most interesting early salvage cases involved a famous ship of the U.S. Navy and deserves a place in the history of Navy salvage, although the work was not done by the Navy.

On 15 February 1889, as a precursor to the Spanish-American War, the 6,682-ton, 319-foot, second-class battleship *Maine* experienced a major explosion and sank in the Havana harbor. The wreck was inspected by divers but lay essentially undisturbed until 1909, when increased traffic in the harbor made its removal or dispersal desirable. Although cutting the ship by using explosives and subsequently removing the pieces would have been the simplest solution, the desire to examine the wreck to determine the cause of the explosion provided a sound reason to expose the hull without imposing further damage.

The Navy had no central organization for salvage and the work was a heavy engineering effort. It was quite logically assigned to the Army Corps of Engineers, who had the means to accomplish it as well as a responsibility for maintaining navigable waterways. This job marked the beginning of a long and harmonious relationship between the Navy and the Corps of Engineers in the field of wreck removal in inland waters. How this relationship changed as Navy salvage developed will be discussed later.

The damage to the hull of *Maine* was so extensive that underwater repairs to allow dewatering and refloating the hull intact were not practicable. To permit examination of the wreck as she lay, the salvage plan called for construction of a watertight cofferdam around the entire ship. Then experts could examine it and determine the best method of clearing it. The construction of the cofferdam was a major engineering effort, beginning in 1911 and lasting almost a year. Interlocking sheet pile cylinders, each 54 feet in diameter, were driven into the dense, blue clay harbor bottom and filled with similar clay from other parts of the harbor. When the cofferdam was watertight, the water was pumped out of the basin, leaving the hull dry and available for examination on the harbor bottom. These examinations showed the damage to the hull to be so extensive that repairing it "in the dry" and refloating the ship was not possible. The hull was cut into two sections; each was subsequently made water-

Earth-filled cofferdams 54 feet in diameter provide access to the wreck of the battleship *Maine* on the bottom of Havana harbor.

tight, refloated, and sunk in deep water.

The operation had accomplished all its goals. The hull had been examined; the harbor was clear. Based on examination of the wreckage, the finding of a previous investigation of the cause of the accident was confirmed. However, the cause of the loss remained controversial and the findings of the investigation were later refuted in a carefully documented 1976 study made by Admiral Hyman G. Rickover.[2] The original investigation, and the one undertaken when the hull was examined, concluded that the ship had been destroyed by an external explosion, probably a Spanish mine. The Rickover analysis demonstrated that an internal explosion caused the loss of the ship.

Inevitably a few Navy ships required salvage, some in remote regions where facilities were limited. With no salvage organization in the Navy, operations were undertaken by those on the scene with the resources they could muster. Two incidents in the Pacific, the salvage of the floating drydock *Dewey* at Subic Bay, Philippines, and the salvage of *Princeton* (PG 13) at Pago Pago, Samoa, illustrate salvage operations carried out by such ad hoc organizations.

---

[2] H. G. Rickover, *How the Battleship Maine Was Destroyed* (Washington: Naval History Division, 1976).

In May 1909, when the 500-foot floating drydock *Dewey* sank in Subic Bay, a salvage team was assembled from divers assigned to ships in port. Two unsuccessful attempts to raise the dock by two different methods were made; a third attempt using yet another method was successful. In the first attempt, compressed air was blown into the 100-foot-high wing walls to force water out. Because of defects in the *Dewey*'s workmanship and deterioration of structure and piping, air leaked from compartment to compartment into the high side of the dock. The low side was left without buoyancy. In the second attempt the drydock's pumps, because of their arrangement, would take water from the high side only. For the final attempt, cofferdams were built on the drydock's hatches. With steam for the dock's machinery provided by a ship alongside, *Dewey* was pumped out and successfully raised after five weeks of work. In retrospect the effort was notable in that it was a conventional salvage operation done without experienced salvors. (One suspects that experienced salvors would have recognized the inherent problems of the first two refloating attempts and avoided them.)

Princeton, returning to the naval station at Pago Pago on the evening of 11 July 1914, struck an uncharted pinnacle and holed herself. With no suitable place for an intentional beaching to prevent sinking, the vessel was brought into the naval station and placed alongside the pier, where she promptly sank. As soon as the ship was alongside the pier, anchors were put out and lines run ashore to trees and deadmen to prevent her sliding down the reef, and a pump suction was run to the nearby power-house. When pumping started, the ship rolled to starboard, uncovering the hull damage.

More deadmen, consisting of cast-iron-and-concrete pedestals intended for the steel dock, were buried, and lines with purchases were run to the mastheads. Divers lightened the ship. Anyone who has done salvage work in the islands of the Pacific can testify to the shortage of the most basic materials for salvage. To salvage *Princeton* it was necessary to order pumps, hoses, plate, lumber, and patching materials from the United States.

While waiting for the material, salvors closed all openings in the ship's hull. When these had been secured, the damage covered by a wooden patch, and the pumps placed, pumping and heaving on the masthead tackles started. Pumping was slowed by the need to patch undiscovered openings and to replace failed patches. While pumping was in progress, divers opened doors to assure the continuous flow of water to the pumps. The ship was raised without further incident. *Princeton* salvors were fortunate. We shall see later how the free longitudinal flow of water hindered the salvage of one of the ships sunk in the 1941 Pearl Harbor attack.

The First Deep Salvage (F–4)

Less than a year after *Princeton*'s salvage, a very different salvage operation, also in the Pacific and also undertaken solely by naval forces, set precedents for similar operations. The operation was so unusual that the lack of experienced salvage people and conventional salvage gear was no handicap. What was needed was sound engineering backed by sound seamanship and common sense.

On 15 March 1915 the F-class submarine *Skate*, or F–4 (SS 23), was lost in approximately 51 fathoms of water while making a short submerged run off the island of Oahu, Hawaii.[3] The submarine was 142 feet, 9 inches long, with a submerged displacement of 400 tons and a designed depth of 200 feet. An oil slick and air bubbles about 2 miles from the harbor entrance led to dragging operations that positively located the boat; there were no apparent signs of life. The submarine lay far deeper than divers had yet descended with existing equipment and methods. In an effort to reach the boat on the day of the loss, Chief Gunner's Mates Evans and Agraz dived to a depth of 190 feet and Chief Agraz later dived to 215 feet; they neither reached nor sighted the vessel.

The only possible chance of saving any survivors was to drag the boat into shallow water because no lifting gear could be made and rigged in the time available. Dragging would work only if the boat was not completely flooded. Sweeps were made by the tugs *Navajo* and *Intrepid* to pass a wire rope sling around the hulk and drag it into shallow water. The sling was passed on the day following the accident, but even with two additional tugs the boat could not be moved. Rescuing the crew appeared hopeless, but one more attempt was warranted. A dredge was brought to the scene; a wire was swept under the submarine, its ends taken to heavy purchase rigged for heaving. If a portion of the submarine remained unflooded and buoyant, there was a possibility of moving the boat into shallow water by heaving with the dredge and towing with tugs. No progress could be made. One of the wires parted at its maximum load. There was no question but that the F–4 was filled with water. The rescue attempt was necessarily, but regretfully, concluded.

Because *Skate* was the Navy's first submarine loss, there was an intense desire within the Navy to determine the cause of the casualty. In addition, there was public interest in the recovery of the bodies of the crew. Naval Constructor (Lieutenant Commander) Julius A. Furer, who was in Hawaii for construction of the new naval station at Pearl Harbor,

---

[3]Early U.S. Navy submarines were given both names and numbers that designated their class and their order in the class. Names were later discontinued, and the names previously given were taken away. No names were given to submarines through the S class of World War I; they were known only by a letter and number designation.

On 15 February 1929, President Calvin Coolidge presented the Medal of Honor to Chief Petty Officer Frank W. Crilley for his heroism in the rescue of Chief Petty Officer William F. Loughman during salvage operations on the submarine F–4. Left to right: President Coolidge, Chief Crilley, Ensign Loughman, Secretary of the Navy Curtis P. Wilbur, and Chief of Naval Operations Charles F. Hughes.

was placed in charge of the technical side of salvage. Eventually total responsibility for the work was Furer's. After evaluating the situation, Furer determined that multiple short lifts and tows were the only feasible way of raising the boat.

Faced with a lack of specialized equipment for the job and an industrially unsophisticated base in Hawaii, Furer demonstrated one of the essential characteristics of a salvor—the ability to improvise with the materials and vessels at hand. Two sturdily constructed 104-by-36-foot mud scows belonging to a local dredging company had the strength to carry the suspended weight of the submarine. A lifting system was built from these scows using I-beams planned for a coal storage facility, sugar mill shafts for windlasses, and miscellaneous machinery that was either available or made for the job.

Knowing that the position of the lift slings was critical to the salvage and that their positions could be verified only visually, Furer requested the best divers available. Gunner George Stillson, the Navy's expert on diving, was ordered to the scene from the New York Navy Yard, where he had been assigned to test and review all existing diving apparatus and techniques for the Bureau of Construction and Repair. Gunner Stillson brought with him his team of four divers—Frank Crilley, Stephen Drellishak, Frederick Nilson, and William Loughman—along with diving physician Dr. George R.W. French, their diving gear, and recompression chamber. The team arrived in Hawaii on 14 April aboard the armored cruiser *Maryland* (ACR 8) and set to work immediately.

Chief Crilley made the first dive just two days after arrival. He reached the F–4, more than 300 feet down, and reported that the boat was upright but that the slings would have to be moved. The first dive demonstrated that divers would be invaluable. Because of the depth of the water, dives were short and diving work limited to observation, but observation of the position of the lift slings and the condition of the wreck was critical to the success of the operation. The futility of attempting work at the lower depths was illustrated when a diver remained on the bottom for thirty minutes trying to pass a small reeving line. He was not aware of fatigue on the bottom but collapsed from exhaustion on the surface and did not regain his strength for several days. Except for one incident in which Chief Loughman became entangled and was rescued by Chief Crilley, the divers, working with long decompressions on rudimentary schedules, reached record open-sea depths and suffered only mild occurrences of decompression sickness.

The final lift of the submarine F–4 was made using these submarine salvage pontoons designed by Naval Constructor Julius A. Furer.

A dredge with its boom and bucket gear removed was selected as the central salvage unit because it had a winch with six independently operated drums. After lifting wires were swept under the submarine, they were taken to the dredge for hauling, then passed to the windlasses on the mud scows. When the wires had been passed, a series of lifts and moves were made. Because the wire-rope slings chafed on the submarine's hull during the early lifts, a portion of the *Maryland*'s anchor cable was used to make composite chain and wire-rope slings. After nine lifts of between 8 and 55 feet in an operation dogged by bad weather, the boat was moved into 48 feet of water on May 25.

A diving inspection of the hull showed severe hull damage and the likelihood of fracture if the same lifting method was continued. If the hull fractured and the boat was lost, the channel into Honolulu could be blocked and the opportunity to determine the cause of the casualty would be lost. The problem now was to lift the submarine in one step from its depth to a draft of not more than 25 feet, the maximum for the Honolulu dry dock.

To accomplish this, Furer developed what became known as the Submarine Pontoon Salvage Method. In this method, chains are worked under the wreck and secured to flooded pontoons alongside the sunken submarine. The pontoons are blown with compressed air, and the wreck, supported by the cradle of chains, rises. Furer designed six 32-foot-long, cylindrical, wood-sheathed pontoons with a total lifting capacity of 420 tons, and supervised their construction at Mare Island Navy Yard in California. The wooden sheathing was one of the most important features of the pontoons' design because it allowed their use in situations where heavy and frequent impact could puncture an unsheathed steel hull.

When Furer returned to Hawaii with the pontoons, Chief Gunner's Mates Agraz, Evans, O'Brien, and McMillian from the Submarine Division began the heavy work of rigging the pontoons. This task required many hours of heavy underwater work that could not have been performed in deeper water. On Sunday morning, 29 August, the pontoons were blown dry from air flasks installed on a coal barge, and the submarine was raised and towed into the harbor. It was placed in drydock the following day. A minute examination of the hull revealed the cause of the accident to be leakage through rivet holes where the rivets had been eaten away by battery acid. The holes were not accessible for inspection. Determination of the cause of the loss of F–4 resulted in design changes to U.S. Navy submarines.

The Navy had responded to its first submarine disaster by diving to unprecedented depths, developing the basic design of its submarine salvage pontoons, and employing a system of lifting with pontoons that would serve well in future submarine salvage operations.

A Different Kind of Submarine Salvage (H–3)

The submarine *Garfish*, or H–3 (SS 30), figured in another classic but very different type of Navy salvage operation.

In the early morning fog of 14 December 1916, H–3 grounded on Samoa Beach near Eureka, California. The crew was taken off in a dramatic and heroic rescue operation by the U.S. Coast Guard. An unsuccessful salvage attempt was made by the monitor *Cheyenne* (BM 10) and the tug *Iroquois*. Shortly after Christmas, following standard practice, the commandant of Mare Island Navy Yard, who had responsibility for the salvage, called for bids to refloat the stranded submarine. Six bids ranging from $18,000 to $72,000 were received. Most were considered too high. The $18,000 bid from Mercer-Fraser Company, a Eureka construction company, was worrisomely low; it was so much lower than the others that the government was skeptical that the contractor could do the work. Accordingly, the Navy decided to undertake the salvage itself.

Now supplemented by the 9,700-ton flagship of the Coast Torpedo Force, the armored cruiser *Milwaukee* (C 21) with 21,000 indicated horse-power, *Iroquois* and *Cheyenne* were brought to Samoa Beach to pull the stranded submarine free. Two 2-inch-diameter wire ropes 4,000 feet long were attached to the submarine and to the stern of *Milwaukee*. A ship not designed for towing, with a heavily loaded tow wire made up near

The grounding of the submarine H–3 at Samoa Beach in northern California resulted in a spectacular salvage. Note the cruiser *Milwaukee* in the background.

The greatest cost of the H–3 salvage operation was the loss of the cruiser *Milwaukee*, which found herself in irons and was forced ashore while pulling on H–3.

her stern, can easily find herself "in irons"—unable to maneuver. To prevent this, *Iroquois* and *Cheyenne* were made up on *Milwaukee*'s bow with long towlines. In dense fog the night of 13 January 1917, after pulling two days, *Iroquois*'s towline parted. Before another towline could be rigged, the cruiser, unable to maneuver and at the mercy of a strong current, was forced ashore. She grounded hard and later broke up, a total loss.[4]

As ships stranded on sandy beaches will do, H–3 had worked her way 300 feet north and buried herself 6 feet deeper in the sand, still some 250 feet below the high-water mark. The naval units were removed from the salvage work and a contract was negotiated with Mercer-Fraser[5] for their original bid price of $18,000.

The imaginative salvage plan called for moving the submarine overland more than a mile and launching her into Humboldt Bay. In the first of two phases, pilings were driven around the ship to support jacks used in conjunction with a timber crib and lifting slings to raise the submarine and lower it onto rollers. Once she was on the rollers, a short move was

---

[4] *Milwaukee* was later stripped by building a pier to the ship from the beach and removing salvaged equipment across the beach. Among the items removed was the parted towline, which was dragged ashore in a great bight to overcome the friction encountered when dragging a wire lengthwise through sand.

[5] Mercer-Fraser remains in business at this writing as a general construction contractor in Eureka, California.

H-3 is moved overland on wooden tracks for launching in the calm waters of Humboldt Bay.

made to above the high-water mark. There work to prepare for the move to Humboldt Bay could be done without concern for the tide.

In the second phase, the wooden cribbing necessary to the jacking was removed and pine logs 80 feet long and 40 inches in diameter were placed on each side of the ship. Heavy wire ropes were wrapped around these logs and timber bobbers—bolted balks of four 14-by-14-inch timbers each 20 feet long and shod with hard wood—were placed under them. All the weight coming on the bobbers was carried at the center, permitting them to equalize when the grade changed. Rollers of California laurel 4 feet long and 8 inches in diameter were placed 4 inches apart under the bobbers. The submarine was hauled along a pine track by a winch working through two fivefold purchases. H-3 moved along at an average rate of 550 feet per day and was launched into Humboldt Bay on 20 April 1917.

A submarine had been salvaged by a skilled and imaginative effort, but the cost—the loss of *Milwaukee*—was high. The difficulties of the salvage problem presented by the H-3 were not fully appreciated by the naval officers involved, because they lacked experience in salvage seamanship and took action that, however well intentioned, proved costly.

World War I

The entry of the United States into World War I found the Navy with some broad experience in salvage, but with no permanent organization for salvage operations. The economics of the salvage business in the early twentieth century had left the United States with three major salvage companies—Merritt and Chapman of New York, Yankee Salvor of Boston, and T.A. Scott of New London. Each maintained ships and facilities along the Atlantic Coast. With the entry of the United States into the war, a salvage corps was founded under the direction of the Chief Constructor, the head of the Navy's Construction Corps (CC). The diving school in Newport was disbanded so that its men, along with civilian salvage masters who had been enrolled in the Construction Corps, could be sent to France to assist with salvage operations there. These forces joined British, French, and Italian salvors to form an Allied salvage force.

Because World War I was primarily a land war on the European continent, the requirement to clear numerous harbors blocked by a retreating enemy or by heavy air attacks, common in World War II, did not exist. But cases of salvage from maritime accidents had to be handled, and a few cases of intentional blockage had to be cleared. Huge quantities of shipping flowed into European ports to transport the American Expeditionary Force and give it logistic support. This sea transport, operating with U-boat opposition, required that shipping lanes and ports be kept open and that salvage forces be available and ready.

In 1917 the British, with the full support of Vice Admiral William S. Sims, petitioned the United States to provide ships to help refloat merchant ships grounded on the French coast. The British ships engaged in this work were privately owned and had civilian crews, but their work was assigned and coordinated by a newly created Admiralty Salvage Section led by the renowned salvor, Sir Frederick Young, under the Director of Naval Equipment.

The U.S. Navy had no salvage ships of its own, so the British request was passed by the Chief Constructor to the three American salvage companies. None of the three felt that the financial risk was justified. Resolution of the problem fell to the Assistant Secretary of the Navy, the official who traditionally dealt with civilian labor and contracting for the Navy. The Navy was fortunate to have the vigorous and imaginative Franklin D. Roosevelt as its assistant secretary.

Roosevelt called one ship each from T.A. Scott and Merritt and Chapman into government service and rented equipment for overseas service from them. The two ships were manned by naval reservists with salvage experience. They sailed for Europe under the direction of two

Naval Reserve commanders—Walter Davis, manager of the offshore division of Merritt and Chapman, and Harold Witherspoon, an owner of Yankee Salvor. A third Reserve officer, T.A. Scott, remained in the United States as Assistant for Salvage Affairs to Roosevelt. The ships arrived on the French coast in time to join the British in numerous salvage efforts, which saved significant amounts of money and cargo. Unfortunately, complete records of these operations were not kept or have been lost.

Meanwhile, in American waters, the winter of 1917–18 in the North Atlantic was particularly cold. With the commercial salvage ships overseas, salvage responsibilities along the northeastern coast of the United States fell to a hastily recruited minesweeper squadron made up of trawlers and menhaden fishing boats. These boats gave salvage assistance to both naval and commercial vessels. With the extreme weather there was no shortage of work. Among the vessels assisted were the battleship *Texas* (BB 35) when she grounded off Clay Head on Block Island, and the gunboat *Don Juan d'Austria*, which grounded entering Woods Hole when she miscalculated the set of the current.

One of the largest salvage operations of the war years was carried out by the Merritt organization in New York harbor when the steamer *St. Paul* capsized between Piers 60 and 61 in the North River on 25 April 1918.[6] The vessel was refloated in a pulling and pumping operation that provided an interesting preview of a much larger operation, the salvage of *Lafayette*, that would take place nearby in a much larger war some twenty-three years later. The *St. Paul* salvage operation, as well as the operations off New England the preceding winter, emphasized that during periods of mobilization all resources cannot be sent overseas; some personnel, ships, and equipment must be retained for salvage in home waters.

Although few records remain of the Navy's salvage operations in World War I, its effort surely contributed to victory by saving ships and cargoes that would otherwise have been lost. Though vital at the time, the total salvage activities were too restricted in quantity and geographic area to have significant value in future planning. When the war was over and demobilization was complete, the Navy maintained no permanent salvage organization.

---

[6] *St. Paul* had been requisitioned from the International Navigation Company for service as an armed merchant cruiser in the Spanish-American War. In this capacity she drove off the Spanish destroyer *Terror* at San Juan. She later served as a transport. Restored to her owners in the fall of 1898, she returned to trade. She gained some notoriety in 1908 when she collided with and sank the British cruiser *Gladiator* in The Solent off south England. *Gladiator* subsequently became the object of a noted salvage operation conducted by Captain Frederick Young of the Liverpool Salvage Association. *St. Paul* was again in government service as a transport when she capsized.

SQUALUS

CHAPTER TWO

Between the Wars

After World War I, when the Navy attempted to return the salvage ships to their owners, trouble developed quickly. The owners claimed that such severe damage had occurred during the Atlantic crossings that major reconstruction was necessary; the Navy felt the ships were beyond economic repair and that their condition stemmed from age and prior service. Merritt and Chapman and Yankee Salvor also believed that T. A. Scott, acting in his capacity as Assistant for Salvage Affairs, had looted their warehouses, sending good equipment to his own New London warehouse and replacing it with worn and damaged equipment returned from overseas. It appeared that the claims would have to be settled by the courts.

Acting with considerable foresight, the Assistant Secretary of the Navy, Franklin Roosevelt, again intervened. He invited Ralph Chapman and Scott to meet him in his suite at New York's Powhatan Hotel to have an after-dinner drink and discuss the future of the salvage industry and the best interests of the United States. Seeing the long-term value of an industry that could be called into service to support the Navy and realizing that it was not in the Navy's current interest to acquire large stores of expensive and seldom-used salvage equipment, Roosevelt was seeking a way to provide salvage protection to the Navy while preserving the industry.

Business planning for the salvage industry has always been difficult, for there is no method of predicting when and where casualties will occur. Roosevelt felt that the general business climate was not propitious for salvors. The three salvage companies had not been making adequate profits in recent years, and prospects for the future were not good; in fact, Yankee Salvor went into bankruptcy shortly after demobilization. Casualties were expected to decrease because ships were better built and more efficient than before, crews were better trained, and navigation aids were better and more numerous. A decrease in casualties is good for shipping, but not for those who make their living from salvage. Seeing too little work to justify a number of companies, Roosevelt proposed that the salvors devise a plan for consolidating their resources. He believed that one company with a virtual monopoly on salvage in American waters could operate profitably and still provide a base for wartime expansion.

From a business viewpoint the proposal made sense. When the pot was sweetened, it became inevitable. Roosevelt suggested that, given its interest in the viability of the American salvage industry, the Navy would pursue a policy of contracting for everything but submarine salvage through the Bureau of Construction and Repair. Business would be conducted on the no-cure, no-pay basis traditional for salvage (the salvor could refuse if the risk was too great), and the newly formed company would agree to send help immediately to any distressed Navy ship in American coastal waters.

The Navy had on hand a surplus of Bird-class minesweepers. These 180-foot, 950-ton, single-screw, steam-propelled combined tug/minesweepers had been built in a wartime shipbuilding program that had enjoyed a higher priority than the destroyer-building program. They were excellent candidates for conversion to salvage ships. Some of the ships were in commission and some were not yet completed; a number were scheduled to be cut up for scrap. Roosevelt proposed that some of the uncompleted ships be sold to the salvors for what they were worth to the Navy, that is, their scrap value less the cost of cutting them up.

The meeting lasted through the night. Scott and Chapman, seeing the worth of Roosevelt's proposals, left the Assistant Secretary's suite for an early breakfast and made their plans. Thus the Merritt-Chapman and Scott Salvage Corporation was born. The new company purchased four Bird-class minesweepers and fitted them out as salvage ships. Combined with those they already owned, these ships gave the salvors sufficient resources to base four ships along the Atlantic Coast and a fifth on the Pacific Coast. Salvage stations with reserve equipment and repair ships were set up at New London; Staten Island; Key West; Kingston, Jamaica; and San Pedro, California.

A New Navy-Industry Relationship

A series of contracts, designated NOd–210, existed between the Bureau of Construction and Repair and Merritt-Chapman and Scott in the years between the two world wars. These contracts carried no annual fee but provided that upon the orders of a naval district commandant, the company would undertake the salvage of a naval ship on a no-cure, no-pay basis with provisions that the salvor had the right to refuse work if the risk appeared too great. If the work was successful, a board composed of one member from each organization involved would determine the salvor's compensation based on the value of the ship and cargo and the risks taken by the salvor. The final payment was subject to the approval of the Secretary of the Navy.

The Bureau of Construction and Repair, the forerunner of the Bureau of Ships and today's Naval Sea Systems Command, was the Navy's technical agency responsible for the design, construction, and maintenance of warships. It was staffed largely by officers of the Construction Corps (CC), known as naval constructors, who, because of their technical training and expertise, were also active in salvage. The bureau had no direct military responsibilities for undertaking salvage operations, but it could arrange for salvage work by contractors and could provide technical assistance for salvage work by naval forces. With the designation of the Bureau of Construction and Repair as the contracting agency for salvage and for the regular letting of salvage contracts, the seeds were sown for a permanent Navy organization devoted to salvage.

Policy that would affect Navy salvage for the next eighteen years was set. The arrangement was totally satisfactory for all parties. The new company had a close working relationship with the Navy that enhanced its business; the Navy was relieved of the responsibility for maintaining expensive salvage stores for infrequent operations; and, because of wartime cooperation between the two, the nation had the basis for a military salvage capability.

Other than administration of the salvage contract by the Bureau of Construction and Repair, there was little active Navy involvement in salvage management or routine minor salvage operations immediately following World War I. When the Navy did become involved in salvage between the two world wars, however, there was a sharp, intense peak of activity.

DeLong: A Joint Salvage Effort

The salvage of the destroyer *DeLong* (DD 129) in 1921 was one of the first examples of a salvage conducted jointly by the Navy and its salvage contractor and demonstrated the effectiveness of the combination.

Running in a fog at 10 knots en route from San Diego to San Francisco, the ship grounded in Half Moon Bay, California, in the early morning of 1 December 1921. Under the impetus of the surf, *DeLong* moved inshore until her bow was at the low-water mark, well within the rock strata that lie at an angle to the beach in the bay. She moved so far inland that it was not possible to get alongside in a shallow draft vessel, making it necessary to work from the beach. In accordance with Murphy's Law this was not to be easy, because the ship was grounded near the base of a 50-foot-high bluff.

A major factor in the successful salvage of *DeLong* was the prompt arrival at the site of experienced salvors who could evaluate the situation and take the initial action often critical in stranding salvage. One of the most important early actions was weighing the ship down by flooding enough compartments so that she would not be driven further inshore. This work was done by the ship's crew, with some of the flooding done by bucket line, a slow and laborious process. To prevent breaching, anchors were laid to seaward and led to deck purchases. A salvage tug laid 5,000-pound anchors, and messenger lines were passed by a Coast Guard launch firing shot lines.

Meanwhile, salvage equipment had been trucked in and sheer legs rigged on the bluff for putting pumps, hauling purchases, and other equipment on board. Trucks connected to purchases hauled the gear on board and later hauled the deck purchases. There were some problems connected with the trucks: one was arrested for being overloaded, another smashed a bridge that had to be rebuilt, and several had to be towed over poor sections of road. Because of the slack in the rigging, the face of the bluff had to be modified for some of the heavier loads. Black powder charges were tried, but when reasonably sized charges failed to do the job, sailors with picks and shovels took over and did it.

The calculations of the salvage engineer, Lieutenant William Nelson (CC), showed that both stability and pumping capacity were adequate. As is usual in salvage operations, not all the information needed for precise calculations was available and Lieutenant Nelson had to rely on soundly based assumptions.

Weather along the California coast can be unpleasant in winter. Heavy seas washed over the ship, breaking lines, making it necessary to build houses over pumps to protect the magnetos, and delaying operations on several occasions. The ground swell and heavy breakers offshore presented a hazard to the pulling operation, and delayed it. When everything was ready, one pulling attempt was aborted with some damage.

On 15 December, two weeks after the grounding, the sea was moderate and all equipment was set for a pull. The pumps were started, the purchases hauled, and a Navy tug and a commercial salvage tug began to pull. But as the pumps lowered the water level in the ship, she started to heel to starboard, reaching 19 degrees before suction was lost. The refloating effort was stopped and the pumps rerigged. By 17 December everything was again ready. The sea was smooth. Three hours before high water the pumps were started, purchases hauled, and the tugs began to work up their pull. *DeLong* moved off her strand and swung clear of the rocks, afloat again.

DeLong was towed to the Mare Island Navy Yard, where she was docked for thorough inspection. The damage to her hull was found to be both extensive and severe. She was not repaired but was stricken in 1922.

Removal of *DeLong* from her strand in Half Moon Bay was a noteworthy salvage operation because of the need to operate from ashore and the measures that had to be taken to get equipment aboard. The most significant thing about the operation was the thoroughly professional response of the commercial and naval salvors, who took exactly the correct action in time to limit the damage and make the salvage possible. We shall see later that prompt correct action is always important in stranding salvage, particularly on the west coast of the United States, where environmental conditions cause rapid deterioration of casualties.

Submarine Salvage

During the period between the two world wars, submarine salvage provided many peaks of Navy salvage activity. Just as submarines are unique to navies, so is most submarine salvage knowledge. Because they navigate beneath the surface of the sea, submarines are different from surface ships not only in their construction, but in the kinds of accidents that threaten them, and in the motivation and means for their salvage. In addition to the hazards of subsea navigation, submarines are exposed to all the hazards of ships navigating on the surface. We have seen earlier how the submarine H–3 became the subject of a successful major salvage operation following an accident that occurred while she was navigating on the surface. In 1920 another submarine, H–1, grounded on the coast of Colombia during a storm and was lost when she sank during the salvage operation.

Submarines, however, have unique design features that may make their salvage easier. Neither the H–3 nor the F–4 salvages took advantage of these features. H–3 was moved overland cleverly, but any object of the same size might be moved in the same manner. Naval Constructor Furer lifted F–4 from the bottom by a pure dead lift and the application of external buoyancy, techniques suited to lifting any object off the ocean floor. The choice of salvage method and the practicality of using the design features of submarines are functions of the nature of the casualty, the depth of the water, the equipment that can be brought to bear, and the background and experience of the officers directing the salvage. The cases that follow illustrate how features not found in surface ships can enhance the salvage of submarines.

Stranded Submarines (S–19 and S–48)

A grounding on 13 January 1925 vividly demonstrates the value of perseverance when success seems elusive in salvage operations. On that date the submarine S–19 (SS 124) ran ashore on Nauset Beach near Orleans, Massachusetts, on the eastern shore of Cape Cod. Shortly after S–19 ran aground, the Coast Guard cutters *Acushnet* and *Tampa* left Woods Hole and Boston, respectively, to stand by the stranded submarine. Commander R.B. Hilliard (CC), and Tug Master B.F. Kemp left Boston Navy Yard in *Wandank* (AT 26) with orders to do whatever was necessary to salvage the submarine. Finding the submarine secure but hard aground, *Wandank* anchored close in and attempted to pass a wire rope to S–19. The attempt failed.

By now help was on the way from Merritt-Chapman and Scott. The work was undertaken on a per diem basis rather than the no-cure, no-pay basis envisioned by Roosevelt. There was some question that the government could legally contract on such a basis.

The tug *Resolute*, with Salvage Master Foster on board, arrived. A 10-inch manila line was passed and *Resolute* pulled for an hour with no result other than to heel the submarine 13 degrees. The crew was taken off the submarine, and *Resolute* and *Wandank* pulled in tandem, parting an 8-inch line. A second Merritt-Chapman and Scott tug, *Merritt*, arrived and joined the operation, taking *Wandank's* place in the tandem pull when the latter parted a towline. The submarine still had not been moved but now heeled about 40 degrees—a condition dangerous for a surface ship but acceptable because of the submarine's shape and the tightness of her hull. About 40 tons of liquid load was removed from the submarine to reduce the pulling force required. *Merritt* continued on almost every high tide to pull with her engines and two purchases[1] rigged to a heavy anchor, without any effect other than to shift the S–19's head two or three points. Near the end of January the manila lines carried away in heavy weather, and the submarine moved 150 feet inshore, nearly 70 percent of her length. It was obvious the pulling arrangements had to be modified.

The submarine now rested inside a sandbar with her bow to seaward buried about 8 feet in the sand. She would have to be moved about 600 feet to seaward to refloat. A shore tackle, consisting of a large buoy moored with four anchors, was rigged to assist in the pulling. A wire-rope line was led from the submarine through a block on the buoy to a purchase ashore. The purchase was hauled with a winch that, in turn, was secured to a deadman (buried log or other object) sunk in a trench. Tension was kept on this line constantly, slack being taken in whenever tension appeared.

---

[1] The purchase used for pulling S-19 was typical of salvage pulling arrangements of the day. Four hundred fathoms of 15-inch-circumference manila was secured to a pulling point on the submarine; the other end was made up on *Merritt's* aft bitts. *Merritt* was moored with her anchors and a 200-fathom length of 15-inch manila carried to a 7,000-pound salvage anchor. This line was taken to a seven-part purchase on *Merritt's* deck. The purchase was rove with 5½-inch manila with the bitter end carried to a windlass.

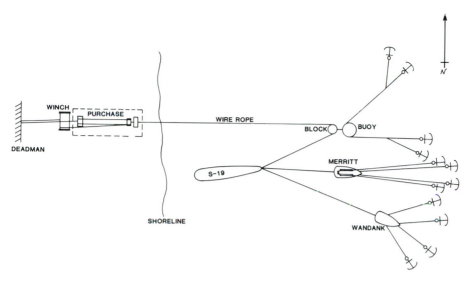

Pulling arrangement for refloating submarine S–19.

Merritt remained rigged as before and *Wandank* was moored with her own and two additional anchors. She pulled with her engines and towing engine. S–19 began to move slowly, heeling at up to 90 degrees—an impossible list for a surface ship—during the pulls. She gave ground hard, coming free on the evening of 18 March 1925 after many short moves. *Merritt* took S–19 into Provincetown on 20 March. Perseverance and patience in making many pulls and in constantly seeking ways to maximize the available pull had paid off, as did the toughness that permitted the submarine to survive being inclined to extreme angles.

Barely two weeks after S–19 grounded, on the evening of 29 January 1925, the submarine S–48 (SS 159) grounded on the rocks a few hundred yards off Jaffrey Point while entering the harbor at Portsmouth, New Hampshire. The submarine lay across the sea in a sort of basin with rocks outboard on the seaward side. She was apparently hung up on a single rock under the port side. During the night, before high tide, the boat came free of the rock and drifted stern-first around the breakwater into Little Harbor, where it grounded firmly in sand with a list of 34 degrees. The submarine's hull had taken a beating during the grounding and was leaking in a number of places. Commander Harold E. Saunders (CC), took charge of the salvage. Saunders had available to him the resources of the Portsmouth Navy Yard.

Navy yards are unsurpassed as bases for salvage operations and, as will be seen, have figured prominently in a number of them. In addition to industrial shops that can make almost anything required by salvors, navy yards have a variety of floating equipment, tugs, cranes, and barges.

Equally important, they have people experienced in the trades useful for salvage.

Working in wet, freezing weather, the salvors laid an anchor to hold the submarine and began to pump out the hull. It quickly became apparent that pumping would not be practical because of the number and location of leaks. While high-pressure air flasks were installed on the tug *Penacook*, salvage crews made the upper portions of the S–48's hull and ballast tight. *Penacook* shuttled from the sister submarines S–49 (SS 160) and S–51 (SS 162) at the Portsmouth Navy Yard, where air flasks were filled, to the S–48, where the air was blown into the grounded submarine. By blowing air into the hull and ballast tanks, Saunders was able to control the list of the boat and refloat her. With *Penacook* alongside controlling the list, trim, and buoyancy of the submarine with air, S–48 was towed stern-first to the navy yard.

Saunders used the facilities of the navy yard to salvage the S–48. He also took advantage of the basic design philosophy of submarines, namely, that the total buoyancy of the hull can be controlled by air. In doing so he accomplished an unusually economical salvage. The cost of the entire operation was only $3,400.

Sunken Submarines

As soon as submarines began to go to sea, the navies of the world realized that they were more vulnerable to accidental sinking than were surface ships. Because of their relatively closed atmospheres and limited reserve buoyancy, explosions and flooding presented special hazards. Subsequent experience showed that flooding by breaching the hull or through an improperly positioned hull opening was by far the greatest hazard to the undersea boats. Accidental, noncombat sinking of submarines generated some of the most difficult and technically interesting salvage operations undertaken between the world wars.

Just as the operation of submarines in those days was uniquely naval, so, too, was raising them when they sank. Techniques and the means of applying them were developed in the U.S. Navy by Navy people. Thus the Navy's special interest in and expert knowledge of submarines were recognized from the outset in the arrangements between the Navy and Merritt-Chapman and Scott.

Submarine salvage operations are motivated not only by the traditional purposes of saving property or returning a ship to service but also by two other purposes. The first is determining the cause of the accident to prevent reoccurrences. This was the primary motivation for the salvage of the F–4 and has continued to be a driving motivation in submarine and deep-ocean salvage. The second purpose is rescue by salvage of the crew trapped within the hull or the recovery of the remains of those who perished in the accident.

Early submarine salvage was conceived primarily as a rescue effort to be accomplished by lifting the ship. In some foreign navies, vessels designed to lift entire submarine hulls were commissioned for the joint purposes of testing the submarine hulls, rescuing survivors of a casualty, and salvaging the hulls. The first of these vessels was *Vulkan* of the Imperial German Navy. *Vulkan* salvaged U–3 at Kiel in 1911. A variety of other schemes for raising submarines were tried; few had much success.

As shown in the table, noncombat submarine sinkings between the two world wars were not rare and had various causes. Most resulted from inadvertent flooding; some were in port, some in the deep ocean; some did not result in the salvage of the ship. When salvage operations were mounted, they were usually major operations and, without exception, were done with organizations and equipment assembled and tailored to the particular job. Following each operation the organization was disbanded and the equipment stowed. Maintaining a specialized permanent organization in a high state of readiness for an event that—though not

U.S. Navy Noncombat Submarine Sinkings
Prior to World War II

Date	Ship	Type of Accident	Salvaged
1915	F–4	Flooding, hull failure	Yes
1917	D–2	Flooding, in port	Yes
1917	F–1	Flooding, collision	No
1919	G–2	Flooding, leaky hatch	No
1920	H–1	Grounded, sank during salvage	No
1920	S–5	Flooding, open main induction	No
1921	R–6	Flooding, open torpedo tube	Yes
1921	S–48	Flooding, manhole cover	Yes
1923	S–38	Flooding, motor room	Yes
1923	O–5	Flooding, collision	Yes
1925	S–51	Flooding, collision	Yes
1927	S–4	Flooding, collision	Yes
1939	*Squalus*	Flooding, main induction open	Yes
1941	O–9	Flooding, exceeded test depth	No

rare—occurred as infrequently as noncombat submarine accidents simply was not an effective use of people and material.

Four U.S. noncombat submarines sank between the loss of F–4 in 1915 and the S–5 (SS 110) accident in 1920. One of these, D–2, was in port and simply required pumping out. Two were deep-water losses, F–1 from collision, G–2 from a leaky hatch. The fourth, H–1, was lost during a salvage attempt following a grounding.

AN IMPORTANT FAILURE (S–5)

Sometimes a failed effort can teach more than a successful one. Such was the case with the salvage of S–5. The S–5 sank during the afternoon of 1 September 1920, 32 miles off the Delaware capes, because she submerged with her main induction and hull valves open. The torpedo room was filled, and some flooding occurred in the control and engine rooms, but by pumping out ballast, fuel, and some floodwater, the crew was able to bring the stern to the surface. With the assistance of two passing ships, *Atlantis* and *George W. Goethals*, the crew was rescued by cutting a hole in the exposed stern.

S–5 was an excellent candidate for salvage; she was a new submarine of the latest type, and hull damage was limited to the hole cut for the rescue of the crew. Interior bulkheads were reported secure; the hole in the stern was in a small compartment that was still above the surface.

Because the submarine was light, dragging it into shallow water was the first choice of the salvors, just as it had been in the case of F–4. The predreadnought battleship *Ohio* (BB 12) was selected as the towing ship. A towing connection was made by taking nine wraps around the stern of S–5 with one-inch wire rope and shackling it to a 2-inch wire rope towing hawser. The hole in the stern was not closed. *Ohio* towed for three hours, moving some 3 1/2 miles into 144 feet of water. The error of taking a shortcut in salvage was again made clear. The stern pulled under; S–5 flooded through the unsecured access hole and sank.

Merritt-Chapman and Scott was called in to provide technical assistance in raising the submarine. Its opinion was that submarine salvage pontoons, like those that Furer built for F–4, were impractical in the open sea and that the only practical means of salvage was to blow the hull and ballast tanks with compressed air.

The salvage plan then became making the top of the ship watertight, providing spill pipes or spill holes in the bottom, and blowing the ship dry. Work began immediately from the Bird-class minesweeper *Mallard* (AM 44). Little progress was made during 1920, and the operation was closed down for the winter in November.

The salvors returned in the spring of 1921 with another Bird-class boat, *Falcon* (AM 28), that had been fitted out for salvage during the winter. Explosives cut off hatches and blew holes in the bottom of the ship. Initially, hatches were fitted with wooden plugs that contained blow and spill pipes and were covered over with concrete. These were not successful and were discarded in favor of steel hatches. Difficulty in making the hull airtight occurred at every stage; the job was going far slower than had been predicted. By late August it was apparent that work would not be complete by the end of good weather and that damage during the salvage attempt had left the boat in far worse condition than had the original accident. On 29 August 1921 the Secretary of the Navy ordered that work be discontinued and S–5 be stricken from the Navy list.

As with every failed salvage job, there were lessons to be learned from S–5. Its condition and location favored salvage, but the use of pontoons, and apparently of any other type of external lift, was excluded from the outset. That was a mistake. External lift would have provided the margin that could have made the difference between success and failure. Explosives, effective for opening the hull and removing hatches, were used inexpertly. The resulting damage multiplied the work necessary to make the hull tight and rendered the salvage impracticable.

The lack of a salvage air system on the boat made the fitting of air supply and water spill connections on the hatches necessary. The experience gained on S–5 and other sunken submarines led to the installation of salvage air systems in later submarines.

The attempted salvage of S–5 shared one characteristic with the salvage of F–4; the work of the divers was exceptional. A total of 479 dives were made with only 10 percent resulting in decompression sickness, a remarkably low percentage for the diving conditions.

Immediately following the successful rescue of the crew of S–5, Commander Submarine Flotilla recommended that one Bird-class minesweeper on each coast be fitted out and kept available for submarine rescue. This recommendation was unheeded; some years later in 1929, when more practical and dependable means of submarine rescue were available, the first six submarine rescue ships, all Bird-class minesweepers, were commissioned. Two of them were veterans of the S–5 salvage, *Mallard* and *Falcon* (renamed ASR–4 and ASR–2).

A 'TYPICAL' SUCCESS (R–6)

On the evening of 26 September 1921, less than a month after the attempted salvage of S–5, R–6 (SS 83) sank at her moorings alongside her tender *Camden* (AS 6) at San Pedro, California; a torpedoman had opened a torpedo tube inner door while the outer door was still open. R–6 provides an excellent example of a straightforward submarine salvage undertaken by an ad hoc organization with no outside assistance.

The conditions favored salvage. R–6 lay on an even keel and trim in 32 feet of water inside San Pedro harbor breakwater; all hatches were open except for the torpedo loading hatch. The main induction and inner and outer lower starboard torpedo tube doors were also open. The crew was available for salvage work. Among them were three divers, including one Chief Petty Officer. The *Camden* was available for assistance with material, ships, additional divers, a diving boat, and pumps. Other submarines in the division were available to furnish compressed air.

Three methods for salvage were available:

1. Sinking two pontoons alongside the ship, forming a cradle with the chains, and pumping out the pontoons. This method was held in reserve because it would require considerable outside assistance and equipment.

2. Sealing all the openings and putting air on the boat through the salvage lines. This method was rejected because of the large amount of diving work that would be required both inside and outside the boat to make it tight and the difficulty in providing exits for the water and keeping them clear.

3. Sealing the vessel and conducting a pumping operation by plugging hatch openings with plugs through which pump suctions and compartment vents would pass, then pumping with air-driven pumps placed on the submerged deck.

In selecting a salvage method, time is given considerable weight; the sooner the work is completed, the less the damage from submergence. By choosing the simpler pumping method, the R–6 salvors planned to complete the work in ten days.

Salvage work began the morning following the sinking. Divers entered the boat and secured as many openings as possible. The tender *Camden* manufactured wooden plugs for the torpedo and engine room hatches. The plugs had a vent pipe to the surface and two suction lines for each pump. The plugs were first carefully fit on a sister submarine. When the plugs were in place, sea pressure would help hold them in, and they would swell to ensure a good seal. Reciprocating steam pumps were set up on the deck of R–6, secured in place, connected with air lines, and tested. Air to operate the pumps was provided by the R–10 moored alongside. Under the direction of the salvage officer, Lieutenant Frederick C. Sherman, pumping began about six days after the sinking. Apparently the leakage continued at a rate that the pumps could not overcome, for the water level in the vents did not drop. Because leaks could not be found,

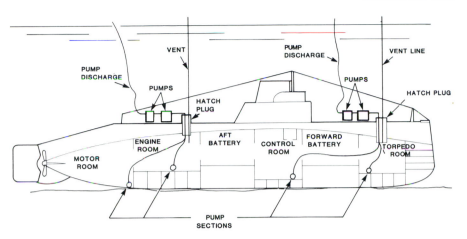

Salvage of submarine R–6; first pumping arrangement.

an attempt was made to seal the vents and blow air into the boat while pumping. This was not successful.

To increase the pumping capacity enough to overcome the leakage, a cofferdam was built on the repair ship *Vestal* (AR 4) and fitted to the conning tower hatch. The suction line from a 6-inch salvage pump borrowed from the tug *Sonoma* (AT 12) was led through this hatch, as were the discharge hoses and leads for two electric submersible pumps borrowed from *Arizona* (BB 39).

With the pumping power significantly increased, pumping started and progressed well. Then a problem arose that has plagued every salvor who has ever used an electric submersible pump. The pump motors flooded out. The pumps were repaired on *Vestal* and water was pumped down to the door sills.

With main ballast tanks flooded to keep the boat securely on the bottom, divers entered the hull, secured more leaks, and blew the auxiliary ballast tanks. Main ballast was then blown and the boat began to rise, hard down by the stern. The extreme trim caused all the water to run aft, leaving the pump suctions dry. An attempt to drag the submarine into shallower water failed because the boat was too heavy for the tender *Kingfisher* (AM 25) to move.

In a heroic effort, salvors entered the sunken hull to blow the fuel tanks, close off the engine, check the pumps, and seal all air outlets so the engine room could be blown. Pumping and blowing caused an almost imperceptible rise in the hull. To prevent sinking in the event of another pump failure, the tender *Alert* and the tug *Cardinal* were brought alongside and rigged for lifting with their anchor chains. By blowing, pumping, and lifting, the R–6 was floated on the afternoon of 13 October 1921, seventeen days after her sinking.

The salvage of R–6 could almost be called a typical salvage operation. Diving conditions were miserable; conditions arising during the operation caused changes in the salvage plan; many techniques were tried; many things went wrong. Frustration levels were surely high, but no higher than the euphoria brought about by final success. The initial rise of the submarine demonstrated the necessity of maintaining strict control of buoyancy and trim. The problem of inadvertent or uncontrolled rising of a sunken submarine was to plague other salvors as well.

The R–6 salvage is notable for its use of advance planning and testing that helped ensure the success of the operation. Because of the hard diving conditions on the R–6, the divers received special training. They were taken into other submarines first to learn their way around blind-folded and to practice their tasks. In the quality of work, safety, and the time saved, these methods proved valuable not only on the R–6, but also on many subsequent salvage operations. Equipment to be fitted to R–6, for example, was prefitted on other submarines, a sound practice that continues to avoid many on-the-scene problems.

MINOR SUBMARINE SALVAGE (S–48, S–38, and O–5)

Not all submarine sinkings required major salvage operations. On 7 December 1921, S–48 (SS 159) sank during a trial run. As the bow was above the surface, the crew was easily rescued. The ship was subsequently refloated and returned to service.

The year 1923 saw two such minor submarine salvage operations. On 17 July, S–38 (SS 143) sank alongside her tender *Ortolan* (AM 45) at Anchorage, Alaska. There was no loss of life, and the ship was raised without difficulty.

On 28 October, O–5 (SS 66) sank in the Panama Canal after colliding with a merchantman and provided an unusual example of rescue by salvage. Fortunately, the Panama Canal Company owned what were, at the time, the world's largest floating cranes, *US Ajax* and *US Hercules*. Midgets by today's standards, these cranes were capable of lifting 250 tons each. Thanks to a superhuman diving effort by Canal Company Dockmaster and Foreman Shipwright Sheppart Shreaves to rig the lifting gear and the compressed air to lighten the boat, the bow of O–5 was lifted clear of the water and the two crew members trapped inside the hull were saved. The submarine was subsequently cofferdammed, re-floated, and scrapped. The concept of rescue-by-salvage had proven viable in this case only because of the immediate presence of extraordinary lifting equipment and extraordinary people.

MAJOR OPEN-SEA SALVAGE (S-51)

Three submarines were salvaged following noncombat sinking in the open sea in 1925, 1927, and 1939. All were salvaged with pontoons, the method pioneered by Furer in 1915. These three submarine salvage operations were the largest and most complex salvages undertaken by the Navy prior to World War II. Each was an example of seamanship and engineering excellence that demonstrated the value of careful and complete engineering and planning for ocean operations. Each salvage effort also demonstrated the tremendous effect that weather has on operations at sea and emphasized that despite the best-laid plans, Murphy makes the laws of salvage operations. There will always be a need for the salvage officer to react to the unexpected.

The operation to save the S–51 illustrates all the challenges of open-sea salvage. The S–51 (SS 162) sank in 132 feet of water following a collision with the Ocean Steamship Company's *City of Rome* on the night of 25 September 1925, 14 miles east of Block Island off the coast of Rhode Island. Of the six officers and thirty-one men aboard, there were three survivors. An immediate effort was made to rescue other men who may have been trapped in the hull. A collection of vessels from both the Navy and Merritt-Chapman and Scott, including the heavy-lift derricks *Monarch* and *Century* (combined lift about 270 tons), assembled at the scene. Dives were made on the submarine by the Navy and Merritt-Chapman and Scott divers. Slings for the derricks were rigged and, as soon as weather permitted, an attempt was made to lift the stern. It failed. No air escaped when small holes were burned in hatches. The entire boat was flooded; rescue attempts were abandoned.

The decision was made to salvage the submarine. Whether it was a wise decision can be argued in retrospect. There were strong reasons not to try salvage. No sunken submarine had been raised from the open ocean. The damage to S–51 was likely to be so great that the hull would be of little, if any, future value; there was no need to determine the cause of the loss, as there had been with F–4. At the time, however, the decision to go ahead was influenced by heightened public and congressional attention to Navy casualties brought on by a series of recent naval aviation accidents.

As difficult as was the question of whether to salvage, deciding who would do the salvage was equally taxing. Though Merritt-Chapman and Scott was the Navy's salvage contractor and the nation's leading salvor, it had no special expertise in submarine salvage, which was not included in its contract. The Navy had little salvage expertise either, but was long on resources and engineering talent. A contract was proposed whereby Merritt-Chapman and Scott would provide a salvage master, divers, and one tug. The remainder of the personnel and equipment would be provided by the Navy.

Because of the uncertainty of the operation, no-cure no-pay was not deemed appropriate; a daily-hire-plus-bonus contract was anticipated. A Navy faction led by Rear Admiral Charles P. Plunkett, Commandant of the Third Naval District, argued that the proposed contract was too generous and that the Navy should be able to salvage the submarine itself. This faction was successful, and on 10 October the work was assigned to the Third Naval District. Preliminary funds were allotted, and orders for ships, materials, and equipment were issued. Captain Ernest J. King, commanding officer of the submarine base at New London, was assigned as officer-in-charge and Lieutenant Commander Edward Ellsberg (CC) of the New York Navy Yard was assigned as salvage officer.

A considerable fleet was assembled consisting of the repair ship *Vestal* (Captain Tomb); the minesweeper-cum-diving-ship *Falcon* (Lieutenant Henry Hartley); seagoing tugs *Iuka* (AT 37), *Sagamore* (AT 10), and *Bagaduce* (AT 21); the tug *Penobscot*; and the submarine S-50 (Lieutenant Commander Lenney). The role of each ship was clearly defined.

- *Vestal* was to act as a supply vessel and mother ship.
- *Falcon*, equipped with a recompression chamber and air banks, was to be the principal player as she supported the diving operations.
- *Iuka* was to attend *Falcon*.
- *Sagamore* and *Bagaduce* were to bring out pontoons and assist with the moorings.
- *Penobscot* was to make daily runs to New London to maintain communication with the submarine base.
- S-50 was to be available as a model and rehearsal platform for divers.

S-51 lay on a northwesterly heading with a port list of about 12 degrees on a bottom of friable clay mixed with sand and gravel. The boat was imbedded about 5 feet into the bottom. There was considerable damage to the hull from the collision and from impact with the bottom. The salvage plan called for placing pontoons for external buoyancy, coupled with restoring internal buoyancy. A total of 1,000 tons of lift was planned, 650 from pontoons and 350 from internal buoyancy. The 1,000-ton total gave a margin of 25 percent over the calculated value of 800 tons required to raise the hull, a margin needed to cover unknown quantities and to overcome the probable suction force of the bottom.

Collision damage precluded restoration of buoyancy in the forward part of the hull, but the three aft compartments could be isolated by securing external hatches, internal doors, and ventilation and piping systems.

How to obtain buoyancy was a major problem. Study of the submarine's systems showed the hull was not well suited to holding internal air pressure. The access hatches were not designed to remain seated under internal pressure and could not be effectively secured with strongbacks. Available pumps had insufficient lift. A method using both air and pumps was planned but proved impractical, so a means of blowing the compartments was developed. Sealing of accesses and piping systems required many hours of underwater work to remove interference and piping, and to seal systems with cement.

Two of the 60-ton pontoons and two of the 80-ton pontoons from the F–4 job were available in the Norfolk Navy Yard. These pontoons, which had been built for a depth of 45 feet, required strengthening for use on the S–51 at 132 feet. Six new 80-ton pontoons were also built at the New York Navy Yard. The new pontoons were equipped with relief valves that kept the internal pressure 5 to 10 pounds above ambient, obviating the need for heavy structure.

Diving from the *Falcon* was to be the key to the operation. A special mooring consisting of six (later seven) buoys with chain attached to 4- to 8-thousand pound anchors was laid in a 1,000-foot-diameter circle, centered on S–51. It was mandatory that *Falcon* remain accurately positioned so that divers would not be dragged away from their work. Tugs were often needed to help hold *Falcon* in position. Anchoring ships, including *Vestal*, to windward to help form a lee for *Falcon* had limited success.

Work commenced on 15 October and continued until 7 December when winter weather and water temperatures prevented any further work. During this period weather was bad enough to prevent diving about half the time; this was reduced to half again following a gale on 13 November. On 30 November divers experienced freezing and blockage of their air lines. Study showed that this could be prevented only by extensive modifications to *Falcon*'s air system. Weather had won. Work was suspended until the following April.

The time on site had been well spent—both in terms of work accomplished and lessons learned. Divers had cleared away interference and, working inside and outside the sunken submarine, had sealed the aft section of the boat. Attempts to pass lines for pontoons under the hull had been frustrated by the bottom soil and the reaction generated when trying to tunnel with a high-pressure water jet and a conventional nozzle. No pontoons had been placed, but much had been learned about how to handle them; even more had been learned about how not to handle them. Problems with tools and equipment, especially the underwater cutting torch, had also been identified.

No sailor likes to walk away in the middle of a job, but a break forced by weather or other uncontrollable causes offers the opportunity to rethink the salvage plan, hone necessary skills, and make and mend both tools and salvors. In the winter of 1925–1926 the S–51 salvage crew increased the cutting rate of the underwater cutting torch, improved underwater lights, developed the nonreactive nozzle for tunneling—a tool known in the Navy as the "*Falcon* nozzle"—and trained new divers specifically for the S–51 operation.

Operations were resumed in April 1926 with essentially the same salvage plan. The most important task was to place the pontoons. Several arrangements for pontoon placement were considered; the simplest was chosen. Eight pontoons were placed in pairs along the length of the submarine. Because the forward section of the submarine was still flooded, three pairs of pontoons were placed forward. A method of accurately placing the pontoons on the bottom was worked out empirically in Narragansett Bay. The method consisted of flooding each pontoon until it had about 10 tons of negative buoyancy and controlling its descent and final position by lines tended from the surface and under the submarine. Each pair of pontoons was troublesome, as only an inanimate object resisting human endeavor can be.

When all the pontoons were in place, preparations were made to raise the S–51. The attempt was scheduled for 22 June 1926. That morning the weather had so deteriorated that the only course open was to boost the pontoons to keep them slightly buoyant and lie clear until the weather moderated. Some of the pontoons had been boosted when huge bubbles began to break the surface and the bow of the S–51 and the two forward sets of pontoons appeared on the surface. A loss of control and buoyancy had occurred, causing the worst possible situation. With the bow up sharply, the aft compartments could not be dewatered and the chains would tend to ride forward, exacerbating a bad situation.

With the bow up and the sea rising, Captain King and Lieutenant Commander Ellsberg had a tiger by the tail. There was no choice but to blow the stern pontoons and the three stern compartments to bring the stern up. What happened has been described by Captain King.

> In about three quarters of an hour, ebullition over the stern of the wreck began and presently the stern pontoons appeared, and floated off with the wind and sea, as the pontoon chains ($2^{1}/_{2}$ inch) had parted, probably in succession. While blowing on the three compartments was continued some time longer, it was obvious that the stern could not be raised at that time.
>
> The wind and sea were still rising and the four bow pontoons were crashing and booming and battering each other badly. Consideration was given to attempting to drag the wreck but this was seen to be useless.[2]

---

[2] Captain Ernest J. King, USN, "Salvaging U.S.S. S–51." U.S. Naval Institute *Proceedings* (February 1927), p. 146.

Divers Smith and Frazier display the induction valve that they removed from the submarine S–51 after 4½ hours work on the bottom.

The pontoons were flooded and the wreck put back on the bottom.

The pontoons and rigging forward were such a mess that they were raised to the surface. The derrick barge *United States* was brought to the scene as a platform for repairing and making ready the pontoons.

The second attempt used a simplified method of pontoon placement. The chains were passed under the hull, centered and laid out with one-inch wires shackled to each end. The wires were passed up through the pontoon hawses and the pontoon placed as the mate pontoons had been previously.

On 5 July, with everything ready, S–51 was raised as per plan and lay in a chain cradle supported by pontoons. Tow toward the New York Navy Yard began, but was interrupted when S–51 struck Man-of-War Rock and broke her tow. The tow and pontoons that had broken loose were rerigged and S–51 was delivered into the New York Navy Yard at 11:30 p.m. on 7 July 1926. The salvage was complete. While the boat was on dock, the remains of the crew were recovered, but no repairs were undertaken; the hull damage was too severe for economic repair.

Salvage of the S–51 depended on diving. More than 500 dives were made on the S–51 in a depth—132 feet—that was considered quite deep. Much of the work required the divers to enter the sunken submarine. Tasks inside the submarine were practiced in full diving dress in the S–50, just as diving tasks had been rehearsed in a sister ship during the R–

6 salvage. At the time of the S–51 salvage, diving physiology was poorly understood and decompression schedules were rudimentary; in fact, decompression schedules were very different and much shorter than those in use today. Decompression sickness, the bends, was a major cause for concern, although only one serious case occurred during the operation. Extraordinary measures to care for the divers were taken. A physician experienced in hyperbaric medicine was on site, and a device developed at the Bureau of Mines to permit breathing of helium-oxygen mixtures for the treatment of decompression sickness was used on board *Falcon*.

Salvage of S–51 was the most complex and difficult salvage undertaken by the Navy to date and was comparable in difficulty to any salvage ever undertaken. Why did it succeed when the S–5 salvage—quite similar in depth of water, submarine type, availability of divers, suitable support ships, and salvage equipment—did not? The S–51 salvage succeeded for four reasons:

1. A well-conceived plan had been laid.

2. Leadership was strong and technical competence great; problems with both equipment and techniques were diagnosed and solved when they occurred.

3. The salvage plan was adjusted as the job proceeded and as difficulties were encountered, but the basic salvage plan and the operational goal was never altered.

4. The salvage force had competence, courage, skill, gumption, perseverance, and serendipity, and they worked hard.

After the salvage of S–51, a thorough technical report was prepared by Lieutenant Commander Ellsberg that analyzed both what went right and what went wrong in the operation. This meticulously detailed report was of great use to other salvors in future operations.

BENEFITS OF EXPERIENCE (S-4)

In an accident strongly reminiscent of S–51, S–4 (SS 109) sank after collision with USCGC *Paulding* (DD 22) on 17 December 1927, off Provincetown, Massachusetts. The submarine sank in 102 feet of water on a soft mud bottom. The tragedy of S–4 was that six survivors were trapped in the sunken hull but could not be rescued even though salvage forces were on scene just above.

This salvage effort was again under the direction of Captain Ernest King, but Commander Harold E. Saunders of the Portsmouth Navy Yard was assigned as salvage officer. Commander Saunders had been salvor of S–48 when that boat grounded in Portsmouth harbor. He was an unusu-

The salvors of submarine S–4 include (front, left to right): Commander Harold E. Saunders, Captain Ernest J. King, and Lieutenant Henry Hartley.

ally skilled naval architect and a meticulous planner. The salvage operation was headquartered on the *Falcon*.

The decision was made to proceed with the salvage immediately, although it was winter and weather delays would be frequent. The salvors were blessed with a somewhat sheltered position and, although it could not have been known when the decision to go ahead was made, an unusually mild winter. Undoubtedly influenced by King's experience with S–51 and Ellsberg's excellent technical report on the use of pontoons, the salvors decided to raise S–4 much like S–51. Many elements were alike in both efforts.

• The task force organization was virtually the same. *Falcon*, the only ship in both operations, was again the primary work platform.

• A similar mooring plan was used for *Falcon*.

• The salvage plan was similar in the use of pontoons and internal buoyancy to raise the submarine. The six pontoons built for the S–51 operation would raise S–4.

• The method of placing the pontoons was the same as the second method used in the S–51 salvage.

• A rehearsal model, in this case S–6, was available for all diving operations.

The lessons of S–51 had been learned well. The careful attention to detail in planning and use of techniques and procedures proven on S–51 ensured a smooth operation. The ship was raised and towed into Boston just three months after her sinking.

The loss of all hands on S–4, however, especially those surviving the accident only to be lost because there was no way to rescue them, gave impetus to the development of submarine escape and rescue techniques. This development, as well as confirmation of the value of thorough planning and detailed study of similar operations, were the legacies of the S–4 salvage.

Unlike S–51, which was scrapped after its salvage, S–4 was returned to service and served until 1936 as an experimental submarine for the development of rescue and salvage procedures.

DEEP-SEA SALVAGE (*SQUALUS*)

The best known of the U.S. Navy's submarine salvage operations was conducted on *Squalus* (SS 192) in 1939. Like S–51 and S–4, *Squalus* was salvaged by lifting with pontoons, but there are some significant differences that make the *Squalus* operation noteworthy. The boat was sunk in 240 feet of water, significantly deeper than any previous submarine salvage. Better equipment was available in the form of the McCann Submarine Rescue Chamber, which was used to rescue crew members, and helium-oxygen diving equipment that allowed divers to work more effectively in the greater water depths.

The salvage was planned and conducted in three distinct stages. Unlike previous pontoon salvage operations, control pontoons limited the distance the ship was lifted in any single lift and no water was removed from the hull in deep water.

A new submarine, *Squalus* (Lieutenant Oliver F. Naquin) submerged with the main engine air induction valve open and flooded the aft compartments on the morning of 23 May 1939 off Portsmouth, New Hampshire. *Falcon* (ASR 2) (Lieutenant Grant A. Sharp) was on site within twenty-four hours. On 24 May 1939, in the first and only use of the McCann Rescue Chamber, thirty-three men were rescued from the forward compartments in four trips. Although there was no reason to believe anyone was alive in the aft part of the ship, a fifth run was made to the aft torpedo room hatch on May 25. This run confirmed the flooding of the entire aft portion of the ship.

The decision to salvage *Squalus* was made immediately. Rear Admiral Cyrus W. Cole of the Portsmouth Navy Yard was designated commander of the salvage unit and Lieutenant Floyd A. Tusler (CC), was named salvage officer. A task unit similar in composition to those of the S–51 and S–4 salvages was organized, again with *Falcon* as the primary work platform. *Sculpin* (SS 191) was the practice submarine.

Because of the Navy's experience in submarine salvage and the availability of sufficient equipment, the salvage plan called for raising the *Squalus* with pontoons and her internal buoyancy, basically the same method used with S–51 and S–4. The depth of *Squalus* complicated the salvage problem. When pontoons and the vessel's own buoyancy are used, the exact locations of the centers of gravity and buoyancy cannot be determined; thus one end always rises first. If the rise of the upper end is not constrained, a sharp angle will result and air will spill from open bottom ballast tanks. To prevent a sharp angle, *Squalus* would be lifted a short distance, towed submerged to shallow water, and lifted again.

To limit the distance the submarine was raised on each lift, the pontoons were arranged at different levels between the surface and the submarine. When the uppermost pontoons reached the surface, their lift would be lost and *Squalus* would hang in midwater, supported by her internal buoyancy and that of the submerged pontoons. The upper pontoons were known as the control pontoons because they controlled the height of the lift. The pontoons were to be arranged athwartships at the bow and stern, with the greatest number supporting the flooded stern. Pontoon placement was handled by methods similar to those used previously, guided down wires that had been passed to chain slings passed under the hull.

The initial depth of *Squalus* sharply limited the amount of work that could be done by divers. The early days of the operation showed that air diving at this depth was not effective because of inert gas narcosis. The Navy Experimental Diving Unit had done a great deal of research work and some field work with helium-oxygen breathing mixtures. Navy Experimental Diving Unit divers, led by Commander Charles B. Momsen and Dr. A.R. Benhke, came to the scene with helium-oxygen diving equipment. As with any new or experimental technique, there were problems with the equipment, but they were solved and almost all diving was done with helium-oxygen equipment. A total of 648 dives were made during the *Squalus* salvage operation; there were only two cases of decompression sickness.

Even with the helium-oxygen equipment, diving time and the diving work was limited. The decision to lift with pontoons and ballast tank buoyancy only, and not to restore the buoyancy of the aft compartments, was based on limiting the diving work. A tunneling lance was developed for reeving the lifting slings under the hull, eliminating much of the hard diving work of tunneling. The lance, outfitted with a Falcon nozzle and

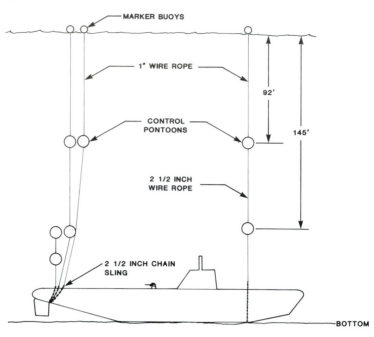

First lift.

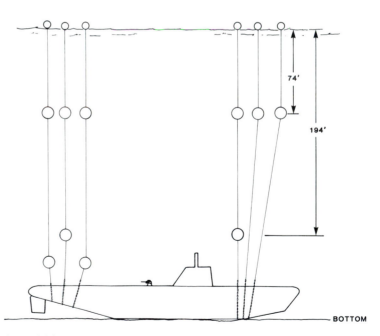

Second lift.

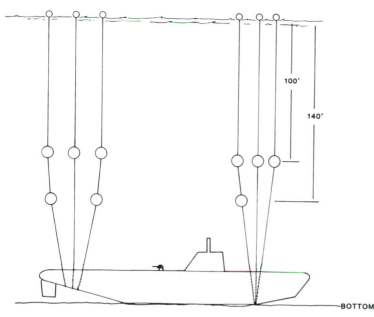

Third lift.

Pontoon arrangements for lifting *Squalus*: first lift, 13 July 1939; second lift, 13 August 1939; third lift, 17 August 1939.

its pipe sections curved to fit the hull, was guided by a diver on the deck of *Squalus* into the hole its water jet dug. Experience showed that the threaded connections between pipe sections tended to loosen, causing the tunnel to head off in directions unknown. This was solved by toggling the sections together. When the lance was completely around the hull, a wire snake ran through the lance and carried the reeving lines around.

All was ready for the first lift. Commander Momsen described what happened:

> At the end of fifty days work, connecting hoses, rigging pontoons, attaching bow and stern towing cables, the first lift was attempted. We raised the stern successfully then the bow. The bow came up like a mad tornado, out of control. Pontoons were smashed, hoses cut and I might add hearts were broken. It was the 13th of the month, July. Another 20 days of mopping up was required before we could again rig for another try. The second try was successful.[3]

---

[3]Commander Charles B. Momsen, USN, "Rescue and Salvage of USS *Squalus*." (Lecture to the Harvard Engineering Society, Cambridge, 6 October 1939).

Pontoons were rerigged for the second lift so that more positive control over the bow was maintained. *Squalus* was raised 70 feet and towed toward Portsmouth until she grounded. The pontoons were rerigged for lifting in the shallower water and *Squalus* was lifted successfully and towed to the final grounding site in 92 feet of water.

At this location all chafed hoses were renewed and two pontoons were rigged fore and aft at the stern. When the submarine was raised bow first, she was found to be transversely unstable. She listed heavily to port, dumped air from her ballast tanks, and sank. An attempt to lift the stern first failed because free water ran forward, making the bow too heavy. Two additional pontoons were rigged at the bow. *Squalus* was lifted and towed to Portsmouth where she was drydocked. Recommissioned as *Sailfish*,[4] she served in the Pacific throughout World War II.

Squalus was the last submarine salvage operation undertaken by the Navy before World War II. Among the many submarine salvage efforts up to this time, the deep-ocean raisings of F–4, S–51, S–4, and *Squalus* were truly remarkable operations that demonstrated expertise in seamanship, engineering, and diving. They were all independent events with no real thread connecting them. There was no permanent organization for marine salvage, particularly the salvage of submarines. The organizations put together for each operation were disbanded after the operation. There was no central office to analyze the work and formulate a program to ensure mistakes were not repeated or to advance salvage technology and readiness.

The greatest legacy of this work between the wars was the almost accidental establishment of a tradition of conducting complex salvage operations totally within the Navy and producing excellent technical reports. The latter allowed those who were interested to study the operations and to learn what did work and what did not. The experience gained in submarine salvage also provided background in the organizational and logistical requirements of salvage operations that would prove invaluable in developing World War II salvage forces.

Prelude to World War II

The number of technical articles published in professional journals gives evidence that the officers of the Construction Corps had considerable interest in salvage; however, the Navy continued to rely heavily on its contractor for salvage services. This situation appeared suitable be-

---

[4] Because of her origins, *Sailfish* was known among submariners as "Squailfish." Ironically and tragically, crew members of the sunken *Sculpin*, the submarine that had stood by *Squalus*, were aboard a Japanese transport sunk by *Sailfish*.

Four divers won the Medal of Honor for their heroism during the rescue and salvage operations on the submarine *Squalus*. Clockwise, from top left: Chief Petty Officers John Mihalowski, James H. McDonald, William Badders, and Orson L. Crandall.

cause, until just before World War II, the Navy was primarily a home fleet that, with a few notable exceptions, operated close to the United States. There was no apparent need for an extensive system of overseas bases, a complete Mobile Logistic Support Force, or integral salvage forces.

With the clarity of hindsight, it is now apparent that there was a costly drawback to the arrangement. With no integral salvage forces and only a limited towing capability (in 1925 there were only eight fleet tugs), the Navy did not develop a doctrine for supporting combat forces with salvage forces. As we shall see, without the doctrine and its own forces to implement it, the Navy lost too many ships early in World War II.

Omaha: Navy-Contractor Success

There were some successes for the system. The grounding of a cruiser in tropical waters illustrates how the Navy worked with its contractor during the pre-World War II years.

On 19 July 1937 the cruiser *Omaha* (CL 4), making 15 knots, grounded on a coral formation called Castle Island in the Bahamas, 389 miles from Miami. The *Omaha* salvage was a classic in the techniques used and in the cooperation among marine organizations. *Omaha* was in a hurricane area during hurricane season. The tide range was small and the tide difficult to predict. *Omaha* grounded on a typical reef, one made of a soft, porous material with no binding power that dropped sharply a few hundred yards offshore. The vessel was firmly aground, bearing on the reef along half her length with very little hull damage. She lay upright with a calculated 2,453 of her 8,993 tons supported by the reef. Although she had grounded at high tide, it did not make much difference.

The Technical Salvage Officer, Commander Melville W. Powers (CC), calculated that if 1,500 tons could be removed, the ship could be refloated by pulling. The forces began to gather. There were soon on the scene the Navy ships *Texas*, *Salinas* (AO 19), *Patriot* (a 98-foot tug), several destroyers, two Bird-class minesweepers, the seaplane tender *Lapwing* (AVP 1), and the submarine rescue ship *Mallard*; five Coast Guard ships; and two Merritt-Chapman and Scott salvage ships, *Killerig* and *Warbler*.

The salvage plan had three parts: (1) The ship would be stripped of all nonessential weight; (2) *Mallard*, *Warbler*, *Killerig*, the Coast Guard ship *Tampa*, and eight legs of beach gear would pull the ship; and (3) the destroyers would make high speed runs to generate waves that would cause *Omaha* to roll, both breaking the friction with the bottom and causing her to crush the coral, settle deeper, and gain buoyancy.

Beach gear is a standard tool for stranding salvage. One shot (15 fathoms) of heavy chain is bent onto a heavy anchor such as an Eells anchor, a special salvage anchor. The chain, in turn, is bent onto several

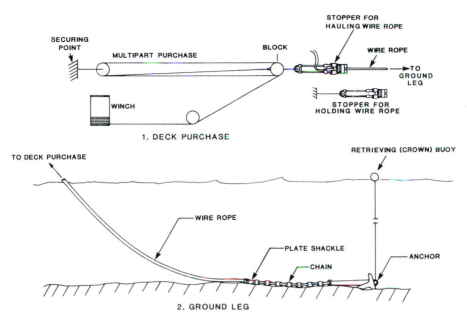

Typical beach gear leg.

hundred fathoms of 1⅝ inch-diameter wire rope. The anchor is laid in the direction toward which the grounded vessel is to be pulled, and the wire rope is taken aboard the grounded vessel or the salvage ship, where it is held on board by a wire rope stopper. Near this stopper a second stopper is passed on the wire. The second stopper is bent onto the moving block of a fourfold purchase rove with 5/8-inch wire rope. The purchase is firmly secured and hauled. When the purchase is hauled, the wire rope pulls up to 50 tons on the anchor.

The three-part salvage plan worked exactly as anticipated. All movable weight was removed from *Omaha* and taken on board *Salinas*. The destroyers found the optimum course and speed for wavemaking, and the salvage ships laid their beach gear and hooked up to pull. When all was ready on high water late on Tuesday, 27 July, the beach gear was set up tight and a pull was made while the destroyer *Mahan* (DD 364) steamed by rapidly as a wavemaker. *Omaha*'s head changed and the ship moved slightly.

The following day, with the destroyer squadron that had arrived in the early morning and the *Mahan* making waves, another pull was made. The vessel moved again, then stopped as the slight tide ebbed. Pulls on high water, each with some slight movement, were continued until the morning high water on 29 July, when *Omaha* floated free. The combined efforts of the Navy, Coast Guard, and a commercial salvor had been successful. *Omaha* got underway for Hampton Roads, Virginia, under escort of *Texas* and *Mallard*.

Of the four significant stranding salvages described above, three were difficult: *DeLong*, S–19, and *Omaha*. The fourth, the 1925 stranding of S–48 was relatively easy. For all, the Navy had provided engineering expertise in the persons of Commanders Hilliard, Saunders, and Powers, and Lieutenant Nelson, as well as much of the logistics support for the work. In the more complex jobs, a vital element in the equation for success—the specialized knowledge of salvage techniques and seamanship—was not resident in the Navy but was provided by a contractor with whom the Navy had a long and close relationship.

Toward a Permanent Navy Salvage Organization

Shortly after the refloating of *Omaha*, but completely unrelated to it, Merritt-Chapman and Scott made a business decision that would have far-reaching implications for the Navy. The Pacific Coast of the United States had always been hostile country for salvors. Geographic and sea conditions—the long, sloping beaches, treacherous bars, rocky coasts, heavy ground swell, offshore surf, and long-period seas—cause ships that go ashore to break up quickly. To be effective on the Pacific Coast, salvage assistance must arrive quickly and free the casualty without delay. For instance, when seven destroyers ran aground off Honda Point, California, on 9 September 1923, no attempt at salvage was made; no help could be provided in time. In 1938 Merritt-Chapman and Scott, after operating a salvage station at San Pedro for twenty years, announced to the Bureau of Construction and Repair that it was forced to close that station. T.A. Scott, then chairman of the company, explained that the company had lost money on the Pacific Coast for years and could no longer afford to maintain the ship and station there. The salvage ship stationed at San Pedro would be moved to the more lucrative Atlantic Coast to replace a ship recently lost at sea.

For the Navy the implications of this move were grave. In 1938 the bulk of the U.S. Fleet was concentrated in the Battle Force and the Scouting Force homeported in San Pedro and San Diego. The closing of the Merritt-Chapman and Scott salvage station at San Pedro and relocation of its salvage ship to the Atlantic Coast would mean that the bulk of the fleet would be without protection; no other company on the Pacific Coast was in a position to take up the slack.

The responsibility for negotiating with the salvors to remain on the Pacific Coast fell to the Assistant Chief of the Bureau of Construction and Repair, Captain Henry Williams. Captain Williams had the assistance of now-Captain Julius Furer, who had raised the F–4, and Captain Lewis

McBride. Captain Furer had become friends with Scott while both were on duty in Washington during the war. Despite direct negotiations between Scott and Furer and the offer of subsidies, Merritt-Chapman and Scott refused to reconsider its decision to withdraw from the Pacific. If the Navy was to have a salvage capability on the Pacific Coast, it would have to develop it internally. Scott himself supported this move and offered to assist the Navy in becoming familiar with the equipment and techniques of commercial salvage.

The development of a naval salvage organization requiring the commitment of personnel, equipment, and funds was beyond the authority of the Bureau of Construction and Repair. The participation of the Chief of Naval Operations and the Secretary of the Navy was required if salvage ships and naval personnel were to be provided. The advice of the Bureau of Construction and Repair was needed to answer the myriad of technical questions that would accompany establishment of a salvage force. The Navy purchased Merritt-Chapman and Scott's Pacific Coast salvage equipment and established the Navy Salvage Base, San Diego. The concept was that when the equipment was required, it would be loaded onto available tugs and minesweepers, while salvage personnel would be drawn from various commands. The base was established at the Naval Fueling Station at LaPlaya, where there were good pier and storage facilities and easy access to the sea. At the suggestion of Captain Furer, Lieutenant Commander William A. Sullivan was assigned as commanding officer of the new salvage base. He was an experienced naval engineer with some salvage experience, much of it obtained while he was assigned as Superintending Constructor, Shanghai. To assist him, and to form the basis of his salvage team, Sullivan had three men trained as divers.

Despite its long record in salvage the operation of a full-time salvage organization was a new Navy venture with many new problems. Merritt-Chapman and Scott had been handling the Navy's requirements for offshore salvage so well that the Bureau of Construction and Repair had little technical information on the subject. Starting from scratch, Sullivan studied salvage problems on the Pacific Coast and proposed methods for dealing with them. He developed an inventory of existing equipment along the coast suitable for salvage and the means for transporting it to salvage sites. Personnel to staff and operate the salvage system, however, were a problem. The rolls of the Naval Reserve were searched for qualified salvage officers. There were none. Recalling salvage officers on active duty in World War I was considered, but they were not only too few, but also believed to be too old for the rigors of salvage. If the Navy was to have salvors, it would have to grow its own. Meanwhile the clouds of war were darkening both the eastern and western skies and would soon place unprecedented demands for salvage on the Navy.

PEARL HARBOR

CHAPTER THREE

World War II Begins

Duraing World War II the United States built the most powerful land and naval force the world has seen. As part of the logistic support, the salvage forces were likewise the largest and most effective ever assembled. The sea was the means for moving men and material, its routes contested by powerful and determined enemies. Throughout the war thousands of salvage operations were undertaken, some huge and spectacular, some so small they scarcely rated a note in the ship's log, but all were important and all contributed to victory.

The United States projected its military and industrial power overseas into Africa and Europe and throughout the Pacific. As a result ships were damaged, and they, their cargoes, and crews had to be saved. Naval forces engaged the enemy and were hit; fires had to be put out, damage controlled, and damaged ships taken to repair bases. Troops were put ashore in huge amphibious assaults, and the transporting ships and craft sustained damage and required salvage service. Landing craft and ships required an entirely new kind of salvage. Retreating enemies left systematically blocked harbors that had to be cleared so material could move to Allied armies. Coastal shipping in the Americas needed salvage protection against normal seagoing hazards as well as the U-boat. Harbors and waterways in the United States had to be kept open so that the flow of material was not impeded.

Preparation for War

Since its early days as a modern naval force, the U.S. Navy had depended heavily on contractors for all but submarine salvage. During the mobilization for World War I, there was no coordinated and lasting development of naval salvage forces. Nor was there developed a doctrine for using salvage forces to support the fleet, tow damaged units to ports of refuge, and free blocked harbors. In the years before World War II, although some naval officers had salvage experience, when a casualty

51

occurred there was no expert to call. Those on the scene handled it as best they could.

When war is imminent, salvage of ships becomes a matter of vital national interest and thus a responsibility of the Navy. In full mobilization a maximum effort is required by the naval and merchant services. This effort cannot be made with the ships on hand for peacetime operations. A massive effort must be undertaken to put reserve ships in commission, build new hulls, and scrape the back channels for every floating object that can be used. The dramatic increase in shipping during wartime brings a concomitant increase in casualties from navigation accidents and especially from hostile action. The function of the ship salvage forces is to reduce the effect of these casualties by preventing the loss of the ships, their cargoes, and trained crews. It is far cheaper and quicker to refurbish damaged ships and return them to service than it is to build new ones. Through salvage thousands of tons of cargo may be saved for the war effort rather than lost to the sea. Through rescue, trained, seasoned seamen may be saved to carry the fight to the enemy.

The experience of the British early in World War II illustrated the value of salvage. The Royal Navy salvage operation started with few experienced people and so little equipment that pumps were rushed by escorted truck convoys from one casualty to another. There was strong opposition to salvage efforts from those who saw direct action against the enemy as the only worthwhile activity. Fortunately, the value of salvage was appreciated by those who knew that logistics is the key to sustaining a modern war. By the end of 1941 the British salvage force had saved more than twice the tonnage delivered in the same period by a fit and well-supported British shipbuilding industry. The lesson learned by an ally in the hardest school was there for the United States to see.

In addition to illustrating the value of ship salvage to waging a maritime war, the British experience also demonstrated the opposition put forward by those who understand neither the value nor the mechanics of salvage. Ship salvage services required in wartime are similar to the services salvage companies render in peacetime. There are, however, two important differences: (1) the wartime scale is much greater, and (2) the motivation is far different. In peacetime, the motivation for a salvage company is purely economic, and economic incentive governs the resources on hand, the areas of operation, and the jobs undertaken. For a nation at war the motivation for salvage is the saving of ships, cargoes, and crews—the economics of salvage be damned! Maritime operators and government officials, uneasy dealing with ship salvage in peacetime, have even more difficulty dealing with the overnight change in motivation and the new urgency for wartime ship salvage.

The scale of operations and the need to save ships and cargoes spurred the U.S. Navy's development of a salvage organization and its undertaking of salvage operations in World War II. The Navy involvement began shortly after German forces moved into Poland on 1 September 1939. Beginning on 2 October the Neutrality Patrol was initiated in a line roughly 300 miles off the coasts of the Americas. It grew in geographical extent and activity until the United States officially entered the war more than two years later. U.S. Navy ships, on a war footing, were placed in a combat zone with the task of preventing combat past an arbitrarily drawn line in international waters. These ships were truly in harm's way.

When the war in Europe started, the U.S. Navy had no salvage forces other than the hastily organized group that manned the San Diego Navy Salvage Base. In the international waters of the Atlantic, the core of what would later become the Navy Salvage Service—Merritt-Chapman and Scott—was insulated from the wartime increase in salvage activity. Enforcement of the Neutrality Act prevented combat operations and combat casualties in the primary area of operations, American waters, and contiguous international waters.

Those concerned with Navy salvage were not idle. Commander Sullivan and his group in San Diego, in cooperation with the Bureau of Construction and Repair, had drawn up specifications for virtually all important pieces of salvage equipment. Sullivan gave these specifications to the British who, in turn, placed large orders in the United States. Because of these orders U.S. manufacturers were tooled up and producing salvage equipment before the United States entered the war. As will be seen later in this chapter, industry was further stimulated in the summer of 1941 when Merritt-Chapman and Scott, acting under the authority of a Navy contract, placed large orders for salvage equipment.

The Bird-class minesweepers *Warbler* and *Willet*, operated by Merritt-Chapman and Scott as salvage ships since 1920, were reclassified and designated as salvage ships (ARS 11 and 12) by the Navy. Three other Bird-class ships were recalled from the Coast and Geodetic Survey Service and converted to salvage ships in anticipation of the yet unformed Navy Salvage Service. Two Navy-manned ships also entered salvage service: *Redwing* was recalled from the Coast Guard, designated ARS 4, and dispatched to Iceland; *Brant* went to Argentia, Newfoundland, for salvage service, forgoing formal conversion and redesignation to ARS 32 until after the start of hostilities. The groundwork was also laid for the shipbuilding programs that would build wooden- and steel-hulled salvage ships and several classes of seagoing tugs. Not the least important of the construction programs was the one that would produce salvage ships and tugs for the British under Lend-Lease through Maritime Administration contracts.

The fleet's logistic forces had had seagoing tugs for years. They were tugs of various designs and modified or converted Bird-class mine-sweepers, not a homogeneous class of ships operated according to a specific doctrine. In the 1930s it had become apparent that to fight a war in the Pacific, the area where the threat was thought to be the greatest, the U.S. Navy needed capable seagoing tugs to provide salvage services and undertake ocean tows that would be part of the logistics effort. It was with considerable foresight that the design of the *Navajo* (ATF 64)[1] class of fleet tugs was undertaken. The expertise of naval officers and the Bureau of Construction and Repair's naval architects was applied, and design recommendations were actively sought from industry. The result was a 3,000-shaft-horsepower, diesel-electric ship with an automatic tensioning towing engine—a large and powerful oceangoing tug that would serve the Navy well for many years. Three of these ships were authorized for the 1939 shipbuilding program. Almost seventy were built before the end of the war. They saw service in every theater. World War II was just the beginning for these ships; some remain in service at this writing, nearly fifty years after *Navajo* slid down the ways.

As the *Navajo*-class oceangoing tug was under design and construction, the Chief of Naval Operations took another step toward providing the salvage forces the Navy would need for the war. He directed the Chief of the Bureau of Ships (recently formed from the Bureau of Construction and Repair and the Bureau of Engineering) to do what was necessary to provide sufficient salvage services on the coasts of the United States and in the Atlantic and Caribbean. Commander Sullivan, who had established the salvage station on the Pacific Coast, was ordered to England in 1940 to survey the salvage situation and report how the British were coping with the salvage problems of the war. In what was expected to be Sullivan's temporary absence, Mr. Lebbeus Curtis, an experienced salvor who had recently completed building the harbor in Port Hueneme, was hired under a special contract to relieve Sullivan at the San Diego salvage base. While in Britain, Sullivan made an exhaustive investigation of the Admiralty salvage organization, and its facilities, ships, personnel, equipment, techniques, and industry arrangements.

The results of the investigation were a clear warning to the United States. The Admiralty lacked sufficient salvage ships, salvage equipment, and trained crews to deal with the casualties caused by having more ships at sea and by the U-boat war. Only those operations that could be accomplished promptly with high expectations of success were undertaken. Complicated or high-risk jobs were left undone despite the high cost of writing off the ships and cargoes. The greatest problems lay in

---

[1] This class of ship was originally designated as AT. The designation was changed to ATF on 15 May 1944 and has been ATF since that date. For simplicity ATF is used throughout this book.

people and ranged from a shortage of trained salvors to a lack of understanding of salvage by shipowners and government officials.

Prior to the war, the Royal Navy, like the U.S. Navy, had relied on commercial salvors to do most of its salvage work. As in the United States, the salvage industry in Britain was small. When war broke out, the Royal Navy found it necessary to take control of civilian salvage firms but allowed them to operate much as they had before the war. (A similar arrangement in the United States would later also solve a portion of the wartime salvage problem).

A comprehensive survey of salvage capability in the United States in 1941 showed that only one firm, Merritt-Chapman and Scott, was equipped to do offshore salvage on ships of any size. The company now operated five salvage ships and maintained five salvage stations, all on the Atlantic Coast. It was to the Navy's advantage to control these facilities. Thus a contract was required to allow the Navy to have its contractor conduct salvage operations on all ships under the control of the Department of the Navy, whether they were naval ships, public ships of the United States, or American or foreign merchant vessels. This would be a great expansion over previous contracts, which had covered only naval ships, but the Navy was without authority to make such a contract. Enabling legislation was rushed through the Congress and signed by President Roosevelt on 24 October 1941. This legislation allowed the Secretary of the Navy during war or national emergency to "provide, by contract or otherwise, necessary salvage facilities for both public and private vessels upon such terms as he may, in his discretion, determine to be in the best interests of the United States."[2]

The way was now clear to negotiate a contract for a Naval Salvage Service. But the storm of war broke upon the nation before the service could be established.

Wartime Salvage Requirements

Before examining the salvage work that the Navy carried out during World War II, it is well to look at the numerous conflicts that made up that war and the particular demands they made upon salvage forces. The wars in the Atlantic and Pacific were quite different, and these differences dictated the type and composition of salvage forces needed. In both areas the United States was projecting its power over long distances with complex logistics systems. Raw materials had to be taken to the places where they could be turned into the manufactured goods that would be transported to forward areas for direct support of combat operations. The sea

---

[2] Public Law 280, 77 Cong. 1st sess., 1948, Chap. 458.

was the only practical means of providing the logistic support. Except for a few attacks on shipping on the West Coast of the United States and on merchantmen that presented targets of opportunity, the Japanese directed their submarines against warships and made little effort to disrupt logistic efforts in the Pacific.

In the Atlantic, however, the Germans made a concerted effort to interdict and disrupt this support with their U-boats. Operation *Paukenschlag*, the German campaign against shipping on the American coast, began in January 1942. It was particularly effective in April, May, and June 1942 when U-boats in their "Happy Time" sank 120 ships, a fact not made public but generally known along the East Coast. Opposition of logistic shipping by an effective and determined German submarine force kept salvors busy with casualties. The U-boat campaign and the need to salvage casualties on the North Atlantic convoy routes resulted in the establishment and operation of salvage bases in Iceland and in Argentia, Newfoundland, and the development of the rescue tug as a distinct ship type.

The war in Europe was primarily a land war supported in traditional ways by naval forces. While Italian naval surface forces were effective early in the war, after the Battle of Cape Matapan in March 1941 they refused engagement and were essentially no threat. The potentially dangerous German surface navy was, in general, ineffective and well contained by the Royal Navy. The result was that the gun, torpedo, and air actions between warships that occurred throughout the war in the Pacific were not a salient feature of the naval war in the Atlantic. Salvage needs also differed. Ships were lost early in the war in the Pacific because salvage forces were limited and the understanding of how to use them to support combat operations virtually nonexistent. The need for salvage forces to directly support combat surface naval forces and their supporting air forces led to the development of doctrine in the Pacific that simply was not required in the Atlantic.

In both theaters, however, large-scale amphibious invasions were carried out. With the exception of the initial landings in North Africa, the invasions in the Atlantic and the Mediterranean were supported from reasonably close shore bases. In the Pacific distances from shore bases were much longer, requiring more mobile support, including salvage and emergency repair forces. Support of amphibious assaults in all theaters required salvage services for supporting ships and for the amphibious assault ships. A type of salvage that was new but common to both theaters was the salvage of landing ships and craft for the purposes of returning them to service and keeping the beaches clear for subsequent traffic. Because concentrations of ships were high and landings usually fiercely opposed, fire fighting was a common requirement during amphibious assaults and led to development of special fire-fighting teams. In amphibious operations, perhaps more than in any other type of operations, salvage was an extension of damage control beyond the ability of ships' crews.

Following amphibious assaults, great quantities of materials must be moved inland to support the assault forces. In the island campaigns of the Central and South Pacific, material could move inland across the beach. In North Africa and Europe the ancient and well-developed port system could be used for logistic support of assault forces. Retreating armies systematically blocked ports to deny their facilities to the advancing Allies. Early in the war, it was realized that harbor clearance would be a major activity of the salvage forces in direct support of combat. The organization and methods of harbor clearance, developed and honed in the European theater, were employed later in the war at Manila and Naha, where the Japanese were even more efficient at blocking harbors than the Germans.

One of the war's largest and most important harbor clearance operations was at Pearl Harbor, where casualties of the 7 December 1941 attack were salvaged for return to service or removed to clear valuable harbor space. Like the *Lafayette* salvage discussed later, the Pearl Harbor fleet salvage stands as a unique salvage operation not directly tied to the development of salvage doctrine. The importance of the Pearl Harbor clearance lies not only in the value of the ships salvaged and the base cleared of wrecks but also in the salvage experience gained by the U.S. Navy early in the war.

The Pearl Harbor Fleet Salvage

The Japanese air attack on Pearl Harbor left the U.S. Navy with a huge salvage problem. The sinking of or serious damage to the majority of the battleships present, as well as of numerous other combatants, left the United States vulnerable to further attack and unable to take offensive action against the powerful Imperial Japanese Navy. Priority at Pearl Harbor was given to salvage of ships that could be returned to the fleet quickly.

Despite the disheartening sight of a harbor filled with sunken, beached, burned, and damaged ships, there were some positive aspects to salvage work at Pearl Harbor.

• The shops and facilities of the navy yard were virtually undamaged.

• The naval staff that supported the operation for its duration was intact and functioning.

• Senior engineering officers and adequate junior engineering officers were available to give technical support to complex salvage operations.

• A major heavy-engineering contractor with special expertise in the underwater use of concrete, Pacific Bridge Company, was working for the Navy in Hawaii.

• Excellent local industrial support was available from Mr. Dillingham of Honolulu, who had hoisting barges and other waterfront equipment.

• Salvage equipment purchased by Merritt-Chapman and Scott under contract NOd–2263 was available for shipment to Pearl Harbor.

To these assets was added a fortunate coincidence. One of the few experienced salvage officers in naval uniform, Lieutenant Commander Lebbeus Curtis, USNR, who as a civilian had earlier been hired to run the San Diego salvage base in Commander Sullivan's absence, had arrived in Hawaii on 6 December en route to the Middle East for salvage work. Awakened by the bombing, Curtis dressed in his whites and hurried to Pearl Harbor; he was still working three days later in the same now-not-so-whites. His travel was discontinued and he remained in Pearl Harbor for several months until he was assigned theaterwide responsibilities as salvage officer on the Service Force Commander's staff.

The Pearl Harbor salvage efforts, under Rear Admiral William L. Calhoun, the Base Force Commander, began with fire fighting and pumping during the attack. The formal salvage organization was put into effect on 14 December under Commander James M. Steele. The salvage organization continued to be part of the Base Force until 9 January 1942, when Captain Homer N. Wallin, who was to remain in charge until completion of the salvage work, relieved Commander Steele, and the Salvage Division became part of the navy yard.

Rear Admiral William R. Furlong, who was made Commandant of the Navy Yard, took a great interest in and supported the salvage operations. The Salvage Division was given working space on the waterfront in the navy yard. Project officers were put in charge of each ship; specialists were put in charge of functions such as diving, ammunition handling, ordnance material removal, and administration. A staff of general assistants was formed.

The thrust of the effort immediately after the Pearl Harbor attack was to repair the slightly damaged ships and return them to service. This effort was undertaken by the Salvage Division, the navy yard, ships' forces, and the crews of the repair ships. By the middle of February the battleships *Pennsylvania* (BB 38), *Maryland* (BB 46), and *Tennessee* (BB 43);

the cruisers *Honolulu* (CL 48), *Helena* (CL 50), and *Raleigh* (CL 7); destroyer *Helm* (DD 388); seaplane tender *Curtiss* (AV 4); and repair ship *Vestal* (AR 4) were salvaged and in service or on their way to the West Coast for permanent repair. While the lightly damaged ships were being taken care of, work had begun on some of the more complex salvage problems. The same basic doctrine, namely, that ships that could be returned to service would be salvaged first, applied throughout the salvage work. Each ship was studied by the Salvage Division, which laid out the job, determined its requirements, allocated resources, and established priorities. Because the planning was thorough and all interested parties participated, there was little difference of opinion and friction as the work was accomplished.

The salvage problem as a whole in Pearl Harbor was complex, because most of the ships were large warships, minutely compartmented and filled with a variety of materials, many of which were inherently dangerous. As with most complex problems the solution lay in a series of straightforward steps.

The destroyer *Shaw* (DD 373), for example, in *Floating Drydock Number Two*, which sank beneath her, remained afloat with her bow blown off by a magazine explosion. Salvage required only cutting the bow away and pumping to control flooding through leaking bulkheads before drydocking. A false bow was fitted and *Shaw* sailed for Mare Island on 9 February 1942.

Floating Drydock Number Two had been sunk to protect her during the attack and suffered bomb-fragment and fire damage. She was patched, pumped, and returned to service by 25 January 1942. Full operation was achieved 15 May 1942.

The battleship *Nevada* (BB 36) was beached and flooded throughout after taking bomb, torpedo, and fire damage. Weight was removed and the hull was patched and pumped. *Nevada* sailed for Puget Sound under her own power on 1 May 1942.

The hulls of the destroyers *Cassin* (DD 372) and *Downes* (DD 375) were so badly damaged in the drydock where they lay that they were scrapped. Machinery and equipment were salvaged from the ships, sent to the Mare Island Navy Yard, and used in new ships with the same names and hull numbers.

California (BB 44) was partially cofferdammed, weight was removed, and the hull pumped out. She entered drydock on 9 April 1942, and sailed for Puget Sound on 10 October 1942. *West Virginia* (BB 48) was also partially cofferdammed by extending the shell and was extensively patched with concrete. Weight was removed and the ship floated with compressed air and pumping. *West Virginia* was drydocked for temporary repairs on 6 September 1942.

When *Plunger* fell off marine-railway blocks in an industrial accident, she presented a difficult problem for Pearl Harbor salvors. Photo courtesy David W. Genereaux.

The sunken harbor tug *Sotoyomo* was raised and returned to service by late summer 1942.

The submarine *Plunger* (SS 179), which was not present during the attack, fell off the blocks in the marine railway as the result of an industrial accident. She was hauled back into the water after removal of weight.

As the first major salvage operations at Pearl Harbor, *California* and *West Virginia* were important. They provided needed experience for the salvors and helped establish effective working relationships between the Navy and Pacific Bridge.

Two operations are particularly noteworthy: the salvage of *Oglala* (CM 4) and the righting and refloating of *Oklahoma* (BB 37). *Oglala*, flagship of the Mine Force Commander at the time of the attack, had a most colorful history. Launched in 1907, she had started life as the Fall River Line steamer *Massachusetts*; called into service during World War I, she became the minelayer *Shawmut*. In this role she participated in the North Sea Mine Barrage. After the war she was converted to a seaplane tender. In 1928 she was reconverted to a minelayer and given her final name, *Oglala*.

During the attack on Pearl Harbor, *Oglala* gradually flooded from concussion damage when a torpedo passed under her and exploded against the cruiser *Helena* (CL 50) moored inboard of her. The *Oglala* capsized to port with her masts and tophamper resting on Ten-Ten dock—some say the old lady sank from fright.

Oglala was considered a total loss and plans were made for her disposal. Three were rejected. Dewatering and floating the ship on its side with compressed air was rejected because the hull would not hold the air pressure required. Cutting her up using explosives was rejected because too few divers skilled in explosive cutting were available, crane services were better employed elsewhere, and there was danger from side effects of the explosives. Lifting with four barges was rejected because personnel and materials would have to be diverted to make the barges suitable for use as lifting vessels. The most practical scheme was to right *Oglala* and float her. *Oglala*'s behavior during the salvage showed she was no dignified elderly lady, but a cantankerous old harridan.

For the righting operation, ten 80-ton submarine salvage pontoons were sunk inboard; chains from the pontoons were passed under the hull and attached above water on the starboard side. Compressed air at 3 pounds per square inch was pumped into the hull and jacks positioned between the dock and the deck edge. *Oglala*'s cantankerous nature exerted itself on the first righting attempt. In full view of a number of distinguished observers, including Fleet Commander Admiral Chester W. Nimitz, chain connections to the hull failed, and several of the pontoons rose to the surface when they were blown. The pontoons were rigged more securely and a second try made. This try was successful and *Oglala* was rotated to a position from which she was righted to a list of about 7 degrees. (The method used to refloat *Oglala* was essentially the same as that used on *California* and *West Virginia*.)

The shell was extended upward with a deck edge cofferdam. Unlike the partial cofferdams on the battleships, that on the old minelayer extended around the entire deck edge. The timber fence was extensively shored from the inside by divers. Pumps were placed, and pumping began. The water level was being reduced satisfactorily when a butt joint in the cofferdam failed because the construction crew had not followed the design specifications. The cofferdam was repaired and the ship floated. The salvors expected that both longitudinal and transverse stability would be critical when the ship was afloat. Although steps were taken to improve stability, little could be done. Two days after the ship was raised, a pump stopped in the middle of the night; inflow exceeded outflow. The ship went down by the bow, water rushed forward, debris blocked other pump suctions, and *Oglala* settled to the bottom again. Shores were tightened, leaks patched, and the ship floated, only to have another field deviation

The minelayer *Oglala* proved one of the most difficult salvages at Pearl Harbor.

from design specifications cause the cofferdam to fail once more. The damage was repaired and the ship refloated a third time.[3]

Oglala had one more trick up her sleeve. A fire broke out when fuel for a gasoline-driven pump splashed on a hot exhaust line during refueling. The fire quickly spread to the oil-soaked cofferdam timbers and was extinguished only by efficient fire fighting. After this final mishap *Ogala* was drydocked in Pearl Harbor for temporary repairs. She later sailed to the West Coast under her own power, where she was converted to a diesel engine repair ship.

If the salvage of *Oglala* was the most unpredictable operation, the salvage of the battleship *Oklahoma* was certainly the largest and most complicated salvage job undertaken at Pearl Harbor and possibly anywhere during World War II. Unlike the majority of ships sunk in the

---

[3] Because of her ups and downs, the salvors had begun to call *Oglala* "Otis" after the famous elevators.

attack, the *Oklahoma* was not intended to return to service. During the attack the ship had capsized to port after taking several torpedo hits, and had come to rest 151 degrees 30 minutes from upright in about 40 feet of water with the starboard bilge above water and the upper portside embedded 20 to 25 feet in the mud. The aft two-thirds of the ship lay on firm soil; the forward one-third floated in soft mud.

The decision to salvage was based on the need to clear the berth and to use material from the ship. As with *Oglala* the only feasible method of removal was to right and refloat the vessel. To do this, the work was divided between the Navy and the heavy engineering contractor, Pacific Bridge Company, with the Navy retaining overall responsibility. The contractual arrangements allowed Pacific Bridge to get suitable priorities on material and hire the right people for the job. The work was carefully planned before starting. Models were used extensively during planning and throughout the salvage both to simulate the behavior of the ship and to plan internal work.

The primary force for righting was to be applied by twenty-one electric winches anchored on concrete foundations on Ford Island and hauling on thirty-four part purchases. The purchases pulled 3-inch wire ropes that were led over headframes about 40 feet high. The wire was

The capsized battleship *Oklahoma* was righted by building headframes on her side and pulling with purchases and winches mounted ashore on Ford Island.

then divided into four one-inch "cat tails" and secured to strong points on the hull. The function of the headframes was to increase the righting arm during the initial part of the righting operation. Martin-Decker strain gauges on the hauling part of the righting tackles determined the pull being exerted and allowed the pull on the twenty-one purchases to be balanced. Placing pontoons on the outboard side to increase the righting moment was considered but rejected because the advantage gained did not justify the work necessary to rig the pontoons.

Calculations and model tests had shown that it would be necessary to reduce the weight and provide buoyancy with its accompanying righting moments during the righting operations. Fuel was removed. The hull was divided into seven zones, each of which was secured by divers entering through the bottom. Because of the extreme difficulty of diving in the interior of an inverted ship, dives were carefully planned, with routes and tasks worked out on models. Air locks were fitted over the access openings in each section; hull openings were made tight; and water was forced lower by compressed air. Salvors could then enter the hull and do additional securing work that was not practical for divers. The air locks were removed and fittings and manifolds for control of air pressure in the hull were installed before righting. The air bubble in the hull would be effective until the ship had reached an inclination of 108 degrees.

To reduce the possibility that the hull might slip sideways rather than rotate, 2,200 tons of coral soil was deposited near the bow section to stabilize the soft mud. When all systems and their controls and monitoring devices were in place, righting began on the morning of 3 March 1943. The righting of *Oklahoma* by parbuckling was a controlled, orderly process that proceeded with care and deliberation. During the pulling process stops were necessary for repairs, clearing of wire from the winch drums, and airlifting soil from the inboard side. When the hull had reached an inclination of 68 degrees, the wires were clear of the headframes; the headframes were removed and floated clear. At about 40 degrees, wire terminations were rerigged from the hull strong points to multiple straps around heavy shipboard structures.

As the ship approached the upright position, divers jetted away soil under the starboard side and salvors topside began to remove weight and prepare for pumping. On 6 June, with the ship inclined at 2 degrees 10 minutes, the righting effort was declared complete and the refloating phase of the work began.

This stage of work resembled that required for *California* and *West Virginia*. A battleship with extensive torpedo damage was essentially upright resting on the bottom; the problem was to restore buoyancy and float the ship. Patching included large steel and wood open-topped cofferdam patches with the bottom sealed with concrete, as well as more

Rear Admiral Furlong (left) and Captain Francis H. Whittaker inspect the purchases used to haul *Oklahoma* upright.

conventional types of patches. To assist in establishing transverse stability during refloating, a wooden-shell extension cofferdam, which had been effective on other battleships and on *Oglala*, was built around a portion of the main deck. The hull was pumped and came afloat on 3 November 1943. Excluding the drydocking that followed, the salvage of *Oklahoma* took eighteen months. That this mammoth job was a success is a testimonial to the men who carried it out with care, deliberation, and confidence, particularly Captain Wallin, the Salvage Officer; Captain Francis H. Whitaker, the Salvage Superintendent; Lieutenant Commander James W. Greely, Ship Superintendent; and Lieutenant Commander H.E. (Pappy) Haynes, Diving Officer.

Only two victims of the Pearl Harbor attack remained unsalvaged: *Arizona* (BB 39), whose forward magazine had exploded during the attack, and *Utah* (AG 16).[4] The latter had capsized and presented about the same

[4] Formerly BB 31.

The new fleet tug *Navajo* and the older tug *Tern* fight fires on the doomed battleship *Arizona* two days after the attack on Pearl Harbor. *Navajo* and her sister *Seminole* provided salvage services around Pearl Harbor early in the war.

salvage problems as *Oklahoma*. There was no thought of raising *Arizona* because her military value was now slight, but a large amount of material including ordnance material and stores were removed. She remains in Pearl Harbor as a memorial to the men who lost their lives in the attack.

Utah was scheduled for salvage following *Oklahoma*, and usable materials were removed. The wreck was partially righted with the same parbuckling system as employed on *Oklahoma* when reevaluation of the work showed that the gain was insufficient to justify the work. Salvage was abandoned and *Utah* left where she lay. In 1956, when a new carrier berth was needed, consideration was given to removing *Utah*. However, the heavy funding requirement, and lack of material, proper personnel, and time required militated against the work and nothing was done. *Utah* also remains in Pearl Harbor.

The contribution to the war effort made by the ships salvaged at Pearl Harbor, well-documented in many publications, is the best known and most important result of the huge salvage effort there. Other benefits, equally important in the narrower context of naval salvage, and perhaps more subtle, came from the work. An unusual feature was the concentration from the outset on removal of ordnance material. There was little or no air defense in Pearl Harbor on 7 December and the attack vividly demonstrated the potential of air attacks. The removal of antiaircraft batteries and ammunition from the sunken ships for installation around the island was a necessary step in building an air defense system for the island. In addition to putting the salvaged antiaircraft batteries to immediate use, directors, ordnance instruments, small arms, and the like were removed from the casualties and preserved.

Because all the ships salvaged, with the exception of *Oklahoma*, were to see war service, care was taken in cleaning the interior of the hulls. A caustic solution was found effective in washing down compartments and removing the fuel oil coating the interior of the reclaimed ships. Particular care was given to preserving and restoring electrical equipment, especially the electric drive on a number of the battleships. A great deal of experience was gained quickly in methods of preserving such equipment.

A number of problems encountered in the Pearl Harbor salvage occurred because the ships were warships, outfitted and provisioned for war and sunk in combat.

• Fuel escaped in great quantity, either burning and causing extensive damage or coating the interior of spaces, thus presenting a fire hazard and requiring removal.

• Volatile liquids, including gasoline fuel for boats and airplanes, was another problem. As is too often the case, the lesson was learned the hard way with a vapor explosion aboard *California*.

• Other fire hazards existed among the ships' normal stores and the materials that sailors, pack-ratting anything potentially useful, had aboard.

• The ships all contained ammunition, some of major caliber, that had to be removed; fortunately, because of long experience and extraordinary care, no mishaps in handling ammunition occurred.

• Unexploded Japanese ordnance, particularly bombs converted from armor-piercing shells, were on board and in the vicinity of the salvage work, and had to be dealt with.

• A particularly unpleasant aspect of the salvage was the presence of human remains, which were located and removed throughout the work. Methods were devised for the removal of remains with as little disruption of work as possible.

During the salvage of *Nevada*, two men were lost to toxic gases generated by the decay of organic matter. After this incident, steps were taken to warn of the presence of toxic gases, particularly hydrogen sulfide, and to protect workers from them. Steps were also taken to guard personnel from exposure to hypoxic atmospheres in the interiors of ships. The toxic gas lessons learned in *Nevada* were widely disseminated, and measures were taken in salvage operations around the world wherever the situation recurred.

The sunken ships at Pearl Harbor became a testing ground for salvage equipment and techniques. Deep-well pumps proved to be very useful in the battleship salvage, particularly because the battleships were fitted with trunks into which the pumps could be lowered. It was brought home clearly that the watertight subdivisions in older ships and in ships that have experienced heavy shocks cannot be depended on. Many long hours were spent chasing down leaks. The hazard that large undivided spaces present to longitudinal and transverse stability was shown in *Oglala*, especially on that ship's open mine deck. The uncontrolled movement of a large mass of water contributed to one of that ship's resinkings. Fortunately, the battleships were finely divided and free surface could be controlled with some precision.

The salvor's maxim that safety precautions are written in blood has been proved many times over. It is nowhere more true than in salvage operations where safety margins are smaller than in ordinary heavy engineering work. The necessity for field personnel to follow all design and safety specifications exactly was graphically demonstrated when deviations from design specifications caused *Oglala* to sink twice and when varying from safety specifications resulted in an explosion with loss of life in *Oklahoma*.

Primarily due to the insistence on safety of Lieutenant Commander "Pappy" Haynes, almost 20,000 hours spent underwater by Navy and contractor divers during Pearl Harbor salvage operations resulted in no serious Navy casualties and only one contractor casualty.

Because Hawaii is basically a nonindustrial island group more than 2,000 miles from the mainland and the naval base at Pearl Harbor was comparatively new, there was a general shortage of materials throughout the salvage operation. Shortages of proper pumps at the outset, and lumber and fastenings throughout were particularly acute. Civilian engineers and mechanics were in short supply in Honolulu and at the navy yard. The shortage of personnel was most strongly felt in the welding and carpentry trades. Had all the needed people and materials been readily available, the salvage work would have been much easier, just as the salvage of F–4 in these same waters would have been enhanced by a well-developed industrial base. Few salvors, however, have found themselves with all the resources required to do a job without some improvisation. The ability to make do and exercise imagination achieved the desired result for those who completed the salvage work at Pearl Harbor.

The numerous lessons of the Pearl Harbor salvage were universally applied throughout the war and undoubtedly prevented the costly experience of relearning them in later operations. Fortunately, this extensive and complicated work came at the beginning of the war and the Navy's salvage forces were organized so that dissemination of information was rapid.

The Navy Salvage Service

While Pearl Harbor was still reeling from the 7 December attack and the huge salvage operation was getting started, events were in progress that would bring about establishment of the Navy Salvage Service and profoundly influence the structure and development of the American salvage forces during World War II.

On 11 December 1941 contract NObs–36 establishing the Navy Salvage Service was signed between the Bureau of Ships and Merritt-Chapman and Scott. This contract provided that:

- The contractor's ships would be chartered to the Navy.

- The contractor's salvage equipment and salvage stations, other than the Staten Island station, would be leased to the Navy.

- The facilities of the Staten Island station would be available to the Navy.

- The contractor would operate the chartered ships and equipment and any other ships and equipment it was assigned.

- The contractor would train salvage personnel.

- The contractor could conduct its customary harbor clearance and inland salvage operations independent of this contract. However, if the Navy felt such an operation was in the interest of national defense, it could be conducted under this contract.

- All salvage operations would be carried out on a no-cure, no-pay basis unless specifically directed otherwise. A fixed price would be paid for the charter of the ships and lease of the equipment, management and consulting services, and the use of the Staten Island station.

- The contract would be managed by a naval officer reporting to the Chief of the Bureau of Ships. This officer, to be known as the Supervisor of Salvage, would be colocated with the contractor and would have the right to attend meetings of the contractor's board of directors and to convene meetings of the contractor's executives and technical employees.

With the contract in place, Commander Sullivan was designated Supervisor of Salvage on 13 December 1941, and an office established adjacent to the contractor at 17 Battery Place, New York City.[5] In Novem-

---

[5] Ironically, these were the former German consular offices.

ber 1942 now-Captain Sullivan was temporarily ordered overseas to take charge of harbor clearance operations in North Africa. Commander Bernard E. Manseau was appointed to act in his absence. Two years later, as a captain, Manseau became the Supervisor of Salvage and held the position until it was reclaimed by Commodore Sullivan in early 1946.

Range of Operations

The basic operating policy of Navy salvage had three primary parts. The Navy Salvage Service was responsible for offshore salvage operations along the Atlantic and Pacific Coasts, in the Caribbean, and off Panama and Alaska. The naval districts were responsible for salvage operations in inland waters. The fleets were responsible for overseas operations.

To utilize all available resources most effectively, the Navy Salvage Service, basically an operator of fully equipped and specialized salvage ships, worked primarily in offshore salvage. Its salvage ships did no harbor or inland salvage and towed no disabled ships into port unless other facilities were unavailable or inadequate. The important function of towing into port ships damaged or distressed at sea was initially performed by tugs attached to the naval districts.

The distribution of tugs under this system made it impossible to bring the correct quality and quantity of resources to bear on the large groups of casualties that sometimes resulted from submarine attack. In addition, the wrong type of tug was frequently put on a job. To correct the problems, which were inherent in this type of organization and had caused the loss of ships and cargoes, all available tugs were organized into the Navy Rescue Towing Service. The service, operating only on the Atlantic Coast, was under the direction of Mr. Edmond Moran of New York's Moran Towing, an experienced towing industry executive who had been enrolled in the Naval Reserve for this purpose. The service functioned under the command of Commander Eastern Sea Frontier. With the centralized control of rescue tugs under an officer who knew tugs and their capabilities, conditions rapidly improved and successes grew.

Fighting the major fires at sea that accompany salvage in wartime was not the responsibility of the Navy Salvage Service. When fires were beyond the capacity of the salvage ships to control, fire fighters were provided from centralized groups available at short notice from fire-fighting schools. Joint wartime naval and civilian fire-fighting efforts are described later in this chapter.

During the war the Navy Salvage Service operated twelve salvage ships. Three of these—*Relief*, *Resolute* and *Killerig*—were owned by Merritt-Chapman and Scott. Five others were converted Bird-class minesweepers: *Warbler* (ARS 11) and *Willet* (ARS 12) had been on bare boat

The Navy Salvage Service salvage ship *Rescuer* was wrecked during salvage operations on the Soviet ship *Turksib* at Seal Cape, Alaska.

charter by Merritt-Chapman and Scott for some time; upon execution of NObs–36 they were transferred to the Navy and placed in the custody of the contractor. *Viking* (ARS 1), *Crusader* (ARS 2), and *Discoverer* (ARS 3) had been operating with the U.S. Coast and Geodetic Survey before the war. *Accelerate* (ARS 30), *Harjurand* (ARS 31), and *Rescuer* (ARS 18) were privately owned ships requisitioned by the War Shipping Administration. All were in constant service throughout the war except *Rescuer*, which was wrecked near Seal Cape, Alaska, during salvage operations on the Russian ship *Turksib* in December 1942.

When *Viking* went into service early in 1942, Merritt-Chapman and Scott again found itself with a West Coast salvage station. *Viking* operated from San Diego and San Pedro throughout the war. Additional West Coast stations operated at Port Angeles, Washington, with *Discoverer*, and at Kodiak, Alaska, until the loss of *Rescuer*.

The Navy Salvage Service handled over 700 assignments including 498 major salvage operations. The bulk of this work was conducted during the height of the German U-boat campaign in old and slow ships carrying little or no armament. The jobs involved such diverse types of salvage and encompassed such diversity that no job was typical. Several operations illustrate the magnitude and complexity of the work.

In the morning fog on 28 June 1942, SS *Stephen R. Jones* (4,387 gross registered tons, 354.2 feet), en route to a convoy assembly point with a cargo of coal, struck riprap on the bank of the Cape Cod Canal. The vessel swung across the canal, capsized, and sank. The canal was effectively blocked, and shipping was forced to make the trip through U-boat infested waters outside the cape.

The following day the Navy Salvage Service undertook the clearance at the request of the Army Corps of Engineers. Commander Sullivan and Captain W.N. Davis of Merritt-Chapman and Scott flew to the scene. What they found was disheartening. The swift currents in the canal made diving impossible except for very short periods at slack water. To cut up the wreck and remove it conventionally would take at least eight months, an unacceptably long time. An alternative method was to flatten the wreck with explosives and pound it to the bottom to below the project depth. This method would be fast, but it threatened the nearby Bourne Bridge. Nevertheless, divers placed charges at slack water from dawn to dusk. The first charge was fired on 4 July. Bourne Bridge was carefully monitored, and charges were gradually increased from the initial 350 pounds to 1,450 pounds.

By 11 July there were 28 feet of water over the wreck and about half of the canal could be navigated by small vessels. While work continued during July, seven hundred twenty-two vessels made transits of the canal. The job was declared completed on 31 July; the entire wreck was blown down to 32 feet. The rapid removal of Stephen R. Jones as an obstruction was commendable, but proving the utility and efficiency of explosives for such work was an even more important result. The technique pioneered would soon prove itself in harbor clearance overseas.

An operation in New York harbor found the Navy Salvage Service employing more conventional techniques. SS El Estero with 1,400 tons of explosives on board caught fire on 24 April 1943 and was scuttled by the Coast Guard in Upper New York Bay near Robbins Reef Lighthouse. The Navy Salvage Service entered the picture the following day. They found the wreck with only her superstructure above water, across the tide and listing 18 degrees.

The salvage plan called for a cofferdam completely around the deck of the vessel and removal of all masts, sampson posts, houses, and obstructions to a height of $7\frac{1}{2}$ feet above the main deck. Only as much cargo as was necessary to place the pump suctions in the holds would be removed. Work on removals and cofferdam fabrication at the Staten Island station began on 3 May. By 7 September removals were complete and the cofferdam was installed. In the early morning of 10 September pumping began with six 10-inch pumps suspended from gallows frames. As the ship became buoyant and righted herself, she was pulled toward the shore with two legs of beach gear. Difficulties with stability, which occur when a ship with its deck completely immersed refloats, were avoided by keeping the ship in contact with the bottom. At the end of the day *El Estero* rested securely on a shoal with more than 6 feet of freeboard. The cofferdam was removed, the pumps relocated, and the ship floated and delivered to the War Shipping Administration on 17 September.

This job could be accomplished quickly with the optimum salvage plan because the work was located close to a major industrial center where all sorts of materials were available and facilities existed for building and handling the cofferdam sections. If the job had been in a remote location, a different approach, probably one that had a lower chance of success and was more time consuming, would have been required. The work on *Stephen R. Jones* and *El Estero* was in relatively protected waters. That was not the case with most of the wartime salvage work.

Fully one-third of the operations of the Navy Salvage Service involved tankers. Typical was the operation on the SS *Oklahoma*. The Texas Company tanker *Oklahoma* was almost new when she was attacked with torpedoes and gunfire by a submarine on the night of 9–10 April 1942. The 9,624-gross-tonnage, 510-foot ship carried a mixed cargo of petroleum products—low- and high-octane gasoline, kerosene, fuel oil, and diesel oil. She was left stern down and bow afire 5 miles from St. Simons Island, Georgia. When the salvage ship *Willet* arrived on 11 April, the salvors found the forecastle still burning and the stern resting on the bottom in 66 feet of water. She was listing 38 degrees to starboard. Salvors boarded on 13 April, put out the fires, and began to rig portable air compressors. The salvage plan was straightforward: hold the wreck with beach gear; patch the holes; cofferdam pumproom doors; and tap into the cargo piping to blow air into enough tanks to raise her for towing into sheltered waters.

The salvage plan worked as expected and the vessel was delivered to her owners on 25 April, even though the salvors had taken two days away from the *Oklahoma* to assist another tanker. During the salvage a particular effort was made to save the scarce cargo of refined petroleum products; some had to be jettisoned but the majority was saved by blowing it into tanks that were still intact.

The increase in wartime shipping meant that more ships were at sea; and larger numbers of ships required more trained and experienced seamen than were available. Many farm boys were at sea. The large number of ships with low levels of crew experience led to larger numbers of noncombat salvage cases. Typical of these was the new Liberty ship *Gaspar De Portola* on the last leg of her voyage from India to New York. *Portola* grounded on Quena Suene Bank in the Caribbean. After jettisoning 1,500 tons of ore and discharging 1,600 tons of jute, burlap, and hides to another vessel, she was freed by the tug *Arsiz* and the Navy Salvage Service ship *Killerig*.

Throughout the war the Navy Salvage Service performed every kind of salvage service with every possible technique. The service also performed two additional functions. The first of these was the removal of menaces to navigation along the Atlantic and Gulf Coasts. This work was normally the responsibility of the Army Corps of Engineers, but the large number of shipping losses exceeded the capacity of the corps. Arrangements were made for the Navy Salvage Service to handle the problem. Salvage of the wrecks and obstructions was not required; they were to be demolished. So that salvage ships would not be diverted from their normal duties, the Chief of Naval Operations assigned a number of small craft to the Salvage Service. A total of sixty-four assignments were completed, resulting in the elimination of the most serious menaces to navigation.

For its second additional function the Navy Salvage Service kept several experienced salvage men standing by in New York City. When vessels were in distress in remote places where assistance could not easily be provided, or when information was so sketchy that critical decisions could not be made, one of these troubleshooters was dispatched to the scene. They ranged from Brazil to Newfoundland and from England to Tokyo Bay, often taking charge at the scene and doing the job with the resources at hand. Typical of their work was the case of SS *Warren Delano*. This ship grounded near Buoy 8 in the Houston Ship Channel carrying a cargo of ammunition. Salvage operations by the War Shipping Administration succeeded in moving the ship 100 yards but left her hard aground. The Supervisor of Salvage dispatched a Navy Salvage Service trouble shooter. Upon arrival the salvor began to assemble from local sources the heavy ground tackle needed to float the ship. Using this improvised beach gear and scouring with the tug *Sands Point*, he had *Warren Delano* afloat a little more than two days after his arrival.

A few months before the establishment of the Navy Salvage Service, contract NOd–2263 was let to enable Merritt-Chapman and Scott to purchase with Navy funds the additional equipment that would be needed. This method of procurement took advantage of the contractor's experience, business contacts, and sources of supply. From the material and purchases made under contract NObs–2263, two carloads of salvage equipment were drawn for delivery to Pearl Harbor in December 1941 and January 1942. Salvage equipment was provided by the same means for outfitting the first four commissioned naval salvage vessels: the fleet tugs *Cherokee* (ATF 66) and *Menominee* (ATF 73) and the salvage ship conversions *Redwing* (ARS 4) and *Brant* (ARS 32). As the war continued, the demands for salvage equipment became too great for the contractor's sources of supply. The Bureau of Ships, therefore, undertook the acquisition of specially designed salvage equipment, while the contractor continued to acquire commercially available items. The Supervisor of Salvage then supplied materials on request to the contractor.

Organizational Problems

In general, personal relations between the contractor and Navy people were harmonious and fruitful to both. Each side made an effort to understand and accommodate the other. However, there were some problems in operating a large-scale contractor effort in support of a huge naval endeavor.

On only one occasion did the conduct of the contractor's people require disciplinary action. *Rescuer* (ARS 18) was wrecked following a party on board while the ship was engaged in salvage operations in Alaskan waters. Although the Bureau of Marine Inspection investigated the incident and saw fit to take no action, the master and salvage officers were nonetheless discharged. Following this incident, the Navy Salvage Service was withdrawn from Alaskan waters, and work there was carried out by Navy vessels.

Problems with communications were also encountered. The contractor's communications procedures and private coding were not compatible with naval practice. There was some contention over the responsibility for sending Naval Salvage Service messages, and in certain areas local commanders forbade the salvage vessels from breaking radio silence under any circumstances. The problems, which were largely in the nature of growing pains, disappeared when the Chief of Naval Operations directed the Navy Salvage Service to use the wartime communications procedures that had been standardized for merchant ships.

The no-cure, no-pay system, intended as the primary means of compensating the contractor, didn't work. The War Shipping Administration underwrote most of the wartime risk insurance on American hulls, while commercial insurers carried marine risks on hull and cargo and some cargo war risk. In November 1942 an agreement was reached that all Navy claims against the War Shipping Administration would be waived. American commercial underwriters then refused to negotiate claims because of the lack of information about War Shipping Administration interest in various shipping ventures. Further, the underwriters took the position that, because salvage was being undertaken as part of the war effort, the elements of risk by the salvor and encouragement to continue—traditional in determining salvage awards—ought not be considered. Underwriters also reasoned that the government's need for the cargoes outweighed the value of the cargoes themselves; thus costly attempts at salvage were warranted although they were not in the interest of private owners. There was even an argument that, because the Navy had an overriding interest in all maritime matters, there should be no charge for Navy services. The Navy could not assent to this for two reasons: (1) underwriters, whose premiums already took into account contractor payments for salvage, would be unduly enriched if all claims were waived, and (2) the Navy had no legal authority to waive claims.

On 9 January 1943 the Supervisor of Salvage was directed to institute a new system that allowed claims to be settled according to standard per diem rates. Underwriters formally accepted the procedure in June and established the Special Salvage Committee to deal with the claims of the Navy Salvage Service.

The Navy Salvage Service quickly provided a professional salvage organization for home waters. It made a definite contribution to the war effort by salvaging ships and cargoes under terms fair to the government and to industry. It operated in a constantly expanding role because it was managed with flexibility and a desire to get on with the job. The Navy Salvage Service, the Navy Rescue Towing Service, and the use of fire fighters to combat fires at sea—all dispatched from a single headquarters— demonstrated the effectiveness of centralized control of limited resources to assure that assets appropriate in both size and ability were assigned to a task.

The Salvage of *Lafayette*

Undoubtedly the largest, best known, and arguably most important single-ship job undertaken by the Navy Salvage Service was the salvage of *Lafayette* at Pier 88 in New York City.

The French liner *Normandie* (1,029 feet overall, 65,000 displacement tons) had been requisitioned by the United States on 16 December 1941. Later that month she was transferred to the Navy Department and renamed *Lafayette*. While work was underway to convert her to a troop transport, she caught fire on 9 February 1942. The New York Fire Department was competent at fighting both land and shipboard fires, but there was serious concern that the fire would spread to the city. Captain Simmers, the Naval Engineer on the Third Naval District staff, and Captain W.N. Davis of Merritt-Chapman and Scott made a plea that the fire be allowed to burn itself out and that the New York Fire Department stop pouring water into her. Fire Commissioner Walsh understood the problem, but declined to take action without the concurrence of Mayor La Guardia. The mayor, in turn, wanted to hear from the Naval District Commandant, Rear Admiral Adolphus Andrews. Admiral Andrews could not personally state that the ship would capsize and declined to take responsibility for the decision to stop fighting the fire.

Captain Simmers and Fire Commissioner Walsh made another strong plea to the mayor, who now became convinced that the ship might well capsize. La Guardia went to the telephone and called President Roosevelt. After hearing the story, the President replied hotly that he couldn't make the decision from Washington. That did it. The mayor said, "The Navy won't take responsibility for the possible spread of the fire. The President won't take any responsibility. Put the fire out." The Fire Department did.[6] The ship capsized during the fire-fighting efforts, coming to rest that evening on her port side at an angle of just under 80 degrees. The 400-foot-wide slip in which the ship lay was between two 1,100-foot piers. The bow lay 180 feet north of Pier 88, and the rudder was slightly under the pier, having broken some pilings during the capsizing. The forward third of the ship rested on a rock ledge; the aft two-thirds was in mud of various densities. She was flooded up to her waterline. The wreck was in a position where it inspired considerable comment from the press and the public, and made two of the longest berths in New York harbor useless. Expert testimony given in subsequent litigation and based on close examination of the ship during salvage indicates that had the fire been left alone, damage would have been limited to portions of the upper three decks.

On 24 February 1942 jurisdiction over the wreck was assumed by the Bureau of Ships and immediately assigned to the Supervisor of Salvage, who began to investigate the feasibility of salvage. Captain John Tooker, a salvage master with long experience with capsized ships, was assigned as salvage officer by Merritt-Chapman and Scott.

Because of the public interest in the wreck, its potential contribution to the war, and the critical position in which it lay, the Secretary of the Navy appointed a special nine-member commission to make recommendations concerning the disposition of the wreck of *Lafayette*. The commission was requested to answer two questions:

> Should this vessel be raised or should it be disposed of as scrap in her present condition, and, if the latter, what method is considered most practical?
>
> If it is determined to raise the vessel, when she is afloat should she be scrapped or should the consideration of her disposition after raising be left for study until she is afloat?[7]

---

[6] Shortly after the call to the President, Captain W.N. Davis, head of Merritt-Chapman and Scott's Salvage Division, not knowing what had gone before, found the Mayor and demanded they stop pouring water into the ship. La Guardia, in no mood to listen, refused to respond. Davis, a crusty seaman and man of action, grabbed La Guardia by the lapels and lifted him off the ground. This was a mistake. The mayor had a policeman lock Davis in a nearby cold storage room, where he was forgotten until after dark. When he was released, Davis walked off the pier and returned to his office. He refused to have anything to do with the *Lafayette*, its salvage plan, or refloating.

[7] Bureau of Ships, *Salvage of* Lafayette, NAVSHIPS 250-880-21 (Washington: Navy Department, 31 October 1946), appendix C, p. 7.

The commission received thousands of suggestions on how the vessel should be raised. The letters were reviewed by engineers who found that many of the ideas were good, but that most recommendations were made either without complete knowledge of the conditions or required a temporary repeal of the laws of physics. Salvors have found it wise not to count on such suggestions.

Many bona fide experts in salvage, construction, and related fields were asked to explore all possibilities to arrive at the soundest solution. A number were discarded as impractical. It was determined that the vessel could be raised, and that the cheapest, fastest, and most certain method to do so was to right and refloat her in one operation by pumping. It was estimated that the operation could be completed in less than two years for about $5 million. On 1 May 1942 the commission reported:

> The vessel should be raised.
>
> Considering the uncertain future needs of the war effort, the committee feels that a decision as to whether the ship should be reconditioned and for what purpose should not be made at this time. Such a decision should await the development of future war conditions and needs as the salvage of the ship grows nearer. Since there is a possibility that the war emergency may make the reconditioning of the ship desirable, every reasonable effort should be made to expedite the salvage.[8]

---

[8] Ibid.

Lafayette, formerly the French liner *Normandie,* lies capsized in her ice-filled berth at Pier 88, New York City.

The Supervisor of Salvage was directed to begin work on the salvage of the *Lafayette* on 17 May 1942. Since the capsizing, work on the ship had been restricted to removing the superstructure, installing scaffolding, removing fire hazards, and defining unknown conditions. The size of the job dictated that special measures be taken to prevent overloading the resources of the Navy Salvage Service and detracting from its mission of offshore salvage. The job was performed under contract NObs–36, but an independent organization was set up using as few of the Merritt-Chapman and Scott staff as possible and actively involving the Supervisor of Salvage in the management of the job.

Two factors were critical to the salvage plan. The first was the bearing strength of the soil under the vessel. Bearing pressures had to be kept low enough during the operation, especially during the righting, to prevent the ship from settling deeper into the mud. Comprehensive analysis of soil samples under Professor Karl Terzaghi at Harvard University showed that the ship rested on sufficiently strong material to prevent anything other than minor settlement. The second critical factor was the ability to divide the ship into compartments and to make them sufficiently watertight for pumping. Hundreds of open ports on the port side had to be closed from inside the ship because the fluidity of the mud made closure from the outside impossible. Only after four months of removing mud by airlifts did the soil become firm enough so that a hole dug under a port would last long enough for the port to be patched.

Chemical and biological hazards were of particular concern. Asphyxiating and toxic gases generated by decaying organic matter have often been a problem in ship salvage; a large amount of such material was left in *Lafayette* when she capsized. In addition, city sanitary sewers discharged into the river near the location of the ship, but shutting the sewers down would be impractical and prohibitively expensive. The chemical firm of Bull and Roberts was hired to monitor bacterial pollution and assess the danger of infection to divers. Based on the experience with gases gained in the ships being salvaged at Pearl Harbor, the salvage team established a program to ventilate, monitor, and clean compartments. The precautions were extremely effective. Because of the experience at Pearl Harbor and with *Lafayette*, the Bureau of Ships contracted with Arthur D. Little, Inc., to produce a *Safety Manual for Ship Salvage Operations* that found wide application in training and in the field.

The plan for righting and refloating *Lafayette* by pumping had thirteen general operations.

1. Removing the superstructure and the promenade deck.
2. Trimming the promenade deck in preparation for patching.

Captain John Tooker, a veteran salvage master with Merritt-Chapman and Scott, was assigned responsibility for the salvage of *Lafayette*. Captain Tooker's folding patch, developed on this job for the many ports in *Lafayette*, is known to generations of Navy divers.

3. Removing all joiner work bulkheads, movable equipment, woodwork, and inflammable material inside the ship.

4. Closing, concreting, and bracing sixteen cargo ports and three hundred fifty-six air ports.

5. Removing approximately 10,000 yards of mud.

6. Cleaning out all machinery spaces.

7. Ascertaining the strength of all decks and bulkheads.

8. Installing timber and concrete bulkheads.

9. Shoring decks.

10. Making the intermediate deck tight.
11. Removing part of the pier and driving fender piles.
12. Making detailed strength and stability calculations.
13. Installing and arranging ninety-eight pumps.

During the righting operations it was necessary to control the relative positions and movements of the ship's centers of gravity (including entrained water) and buoyancy. It was also necessary to control trim, safeguard transverse and longitudinal stability, and limit bearing pressure. This task required fine control of the pumping. It was accomplished by constructing bulkheads to divide the ship into fourteen watertight compartments, making the hull as tight as possible, and removing all loose material. Closing the hull required hundreds of patches, ranging from the folding Tooker patches, developed especially for the *Lafayette*'s ports by veteran salvage master John Tooker, to some of the largest patches ever used in salvage. Throughout the operation, care was taken to reduce infectious and toxic pollution in the ship caused by nearby dumping of sewage and the decay of organic material in the ship. A tremendous amount of construction, patching, and shoring work by divers was required under conditions that were hazardous and generally undesirable.

To secure absolute control of the longitudinal movement of the ship, special moorings were installed. In these moorings 5-ton, 2-drum winches hauled standard beach gear purchases to pull 40 tons on each of the twelve mooring lines. The mooring lines did not help in righting the vessel, but controlled and positioned her during refloating.

As compartments were made watertight, they were pumped slightly to determine the extent of leaks. Despite the careful preparation, long hours of searching out and stopping leaks were required in almost every compartment. Most of the troublesome leakage developed through scupper and plumbing drains. The last stages of making the compartments watertight merged into the final pumping operation.

Compartment testing continued through July 1943, and on 2 August an overall pumping test was made. On 4 August the final pumping began. There was no urgency to rush the operation, so pumping proceeded deliberately with constant checks and repairs, some of them major. The ship was afloat by 15 September. Thereafter, pumping continued to remove as much water as possible from the ship, to control massive leakage that had developed in one compartment, and to prepare the ship for delivery to the naval district commandant.

Following her delivery the decision was made not to refurbish *Lafayette* for use as a transport, and the ship was eventually scrapped. One of the factors that influenced the decision was the size of the ship. Many

Captain Bernard E. Manseau (left) shows Rear Admiral E.L. Cochrane (center), Chief of the Bureau of Ships, and Rear Admiral Joseph J. Broshek (right), Chief of the Maintenance Division, around the *Lafayette* salvage site during the first stages of the righting operation.

believed it unwise to transport an entire infantry division in a single ship as the Cunard liners *Queen Elizabeth* and *Queen Mary* were doing because the potential for loss if the ship was attacked was too great.

The salvage of *Lafayette* was a huge job, skillfully done with a minimum of interference with other work and at a reasonable cost. But the most important product of the salvage was its contribution to the development of skilled Navy and civilian salvage officers and divers.

The projected manning of a large force of commissioned U.S. Navy salvage ships and harbor clearance units required a large number of trained Navy salvors. The salvage of *Lafayette* also required large amounts of manpower. A logical solution to the problem was to establish schools for training both Navy and civilian salvors at Pier 88, where classroom and administrative facilities existed in the pier buildings, and to use *Lafayette* as a training aid. Trainees could supply some of the job's manpower while they gained practical experience. These salvors ultimately played leading roles throughout the war in clearing harbors, salvaging warships and merchant vessels, and carrying out emergency repairs in forward areas.

Navy Salvage Training

Through its contract (NOd–2263) with Merritt-Chapman and Scott, the Navy had already acquired one of the four elements its salvage force needed for a worldwide naval war—equipment. The most important element, human resources, was not so easily come by. The conventional wisdom of the day argued against any attempt to train salvors in a brief period. The only way to train salvors, the thinking went, was in the school of experience, with about twenty years required to produce a salvage officer. But the luxury of time was not available to the Navy; extraordinary steps to produce salvors were necessary.

Although the Navy had trained salvors for many years and was a world leader in diving technology, there was no formal salvage training. The small group that established the San Diego salvage base in 1938 had collected a quantity of salvage information from various sources, classified it, and prepared a series of lectures on salvage and underwater work. There was, as yet, no forum for its use.

In 1939 the Navy had decided to establish a salvage school to train experienced engineering graduates from the Naval Reserve and artificers in salvage. Equipment was assembled and candidates selected. Pearl Harbor was chosen as the site for the school, but its establishment was delayed by concern that support of the facility would tax the capabilities of the relatively small naval base on the island. On 7 December 1941 sixty prospective salvors in San Francisco were awaiting a decision on where their training was to take place. Forgoing formal training, these officers and men were immediately shipped to Pearl Harbor to begin work on the casualties of the attack. In addition, officers with the requisite technical background were assembled from other stations and shipped to Pearl Harbor in early January.

The need for large numbers of trained salvors was now urgent. Taking advantage of the opportunity presented by the *Lafayette* salvage, schools for both civilian and Navy salvors were established at Pier 88 in New York City. Initially, one civilian salvage master was called back from offshore work, and two officers were brought in from the Pearl Harbor clearance to form the nucleus of the faculty. Commander Sullivan assisted by giving lectures at the school. With the demand for salvors developing rapidly, the school was soon operating twenty-four hours a day, seven days a week. Training was sometimes terminated abruptly and a class ordered into the field in response to an immediate need; at other times students awaiting assignments participated in ongoing diving and salvage work, and on a number of occasions assisted the Navy Salvage Service with removal of menaces to navigation.

The students were given a combination of classroom and practical

Commander Carl Holm (left) discusses the *Lafayette* salvage with Lieutenant Clarence M. Hart, a member of the first graduating class at Pier 88. Photo courtesy Rear Admiral C.M. Hart.

training in basic naval architecture, blueprint reading, ship construction, salvage seamanship, salvage techniques, demolition, diving physics and physiology, and underwater work methods. All were trained as divers and made qualifying dives to at least 150 feet. The curriculum was constantly updated by reports from the field, since lessons learned in salvage operations were passed on immediately.

Initially, officer trainees were engineering graduates with several years' field experience and a Naval Reserve background. No significant problems were encountered in training these officers. Later, when the demand for

Officers of the first class of the Navy Salvage School at Pier 88 gather before scattering to all theaters of the war. Photo courtesy Rear Admiral C.M. Hart.

salvage officers required the training of less technically oriented or less-experienced people, the curriculum was modified. Two of the problems in training enlisted personnel are worthy of note. The Bureau of Medicine and Surgery first set age 28 as the maximum age for entering salvage training. This proved unrealistically low, both in terms of the availability of qualified candidates and the untapped ability of older candidates to handle the physical demands of diving. The limit was subsequently raised to age 35.

The other problem had no easy solution. Candidates for salvage training were taken from deck and artificer ratings, and continued to hold these ratings after receiving salvage training. Enlisted salvors were assigned and advanced mostly through their rating rather than by their knowledge and skills in salvage, their actual primary job. Attempts to establish a salvage mechanic rating were not successful until after the war. An emergency service rating of Salvage Mechanic was established, but was suspended a short while later. Debate on whether or not to establish a diver rating continues even today.

During World War II the Naval Training School (Salvage) at Pier 88 trained more than twenty-five hundred officer and enlisted salvors at a cost of about $320,000. Most of the graduates were Navy men, but there were some Army and Coast Guard personnel, and officers and men from Allied navies. The Bureau of Ships kept a record of the training and experience of the graduates so that when particular skills were needed, the most qualified men could be nominated. These salvors participated in operations in every war theater and made an immeasurable contribution to the Allied victory.

Fire Fighting

Fighting fires caused by battle damage was another task that required direct attention. Early operations showed that fire, especially fires resulting from battle damage, would be a major problem. In the first days of the war, the New York Fire Department interested Rear Admiral Edward L. Cochrane, Chief of the Bureau of Ships, in a new fire-fighting development—a nozzle that atomized the water stream into a fine spray or fog and cooled the fire more efficiently than a solid stream. This nozzle was a weapon of great effect against shipboard fires.

In addition to providing the Navy with the most modern fire-fighting technology, the New York and Boston Fire Departments formed cadres to establish fire-fighting schools at naval bases in the United States and overseas, much as Merritt-Chapman and Scott had provided the cadre for establishing the Salvage School at Pier 88. The schools trained fire fighters to professional standards for the fire-fighting teams on the salvage ships, and also trained sailors who served on the damage-control parties of every ship in the fleet. The civilian fire departments worked with the Bureau of Ships to develop portable fire-fighting equipment and chemicals for carrying on ships and to fit out the various classes of salvage ships and tugs with off-ship fire-fighting tools. The program was remarkably successful. In the latter part of the war, ships survived after much more damage than those lost in the early months.

Salvage Ships

A third element the salvage force needed was ships designed and outfitted for salvage. Salvage ships and their characteristics had been discussed by Commander Thomas B. Richey (CC), in his 1925 monograph, *Ship Salvage*;[9] however, the Navy had not developed a program for salvage ship construction. A survey made shortly before the war among flag officers to determine their ideas on salvage ships revealed there was no consensus. The need to develop and construct the different types of ships required for various tasks led to the initiation of a major design and shipbuilding program. An important feature of the program that constructed salvage ships was the close cooperation and sharing of designs and construction priorities between the British and Americans.

---

[9]Richey, Commander Thomas B. *Ship Salvage*, Technical Bulletin No. 2–25 (Washington: Bureau of Construction and Repair, 1925).

Eight main types of salvage ships were built during World War II. The first step toward the development of a salvage fleet had actually been taken with the authorization of the initial group of the *Navajo*-class fleet tugs (ATFs) for the 1939 shipbuilding program. These ships were all-purpose, long-range, seaworthy, powerful, diesel-electric[10] tugs well suited for operations with combat forces. Their automatic tensioning towing winch made them particularly suitable for taking in tow ships that had been disabled at sea. They were also good for long-distance towing of all types of ships and craft. For fire-fighting and combat operations they were generally provided with additional salvage equipment and crew.

These fleet tugs were built in two classes: twenty-eight *Navajos* and forty-one near-sisters—the *Abnakis*. The two classes were distinguishable primarily by their outer appearance, the *Abnakis* being stackless. These ships proved to be an outstanding design. Because they were available throughout the war, they were the primary salvage ships in all theaters. The only criticism leveled at these ships was that they were too good. Some felt that because their specifications approximated those of warships, the tugs were unnecessarily large and powerful and their equipment of too high a standard, making them more expensive than necessary. If cheaper ships had been designed, it was argued, it would have been possible to build more and alleviate the tug shortage in all theaters. To this day the question of proper specifications for Navy salvage ships remains open as nonsalvage-experienced engineers and operators continue to drive the operational-requirements process.

Auxiliary tugs (ATAs) were steel-hulled, single-screw, diesel tugs with approximately half the horsepower of the fleet tugs.[11] They were designed for major towing operations and had a large radius of action and considerable endurance. These ships were fitted with the minimum facilities for fire fighting or salvage expected of a seagoing tug, and were best suited for use in reserve areas or just outside a combat zone. In this service they could relieve fleet tugs towing disabled vessels to a repair base, thus enabling the more salvage-capable ship to return to the combat zone.

Similar in size to the auxiliary tugs, rescue tugs (ATRs) were wooden-hulled, single-screw, steam tugs originally designed to assist vessels disabled at sea and in submarine-infested coastal waters. These ships were extremely well fitted for fire fighting, with moderate salvage facilities and extra accommodation for rescued crews. They were excellent sea boats

---

[10] When the *Navajo* class of fleet tugs was designed, the use of diesel propulsion for tugs was in its infancy; tugs had previously been steam powered. The Dutch firm L. Smit commissioned four tugs, including the then world's largest tug, *Zwarte Zee*, that demonstrated diesel-powered tugs were superior in power, endurance, and economy.

[11] Auxiliary tugs (ATA) were originally built as ATs in the same numerical series as the fleet tugs (ATF). They were designated ATA on 15 May 1944. Except for two ships, auxiliary tugs were not given names during the war.

with good towing power, but were sharply limited in their radius of action. These rescue tugs were well employed in supplementing fleet tugs in combat areas where fire was a major hazard and cruising endurance was of secondary importance. Fifteen were transferred to the Royal Navy.

Perhaps the most important wartime salvage ship program was that which developed the ARS type of salvage vessel. Converted Bird-class minesweepers and other suitable hulls acquired from various sources comprised one group of these ships. Most were operated by the Navy Salvage Service because they lacked sufficient accommodations for naval manning. They were fitted out for the specialized work of ship salvage in coastal waters and were not especially suitable for towing. Two ships, *Redwing* (ARS 4) and *Brant* (ARS 32), had Navy crews. For salvage operations using these two ships, it was necessary to put additional salvage crew on board and provide sleeping accommodations on deck or wherever else possible.

Nine salvage ships of the *Anchor* class (ARS 13 through 17, 28, 29, 35 and 36) were 183-foot, twin-screw, diesel-electric, 1,200 horsepower, wooden-hulled ships. The first wooden salvage ship, *Anchor*, was commissioned in March 1943; the last, *Vent*, was commissioned just thirteen months later. They were built as salvage ships for service in distant waters and carried a full salvage crew and allowance of salvage equipment. They were somewhat limited by a small cruising radius and wooden hulls, but served in all theaters. Several wooden-hulled salvage ships were built for Britain as BARSs; two of these, *Weight* (ARS 35) and *Swivel* (ARS 36), were commissioned in the U.S. Navy.

The steel-hulled salvage ships (ARS 5 and 38 classes) were built in the United States to both American and British specifications. They were 213-foot, 3,000 horsepower, twin-screw, diesel-electric ships with a long cruising radius, quite different from the contemporaneous British *King Salvor* class. They were designed as salvage ships with adequate storage for salvage machinery and equipment. Initially, they were equipped with a powered wire reel for towing, but when it was found that the ships could be used interchangeably with fleet tugs for all towing, automatic towing winches were diverted from the auxiliary tug (ATA) program and installed on the steel-hulled salvage ships.

In addition to features for offshore salvage, these ships were fitted with rollers and tackle for lifting over the bow, making them useful in harbor clearance. The steel-hulled salvage ships were considered so valuable that operational doctrine developed during the war called for stationing them outside the combat zone where they would not be exposed to unnecessary hazard but would be available for any major salvage situation. Twenty-two of these ships saw service in the U.S. Navy. Fourteen were of *Diver* (ARS 5) class, and six of the slightly wider *Bolster* (ARS 38) class. The latter, with a greater beam, was more stable, had a larger lifting capacity, and had more room for stowage of salvage equipment. Two of four ships built for the British[12] were retained and commissioned in the U.S. Navy as *Clamp* (ARS 33) and *Gear* (ARS 34). After the first steel-hulled ARS, *Clamp*, was commissioned in August 1943, the ships saw service in the Mediterranean, Atlantic, and Pacific theaters. Like the fleet tugs, the steel-hulled salvage ships were an extremely successful design, remaining in active service well into the late 1980s, when this chronicle ends.

Although not constructed expressly for salvage, the various classes of net tenders found considerable utility in salvage operations. These vessels, which were wooden or steel hulled, with some British designs among them, were intended to lay and tend submarine nets protecting harbors and anchorages. They were never fitted out with salvage equipment but operated extensively placing moorings and making lifts over their horns in harbor clearance operations.

Four ships were converted from landing ship, medium (LSM) hull to salvage-lifting ship (ARS(D)), especially suited for harbor clearance operations. These ships were given full suits of salvage equipment and fitted with horns and purchases for lifting up to 365 tons in harbor clearance work. Additionally, the bow doors were welded shut, and salvage shops were laid out on the former vehicle deck. The salvage-lifting ships were intended for harbor clearance operations expected to follow the invasion of Japan. They were not completed in time for war service.

Three ships were converted from LST hulls to salvage base ships (ARS(T)s) designed to function as mobile salvage bases. These ships, which mounted 25-ton cranes and carried over 300 tons of salvage equipment, were assigned to combat salvage and harbor clearance units. Additionally, ex-*W.R. Chamberlain*, later *Tackle* (ARS 37), was briefly designated ARS(T) 4 in 1945.

Submarine rescue ships had first been commissioned in the Navy when six Bird-class minesweepers were fitted for submarine rescue service in 1929. The rapid expansion of the submarine force and the development of more complex technology for submarine rescue led to the design of a class of submarine rescue ship in the 1930s. Five ships of *Chanticleer* (ASR 7) class were ordered in 1940 and six additional ships were ordered in 1944. These eleven ships were the largest tug-type vessels operated by the Navy; not all were completed before the war ended. Because of the

---

[12] Two ships, *Caledonian Salvor* (BARS–1) and *Cambrian Salvor* (BARS–2), were transferred to Great Britain under Lend Lease and assigned to Australia. The names of the ships reflected the Scottish and Welch backgrounds of Judge Thomas Clyne and Captain Sir John P. Williams, who were leaders of the Australian salvage effort. Both ships had long careers in commercial salvage in other parts of the world after the war.

demand, three ATF hulls were also completed as submarine rescue ships. The principal value of these ships in salvage lay in their ability to support deep diving with helium-oxygen breathing mixtures. During the war they primarily supported submarine operations.

With amphibious assault one of the prime characteristics of World War II, the salvage of landing craft became important—either to repair and return the landing craft to service or to remove them from the beaches so they did not block across-the-beach movement of men and material. No ships or craft were developed specifically for landing craft salvage; however, several 157-foot oceangoing ships—landing craft, infantry, large (LCI(L))—were modified for fire fighting and salvage work. In the Atlantic these were dual-purpose vessels that sometimes delivered assault forces and then turned to salvage work. In the Pacific they carried so much salvage gear that the dual role was impractical; they were strictly salvage craft. Larger landing craft were also fitted out for salvage. Landing craft-tanks (LCTs) were fitted with shear legs to assist in lifting or righting landing craft and one landing craft, mechanized (LCM) in each group carried patching and pumping material and a salvage crew.

Salvage Doctrine, Organization, and Management

By the time the United States entered the war, the development of three of the four necessary elements of salvage—ships, men, and equipment—was well underway. A varied and successful program to meet these needs would continue throughout the conflict. The shipbuilding program had begun building and converting ships, and would adapt them as lessons were learned in the hard school of combat salvage. The practical salvage experience and training at Pearl Harbor and New York's Pier 88 were producing the critical nucleus of men. The Bureau of Ships and Merritt-Chapman and Scott, working closely with industry, were developing and procuring needed equipment. For the salvage forces to be fully effective, however, much new ground had to be plowed. The expectations for this new component of the fleet, the doctrine for its operation, its organization, and its management procedures had yet to be determined.

In the days immediately preceding the war, salvage responsibility was concentrated in the Bureau of Ships. In the spring of 1941 Admiral Samuel M. Robinson, Chief of the Bureau, and Rear Admiral Joseph J. Broshek, Chief of Maintenance, assigned Commander Sullivan as head of the Navy salvage effort with the title Chief of Navy Salvage. In his new capacity, Sullivan set out to organize the Navy salvage effort and to incorporate engineering as an integral part. Sullivan later took on additional duty as Supervisor of Salvage and managed the Navy Salvage Service. Thus Sullivan wore both the technical- and operational-management hats. As a natural outgrowth of this arrangement, and of Sullivan's later personal involvement in salvage operations primarily in Europe, a close relationship developed between the Bureau of Ships and operational salvage forces in the European theater.

The same close relationship did not exist between the Bureau of Ships and salvage forces in the Pacific. As soon as he could be spared from Pearl Harbor salvage work, Commander Lebbeus Curtis was designated Mobile Salvage Engineer on the staff of Rear Admiral William L. Calhoun, the Service Force Commander. There was no corresponding position in the Atlantic Fleet. From the time the commands of Commander in Chief, U.S. Pacific Fleet, and Commander Service Force, U.S. Pacific Fleet, were established in nearby buildings at Makalapa overlooking Pearl Harbor, many officers, including the salvage officer, occupied positions on both staffs. This symbiotic relationship between the staffs continued until the newly established Naval Surface Force absorbed the Service Force in 1975.

In both theaters the principle of centralized control of salvage was established. This approach made the most effective and economical use of men and equipment because it permitted:

• Coverage of an extremely large geographic area by a relatively small organization.

• Rapid delivery of men and equipment to handle short-duration jobs.

• Assignment of the best-qualified men and most suitable equipment to specific jobs.

• Development of a corps of trained and dedicated salvors by providing a workload sufficient to hone skills through experience and to prevent diversion to other activities.[13]

• Allocation of resources commensurate with changes in location and intensity of activity.

Each salvage job presents its own unique problems requiring specialized equipment and skilled personnel. Experience during the war showed that distribution of skilled personnel and equipment was not likely to be uniform. For instance, an abundance of personnel skilled with explosives might be needed to clear one port while another port might require those skilled in heavy rigging. Highly specialized equipment is needed only for particular conditions. Centralized control and assignment of assets during

---

[13]During the war, if specialized manpower was not kept fully employed in its specialty, it would be diverted or shanghaied to other uses. Salvage organizations were known to engage in this practice.

the war allowed a small inventory of such equipment to be maintained and transported where it was required. Similarly, while all salvage people received general training in the basic techniques and principles of salvage, many became highly specialized as their skills, interests, and experience grew; careful and continuous tracking of key people and their assignments meant the best available human assets from a relatively small pool could be assigned to the right job. Thus efficiency in handling men and resources assured that salvors' skills were maintained and that the salvage organization did not use manpower in one place that could be employed more effectively elsewhere. The salient advantage was extreme mobility.

As the war progressed it became apparent that amphibious assault would be a major naval emphasis in both major theaters.[14] Salvage forces supported amphibious assaults in four principal ways. First, salvage ships assisted assault-group vessels damaged by attacks en route to invasion sites. Second, during and after an assault, salvage forces assisted ships damaged by the opposing forces. Third, salvage forces recovered landing craft from invasion beaches both for repair and to clear the beaches for across-the-beach movement of supplies for invasion forces. Fourth, salvage forces cleared captured harbors of obstructions so that supplies could flow through for the land campaigns that followed.

As the requirements for salvage were learned through experience in the field, salvage organization took on a definite structure. The precise composition of a specific salvage force depended on many factors: geography, distance, the type of action expected, and the needs of the particular assault. However, all operations followed a general pattern.

Salvage forces were most effective when they were nearly autonomous and the only directions they received for doing their work were the location and priority of vessels and craft to be salvaged. This practice decreased the confusion that naturally attends combat and reduced work interruptions, because the salvors, the experts in the work, made the decisions rather than commanders who had many other concerns.

In the best possible situation, the salvage commander worked from a ship that had complete communications facilities and served as his headquarters. This ship, usually a salvage vessel, would act primarily as a command ship, becoming a salvage ship only to support other forces or when all forces were engaged.

When they were available, each assault group had three tugs—either fleet tugs (ATF) or rescue tugs (ATR). They were equipped with fire-

---

[14] Following the disastrous Gallipoli assault in World War I, amphibious assault against a prepared position was deemed infeasible by military thinkers. In World War II the United States had no other option. Its tactical expertise evolved to the point where, late in the war, the Japanese refused battle on the assault beaches and waited in selected and prepared positions inland.

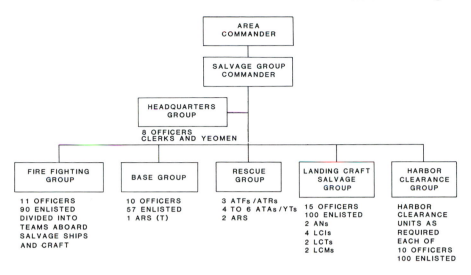

This basic Salvage Group organization was tailored to the work being undertaken.

fighting and salvage gear and manned with a combat salvage team of one officer and ten men and a fire-fighting team of one officer and eight fire fighters. These ships accompanied the assault group from the departure point and were prepared to undertake salvage and fire-fighting work on the ships of the group. The three fleet or rescue tugs were supported by four to six seagoing tugs, preferably auxiliary tugs (ATA), who could tow ships damaged by enemy action clear of the combat area. The auxiliary tugs were also ready to relieve the fleet tugs as soon as emergency fire-fighting or salvage work was completed.

Two fully equipped salvage ships (ARS) were stationed in a nearby reserve area where they would not be exposed to attack but would be available to deal with operations beyond the ability of the tugs, primarily ships towed out of the combat zone or beached for further salvage.

Like the fleet tugs, specially equipped landing craft attached to the amphibious ships provided immediate salvage assistance to stricken craft and passed on jobs beyond their capacity to salvage forces with greater capability. Landing-craft salvage required a great deal of attention during each assault. Experience early in the war showed that prompt action in landing-craft salvage was necessary if the work was to be effective. Craft left on landing beaches deteriorated quickly in salvageability and value. The landing-craft salvage officer, working directly for the Salvage Force Commander, supervised their salvage.

The policy and practice was to salvage landing craft from seaward. Net tenders laid heavy moorings on the first day of the assault so heavy pulls could be made directly from these moorings. When it was necessary to salvage from the beach, the beach battalion made personnel and equipment available to the landing-craft salvage officer so work could be performed under his supervision.

The dedicated landing-craft salvage forces consisted of about four LCIs fitted for fire fighting and salvage. In some assaults these craft went in as assault craft in the initial landing, then reported to the landing-craft salvage officer for fighting fires in shore, scouring around stranded vessels, and removing sandbars. As the salvage outfits of these ships became more extensive and took up more space aboard, their role was limited strictly to salvage, especially in the Pacific.

Two smaller types of landing craft supported the LCIs. LCMs were fitted with welding machines and carried tools, patches, pumps, and other materials for patching and pumping landing craft. The larger LCTs were fitted for fire fighting and diving. They were also equipped with extra generators, capstans, cordage for heavy pulling, and shear legs for lifting small landing craft off the beach or out of the water, raising the outboard side of beached craft for pumping, and raising pontoon causeways.

Organization, communications, and rapid response were the major requirements for landing-craft salvage. Experience had shown that the work accomplished in the first five hours determined the scope of the work for the first five days.

Always in Europe and sometimes in the Pacific, the initial assault was followed by a harbor clearance operation to clear blocked channels and berths for shipping. It soon became routine practice for Harbor Clearance Units of about 10 officers and 100 men to be held in readiness for movement into ports as soon as practicable. These units were self-supporting and were composed of men who had not taken part in other portions of the salvage operation. Harbor clearance constituted some of the most important and concentrated salvage work during the war. It required men who were fresh and not recently exposed to the wearing work of combat salvage.

The salvage base provided administration and specialized logistic support for the salvage group. The base not only took care of the everyday needs of the men in the units, it also served as a store to replace material damaged in operations and included repair facilities for damaged machinery and equipment.

The overall organization described above was tailored to each operation's specific requirements and reflected the lessons learned in previous campaigns. The guiding principles for salvage organization were centralization of control, flexibility, and responsiveness to the needs of the forces being served. Their application resulted in effective salvage operations during the war in both the Atlantic and Pacific theaters.

This chapter has explained the World War II genesis of ships, men, and equipment, and how the fourth element of salvage, doctrine, would evolve as the war progressed. Now it was time for Navy salvage forces to roll up their sleeves and go to work around the world!

Harbor Clearance

CHAPTER FOUR

Fleet Operations in World War II: The European Theater

W hen the United States entered World War II, the Navy had in the Atlantic only two fleet-manned salvage ships, *Redwing* and *Brant*, and the new fleet tug, *Cherokee* (ATF 66). Both salvage ships supported the Neutrality Patrol, while *Cherokee* provided towing services to the fleet. Although the foundations for the worldwide U.S. Navy salvage force had been put in place, it would take time for it to become fully operational and effective. As salvage forces were being assembled to support the projection of U.S. power overseas, the Navy Salvage Service held the line in American waters, especially during the dark days of the U-boat campaigns and shipping shortages of 1942.

Salvage is most important to the side whose production and transportation is under attack, for ships and cargoes that are salvaged do not have to be replaced. They can further the war effort by allowing production facilities to turn out more guns and shells rather than replace ships and cargoes at the bottom of the sea. Salvage, therefore, assisted materially in the effective use of the nation's huge industrial potential.

The requirements and urgency for salvage in the Atlantic and Pacific were quite different. Other than the unique problem at Pearl Harbor, no immediate need existed in the Pacific for salvage forces of the size required in the Atlantic. The decision to hold the line in the Pacific theater and concentrate on the defeat of Germany amplified the necessity for rapid development and deployment of salvage forces in the Atlantic.

First Blood

When the British took Mesewa in Italian Eritrea[1] early in the war, they found that eighteen major wrecks had been sunk, bow to stern, by

---

[1] Now Massawa in Ethiopia.

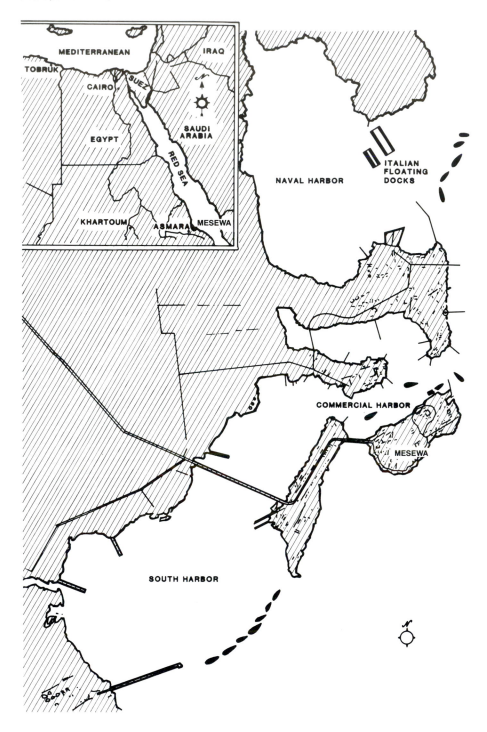

Mesewa harbor.

Captain Edward Ellsberg surveys the blocked harbor of Mesewa from atop a wreck. Photo courtesy the Bettman Archive.

the Italian defenders, who wanted to block the harbor entrances to the British. The primary importance of this Red Sea port lay in its potential as a repair base for the Royal Navy operating in the Mediterranean.[2] Because British salvage facilities were already stretched thin, the United States agreed to provide one salvage officer under the provisions of the Lend-Lease Act. He would oversee a contractor effort to clear the harbor and get the repair facilities back in service. Lieutenant Commander Lebbeus Curtis had been on his way to the Middle East when he was detained in Pearl Harbor. With the United States fully in the war and Curtis occupied in the Pacific, no one was available to oversee the work in Mesewa. Then, Commander Edward Ellsberg, USNR, who had left active duty following the S–51 salvage but remained in the Naval Reserve, volunteered his services to his old boss, Admiral E.J. King, and returned to active duty.

---

[2] The only other ship repair base in the eastern Mediterranean available to the Royal Navy was at Alexandria. The Mesewa operation was designed as a backup to these facilities should the Germans break through the British lines in Egypt. The German forces never made a breakthrough, but the frequency of air attack when the Afrika Corps had penetrated as far as El Alemain was sufficient to close the port of Alexandria.

Some suggested that Ellsberg join Sullivan in the Navy Department. This team would have been powerful indeed, but the combination was not in the cards. The organization of Navy salvage for the war required the particular vision and genius of William Sullivan in the Navy Department position. Ellsberg was needed elsewhere.

Ellsberg went to the Red Sea as Officer-in-Charge, U.S. Naval Operating and Repair Base, Mesewa. His work in Mesewa showed tremendous ingenuity. He had virtually no salvage equipment available and only a handful of capable divers. Workers in the port were limited to malnourished Eritrean laborers and some Chinese deckhands. Nevertheless the harbor entrances were cleared, the harbor opened, and the shops and much of the floating industrial equipment returned to service in a short time. This success came largely through the personal efforts of Ellsberg and Lieutenant Byron Huie, who joined him near the end of the operation and remained after Ellsberg's departure. One of the more notable efforts during Ellsberg's stay in Mesewa was the emergency repair of the severely battle-damaged cruiser HMS *Dido* in a salvaged drydock.

In the first year of the war the Navy's meager Atlantic salvage forces found ample employment along the convoy routes to the North. *Brant* (ARS 32), operating out of Argentia, Newfoundland, and *Redwing* (ARS 4), working from the salvage base in Iceland, provided towing and salvage assistance to casualties in the North Atlantic. Some of the jobs were unusual. In January 1942, for example, a fuel barge belonging to Polling Brothers of New York broke loose and drifted 2,400 miles before it grounded near Reykjavik and was salvaged by *Redwing* and Commander Kaplan, the Iceland salvage officer. The majority of the jobs, however, involved the arduous, dangerous, and important work of assisting and towing to safety ships stricken at sea. Unfortunately, few diaries, reports, or logs survive from this phase of the war. Thus the details of the salvage work undertaken early in the war are largely lost, and the heroes remain unsung.

The year 1942 was one of intense training and procurement for the United States. The war in the Atlantic was primarily a logistics war, with the Allies producing and transporting war materials and the Germans attacking sealift facilities. Salvage operations were not limited to dedicated salvage forces. Ships of many types took part in salvage operations. An incident in May 1942 illustrates the effectiveness of salvage-forces-of-opportunity and helped cement U.S. relationships with our soon-to-be ally, Brazil. A U-boat torpedoed the Brazilian steamer *Commandante Lyra* near Cape São Roque. Brazil was still neutral. The cruiser-destroyer team of *Milwaukee* (CL 5) and *Moffett* (DD 362) responded to the SOS at high speed. They reported the location of the burning steamer and set off to find survivors.

Meanwhile, another team, *Omaha* (CL 4) and *McDougal* (DD 358), arrived at the scene, put a salvage party on board, and started fighting the fires and securing the ship. A tow was needed. It did not make sense to tow with a cruiser where submarines were known to be operating. *Thrush* (AVP 3), originally one of the ubiquitous Bird-class minesweepers and now a small seaplane tender, sailed from the nearby Brazilian port Natal as a towing ship. *Thrush*, guarded first by one cruiser-destroyer combination and then the other, started the voyage north towards Fortaleza. The Brazilian tug *Heitor Perdigao* soon joined the group. Upon successful completion of the salvage, the Brazilian government presented a letter of thanks to the American ambassador, and the ship's owners donated $50,000 to the Navy Relief Society.

Operation Torch—The North African Campaign

Navy salvage forces began to take the form and function they would have throughout the war starting with the campaign in North Africa, the first movement of U.S. combat troops across the Atlantic. The main object of the North African invasion, Operation Torch, was to put American and British armies ashore along the Atlantic Coast in French Morocco and along the Mediterranean in Algeria. The Atlantic Coast invasion was to be a purely American show; the Mediterranean landing was to be a joint operation, with the British providing much of the naval support and having overall naval command. The U.S. Navy had three missions: to provide for the sea defense of the forces ashore, to operate naval bases and harbors, and to provide logistic support for all U.S. forces. Salvage had a role in each mission.

Neither the planning for Operation Torch nor the composition of the naval logistics forces showed much understanding of the importance of salvage forces in amphibious assaults. Only one American salvage ship, the fleet tug *Cherokee*, accompanied the invasion fleet to the coast of French Morocco. The salvage ships *Redwing* and *Brant* sailed from the United States two days before the initial assaults, far too late to provide salvage support to transports and combatants either during the transit from the staging areas or during the invasion itself. Their primary mission was intended to be harbor clearance. Fortunately, the opposition to the landings was relatively light at all sites. Gunfire from shore batteries or French naval vessels damaged only six ships[3] during the Casablanca attack. None of the damage provided much work for the *Cherokee*.

---

[3] One battleship, *Massachusetts* (BB 59); two cruisers, *Augusta* (CA 31) and *Brooklyn* (CA 40); and two destroyers, *Murphy* (DD 603) and *Ludlow* (DD 438).

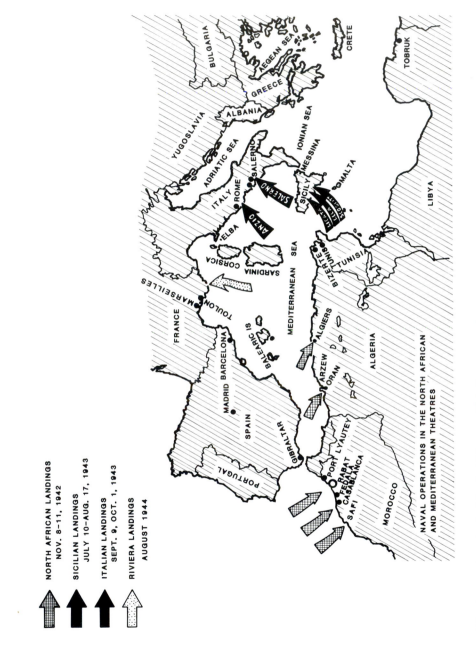

Naval operations in the North African and Mediterranean theaters.

NORTH AFRICAN LANDINGS
NOV. 8–11, 1942

SICILIAN LANDINGS
JULY 10–AUG. 17, 1943

ITALIAN LANDINGS
SEPT. 9, OCT. 1, 1943

RIVIERA LANDINGS
AUGUST 1944

The situation differed somewhat in the Algerian invasion. The British destroyer *Cowdray* took a bomb hit in the fireroom, the transport *Leedstown* (AP 73) was torpedoed, and SS *Exceller* developed leaks from a near miss. The Transport Division Commander requested a British tow for the badly damaged *Leedstown*, but the transport was torpedoed again and sank before effective salvage assistance could be provided.

One transport bound for Algeria, *Thomas Stone* (APA 29), was disabled in the Mediterranean by a mine or torpedo explosion near her stern. In a saga of seamanship and improvisation, 741 of the 1,400 soldiers were embarked in the ship's landing craft and sailed 160 miles to Algiers under escort of the British corvette *Spey*. *Stone* was towed in by two British destroyers, *Velox* and *Wishart*, and the small tug *St. Day*. The incident demonstrated great bravery and tenacity. But it should not have happened. The drama-filled adventure would have been a minor incident had adequate salvage forces accompanied the invasion fleet. It certainly does not reflect well on the planners of the transit, who neglected to provide salvage protection for amphibious assault forces in a combat zone. Because salvage forces were new in fleet operations, only the most elementary doctrine had been developed.

If the landings and transits of the North African invasion had been more vigorously opposed, it is likely that the losses would have been much greater, perhaps even unacceptable. Nevertheless, the losses in transports alone[4] were greater than in any other campaign. Based on the results of later landings, it is fair to assume that some of these losses could have been prevented if salvage ships had been an integral part of the invasion forces and could have given immediate assistance to casualties. However, the lesson had been learned: Naval forces of all kinds in combat areas must be supported by effective salvage forces to prevent unnecessary losses. Future transits had salvage protection.

Landing Craft Salvage

Experience taught another lesson on the North African beaches. Huge numbers of beached, broached, and damaged landing craft hampered over-the-beach movement of men and equipment. This situation came about from insufficient attention to landing-craft salvage and the absence of dedicated, trained, and equipped salvage teams.

---

[4] In addition to the *Leedstown*, the transports *Joseph Hewes* (AP 50), *Tasker H. Bliss* (AP 42), *Hugh L. Scott* (AP 43), and *Edward Rutledge* (AP 52) were sunk by torpedo attack within four days of the initial landings. Their cargoes were mostly lost, and over 100 men were killed outright or died of wounds.

In both Algeria and Morocco the initial landings were made on a day when the surf was reportedly the calmest in many years. Only two boats of the Northern Assault Group in Morocco were unable to retract themselves from the beach on the first morning of the landings. The surf began to rise on all beaches, and the number of boats returning from the beaches for more loads began to decrease. The growing scarcity of landing craft hampered the movement of men and material ashore. Captain Allan P. Mullinnix, Chief Staff Officer to the Commander of the Center Attack Group, describes what he saw:

> As I walked along the beach [on November 9] I counted 169 wrecked boats, and as I went along the aspect got progressively worse, and toward the end I found myself counting engines instead of hulls. The landings had cut our boats in half—we had 330 originally, now half of these were on the beach.[5]

The same situation existed on all the landing beaches. Salvage groups, organized hastily at the scene with whatever men and equipment could be found, were unable to cope with the problem. A large number of landing craft were lost. Most could have been salvaged if work by competent and properly equipped salvors had begun in time. The size of the loss not only hampered the ship-to-shore movement of men and material but created a demand for replacements. Building and transporting the replacement craft took up production and transportation capacity that could have been better used. Another lesson was learned the hard way: landing-craft salvage must be an important part of amphibious and logistic doctrine.

Harbor Clearance

The eighteen wrecks sunk systematically by the Italians to block the Eritrean port of Mesewa gave notice to the Allies that the same tactic would be employed in other harbors. To minimize the effect, planning for the capture of the Algerian city of Oran and its subsequent use as a major logistics port included a British operation to prevent the harbor from being blocked by retreating forces. The operation was carried out despite objections of Rear Admiral Andrew C. Bennett, who had responsibility for the development of the harbor for Allied use. The Royal Navy ships *Hartland* and *Walney*, formerly the U.S. Coast Guard cutters *Pontchartrain* and *Sebago*, with antisabotage parties embarked, entered Oran

---

[5] Rear Admiral Worral Reed Carter, USN, and Rear Admiral Elmer Ellsworth Duvall, USNR, *Ships, Salvage, and the Sinews of War* (Washington: Department of the Navy, 1954), p. 170.

two hours before the initial landings. Their mission was to gain control of the waterfront and prevent blockage of the harbor by sunken ships. The ill-conceived operation ended in disaster. It contributed two more wrecks to the harbor, resulted in heavy casualties, and did not prevent systematic destruction in the harbor. Needless to say, no similar operations were undertaken.

At Port Lyautey, on 12 November, four days after the initial landings, the first clearance operations got underway when Lieutenant Commander Domenech and a party from the battleship *Texas* went ashore to salvage scuttled ships blocking the Wadi Sebou River and the port. In contrast to the ill-fated British effort at Oran, this group did their work well. Before they had to be recalled to *Texas* on the fifteenth, they salvaged and returned to service the steamer *Export* and had three other small ships well on their way to being ready for service.

This operation taught two lessons. The first was that providing salvage units would eliminate the need to take men away from combatant ships where they are needed. The second, more subtle lesson affected the nature of harbor clearance work throughout the war. In peacetime, salvage of a ship implies that it will be returned to service. Following this philosophy at Mesewa and again in the first days at Port Lyautey, ships that could be put back in service received priority attention. However, those in touch with the broad picture saw that the military task of harbor clearance differs from standard harbor salvage. The wartime clearing of a blocked harbor changes normal salvage priorities, and the primary goal becomes making the harbor usable.

With an important exception, the fate of ships and craft blocking the harbor is unimportant; they are simply unwanted obstructions that must be removed as quickly as possible. The exceptions are craft such as drydocks, tugs, and floating cranes that can be used in the clearance operations or in the operation of the port. Many times during harbor-clearance operations in the war, ships that could have been returned to service were demolished because salvage would have impeded clearance. This change in priorities brought a new dimension to the clearance operations. In a process not unlike medical triage, each casualty had to be examined to determine its priority and disposition. There is not a great deal of finesse in harbor clearance. Many operations, for example, used three or four times the normal number of pumps or compressors and allowed ships with considerable leakage to be raised without spending endless hours looking for and sealing leaks.

The thorough blockage of ports on both the Atlantic and Mediterranean coasts of North Africa called for immediate salvage action. It was taken. On the morning of 16 November 1942, Captain Sullivan, accompanied by six salvage officers, six salvage divers, and a diving doctor, boarded a plane in New York bound for Casablanca on the Atlantic.[6] Salvage gear was shipped separately.

Shortly thereafter, in an action he neglected to coordinate with the American naval authorities, Admiral Sir Andrew Brown Cunningham, GCB, RN, commanding the Allied naval forces in the Mediterranean, summoned Captain Edward Ellsberg from Mesewa. Impressed by the work that Ellsberg had done in Eritrea, Cunningham wanted him as the principal salvage officer in the Mediterranean. At Cunningham's request General Eisenhower appointed Ellsberg to that position.

CLEARING THE ATLANTIC PORTS

The harbor clearances in the Atlantic ports of North Africa provided valuable lessons for the Americans who were to be instrumental in clearing many other blocked harbors as the war continued. Nowhere was a greater variety of technical problems encountered than at Casablanca.

Casablanca

When Sullivan and his team arrived in Casablanca, they found *Cherokee*, *Redwing*, and *Brant* in the harbor. Their first job was to make a quick survey of the port and determine the need for additional people and equipment. They found that all but one of the berths in the harbor were blocked, and that the salvage gear shipped over had either been lost in a torpedoed ship or landed by the other ship at Safi and lost in the Army supply dumps. It is probably just as well the equipment was lost. Experience had shown that the particular equipment and special skills required in a port could only be determined after an initial survey.

A salvage group of about 125 men was assembled from the first class of the salvage school at Pier 88, survivors of ships sunk in the landings, and the brig. As the salvage ships could do little in the clearance work[7], Sullivan stripped them of equipment not needed for emergency work offshore and set about clearing wrecked vessels from blocked berths.

---

[6]The thirteen were all students at the Pier 88 salvage school. They left on less than twenty-four hours notice in a hastily converted Pan American flying boat. Because routing via the Azores was infeasible in the bad weather, they flew to Gibraltar via Trinidad; Natal, Brazil; and Bathhurst, Union of South Africa. The trip took four days.

[7]Although planners had envisioned the use of the salvage ships for harbor clearance, ships like the fleet tugs and the converted Bird-class minesweepers were of little use in these operations. They occupied valuable harbor space and had such congested holds and storerooms that it was impractical to use them as floating bases. Salvage ships were designed for dealing with a single moderate-sized ship offshore; they did not carry sufficient equipment to support harbor clearance operations. Fleet tugs and Bird-class minesweepers had no heavy lift capability. This was corrected in the British *King Salvor* class, which was designed for belly lifts, and in the American steel-hulled ARS, which was designed for heavy bow lifts. When these ships became available, they were used in this manner. One salvage ship was generally kept available in the harbor for fire fighting.

Four major jobs in Casablanca are of particular interest. The first was salvage of a floating drydock needed for docking a badly battle-damaged destroyer. The raising of this dock is an example of salvaged craft being used in port operations. Salvage had begun under the supervision of an expatriate Danish salvage officer before Sullivan arrived in Casablanca, but Sullivan, noting no progress after a few days, inspected the operation. He found that the salvage pumps had been connected to the drydock's main drain, and the main drain was open to the sea. The salvors were, in effect, pumping the sea through the drydock. Further investigation showed that there had been no presalvage survey and no attempt to determine what had sunk the dock. The salvage officer, an elderly man whose abilities had been affected by privations suffered before the Americans arrived, was relieved of his assignment.

A survey revealed that the dock had been holed by hundreds of fragments. These holes could be plugged with wooden plugs, but with pumps on the side wall—about a foot above water at low water—the pontoon deck of the dock could not be brought above the surface. The suction lift was too great for the pumps. To solve the problem, pumps were placed on floating platforms, and pump suctions were led to the bottom of the pontoon through manholes. This work required divers to remove the access plates, place the suction pipe inside the drydock pontoon, replace the covers—now cut to accommodate the pipe—and weld up the joints. The dock was floated in one operation. More than 200 additional holes were found when the dock was afloat, along with an unexploded 16-inch shell from the battleship *Massachusetts*.[8]

The two largest jobs in the harbor at Casablanca were the French passenger liners *Lipari* and *Savoia*. Both ships had been badly holed when 8- and 16-inch shells passed completely through them, penetrating the rock bottom of the harbor before exploding. The explosions blew numerous rock fragments through the hulls. Large quantities of decomposing organic matter on board generated noxious gases. These gases caused frequent interruptions of the salvage work in order to aerate the water in the holds. The release of gases generally cleared the piers, much to the chagrin of the Army trying to move supplies across them.

Lipari had broken in two except for some badly burned bottom and tank top plating. *Savoia*, not quite so badly damaged, lay directly astern of *Lipari*. The work on both ships was exasperating. Each time all the known holes in a compartment were plugged, a pumping test was made. Sometimes it showed more holes; sometimes the flow caused by the

---

[8]This shell had apparently struck the forward barbette on the French battleship *Jean Bart*. The glancing blow destroyed the shell's fuse but the shell rebounded, coming to rest on the dock floor.

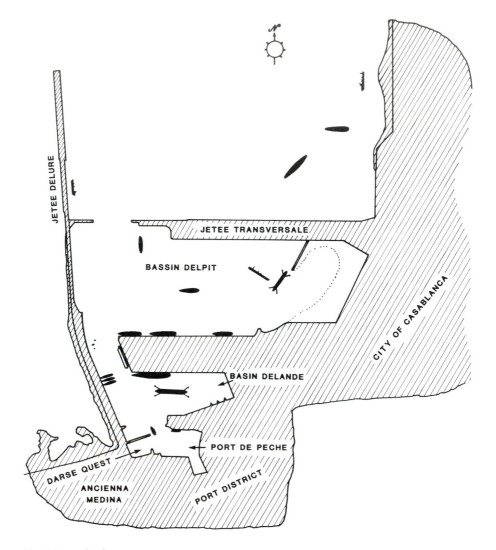

Casablanca harbor.

pumping broke down the clay domes that plugged some of the holes. Some compartments required as many as a dozen pumping tests.

The poor condition of the ships presented a problem. The water level could be taken down only 8 or 10 feet in pumping tests because of the deteriorated bulkheads. This same deterioration made it necessary to pump several adjacent compartments simultaneously, presenting stability problems from the large free surface. Water levels in adjacent compartments on *Savoia* could be stepped no more than 5 or 6 feet so that the

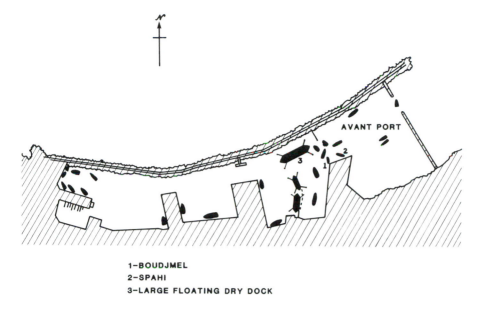

1—BOUDJMEL
2—SPAHI
3—LARGE FLOATING DRY DOCK

Oran harbor.

hydrostatic head would not collapse the bulkheads. She was finally raised by carefully controlled pumping.

The problem of raising the nearly broken *Lipari* in one piece required an innovative approach. To reduce the total weight, the superstructure was cut down and removed piecemeal. The gaps in the deck and shell plating were first bridged with six heavy girders. This didn't work because, as soon as one end lifted, the weakened structure at the other end failed. Next, anchor chain was run along both sides of the ship and secured wherever evidence of strength remained. This arrangement provided good tensile strength across the break, but did not ensure that the main deck would remain in tension. Finally, to provide compressive strength, wooden shores were wedged in the gap where feasible. This approach was successful, and the ship was refloated with the ends hanging together.

One of the most technically interesting jobs at Casablanca had practically no military value. A lift craft had been built early in the century to salvage sunken submarines; it had not been a success, and the French Navy had relegated it to an out-of-the-way mooring, where it sank. The structure resembled a drydock, and the salvors were under constant pressure from visiting firemen to raise it to add to the docking facilities in the port. The salvors knew the badly deteriorated lift craft was useless. Technical problems abounded. The craft could not be pumped because water pressure would crush the deteriorated sides of the craft. Shoring the sides would require too much timber.

Hard quarters and dead tired: a condition every salvor knows. In the rudimentary officers' quarters at the first salvage base in Casablanca Dr. George Schlessinger sits on his cot as Lt. Commander Wiley Wroten looks for an empty cot. Another officer lies collapsed in welcome sleep. Photo courtesy Vice Admiral Bernard E. Manseau.

The lift craft, however, did seem to be an appropriate training project for a new program just getting underway to restore French salvage forces so they could be of service to the Allies. The hull, therefore, was tightly sealed, water pumped out, and air simultaneously pumped in to keep the differential pressure at a level the sides could tolerate. The salvage method worked, but when the vessel floated, no practical use for it could be found. Thus the operation served only for training and to stop pressure from the port authorities for raising it.

The Casablanca harbor clearance removed or salvaged thirteen wrecked ships, including five large cargo or passenger ships, the French battleship *Jean Bart*, a French destroyer, and two floating drydocks. Along with the technical expertise gained, some very important lessons were learned about the mechanics of running harbor clearance operations. It became obvious, for example, that harbor clearance units must be self-sufficient. The work required shifts starting at all hours of the day and night. To accommodate these shifts, berthing with a round-the-clock messing near the waterfront was a necessity.

Normal rations, moreover, were inadequate for divers and salvors doing 12 to 16 hours of heavy labor. The choice was simple: better rations or less work. But appeals through the proper chain-of-command inevitably generated the response that what was good enough for fighting men was good enough for divers. Furthermore, cooks and bakers assigned to the salvage unit were often shanghaied into other units. The handling of another problem turned what could have been a hardship into a true gain for the salvors. They simply hired excellent and very capable local cooks with the wherewithal to satisfy the salvors' appetites.

The heavy demand for patching and cofferdamming material including lumber, steel, cement, and corrugated sheet metal posed additional problems and stimulated further creative solutions. Guards had to be stationed to prevent the material finding its way into some informal barracks-improvement program. Good scrounges, an invaluable asset for any salvage effort, were an integral part of the Casablanca operation, and salvors near the waterfront laid first claim on dunnage lumber from arriving ships, material quite suitable for patching and cofferdamming.

Port Lyautey

Lieutenant Robert Helen—one of the officers who had flown over with Sullivan—ten men, and *Redwing* were sent to Port Lyautey[9] to deal with the eighteen wrecks that were still there. The French had tried to block the harbor with interned ships, mostly vessels of Scandinavian and Belgian registry. The strong river currents gave them fits when they tried to position the ships, resulting in a scattered mess of ships. The clearance plan included opening the port, which lies 8 miles up the Wadi Sebou River, to marine traffic; making the river safe for antisubmarine seaplane operations from the old French seaplane base down river from the main port; and returning as many ships as possible to war service.[10]

The crews of the sunken ships were also interned, housed in prison camps not far from the port. Helen arranged for these men to augment the harbor clearance workforce. The first wreck, *Nihorn*, a diesel-electric ship with no major hull damage, was raised quickly and towed to the United States for refurbishment. Lieutenant Helen faced some difficult stability problems in some of the other wrecks. Several were four-hatch, two-hold coasters of a type that, unless sunk in very shallow water, would become buoyant enough when pumped to float before becoming stable enough to stay upright. Stability was maintained by controlled pumping and warping the ships to the river bank, keeping them on the bottom while beach gear and tractors prevented listing. When a ship had been moved to shallow water, one end was pumped while the other end re-

---

[9] Now called Kenitra.

[10] Returning ships to service early in the war was always of concern. It was practical at Port Lyautey because most of the ships were steam propelled. Their machinery could easily be put back in service after being thoroughly cleaned. The Wadi Sebou carried so much silt that cleaning the ships was nonetheless a major job.

mained on the bottom until the ship became sufficiently stable to raise it.

One wreck was a large yacht belonging to Madame Coty, at that time one of the most famous ladies of the fashion world. Hanging on a projection from a pier at a list of about 40 degrees toward the channel, the ship would have blocked the channel had it capsized. With extreme care to prevent capsizing, the yacht was refloated.

The most difficult wreck in Port Lyautey was sunk in the middle of the river with a list of 15 degrees. At low water, half the main deck was exposed. The salvors built a timber cofferdam on the low side of the ship, removed mud, and patched holes in preparation for pumping. Beach gear and tractors dragged the ship toward the bank as she became light. She gradually righted, rotating on her keel, and refloated.

Lieutenant Helen, ably assisted by Lieutenants Whitmyre, McCaffrey, and Sibitsky, the latter commanding the *Redwing*, had done fine work clearing the wrecks in Port Lyautey.

CLEARING THE MEDITERRANEAN PORTS

As the Casablanca operation shows, the lessons of wartime salvage are not all technical, and the lessons of salvage do not apply only in war. Through the Strait of Gibralter into the Mediterranean ports of North Africa, harbor clearance operations took place that reinforced and expanded these lessons.

Though the abortive adventure of *Walney* and *Hartland* at Oran showed that the Allies knew there would be attempts to block North African ports, little was done to provide forces and equipment to clear these ports efficiently. In fairness to the operational planners, it must be understood that salvage equipment was still in short supply in late 1942. Despite the efforts of a small Navy cadre who understood salvage and its requirements, it is doubtful that enough equipment could have been provided simultaneously to cover the requirements of the Atlantic submarine war and a major harbor clearance.

One salvage officer, Lieutenant George Ankers, USNR, a veteran of the Pearl Harbor salvage work, and ten divers were made available to Admiral Bennet's force in the Mediterranean. The force also included the British salvage ship *King Salvor* and a small contingent of poorly equipped French divers. They set to work as soon as practicable, but efforts were not well coordinated until Captain Ellsberg arrived in Oran on 29 November.

As he described it, Ellsberg found a mammoth clearance problem:

There were twenty-seven French wrecks littering the harbor. Masts and stacks at crazy angles broke the surface . . . wherever one's eyes lighted—in most cases, the hulls, whether right side up, upside down, or on their sides, were wholly submerged and invisible. A string of masts and smokestacks lay across the entrance to the inner harbor. There six ships, anchored in two lines nearly bow to stern, had been scuttled to block the port. Inside there were sunken destroyers, sunken submarines, sunken freighters, sunken passenger ships, sunken drydocks. Everything in the port had been scuttled before the surrender—across the entrance, in the fairways, alongside the quays—wherever in the opinion of the French commandant at Oran they would cause us the most trouble in reopening the port.[11]

The outer port of Oran, the Avant Port, had not been blocked and could be put into service immediately. Six blockships sunk across the entrance impeded access to the main port. Just as ships being raised do not always behave in accordance with the wishes of the salvors, blockships also show an independence and often fail to go where they are wanted. This had happened at Oran, and the six blockships at the entrance to the main port were badly placed. HMSV *King Salvor* had pivoted one of these blockships, *Boudjmel*, on its stern, thus clearing a channel deep enough for partially laden Liberty ships[12] to pass.

While the overall problem was formidable, many of the wrecks could be left alone while those of higher priority were cleared. Ellsberg attacked the wrecks at Oran like a man eating an elephant. His first bite coordinated the activities of the three salvage groups so that all were working toward a common goal. His second bite widened the harbor entrance. To do this he patched the *Spahi*, a freighter laden with hogsheads of wine, lightened her with compressed air, and pivoted the stern, more than doubling the width of the channel.

As at Casablanca, a large floating drydock that had been sunk was urgently needed for battle-damaged ships. By the time Ellsburg turned his attention to the dock, he had a salvage master and a group of divers from Mesewa. These men quickly had the dock afloat in Oran by patching and pumping. The opening of the entrance and the salvage of the drydock completed the urgent clearance work. The remainder of the wrecks were attacked systematically, and the port continued to develop as the primary logistics port in North Africa.

In both the Atlantic ports and in Oran, harbor clearances had been carried out by small, hastily organized, but well-led ad hoc groups of

---

[11] Edward Ellsberg, *No Banners, No Bugles* (New York: Dodd, Mead and Son, 1949), p. 49.

[12] The Liberty ships, Maritime Commission hull-type EC2-S-C1, were the dominant Allied merchant-ship type during World War II. The 1879 British design was chosen for the emergency shipbuilding program because of its simplicity and adaptability to mass production. Between September 1941 and October 1945, 2,742 of these ships were built. They were 414 feet long, and had an extreme beam of 57 feet and a maximum draft of 27 feet 9 inches; their deadweight tonnage was 10,920. The ships became the standard in planning berthing and passage facilities in harbor clearance. Because of the dominance of the Liberty type, the term "Liberty" was often used to mean any merchant ship.

salvors. It was now apparent that salvage and harbor clearance were to be major factors in the logistics of the war.

Although Ellsberg was appointed Principal Salvage Officer for the Mediterranean, Admiral Cunningham and General Eisenhower had not been kept advised of the Navy's overall salvage plans. Although he had gotten out of the mainstream of the American salvage effort while in Mesewa, Ellsberg did some excellent work in the Mediterranean and in the Oran harbor in the winter of 1942–43. But as principal salvage officer in the Mediterranean, he fit neither the plans of the Navy nor the desires of Admiral King. Ellsberg, whose health had suffered under the Red Sea sun, was ordered back to the United States early in 1943 and participated no further in Navy salvage.[13]

Edward Ellsberg's contribution to Navy salvage was significant. An extremely competent engineer himself, Ellsberg saw salvage as primarily an engineering task. Not the first to apply engineering principles to solving salvage problems, he nevertheless raised the standards of that art. He also wrote well, and his detailed technical report of the S–51 salvage enabled Harold Saunders to salvage the S–4 without having to repeat the hard lessons of the earlier job. Ellsberg's technical writing set a high standard for reporting of salvage work that has continued to the present. In an entirely different vein, Ellsberg's popular accounts of salvage work, books that today seem curiously simplistic and quaint, captured the public imagination and served as excellent publicity for the Navy and its salvors.

As a hands-on engineer Ellsberg was often too close to his work to see it as part of a larger pattern. However, he clearly recognized the need for continuity in a Navy salvage organization and for both peace and wartime readiness. His attempts to communicate this ongoing need to higher authorities, though largely futile, were perhaps Edward Ellsberg's greatest contribution to Navy salvage. He saw and had the courage to put forward a truth too often forgotten—that salvage and preparation for salvage pays large dividends on a small investment.

In February 1943 Captain William Sullivan reported to Algiers. There Admiral Cunningham informed him that he would command a combined salvage force for the Mediterranean with the titles Commander Task Force 84 and Principal Salvage Officer.[14] The original intention was that

---

[13] Ellsberg's excellent engineering talent, however, was used by the Navy throughout the war, first as an inspector of shipyards in the Third Naval District and later in the European theater, where he was instrumental in the success of the artificial harbors in Normandy. He retired as Rear Admiral, USNR.

[14] In a letter dated 5 May 1943, Rear Admiral H.K. Hewitt, Commander Western Naval Task Force, assigned Captain Sullivan as Commander Task Force 84, the U.S. naval salvage force in North African waters. Sullivan was directed to organize U.S. salvage vessels, forces, and depots, and to keep them in a constant state of readiness, as well as to cooperate closely with forces under the Commander in Chief, Mediterranean.

Lieutenant W.A. Reitzel found the harbor at Dellys and the yacht club at right an ideal headquarters for Task Force 84 in North Africa. The small harbor could accommodate two salvage ships.

British salvage ships would take care of all offshore salvage while the United States would organize and equip shore-based and mobile harbor clearance units. Sullivan asked that the British salvage officer Captain W.A. Doust, RNVR, with whom he had become friends in London, join him. The request was at first denied, and Sullivan worked with a series of other British officers until the Admiralty relented. Alec Doust joined his friend in North Africa in June 1943 as his principal assistant.

Initially the salvage force had an office in Algiers set up by Lieutenant W.A. Reitzel, USNR, and staffed by the lieutenant and a member of the Woman's Army Corps (WAC) who had survived a torpedoing and was later highjacked to the salvage office. In short order Reitzel found a more suitable headquarters at Dellys, a pleasant little town with a miniature harbor some 60 miles east of Algiers. The French made Dellys available, and the Americans set up a salvage base there. The salvage force based at Dellys initially numbered about 350 officers and men, had a large amount of equipment, and could expect more coming in each day. The base had berthing, messing, and recreational facilities, as well as repair shops and warehouses. Dr. George Schlessinger, the unit's medical officer, fitted out a small hospital. Lieutenant H.M. Andersen, the commanding officer of *Brant*, came in as commanding officer of the base.

The original clear division of offshore salvage responsibility to the British and harbor clearance to the Americans did not last long. American ships began to appear in the Mediterranean, and British salvage units

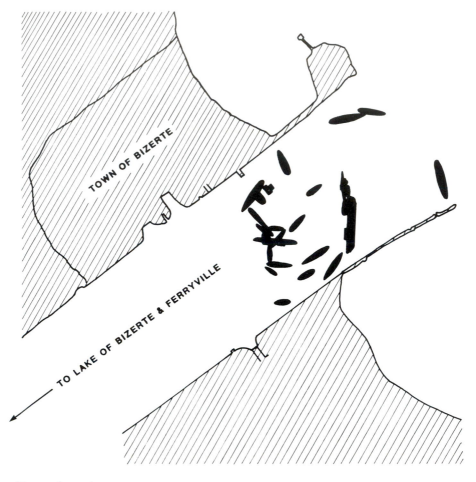

Bizerte channel entrance.

cleared the ports of Philippeville, Bone, and Bougie as the Allied advance moved eastward.

Bizerte, the principal port of Tunisia, was the last large harbor clearance in North Africa. Even before Bizerte was captured by the Allies the decision had been made to use the Lake of Bizerte as a staging area for the next major invasion, Sicily. Some had expressed concern that the channel to the lake and the French naval base at Ferryville would be blocked. Intelligence sources, however, revealed that there were tidal currents up to 6 knots in the channel and that at least 40 feet of fine sand lay under the channel bottom. These conditions made it suitable to use explosives to lower and flatten the wrecks as had been done with the wreck of *Stephen R. Jones* in the Cape Cod Canal the previous year.

Sullivan sent Lieutenant Commander Walker to Port Lyautey, where conditions simulated those in the Bizerte channel, to practice explosive demolition on two old wrecks. Unfortunately, while Sullivan was in the United States and before any tests were made, the Army became worried about Walker's being in Port Lyautey and ordered him back closer to the action. Following Sullivan's return to North Africa, Walker was wounded during an air raid. George Ankers took command of the salvage caravan, which was part of the invasion force advancing toward Bizerte.

Ankers's caravan became separated from the main column during the advance, and he and his men entered Bizerte ahead of the assault troops.[15] They found that twenty-eight blockships sunk by the Germans blocked the channel into the Lake of Bizerte. These wrecks were arranged more or less in four rows across the channel, but the current had twisted them around and piled them together so that in some places they were three deep. There had been concern that the Germans would fill the ships with concrete or a mixture of cement and sand that would set up and make their clearance much more difficult. Fortunately, all the ships were empty.

To clear the channel, the ships were cut into sections with high-grade explosives, then pounded below the channel bottom with low-grade explosives. Shots were made in periods of maximum current so that the material loosened by the explosive shock would be carried away. The scheme worked well. The wreck sections were lowered 3 to 5 feet with each shot. Three factors hindered the work: the short periods of slack water for diving, German air attacks, and sightseers. After Tunisia fell, the Army had little to do until ships could enter the Lake of Bizerte and preparations for the invasion of Sicily could begin. There were many senior officers hanging around watching the operation and offering free advice—much of it similar in quality to some of the suggestions for raising the *Lafayette*.

Within a week a channel had been cleared for the first ships. It had taken more than 100 tons of explosives. Passage of LSTs, then Libertys moving supplies into the staging area began as soon as there was sufficient clearance. These passages slowed down the operations on the wrecks, but quite correctly had priority.

Clearance of the channel into the Lake of Bizerte provided access to

---

[15] Salvors are resourceful people capable of looking out for themselves. The story is told that an Army colonel entered Bizerte with the first troops and was instructed by his general to find a suitable building for his headquarters. While his troops were clearing snipers, street by street, the colonel found a fine, undamaged building near the waterfront. There was a sign on the front door:

US NAVY SHIP SALVAGE
George Ankers, LCDR, USNR
O-in-C
Bizerte Group

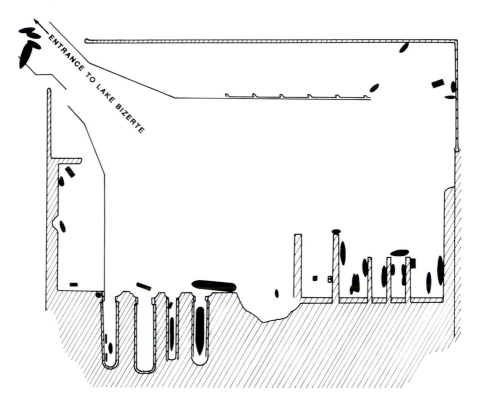

Ferryville harbor and docks.

the modern French naval base and dockyard at Ferryville with its excellent potential as a landing craft and general repair base. Before the facilities could be used, however, wrecks blocking them had to be cleared. Three small wrecks and the caissons for six graving docks were removed immediately to give access to the yard.[16]

There was only one difficult job at Ferryville. An Italian ammunition ship, converted from an old French ship, had been blown up during an American air raid. Ammunition had filled the forward three holds, and no trace of this portion of the ship remained. The stern section had been blown across the harbor, blocking access to the drydocks. This section could be pumped out and floated clear only after a considerable amount of work by divers who patched the holes in the shell plating and bulkheads. The number six hold of the ship contained a cargo of medical brandy. Through some fluke the bottles had remained intact. The ship was immediately lightened by removal of this cargo, which the salvors undoubtedly used for its proper purpose. The remainder of the work in Ferryville was not urgent and was accomplished on a long-term basis.

In preparation for the invasion of Sicily, American forces also cleared the port of La Goulette and the channel across the Lake of Tunis leading from La Goulette to Tunis.

The North African campaign taught the Allies a number of things about harbor clearance. Harbor clearance would be a major factor in the projection of power onto the European continent. The huge logistic effort to support modern warfare required that harbors be at least partially cleared before they could be used as supply ports. Organization for harbor clearance went quickly from infancy through adolescence in North Africa; it matured further when the Allies invaded Sicily.

Offshore Salvage

Even before the establishment of Task Force 84, neither Sullivan nor Ellsberg had been allowed the luxury of concentrating entirely on harbor clearance; both had to give time to offshore casualties as they occurred. These casualties in the North African campaign taught some valuable lessons about offshore salvage that would affect the Allied approach to this subject during the remainder of the war.

A major offshore casualty occurred when the Navy cargo ship *Electra* (AK 21)[17] was torpedoed by U–173 about 17 miles from the Moroccan

---

[16] Of the six drydocks at Ferryville only one had damage to the stone sill. This damage rendered the dock inoperative for eighteen months while repairs were made. This was the only damaged drydock sill encountered in the European war and may have resulted from bomb damage rather than from intentional destruction.

[17] Later AKA 4.

city of Fedhala. Effective damage control measures stabilized the ship and allowed her to be brought into Casablanca, where salvors began getting her ready to sail to a repair yard in the United States. *Electra* had a 48-by 21-foot hole in the port side of number four hold; that hold and the main machinery space were flooded. *Cherokee* came alongside to furnish power and construction was started on a large steel patch. Structural steel was in short supply in Casablanca, so the ship's steel hatch covers, stiffened by girders of material cut from wrecks in the harbor, served as construction materials. Because simultaneous pumping of the machinery space and hold would have generated a large, stability-destroying free surface, the bulkhead between the two spaces had to be made tight enough to allow the spaces to be pumped independently. This entailed removal of wreckage by divers to give access to the bulkhead, then plugging or patching the holes that were found.

As soon as the bulkhead held, the machinery space was pumped dry and attention turned to overhauling the machinery. With the hold dry, salvors replaced the steel salvage patch with a reinforced concrete patch extending from tank top to 'tween deck. *Electra* went home under her own power with an absolutely tight patch.

SS *Lancaster*, a World War I Hog Island ship[18] with an unusually valuable cargo—teletypes, howitzers, motor vehicles, radar equipment, airplanes, food, and ammunition—ran aground on the rocks off El Hank Light on New Year's Eve 1942. Seventeen of the crew were lost when the ship was abandoned. The ship lay broadside to the reef and inside the breakers except at low water. Salvage of the old, now badly damaged hull, did not seem feasible, but the cargo was too valuable to be written off.

Captain Sullivan and Lieutenant Andersen surveyed the ship at various stages of the tide and found they could work three LCTs between the ship and the shore at low water and keep them there in the lee during the full tide cycle. The salvors tried to load air compressors for running the ship's steam winches on the boat deck, but seas breaking over the ship carried them away. The compressors were then placed in the LCTs; *Lancaster*'s boilers became air reservoirs. Army stevedores began discharging the cargo into the LCTs under Andersen's supervision. All of the deck and 'tween-deck cargo and some of the hold cargo had been discharged before the ship's winches and parts of the deck houses were lost to heavy seas. The last of the discharging was done with portable, air-driven winches strapped to the booms. Several booms broken by the sea were replaced by booms salvaged from wrecks in the harbor.

The results of the cargo salvage justified the effort. Cargo was dried

---

[18] A 380-foot dry cargo ship built at Hog Island, Philadelphia, in a World War I construction program.

Redwing, now ARS–4, sinks by the bow after hitting a mine off Tunisia in June 1943. The former Bird-class minesweeper was the first salvage ship lost in the Atlantic theater.

and preserved at a station ashore. The airplanes were further salvaged for spare parts; most of the vehicles, all the artillery, communications and electronics gear, and much of the food and ammunition proved usable. Though the ship was lost, the cargo—far more valuable at the time—was not.

The casualties around Casablanca continued. A high wind one night roused the entire salvage force to secure several Libertys that had broken loose from their moorings and were in danger of grounding. Another night, tankers grounded and were refloated the following day. One of those appeared to belong to the fleet of ghosts that sometimes haunt salvors. Sullivan had already salvaged the same ship twice the week before at Port Lyautey.

Sullivan and Lieutenant Wiley Wroten had traveled by jeep to Port Lyautey after receiving a late-night telephone call that a ship had stranded on a shoal off the mouth of the river at Port Lyautey. With two tugs and a dredge they refloated the ship and returned to Casablanca in the afternoon. After dinner the phone rang. The tanker was stranded again— this time on rocks at the other side of the river—and there was danger of its breaking up. Because of dense fog the 135-mile drive to Port Lyautey took all night. The ship was refloated in the afternoon.

Similar casualties with both American and British ships also occupied Ellsberg and George Ankers at Oran. Among the most notable were HMS *Porcupine*, a destroyer that was successfully salvaged, and the British troopship *Strathallan*, torpedoed and lost after a long struggle.

121

The salvage ships were kept busy assisting battle-damaged ships and marine casualties. When not attending casualties they engaged in towing operations, moving supplies and equipment as needed. The forces were augmented by new fleet tugs that began arriving in the spring of 1943 and were assigned mostly to the Mediterranean ports. The Army ship *W.R. Chamberlain*, requisitioned from her owners by the War Shipping Board, was turned over to the Navy. She became *Tackle* (ARS 37)[19] and served as a base ship for the Harbor Clearance Units.

On 27 June *Redwing* departed Algiers for Bizerte with four harbor tugs (YT) in tow. About 10 miles short of her destination, she struck a mine that blew a large hole just below the bridge. She began to take on water and list heavily. The order to abandon ship was given. The towed vessels became the towing vessels as *Redwing*'s towing hawser was cut and the small tugs took her in tow. Near the channel entrance a British destroyer passed close aboard. The destroyer's wake capsized *Redwing* and she sank in 27 fathoms—the first combat loss of a U.S. Navy salvage ship in the Atlantic theater.

Operation Husky—Sicily

The planners of Operation Husky, the invasion of Sicily, had a much better appreciation of potential salvage needs than they had in North Africa. They also had better resources for both offshore salvage and harbor clearance. Fleet tugs were available, Harbor Clearance Units had been formed and were in a high state of readiness, and fire-fighting units and Task Force 84 were organized.

The original plan called for the fleet tug *Hopi* (ATF 71) and the salvage ship *Redwing* to accompany the DIME Attack Force at Gela. This plan had to be modified when *Redwing* sank. *Brant* replaced *Redwing*, joining the force on 9 July. *Narragansett* (ATF 88) and *Nauset* (ATF 89) were with the CENT Attack Force at Scoglitti, and *Moreno* (ATF 87) with the JOSS Attack Force at Licata. In addition, two 275-ton harbor tugs, *Intent* and *Resolute*, and several 65-ton harbor tugs were assigned to the Task Force Commander for salvage and fire fighting.

Salvage During the Invasion

Unlike the landings in North Africa where opposition, primarily from the French, had been relatively unenthusiastic, the landings in Sicily were strongly opposed by the Germans and led to intense offshore salvage activity.

---

[19] Later ARS(T) 4.

122

Early on the morning of 11 July, a German air attack damaged *Barnett* (APA 5), anchored off Gela. Bombs exploding close aboard caused flooding and started fires in the ship. Within twenty-five minutes *Hopi*, which had started the day by pulling LST–312 off the beach and already had a party ashore salvaging landing craft, came alongside to port with her hoses, and a fire-fighting party led by Lieutenants Burns and McConnell boarded *Barnett*. The fire was brought under control. *Hopi* shoved off within the hour to continue her day by refloating LCI–220 and a number of landing craft, steaming to assist a Liberty ship, and finishing up by refloating another dozen landing craft. The small job on *Barnett*, an emergency response to battle damage, was typical of the services rendered by afloat salvage forces in support of amphibious attacks throughout the war.

In the early evening of 15 July, while clearing a channel and engaging enemy shore batteries, the fleet minesweeper *Staff* struck a mine. The ship listed to starboard, fires broke out throughout the vessel, and she went down by the bow. YMS–63 provided immediate assistance, put out the fires and removed the casualties. *Staff's* sister ship *Skill* (AM 115) took her in tow, then passed the tow to *Moreno*. *Moreno* took *Staff* to the harbor at Licata, where *Brant* fabricated a patch for her side, installed the patch, and pumped the engine room. Like the large majority of patches, this patch leaked and pumping had to continue.

Hopi took *Staff* in tow for North Africa. During the tow the leakage increased, and the submersible and light gasoline-driven pumps failed. *Hopi* put a 6-inch salvage pump aboard and completed the tow. Another ship had been saved by prompt, thorough salvage action. These and other offshore salvage operations during the Sicilian invasion gave a preview of the intensity of work to come.

The landing-craft salvage problem, on the other hand, was not nearly so severe during the landings in Sicily as in North Africa. In part, this was because the planners for the Sicilian invasion were aware of potential problems and planned accordingly. Each transport, for example, had one LCM designated as a salvage boat, though its equipment left much to be desired. LCI(L)s pressed into service as tugs for removing landing craft were so successful that, after the assault, a recommendation was made to equip them as salvage boats.

The tugs under the direction of now-Lieutenant Commander Andersen, the senior salvage officer in the Gela area, did excellent work in the salvage of landing craft. Andersen took charge of landing-craft salvage on the afternoon of D-Day. The salvage crews of the tugs were landed and both fleet tugs and harbor tugs engaged in landing-craft salvage. The results were spectacular: Almost 200 landing craft were salvaged and returned to service; less than 100 were left on the beach as unsalvageable.

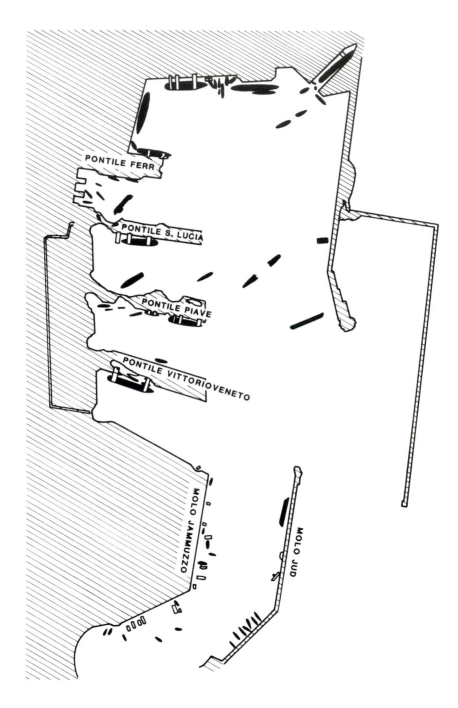

Palermo harbor.

Engines and other parts from wrecked craft were salvaged as well. Centralized control and attention to the lessons of earlier operations enhanced the effectiveness of the work.

The Palermo Harbor Clearance

The original preparations for the campaign in Sicily envisioned giving priority to clearance of the harbor at Trapani. However, the damage there turned out to be much greater than anticipated. Thus, when Palermo was captured, the harbor clearance units were concentrated there and Trapani was abandoned.

The harbor entrance at Palermo was not blocked, but numerous ships sunk by bombers lay alongside piers. Most of these ships were so badly damaged that salvage would have been a major effort. It was more expedient and effective to simply cut the tophamper away and extend the decks of the piers over the wrecks.

Opening the repair facilities at the Sicilian port presented a particular challenge. The caisson of the graving dock had been split by a bomb, allowing a great inrush of water. The water knocked over the spare caisson and carried it forward, then lifted a destroyer from the blocks and capsized it on the spare caisson. The destroyer could not be cut up with either torches or explosives because ammunition remained on board. Lieutenant Commander Bob Helen dived on the wreckage for a personal survey and devised the salvage plan. The blocks were cut away so the caisson could be dragged clear of the destroyer. The spare caisson was seated in the sill, the destroyer was patched, pumped, and removed, and the dock was restored to service.

A small Italian steel schooner was, literally, the catalyst for another series of problems at Palermo. The schooner lay across the slip between Pontile St. Lucia and Pontile Piave. Because the completely submerged wreck had too much damage to be removed intact, it was cut into sections with explosives. The job proceeded routinely with charges of no more than 100 pounds.

One of these shots produced an enormous explosion that shook the town, dumped a section of a damaged pier into the water, tore a Liberty ship loose, caused *Philadelphia* (CL 41) to roll violently, and blew the Admiral's aide off the pier into the harbor. The schooner disappeared, leaving a hole about 50 feet deep where it had been.

This violent chain reaction could be traced back to three ammunition ships that had exploded in Palermo harbor prior to the American occupation. When ammunition ships explode, large amounts of munitions are not detonated but are flung about intact. Some of these explosives, particularly land mines and cased explosives, are nearly neutrally buoyant and tend to be washed about the harbor bottom by currents until they eventually pile up in banks. One of these banks apparently had formed near the schooner and was detonated by the small demolition charge. A more complete survey of the harbor bottom showed it to be literally covered with unexploded ordinance which was then methodically disposed of or detonated.

Salvage operations and the salvage organization had continued to grow and mature during the Sicily campaign and in related operations in the Mediterranean. They would be further tested on the Italian peninsula at Salerno.

Other Mediterranean Salvage

In wartime, as in peacetime, three levels of salvage activity are maintained: planning and preparation, routine operations, and high points of major jobs. The high points were provided by amphibious assaults and other contact with the enemy when casualties were heavy. There was no shortage of routine jobs, and many ships at sea were doing the myriad tasks and hauling the huge quantities of goods needed for modern war. Many of these ships were manned by crews with limited experience. All the ships in the Mediterranean were subject to U-boat and aerial attack as well as the normal hazards of the sea. The routine work and the casualties that inevitably came day after day and week after week kept the salvage ships busy.

The exploits of *Nauset* for eight days in August are typical of the work of the salvage ships in the Mediterranean. On 21 August 1943, *Nauset* got underway from Licata with two pontoon causeways in tow. After delivering the causeways, she was in Palermo on the morning of 23 August when a German air attack damaged two subchasers and set fire to the British cargo vessel *Speedfast*. While her sister ship *Narragansett* assisted the submarine chasers, *Nauset* put a fire and rescue party aboard *Speedfast*. With the fire extinguished, *Nauset* got underway for Bizerte in the afternoon of the same day. En route, SS *Pierre Soule* hit a mine and had to be taken in tow.

The day following her arrival at Bizerte with *Pierre Soule*, *Nauset*, along with *Moreno*, tried to haul the tanker *Empire Fay* off a shoal near the channel entrance. Both ships pulled until their tow wires parted. *Nauset* subsequently made two attempts to free the Liberty ship *Jeremiah Black* grounded on a shoal. The end of this busy but typical eight days saw her tow *Pierre Soule* to the outer harbor. Such constant and varied work, some of it in vain, all of it hard, occupied most of the salvage ships in the Mediterranean during 1943.

One of the Mediterranean salvage jobs that perhaps received more than its share of publicity was that of the destroyer *Mayrant* (DD 402). The ship took a near-miss that flooded two main machinery compartments and caused leakage in other spaces. She received first aid in the form of pumps and a tow into Palermo harbor, where topside weight was removed for a tow to Malta. The damage attracted much attention and brought many distinguished visitors to the ship, including Generals Patton and Montgomery. The attraction may have been *Mayrant's* executive officer, rather than the damage. He was Franklin Delano Roosevelt, Jr.

Salvage forces continued to increase in the latter half of 1943 as the first of the wooden-hulled salvage ships began to arrive from the United States and additional *King Salvor* class ships came in from the United Kingdom. A setback occurred on 10 August when, because of faulty recognition signals, Allied naval forces fired on *Brant* and damaged her. She was repaired and back on the line in short order.

The Italian Campaign

The need for salvage forces in support of amphibious assault had been established during Operation Torch in North Africa; their efficacy had been proven in the Sicilian invasion. They were now an established part of the Allied assault forces. The landings at Salerno would show even more signs of their maturation.

Salerno

For the invasion of the Italian mainland at the Bay of Salerno, by the mixed Western Naval Task Force under Vice Admiral Henry K. Hewitt, *Hopi* and *Moreno* accompanied Rear Admiral Hall's southern attack force. *Nauset* and *Narragansett* accompanied Commodore Oliver's northern attack force. The British salvage ships were to be held in Sicily. *Brant*, repaired after being shot up, had since collided with a wreck and was not in good condition. Captains Sullivan and Doust felt that combat salvage work could be done with the personnel and gear aboard aided by fleet tugs, auxiliary tugs, and rescue tugs. They decided that the American salvage ships and the British *King Salvor* class ships should not be exposed in the primary combat zone. An additional eight British tugs had been fitted with fire-fighting pumps for emergencies. These tugs would take damaged vessels handed off by the fleet tugs and tow them to the salvage ships while the fleet tugs returned to the fray.[20]

---

[20] The operations officer felt that Sullivan and Doust were building too big an empire and that so many tugs were not necessary. The two captains appealed to Admiral Cunningham, who approved the plan. In this and in other matters throughout the war, Admiral Cunningham showed an extraordinary grasp of the requirements and details of salvage.

Captain Alec Doust, a leader of the British salvage effort during World War II, worked closely with his American colleague and friend Commodore Sullivan throughout the Mediterranean. Captain Doust's autobiography, *Ocean on a Plank*, is dedicated to "Sully."

During the assault Sullivan ran salvage operations in the American (southern) sector from Admiral Hewitt's flagship, *Ancon* (AGC 4), while Doust joined Commodore Oliver in HMS *Hilary*. The salvage ships had plenty of work and proved their worth frequently in the hotly contested landing. From Algiers, Captain Donot and Commander Andersen had been working on plans for landing craft salvage. A number of LCIs had been fitted for inshore fire fighting and salvage and some LCMs were also equipped for salvage.

The preparation for harbor clearance was more thorough than in the past. A major clearance operation was anticipated at one of the major objectives of the Salerno landings, the harbor at Naples. For the first time clearance would be done by fresh men, held in reserve in Sicily until needed, rather than by men worn down by salvage work during the assault. The Navy harbor-clearance forces and the Army Corps of Engineers planned to cooperate more closely than they had in the past. Commander Wroten and Colonel Martin of the 1061st Engineers set up a joint office in Palermo to plan the harbor clearance and rehabilitation and to establish joint priorities. Because definitive plans could not be made until the situation had been assessed, the planning was only rough and preliminary, but it assured the elimination of conflicts between the Harbor Clearance Units clearing the port and the Corps of Engineers rehabilitating and putting it in service.

The cooperation was not limited to planning. *Tackle* had been sent to Algiers to load up with salvage material and bring more people forward. The entire reserve filled up *Tackle*. The loss of the ship with that much specialized equipment would be grave. In an excellent example of interservice cooperation, half of *Tackle's* load went in two LSTs allocated to the Army engineers and *Tackle* carried a half-load of Army engineer equipment.

Because the Army hoped to achieve tactical surprise with the attack, they chose to forgo the usual preinvasion bombardment, feeling it would alert the Germans unnecessarily and cause them to move more troops into the area. In addition, the announcement of the armistice with Italy two days before the invasion created a relaxed attitude among the Allied troops not warranted by the situation. The invasion at Salerno turned out to be one of the most fiercely opposed of the war.

In the early morning light of D-Day, *Narragansett* saw heavy gunfire and flares from the beaches. She steamed toward a burning ship to render assistance, soon recognizing it as her sister ship, *Nauset*. *Nauset* had gone in earlier with a special assault craft; while she was waiting for the craft to return from its mission and rearm, a stick of bombs scored several hits and near misses. Fires enveloped the ship. Power lost, she took on water. While the harbor tug *Intent* fought the fires and attempted to beach the grievously wounded ship, *Nauset* struck a mine. She broke in half and sank within 10 seconds. *Narragansett* picked up wounded and steamed away. Before transferring the casualties to LST 351, *Narragansett* engaged enemy aircraft and claimed one hit.

On D+2 the British hospital ship *Newfoundland* was torpedoed. Fortunately there were no wounded on board, but casualties among the staff were high. Fire spread over the entire midship portion of the ship and she listed heavily. The destroyers *Mayo* (DD 422) and *Plunkett* (DD 431) went alongside and began fighting the fire, but met with little success.

Moreno arrived and took the destroyers' place, fighting the fire with fog and pumping out water from the low side.

Moreno's crew battled the fire down to one location, cut away debris topside, patched the hull, and pumped out flooded spaces. The one remaining fire burned in a coal bunker that had been installed for the galley when *Newfoundland* was fitted out as a hospital ship. The coal bunker lay atop a fuel oil tank. The deck of the bunker threatened to carry away, dumping the fire into the partially filled oil tank. Salvors poured water into the bunker. The additional water increased the list, presenting another problem.

Preparations were being made to take the ship in tow when the order came to sink her. Sullivan, feeling she should be saved, sent a message recommending that she be left until a tug could be spared to get her. No answer came after two hours, so the destroyer commander sank the ship. It was later learned that both Admiral Hewitt and Admiral Cunningham had approved Sullivan's recommendation. Neither message was received.

Action was equally intense in the Southern Attack Force's area. On D-Day the British monitor[21] *Abercrombie* struck a mine and asked *Moreno* to stand by. The ships steamed to the southern edge of the transport area and lay to. *Moreno*'s salvage officer went aboard *Abercrombie* for a survey. There he found the starboard blister ruptured and flooded. *Abercrombie* had taken a 6-inch shell hit in Sicily. There had been no drydock available for proper repair, so a patch had been installed with a velocity impact tool.[22] The patch leaked considerably so that when the ship was hit at Salerno, the forward void tanks were already flooded. The new hit blew away a sizable portion of the starboard blister. A salvage party from *Moreno* cut away loose plating and secured the remainder with lashings and turnbuckles. The ship could have been made more seaworthy for the trip home if lost buoyancy had been restored. However, casualties were happening rapidly and the demands for immediate salvage assistance were frequent. Rather than tie up salvage ships in the forward area, *Abercrombie* was headed toward Palermo in marginal condition; there the *Brant* crew performed additional repairs before she went on to Malta.

The following morning *Moreno* went to the assistance of the Dutch gunboat *Flores*, towed her to a safe anchorage, and assisted with repairs

---

[21] The monitor type, introduced by the U.S. Navy during the War Between the States, persisted in the Royal Navy long after being abandoned by the U.S. Navy. *Abercrombie* was the last monitor built, completed in the Vickers-Armstrong yard at Tyne on 5 May 1943. She was armed with two 15-inch guns, eight 4-inch ones, and antiaircraft weapons. The ship had a 17-foot-wide blister on each side for torpedo protection. The blister was a sandwich of one water-filled compartment between two air-filled voids intended to defeat a torpedo with a 1,000-pound warhead.

[22] The velocity impact tool in use during World War II was the British-made Cox submerged bolt driving and punching gun. This gun drives a threaded bolt into steel plate by means of an explosive charge. The bolt is driven in such a way that it is gripped firmly in the plate and the threaded portion left protruding ready to take the patch and nut.

that allowed her to get under way under her own power. *Moreno* suffered a heavy casualty while the Dutch captain was bargaining with Captain Kyllberg of the *Moreno* for two valuable crates of potatoes. A German air raid abruptly interrupted the negotiations.

The Germans introduced a new weapon at Salerno, a glide bomb that could be guided to its target by a high-flying aircraft. One of these bombs struck the cruiser *Savannah* (CL 42) on her number three turret, just forward of the bridge, causing considerable damage. Sullivan and Commander Burns, who were nearby in *Ancon*, went aboard immediately and took charge of fire-fighting efforts. German aircraft had been attacking the cruiser all morning, and commanding officer Robert Carey wanted to keep the ship under way to make her a more difficult target. Initial efforts were devoted to fire fighting, containing the flooding, and shoring bulkheads to prevent their collapse. With the ship still under way, men went into compartments below the forecastle to plug sprung doors and hatches with mattresses, pillows, and life jackets.

After some time the ship anchored. *Hopi* and *Moreno* came alongside; they put crews, pumps, and pump suctions aboard and were able to help stabilize the cruiser. *Savannah* planned to leave as soon as possible for Malta at whatever speed would not put the forecastle under. This speed turned out to be a rather respectable 18 knots. Apparently at that speed the damage on the bottom caused the water to be sucked out, allowing men to enter and further secure compartments.

The rapid assistance provided to *Abercrombie* and *Savannah* and their immediate dispatch out of the combat zone were prime examples of the salvage operations conducted by fleet tugs supporting the landings. The planned operation suffered, however, because the tugs designated to take damaged ships from the fleet tugs didn't show up. Doust and Sullivan, out of contact for some days following the landings, each thought the other had captured the escort tugs all for himself. Neither was right; the tugs had been mistakenly held at Bizerte.[23] Lacking them, Doust ordered the salvage ships forward, leaving only *Brant* at Palermo to take care of the returning casualties.

The absence of tugs presented a major problem when the British battleship *Warspite* was hit in an aerial attack. The hit flooded five of her six firerooms. Six minutes after the attack *Hopi* headed to *Warspite* and soon had the battleship in tow. *Moreno* joined them, and the two tugs began towing the battleship in tandem. The commanding officer of *Warspite*, Captain H.A. Packer, RN, wanted the two fleet tugs to take him all

---

[23] Sullivan was quite perturbed by the failure of the tugs to show up at Palermo. He notified Algiers that he intended to resign as principal salvage officer unless the matter was thoroughly investigated. Almost all the staff concerned were transferred after the fighting at Salerno ended, and the messages that kept the tugs at Bizerte were never found.

the way to Malta. Devoting these two tugs to the damaged battleship would denude the American sector of salvage ships. Had the escort tugs not been held in Bizerte by mistake, they would have been available for the *Warspite* tow.

But *Warspite* was an important unit and deserved special consideration. The 300-mile trip to Malta began with *Hopi* and *Moreno* towing in tandem with an escort of British cruisers and destroyers. British tugs were to come out and pick up the tow halfway. In the first watch on the first evening of the tow, the cruiser *Delhi* passed between *Warspite* and *Hopi*; *Warspite* slipped the tow and *Hopi* slipped *Moreno*'s wire. The tow was made up again—a laborious process—and the trip set off again.

At the beginning of the midwatch *Hopi*'s wire parted at the shackle, and the tow had to be made up once more. In the morning two British tugs, W123 and W117, joined. Even with all four tugs towing and the sea smooth, *Warspite* was difficult to tow. She tended to take charge and sheer wildly. The Strait of Messina with its strong currents lay ahead. The cruiser HMS *Euryalus*, in a beautiful demonstration of seamanship, held station on the bow of *Moreno* and guided the tow into the Strait. Not long after entering the strait in the dark of the midwatch, one of the British tugs fell off her course, crossed *Hopi*'s tow wire, and parted it. This was the third break; all had come in the middle of the night. Making up the tows again and again was back breaking, dangerous, and frustrating.[24] No doubt the Strait of Messina heard some basic Anglo-Saxon language.

Narragansett, which had taken the damaged cruiser HMS *Uganda* to Malta, came out and took *Hopi*'s place while the latter, all her tow wires broken, made up alongside. The difficult and trying tow was completed without further incident.

Once the Allies established control of the air over the Salerno beachhead, the German air raids ended. The number of casualties and the tempo of salvage operations declined drastically. Allied troops began to move north toward Naples, where one of the largest harbor clearances of the war would soon take place.

The Naples Harbor Clearance

Before the Allies entered Naples, a series of conferences was held on Capri to make plans to clear and rehabilitate the harbor. The work that had been done by Colonel Martin and Commander Wroten in Sicily paid off. They had much knowledge of the harbor and the construction of the waterfront facilities. A committee consisting of Commodore Sulli-

---

[24] *Warspite* never was a ship to tow docilely. En route to the breaker's yard in April 1947, she broke her tow and grounded at Prussia Cove, Cornwall. She was scrapped in place.

van,[25] Colonel Martin of the Army Engineers, and Colonel Clarkson of the Transportation Corps was established to meet daily and decide what work would be done and what priority it would have. Admiral Marne and General Pence agreed to run interference for the committee and give it sole responsibility for the success of the operation. This system worked so well in Naples that it became the standard for other operations.

Naples harbor was a mess. The combination of Allied bombing and systematic destruction by the retreating Germans had left over eighty major pieces of wreckage in the harbor. All harbor installations were completely wrecked; all berths, save one, capable of taking a ship the size of a Liberty, were blocked. The wreckage consisted of cranes and dockside installations that had been blown into the harbor, barges, fishing boats, small craft, merchant ships, and warships. Most were so heavily damaged that they could not be quickly cleared by refloating; and conditions were not good for blasting. Lifting the wreckage or dragging it clear had to be the primary techniques employed at Naples. These jobs called for extensive diving and heavy-rigging skills.

Eight berths were clear and ready in fourteen days. British boom defense vessels, similar to the U.S. Navy's net tenders specially rigged for lifting over the bow, accomplished much of the work in the early days. Later these ships were supplemented by British wreck dispersal vessels, which had a larger lift capacity; a variety of pontoons and derricks; and the first new construction salvage ships to arrive in European waters—the wooden-hulled *Extricate* (ARS 16) and her sister *Weight* (ARS 35).[26] Within three weeks, twelve berths were available. Within two-and-a-half months, thirty berths, more than existed before the war, were operating. Although most of the berths were cleared by lifting out the wreckage, many were improvised by bridging over wrecks as had been done at Palermo.

There were several reasons the harbor clearance worked particularly well at Naples.

- Relationships with the customers, the Army people who would use the harbors, were established beforehand and systems for establishing mutually agreeable priorities worked out.

---

[25] On 28 May 1943 Sullivan was designated Chief of Navy Salvage, Office of Chief of Naval Operations, Navy Department, with the rank of commodore.

[26] *Extricate* and *Weight* were brought to Naples when the value of salvage-lifting had been demonstrated by the British ships. Bow-lifting equipment was not used by American commercial salvors prior to World War II and was included in salvage ship design only after Sullivan saw its usefulness in Britain before the United States entered the war. When the two salvage ships arrived from Bizerte on 29 November, Sullivan found that one of the pair of heavy lift chocks had been removed on the recommendation of an American civilian salvage authority. The ships were useless for lifting but proved valuable for fire fighting. The wooden-hulled salvage ships were better for fire fighting than steel-hulled ships because they could remain alongside the burning ship without their interior becoming hot. A hose on deck kept the wooden deck and hull from catching afire.

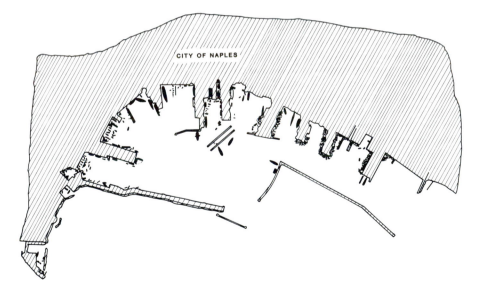

Naples harbor.

- The operation was controlled by a single directorate concentrating command, control, and responsibility.

- The salvors, as they must, gave their imaginations free rein and were willing to try innovative techniques.

- The salvage force was a self-sufficient organization with its own berthing, messing, medical, and support facilities, all located near the work.

- The men engaged in harbor clearance were fresh, not worn down by working in salvage operations during the assault.

- The close personal relationship between Sullivan and Doust affected the entire organization and ensured harmonious relationships between the British and Americans.

During the harbor clearance, air raids continued and fires on Libertys were frequent. The salvage ships were instrumental in fire fighting. An incident during one of the fires illustrates a problem that has often plagued salvors. A Liberty's cargo of 5-gallon gasoline cans was afire. The crew, except for two men, abandoned the ship. *Extricate* and *Weight* came out to fight the fire and fire-fighting crews went aboard. Finally *Brant* cut the anchor chain, towed the ship out of the harbor, and beached it so that its holds could be filled with water. It looked like another salvage job well done, but when Commodore Sullivan returned from the ship he found that the master had filed a complaint accusing the salvors of looting. Although the items reported stolen were later found on the ship which the Liberty crew had boarded after abandoning their own, and the master was prosecuted, the story circulated widely. After this experience, it became the policy for Navy salvage crews boarding merchant ships to call Military Police to act as ship's police.

To ensure that all underwater obstacles had been removed in Naples and nearby harbors, a Royal Navy lieutenant and hydrographer, Lieutenant Hutchinson, with a group of enlisted specialists was assigned to the salvage group. Using a DUKW, a specially fitted Army amphibious vehicle, Hutchinson became the busiest man in the area, surveying and charting harbors up and down the coast. He was an important part of the salvage team.

At this stage of the Italian campaign the salvage organization had reached full maturity and was ready for the tasks ahead.

Anzio

The Anzio landing, the last in Italy, met opposition from competent and determined German forces. The offshore salvage situation was much as it had been at Salerno. British tugs and *Edenshaw*, a large American harbor tug, made up the salvage forces that accompanied the invasion fleet. *Hopi* and ATR–1 joined after the assault. The work was similar to that of previous assaults: freeing grounded landing craft, responding to ships hit by gunfire and aerial attack, fire fighting, taking care of the casualties that occurred when large numbers of ships had to operate in a confined area under confused circumstances. The jobs were numerous and they followed one another rapidly. There were some successes, some failures, a great deal of sweat, some blood, some heroics, and more heroism. Although the salvage work at Anzio did not differ in nature from work at the other landings, it was unique in its duration. The siege-like character of the combat that developed at Anzio kept the Allied troops contained in a beachhead where support from the sea was an integral part of the operation for a long time. With sea forces closely involved in support of the troops on the beach, there were ship casualties from enemy action far longer than in prior operations.

Very shallow water made landing-craft salvage at Anzio difficult. To facilitate these salvage efforts Doust and Sullivan had an idea for shear legs for an LCT. The two men sat down one night and designed a set. With scrounged materials they built one that lifted over 20 tons. Using the direct line of communication that existed with the Bureau of Ships, Sullivan sent Captain Manseau the sketch and asked that a standard design be worked up. Craft fitted with the improved standard model could lift 40 tons. These craft would do excellent work later in the Pacific—another spin-off from the salvors' combat experience.

Operation Overlord—Normandy

The Allied landing in Normandy, one of the most complex military operations ever undertaken, involved an assault on a hostile shore and the transportation of huge numbers of troops and their supplies by sea. Commodore Sullivan reported to London in April 1944 to participate in planning the invasion. He left Captian Doust in the Mediterranean commanding the Allied salvage force, with Commander Andersen as Commander Task Force 84. Commander Helen was in Algiers working with the Army on plans for the clearance of Marseilles harbor. Lieutenant Commander Whitmyre was in charge of the group still working at Naples.

Planning and Preparation

Despite the overwhelming need for salvage forces in amphibious landings that had been demonstrated during the North African, Sicilian, and

Italian invasions, as late as two months before Operation Overlord there was no salvage and fire-fighting plan. A study of the conditions and probabilities for the invasion of Normandy led to the conclusion that the salvage requirements would be much like those for the Mediterranean invasions. A nucleus of experienced officers and men could be brought in from the Mediterranean and augmented by graduates of the Salvage School at Pier 88.

The salvage people who arrived in Britain for Overlord were concentrated at Base II on the Roseneath peninsula on the northern side of the Firth of Clyde in Scotland. All their salvage gear was also there, along with a lot of other equipment turned over to the salvage group by various military and naval units. In fact the salvors had far more equipment than they needed.

Fire fighters were mostly at Base II also, although some had been scattered around the isles at fire-fighting schools. Their equipment had been liberally distributed to ships so that an inadequate amount remained for the invasion.

Most alarming to the U.S. Navy, the American salvage ships (which, unlike the British salvage ships, were equipped for towing) as well as the American tugs had been requisitioned for the Allied tug pool and would not be available for salvage until sixty days after the assault. The British salvage ships were to be dedicated to the clearance of Le Havre, while the Normandy landings were to be supported by Dutch tugs. The Dutch ships were fine towing ships but were not well equipped for fire fighting or for assisting sinking ships. Another disturbing factor was the possibility that the Dutch crews might not understand or be able to make themselves understood in English. Clear, concise communication between the casualty and salvage crews are of utmost importance in combat salvage, where mistakes or inaction caused by language problems can be disastrous.

Commodore Thomas McKenzie, CB, CBE, RNR, had been assigned as the principal salvage officer on the staff of Admiral Sir Bertram Ramsay, RN. He had been the manager of Metal Industries, Ltd., a salvage firm, before the war and had supervised much of the salvage work on the German fleet at Scapa Flow. Commodore Sullivan was concerned that McKenzie did not have sufficient experience with the salvage requirements of a large, opposed amphibious operation or with wartime harbor clearance. On his arrival in Britain as deputy to McKenzie, Sullivan strongly supported the idea of an Allied salvage and fire-fighting force, the concept that had worked well in the Mediterranean. He soon reversed this position because he found conditions and arrangements that he believed were unsatisfactory. He may have felt that, given his recent experience in the Mediterranean, he should have been the principal salvage officer.

After an acrimonious exchange, American salvage ships and tugs were returned to the salvage force. Captain Edmond J. Moran, USNR, an executive of an American towing company who had solved the early problems of the Navy's Rescue Towing Service and made it effective, was brought over to organize and manage the American towing forces in the Normandy invasion.

Despite preinvasion wrangles over authority and organization, the American and British salvors worked together as a joint force once the action started. Commander Huie commanded the salvage forces at Omaha Beach and Commander McClung covered Utah Beach. The fleet tugs *Pinto* (ATF 90), *Kiowa* (ATF 72), *Bannock* (ATF 81), and *Arikara* (ATF 98) and rescue tugs ATR–2 and ATR–3 accompanied the invasion force. In addition to their normal crews each tug carried two salvage officers, a fire-fighting officer, twelve salvage mechanics, and eight fire fighters. Salvage ships *Diver* (ARS 5), *Swivel* (ARS 36)[27], and *Brant* were to stand by in Falmouth to protect the Channel. One of the salvage ships was fitted out for blasting through the entrance of the breakwater at Cherbourg should the Germans block it. All the tugs and salvage ships were equipped with large amounts of material for landing-craft salvage. Half of the equipment and the personnel from the Roseneath Base were gradually trucked to the south coast of England where they would be close to the invasion area and could quickly augment the forces there.

The American salvage forces were to have responsibility for clearance of the harbor at Cherbourg with Commander Wroten in charge. Commodore Sullivan gave a series of lectures to the Army Engineers in Wales stressing the necessity for close cooperation between the engineers and the Navy in harbor clearance and rehabilitation. As a result a plan was drawn up almost identical with that which had worked so well at Naples. Colonel Sibley, the Port Commander and an Army Transportation Corps representative; Colonel Cross, the engineer for the port, and Commodore Sullivan formed a committee to survey the port and make a joint priority list for the work.

The Normandy Landing

The salvage problems experienced off the beaches of Normandy were quite different from those in Sicily and Italy. The Allies had almost complete control of the air in Normandy, German air attacks were nonexistent during daylight, and night attacks were generally limited to bombing. Bombs sank only one ship in the American sector. The absence of bombing attacks meant an absence of fires, the only serious fire in the

---

[27] *Diver* was the first of the steel-hulled ARSs to arrive in European waters. *Swivel* was a wooden-hulled sister to *Weight* (ARS-35) and, like that ship, was a former BARS.

Captain Edmond J. Moran, seen here in the uniform of Rear Admiral, was prominent in the towing industry before and after World War II. During the war he organized and oversaw the Navy Rescue Towing Service and the towing operations that supported the invasion of Normandy.

American area occurring when a ship struck a mine and started to sink. The mine damage at Normandy, however, was greater than in all the other invasions. Each of the many ships mined had serious damage, though only four were lost.

The storms that struck after the invasion, combined with the German opposition and the heavy traffic, made the general salvage workload off Omaha and Utah beaches heavier than in other invasions. To handle the huge workload, the salvage ships were called over from their reserve location at Falmouth. But none of the jobs required outstanding efforts or were of great technical interest.

Landing-craft salvage made up much of the work for the salvage forces. The amphibious forces had been organized to conduct their own landing-craft salvage without any assistance from the salvage forces and refused help when it was offered in the planning stages. The salvors attached to the amphibious forces were a well-trained, hard-working lot, but in salvaging landing craft they made the mistake of doing too thorough a job. Time-consuming permanent repairs were made when all that was needed was a temporary repair so that the craft could be moved to permit more material to come ashore through its berth. After a short time the amphibious force personnel were augmented by fire fighters and salvors from the salvage force, who showed them how well the techniques used in previous invasions worked.

The Cherbourg Harbor Clearance

Harbor clearance units were brought into Cherbourg shortly after the port was captured. Clearance work in the badly blocked harbor was relatively straightforward. Commodore McKenzie had made a number of the British lifting ships available to the American salvors because it looked as if Cherbourg, like Naples, would require numerous lifts. Thus even the largest ship sunk in the harbor, a 17,000-ton whale factory, presented no particular problems. A number of concrete barges did give some trouble because they tended to break up when lifted. The harbor had been thoroughly mined, and removal of the mines delayed the clearance work. The first wreck was not removed until a month after the capture of the harbor.

Shortly after the Americans arrived, an engineer poking around a German office found a large detailed, colored chart showing all the demolition in the harbor. The work had been completely executed, but the plan was flawed because the wrecks were not located where they would be most effective in blocking the harbor.

While most of the clearance work at Cherbourg was routine, a few jobs had some novel aspects. One barge, for example, carried a cargo of all types of naval mines: acoustic, magnetic, contact, and snag. The mines had spilled and piled up as the barge capsized. An operation that promised to be long and dangerous was started. A Canadian lieutenant commander qualified in explosive ordnance disposal dived in the muddy water where, working in zero visibility, he began removing the individual detonators. It was slow work. Then someone noticed that the detonators were in the retracted position, and the mines could be lifted without removing them. The detonator might explode when the mine came clear of the

Two types of lifting ships at Cherbourg: Lift ships such as these proved invaluable in the harbor clearances of the European war. The boom defense vessel on the right, a self-propelled ship, makes lifts over the bow horns. LC–21 on the left, a dumb barge, makes either belly lifts or bow lifts. Four sister craft of LC–21 were later leased from the Royal Navy for use in Vietnam. Photo courtesy Vice Admiral Bernard E. Manseau.

water, but the mine would not explode. There was considerable trepidation when the first armed mine came clear of the water,[28] and an equal amount of relief when the barge was finally dragged out to sea.

Another unusual problem was posed by an old coaster sunk before the war. Lifting augmented by compressed air seemed to be the only practical way to raise the ship. The coaster's plating was so badly deteriorated that the hull could not be made airtight, and the air leaked out through thousands of tiny pinholes and one large hole. The large hole was patched easily enough with concrete, but the small holes were a problem requiring special logistics effort. They were plugged with toothpicks, a luxury item in short supply in the war-ravaged port. The hull finally became tight enough to build up an air bubble, and three lifting ships dragged it away.

A third interesting wreck at Cherbourg was reminiscent of Casablanca. A double-hulled craft for lifting sunken submarines had been built by the Germans early in the century and given to the French as

---

[28] When the first mine was being lowered onto the dock, the detonator did explode. The mine did not. The theory was proven.

part of the World War I reparations. The French took it to Cherbourg but found it of no value. As they had done with their own early submarine lift vessel in Casablanca, they put it in a back channel with no maintenance. Before the invasion, the Germans brought it out and sank it in the entrance to the outer port. The sinking of the vessel tore the structure so badly that the only way to clear it was to cut it up with torches and lift out the pieces. The cutters worked while the mines were being removed from the harbor. Bit by bit, the old lifting ship was dragged out of the way and disposed of, opening the entrance to the harbor. If the Germans had piled ten or twelve ships atop one another where the lifting ship had been sunk, the harbor would have been closed for a long time indeed.

The Invasion of Southern France

The second chapter of the Battle for France opened on 15 August 1944, when a force of almost 900 ships struck on the Mediterranean coast. Included in this force were salvage forces under the command of Commander Andersen. The task group had learned much in the almost two years of constant salvage operations in the Mediterranean, and its organization and equipment reflected those lessons.

Salvage forces for this invasion were divided into four categories: (1) shallow water salvage and fire-fighting units, (2) deep water salvage and fire-fighting units, (3) reserve units, and (4) harbor clearance units. They saw little action. As in Normandy, there were no daylight air attacks and few at night. The Germans no longer had the capability to resist the invasion with the force they had applied at Salerno and Anzio.

During the months preceding the invasion, fire-fighting schools were held in North African and Sicilian ports, and three experienced fire-fighting officers were ordered to the Eighth Fleet specifically to advise task force commanders. A number of LCI(L)s in each group were designated for fire-fighting and salvage duties. They were fitted out with fire-fighting equipment, heavy bitts, stern chocks, stern anchors, heavy wire ropes, and other miscellaneous gear and manned with trained salvors and fire fighters. LCTs and LCMs were also fitted out for salvage; some of the LCTs were fitted with shear legs capable of lifting 30 tons.

The shallow water units arrived off the assault beaches at first light on D-Day and turned to salvage work after delivering their loads of troops and vehicles for the assault. They hauled beached craft back into the water, cleared craft from underwater obstacles, raised sunken landing craft, and made emergency repairs. All damaged landing craft were cleared from the beaches in the first fifteen days.

The deep water units were two fleet tugs (*Moreno* and *Arikara*), an

142

auxiliary tug, two British rescue tugs, and a boom defense vessel. An American fire-fighting officer and men with additional gear were assigned to the British ships. Unlike other invasions, there were no major fire casualties that called for the services of the deep water units, but there were numerous towing jobs and in one area a number of ships were blown ashore in a storm and had to be hauled off.

The reserve units—three American salvage ships (*Extricate*, *Restorer*, and *Weight*) and one British salvage ship—were held in Corsican ports, removed from the assault area, but within easy reach. Except for a few minor repair jobs, the reserve forces had little to do until the harbor clearance work started.

The harbor clearance units did not lack work. These units, on the venerable *Tackle* and some merchant ships, moved into the ports of Toulon, Marseilles, and Port du Bouc to make them ready for the shipping needed to support the Army ashore. The salvage ships were brought forward to assist in the harbor clearance.

Toulon harbor was a shambles. The damage came from a variety of sources: the scuttling of the French fleet, Allied bombs, and the demolition of piers and ships. Removing a wrecked bridge, lifting three sunken tugs, moving the 12,000 ton passenger ship *Andre Lebon* and a damaged caisson, and shifting the destroyer *Vauban* made up the high-priority work. Each of these jobs would provide an unloading berth. Refloating wrecks, demolishing them with explosives, or bridging them over made portions of six piers usable. By 15 September, six-and-a-half berths were available; by the end of the month two more. The effort demonstrated the need to remain flexible and adjust priorities to fit existing conditions. For example, when work on the *Vauban* looked as though it would take too long, it was stopped and the manpower was applied to clearing Drydock Number One quickly in order to add another berth.

Meanwhile, a few miles to the west at Marseilles, one of the most effectively blocked harbors of the war was being cleared. The man who had carried out this blockage knew his business. The block ships had been sunk both athwart and parallel to the axis of the channel, and were jammed tightly together in lines. To complicate matters, harbor mining had been complete—in the outer channel, past the breakwater, and between the piers. Quayside demolition was equally thorough; the outer legs of cranes were blown, causing them to topple into the berths alongside. As many as five cranes had been dumped into a single berth. The harbor clearance units went to work and by early September fifteen berths for ocean-going ships were ready. By the end of the month an additional eighteen full berths, six partial berths, a coaster berth, and two tanker berths were also ready.

Further west, in Port du Bouc, small tankers were able to enter the excellent oil storage facilities two days after the salvage forces began work. This port had also been heavily mined, but minesweeping operations had been thorough and the hazard was believed to be eliminated. *Tackle*—along with *Brant*, the hard-luck ship of the salvage forces—was going to the fuel pier assisted by the tug *Provencal* when the tug brushed a buoy and detonated a mine attached to it. *Provencal* sank, and there were also casualties in *Tackle*. The ship was first towed to Toulon for emergency repairs, then to Palermo for permanent repairs. She served out the war and returned to the States before being declared unfit for further naval service.

Le Havre

The Allies' schedule called for the port of Le Havre, captured by Canadians on 12 September 1944, to be cleared by the British without American involvement. The port had been stubbornly defended by the Germans, who appreciated its potential as a logistics port, and carefully blocked it when surrender became inevitable.

The port at Le Havre is unusual because it consists of both a tidal port and also a port composed of basins isolated by locks from the effect of tides. The tidal harbor is difficult to use in inclement winter weather. Damage in the harbor had effectively destroyed the usefulness of the locked harbor. When the port was captured, barges had to transfer cargo from the anchorage.

Commodore MacKenzie, with limited experience in harbor clearance, had little to offer for the solution of what seemed an insurmountable problem. Commodore Sullivan, with his unsurpassed experience in getting badly blocked harbors back into service, took a look. Although faced with huge problems elsewhere, Sullivan agreed to apply his organization to the problem. The same experience that led the British to ask for Sullivan in the first place enabled him to see the deficiencies in the Germans' work of blocking the harbor. As soon as he had accepted responsibility, Sullivan requested that *Brant* plus two 900-ton lifting craft and a variety of other salvage equipment be sent to Le Havre immediately.

Colonel W.F. Way, U.S. Army, attached to the Navy salvage forces, became the senior salvage officer for Le Havre. He arrived three days after the capture of the city, with a survey party. The tide range in Le Havre is about 24 feet. This was enough to uncover or at least expose most of the wrecks at low water, enabling the party to locate the wrecks they would be dealing with and get a preliminary idea of the problems.

Brant was the first ship into Le Havre. A variety of equipment followed in short order. Two net tenders managed to remove eighteen wrecks even before the rest of the salvage equipment arrived. Some of the equip-

Supported by pontoons, a submerged tug is towed out of Le Havre under the direction of Lieutenant Frank N. Oberle. Photo courtesy Vice Admiral Bernard E. Manseau.

ment, such as floating cranes that had countless uses around the harbor, had been shanghaied and so were unavailable or only partly available to the salvors. Lifting craft were sent to Le Havre when their work in Cherbourg was finished and after a brief overhaul in Britain. Salvage ships also began to straggle in. HMSV *Abigail*[29] arrived in early November; *Diver*, HMSV *Help*, and several lifting craft arrived shortly thereafter.

The work in Le Havre was not technically difficult and the salvors eventually had all the equipment required to deal with it. Through their efforts, the capacity of the port grew until it became a major supply port handling a far greater tonnage of cargo than it had before the war.

The Western Atlantic

While the war in Europe raged, the war in the western Atlantic continued. The Navy Salvage Service had the chief responsibility for

---

[29] *Abigail* may seem a strange name for a salvage vessel, and so it is. When Alec Doust was Chief Technical Officer for Salvage in the Admiralty early in the war and specifications were being drawn up for salvage ships, he also drew up a list of suitable names for salvage ships. He realized that there was a strong psychological value in names that suggested power, endurance, and capability. When the approved names came back from the Admiralty, the first ship—a converted dredging support vessel that bore the unglamorous name *Hopper No. 4*—was to be renamed HMSV *Abigail*. Perhaps it was named for the handmaiden of King David, perhaps for Mrs. Abigail Smith, the most prized office-cleaner in the Admiralty.

salvage in this area, and the Navy Rescue Towing Service bore the responsibility for ships disabled at sea. As the war dragged on and the shipbuilding and training programs began to turn out excellent salvage ships manned by trained salvors, the fleet began to play a larger role in salvage in the western Atlantic.

As Newfoundland and Iceland were important stations for the North Atlantic routes, so was Bermuda important to the more southerly sea lanes between Europe and the United States. Lying almost equidistant from New York and Norfolk and almost directly astride the sea lanes between those ports and Europe, Bermuda is a natural location for a salvage station in peace or war. In World War II it became a major base for support of convoy operations.

Navy Salvage Service ships were frequent callers at Bermuda, sometimes taking up salvage station there. For Navy tugs the island was both a way station and a salvage station. The ships stationed there, including *Escape* (ARS 6) and *Chain* (ARS 20), did excellent work during the war. The station was so important that the Navy kept *Restorer* (ARS 17) on salvage station there for several months following the end of the war.

Salvage ships and tugs operated throughout the western Atlantic and Caribbean, as far south as the coast of Brazil. The work they did had no glamour, and it did not deliver fire upon the enemy, but it was an important part of the logistic effort and thus, by definition, an important part of the war.

Notable work in the western Atlantic included *Escape*'s rescue tow of *Georgeade* in the fall of 1944 during a storm; *Escape*'s tow of three disabled ships into Bermuda; and *Choctaw*'s (ATF 70) tow over twenty-four days of the tanker *Murfreesboro* stern-first to an American port.

The War in Europe Ends

The war in Europe was essentially over for the salvage forces by 1944. The need to put salvage ships alongside burning and sinking ships diminished greatly following the last amphibious assault. There were still the casualties that inevitably accompanied an unprecedented volume of shipping, and U-boats still posed threats, though not as deadly as in 1942. There were no more harbor clearances driven by the terrible need to open berths so that supplies could be discharged and moved forward to troops at the front. What remained were large amounts of wreckage in European waters. Much of this had to be moved before the harbors would be fully functional. With no urgent military necessity driving salvage operations, however, local people did the work, with the U.S. Navy providing equipment and technical assistance.

As soon as the ports on the Atlantic Coast of France had been cleared, an effort began to clear commercial ports like Bordeaux, La Rochelle, St. Nazaire, Brest, and Lorient. Bordeaux, on the Gironde River, had the highest priority. Commodore Sullivan arranged with Admiral Kahn of the French Navy for the transfer of salvage equipment under Lend-Lease. To assist the French, a small crew that included a salvage officer was located in each port. Two salvage officers billeted in Paris oversaw the work of the field teams and conducted liaison with the French Navy. The program lasted from December 1944 until September 1945 and produced worthwhile results.

Throughout the war the Navy had responded to its salvage needs in a typically American way. The leadership had been strong, the technical ability great, and the ingenuity unsurpassed. Solutions usually fit the problems exactly. When mobilized, the huge industrial capacity of the United States produced not only an extraordinary quantity and variety of materials for war and the bottoms to ship them in, but also the salvage ships and craft to conserve them when casualties were inflicted by a determined and skillful enemy. Massive harbor clearances, a new requirement generated by the techniques and logistics of modern war, were undertaken successfully. If they had not been so successful, the ability of the Allies to supply their armies would have been seriously reduced, and the overall history of the war might have been quite different. However, the job had been done; all who were associated with it could be proud.

Without doubt the dominant figure in the American salvage effort during the war in Europe was William A. Sullivan. He developed the necessary organization and led it effectively. He recognized wartime harbor clearance as vastly different from harbor salvage. He was effective in working with both Allied and other American services. He seemed to be the right man in the right place at the right time. Or was he? As Chief of Navy Salvage, Sullivan's responsibilities were global. Except for a couple of brief trips to the United States and one to Australia about the time of the Anzio invasion, Sullivan was in the Afro-European theatre for almost the duration of the American involvement. Was this the right place for the Chief of Navy Salvage?

A salvage man is attracted to a wreck like a fly to a honey bucket. By nature he wants to be involved in the action. But sometimes the senior salvage officer must stand back and tend to the total, often less glamorous responsibilities of his job. In retrospect, however, it seems clear that the Afro-European theater was the appropriate place for the Chief of Navy Salvage to be for more than two years for a number of reasons:

- The war in Europe was the highest U.S. priority.
- The Navy Salvage Service in American waters and the Bureau of Ships Salvage Section, both direct responsibilities of the Chief of Naval

Commodore William A. Sullivan, the Navy's first Supervisor of Salvage, led the salvage and harbor clearance efforts in the Mediterranean and European theaters and in the Philippines.

Salvage, were in the hands of Captain Bernie Manseau, a brilliant officer supported by a capable staff.

• Salvage in the Central Pacific was in the hands of Lebbeus Curtis, a competent salvor, completely able to deal with the situation there.

With other priorities, or, more significantly, without men of the caliber of Manseau, Curtis, and many others to look after particular aspects of the wartime Navy salvage effort, the lengthy commitment of its chief to one theater would probably not have been desirable or possible.

While the war in Europe was being fought and won and a salvage force was being tailored to its requirements, a very different war was being waged in the Pacific. Determined, imaginative men there were solving very different problems.

Under Tow

CHAPTER FIVE

Fleet Operations in World War II: The Pacific Theater

W orld War II salvage operations in the Pacific differed significantly from those in the Atlantic, as did the war itself. Combat areas and logistics routes in the Pacific extended over thousands of miles of ocean with few developed harbors for either refuge or terminals. In opposing U.S. forces, the Japanese Navy had used its balanced air-surface-submarine force quite differently from the German forces in the Atlantic.

Key to the difference was the lack of a concentrated campaign against strategic lines of communications, despite Japan's excellent submarine force. Logistics forces in transit needed less elaborate defensive methods in the Pacific. U.S. offensive naval operations consisted either of operations to keep unrelenting pressure on the Japanese, or amphibious assaults to move Allied forces nearer the Japanese homeland. Logistics operations, by contrast, became mammoth. The number of noncombat ship casualties grew almost inconceivably large. Operating only in U.S. waters in the Pacific, the Navy Salvage Service had slim resources and an area of operations proportionately much smaller than in the Atlantic. The brunt of salvage work for the huge American naval effort in the Pacific thus fell upon the U.S. Navy.

At the outset salvage forces in the Pacific essentially did not exist, but building and procurement programs had been started. The salvage work at Pearl Harbor had tied up whatever forces and equipment could be mustered quickly. Although the two lead ships of the *Navajo* class of fleet tugs, *Navajo* (ATF 64) and *Seminole* (ATF 65), were operating out of Pearl Harbor, the U.S. Navy had an acute shortage of tugs throughout the Pacific. Admiral Thomas C. Hart's Asiatic Fleet had only one, *Whippoor-will* (AM 35).[1] Hart sent *Whippoorwill* to Darwin, Australia, with the

---

[1] Later ATO 169.

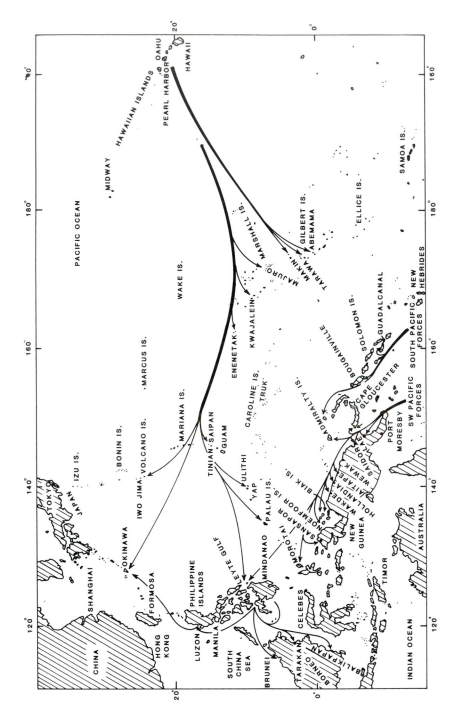

The dual drive across the Pacific.

other auxiliaries in late December 1941, leaving the fleet with no tug support for the actions that followed.

The Asiatic Fleet was not unique. Construction of all types of auxiliary forces had lagged behind the building of combat forces in the fifteen years before the war. After the Pearl Harbor attack U.S. battleships sailed from California on their first voyage to the South Pacific with no logistic support whatsoever. No salvage ships or tugs supported the initial raids by carrier groups in the Marshall and Gilbert Islands. Combatants in the Battles of Coral Sea and Midway had no salvage or tug support either, and few support forces were present during the naval battles off Guadalcanal. Ships, notably *Hornet* (CV 8), *Porter* (DD 356), *Atlanta* (Cl 51), and *Yorktown* (CV 5), sank either because tugs and salvage ships were not available or because the doctrine for salvage in combat support had not been developed. Fortunately neither situation would continue for long.

The year 1942 saw much regrouping and containing of the Japanese thrusts into the eastern and southern Pacific and the Aleutian Islands. The assault on Guadalcanal, the first major American amphibious operation of the war, was not a part of a planned movement against the Japanese homeland. Its purpose was to prevent the Japanese from using the island as a base on the flank of the operations in New Guinea. The Pacific War was the poor relation; the lion's share of war production went to Europe in accord with the Allies' policy of "Beat Germany First." Until the industrial output of the United States could reach a level that would support both theaters, the Pacific waited for material. The absence of an intense logistics war like that in the Atlantic was a boon for the salvage forces, because coastal and overseas convoys in the Pacific required neither elaborate warship escorts nor constant salvage protection.[2] In fact no definite U.S strategy for the Pacific War existed until mid–1943 when ships, men, and equipment began to be available in great quantity.

General MacArthur, thinking like a soldier, supported a single advance toward Japan through the land masses that border the southwestern and western Pacific. In such a strategy the Navy would take on the secondary roles of providing transport, convoy, and security on the flank of the central drive. Naval leaders, although recognizing these as traditional fleet missions, saw the potential of carrier air power in gaining control of the huge areas of the central Pacific. They supported a dual thrust with seaborne forces pushing through the central Pacific while

---

[2] The failure of Japan to use its excellent submarines against logistics shipping can be characterized as a major mistake. Whether it was a strategic blindness to the value of logistics in modern warfare or the Japanese warrior code that prevented a systematic attack on merchant shipping will long be argued. Whatever the reason, the result was that Japanese submarines were sent after well-protected warships rather than the more vulnerable tankers and cargo vessels upon which the warships depended.

MacArthur, also seaborne, drove northward in the west. The naval leaders' views prevailed; the Combined Chiefs of Staff approved the two-pronged attack in May 1943.

The delay in determining a strategy for the war allowed American production to come up to speed, ships to be built, and men to be trained. When the moves toward Japan began, the Navy had not only salvage ships and tugs, but experience derived from action in the Mediterranean.

The First Days

The immediate attention of salvors in the Pacific focused on salvaging the ships sunk at Pearl Harbor. The work required the full-time attention of all the experienced salvage men and of those who had the background to acquire salvage skills quickly. It soon became apparent, however, that salvage would not be limited to a single area but would become a theater-wide activity. Development of a Pacific salvage force became a priority. Commander Lebbeus Curtis was pulled away from the Pearl Harbor work and assigned as Mobile Salvage Engineer on the staff of the Service Force Commander, Rear Admiral William L. Calhoun. Curtis ranged over the Pacific, taking his skills and experience wherever needed.

In the South Pacific

Navajo and *Seminole* operated in the central and eastern Pacific until February 1942, when they embarked salvage teams and attempted to salvage the SS *President Taylor* at Canton Island. *Navajo* got underway shortly thereafter for the South Pacific, where she performed towing and salvage operations in the Solomons and Fijis. She made the long tow to Sydney with the *Portland* (CA 33) after she became crippled at the naval battle of Guadalcanal.[3]

Seminole, too, sailed to the South Pacific but did little salvage work.[4] Along with YP–284, she was pressed into service as a supply ship in the frantic effort to move men and material into Guadalcanal, and was discharging marines, howitzers, and gasoline off Lunga Point on the morning of 18 October 1942 when three enemy destroyers appeared in the northwest. The Japanese ships broke contact with two American

---

[3] On *Portland* and other long tows of damaged ships, a salvage officer rode the tow. In the case of *Portland*, that salvage officer was Lieutenant W.N. Bjork, a veteran of Pearl Harbor salvage and a future Supervisor of Salvage.

[4] *Navajo* now disappears from this account. She continued to participate in salvage and towing operations and made one trip to the United States to be overhauled. On 12 September 1943, while towing YOG-42 from Pago Pago to Espiritu Santo, *Navajo* was rocked by a heavy explosion, probably a mine or torpedo, and sank quickly, taking seventeen of her crew with her.

destroyers and pursued *Seminole* and YP–284, sinking them both with gunfire.

Much of the salvage work in the first part of the war was done by on-the-scene forces with assistance from the few available trained salvors. Such joint and innovative efforts were needed for temporary repairs when the bow of *Minneapolis* (CA 36) was blown off at the Battle of Tassafaronga. Captain Homer Wallin sent Commander Floyd Schultz, who had worked on the Pearl Harbor salvage, to Tulagi to oversee the job. *Ortolan* (ASR 5) assisted. Native labor cut coconut logs to build a temporary bulkhead that replaced the bow of the cruiser.[5] The *Minneapolis* then steamed to Espiritu Santo for additional repairs before heading to the navy yard facilities in Pearl Harbor.

Menominee (ATF 73) was commissioned on 25 September 1942 and outfitted with equipment purchased by Merritt-Chapman and Scott under their prewar procurement contract. It was one of the first of the wartime construction fleet tugs to reach the South Pacific. She was commanded by Lieutenant Commander Emile C. Genereaux, USNR, a professional mariner who had participated in the salvage of *Nevada*, *California*, *West Virginia*, and *Plunger* at Pearl Harbor. The new tug arrived in Suva, Fiji, on 12 December and began a full career of wartime salvage three days later when she was sent to the grounded British Liberty ship *Thomas A. Edison* at Vuata Vatoa, Fiji. Commander Lebbeus Curtis was on the scene because the cargo included badly needed torpedoes bound for the submarine base at Brisbane. *Grebe* (ATO 134) also participated in the salvage operation. There was no thought of saving the ship, which was hard aground and broken in two, but over 500 torpedoes were removed and sent on to their destination before the wreck broke up in a typhoon. Unfortunately the same storm also put *Grebe* ashore and destroyed her.

Immediately afterwards *Menominee* headed towards Bulagari Passage, where the destroyer *Shaw* (DD 373), the Pearl Harbor attack veteran, had run aground at 25 knots and badly holed herself. Genereaux attacked the problem with vigor, beach gear, patching materials, and fourteen pumps. The ship refloated and, with the pumps controlling the constant leakage, was towed to Noumea, New Caledonia, and drydocked.

While in Noumea *Menominee* and Genereaux received one of the most

---

[5] The natives were hired through the military governor of the island, a New Zealand major, to cut the logs for three dollars. The natives appeared, a ragtag bunch dressed in cast-off marine clothing—the one wearing sergeant's stripes worked for the one with corporal's stripes—and set out to do their work. The next morning there were no logs in sight. The natives took the naval officers into the woods where the logs lay and where they would continue to lie because they were too large to move to the beach. A second deal was struck and more logs near the shore were cut. Coconut is a very dense wood; it does not float. The tide came in and submerged the logs. The logs were finally floated to *Minneapolis* with empty 8-inch powder cases used for buoyancy.

unusual salvage assignments of the war. The small Japanese destroyer *Yayoi* had been sunk by air attack on 9 November 1942.[6] A scheme was afoot to raise the ship and use it as a decoy, but first the salvors had to find the wreck. Analysis of charts of the area around Halava Bay, Tulagi, where ships would lie at anchor, gave likely places to start the search. Divers began the tedious business of searching the bottom. Owing primarily to careful work in determining search locations, the wreck was located quickly. The salvors made a careful survey and developed a salvage plan using equipment that could be provided reasonably soon. After a few months and some effort, the necessary equipment was assembled.

During the wait, Genereaux and *Menominee* did not lie idle. They attempted the salvage of SS *Lipscombe Lykes* grounded on Durand Reef. The effort failed because the ship broke up in the heavily pounding surf. They refloated *Delphinius* (AF 24) from South Reef, New Caledonia, SS *Robert Coulton* at Noumea, and the *Buchanan* (DD 484) from a reef near Lengo Channel.

With equipment finally on hand, the salvors tackled *Yayoi*. The Japanese destroyer lay on her starboard side in 12 fathoms of water. The first part of the salvage plan called for lifting and dragging the wreck to the beach. A 500-ton lighter was rigged as a lift craft. The lighter was positioned over the wreck and flooded down some 7 feet. Twelve chains were rove around *Yayoi* and the barge then hauled tight. With the chains tight, the lighter was pumped out to give 500 tons of lift. The lighter could not lift the ship clear of the bottom, but was able to reduce the ground reaction while the ship was dragged into shallow water.

Purchases rigged to anchors ashore provided the main pulling force to move the destroyer and lift barge. Wire ropes from the anchors led to purchases laid out on the deck of a second barge. The other end of the purchases were attached by wire ropes to the bow of *Yayoi*. Winches on the barge hauled the purchases.

Menominee moved ahead of *Yayoi* using both of her bow anchors and long scopes of chain. Additional chain was rigged from the tug around the stern of the destroyer and back to the deck of the tug, where the bitter ends were hauled with *Menominee*'s deck machinery.

Yayoi moved into shallow water until the bow came above water. The ship was then righted with pontoons. With the ship upright, the pontoons were shifted to place three on a side to provide additional stability. The ship was still partially sunk, her stern at least 20 feet under the surface.

---

[6] *Yayoi* (Destroyer No. 23) was a *Mutsuki*-class destroyer built at Uraga, Tokyo, in 1925. The ship had a length of 320 feet, a beam of 20 feet, and a full-load draft of 9 feet 9 inches. Standard displacement was 1,315 tons. All twelve of the ships of this class were lost in the war, most from air attacks in the Solomons.

With the destroyer still resting on the bottom in shallow water, a 30-by-60 foot torpedo hole had to be patched before the ship could be floated. A 15-ton steel patch was made up and attached by drilling holes on one-foot centers around its periphery and securing it to the hull with toggle bolts.[7] With the patch in place and cofferdams built around deck openings, one barge was positioned to lift the stern of *Yayoi*. Sixfold purchases, led around the stern from the barge, were hauled to lift that section. With the barge lifting and numerous pumps pumping, *Yayoi* was brought afloat, dried out, and drydocked. A subsequent survey showed that the hull was so badly damaged it could not be restored. The project was abandoned—clearly a tactical victory but a strategic defeat.

Casualties frequently interrupted the effort to salvage *Yayoi*, as they did other long salvage operations throughout the war. Japanese air raids every night for over four months caused damage requiring the attention of the few available salvage ships. As the quantity of shipping in the South Pacific increased with the war, so did the casualties. The South Pacific is not the easiest place to navigate in the best of times because of the numerous islands and reefs and the lack of navigational aids and good charts. During the war ships lay offshore, anchored in generally poor holding ground, exposed to the vagaries of fickle and wicked weather. As a result they were often driven ashore. Seamanship was in short supply, further contributing to many of the casualties. The shipyards could and did turn out thousands of new hulls, but the men to operate them skillfully were not so easily produced. The judgment and experience of years at sea cannot be replicated in a classroom. Although the men operating ships during the war did well, the standard of seamanship was not high.

The increasing number of casualties stretched the limited salvage resources, as did the failure of operational commanders to use their tugs to best advantage. Many commanders considered all tugs more or less equal, not recognizing that these small ships are of quite complex designs and have characteristics that must be matched to the task. The same operational mistakes in matching tugs to the job made in the early days of the Rescue Towing Service and in preparation for the Normandy invasion were also made in the Pacific. The situation improved as the war went along, particularly after the assignment of Commander Henry Foss, a West Coast towing company executive, to the Service Force Comman-

---

[7] The steel for this patch had been ordered quite a long time before it was required, but it failed to show up. Tracers put out through the supply system failed to locate the steel. Genereaux was ashore on Guadalcanal checking on material when an air raid occurred. While sheltered from the raid in a bunker, Genereaux happened to look up overhead. The following day he made a survey of other bunkers. Shortly thereafter the plate ended its temporary duty as overhead air-raid shelter material and reported to its intended assignment as hull-patching material.

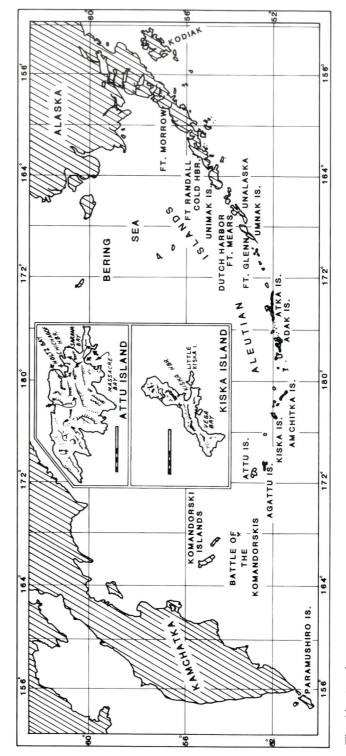

The Aleutian theater.

der's staff. Tug operations in the Pacific, however, never reached the level of effectiveness they did in the Atlantic.[8]

In the Aleutians

The Aleutian Islands are a nasty place to fight a war at sea. The weather changes quickly and can be as violent as any place on earth. Fog is common and dense; distances are great. Nothing that happened in the Aleutians in World War II, other than the diversion of men and material from other theaters, had any influence on the outcome of the war, but the conflict made heavy demands on the men and equipment operating there. Shipping in the Aleutians increased dramatically as it did in all war theaters. Soviet ships carrying Lend-Lease goods from the West Coast to Vladivostok added an unusual twist to the shipping problems in the Aleutians. The Japanese, carefully avoiding trouble with the Soviet Union, did not attack these ships, but the ships sometimes became casualties of the difficult sailing in the area.

The resources applied to the Aleutians were even more meager than in the South Pacific. Tugs were scarce; the few that were there operated constantly, dividing their time between towing and salvage operations. The Navy Salvage Service ran salvage stations at Port Angeles, Washington, and Kodiak, Alaska, for operations in the Aleutians until *Rescuer* wrecked at the end of 1942 and Navy Salvage Service ships were withdrawn from Alaskan waters. In late 1942 the Commander of the Alaskan Command requested help from the Chief of Naval Salvage. Commander Burris D. Wood, who had recently trained at the Pier 88 salvage school, was sent to the northern Pacific to coordinate and direct salvage operations.[9]

The surface ship operations that climaxed in the Battle of the Komandorskiyes (Commander Islands) had virtually no salvage ship support; only the old tugs *Tatnuck* (AT 27) and *Oriole* (AT 136)[10] were available until the newly built *Ute* (ATF 76) arrived in Dutch Harbor early in 1943. *Ute* went into action soon after arrival when, teaming with *Tatnuck*, she freed the grounded transport *Arthur Middleton* (AP 25). Like her sisters

---

[8]To provide guidance for officers concerned with the operation and administration of tugs, the publication *Navy Seagoing Tugs and Related Craft—General Characteristics and Considerations Governing Use of* (COMINCH P-03) was prepared from notes made by Commodore Sullivan and distributed by the Commander in Chief, US Fleet on 21 June 1944. This pamphlet was a forerunner of the *U.S. Navy Towing Manual*. On 15 May 1944 an attempt to clarify the capabilities of tugs was made by breaking the designation AT—Ocean-going Tug into two groups: ATF—Fleet Ocean Tug, for the new *Navajo*-class ships, and ATO—Old Ocean Tug, for the older tugs and converted Bird-class minesweepers.

[9]Commander Wood and those who accompanied him and worked with him did a remarkable job in the northern Pacific. Commander Wood became well known and was requested by name for the invasion of Guam and Saipan.

[10]Originally AM 7, later ATO 136.

to the south, *Ute* found it difficult to complete a long salvage job. She was called away from the *Middleton* to salvage the stranded merchantman *Wallace*.

As the only salvage unit that accompanied the task force in the invasion of Attu, *Ute* could do no good in the early stages of the invasion. Lacking adequate radar equipment, she could not take her proper station in the foul weather. The day following D-Day she went to the assistance of *Perida*, the only Army ship in the operation. *Perida* had hit a pinnacle and holed two compartments. *Ute* beached her to prevent sinking, and patching, pumping, refloating, and cargo discharge operations were carried out simultaneously. *Perida* was subsequently towed to Adak and returned to service.

Ute and the older and smaller tugs participated in numerous salvage operations on both merchant and naval ships in the area during the next few months. *Ute* sailed to Kiska with the invasion force but did no combat salvage operations because the Japanese had departed. *Cree* (ATF 84) joined the Aleutian salvage group and assisted *Ute* with the salvage of the Soviet merchantman *Valery Chkalov* that had broken in half in heavy seas. *Cree* took the forward half of the ship in tow and *Ute* picked up the stern. When the towline to the Russian ship failed, *Ute* sailors reconnected the tow by a novel variation on the traditional line-throwing gun. To make the initial connection, they lashed a 400-pound anchor to a depth charge arbor and fired it with a depth charge projector toward the drifting stern section.

Cree, *Ute*, *Tatnuck*, and *Oriole* continued salvage operations throughout Aleutian waters and accompanied raids against Paramushir as standby salvage ships. By mid-1944 the tempo of operations in the Aleutians had slackened to the point where keeping valuable ATFs there was no longer justifiable. *Cree* and *Ute* headed for other areas of the Pacific. Salvage forces did not abandon Alaska entirely. The newly built, wooden-hulled ARS *Protector* (ARS 14) took up salvage station in Alaska before the departure of *Cree* and remained there until the spring of 1945. *Protector* left in the spring, but *Gear* (ARS 34) arrived before the harsh winter weather set in.

The campaign in the Aleutians may have been merely a sideshow of the total Pacific war, but it was a major effort for the salvage forces there. Their work was hard, dangerous, valuable, and done under extreme conditions of weather. Although all maritime operations in Aleutian waters are hard, salvage operations there are particularly difficult. The Navy salvage forces operating in Alaskan and Aleutian waters did an excellent job of supporting fleet operations and of providing assistance to the numerous casualties caused by the high level of Lend-Lease shipping going to the Soviet Union.

The Drive Across the Central Pacific

For the drive through the Marshall and Gilbert Islands into the Marianas, the Navy needed the mobility and longevity at sea that fleets enjoyed in the days of sail. Amphibious assault operations took place thousands of miles from the nearest permanent base and were made possible only by the Mobile Base concept. Hundreds of ships supplying all the logistics needs of the fleet established bases at places such as Funafuti in the Ellice Islands, Efate, Espirito Santo, and Ulithi. The Mobile Bases formed an integral part of the fleet and allowed fighting ships to remain deployed almost indefinitely without shore-based support. Salvage forces formed an integral part of the Mobile Base concept. Not only did they provide salvage support for combat operations, but they also filled the salvage requirements of the bases and the endless chain of ships that supplied the bases from the United States.

A harbinger of the series of island invasions that followed strikes against the Japanese started in the summer and fall of 1943 as new salvage ships began to join the growing stream of fleet tugs arriving in the Pacific. *Clamp* (ARS 33), the first steel-hulled salvage ship to enter service, arrived in Funafuti on 8 November 1943, in time to support the invasion of Tarawa. Along with *Tawasa* (ATF 92), *Clamp* stayed busy during the invasion. Under air attack five times on 10 December alone, she earned her keep during the invasion by hauling LST–34 off the beach and refloating *Hoel* (DD 533) at Betio Point.

Salvage operations supporting amphibious assaults in the central Pacific began to take the same general form they had in Europe. Salvage ships and fleet tugs, augmented by teams specially trained in salvage or fire fighting, closely supported amphibious forces and provided assistance to ships damaged during the assault. LCI(L)s fitted out for towing and fire fighting, and LCTs with the shear legs derived from Sullivan and Doust's late-night design, carried out salvage operations on landing craft and amphibious vehicles during and immediately after the assault. The relatively short island campaigns generated salvage work to be done after each island was secure. This work included recovery of landing craft too badly damaged for immediate salvage, salvage of ships beached to prevent sinking, and removal work.

The salvage of SS *Sea Flyer* was a routine after-the-assault operation. *Sea Flyer* grounded on the south side of the east channel at Eniwetok[11] atoll at 2:30 in the morning of 21 July 1944. Salvage operations began immediately under the direction of Captain Worral R. Carter, Commander Service Squadron Ten. Preparations for disembarking troops and

---

[11] Sometimes spelled Enewetak at the time.

discharging cargo started. Lieutenant Robert K. (Bulldog) Thurman, the commanding officer of *Tawasa*, laid out beach gear. Commander Curtis flew in to supervise the operation. Tugs initially tried to haul the ship off before all the beach gear was laid and set—an exercise in futility and a waste of time. In the end, after 1,900 tons of cargo had been discharged and the beach gear properly set, *Sea Flyer* was hauled off and returned to service.

Salvage forces in the Pacific worked for the Service Force Commander throughout the war rather than being organized into their own task force. As part of the Service Squadrons, salvage ships reported directly to the service and salvage group commander in each operation. Salvage commanders were usually given a great deal of autonomy in their operations and in deciding the details of resource allocation. This is not to suggest that the confusion of combat did not affect Pacific salvage operations, as it affects all combat efforts. However centralized salvage control operations helped minimize the confusion because assignment of priorities and allocation of resources was done by a single commander rather than fragmented throughout the assault force.

The same salvage pattern continued during the invasions of the Marianas and the western Carolines. New salvage ships began pouring into the area. *Apache* (ATF 67), *Yuma* (ATF 94), ATR–33, and ATA–123 assisted the grounded Army ship FP–147. *Yuma* refloated the hospital ship *Samaritan* (AH 10), which struck a reef while carrying more than 600 battle casualties. *Apache* assisted the mined Liberty ship *Elihu Thompson* and towed her to Noumea. *Grapple* (ARS 7) put a fire-fighting and salvage crew aboard the destroyer *Wadleigh* (DD 689). *Quapaw* (ATF 110), the venerable *Sonoma* (AT 12), and *Lipan* (ATF 85) hauled landing craft off the beach at Morotai. Fleet tugs undertook the highest-value tows on the moves of the Mobile Bases. Salvage ships acted as retrievers of lost tows on the same moves.[12] The jobs went on and on—most small, none glamorous, but a huge cumulative benefit.

While the amphibious forces captured island after island and steadily reduced the size of the Japanese holdings in the Pacific, Fast Carrier Task Forces kept pressure on the Japanese by striking at their bases. Much had been learned about conducting these strikes since the initial raids in the Gilberts and Marshall Islands in 1942. One important lesson was that losses could be prevented by stationing salvage and towing ships along the anticipated withdrawal route to assist ships damaged by the Japanese.

---

[12] Wire rope and heavy manila towing hawsers were in short supply throughout the Pacific, as were shackles, flounder plates, and other towing hardware. Tow rigging often showed more ingenuity than technical sophistication. Lost tows were not uncommon. It became a matter of practical necessity to have a ship designated to assist in recovering lost tows.

Salvage ships and tugs were allocated for this purpose during the drive across the central Pacific.

Just how valuable these preparations were was proven after the 13 October 1944 torpedoing of the cruiser *Canberra* (CA 70) 85 miles off Taiwan.[13] *Canberra* was seriously wounded. She lost propulsion, and both firerooms and an engine room flooded. There were 4,500 tons of flood-water in her. *Wichita* (CA 45) took her in tow and headed for a rendezvous with *Munsee* (ATF 107). *Munsee* put a salvage crew aboard *Canberra* and took over the tow. The salvage crew turned to repairing the torpedo damage to the cruiser's hull and preparing to pump her out. During the repairs Ensign P.S. Criblet, the tug's salvage officer, died in a diving accident in the engine room. After almost a week of towing toward Ulithi Island, the group was joined by the tug *Watch Hill*, which had been leased by the War Shipping Administration. *Munsee* and *Watch Hill* towed in tandem for another week until they reached Ulithi and delivered *Canberra* alongside the repair ship *Ajax* (AR 6).

While the damaged *Canberra* withdrew, the Fast Carrier Task Force, Task Force 38, shifted its movements to protect the damaged cruiser. The cruiser *Houston* (CL 81), part of the task force covering the withdrawal, was hit by an aerial torpedo on 14 October. Having lost all propulsion and steering power, the ship listed heavily. Excess personnel were removed and the damage seemed fatal. The cruiser *Boston* (CA 69) made up a tow and got underway at 3 knots. The following morning a fire in *Houston*'s engine room caused a loss of power in the forward part of the ship, making the anchor windlass inoperable and delaying passing the tow to *Pawnee* (ATF 74), which had joined in the early morning hours. The tow was passed by midmorning. Early afternoon brought warning of an approaching air raid. A persistent and courageous Japanese pilot bored in on *Houston* and, despite suffering many hits, dropped his torpedo; it struck the cruiser in the stern, starting a raging gasoline fire. *Pawnee* held on and kept towing while salvage crews and the ship's force fought to extinguish the fire and keep the ship afloat.

Pawnee held on for six more days and then passed the tow to *Zuni* (ATF 95) and *Current* (ARS 22) towing in tandem. In another six days the two tugs brought *Houston* into the lagoon at Ulithi where she came alongside the repair ship *Hector* (AR 7)—1,250 miles from where the damage had initially occurred.

It was the season for torpedoing and towing cruisers. A week after *Houston* arrived in Ulithi, *Reno* (CL 96), while operating east of the Philippines, was torpedoed in the port side aft. *Zuni* arrived the following day, put a salvage crew on board, and commenced the tow. Both tug and

---

[13] Then known as Formosa.

cruiser crews worked with courage, skill, and determination to keep the badly damaged warship afloat. They succeeded.

The rescue tows of the battle-damaged *Canberra*, *Houston*, and *Reno* demonstrated the value of tugs supporting far-ranging Fast Carrier Task Forces. Three warships had been saved for repair and return to service. Support of strike forces by salvage ships stationed along expected withdrawal routes continued as a routine practice through the war.

Salvage in the Rear Areas

The very nature of the Pacific war—with operations over great areas of ocean and on innumerable islands and huge quantities of material and numbers of men moving by ship—meant that salvage efforts had to extend throughout the entire Pacific.

The large wartime shipbuilding program that was needed to support such extensive operations introduced ship types previously unknown into the U.S. Navy. Nowhere was this truer than in the Service Force. The prewar logistics arm of the fleet, the Base Force Train, had 51 ships in 1940; its wartime successor, the Service Force, Pacific Fleet, had 2,930 vessels of all types in July 1945. Many of these ships had missions generated purely by the nature of the war being fought. Of all the ships in the Service Force, none had more specialized missions or demanding seamanship requirements than the salvage ships and tugs.

As we have seen, salvage experience in the Navy at the beginning of the war was limited to a small number of officers and a somewhat greater number of warrant officers and enlisted men. Field experience grew quickly in the war. The salvage school at Pier 88 proved invaluable for training men in the fundamentals of salvage. It remained to match the men and equipment, especially the fine, steel-hulled salvage ships being built by Basalt Rock Company of Napa, California.

Commander Emile Genereaux who, after being relieved as commanding officer of *Menominee* had been serving as a staff salvage officer in the South Pacific, returned to the United States. He was given the job of setting up a salvage training course for the new salvage ships and their crews. Another experienced salvage officer, Lieutenant Commander Ray Chance, served as Genereaux's principal assistant.

An intensive course was set up incorporating salvage training in the shakedown training of the newly built ships. Initially located in San Diego, the training soon moved to the Roosevelt Base on Terminal Island. Particular attention was paid to those salvage skills that had proven most valuable in wartime operations—laying and retrieving beach gear, patching and pumping, and towing at sea. Eleven ships went through a tough eleven days of salvage training before being sent on to forward areas. Fire fighting on damaged vessels, a major function during combat support operations, was conspicuous by its absence from the salvage training for two reasons. First, fire-fighting crews aboard salvage ships were not part of the regular complements of the ships, but were specialists assigned temporarily to supplement the ships' crews. Second, the operational concept for salvage forces called for tugs—fleet tugs, auxiliary tugs, and rescue tugs, augmented by salvage and fire-fighting specialists—to provide prompt assistance to damaged ships while the salvage ships were held outside the immediate combat zone. The salvage training instituted at San Diego as part of the shakedown has provided the basic pattern for the training of salvage ships and crews ever since.

All was not success and glory, nor even sweat and hard work, for the new salvage ships. There were some embarrassments. *Seize* (ARS 26), fresh from the builder's yard and on her first salvage assignment, went to Clipperton Island to refloat LST–563 stranded there. *Seize* put her towing hawser aboard and maneuvered to take position for a pull, but wrapped the wire rope hawser in her starboard screw. Like the *Milwaukee* during the H–3 salvage, *Seize* found herself in irons, and, like the *Milwaukee*, *Seize* grounded and broached. *Tenino* (ATF 115), with Commander Genereaux aboard, sailed from San Diego in company with the Navy Salvage Service ship *Viking* (ARS 1).

Clipperton Island is a typical Pacific atoll, about two miles in diameter. It has an average elevation of only 20 feet, sparkling white sand, and sparse vegetation. *Seize* was well and truly grounded there, high and dry, her starboard side to the beach, her bottom holed, and her double bottoms flooded. The hawser was still connected to the LST and still wrapped around the salvage ship's wheel. The surf was vicious; the landing craft with the salvage officer aboard capsized on its way in to the beach.

Four legs of beach gear were laid out and anchors were set ashore to hold *Seize*, pivot her into the sea, and haul her off. To reduce the ground reaction, all possible weight was discharged onto the island, and air at 3 pounds above sea pressure was blown into the damaged tanks. On the eleventh day after the arrival of the salvage forces at Clipperton Island, *Seize* came off the beach and headed for San Diego, towed by *Viking*.[14] *Tenino* continued trying to refloat LST–563, but to no avail; the badly damaged ship would have sunk if refloated. The attempt was abandoned.

---

[14] After being hauled off Clipperton Island, *Seize* was repaired and joined the salvage forces in the western Pacific, where she had a productive, if undistinguished, career for the remainder of the war and also in China after the war. *Seize* was transferred to the Coast Guard in 1946. The grounding did not seem to hurt the ruggedly built ship. Recommissioned as USCGC *Yocona* (WAT 168, later WMEC 168), after four years at Eureka, California, she served in Oregon at the mouth of the Columbia River for more than thirty years.

Another salvage ship operating in a rear area got into trouble with not so happy results. The channel entrance to Midway Island is treacherous, a hard passage for the most seasoned navigator. When the submarine *Flier* (SS 250) stranded there in early 1944, the submarine rescue ship *Macaw* (ASR 11) came in and refloated her. Submarine rescue ships are fitted with deep-diving equipment and the specialized rigging that allows them to lay and go into multiport moors; they are not well equipped, nor are they well suited for conventional salvage operations. *Macaw* found herself hard aground. *Clamp* came up immediately from Abemama atoll to Midway where she arrived in the midst of some particularly foul weather. She laid her beach gear when the seas subsided and pulled for two days. *Macaw* didn't budge. *Clamp* then hauled off to regroup and rethink the operation. More attempts were made and, in the teeth of a howling gale more than three weeks after her arrival, *Clamp* hauled *Macaw* off. The elation was short lived. The badly holed *Macaw* sank in the entrance channel, taking much of *Clamp*'s salvage gear with her. In the spring of the same year, *Shackle* (ARS 9) removed much of the wreckage of *Macaw* that had made the entrance into Midway even more treacherous.

As in the other theaters of the war, not all salvage in the rear areas of the Pacific involved the salvage forces. Some was done on an ad hoc basis by whatever forces could be mustered. When the new Liberty ship *M.H. Deyoung* took a torpedo en route from San Francisco to Australia, no salvage ships were available to assist. The ship was seriously damaged and without power, but in no immediate danger of sinking. A naval engineer, Commander Arthur Bushey, went to the scene with instructions to save the cargo. Fortunately, the cargo contained the material that would be required for the salvage operation. Commander Bushey evaluated the remaining strength in the hull and opted not to expend time and manpower in strengthening the ship. He directed effort to the more important matter of ensuring that no dangerous flooding could occur.

SS *Mark Hopkins*, en route in ballast back to San Francisco, was brought alongside. The salvors ran a steam line from *Hopkins* to provide steam for *Deyoung's* winches. Preparations were made to discharge cargo into *Hopkins*. The task became a competition as merchant seamen and Navy sailors vied to discharge the most tonnage during their shifts.

As the cargo discharge operation began, an incident occurred that demonstrated the difference between mariners engaged in normal operations and salvors, particularly Navy salvors, who have a different rulebook.[15] With hatches open and preparations being made for the first lift,

---

[15] The ship had been loaded and would have been unloaded by shore cranes, which have a greater capacity than ships' booms.

The salvage ship *Seize* lies hard aground on the white sand of Clipperton Island after getting her tow wire in her screw while trying to salvage LST–563. After the successful salvage *Seize* saw war service in the Pacific and more than forty years duty as USCGC *Yocona*. Photo courtesy David W. Genereaux.

From the bridge of *Tenino*, Commander Emile C. Genereaux directs salvage operations on *Seize*. Photo courtesy David W. Genereaux.

it was discovered that the first heavy piece of machinery to be lifted exceeded the capacity of the jumbo boom. The master, forbidden by law from permitting a lift greater than the boom rating, stopped the operation. The salvage officer gave the master the option of accepting one of two letters. The first letter would relieve the master of all responsibility for making the lift and place that responsibility on the salvage officer. The second letter stated that the ship would be taken over by the Navy.

The master accepted the first letter, thereby resolving a sticky problem. Although the master and the salvage officer responded differently to the same situation because they operated under different mindsets, a mutually satisfactory solution was found. The discharge of *Deyoung*'s cargo, passengers, and most of her complement proceeded smoothly. *Mark Hopkins* soon left the scene to return to Australia. A War Shipping Administration contract tug shortly arrived and took *Deyoung* in tow for Espiritu Santo, where she became a hotel ship.

An almost infinite variety of salvage efforts continued throughout the war in the Pacific. Even the rear areas required harbor clearance. Pearl Harbor, the site of the largest harbor salvage job of the war, was also the site of an important harbor clearance operation.

On the morning of 21 May 1944 an accidental explosion in LSTs loading ammunition in West Loch for the invasion of Guam triggered a series of explosions and fires that sank five LSTs and blew the deck-loaded LCTs off, sinking them and a number of smaller craft. Fortunately, *Valve* (ARS 28) and *Vent* (ARS 29) lay in the harbor at the time. These ships fought the fires until exploding ammunition forced them to clear the area. As soon as possible, *Valve* returned to the scene and extinguished the fire on LST–480.[16] When all fires were extinguished and the situation somewhat under control, *Valve* began to clean up the mess. She continued her work, picking up live ammunition, recovering ten LVTs, removing wreckage, and setting the ships up for explosive cutting until September 5, leaving the scene only once to refloat LCI(G)–566, grounded off Wahie Point, Lanai.

The work continued under the overall direction of Commander Henry Foss at Service Force Headquarters at Makalapa. Lieutenant Commander Jim Greely, in charge at the scene, had Lieutenants Charles Bisordi, Charles Koener, and John M. Ephland and Chief Carpenter Thomas to assist him as salvage officers. The Salvage Base at Waipio Point, conveniently located at the entrance to West Loch, provided enlisted salvors. The work included hauling one LST onto the beach with beach gear and lifting out an LCT with a battery-operated, 200-ton crane of World War I vintage. An unusual aspect of the operation was an attempt to cut up

---

[16] *Vent* sailed 23 July on a previously scheduled, high-priority deployment to Funafuti.

LSTs burn in West Loch, Pearl Harbor, after the explosion on 21 May 1944. A salvage ship, center, goes to fight the fire.

an LST with shaped charges, the first time this technique had been used in the Navy. It produced mixed results then, just as attempts to use shaped charges to cut ships do today.

In the Pacific war the delineation between forward and rear areas was not always clear. The Advanced Base at Ulithi came under enemy attack at irregular intervals. Some of these attacks resulted in damage to the ships there and, consequently, work for the salvage forces. Fortunately, because Ulithi was a major Advanced Base, the harbor usually sheltered salvage ships. When a midget submarine attack badly damaged *Mississinewa* (AO 59) and set her afire on 20 November 1944, *Munsee, Menominee, Extractor* (ARS 15), and ATR–51 did excellent fire-fighting work, going alongside the ship with its burning cargo, mainly of aviation gasoline. That work was to no avail, however, and *Mississinewa* sank.

There was success, however, at Ulithi on 11 March 1945 when a suicide plane struck the carrier *Randolph* (CV 15), doing substantial damage and setting the ship on fire. *Current* went alongside to port and *Chickasaw* (ATF 83) to starboard, both fighting the fire effectively. When the heat became too intense for *Current, Munsee* and the large harbor tug YTB–384 replaced her, pouring six streams on the fire. *Apache, Molala* (ATF 106), *Grapple* (ARS 7), and several harbor tugs also moved in to assist. The salvage ships and *Randolph*'s crew, working through the night, extinguished the fire.

The vastness of the Pacific war often called for salvage ships to be everywhere at once. Jobs were not limited to combat areas but, as the few examples above indicate, were spread all over the ocean. Nor was the Pacific simply a *mare nostrum* for U.S. Navy salvors. Australia's Commonwealth Marine Salvage Board operated two BARSs, three BATs,[17] and various leased tugs on salvage operations, mostly in the waters around Australia and New Guinea. They did excellent work, and many of the ships they assisted flew the U.S. flag.

The Philippine Campaign

The two thrusts of the Pacific war, one across the central Pacific and the other through the southwest Pacific, joined for the first time in the Philippine campaign. This campaign had many other firsts, including some notable ones for the salvage forces. The Allied forces operating offshore saw the introduction of a new weapon—suicide aircraft, or kamikazes—that caused much ship damage and provided much work for salvors. The large, well-developed harbor at Manila—no stranger to naval action—was to be the first major harbor recaptured and the location of the first major clearance of a harbor blocked by the enemy in the Pacific theater.

The Japanese heavily opposed the approach to the Philippines with

---

[17] The BARSs (steel-hulled ARSs) and BATs (oceangoing tugs) were both intended for Britain. The three Australian tugs—*Reserve, Sprightly,* and *Tancred*—were ATA-type ships. These five ships were responsible for the salvage of more than 600,000 tons of shipping during the war.

frequent air attacks. During one of these attacks, *Grasp* (ARS 24) shot down an enemy aircraft, and *Grasp* and *Chowanoc* (ATF 100) assisted in downing several others. On 20 October a bomb struck *Preserver* (ARS 8) while she was bound from Seeadler Harbor to the Philippines, penetrating her hull and causing the engine room to flood. The hit essentially put the ship out of the war; battle damage repairs took until the following July.

The kamikaze was extremely effective. A successful kamikaze attack on a ship almost always resulted in serious fire and extensive damage. The presence of salvage ships, capable of providing specially trained fire fighters and salvage people and of towing the stricken ship away from the danger area, became a major factor in the fleet's ability to deal with the kamikaze.

Combat Salvage

The numbers of salvage ships and tugs had grown significantly prior to the Philippine campaign, but there were never enough. The ships present were constantly active. The level of activity is apparent in the following excerpts from the report of the Salvage and Rescue Group[18] at the MIKE ONE operation in Luzon for a ten-day period:

> 8 January 1945—Just before dusk on 8 January, CVE–71 (*Kitkun Bay*) . . . was hit by an enemy suicide plane. *Chowanoc* took the CVE in tow. . . .
> 9 January 1945—. . . All units of the group reported to the Group Commander and initially took positions deployed at regular intervals in the sectors of the objective area occupied by the attack forces. . . . At 1300 the *Mississippi* (BB 41) was seen to be burning on the main deck and superstructure amidships on the port side, apparently as a result of aerial enemy attack. *Grasp*, *Quapaw*, and ATR–61 immediately closed on the *Mississippi* but were informed no assistance was needed. . . . At 1400 *Grasp* began a tour of inspection of all beaches running as close to shore as her draft would permit. . . . LCT–1028, badly damaged by an underwater explosion, was beached by *Rail* (ATO 139) and her after compartments flooded to prevent broaching. LCI–865, damaged by enemy action, was taken over by *Hidatsa* (ATF 102) and emergency repairs started.
> 10 January 1945—A heavy swell developed during the night and conditions became bad on the beaches. . . . LSTs 925 and 1028 were severely damaged below their water lines during the night by enemy action. Salvage teams went aboard to inspect the damage and both craft were assisted to the beach. . . . *Chowanoc* retracted LST–567 hard aground and in danger of broaching. *Apache* placed pumps aboard APD 10. . . . LCI–690 retrieved a broached barge. . . . *War Hawk* (AP 168) was severely damaged during the

---

[18] Commander Task Group 77.8, Commander Byron S. Huie, Jr., USNR.

night by a small enemy craft apparently carrying a torpedo. *Grasp* closed on *War Hawk* immediately and placed pumps aboard. . . . With the water under control, *Grasp* was replaced by *Chickasaw* who completed repairs sufficient to enable *War Hawk* to be towed to port for major repairs.

11 January 1945—. . . Salvage units were concentrated in the trouble areas in order to assist wherever possible and without specific orders. . . . The communication burden increased to such an extent that the limited facilities of *Grasp* were inadequate successfully to cope with it. In the confusion, considerable difficulty was experienced in obtaining the location of craft reported needing assistance. . . .

The account of assistance to landing and beaching craft of all types goes on, and larger ships were assisted as well. The report continues:

13 January 1945—. . . At 2230 *Grasp* closed on the Liberty *Otis Skinner* which had received severe damage above the water line on the starboard side forward of the bridge from an enemy suicide plane and was burning. Fire fighters were immediately placed aboard and the fire was brought under control. *Chickasaw* closed on the *Skinner* soon after to assist *Grasp*. . . .

14 January 1945—The fire on the *Skinner* smoldered during the night, but by daybreak was completely extinguished by *Grasp*. *Chickasaw* took over, placing repair parties on board, and *Grasp* resumed her normal function. Fire fighting teams sent by *Grasp* to combat the fire on the *Skinner* displayed outstanding courage and skill. In order to reach the flames, it was necessary for the fire fighters to use masks and to enter the hole made by the enemy aircraft in the side of the ship. Gasoline was stored beneath the hold where the fire was burning and the magazine was situated nearby. . . . The Liberty *Kile V. Johnson* entered the harbor severely damaged and in a critical condition as a result of being hit by an enemy suicide plane in number three hold. *Cable* proceeded to her assistance and placed pumps and a repair party on board. . . .

The report goes on to describe a high tempo of activity by the group through 17 January,[19] concluding with this recommendation:

Any tug or salvage vessel designated as a flagship of a salvage group such as that employed in MIKE ONE, should be furnished an experienced and competent communications officer with additional radio and visual equipment and sufficient radiomen and signalmen to stand constant watches. In the case of MIKE ONE, the flagship *Grasp* could have operated much more efficiently had it been provided a Staff Communications Officer, six radio-

---

[19] The report includes a brief description of the salvage of a small enemy submarine containing cargo and documents of intelligence value. *Rail* and *Grasp* participated in the salvage. The submarine was not a midget, but was probably one of the *Yu1*-class transport submarines designed, built, and operated by the Japanese Army. Twelve of these 130-foot units were built; the fate of ten is unknown.

men and six signalmen.[20] Highly efficient communications are absolutely essential to successful salvage operations. Without such efficiency, immediate response cannot be made to emergency calls; and, in the great majority of instances, time is of the essence. If the salvage vessel arrives on the scene promptly, a major salvage operation, or even a complete loss of a vessel, is likely to be prevented.[21]

The table on the next page summarizes the work of the Luzon Salvage and Rescue group in the ten-day period covered by the report.

The action described above was neither isolated nor unusual, but rather typical of what salvage ships all over the Pacific did during amphibious operations. The U.S. Navy had come a long way in developing a large and proficient salvage force that was making a significant contribution to the war. However there were still lessons to be learned, as there always are in salvage and in war. And there were still many hard knocks ahead.

Three salvage ships became casualties during the campaign in the Philippines. One was the elderly tug *Sonoma*, built in 1912 and a veteran of numerous peacetime and wartime salvage operations. A flaming Japanese bomber crashed into her, two explosions followed, and she began taking water. *Chickasaw* and LCI–72 put the fires out, but the damage was fatal. *Sonoma* sank on the afternoon of 24 October 1944. A second casualty occurred when *Guardfish* (SS 217) mistakenly torpedoed *Extractor* (ARS 15) on New Year's Day 1945 in the Philippine Sea. Finally, on 17 February, while returning from the landing on Corregidor, *Hidatsa* (ATF 102) struck a mine in Mariveles harbor that left several dead and wounded; she was towed to Subic Bay for repairs. The damage was serious enough to put the tug out of the war but she returned to the Philippines for postwar salvage operations.[22]

The Manila Harbor Clearance

Manila Bay in west-central Luzon is the best natural harbor in the Philippines. Manila has a well-developed port facility, and for many years before the war most of the foreign trade of the Philippines passed through

---

[20] The recommendation that thirteen men be added to the staff may have been tongue in cheek. Accommodating this many men aboard a salvage ship would have been difficult.

[21] Ltr, Task Group 77.8 to Commander Task Force 77, 17 January 1945, "Activities of Task Group 77.8 during MIKE ONE Operation, Report of."

[22] One of those wounded was an officer on Commander Huie's staff, Walter L. (Scotty) Marshall. Marshall was to have a long and distinguished career in salvage, becoming Seventh Fleet salvage officer, Pacific Fleet salvage officer, and Supervisor of Salvage. Following his retirement from the naval service, he became vice president of a major American salvage company. Captain Marshall wrote numerous articles on salvage, many of which served as references for this history.

Summary of Work
By Salvage and Rescue Group,
Luzon Attack Force

Stranded or broached craft refloated

LST	23
LSM	6
LCI	2
LCT	4
Pontoon barge	23

Major repair jobs

AP	1
AK	2
APD	2
LST	5
LCI	4
PC	1

Towing

CVE	2
APD	1
LCI	3
PC	1

Minor repair jobs

LSM	2
LCT	1
LCI	5

Craft sunk as a menace to navigation

LCI	1

Craft raised

Submarine	1
LCT	1

NOTE: LCVPs and other small craft were retrieved from various beaches during other operations, but no account was kept of their number.

SOURCE: Report dated 17 January 1945 submitted by Commander Task Group 77.8 to Commander Task Force 77.

Chickasaw and LCI–72 assist the venerable tug *Sonoma* after a Japanese aircraft crashed into her.

the port. When the Japanese left Manila, they did a thoroughly professional job of blocking the harbor and rendering the port useless.

In preparation for the invasion General MacArthur insisted that Commodore Sullivan come to the Pacific to discuss clearance of Manila harbor. Sullivan flew to Australia from the Mediterranean for the initial conferences about the time of the Anzio landings. He did not look forward to working with MacArthur, whom many in the Navy considered to be a prima donna, but he came away impressed with the general's effectiveness and the small size of his staff.

The clearance of Manila harbor was to be quite unrelated to the other salvage work in the Pacific. Salvors from the Atlantic and recent graduates of the Salvage School entirely manned the Salvage Group that worked there. When Sullivan returned to the Pacific for the Manila harbor clearance, he brought some of the most experienced salvors from the European theater, along with Captain Manseau and others from the United States.[23]

The number of ships sunk at Manila far exceeded that in any other harbor cleared during the war. At first it seemed that there were probably not more than about 200 wrecks. But as the work went on, the salvors

---

[23] When the work in Manila harbor necessary for resuming military operations was complete, a large number of wrecks remained. These were removed commercially after the war. After the war Huie returned to Manila and joined the staff of Luzon Stevedoring Company, a participant in this work.

kept finding more, until an estimated 750 ships, barges, and assorted craft had been removed from Manila Bay.

Harbor Clearance Units in Europe had proven their skill at moving in and going to work immediately behind combat forces. In Manila something new was encountered. All Japanese had not been driven away by the assault forces—suicide squads hid in the wrecks until the salvors came aboard, then attacked them with machine guns and hand grenades. Before salvage work or even survey work could begin, the remaining Japanese had to be cleared out. Army troops with flame throwers, supported by PT boats and light aircraft, began sweeping the wrecks to clear them of suicide squads. The sweeps had to be repeated, often several times, for as soon as soldiers cleared the wrecks more Japanese would swim out and form new suicide squads.

When the suicide squads had finally been cleaned out and salvage work began in earnest, salvors found that the entrance to the harbor had been successfully blocked with four ships.[24] These ships, all between 700 and 900 tons displacement, were sunk in exactly the right positions. An unusual procedure in sinking the wrecks reportedly achieved this precision. In most cases when blockships are sunk, time fuses on the explosives allow crews to leave before the charges detonate. Small charges, just large enough to ensure sinking, are used and there is some time for currents and other environmental forces to act on the ship before she hits the bottom. In compliance with Murphy's Law, ships usually move away from the planned positions. The Japanese did not follow this procedure. They blew up the ship's magazines with the crews still on board. The ships sank immediately, positioned precisely.

These blockships presented a tough salvage problem for three reasons:

1. There was 12 to 15 feet of water over the decks, and the hulls were too badly holed to allow the use of compressed air to restore buoyancy.

2. Rough seas at the harbor entrance made it impossible to keep cofferdams in place.

3. Lift craft such as the British had used so well in Europe were not available in this part of the world.

A complete survey of the ships showed that the deck of one had been relatively lightly damaged. Patches were prepared and fit. Air was then blown into the hull. This procedure lightened the ship enough so that it could be dragged away by a salvage ship with beach gear. Removing the

---

[24] Two Filipino coasters, a 210-foot Japanese tanker, and the ex-U.S. Navy gunboat *Luzon* (PR 7) that had been captured at Corregidor in May 1942.

Commander Bradford Huie (without shirt) and Captain Bernard Manseau (with can) enjoy a formal luncheon, salvage style, during the Manila harbor clearance. Photo courtesy Vice Admiral Bernard E. Manseau.

others required pure brute force. This force was provided by lifting the ships with all the pontoons and cranes in the harbor, then dragging them out of the way with the salvage ships. *Cable* (ARS 19) and *Grasp* (ARS 24) assisted with the harbor clearance work for long periods. The salvage ships' mobility, heavy purchases, and bow-lifting arrangements made them valuable assets. However, the variety of lifting craft available in Europe was sorely missed. An attempt to convert two tankers to lifting craft was unsuccessful because men and time for their conversion could not be spared. The work had to proceed without the benefit of lifting craft other than the salvage ships and net tenders.

The variety of ships and salvage scenarios at Manila called upon most of the known salvage techniques—patching, pumping, blowing, piece-mealing. Japanese wooden cargo ships known as "Sugar Charlies" made up almost a hundred of the wrecks. Many were sunk empty and presented no particular problem. But some carried a variety of cargoes including ammunition. These cargoes caused major problems that had to be dealt with on a ship-by-ship basis. Coastal freighters scattered throughout the harbor could not readily be salvaged by conventional means because of

Accommodations for those clearing Manila harbor were far from grand. This Quonset hut served as Commodore Sullivan's quarters. Photo courtesy Vice Admiral Bernard E. Manseau.

their construction. A method similar to that developed during the salvage of the German High Seas Fleet at Scapa Flow was used. The masts and deckhouses were blown off, the ships were capsized, and then they were floated to a disposal site upside down on a bubble of air.

As had been the case during the clearance of Port Lyautey, a number of the coastal trading vessels that had to be removed had poor stability and were subject to capsizing during refloating. An unusual device solved the problem. It was a salvor's delight, innovative and workable, and must have added spice to the operations. Most of the coasters had a heavy list. A large tank, partially filled with water, secured to heavy girders on the high side could be positioned athwartships by hauling with heavy purchases. By moving the tank, the list could be kept between 5 and 15 degrees away from the tank. The process worked and provided a number of thrills for the salvors. As a recommended process, rise of the tank is nearly in the same category as the reported Japanese method of positioning blockships accurately.

Considering the number of wrecks, the port at Manila was opened reasonably quickly. The work of course continued until after the war, both at Manila and, to a lesser extent, northward at Subic Bay. The work was difficult, the conditions not good. However, invaluable experience gained in Europe expedited the clearance. Lift craft would have helped, but the ingenuity of the salvors—now reinforced by experience—along with the new salvage ships and tugs allowed the salvors to overcome the absence of this tool.

The Attack on Japan

By the time final preparations began for the attack on Japan, the U.S. Navy had reached its full fighting potential and had proven itself capable of sustaining operations with a flexible mobile logistics system. Without this level of expertise, the complex two-pronged operation involving Iwo Jima and Okinawa could not have been considered. Strong and effective salvage forces made up part of the logistics system. Possession of Iwo Jima in the Bonins was crucial to the establishment of bomber bases for effective raids on the Japanese home islands. Originally scheduled for January, the attack was delayed until 19 February by operations in the Philippines and the December typhoon. The Okinawa invasion was to follow six weeks later. By that time the kamikaze aircraft had established itself as a forceful weapon, one that would take two carriers out of action at Iwo Jima[25] and have a profound effect on the operations of the salvage forces in both the Iwo Jima and Okinawa campaigns.

Iwo Jima and Okinawa

The salvage forces for the invasion of Iwo Jima consisted of three salvage ships, two fleet tugs, and two rescue tugs, along with several LCIs and LCTs configured for salvage. Captain Lebbeus Curtis, who flew his pennant in *Clamp*, the salvage ship commanded by his son, led this group. The salvage forces on the scene had support from backup forces in the Marshalls and Marianas under the command of Service Squadrons Ten and Twelve. The existence of backup forces must have seemed a luxury to Captain Curtis and the others who had lived through the early days of the war when salvage forces were minimal or nonexistent.

The salvage forces found plenty of work at Iwo Jima, but few jobs of particular note. *Ute*, the Aleutian veteran, headed for *Bismark Sea* when that escort carrier was struck by kamikazes, but knew only the frustration of arriving too late. *Sioux* (ATF 75) and *Molala* towed the destroyers *Ringgold* (DD 500) and *Yarnall* (DD 541) to Ulithi following a collision at sea. All of the salvage ships refloated landing craft and ships broached and swamped on the beach. Soft volcanic sand, not passable by amphibious tracked vehicles, created an unusually large amount of this work at

---

[25] *Saratoga* (CV 3) was hit by three kamikazes and several bombs. She was saved by the damage control and fire-fighting abilities of her crew but returned to the United States for repairs. *Bismark Sea* (CVE 95) rolled over and sank after two kamikazes ignited ammunition that blew off her stern.

Iwo Jima. Vehicles bogged down in the first waves blocked the beaches, so that the following waves of beaching vessels could neither beach securely nor anchor effectively in the poor holding ground.

The fate of *Zuni* at Iwo Jima illustrates how salvage ships working in shallow water routinely stand into danger. *Zuni*, operating aggressively, had deliberately grounded herself to assist an LST in landing ammunition. That grounding caused no damage, but a few days later on 23 March 1945, while attempting to haul LST-727 off the beach, *Zuni* parted her tow line. The broken wire fouled her screw and anchor. She grounded again, breaking her keel and holing herself seriously. She was refloated and towed to Saipan, out of the war, a casualty of the hard, inherently dangerous work of salvage.[26]

The Okinawa campaign, the last of the war, was to be described by Winston Churchill as one of the most intense and famous in military history. No coup de grace delivered to a dying enemy, it was a hard-fought battle against a fanatic and courageous opponent. The capture of Okinawa cost the U.S. Navy thirty-four naval ships and craft sunk and more than three hundred and fifty damaged—many by kamikaze, some by a variation called the "baka bomb."[27] Naval action around Okinawa continued until the Japanese surrender.

The Okinawa campaign saw an imaginative logistics concept. The group of islands known as Kerama-retto lie about 15 miles west of southern Okinawa. The concept called for the capture of these islands as an advanced base and anchorage for fueling and ammunition replenishment. As conceived, the secondary use would be for salvage and repair work. In practice, as Japanese air attacks increased and a large number of damaged ships had to be dealt with, the priorities became reversed.

The islands were captured six days before the main assault on Okinawa in an operation that would have been regarded as a major amphibious assault in 1942. Finding only light Japanese resistance, the Americans secured the islands before the invasion of Okinawa.[28] The anchorage saw no security from either conventional or kamikaze attack, and some casualties occurred there.

On 27 March, four days before the invasion of Okinawa, the first salvage and repair unit set up in the anchorage with the arrival of *Clamp*

---

[26] *Zuni* was out of the war but by no means done for. She transferred to the Coast Guard in 1946 where she was renamed *Tamaroa* and redesignated WAT 166. She was redesignated WMEC 166 on 1 May 1966 and remains on active service in the late 1980s.

[27] The baka bomb was a piloted glider with rocket boosters and a warhead of 2,645 pounds of high explosive. The weapon was carried slung under a conventional bomber and released near the target. It was guided to the target by the suicide pilot, who used the rocket boosters to maneuver and to achieve speeds in excess of 500 knots.

[28] The capture of Kerama-retto was costly to the Japanese defense plans. Several hundred small suicidal motorboats capable of carrying torpedoes or explosives were found hidden in caves and destroyed.

Two generations of an American family with a long maritime history, Commander Lebbeus Curtis V and his son, Lieutenant Commander Lebbeus Curtis VI, served together in salvage during the Pacific war. Photo courtesy Lieutenant Commander Lebbeus Curtis VII.

(still wearing the broad command pennant of Captain Curtis), the fleet tugs *Yuma* and *Tekesta* (ATF 94), the landing-craft repair ship *Egeria* (ARL 8), and a number of LCIs and LCTs fitted for salvage. The ships went to work immediately on the *Kimberly* (DD 521), which had been struck by a kamikaze the day before. After that the work came fast and furious, as did the arrival of more salvage ships. *Gear* arrived before the invasion, *Molala* and *Jicarilla* (ATF 104) soon after.

Rear Admiral Carter, then Commodore Carter, commanding Service Squadron Ten, describes the action:

> The large salvage pumps on the *Clamp* and *Gear* proved valuable in keeping damaged ships afloat until temporary underwater patching was effected. The busy tugs were alerted for service at all times and brought battle-damaged destroyers and other vessels in from picket and screening stations. By night the salvage craft were strategically located throughout the anchorage to aid ships in case of fire or of damage by suicide planes. *During the period of severe enemy activity, twice as many of these ships could have been utilized had they been available.* [italics added][29]

Providing services to ships on the line was only part of the salvage group's work. They also pulled landing ships and craft off landing and supply beaches, and patched and dewatered ships at Kerama-retto to reduce their draft enough to allow them to enter the floating docks. Additional ships, including *Shackle*, *Deliver* (ARS 23), *Lipan*, *Menominee*, *Munsee*, *Tawakoni* (ATF 114), *Vestal* (AR 4), and *Zaniah* (AG 70),[30] joined the group; more came later.

---

[29] Rear Admiral Worral Reed Carter, USN (Ret.), *Beans, Bullets and Black Oil* (Washington: Department of the Navy, 1952) p. 339.

[30] *Zaniah*, classified as a miscellaneous auxiliary, AG, at Okinawa and formerly AK 120, was fitted out as a limited-repair ship. As such she carried a diving crew and could do patching and underwater repair. After the island was secure she was the flagship of the third Salvage Group Commander, Lieutenant Commander J.W. Greely.

The fleet tug *Zuni* lies hard aground on the black-sand beaches of Iwo Jima. She was refloated to enjoy a long career as USCGC *Tamora*.

The level of activity peaked during the month of April, with the salvage force towing battle-damaged ships into Kerama-retto faster than they could be repaired. The majority of casualties were destroyers from the picket line. The salvage ships lay outside the smoke masking the fleet and often served as decoys to draw in the kamikazes. They were in the thick of it.

- *Pakana* (ATF 108) picked up survivors of *Canada Victory*, had three of her crew wounded in a strafing attack the following day, and went to the assistance of *New Mexico* (BB 40) when a kamikaze struck the battleship.

- *Jicarilla* and *Valve* aided *John A. Rawlins* when an aerial torpedo started a roaring fire in the barrels of asphalt and camouflage material in number three hold of the Liberty ship. The crew put the ship aground to prevent her from sinking. Salvors pulled her off the beach, removed the beer cargo from number one hold, and flooded her to put out the fire. The flooding put the ship so far down by the head that the salvage officer cooled his weary feet by dangling them in the water from the bow.

- *Jicarilla* later towed the damaged *Idaho* (BB 42) to Ulithi.

- *Clamp* refloated *Tolman* (DM 28), put out fires on LST–559, and made emergency repairs to *Laffey* (DD 724) after five kamikazes hit that destroyer.

- *Lipan* picked up *Barry* (APD 29) and headed for Kerama-retto among a flurry of kamikaze attacks that sank both her escort, LSM–59, and her tow.

- *Shackle* performed emergency repairs on twenty-one ships during the month of May alone.

- *Tekesta* (ATF 93) hauled in a number of destroyer-type ships from the picket line, among them *Newcomb* (DD 582), *Harding* (DMS 28), and *Oberrender* (DE 344).

- *Yuma* brought in the attack transport *Hinsdale* (APA 120), as well as *Tenino* and *Marathon* (APA 200).

- *Gear* made battle-damage repairs to *Wichita*, *England* (DB 635), and *Ingraham* (DD 694), and to *Aaron Ward* (DD 483), which was barely afloat with three main machinery spaces flooded.

- *Ute* pulled landing craft and ships off the beach. When the *William B. Allison* was hit she assisted her, interrupting that salvage to take *Braine* (DD 630) to Kerama-retto. She also towed in *Butler* (DMS 29), *Haggard* (DD 555), and *J. William Ditter* (DM 31).

- *Pakana* and *Ute* each shot down two Japanese planes. *Tekesta* got an assist on another.

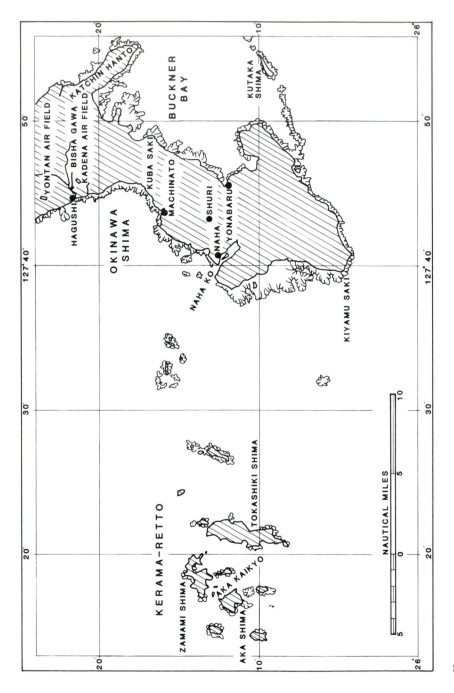

Kerama-retto.

Both Captain Curtis and Commander Carl Holm, his successor as Salvage Group Commander, stressed the need for better communication. All too often information transmitted about damage resulted in the wrong assistance. Often salvage units badly needed elsewhere were sent to deal with minor problems because of a bad or poorly understood description.

Fire-fighting teams and techniques had improved greatly during the war, but at Okinawa the salvage forces were faced with three major stumbling blocks. Smoke and chemical fog masking the anchorage area made maneuvering difficult for the salvage ships. Crowded anchorages resulted in increased maneuvering times for large salvage units. Water depths in a number of areas were insufficient for fleet and rescue tugs. Landing craft, such as LCMs, fitted for fire fighting would have been invaluable. Unfortunately, there were no such craft.

Small craft suitable for passing lines to ships needing assistance at sea or on the beach were in short supply, and several ships suffered additional damage because of the lack of such boats or amphibious vehicles.

Naha Harbor

With Okinawa almost secure, Japanese activity had slacked off, and the backlog of battle-damaged ships at Kerama-retto had been reduced. The salvors' attention turned to the harbor at Naha. Planners anticipated that Naha would be a major staging and supply base for the invasion of Japan, and the harbor there had to be cleared. The job was formidable because almost 200 wrecks of all sizes littered the harbor.

Harbor clearance and rehabilitation was done under the Commander, Naval Forces Ryukyus with assistance from Service Squadrons Ten and Twelve. The salvage group doing the clearance work had participated in the assault operations. Several other units assisted,[31] including Army Engineers and an Underwater Demolition Team that did the initial survey.[32] Despite the relative lack of experience in harbor clearance in the Pacific, after only seven days, ten LCT and fifteen barge berths had been cleared. A report issued on 11 September shows that in June, forty wrecks were removed; in July, thirty-two; and in August, sixty-seven. Another forty were cleared in the first eleven days of September.

---

[31] The assistance of a wide variety of units from all services was common in salvage operations. Particularly notable for their contribution were Army Engineers, Navy Construction Battalions (Seabees), Beachmaster Units, and Underwater Demolition Teams.

[32] The salvage group during the clearance of Naha harbor was under the command of Lieutenant Commander J.W. Greely, a veteran of the Pearl Harbor salvage and the West Loch clearance. In the harbor rehabilitation group that worked closely with the salvors was another Lieutenant Commander Greely, an experienced dredge man and the salvage officer's father. Much to the amusement of the elder Greely, the son was senior in rank.

The diving gang from *Zaniah* exemplify the men who worked at salvage and emergency repair during the Okinawa campaign. Photo courtesy Captain James W. Greely.

The wooden-hulled salvage ship *Valve*, which had performed well during the clearance of West Loch at Pearl Harbor, proved equally effective at Naha. Like *Grasp* in Manila, *Valve* in Naha continued clearance operations long after the heavy concentration of initial effort ended and long after the war was over. *Anchor* (ARS 13) also did yeoman service during the harbor clearance and around Okinawa for some months after the war ended. *Anchor*'s Commanding Officer, Lieutenant J.L. (Jack) Hill, had an especially valuable skill. He knew explosives and could use them effectively. Explosives assisted in removing some of the more difficult obstacles and in sinking refloated hulks at sea. Jack Hill did first-class work as the chief powder man.

During the Naha harbor clearance salvors designed and built on site a useful craft—a 50-ton shear leg mounted on a barge. This shear leg proved to be a fine supplement to the LCTs fitted with the 20-ton shear legs and to the few floating cranes. The combination made up the principal means of lifting for the Naha clearance and compensated in some degree for the lack of specialized lifting craft.

The War Winds Down

Although it was not apparent to anyone at home or in the field, the war began to wind down after the Okinawa campaign. Logistics operations on Okinawa were building toward the invasion of the Japanese

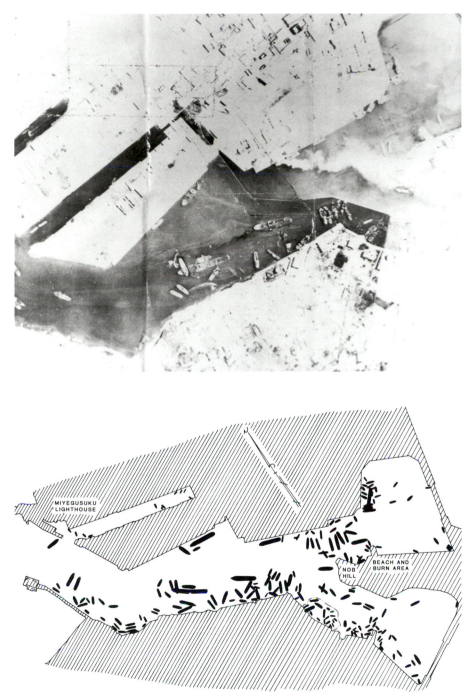

Harbor clearance at Naha, Okinawa.

Lieutenant Commander James W. Greely (center) and two other salvage officers during the Naha harbor clearance.

home islands. The primary logistics base had moved from Kerama-retto to Buckner Bay[33] on the eastern side of Okinawa. Salvage forces around the island kept busy cleaning up the aftermath of the battle and taking care of the casualties that resulted from the heavy traffic of logistics operations, from mines, and from the occasional air attacks that continued until the end of the war.

During the carrier air strikes against Japan, salvage units moved forward along the Task Force's retirement routes, but seldom practiced their trade. Doctrine called for two tugs for battleships and carrier casualties, one tug for other types of ships. Exceptions occurred. When the carrier *Franklin* (CV 13) was seriously damaged by bombs southeast of Kyushu, four fleet tugs, *Cree, Munsee, Sioux,* and *Ute,* headed toward her. *Franklin,* taken in tow by the cruiser *Pittsburgh* (CA 72), regained her propulsion power before the tugs arrived.

Just as the first salvage work of the Pacific war—the Pearl Harbor salvage—had involved battleships, so did one of the final salvage opera-

---

[33]Previously known as Nakagusuku-wan.

tions. Off Okinawa on 12 August 1945, a single Japanese aircraft eluded the warning system, dropped one torpedo, and flew away. The torpedo struck the starboard outboard shaft of the elder sister of the ill-fated *Arizona*. *Pennsylvania* (BB 38) had been virtually undamaged during the Pearl Harbor attack, but now the resulting noncontact explosion blew a 32-by–50-foot hole in the stern, abaft the torpedo protection system.[34] More than 3,400 tons of water poured into the after portion of the ship and reduced her freeboard aft to 6 inches.

Pennsylvania had an unusual shaft arrangement. It was not continuous from the machinery space to the stern tube, but stepped through a gear located just aft of the after magazine spaces. Oddly enough a nonwater-

---

[34]While *Pennsylvania* was being designed, empirical tests were conducted on a specially built caisson to develop her torpedo protection system. When commissioned, her protection was considered to be superior to that of foreign contemporaries. The shape and overall design did not permit carrying the protection system to the ship's ends. *Pennsylvania*'s sister *Arizona* had been sunk by a Japanese weapon that also defeated her protection system, but in a way completely different from the *Pennsylvania* casualty. It is generally believed that the *Arizona*'s loss was caused by a bomb, probably one of the stabilized, large caliber, armor-piercing shells the Japanese dropped as bombs, that penetrated into a black powder magazine in the forward part of the ship.

Salvors pump wreck number 67 during the Naha harbor clearance. Photo courtesy Captain James W. Greely.

When *Pennsylvania* was torpedoed at Okinawa, hoses for pumps were run through her 14-inch guns to reach the magazines. The battleship is not shooting hoses. Photo courtesy Captain James W. Greely.

tight door gave access to the gear room. The torpedo damage left the gear space open to the sea. The magazine spaces flooded through this door and through the ventilation systems. To complicate the situation, the damage could be reached only through very limited access. A recommended trunked access between watertight bulkheads had not been installed. The ship's force began to attack the flooding immediately, dropping submersible pumps down through number four turret with the hoses leading out through the gun barrels, and resulting in the unusual picture of *Pennsylvania*'s 14-inch guns shooting hoses. Salvage forces, including *Shackle* and the Atlantic War veteran *Extricate*, and trained salvage crews quickly came to *Pennsylvania*'s assistance, placed high capacity salvage pumps on board, and began to dewater the battleship.

When watertight integrity and freeboard had been restored, *Serrano* (ATF 112) and *Tenino* towed the badly damaged battleship to Guam for emergency repairs. Lieutenant Bill Horn, a salvage officer, rode the ship during the tow. The rapid response of salvage forces had been instrumental in saving the ship.

When hostilities finally ended on 15 August 1945, the work of the salvage forces did not. There remained considerable cleanup in Okinawa and the Philippines. The harbors of Japan had to be made serviceable. As in Europe, local people did much of this work with American equipment, technical assistance, and supervision. This policy achieved several worthwhile purposes. It opened the harbors for the rebuilding process that followed the war. It provided badly needed jobs for local citizens in war-torn nations, while at the same time taking advantage of a large labor pool that was much cheaper than American military labor. It permitted repatriation of the bulk of the American naval salvage personnel, many of whom had been out of the United States for years.

Typhoons had disrupted operations around Okinawa before the end of the war, causing a number of sorties from the anchorages and storm damage to a large number of ships including at least one fleet tug, *Jicarilla*. The storms did not stop with the end of the war. Buckner Bay had been chosen with the knowledge that it lay particularly exposed to typhoons; however, operational considerations dictated acceptance of the risk.

Typhoons struck the area on 16 and 28 September, and again on 9 October. The October storm was fierce, causing extensive damage and loss of ships. During the typhoon of 16 September, the seasoned wooden-hulled ARS *Extricate* had lost power and both anchors while assisting another ship. She continued salvage operations during that typhoon and the next, but the 9 October storm drove her ashore and badly damaged her. She had to be abandoned and subsequently destroyed with explosives. The same storm drove *Wateree* (ATF 117) ashore and battered her starboard side out against a reef. She too was abandoned. The typhoon also drove *Tenino* hard aground, but *Bannock* (ATF 81) and *Menominee* refloated her. She was repaired on site and joined the salvage operations.

During the October storm *Valve* twice fouled SS *Richard S. Oglesby* and collided with LST–826, but survived. After the storm she removed the wreck of *Wateree* and salvaged *Sacadanga* (AOG 40), two LSTs, and *Vandalia* (IX 191). Meanwhile her sister, *Vent*, refloated a number of small craft and several floating drydocks.

Extricate and *Wateree* were not the only ships to suffer in the aftermath of combat. On 16 October two mines exploded close alongside *Ute* (ATF 76) while she steamed up the Yangtze with a tow of barges. The explosions opened her fuel tanks, dislocated shaft bearings, and caused damage throughout the ship. *Seize*, also operating in the area, towed *Ute* to Shanghai, where she went alongside *Dixie* (AD 14) for repairs. Apparently some people in China hadn't gotten the word about the end of the war, because less than a week later *Seize* came under machine gun fire from a Chinese village. She returned the fire with her 40-mm guns with little apparent damage on either side.

The Wartime Role of Salvage

The U.S. Navy had entered World War II with practically no salvage forces and little expertise in this highly specialized marine field. By the end of the war it had built a large, varied, and effective force. The salvage requirements of the war had ranged from fire fighting aboard battle-damaged ships; dealing with severe hull damage caused by air, surface, and submarine attack and by mines; and clearing harbors blocked intentionally or by combat, to dealing with large numbers of routine marine casualties. Every type of marine casualty had been faced and overcome by Navy salvors. The salvage forces had been in the thick of it, and losses of oceangoing tugs and salvage ships during World War II ranked fourth after those of destroyers, submarines, and mine warfare ships.[35]

The United States was able to build and operate its salvage forces successfully during the war for a number of reasons:

• It had the industrial capacity to produce the specialized ships, machinery, and equipment needed as well as the materials and equipment used in combat. This industrial capacity was able to grow because, unlike that of our enemies, it was not attacked.

• The U.S. Navy had in its ranks a corps of men of the caliber of William Sullivan, Bernard Manseau, Edward Ellsberg, and Lebbeus Curtis with the foresight to predict requirements accurately, the imagination to conceive solutions, and the fortitude and leadership to take a difficult course and hold steady on it.

• Technology and expertise in salvage and towing resided in the United States. It was mobilized and applied to solving wartime salvage and rescue problems. Maritime professionals like Edmund Moran, Henry Foss, Emile Genereaux, and the Curtises were in uniform throughout the war, using their civilian-developed expertise to benefit the Navy and their nation.

• The single, strong marine salvage operator in the country had been mobilized immediately to provide salvage services until the Navy could build up adequate forces. When Navy salvage forces took the load in the combat area, the Navy Salvage Service did the lion's share of the work in American waters.

• The United States had as an ally the most experienced and professional maritime nation in the world, Great Britain. When the United States entered the war the British already had more than two years' experience and many lessons already learned. The United States took

---

[35] This total includes losses of four ATO, four ATF, four ARS, and two ASR from all causes.

advantage of both this experience and Britain's general experience in organizing and building its own salvage forces.

• An effective organization for salvage existed throughout the war. The somewhat free-wheeling organization adapted to the different situations in the various theaters. The specialized business of salvage did not get caught up in the vastness of the U.S. Navy, but maintained its own unique character, methods, and people.

• A centralized system communicated the technical and operational lessons learned in the field to other theaters of war and incorporated them in training programs.

How valuable were salvage forces to the U.S. Navy and to victory in World War II? The question is not easily answered. A purely dollars and cents analysis—the businessman's concern of return on investment—does not provide a comprehensive answer. An accurate dollar value of vessels and cargoes cannot be provided; undoubtedly, it amounted to hundreds of millions of dollars. This figure compares favorably with the total cost of approximately $80 million for salvage ships, equipment, personnel, and training.

Although this differential alone made the effort worthwhile, the matter is far more complex. The United States had won a war. The value of the salvage force to naval operations had been convincingly demonstrated by the number of ships and cargoes saved for future service and the operations that were expedited. No dollar amount can be assigned to this service. Thus by any standard of evaluation the return on the investment the Navy had made in salvage was very high.

The salvage forces of the U.S. Navy in World War II had been built to solve specific problems and respond to specific lessons of the war. However because of the basic nature of the work they were designed for, their widespread application did not end with the hostilities. Not only had forces and equipment been built almost from scratch but, just as important, doctrines had been developed, implemented, modified, and documented as the war progressed.

With the end of the war and the general demobilization that inevitably followed, requirements and emphases changed drastically throughout the Navy. Salvors were faced with a new set of questions:

• What role would salvage forces have in the postwar Navy?

• What should happen to the large numbers of salvage ships and the specialized salvage equipment in Navy hands?

• How should demobilization of the Navy Salvage Service be handled?

- What role would salvage have in the commercial maritime community of the United States?

- How could the Navy ensure adequate salvage resources in the United States for future mobilizations?

Immediately following the war the attention of senior salvage officers turned from intensive combat operations to finding the answers to these questions.

TYPHOON FURY

CHAPTER SIX

Navy Salvage After World War II

From combat to harbor clearance operations World War II repeatedly validated the role of naval salvage forces. The value of that role is not so apparent in peacetime because of the relative infrequency of salvage demands, the cost of maintaining a capability that is only occasionally productive, and the Navy's widespread lack of familiarity with or empathy for salvage. After the war, therefore, most senior salvors felt justifiable concern that without strong and effective measures, the lessons learned from almost four years of combat would be lost and salvage in the United States would revert to its prewar state, or worse.

The demobilization that was proceeding rapidly in all services included trained salvage people. It also included a shift of authority within the Navy salvage organization. The Chief of Naval Operations phased out the Chief of Navy Salvage, and salvage authority was concentrated in the office of the Supervisor of Salvage within the Bureau of Ships. On his return to the United States, Commodore Sullivan relieved Captain Manseau in this position. Salvage ships were being laid up or sold. Many thought the salvage business would no longer be attractive and that no new operators would set up. Some believed that even Merritt-Chapman and Scott might not continue in the business for long.

Government action to ensure the continuation of salvage services in the United States seemed appropriate, but just what specific action should be taken was not immediately apparent. A number of government agencies had an interest in salvage. The Department of the Navy's interests were obvious. The Department of War was involved in salvage because of the Army Corps of Engineers' responsibility to maintain navigable waterways and the Transportation Corps's duty to move material by water. The Coast Guard, in the Department of the Treasury, had responsibilities in the closely related fields of maritime search and rescue; and the Maritime Commission, an agency of the Department of Commerce, had charge of the activities of the merchant marine.

An Interdepartmental Committee on Salvage made up of senior members of these agencies was formed under the chairmanship of Rear Admiral Howard H. Good. The committee's charter required it to look into all aspects of salvage in the United States and to make recommendations for government action. In its report on 5 March 1946 there were four conclusions and recommendations.

The first three statements were broad in scope, but the fourth specifically addressed the Navy's salvage role.

1. Because salvage is of vital interest to the United States, the government should assume responsibility for providing salvage protection for ships in peacetime as well as wartime, and as a matter of policy should encourage other maritime nations to provide salvage protection for American shipping in their waters.

2. Because salvage has questionable commercial viability, the government should encourage and aid reliable and experienced salvage companies to maintain facilities manned by qualified personnel.

3. Legislation should be passed to permit the U.S. Navy to represent the government in salvage matters.

4. When given responsibility for salvage, the Navy should:

Encourage reliable companies to operate salvage facilities.

Provide salvage facilities with Navy resources where adequate commercial resources are not available.

Continue the prewar practice of contracting for the salvage of government ships.

Offer the services of the Navy salvage organization to other government agencies for settlement of salvage claims.

Retain enough surplus salvage ships and equipment to provide to reliable and experienced salvage companies.

Maintain a salvage branch in the Navy to keep abreast of marine salvage at home and abroad and to advise all government agencies on salvage matters.

Use appropriate channels to encourage other governments to maintain salvage facilities in their waters.

Continue to maintain facilities for salvage training and studying salvage methods and make these facilities available to government departments and private enterprise.

In sum, the committee recommended that the U.S. government take an abiding interest in salvage and that the U.S. Navy be the government's executive agent for salvage.

The Navy Salvage Service

The Navy Salvage Service presented an immediate postwar problem. The contract (NObs–36)[1] that established the Navy Salvage Service saw its primary mission to be mitigation of the effects of combat-related casualties along the coasts of the United States. If this had in fact been the case, the service would have outlived its usefulness more than a year before the war ended. By then, the danger of attack in American waters had become almost nonexistent.

Despite the virtual elimination of danger of attack, however, casualties along the coasts persisted because of the large number of ships at sea, restricted channels, blackouts, shutdown navigational aids, and inexperienced crews. The service more than earned its keep until the war's end and beyond. But other than allowing navigation lights to be turned on, the end of hostilities had little immediate effect on shipping. There was every expectation that the contract would run its full course of six months after the end of the national emergency.

By mutual agreement the government and Merritt-Chapman and Scott formulated a system for facilitating the eventual disestablishment of the Service. Under this system the contractor would periodically return excess items, including government-owned ships, to government custody. Handling the return of the material on a long-term basis saved a great deal of confusion and inefficiency.

The report of the interdepartmental committee confirmed the opinion held by Commodore Sullivan that it was in the national interest to continue the service in some form. What the most practical form was became the next question.

On 3 September 1946 the Chief of the Bureau of Ships recommended discontinuing the service of *Discoverer* (ARS 3), which was stationed in Port Angeles, Washington, to protect shipping in Puget Sound and in northwestern waters. Merritt-Chapman and Scott delivered *Discoverer* to Puget Sound Naval Shipyard in November and the salvage station at Port Angeles closed, leaving *Viking* in San Pedro as the only Navy Salvage Service operation on the West Coast. Planning for the future was underway in the offices of Merritt-Chapman and Scott. Its management saw that the government intended to help them stay in the salvage business. They also saw that the majority of ships they operated had grown old in hard service—"rode hard and put away wet." Updating and upgrading their fleet was a matter of high priority.

The Maritime Commission had built a number of excellent tugs during the war. Negotiations began for the purchase of two of these tugs, to

---

[1] Contract NObs–36 between the Bureau of Ships and Merritt-Chapman and Scott had established the Navy Salvage Service and was the foundation for its operation throughout World War II.

be named *T.A. Scott* and *W.N. Davis*, at a reasonable price. In return for favorable purchase terms Merritt-Chapman and Scott would agree to remain in the salvage business for ten years. It appeared that the negotiations would take some time and that the ships would require conversion to make them suitable for commercial salvage service. Until these two ships could enter commercial service, therefore, two others would be chartered by Merritt-Chapman and Scott: *Willet* (chartered since 1920, returned to the government just before the war, then operated by the Navy Salvage Service) and the new salvage ship *Curb* (ARS 21).

Before negotiations could be completed, however, one of the two ships proposed for sale by the Maritime Commission sank following a collision; the other was found to be unsuitable for salvage service. Since no other Maritime Commission tugs were immediately available, other permanent arrangements would have to be made if the company was to update its fleet. In the meantime the government went ahead with the charter of *Curb* and *Willet*, though within six months the aging *Willet* was replaced by *Cable* (ARS 19), a sister of *Curb*. Both *Curb* and *Cable* were on indefinite charter to the contractor. Two years later Merritt-Chapman and Scott purchased *Diver* (ARS 5) from the government and operated her for many years on salvage service as MV *Rescue*. For much of that time *Rescue* was under the Panamanian flag and maintained her salvage station in Kingston, Jamaica.

By early 1947 Merritt-Chapman and Scott was anxious to end its full-time commitment to the government and return to commercial operations. Accordingly, negotiations began to terminate contract NObs–36 and establish new contracts to furnish salvage services to the Navy in the Atlantic and Caribbean. These new contracts would be similar to those that existed before World War II. The first one went into effect at midnight on 10 May 1947. It was supplemented by an agreement to manage and operate the salvage ship *Viking* on the Pacific Coast. *Gear* (ARS 34) replaced *Viking* in 1953. Merritt-Chapman and Scott returned *Viking* to Navy custody on 17 March 1953, and she was sold for scrap soon afterwards. *Gear* remained on salvage station in San Pedro until the early 1970s.

Meanwhile another contract was being let by the Navy for salvage services in another part of the world. There were strong American ties and economic interests in the Philippines. Many in government felt a responsibility to help the newly independent nation develop its industry and economy. The management of Luzon Stevedoring Company of Manila had expressed an interest in making the salvage business a part of their diversified marine operations. Many in the Navy saw the advantages of having a capable salvage contractor in the western Pacific, and a contract almost identical to that with Merritt-Chapman and Scott was let to Luzon Stevedoring. No ships were provided; instead the Bureau of Ships established an Emergency Ship Salvage Material (ESSM) Pool under the company's custody in Manila. This varied collection of salvage equipment was to be husbanded by the company for the Navy and used on commercial as well as Navy jobs. Thus the company was in effect being subsidized by the Navy to compete in the salvage business.

The coexistence of Navy salvage forces and Navy salvage contractors gave the Navy greater flexibility than it had had prior to World War II. However it now became necessary to divide the available salvage work between active-duty salvage forces and contractors and to decide which work could best be assigned to each. Navy forces had to do enough salvage work to maintain their proficiency; nothing decreases salvage skills as rapidly as inactivity. Contractors had to get enough work to ensure the effectiveness of the de facto subsidy. Overall, maintaining a balance of fleet and contractor work would contribute to a close working relationship between the Supervisor of Salvage and fleet salvage officers.

Postwar Navy Salvage Operations

While senior salvors in Washington looked to the future, active duty salvors stayed busy in the field. In both Asia and Europe the Navy was providing technical assistance, supervision, and equipment to local groups cleaning up the detritus of war.

Nuclear weapons had been introduced to the world at Hiroshima and Nagasaki. Prior to their wartime use only one test explosion had been conducted. No information about the effects of nuclear weapons on naval vessels existed. Development of standards for future ship designs and for defensive measures required definition of these effects. The most practical way to do this was by full-scale empirical testing. And the time for such tests would never be better. The fleet had large numbers of excess ships of varying designs, as well as captured units from defeated navies that could become target vessels.

Admiral William H.P. Blandy, as Commander Joint Task Force One, commanded the testing operation called Operation Crossroads. The plans called for two tests. The first was to be a detonation above the ships—an airburst such as had occurred in Japan. The second was to be an underwater burst. Remote Bikini atoll in the northern part of the Marshall Islands would be the test site.

A salvage unit of eighteen ships, formed especially for the operation under the command of Captain Manseau in *Palmyra* (ARS(T) 3), would have a major role. The nature of the operation called for the salvage unit to be structured differently from those in the wartime amphibious assaults. A major pretest task was the installation of moorings for the target ships. Salvage ships with their two booms and bow-lift capability were far better suited for this work than fleet tugs. Therefore the salvage unit had a higher proportion of salvage ships than the wartime assault units had had. The salvage lifting ships *Gypsy* (ARS(D) 1) and *Mender* (ARS(D) 2), both converted from LSM hulls intended for harbor clearances after the invasion of Japan, had been commissioned too late for World War II but were available and suitable for Operation Crossroads.

The salvage unit began preparations for the tests several months before the scheduled detonations. Operations commenced with underwater surveys, obstruction removal, and clearance of evacuation channels. When site preparations had been completed, moors were laid and the ships positioned in the test array. Special subsurface moorings were developed for target submarines. All phases of the operation were carefully rehearsed.

Following the first detonation—the airburst designated "Able"—the salvage unit, led by *Clamp*, entered the lagoon to extinguish the fires and control the damage on the target ships. As many ships as possible were saved for the underwater shot—the "Baker" shot—scheduled for about a month later.

Salvage unit preparations for the Baker shot consisted of making more surveys, gathering and replacing instruments, clearing more channels, laying more moorings, and remooring targets. The work following the second detonation generally resembled the first. Salvage ships entered the lagoon and took the same kind of salvage action they would have taken in dealing with any large number of combat casualties, with one important exception: They had to deal with high levels of radiation in seemingly random hot spots. These hot spots presented a hazard to the salvage crews and divers, but allowed testing of various methods of decontamination. Salvors tried a number of methods of washing away the radiation—high-pressure water, chemical foam, special solutions—with mixed results. Divers photographed the underwater hulls of the target ships to document the effects of the blast.

After the tests were completed and the data gathered, the scientists could go home and begin the analysis that would complete the test program. Not so the salvage unit. They towed radioactive targets that were still afloat to Kwajalein to await ultimate disposal and took less dangerous material to other ports. Moors were recovered and ships and equipment thoroughly decontaminated. Not until all the tools were back in the toolbox and the shop cleaned was the work of the salvage unit complete. The success and importance of this work is indicated by the award of the Legion of Merit to Captain Manseau.

With their work at Bikini and subsequent overhauls completed, the two salvage lifting ships *Gypsy* and *Mender*, commanded by Lieutenant

Commanders Clyde Horner and "Bulldog" Thurman, were available for salvage work in Guam.

The island of Guam, the principal island in the Marianas, lies like Okinawa in the path of many typhoons. Guam had become a major naval base during the war. Because of the large number of ships and craft in the harbor, the typhoon that passed through Guam near the end of the war was particularly destructive. Most of the wrecks that required urgent salvage had been cleared immediately. However, several remained to be cleared before the harbor could be fully developed, such as the bow of the cruiser *Pittsburgh* (CA 72),[2] numerous pontoon barges and landing craft, and a civilian-manned Army FS, a small freighter that sank after an explosion.

The cruiser was the first of the wrecks attacked. Because *Pittsburgh's* stern section remained almost intact, a replacement for the engine room skylight was fitted in order to pump out the engine room and restore the buoyancy of the aft portion of the ship. Beach gear, rigged to deadmen on the beach, helped roll the wreck upright, and a floating crane[3] lifted the bow. Lifts were made slowly. As soon as the main deck came awash, pumps went aboard to pump the forward hold. The ship floated and went to sea for the last time—to be sunk. She did not sink quietly. The towing ships fired at her to hasten the sinking, and gasoline fumes exploded. It was quite a show.

The cruiser's bow presented a more difficult problem. The bow, previously sealed for tow to Pearl Harbor, broke her mooring and sank, partially capsizing during the typhoon. The diving survey showed that a large portion of the section's buoyancy could be restored. The most feasible plan seemed to be to blow air into the bow itself, rig pontoons, and blow the water from both the bow and the pontoons. While *Gypsy* worked on *Pittsburgh's* bow, *Mender* cleared pontoons from the beaches, selected suitable ones for lifting, and fitted them with blow and vent plumbing. As extra margin, *Gypsy* rigged for a bow lift. When all was ready, the bow section was lifted and allowed to stabilize, then lowered until it would just clear the harbor bottom during the tow out of the harbor.

The entrance to Apra harbor is not easy. There are strong tidal

---

[2] *Pittsburgh's* bow was torn off during a typhoon near Okinawa on 5 June 1945. *Munsee* sailed in search of the bow section, found it, and took it in tow. With *Pakana* assisting in the final stages of the tow, the unwieldly tow was taken to Guam.

[3] Commander J.W. Greely, the Pacific Fleet salvage officer was in Guam for these operations. The floating crane, rated at 100 short tons at the required radius, had recently arrived in Guam. The commanding officer of the facility that owned the crane was very protective and would permit only a 50-ton lift—not enough for the job. However, he had gone on a trip before the raising operation. A 100-ton lift was made successfully and Commander Greely left the island before the commanding officer returned.

currents that vary with depth, great surges at the harbor entrance, and heavy offshore ground swells just outside the entrance. *Mender* towed on the hawser while *Gypsy* came astern, keeping a lift on the bow section and stabilizing the tow. When the tow reached deep water clear of the harbor, the bow section would be lowered away. Harbor tugs were available to assist in the tow. Even with such tug assistance, the tow often lay across her intended course while maneuvering in the harbor. Outside the harbor the ground swell was so heavy that *Gypsy* executed the contingency plan—she lowered the heavy lift blocks and released the special, quick-release links. *Mender* kept towing. Other lines and air hoses from *Gypsy* tore away. Finally, *Mender's* fathometer showed over 400 fathoms. Thurman stopped *Mender*, cut her tow wire, then executed the maneuver known as "getting the hell out." It was well he did; one of the pontoons broke loose and surfaced spectacularly.

Both at Bikini and Guam, *Gypsy* and *Mender* established the usefulness of salvage lifting ships. On the East Coast their sisters *Salvager* (ARS(D) 3) and *Windlass* (ARS(D) 4) were likewise proving themselves. These ships worked together in a series of operations that demonstrate the demands of routine peacetime salvage work.

- They lifted the sunken tug *Lone Wolf* (YTB 179) in Narragansett Bay from 130 feet of water.
- At Vera Cruz, Mexico, they raised a couple of sunken barges in a two-week operation.
- Going back north, they located and dispersed the wreck of YP–387 off Hereford, New Jersey.
- Aided by a blimp, they swept wires under the wreck of YTB–274 off Charleston, South Carolina. After going into three-point moors they lifted the wreck to recover a body, then blew the wreck up to prevent its becoming a navigational hazard.

These varied efforts not only proved the worth of salvage-lifting ships in major and minor operations, but also demonstrated something much more important: Salvage forces had a definite place in the much expanded, two-ocean Navy that the United States supported following World War II.

The demobilization following World War II reduced Navy salvage forces to the level needed for peacetime operations. The Harbor Clearance Units were disestablished and numerous ships were taken out of commission and disposed of. Whole classes of ships, notably the wooden-hulled *Anchor*-class salvage ships and the steam-powered rescue tugs, were decommissioned. A number of ships were sold and placed in commercial service in the United States and abroad. Some vessels were transferred to foreign navies; some were transferred to other U.S. government agencies such as the Coast Guard and the Bureau of Mines. The number of salvage ships and tugs retained was a small fraction of those in commission at the end of the war. These ships were kept busy with the routine salvage operations and tows that are the bread and butter of peacetime salvage forces. Sufficient quantities of such work is what keeps salvage forces in a high state of readiness. Unlike structural fleet exercises, there is no simulation for salvage work. Each operation is the real thing with a full ration of hazards and of chances for success or failure.

Besides providing direct support for fleet operations along both coasts and overseas, salvage ships were regularly deployed to Alaskan and Caribbean waters. For several years a salvage ship, first *Recovery* (ARS 43) and then *Paiute* (ATF 159), was homeported at Balboa, Canal Zone, to provide standby salvage services in the Caribbean and to operate a diving school at Rodman. Similarly, *Opportune* (ARS 41) and later *Escape* (ARS 6) were homeported in San Juan for many years.

The Salvage Law

Implementing the recommendations of the Interdepartmental Committee on Salvage occupied a large portion of the time of Commodore Sullivan and his staff. Drafting the legislation that would authorize the Navy to carry out the committee's recommendations formed an important part of the work. On 8 August 1948 Secretary of the Navy John L. Sullivan wrote the Honorable Joseph W. Martin, Speaker of the House of Representatives, a letter forwarding the proposed legislation and describing what the legislation would allow.

• It would authorize the Secretary of the Navy to provide salvage facilities for public and private vessels, by contract or otherwise.

• It would allow the Secretary to acquire ships and equipment for transfer to salvage companies.

• It would permit funds to be advanced to private companies for financing salvage operations.

• It would allow the Secretary of the Navy to settle and adjust claims for Navy-operated salvage facilities.

The letter went on to point out that, for several reasons, the Navy was the logical agency within the government to carry out U.S. responsibilities for salvage. The Navy already had a salvage organization with a full understanding of salvage problems. This organization must continue its involvement in peacetime in order to be prepared for war. In addition, the Navy had sufficient salvage vessels to provide services in U.S. waters where no commercial salvage services operated. Finally, the Navy operated, and intended to continue operating, a school for divers, salvage mechanics, and salvage officers.[4]

The proposed legislation was short, sweet, and simple. There is no need to dig into the dustbins of legislative history to determine what was in the minds of the drafters of the legislation or of the Congress.

Western marine operators who feared the Navy would compete with them for salvage business raised some objections to the bill. To protect the interests of those already in the salvage business, amendments required that contracts could be let only if existing commercial facilities were inadequate for national defense, and that public notice of contracts must be given to ensure competition. Another requirement called for anyone receiving vessels or equipment from the Navy to remain in the salvage business for a specified number of years. The bill passed and was signed into law in 1948 as the Salvage Facilities Act, Public Law 513 of the Eightieth Congress.[5]

The Salvage Act immediately became, and remains, the charter and cornerstone of the Navy salvage organization, giving basic national salvage policy the force of law. It allows the Secretary of the Navy great flexibility in supporting the nation's salvage posture, but it does not require him to do anything. In other words it is permissive rather than commanding; it says *may*, not *must*. The Navy has consistently taken the position that this statutory authority does not obligate it to maintain salvage facilities in excess of its own needs or to render salvage assistance on all occasions. Accordingly, while the Navy maintains close contact with the commercial shipping and international salvage worlds, it does not consider the needs of commercial shipping when deploying its salvage forces and does not inform underwriters and other commercial interests when it changes employment schedules or practices.

At the same time that the Navy's overall role in a national salvage policy was being legally defined, Navy salvors continued to carry out their individual roles in actual operations. The most celebrated of these was the salvage of the "Mighty Mo."

Mighty Mo Hits the Beach

In January 1950 *Missouri* (BB 63)—the "Mighty Mo"—was the only commissioned battleship remaining in the U.S. Navy. A proud ship and

---

[4] The Navy Salvage School, founded at Pier 88 in New York City, gave up that expensive real estate in 1947 and moved to Bayonne, New Jersey.

[5] The Salvage Facilities Act, originally codified in 46 U.S.C. 733–735, was later transferred to Title 10 "Armed Forces" in 1956 and is now 10 U.S.C. 7361–7367.

the last of the great *Iowa* class,[6] she had seen the Japanese surrender signed on her decks. In the public mind the name *Missouri* had become synonymous with seapower.

About 8:25 on the morning of 17 January 1950, *Missouri* grounded near Old Point Comfort. The battleship had just run the degaussing range while standing out to sea from the Naval Operating Base at Norfolk, Virginia. Mighty Mo hit the beach hard. Fully loaded and running at 12 knots, she crossed about 2,500 feet of shoal water before coming to rest on the hard sand bottom nearly at high tide. The Navy faced a major salvage operation that would tax the ingenuity, patience, and skill of all involved. An attempt was made to refloat her on the evening tide with resources that could be hastily assembled. It was fruitless, as such attempts often are. Rear Admiral Allan E. Smith, Commander Cruiser Force, U.S. Atlantic Fleet, moved aboard *Missouri* and settled down for a long job.

Even a cursory look at the grounding showed many favorable aspects. *Missouri* was in no danger of loss or extensive further damage. She lay in protected waters and was not exposed to environmental forces that could damage her or drive her further ashore. The hard sand bottom supported her entire length, preventing the development of high hull-bending stresses or unusual stress distribution patterns. Thus decisions could be made without pressure caused by the potential loss of the ship.

Salvors could take the time to work in a way that would not damage the ship rather than choosing damage from salvage as preferable to damage from the sea. The grounding site was near the Navy's greatest concentration of men, equipment, and floating and shore resources. Special equipment or people could easily be brought in from elsewhere. There was probably no more convenient place for a ship of the U.S. Navy to go aground. *Missouri* carried almost a full load of consumable materials that could be discharged to reduce total weight. No stability problem existed either as the ship lay or in any condition she would pass through during the salvage. The hull had sustained only slight damage. Only three of more than four hundred and fifty double-bottom compartments were open to the sea. On the other hand, the battleship had grounded at high tide, and so she would not benefit from additional buoyancy on the rising tide. The general salvage plan was straightforward. It consisted of increasing the ship's buoyancy and decreasing her displacement, dredging an exit channel, and pulling her off.

The first part of the plan called for removing fluids, ammunition,

---

[6] *Missouri* was commissioned on 11 June 1944. The first officer reporting aboard on the precommissioning crew was Lt.(jg.) A.A. Bartholomew, the author's father. The *Wisconsin* (BB 64) was commissioned on 16 April 1944. The two other ships in the class, *Iowa* (BB 61) and *New Jersey* (BB 62), were commissioned in 1943.

stores, and other weights from the ship. However, removal of these weights would leave her trimmed by the stern, a condition that would complicate refloating. To further decrease the ground reaction and to reduce the trim, pontoons would be placed at the stern. Some dredging and tunneling of the bottom material, which divers said had been compacted to the consistency of a poor grade of concrete, would allow the hull to settle.

A large number of fleet tugs, salvage ships, submarine rescue ships, and harbor tugs were present in Norfolk, as were the salvage lifting ships *Windlass* and *Salvager*. Many of these ships carried several legs of beach gear. The plan called for rigging beach gear to the battleship and rising various ships for pulling and wrenching both alongside and on the hawser.

The salvage lifting ships could be rigged for heavy pulls as well as heavy lifts; they would be in harness. The salvage ships laid beach gear and took it to the battleship for hauling. The large, clear deck areas, adequate deck machinery, and ample places to secure portable salvage winches made the battleship an excellent beach gear platform. The submarine rescue ships' value lay in their ability to provide large quantities of air to blow pontoons and to support the extensive diving operations necessary to observe bottom conditions, tunnel, and pass pontoon messenger lines. Fleet tugs nested together and rigged in tandem, salvage lifting ships in harness, and nine legs of beach gear would pull from astern. The submarine rescue ships and the *Hoist* (ARS 40), all alongside, would work up to full power, and a unit composed first of four harbor tugs [later of *Opportune*, *Recovery*, and *Nipmuc* (ATF 157)], would twist *Missouri*'s head. Harbor tugs would hold all the pulling units in position.

To create trenches parallel to the keel and at a depth well below it, dredging was started alongside almost as soon as the ship grounded. The material on the side of the trench would gradually slough off into the trench allowing the ship to settle deeper. The Army dredge *Comber* did most of the work, but could not approach the battleship closely. To get close to the hull and work under the counter, the dredge *Washington* was hired. *Comber* dredged the escape channel astern of *Missouri*. This channel was 150 feet wide and 40 feet deep. It ran from the stern of the grounded ship to the main channel.

Public relations took on particular importance in this salvage case because of the fame of the ship and its highly visible location. The press understood neither salvage nor the physical forces at work, but that seldom inhibited its members from comment and judgment. Unfavorable press coverage began to appear and gave indications of increasing. There was heavy pressure on the Navy for a public statement regarding a target date for refloating. With the large number of variable factors in salvage, of course, accurate schedules can seldom be laid down. After study of the situation and the work to be done, 2 February was chosen by Rear

Admiral Smith and published as the target date for refloating. If *Missouri* was not afloat by this date, some more drastic action would be forced.

Rear Admiral Smith held a staff conference each morning. Here the day's operations were laid out in detail and problems of coordination addressed. Space alongside the grounded battleship was allocated each day because of potential interference from different operations.

Measurements made during the operation were extensive. Because *Missouri* had run the degaussing range immediately before grounding, salvors knew her precise before-grounding drafts. Gages were built to measure vertical motion, and gunner's quadrants were set up to measure changes in declivity. Other full-scale empirical experiments established the coefficient of friction of the bottom soil. Underwater explosions were tried as a method of squeezing sand into the dredged troughs, but were too inefficient. Throughout the preparations additional beach gear, inflatable pontoons, a barge to lift the stern, and wavemaking destroyers were held in reserve.

An unusually high tide expected on 20 January gave the incentive for a pulling attempt on that date. The premature pull failed; the predicted high tide did not materialize, and everything else was not ready. The failure emphasized the futility of attempting to refloat a stranded ship when preparations are not complete. Hope and luck don't refloat ships; thorough preparation, good engineering, and seamanship do.

The next attempt was a full-dress rehearsal on 31 January. Operations began before sunrise and in heavy fog. Beach gear was hauled taut and the ships began to work up to full power. By 6:00 a.m. all ships were pulling full, and the beach gear wires were singing with tension. Then things began to go wrong. One of the harbor tugs fouled *Windlass*, forcing her to slack off. The twisting unit of four harbor tugs was not effective. The towing hawser of *Mosopelea* (ATF 158), one of the fleet tugs pulling ahead, parted. *Missouri* did not move. The attempt was terminated.

To increase the probability of success on the next pull scheduled for the following day, salvors removed the battleship's anchors and chains, emptied the forward peak tank, rigged two additional pairs of pontoons, and called in the big guns, *Opportune*, *Recovery*, and *Nipmuc*, to form the bow unit.

At 5:30 on the morning of 1 February, the salvors were ready. So was *Missouri*. The weather was cooperating. The tide, scheduled to peak around 7:30, looked as if it had been influenced by the northeast winds that had blown through the night. It would be higher than predicted. The bow unit began hauling to starboard; the port quarter beach gear was set taut. The ship swung slowly right. The twist was reversed, the ship swung back to port and moved astern. By 7:09 the great battleship was again afloat.

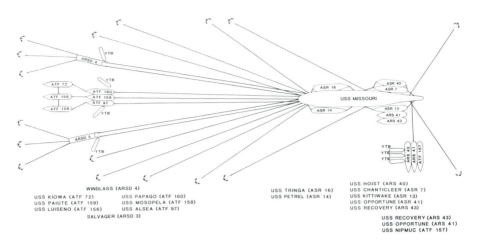

WINDLASS (ARSD 4)
USS KIOWA (ATF 72)   USS PAPAGO (ATF 160)
USS PAIUTE (ATF 159)   USS MOSOPELA (ATF 158)
USS LUISENO (ATF 156)   USS ALSEA (ATF 97)
          SALVAGER (ARSD 3)

USS TRINGA (ASR 16)
USS PETREL (ASR 14)

USS HOIST (ARS 40)
USS CHANTICLEER (ASR 7)
USS KITTIWAKE (ASR 13)
USS OPPORTUNE (ARS 41)
USS RECOVERY (ARS 43)

USS RECOVERY (ARS 43)
USS OPPORTUNE (ARS 41)
USS NIPMUC (ATF 157)

This pulling arrangement finally freed *Missouri*.

Tugs churn the water, vainly trying to pull the grounded battleship *Missouri* on 20 January 1950.

The Navy's largest single peacetime stranding salvage was accomplished using only Navy forces. The response was fast and thorough. The operation was completed without a single personnel casualty. The value of Navy training schools in providing well-trained salvage mechanics and officers, the value of salvage forces ready and able to meet emergencies and adapt to the conditions they find, and the value of salvage equipment located close to the probable point of need and in ready-for-issue condition—all these were demonstrated in the salvage of Mighty Mo. These assets would soon be needed in another war.

War in Korea

Shortly after North Korean forces crossed the 38th parallel on 25 June 1950, the U.S. Navy found itself at war again after less than five years. For salvage forces the Korean War would be very different from World War II. The 1,500-mile-long Korean coastline offered many places for concealment, but few sites for amphibious assaults. Its east coast had few harbors; the west coast was protected by vast mud flats and great tide ranges. The enemy lacked an effective, diverse naval force.

The general pattern of the naval war in Korea established itself quickly as focusing on interdiction of enemy supply routes by air attack and bombardment, and transportation of equipment and supplies to the peninsula. Exceptions to the basic pattern would be the great amphibious landing at Inchon, the much less notable one at Wonsan,[7] and the evacuation from Hungnam. Salvage forces supported all these operations.

In a noteworthy difference from World War II practice, ships went to war in Korea on a series of scheduled deployments rather than on indefinite assignments. The World War II practice of holding salvage ships in reserve while committing fleet tugs to the most forward area was discontinued; the two types of ships became virtually interchangeable. Used in this manner, as they had been in some areas of the Pacific during World War II, the ships complemented each other well. The salvage ship with its shallower draft and twin screws could approach a stranding more closely than the fleet tug. The fleet tug enjoyed a speed advantage and could reach a casualty more quickly; it could initiate operations and hold the fort until the salvage ship arrived.

---

[7] The amphibious landing at Wonsan was planned as a combat assault by the First Marine Division. It turned out to be something different. The situation ashore was so fluid that events outdistanced plans. Wonsan was captured from the rear by Republic of Korea forces before the Marines came ashore. Effective mining of the harbor also delayed the landing. Minesweeping required fifteen days rather than the planned five. When the Marines finally went ashore, they found that not only was the First Marine Air Wing already there, but that they had already been entertained by Bob Hope's USO troupe.

Even with the two types of ships serving interchangeably, the need for salvage vessels was so much greater than in peacetime that ships decommissioned after World War II were reactivated.

Throughout the war a salvage ship or fleet tug accompanied each task group of combatant ships to give the same kind of salvage assistance that had supported fast-carrier task force operations in World War II. With the combatants engaging primarily in bombardment operations and meeting little resistance, however, there was not much for the salvage ships to do other than recover downed aircraft.

Using the lessons learned in World War II, salvage ships were assigned to accompany the assault forces at Inchon. Because the fortresses of Wolmi-do and Sowolmi-do were taken out prior to the main assault, and because the United Nations' forces had complete control of the air, the numbers and types of casualties that had occurred in the Pacific campaigns were not repeated. Salvage ships found their primary work here to be in retracting landing ships left high and dry by the falling tides.

Combat operations and the high traffic density of wartime logistic operations typically occupied the salvage ships in Japanese and Korean waters. For example:

- *Current* and *Ute* refloated LST–578 at Cheju-do.

- *Grasp* and *Reclaimer* salvaged *Muhlenberg Victory* near Sasebo.

- *Mender* hauled *Park Benjamin* off the beach at Pusan,

- *Safeguard* extinguished a fire on *Firecrest* (AM 10) off Sasebo; refloated the Army's concrete hotel barge BH–3067 at Sokcho-do; assisted the battle-damaged *Lewis* (DE 535) at Wonsan; towed the disabled *Electron* (AKS 27), and raised the sunken LST–176 at Sokcho-ri; and in company with *Takelma*, the Army tug LT–1535, and USNS ATA–240, refloated *Park Benjamin* when she grounded at Pohang, her second grounding in Korea.

- *Reclaimer* towed the burning *Plymouth Victory* to Sasebo, escorted the mine-damaged *Wile* (DD 723) to port, pulled the Japanese LST Q–081 off her strand, and towed in the foundering *Gulf Haven*.

- *Conserver*, *Safeguard*, and *Current* refloated USNS LST–623, hard aground at Sokcho-do.

- *Moctobi* refloated the Korean Navy's PF–62 from Abru Somu Island in North Korean waters.

Salvage ships performed a variety of missions in addition to salvage and towing during the Korean War. These included:

- Laying buoys for marking swept channels, for navigation, and for moorings.

Navy salvors pose aboard the wrecked Thai frigate *Prasae* off the coast of North Korea. Left to right: Chief Petty Officer E.P. Wacham, Lieutenant (jg) D. Taylor, Petty Officer C.K. Harvard of the salvage ship *Bolster*, and a Korean colleague.

- Serving as a floating medical laboratory at Ulong-do for doctors fighting a typhoid outbreak.
- Carrying out resupply operations to remote outposts in North Korean waters.
- Patrolling to interdict coastal junk shipping and to prevent mining operations.
- Providing fuel, repairs, and other services to Korean Navy ships.

Occasionally, these missions included the unlikely work of shore bombardment. During one such operation, *Ute* earned the nickname Good Shoot *Ute* when her 3-inch shells started fires that burned all one night near Wonsan. The antimining, antijunk patrols—flycatcher patrols—were especially dangerous for the salvage ships. During one of these patrols on 8 August 1952, *Grapple* took a hit below the waterline from a shore battery, but effective damage control kept the ship on the line. She suffered more serious damage and two of her crew were killed just three days later when *Chief* (AM 315) opened fire on her because of a mistake in recognition signals. A little over two months later, on 27 October, *Sarsi* (ATF 111), conducting a night flycatcher patrol between Wonsan and Hungnam, struck a drifting mine. The damage defeated the damage-control measures and the tug sank in twenty minutes. Four men were lost; the others spent the night on rafts and the ship's motor whaleboat awaiting the rescue that came the following morning.

There were some significant operations. In January 1951 the Thai frigate HMTS *Prasae*, one of the many foreign warships supporting the United Nations operations in Korea, ran aground in North Korean territory. *Bolster*, with the task group, approached and anchored about a mile off the beach. True salvage weather was blowing. It was bitter cold, and the seas were about 6 feet. The frigate had broached and buried herself more than 7 feet into the sand. Salvors managed to get a line on board, but could do little else because the ship had no power and no mechanical assistance for getting lines and equipment to her. A major salvage operation in enemy territory seemed unwise. *Prasae* was abandoned and destroyed by covering warships.

A classic operation followed the stranding of the Republic of Korea's LST M–370 on the rocky island of Taechong-do on Memorial Day 1951. The U.S. Navy agreed to undertake the salvage; *Grasp*, *Moctobi*, and Commander J.W. Greely, the salvage officer of Service Squadron Three,[8] headed for the scene.

LST M–370 lay broached at the base of a rock cliff, cradled in rock with much of the double-bottom open to the sea. Both ends of the ship were damaged beyond the salvors' on-site ability to repair. Because the ship lay starboard side to the cliff, equipment could be loaded aboard only by the port boat davit, a difficult and time-consuming operation. The wisdom of salvaging so severely damaged an LST had to be carefully addressed. After thorough evaluation it was decided to go ahead with the salvage, but not to give it priority over other salvage needs. The basic salvage plan called for making double-bottom tanks tight and restoring buoyancy by either pumping them or blowing air into them. Explosives would remove some rock at the bow and stern. A temporary bulkhead would be built in the tank deck about one-third of the distance from the bow, abaft ruptures in the deck, in order to gain about a thousand tons of buoyancy.

Foul weather canceled work on some days and on others forced the

---

[8]From shortly after World War II until the 1975 organization of the Naval Surface Forces, the salvage officer for Service Squadron Three, homeported in the western Pacific, was also the salvage officer for Seventh Fleet. Similarly, the salvage officer assigned to the Service Force Commander's staff was double-hatted as the fleet salvage officer. With appropriate organizational changes this basic arrangement continued after the 1975 reorganization.

salvage party to abandon the LST over the starboard side and walk to a nearby village where they could be picked up for return to their ships. Plain, hard work continued all during the operation: building the temporary bulkhead, sealing the bottom, plugging vents, making compartments watertight, securing pumps and compressors on board, installing air fittings, and preparing a towing connection. The salvors chose a target refloating date of 21 June to coincide with the month's highest tide.

Pumping tests showed that the engine room could not be pumped nor could the compartment be sealed for blowing with air because the structure around various openings was badly deteriorated. The salvors crossed the compartment off the list of those to be made buoyant. Three days before the target refloating date, *Moctobi* was detached from the LST salvage for a higher priority operation. *Grasp* began an all-hands, round-the-clock operation.

At midnight on 21 June visibility was only 500 yards. The decision was to go ahead with the salvage operation despite the weather. The salvors felt that if every opportunity to make progress was not taken, the probability was quite high that worse weather would set in and the ship would be lost. By the time the ship was ready for pulling, a light wind had blown the fog to seaward. *Grasp*'s log (with the spelling unrevised) tells the story of that morning.

0440—Ship ready for pulling, commenced taking in on tow wire and paying out on anchor chains to get maximum holding power.

0500—Anchors secured with 90 and 60 fathoms of chain, tow wire taught at 1250 feet, waiting for word from salvage officer that the LST was starting to gain buoyancy.

0600—LST starting to roll with the sea, commenced working engines up to maximum speed. Set off four demolition charges on rocks near bow and stern of LST.

0628—Stern of LST commenced moving, anchor chains slacking, commenced heaving in on both anchor chains.

0637—Fog setting in, visibility decreased to 1000 yards.

0639—Salvage officer reported LST stern had swung to port and clear of rocks.

0640—Underway, attempting to swing ship to starboard about 40°.

0700—Fog set in, visibility zero.

The Korean LST M–370 lies hard aground on and against rocks—a difficult salvage case.

Salvors from the salvage ship *Grasp*, assisted by a Korean boy, study a recalcitrant air compressor used to blow air into the tanks of the South Korean LST M–370.

0716—Let go one anchor to hold ship in its present position. Visibility cleared to 1000 yards, heaved up anchor and took in tow wire to 1000 feet, engines slowed to 100 RPMs. Current taking ship to starboard, fog setting in to zero visibility.

0726—Tow wire let out to 1250 feet, let go starboard anchor to hold ship in present position until visibility increases.

0730—LST reported swinging stern to port, commenced taking in on tow wire and maintaining 100 RPM's with engines. The ships position had to be determined before maximum power could be used.

0750—Visibility increased to 1000 yards and showed the ship as being about 200 yards from the beach and in safe water, however, it was unsafe to attempt picking up the anchor and swing away as the current was setting toward the beach. Port anchor was dropped, all engines stopped, Tow wire was again taken in and chain paid out to the anchors to 45 and 60 fathoms.

0810—With both anchors holding and tow wire taught commenced building engines up to maximum power.

0920—Secured from pulling as tide was then ebbing and gone down until the bow of the LST was resting on the rocks. The stern had been pulled 90° to port and in good water.[9]

The first pull had been made in the worst kind of conditions. LST M–370 had been turned and was now aground only by the bow. On the following day the LST came afloat but the tension was only slightly relieved. The badly damaged ship began taking on water, and the auxiliary engine room bulkhead gave way, allowing flooding that grounded out the switchboard and caused power loss all through the ship. The ship took on a list and was in danger of capsizing. All available pumps were put into the engine room, and air was pumped into the starboard side tanks. The ship righted slowly and stayed afloat. LST M–370 was secured for tow and taken to Pusan, where she was returned to the Korean Navy with a recommendation to get her into drydock—quickly.

Throughout the Korean War there was concern at senior military and political levels that the Soviet Union might intervene and greatly escalate the war. Those who understood the Sino-Soviet Mutual Defense Pact of 1950 and its ramifications were doubly uncertain after the Chinese entered the war. The Soviets had then, as they do now, a large submarine fleet that would be a worthy adversary at sea capable of adding a new

---

[9]Ltr, Commanding Officer *Grasp* (ARS-24) serial 014, 16 July 1951.

dimension to United Nations naval operations. In the summer of 1951 an object believed to be a Soviet submarine had been located in about 50 fathoms of water off the Korean coast. A proposed investigation of this object had pulled *Moctobi* away from the salvage of LST M–370.

The submarine rescue ship *Coucal* (ASR 8) joined the operation to provide a mixed-gas diving capability. Working together, the two ships snagged the object and laid a four-point mooring over it. Mixed-gas divers went down for a look. The object turned out to be not a Soviet submarine, but a Japanese merchantman, apparently sunk during World War II. As an intelligence coup the operation was a disappointment, but as a confirmation of the Navy's ability to work in the ocean it was a success. The object had been pinpointed and positively identified at a depth in which few marine organizations could work at the time.

The heavy logistics traffic into Pusan generated some casualties. *Cornhusker Mariner*, one of the new postwar 535-foot, Mariner-class, break-bulk cargo ships, grounded hard on a rocky pinnacle just outside Pusan on 7 July 1953. The ship was refloated under the direction of the Seventh Fleet salvage officer, Commander Albert W. Mott, in a long and difficult operation that was not completed until October.

San Mateo Victory provided additional work for salvors when she ran aground on a rock bottom on Cheju-do near Pusan while making her best speed of 17 knots in a light condition. She was refloated by *Safeguard*, *Grasp*, and *Takelma* under Commander Mott's direction after rock had been blown away with explosives and chipped away with pneumatic hammers.

While Korea placed some heavy demands on salvage forces, other salvage units employed elsewhere in the Pacific and in the Atlantic on bread-and-butter operations conclusively demonstrated that such forces should be a part of a peacetime Navy with worldwide responsibilities. Two casualties occurring in the mid-Pacific near the end of 1952 introduced the Navy to some of the harsher realities of commercial salvage and affirmed some important legal principles that affected the Navy's position.

The first of these casualties was the break-bulk carrier *Andrea Lukenbach*. The ship was on a voyage from the West Coast of the United States to the Far East with a government-owned cargo mainly of foodstuffs and heavy machinery, when the master became ill. The ship diverted to Honolulu, where the master went ashore and the second mate became master. The ship left Honolulu on a course that took her a bit too close to the island of Kauai—especially given the set and drift in those waters. She touched bottom, holed herself, and grounded hard by her stern.

The Navy was asked to assist, but was not placed in charge of the operation. Commander C. Monroe Hart, the fleet salvage officer, left

A salvage conference aboard *San Mateo Victory* includes (left to right): Lieutenant Commander Franklin W. Rogers, Lieutenant Commander J.C. Hale, Commander Warren Mott, Seventh Fleet Salvage Officer, Lieutenant J.D. O'Kane, Lieutenant Commander W.M. Brobston, and Captain E.A. McMichael.

Pearl Harbor with a salvage crew[10] and *Cocopa* started toward the distressed vessel. The underwriter's agent at the scene had little salvage experience and, despite sound advice from Commander Hart to the contrary, tried to refloat the ship before a complete survey had been made and the ship properly secured.

Deliver had also been assigned to the job but was still some days away, so a commercial tug was hired to lay beach gear. The tug skipper had never been on a salvage job before and had never laid beach gear. Men who operate tugs tend to think they can do anything; often they are right, but not this time. Instead of putting the bitter end aboard the wreck, steaming out to stretch out the wire and then dropping the anchor,

---

[10] When Commander Hart and the salvage crew arrived, they found the cargo in number four hold to be heavy machinery tightly packed throughout the hold except in the square of the hatch, where Scotch whisky was loaded. The hold was secure, with the metal hatch boards welded down. Having no delusions about what could happen, Commander Hart realized that removal of the whisky was a matter of highest priority. A Coast Guard buoy tender was present, so Hart asked its commanding officer to place an armed guard on the hatch, trusting the tightly packed heavy machinery to block access from inside.

Commander Hart then went ashore to make some arrangements. When he returned, the Navy salvage crew was very drunk. Hart was furious. The Chief Warrant Officer in charge of the crew would have to be court-martialed. When the man had sobered up, Hart dressed him down royally and asked, "How did you get to the booze?" The warrant officer explained that, because the hatch was welded shut and guarded, they went in from another hold. When asked about the heavy machinery, he explained it had been a problem but had been solved by disassembling three bulldozers and removing them piece by piece. Any thoughts of court-martial were forgotten. These men had the ingenuity and drive of good salvors; the Navy could not afford to lose them.

the tug skipper dropped the anchor first and, hauling the wire, steamed toward the ship. The seas were rough. Working close to the wreck in heavy seas with a long wire to the anchor was not to the skipper's liking. He dropped the wire and steamed away. The wire was eventually recovered and brought on board.[11]

Deliver arrived and some cargo was removed. Mr. Walter Martignoni, an experienced salvage engineer representing the owners and underwriters, also arrived and took overall charge of the operation. Hart was called away on another emergency. All preparations for refloating were made, and calculations showed that the ship would float free when all flooded holds and the machinery space were pumped. However it now became apparent to the owners and underwriters that the hull damage, the numerous broken pipes and valves, the fractured reduction gear casing, and other damage would require long and expensive repairs. When added to the cost of the salvage, these repairs did not make economic sense. The owners abandoned the ship.[12]

The uncompleted salvage of *Andrea Lukenbach* involved a mixture of naval and commercial assets in a commercial salvage operation. It was a revelation to the Navy salvors who took part. In naval salvage the primary consideration always is getting the job done, often without any regard for cost. In commercial salvage, however, cost and the economics of an operation are important factors that often dominate the decisions. Frequently, a hull is not salvaged even though it is technically feasible to do so because the cost of salvage and repair are greater than the insured value of the ship. As is often true in commercial salvage cases, lengthy litigation followed the loss of *Andrea Lukenbach*. The point of contention was the general average[13] claim of the ship's owners and underwriters against the government as the owner of the cargo.

A short while later SS *Quartette*, laden with a cargo of Army-owned grain, grounded on Pearl and Hermes reef near Midway Island. At the time there was no commercial organization in the Pacific that could provide salvage services at the reef. Knowing that salvage time is always of the essence in stranding, Commander Hart dispatched *Current* to the

---

[11] The wire was brought on board in an unusual manner. A few days before, a local man named Bill Pye had showed up at the site and asked the underwriter's surveyor for a job. Pye said he was a diver but needed no equipment because he would breath-hold dive. He was not hired. Several days later he showed up on a small tender with a piece of line and a large shackle. Ignoring the salvors trying to wave him off, he jumped into the water. The people topside were quite anxious when Pye had been down more than a minute and a half, but he surfaced with the bitter end of the line and passed it to the ship. The wire was hauled aboard. Bill Pye was hired.

[12] *Andrea Lukenbach* was later sold as-is, where-is to an adventuresome Honolulu businessman who failed to realize a positive return on his investment. He lost his shirt.

[13] "General average" is a legal principle unique to maritime law wherein cargo owners share with ship owners the risks of the voyage and are liable for a proportionate share of costs if the ship becomes a casualty.

SS *Quartette* when first aground and after some time aground. The fate of *Quartette* vividly demonstrates the dangers of even the simplest grounding. *Quartette* was scarcely damaged in her initial grounding, but after some days' exposure to the force of the sea in conditions her designers never anticipated, she began to break up.

scene without waiting for a request for salvage from the owner or his agent. That request was not forthcoming; what came forth was a court order prohibiting the Navy from touching the ship. *Current* was recalled, while Hart went to see the fleet judge advocate to find out what could be done to get on with the job. The judge advocate took the position that under the law the Navy could salvage the ship to mitigate damages. The salvage officer and judge advocate went to Admiral Arthur W. Radford, the fleet commander, who agreed. *Current* sailed again.

By this time a storm had come through. *Quartette* no longer lay perpendicular to the beach, an easy salvage job; she had now broached and torn her bottom out. It would be a long hard job to patch the hull damage, discharge the cargo, and rig beach gear. The salvage and legal battles went along simultaneously. When the government-owned cargo had been saved, all the beach gear had been laid, and everything was ready for a pull, Hart received a message to stop, pick up the gear, and go home. He couldn't believe it and requested confirmation in a what-the-hell message. He got his confirmation. He was to pick up and go home.

Quartette's owners and underwriters did not want the ship salvaged and had obtained another court order to stop the Navy. As all the salvageable government-owned cargo had been removed, there was no further reason for the Navy work to continue. Hart did as he was directed. The government's right to salvage and to act to mitigate damages had been confirmed, but so had the right of the ship's owner and underwriter to determine the fate of their vessel on purely economic grounds.[14]

Pacific Fleet salvage forces worked all over the Pacific during the Korean War. Along with their regular turn in Korea, ships also undertook salvage at Iwo Jima, Kwajelein, Majuro, Subic Bay, and many other places. Atlantic Fleet units did not deploy to Korea but were kept occupied in responding to casualties in the Atlantic, clearing navigation hazards, cleaning up Navy ports in Operation Chin, installing and maintaining moorings, escorting resupply convoys into the Arctic, and supporting research and development projects. In both fleets, the recovery of aircraft for both the Navy and the Air Force was taking on greater importance.

A particularly significant job started one clear and unseasonably cool night in the summer of 1953, when two ships did not pass in the night as they should have. SS *Pan-Massachusetts*, a tanker fully laden with gasoline and inbound up the Delaware River for Marcus Hook, collided with her empty sister SS *Phoenix*. The explosions could be heard for 20 miles, and fires lit the night. Local fire fighters were not able to do much against the

---

[14] Though there was reason to suspect barratry in the grounding of *Quartette*, the matter was not pursued, and all legal action was dropped.

raging gasoline fires. The owners called the Navy for assistance, primarily because they knew the excellent reputation of the Navy Damage Control Training Center at Philadelphia. Lieutenant Commander Louis O. Lindemann, Jr., the officer-in-charge of the Fire Fighting School and a former lieutenant in the Baltimore Fire Department, grabbed a tug and went to have a look.

Lindemann assessed the situation and returned to Philadelphia. The next morning he was back with the tug *Toka* (YTB 149), a fire-fighting crew, and a full load of mechanical and chemical foam. *Toka* began making passes up and down both sides pouring water on the flaming tanker. After several passes, the fire fighters broke out the foam lines and began pouring foam on the fire. The foam was effective, but *Toka* drifted away on the tide and the fire reclaimed the territory the foam had taken.

There was a brouhaha on the bridge of *Toka*. Lindemann wanted the tug secured alongside the flaming tanker, but the pilot was reluctant to do that. Thus when the tug moved in, the fire fighters gained ground; when the tug drifted back, the fire fighters lost their gains. Gradually, the pilot began to gain confidence and soon was holding the tug alongside. Within two hours Lindemann judged the ship safe to board, and fire fighters went aboard. The decks were so hot that the men stood first on one foot and then on the other. They worked slowly aft, blanketing the tanks with foam and cooling the deck with water. Four hours were lost when the tug left to get more foam. When the fire fighters returned, they found that *Pan-Massachusetts* had swung over against *Phoenix* and many of the fires had rekindled. The crew renewed the battle. In three hours the fires were out and the fire fighters were on their way home. Merritt-Chapman and Scott then moved in and completed the salvage of the two tankers as a commercial salvage operation.

In this case, the system had worked as it was supposed to. A dangerous and expensive ship fire had been put out by Navy fire fighters when no one else could do the job. The Navy's fire-fighting technology and training system was coupled with the expertise of a commercial salvage operator to handle a major marine casualty.

Expertise that the Navy had acquired by assembling the best fire-fighting technology and experience and by analyzing combat fires during World War II had paid off in a casualty that could have had much more serious results. The combat in Korea (and later in Vietnam) did not produce a large number of shipboard fires. Subsequent British experience in the Falklands and American experience in the Persian Gulf, however, have shown the need for sophisticated fire-fighting technology and well-trained fire fighters in modern combat salvage forces.

The Korean War and concurrent salvage operations throughout the world demonstrated the value of having Navy salvage forces available for simultaneous peacetime and combat scenarios. The combat situation itself was very different from any in the major theaters of World War II, and salvage operations reflected this difference. The salvage organization for the Korean War remained a part of the Service Forces supporting combat forces as they had in the Pacific War, but there were no nearly autonomous salvage units as there had been in the earlier and larger war. Not only were fleet tugs and salvage ships used almost interchangeably, but there were no special fire-fighting or harbor clearance units in Korea; they were simply not needed. With a smaller number of salvage ships, a different threat, and worldwide demands for salvage services, the post-World War II salvage strategy proved totally suitable. During the Korean War Navy salvage forces successfully met the simultaneous challenges of supporting a modern limited war, supporting global naval operations, and maintaining the Navy's newly established position as the national agency for salvage.

Peacetime Salvage

With the end of combat in Korea the Navy settled into a peacetime routine. But it was not the routine of the days before World War II. The U.S. Navy now had a constant worldwide presence. The Sixth Fleet in the Mediterranean and the Seventh Fleet in Far East waters were permanent organizations, manned by ships on regular deployments from their homeports in the United States. Salvage ships, like other vessels, made regular deployments. The staffs of Service Squadron Six in the Mediterranean and Three in the Far East were permanently assigned to the deployed fleets. Each of these two staffs had a salvage officer who performed regular ship maintenance duties until a casualty occurred. He then grabbed his bag and headed for the casualty to take charge or to provide technical direction for the salvage operation. Service Force salvage officers in Pearl Harbor and Norfolk operated in a similar manner.

For the salvage establishment in the Navy it was a relatively quiet time. The major portion of the task of salvage management, planning, budgeting, and administration fell on the Supervisor of Salvage, along with the job of managing the Navy's salvage contracts. Despite the experience of World War II and Korea and the relatively constant use of salvage forces in peacetime, the Supervisor of Salvage found that many in the Navy remained unconvinced that salvage should have a permanent role or that money to support salvage was being well spent. Ever since the elimination after World War II of the position of Chief of Navy Salvage on the Chief of Naval Operations Staff, the Supervisor of Salvage had been hard pressed to argue the case for strong salvage forces. Navy salvage lacked an effective advocate in the corridors of power.

Despite some skepticism about their usefulness, the training of Navy salvors continued.[15] Service Force salvage ships and Submarine Force rescue ships were kept in a reasonably high state of readiness by a combination of scheduled training, many small jobs, and regular deployments to the Sixth and Seventh Fleets. Occasional major operations brought together the entire range of salvage resources.

During this period the Navy acquired little salvage equipment and no salvage ships. Ships built during World War II were in their relative youth and large stockpiles of salvage equipment and machinery were also available from the World War II acquisitions.

Increased interest in working in the ocean produced new jobs for Navy salvage ships. The vessels proved to be good, stable platforms with a variety of installed systems for lifting and handling lines. They were crewed with energetic, resourceful, imaginative, capable, and well-trained people. They participated in a variety of ocean research projects, backed the fusion bomb tests at Eniwetok, bolstered several cable-laying operations, participated in the at-sea recoveries of the nation's space vehicles, and recovered aircraft for the Navy and Air Force. Most important, they continued in their traditional roles of supporting the Navy's needs in ship salvage and in filling the gaps in U.S commercial salvage.

There was plenty of traditional salvage work for them to do:

• *Salvager* cleared the wreckage of YFN–6 in Delaware Bay and worked over the wreckage of the battleship *Texas*, which had been a navigation hazard in Chesapeake Bay southeast of Tangier Island since 1911.[16]

• On 5 January 1956 the destroyer *Basilone* (DDE 824) grounded off Fort Storey, Virginia. The grounding was on the Officers' Club Beach, where observers could gather and hoot in well-oiled comfort. Headquarters for the salvage operation was set up in the Officers' Club Game Room. Salvage was undertaken under the auspices of the Service Force Commander; the Supervisor of Salvage provided technical assistance. *Hoist*, *Seneca* (ATF 91), and *Windlass* were on scene in short order. The weather was foul and the seas rough. *Seneca* was driven ashore; wires parted aboard *Hoist*; and *Windlass* dragged dangerously near the de-

---

[15] The Navy Salvage School moved from Bayonne, New Jersey, to the Washington Navy Yard in 1957, where it was combined with the Deep Sea Divers School. In 1970 the name was changed to Naval School, Diving and Salvage to relect its function more accurately. The school continued under this name until 1980, when it moved to a new facility in Panama City, Florida, as the Naval Diving and Salvage Training Center.

[16] *Texas*, completed in 1895, had her name changed to *San Marcos* prior to being sunk as a target by *New Hampshire* (BB 25) in March 1911. Over the years her upperworks were shot away, and she settled into the mud. As a menace to navigation she cost the government over $100,000 until all the structure above the mud line was removed. This wreck was not the *Texas* (BB 35) mentioned several times previously; that ship is now a memorial at San Jacinto, Texas.

stroyer and the beach, but managed to break loose and steer clear. The salvage ships took shelter, their rigging and decks covered with ice. When the weather moderated, the salvors returned with *Salvager*. *Windlass* pulled *Seneca* free; *Salvager* refloated *Basilone*. When the job was done, the salvors picked up fourteen anchors.

• *Reclaimer* refloated a stranded LST at Kauai, Hawaii.

• *Escape* (ARS 6) freed the new destroyer *Jonas Ingram* (DD 938) from her strand on Culebra Island, Puerto Rico.

• In the bitter-cold winter of 1961, reminiscent of the winter of 1917–18, *Recovery* assisted Coast Guard ships in clearing heavy ice congestion and freeing stranded merchantmen in Hampton Roads, Virginia.

• *Luiseno* (ATF 156), *Recovery*, *Salvager*, and *Windlass* combined to haul the Reserve Fleet destroyer *Baldwin* (DD 624) off Montauk Point, Long Island. One man was killed and another injured aboard *Windlass* in the ever-dangerous work of salvage. In an ironic twist to the operation, the salvage ships took the badly damaged destroyer to sea and sank her with gunfire.

• *Shakori* (ATF 162) towed the collision-damaged Norwegian ship *Tarrantel* into Hampton Roads, Virginia, and grounded her to prevent sinking while *Opportune* stood by.[17]

• *Hoist*, *Seneca*, and *Windlass* teamed again to free the grounded USNS *Bluejacket* (T–AF 51), saving a cargo of frozen stores.

• With eight legs of beach gear laid across a pier and hauled by a D–8 Caterpillar tractor, *Opportune* refloated *Duell* (APA 160) after hurricane Carol blew the transport ashore at Davisville, Rhode Island.

Two Strandings

The spring of 1962 saw two major and interesting salvage operations— one in each ocean; one concerned a U.S. destroyer, the other a Panamanian flag freighter.

On 5 March 1962, *Monssen* (DD 798), a Reserve Fleet destroyer, was being towed from the Bayonne Group of the Atlantic Reserve Fleet to the Philadelphia Group by *Penobscot* (ATA 188).[18] Late in the evening, with

---

[17] Despite pressure from the State Department and the Supervisor of Salvage to use fleet assets to complete the salvage of *Tarrantel*, the Service Force Commander, Rear Admiral Dennis Knoll, maintained that this was a case for commercial salvors because *Tarrantel*, unlike *Quartette*, had no government cargo on board. Service Squadron Eight ships provided health and comfort assistance until *Cable* arrived from Key West. The wait left Navy salvors extremely frustrated as they watched the new ship deteriorate.

[18] ATAs were not named when commissioned. The ATAs that were retained in commission following World War II were given names in 1948. Like ATFs, they carried the names of Indian tribes. Many of the names had been previously carried by Navy tugs.

The salvage lifting ship *Windlass* prepares for a pull on the stranded Reserve Fleet destroyer *Baldwin* off Montauk Point, Long Island.

seas building to 15 feet and winds steady at 30 knots and gusting to 50, the tow wire parted. *Monssen* grounded six hours later just south of Beach Haven, New Jersey. The storm continued to cast the destroyer up the beach.

Response was immediate. The assistant force salvage officer, Lieutenant (j.g.) Lewis W. Berke, and Master Diver Jack Kennedy, headed for the scene by land to make an initial survey. *Hoist*, *Windlass*, and *Salvager* loaded out in Norfolk and got under way for Beach Haven. *Papago* (ATF 160) followed them with the Service Force salvage barge YFNB–17 in tow. Captain Norman C. Nash, who was to command the task unit, and Lieutenant Commander Joseph F. Madeo, the force salvage officer, were embarked in *Hoist*. *Luiseno* was held in Newport, Rhode Island, on two hours' steaming notice. It was not an easy trip for anyone; the storm continued with heavy winds, rains and high seas. The storm also continued to drive *Monssen* ashore until she was embedded in sand above the high-water mark. It was going to be a major job.

The initial, detailed survey showed that *Monssen* had moved across the sandbar and lay broached above the high-water mark, 7 feet deep in soft sand with a 5 degree list; she had little flooding or structural damage. The 132,000 gallons of fuel oil on board in two grades, Navy Special Fuel Oil (NSFO) and the heavier Bunker C, could be easily removed to eliminate the hazards of pollution and fire and to lighten the ship. A full set of ship's plans was available, and so precise calculations would be feasible. Perhaps most important, there were extensive salvage assets available to support the effort.

The salvors' basic plan called for holding what they had, getting as much buoyancy as possible, rotating *Monssen* until she was perpendicular to the beach line, and then hauling her off little by little. The large number and variety of Navy resources that could be brought to bear on the *Monssen* meant that several of the salvage tasks could begin and work simultaneously.

It is a firm rule in salvage that to prevent a stranded ship from being driven ashore or broaching, anchors should be planted to seaward. This strategy hardly seemed necessary in the case of *Monssen* since the ship was high and dry and already broached, but the rules of salvage are written by harsh experience. *Luiseno*, which had joined the task group by this time, and *Papago* laid Eells anchors astern of *Monssen* and secured wire rope anchor cables on board with carpenter's stoppers.

With the destroyer secured, lightening could begin. Salvors turned to removing what they could, but major weight and fuel removal had to wait until a road of pierced-steel planking was laid to the highway and trucks and cranes could be brought to the ship. Immediate efforts were made to remove the fuel by taking a suction through the tank manholes with 6-inch and 3-inch salvage pumps. This did not work because the oil was too viscous and cold. While this attempt was in progress, another crew was rigging the ship's fuel-oil transfer pump so it would run on compressed air and hooking up a 3-inch salvage pump to act as a booster. This system worked for the NSFO in the forward tanks, but not for the heavier Bunker C or the NSFO in the aft tanks. Activating the aft fuel-oil transfer pump took care of the problem of the NSFO aft. To reduce the viscosity of the Bunker C, steam from a portable boiler was injected directly into the tanks.

Some tank boundaries had ruptured. The forward bilge pump and portable air-driven pumps removed all the oil. To ensure that there would be no pollution during refloating, all tanks and contaminated spaces were cleaned with an emulsifier and detergent. A few minor spills on the beach were cleaned up so that no trace of oil would remain on completion of the operation.

Weight removal proceeded systematically with small items and pilferable material being removed first. The propellers, rudder, shafting, and struts were removed by cutting with shaped charges and electric-arc and oxyacetylene torches. These removals served the dual purpose of preventing the appendages from digging in and of removing weight from the hull. To facilitate the removal of major topside weights, such as the 5-inch gun mounts and torpedo tubes, sand ramps were built to give cranes and trucks better access to the ship. Over 265 tons was removed from the destroyer, significantly reducing the weight to be dragged back into the water.

The nature of the sea bottom complicated the operation. Never has the term "shifting sands" better described a bottom. Bars, shallows, and pools moved constantly in the offshore area. Each ship's commanding officer kept a constant survey of the bottom in the area where he operated. Inordinately long hauling wires were required between the pulling ships and the destroyer because of the shallow beach approaches. Hauling the heavy, 2-inch-diameter wire rope ashore was hard and dangerous work. On 23 March a nylon line hauling one of the wires through the surf parted and struck Lieutenant (j.g.) Thomas E. O'Malley. O'Malley was immediately treated by a medical officer, who accompanied him on the helicopter to the Naval Hospital at Philadelphia. The injuries were too grave; O'Malley died en route.

The sand on the beach, by contrast, did not shift easily. To rotate the hull so that the destroyer could be pulled directly seaward, large amounts of sand had to be removed near the hull. The sand removal area initially extended from just abaft the stem on the starboard side, around the bow and down the port side to the after stack, and from the starboard quarter to the forward stack. Bulldozers and draglines removed the sand, but the tide really controlled the sand removal operation. During any given tide cycle, the inboard (port) removal area maintained about 70 percent of its depth, the outboard side only about half as much. Jetting pumps and small gasoline-powered pumps kept the sand close to the hull fluid, and eventually the moat grew until it encircled the ship, 20 feet wide and 10 feet deep. In the last stages of the operation, LCMs scoured. They were very effective.

The bar separating the *Monssen* from deep water was attacked with explosives. A channel was cut by over 4,000 pounds of explosive hose charges. In the shifting sands the channel did not remain, but the sand had become loosened and less stable than the normal bottom, and so it offered less resistance to the passage of the destroyer.

Weight removal, bottom grooming, and rotation were needed but were complementary to the main tool—the beach gear. The ship came free in a number of small moves, with the beach-gear hard work. Fortunately, as with the *Missouri*, the operation took place in an area where there was easy access to a variety of industrial services and the huge range of services available in the Navy. In so complex a salvage operation, ready access to such industrial services can spell the difference between success and failure. The Navy brought to the operation more resources and a wider variety of state-of-the-art salvage than any other organization in the world could have done at the time.

Attachment points for the beach gear were a matter of major concern. Destroyers are lightly constructed ships; unless carefully engineered, pulls on the structure of one can cause extensive damage. The strongest points possible, the gun mount foundations, were chosen as attachment points for the beach gear. Because the ship was high and dry, it was possible to attach *Salvager* to the skeg.

Initially, wire ropes from the anchors laid by *Papago* and *Luiseno* were led through the stern chock up both sides of the main deck to purchases hauled by portable winches. Two additional legs, with their purchases and winches on the beach, were led over the shore side to add stability and some rotational force. *Salvager* and *Windlass* were in harness astern and slightly to starboard; *Hoist* lay 90 degrees off the bow, also in harness. A pull was made with this arrangement on 26 March. *Monssen* did not move, but the beach gear anchors did. The fluid sand made poor holding ground. *Hoist* was taken off the bow and put astern between the two. Still *Monssen* didn't move; still the anchors dragged. *Papago* and *Luiseno* were sent to Bayonne to draw more anchors from the Emergency Ship Salvage Material Pool there. *Preserver* joined, laid her beach gear, and went into harness with the others. *Preserver* and *Hoist* had two anchors in each leg, *Windlass* and *Salvager* had four. *Luiseno* and *Papago* helped hold the salvage ships so that their doubled anchors would not drag. Pulls didn't move the destroyer; tow wires parted; heavy weather disrupted work; discouragement and frustration grew; the work went on.

On 7 April *Monssen* moved 15 degrees to port and 15 feet aft. The ship trembled during high water—a movement that indicated the ship was ready to come off her strand. She continued to move slowly. Gear was rerigged to get the best pull as she came around and moved aft. The work was heavy; the weather was lousy; lines parted; pins bent; *Monssen* crept toward the sea.

Gale-force winds blew on 13 April. *Preserver* was driven against a bar; *Hoist* pulled her clear. The anchors laid to seaward early in the operation held; *Monssen* was not driven further ashore—in fact, she moved aft a few more feet. When the strong winds abated, the slow movement seaward continued, until on 19 April *Monssen* slipped slowly across what was left of the bar and floated. *Luiseno* took *Monssen* in tow for Philadelphia with *Preserver* escorting. The rest picked up anchor and cleaned up the beach.

The *Monssen* salvage operation was complete. It had involved a relatively large force of Navy salvage assets, a great deal of planning, careful coordination, and more than a full ration of hard work. Fortunately, as with the *Missouri*, the operation took place in an area where there was easy access to a variety of industrial services and the huge range of services available in the Navy. In so complex a salvage operation, ready access to such industrial services can spell the difference between success and failure. The Navy brought to the operation more resources and a wider variety of state-of-the-art salvage than any other organization in the world could have done at the time.

The salvage of *Monssen* was an excellent example of how the Navy continually adapts a variety of units and techniques to maximize the on-the-job training available from actual salvage operations. For example, the salvage ships had been designed primarily as lifting ships. In the *Missouri* and *Baldwin* salvages, however, they had proved their ability as pulling ships; in the *Monssen* operation they confirmed it. During the *Monssen* operation, helicopters transported both people and equipment—an early application of what would later become an indispensable salvage tool.

Eight days after *Monssen* crept off her strand, and half a world away, the Panamanian-flag freighter *Dona Ouriana* grounded on Pocklington Reef 200 miles south of Guadalcanal. *Dona Ouriana* was a 12,000-ton grain carrier sailing empty except for 1,900 tons of ballast. After several attempts to back off, the crew abandoned the ship. As there were no commercial salvage facilities in the area, assistance was requested from the U.S. Navy. *Bolster* drew the job. She got under way from Yokosuka, Japan, bound for Pocklington Reef by way of Guam, where she picked up the Seventh Fleet salvage officer, Commander Thomas N. Blockwick, and, with foresight, a large load of explosives. *Bolster* arrived off Pocklington Reef on 15 May 1962. Only an Australian surveyor, representing the British owner, and his diver were aboard the stranded ship.

The first 180 of the ship's 483 feet lay on the ground. The ground reaction was 2,000 tons, the center of pressure was just forward of number three hold, and the hull was working heavily. The forepeak and the double bottom under number one hold were open to the sea. There was no question of moving the ship in this condition. The most promising solution seemed to be to remove some of the coral under the ship and even that didn't look too good. The forward part of the ship was hard aground, the reef dropped to great depths, and there was deformation of the ship's structure at the edge of the reef. The tide range was only one foot on a twenty-four-hour cycle. The water was too deep for beach gear.

Divers placed explosives in coral caves and began to blow the coral away from under the ship. The point of action of the ground reaction moved forward. Some of the original crew returned to the ship and put her machinery into operation. *Bolster* hooked up her tow wire. The shots continued. As the point of action of the ground reaction moved forward and the ground reaction lessened, *Bolster* wrenched the hull while *Dona*

The destroyer *Monssen* lies high and dry on a New Jersey beach.

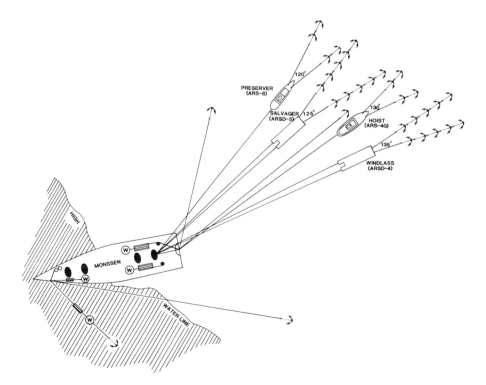

These pulling arrangements freed *Monssen*.

Ouriana backed full. She gradually moved off the reef and followed *Bolster* under her own power to Brisbane.

Using explosives to cut away the coral to refloat *Dona Ouriana* demonstrated a quality always required in salvage—the ability to select the tool, technique, and technology that best fits the situation at hand.

Typhoons Karen and Olive

As typhoon Karen approached Guam in November 1962, senior commanders watched it carefully and prepared to assist the island after the storm passed. Karen struck Guam with fury. The eye of the storm passed just 10 miles south of the island. Sustained winds of 150 knots with gusts to 180 struck the island. Damage was extensive. Eleven wrecks littered the harbor.

The storm provided the Navy with its most extensive harbor salvage operation since the end of World War II. The wrecks were primarily service craft, small tugs, and warships being modernized for foreign navies under military assistance programs. The wrecks were small, but the principles involved in their salvage were the same as for larger ships. Many a salvor has learned the hard way that small ships can be more difficult than big ones; they are not so forgiving or tolerant of error.

In addition to retaining the values in the wrecked vessels, there was another motivation to salvage the wrecks with Navy resources. In the salvage to be done lay an unparalleled opportunity for training, developing new salvage techniques, and field testing new equipment.

The Pacific Fleet salvage officer, Commander Willard F. Searle, Jr., recognized this opportunity and made the most of it. Immediately after the storm, the Ship Repair Facility at Guam had the primary responsibility for salvage. The assets available there included Lieutenant Commander J. Huntly Boyd, an Emergency Ship Salvage Material Pool, and industrial capacity. The work could have been done with these assets alone, but to ensure that it was done as quickly as possible while maximizing training, Commander Blockwick, the Seventh Fleet salvage officer, and the two Seventh Fleet salvage ships *Bolster* and *Reclaimer* were ordered to Guam.

Besides providing the maximum fleet support for the salvage operation, Commander Searle arranged with the Supervisor of Salvage, Commander Theodore F. Bacheler, for a report and analysis of the operation to be published and distributed by the Bureau of Ships. Understanding the importance of politics and semantics in the peacetime Navy, Commander Searle referred to the operations in Guam as "harbor clearance operations," whereas they were in fact "harbor salvage," since all the craft salvaged were intended for return to service. The importance of the term

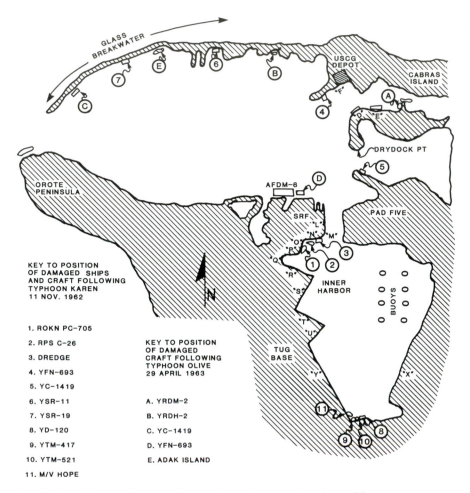

KEY TO POSITION
OF DAMAGED SHIPS
AND CRAFT FOLLOWING
TYPHOON KAREN
11 NOV. 1962

1. ROKN PC-705

2. RPS C-26

3. DREDGE

4. YFN-693

5. YC-1419

6. YSR-11

7. YSR-19

8. YD-120

9. YTM-417

10. YTM-521

11. M/V HOPE

KEY TO POSITION
OF DAMAGED
CRAFT FOLLOWING
TYPHOON OLIVE
29 APRIL 1963

A. YRDM-2

B. YRDH-2

C. YC-1419

D. YFN-693

E. ADAK ISLAND

Apra harbor, Guam, after visits from typhoon Karen and typhoon Olive.

"harbor clearance," and the value of the implicit tie to the great successes of World War II, will become obvious as the story of Navy salvage develops.

The first step at Guam, as in any major harbor salvage or clearance, was to establish a priority for dealing with the wrecks. As noted earlier, the process is analogous to the medical task of triage. Each casualty must be analyzed to determine not only how, but when it should be dealt with and what its importance is relative to other casualties. In Guam those wrecks that could be salvaged and used in the subsequent operations were given priority. Starting with only meager floating resources, the salvors could, in effect, build their own salvage fleet by reclaiming the most useful wrecks first, as Ellsberg had done at Mesewa.

For this reason first priority went to the floating crane YD-120, aground, starboard side to, at the end of wharf V. The salvage plan called for hauling off the wreck with beach gear from the Emergency Ship Salvage Material Pool and the locally based *Wandank* (ATA 204), which had returned after evading the typhoon evasion at sea. Because the working area was limited, the beach gear legs were modified for heaving from the crane pontoon, and *Wandank* was secured to the wharf across from the grounded crane where she could pull most advantageously with her towing winch.

The crane floated on the third attempt and went immediately into service. Before the arrival of the Seventh Fleet salvage ships, two barges, YSR–11 and YC–1419, were also refloated by *Wandank* and the Ship Repair Facility crew using YD–120.

Commander Blockwick arrived in Guam on 15 November, *Bolster* three days later, and *Reclaimer* three days after that. *Deliver* (ARS 23) sailed from Pearl Harbor on 20 November laden with additional salvage and diving equipment. Five divers from units based in Pearl Harbor flew in on 30 November. When *Deliver* arrived in Guam on 2 December, the cast was complete.

Raising the two patrol craft, ROKS *Han Ra San* (PC–705) and RPS *Negros Oriental* (C–26), and the Trust Territories' dredge *John S. Campbell* had first priority. These three wrecks blocked almost half the industrial waterfront of the Ship Repair Facility. They all were light enough to make lifting to the surface and dewatering practicable. The alternative methods of raising by air or cofferdamming and pumping were likely to be time consuming, dangerous, and impractical because of their depth, about 35 feet. The plan for all three wrecks called for lifting one end with YD–120 while lifting the other end with one or more salvage ships. The arrangement of the wrecks and the geography of the wharves dictated the order of the work: the dredge first, then *Negros Oriental*, and finally *Han Ra San*.

The dredge was light enough to be lifted by the crane and one salvage ship, but because of the arrangement of the bow rollers on the salvage ship, the dredge would come up under the salvage ship's forefoot. To correct this situation a set of auxiliary blocks were designed and installed at the extreme bow on either side of the warping posts. With standard beach gear rigging, about 100 tons could now be lifted to the surface under the rake of the bow. Auxiliary rollers were installed on both *Bolster* and *Reclaimer*.

The crane and the salvage ships successfully lifted all three vessels. A variety of gasoline, diesel, electric submersible, and Power-Pack-powered pumps were used to draw the winch out. (Power Packs were diesel engines to which a variety of driven ends—pumps, compressors, and generators—could be fitted.) Pumps were located aboard the wreck or alongside on the pier as appropriate. The dredge returned to service, but the two patrol craft had suffered too much structural damage for further service; they became hulks for salvage training.[19]

Two harbor tugs, YTM–521 and YTM–417, lying together at the extreme southern end of the harbor presented a tough salvage problem. YTM–521 lay almost perpendicular to the beach with a 25-degree starboard list. Her bulwark at the forward part of the house lay under the counter of YTM–521, which lay with her port side on the beach and a starboard list of just over 18 degrees. YTM–521 had some flooding through topside openings. Stability and interference with YTM–417 were major concerns. Prevention of capsizing during refloating required physical restraint as the tug was pumped and retracted. The recently salvaged barge YC–1419, with a crawler crane, generator, and pumps aboard, was brought in to starboard of the tug, YD–120 was placed on the port quarter, and *Reclaimer* was positioned to pull with her main tow wire. With the crane lifting, the hull was pumped out and the entire nest of craft pulled slowly off the beach. With the tug safely afloat, the nest was broken up and the salvaged vessel was moved to a waiting drydock. The second tug was floated by patching her hull and lifting with YD–120 while *Deliver* pulled.

With the bulk of the salvage work done by mid-December, the salvage ships departed. The salvors were still telling stories of the aftermath of typhoon Karen when Olive, an out-of-season typhoon, struck in April 1963. Less severe than Karen, this storm left five wrecks at Guam, two of which had already been salvaged after the previous typhoon.

To assist Lieutenant Commander Boyd and the local salvors, *Safeguard* was ordered to Guam. These forces salvaged the new wrecks handily. The most interesting job lay nearby in Tanapag, Saipan, where the Trust Territories' 182-foot tanker Y–101 had been driven ashore. In response to a request from the U.S. Department of the Interior, *Safeguard* went to Saipan to salvage Y–101 after she had finished work at Guam.

Y–101 lay with her bow on the beach, on a coral bottom between sunken pontoon barges inboard of the island's only pier. The salvage plan called for the following actions:

• Laying beach gear across the pier to pull the grounded tanker straight astern.

• Removing as much weight as practicable.

---

[19] An innovative and unusual salvage operation involving the use of a drydock as a lifting pontoon resulted the first time *Han Ra San* was used for salvage training. The hulk had been inadvertently sunk in water too deep for conventional salvage. YD–120, then under overhaul, could not be used for lifting. Some urgency existed because a harbor dredging-and-improvement project included the area where the hulk rested. The recently activated floating drydock AFDL–21 was positioned over the wreck in the fully raised position. Lifting slings were rigged, the dock flooded down, the slings tightened, and the wreck lifted some 3 feet. The lift allowed moving the wreck clear of the dredged area. It was subsequently lifted and removed, as it had been before, by YD–120 and two ARSs.

The main deck of patrol craft PC–705 is about to break the surface, lifted by *Bolster, Reclaimer,* and the crane YD–120.

- Blasting the coral bottom to make a removal channel.
- Excavating the bottom along the ship's sides.
- Augmenting the beach gear with a bulldozer fitted with heavy tires to prevent penetrating the hull.

The first refloating attempt started just after midnight on 15 June. As the wreck moved 3 inches aft, the towing bitts gave way. The attachment was made again and a strain taken on the beach gear. While both sets of beach gear were singing with strain and a bulldozer was pushing at full throttle, a charge was set off to clear more bottom. Nothing happened. Then one beach gear wire parted; another followed quickly. This refloating attempt was over. It had been a long and discouraging evening.

For the next attempt a third leg of beach gear was rigged, and 24 previously undiscovered tons of water were removed from the wreck. This attempt started in the wee hours of the morning of 16 June. The ship moved, the bulldozer started to push, and an explosive charge was set off. The tanker moved aft in a series of jerky movements as the beach gear, working with no catenary, alternately relaxed and picked up strain and the bulldozer backed off and charged into the ship.[20] The ship moved astern until it was afloat. It was turned, secured for sea, and towed to the Ship Repair Facility at Guam for repair.

Far more resources were used than were necessary to do the harbor salvage work at Guam. But the principal purpose was not to accomplish the task with the minimum force. Rather, it was to train as many people as possible in salvage under the most realistic conditions and to demonstrate the responsiveness and value of the Navy's salvage forces. This purpose was accomplished. The long-term value of the Guam harbor salvage was the excellent report that followed the operation. This report not only discusses the work comprehensively, but also details the reasoning behind it, analyzes the mistakes made, includes a detailed appendix of salvage calculations, and spells out the important lessons learned or relearned. It is the most important legacy of the salvage work that followed the typhoons Karen and Olive.[21]

The Navy's Salvage Posture

Salvage posture is an intangible but real factor. By the late 1950s those most able to judge the Navy's salvage posture began to have concern that it was not as good as it should be, and was, in fact, declining.

At the end of World War II the U.S. Navy had trained salvors, new state-of-the-art salvage ships and tugs, mountains of machinery and equipment, an organization and doctrine that had evolved in combat, and commanders who appreciated the value of salvage forces. Although the demobilization following World War II laid waste the Navy's salvage force as it did all the Armed Services, measures had been taken to ensure that the salvage capability of the Navy did not disappear. Most important was passage of legislation that gave the Navy's role in salvage the force of

---

[20] The Saipanese bulldozer operator was certain that he was moving the ship alone. After all, every time he pushed the ship moved. No one had the heart to tell him otherwise.

[21] "Harbor Clearance Operations in Guam Following Typhoons Karen and Olive; November 1962–July 1963," NAVSHIPS 250–638–5 (Washington: Bureau of Ships), 1964.

law, ensuring its existence as a national rather than solely a Navy resource. Other important decisions included the retention of the most capable types of salvage ships in the active fleets (ARSs, ATFs, and ATAs) and the establishment of Emergency Ship Salvage Material Pools ashore throughout the world so that salvage machinery would be husbanded and ready to use where it was likely to be needed. But two serious mistakes had also been made: (1) No Naval Reserve program had been formed to keep salvage units together so they could be mobilized quickly and so their hard-gained expertise would not fade, and (2) all salvage billets were eliminated in the office of the Chief of Naval Operations.

In the post-World War II years, Navy salvage forces responded to some major salvage cases with huge expenditures of resources and effort—perhaps more than were required to do the job. Problems seemed to be solved more often by throwing money and resources at them and by pure doggedness and perseverance rather than by finesse and skillful salvage. A perception began to develop that the Navy's salvage capability was less real in the field than its paper strength would indicate. This view began to appear in the late 1950s in the correspondence of the Pacific Fleet salvage officer, Commander Walter L. (Scotty) Marshall, and his successor, Commander Frank W. Laessle. It worked its way up through the chain of command, culminating in a joint letter from the Service Force Commanders to the Chief of Naval Operations that addressed a number of problems in the Navy's salvage posture. A salient feature of the letter was the recommendation that a billet be established in the Office of the Chief of Naval Operations with "overall responsibility for maintaining salvage know-how within the fleet and for formulating and assisting in the execution of long-range salvage plans."[22]

The recommendation was favorably endorsed by the fleet commanders. The billet would have filled a void that had existed since the position of Chief of Navy Salvage had been eliminated, and would have helped ensure that salvage was not omitted in budgeting and long range planning—vital functions in the peacetime military. The Chief of Naval Operations, however, while supporting a strong salvage capability in the Navy, felt that ship salvage programs were reasonably focused in his office and declined to provide this billet.[23] Salvage in the Navy would continue to be in the hands of a few individuals in key billets in the fleets and in technical bureaus. Progress—or preservation of existing capability—would depend on their initiative and imagination and the interest and support of their commanders.

[22] Joint ltr, COMSERVPAC FF4–15 9940 serial 70.4–9806, 4 November 1959 and COMSERV-LANT FF4–16/9940 44: (rnp) serial 40/8912, 19 October 1959.
[23] Ltr, Chief of Naval Operations serial 102PO9B1E, 27 May 1960.

By the early 1960s salvors who had stayed on active duty, especially those who had been in policy and decision-making positions during the war, were beginning to complete their service. People who had entered the service following the war had the advantage of training at the world's only school devoted to salvage, but lacked the depth of experience of the wartime salvors. The difficulty in obtaining and keeping officers qualified in this unique field of maritime endeavor was recognized in the Service Force Commanders' joint letter. Fleet commanders and those responsible for training made recommendations for innovative solutions to the problem.[24] Most of the recommendations would have required policies, inconsistent with the larger needs of the Navy, that could not be implemented. Getting and keeping qualified personnel for salvage was to remain a matter of concern to senior salvors.

Realizing the importance of engineering in ship salvage, the Bureau of Ships periodically sent officers from the naval architecture graduate programs at the Massachusetts Institute of Technology and Webb Institute of Naval Architecture to salvage school. These officers were subsequently assigned to shipyards in which there was a Naval District salvage officer billet. It was from this pool of officers who showed unusual interest or ability in salvage that much of the post-World War II salvage leadership emerged. These officers with their superb technical training teamed up with limited duty officers experienced in the art of salvage to create a powerful team that combined the requisites of both engineering and seamanship.

Providing experience for salvors on real salvage jobs rather than in canned exercises under controlled conditions was, as it continues to be, a major problem. Maximum advantage had to be taken of every opportunity to train on real salvage jobs, yet in the peacetime Navy responding to opportunities, which came irregularly and did not fit fleet deployment and operating schedules, was difficult. The disruption caused by assigning ships to jobs as they came up could be serious and had to be balanced against the value to be gained by salvage training. The way the balance was weighted depended on the viewpoint of the people doing the balancing. Fleet commands often were forced by a myriad of considerations to refuse salvage work, particularly if it might tie up forces for long periods. Training opportunities were lost and work that might have been done by fleet units was done by Navy contractors or not at all.

The years following World War II saw an exponentially increasing

---

[24] One of the more innovative ideas was to assign Navy salvage officers to commercial salvage operators for a limited period to see how commercial salvors worked. This assignment would have been supplemented by an orientation with the Supervisor of Salvage's admiralty attorney to provide the salvage officer with a better understanding of the specialized legal environment of salvage and how the Navy works within it.

technology. For many of these years, however, salvage technology did not change. Salvage equipment had been purchased in large quantities to specifications prepared early in World War II. It was essentially 1930's technology. Because this equipment served its purpose adequately, for a considerable period there was neither evolutionary development nor piecemeal replacement of salvage equipment.

The equipment in the Emergency Ship Salvage Material Pools was husbanded by local commands with competing priorities. The condition of the equipment became a function of the level of interest of the local commander and varied widely. Because maintaining such equipment drew on the command's resources and seldom made much contribution to its mission, little attention was generally devoted to it. The result was inevitable. Equipment failures on jobs and equipment that did not work at all or was missing critical components were common, spare parts were difficult to obtain, and repairs were excessively expensive.

Much of the portable equipment purchased during the war was later fitted with gasoline engines. The rationale for this action suited the times. There were no suitable lightweight diesel engines, and gasoline was more likely than diesel fuel to be available for harbor clearance operations.[25] Under salvage conditions, however, it is difficult to protect the fuel and electrical systems of gasoline engines from moisture and to prevent corrosion of vital components.

Diesel engines were the obvious choice for the next generation of salvage machinery, and around 1960 the Pacific Fleet got two diesel-powered units for evaluation: a 6-inch pump and a rotary compressor. These units were kept aboard the salvage ships deployed to the Seventh Fleet and used whenever practicable. The two pieces of equipment hardly filled the need for new equipment. More important they were not part of a planned and structured modernization program. The equipment put into the fleet in this manner did little to solve the long-term problem.

A more effective step was taken when Power Pack equipment was introduced into the Pacific Fleet. The concept was basically good, but there were some drawbacks, notably the difficulty encountered in aligning the driving and driven ends. Power Packs turned out to be only a passing curiosity in the conversion of Navy salvage equipment to diesel power. This conversion process was fairly lengthy; completion had to wait until the early days of the Vietnam War brought money for improving readiness.

Just as there had been no development in salvage equipment for many years after World War II, neither had there been any evolutionary devel-

---

[25] The latter reason had validity, since all U.S. military vehicles during World War II, including tanks, were driven by gasoline engines.

opment of salvage ships or program of salvage ship replacement. The existing salvage ships and fleet tugs were fine ships made to extremely rugged designs, but in 1960 these ships were aging. There were no ships in the merchant fleet, other than the government-owned ships and the MV *Rescue*[26] operated by Merritt-Chapman and Scott, and *Salvage Chief*, operated by Fred Devine Diving and Salvage, that could be mobilized as salvage ships. *Salvage Chief* had been converted from an LSM to a pulling vessel following World War II. Her salvage station was at Astoria, Oregon, near the treacherous Columbia River Bar. She had a number of features that particularly suited her for operation there and along the West Coast. *Salvage Chief* remains in operation at this writing.

No salvage ships or tugs appeared in ship construction programs although some designs, notably a new salvage lifting ship, had been carried out. Suggestions for specific alterations to improve the capability of existing salvage ships originated in the fleets and were integrated into a modernization program. The alterations addressed a variety of areas that took advantage of emerging technology and lessons that had been learned in the commercial salvage community since the end of World War II. One of the most significant parts of the modernization program was replacement of the salvage ships' propulsion engines with Caterpillar engines to significantly improve reliability and maintenance of the propulsion system.

Alteration of existing ships did a great deal to improve them and increase their usefulness, but it was not the total answer for an aging salvage fleet. A new construction program was required. Unfortunately, such new programs have never enjoyed high priority. Combatant ships must come first. Although salvage ships are relatively inexpensive, they are often the victim when the budget axe cuts a predetermined number of ships from shipbuilding programs. To increase the probability of salvage ships being retained in the building programs, the characteristics of the fleet tug and salvage ship were incorporated in a single ship, first called AST, then ATS. The Bureau of Ships and its successors sought the advice of the fleets and of experienced salvage officers on the characteristics and outfitting of the new ships. Eventually, designs for new salvage ships found their way into building programs.

The correspondence that originated in the Pacific Fleet in the late 1950s and early 1960s brought attention to the specific areas of declining Navy salvage capability: lack of focused attention within the office of the Chief of Naval Operations, marginally qualified salvors, obsolete equipment, and aging salvage ships. The problems would require some time to

---

[26] Formerly *Diver* (ARS 5).

solve. While solutions were being sought and implemented, a major and influential operation was conducted in the Pacific.

RPS *Rajah Soliman*—A New Tool

An opportunity to make the Navy's salvage forces more responsive to future needs came in June 1964, when typhoon Winnie battered and sank the RPS *Rajah Soliman* (RPS 66)[27] at the Bataan National Shipyard near Mariveles, Philippines. The vessel lay alongside the pier in 24 feet of water and 8 feet of mud at an angle of about 150 degrees to starboard. Philippine Navy salvors commenced operations and brought the ship up about 10 degrees with large makeshift pontoons. What the next step should be was less obvious. Without doubt, the wreck had to be cleared because it blocked an important industrial berth. But there was uncertainty about whether the Philippine Navy could complete the salvage and whether the salvage was worthwhile because of the extensive repairs required.

The Pacific Fleet salvage officer, Commander Eugene B. Mitchell, immediately saw the salvage training opportunity presented by the wreck. While Commander Mitchell stirred up interest and support from the fleet and Service Force commanders, Lieutenant Commander Huntly Boyd lobbied the Commander Service Squadron Three and Commander Seventh Fleet. To get the U.S. Navy involved, they reminded the Philippine Navy that the terms of the Military Assistance Program required the ship to be returned to the United States when the need for it had expired.[28] The Philippine Navy needed little prompting to tell the U.S. Navy to "come get your ship." It was agreed that after salvage the Navy would sell the hulk for scrap to finance the salvage and obviate the argument that the salvage would require a large unbudgeted expenditure. However the sale-for-scrap requirement complicated the salvage operation. The simplest method of salvage would have been to invert the ship, float it with air, and tow it to sea for sinking. But because the ship was to be scrapped, it had to be floated right side up.

The relative complexity of the operation opened another door for the Navy. After being relieved by Commander Mitchell, Commander Searle had become the Supervisor of Salvage. Well aware of the necessity for a salvage force buildup for Vietnam, he had begun to lay the groundwork while still in the Pacific. Now in Washington, he was in a position to build on the foundations he had laid.

---

[27] Originally *Bowers* (DE 637), later APD–40.
[28] The purpose of these terms was to prevent the transfer of the former U.S. Navy warship to a third nation.

Searle and Mitchell both saw the need for a unit of highly qualified salvors that could keep open the rivers of Vietnam. The key was proper equipment. The tidal range in Vietnam's river deltas makes craft that use tidal lift very attractive. There were no such craft in the Navy's inventory. The salvage lifting ships came the closest, but they were in poor condition, had all but disappeared from the Pacific Fleet, and were scheduled to be retired from the Atlantic. New lifting ships were not in the cards. There were, however, two 750-ton lift craft of World War II construction kept by the Royal Navy in Singapore. If these ships could be shown to be useful lift salvage tools, the groundwork would be laid for leasing the craft to the U.S. Navy. Arguing that they were needed for the *Rajah Soliman* salvage was stretching the point. Strictly speaking, the craft were not necessary; the ship could have been raised without them. But a longer-term need was at stake.

Commander Mitchell, Lieutenant Commander Boyd, and Chief Warrant Officer W.D. Thomas from Ship Repair Facility, Subic, went to Singapore to inspect the lift craft. The officers deemed the craft suitable and negotiations began. The final agreement called for the services of a salvage officer, lift master, and salvage engineer familiar with these craft.

The Philippines released *Rajah Soliman* on 9 December 1964.[29] Shortly afterward preparations for the salvage began. Two salvage ships, *Bolster* and *Grasp*, headed for the scene; *Takelma* (ATF 113) sailed for Singapore to pick up the lift craft; a 100-ton floating crane, YD–127, came in from Sangley Point, Philippines.

Work began on 16 January 1965. The first step of the salvage operation called for *Rajah Soliman* to be parbuckled into an upright position. For the first parbuckling attempt, made before the arrival of the lift craft, the two salvage ships each laid two legs of beach gear and led their tow wires to parbuckling chains that encircled the wreck. The YD–127 was positioned at the bow and a 60-ton shore crane at the stern. Wires to prevent sliding and uncontrolled rolling were rigged ashore. To achieve maximum buoyancy and increase the rolling moment, air was blown into the hull, beginning at 4 on 26 January. The ships began to pull, the cranes lifted, the wreck rolled. By midafternoon the beach gear anchors were dragging in the soft volcanic sand of the bottom, and the rolling stopped. Wires were slacked. *Rajah Soliman* had rolled 35 degrees but

---

[29] Upon his arrival at Manila International Airport to take charge of the operation, Lieutenant Commander Boyd was met on the tarmac by a delegation of Filipino naval officers who asked him to sign a document accepting return of the ship from the Philippines and assuming responsibility. Commander Boyd asked in whose name he was accepting the ship. "In the name of the United States," he was told. He took the document and spelled aloud as he signed it: "L-Y-N-D-O-N B. J-O-H-N-S-O-N." The Filipinos were apoplectic until they looked at the papers and saw that Boyd had signed his own name.

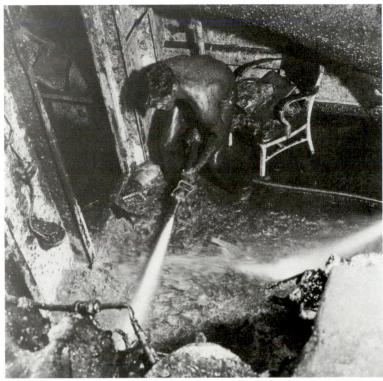

It's a dirty job! A salvor with a fire hose washes mud out of the *Rajah Soliman* to lighten the ship.

Bolster, assisted by a harbor tug, prepares to tow the hulk of *Rajah Soliman* out of Mariveles after the destroyer escort was refloated.

settled back to near her original position. With parbuckling in progress, *Takelma* steamed into the harbor with the leased lift craft.

For the second parbuckling attempt two anchors were put into each leg of beach gear and washed into the bottom or blown into it with explosives. One lift craft was rigged with beach gear between the two salvage ships. The other was placed at the stern in position to make a bow lift, augmented by the 60-ton shore crane. The YD–127 lifted the bow.

On 29 January air was cut into the wreck and all slack taken up. The lift craft at the stern could not be used because the deck edge did not clear the bottom of the lift craft. The lift wire on the 60-ton crane parted. The lift craft picked up the load, but as the load plumbed, the stern slid under the bow of the lift craft. *Grasp's* anchors dragged. The attempt ended.

The third attempt kept the ships and craft in the same position, except that the lift craft at the stern was rerigged to allow it to lift and stay clear. *Rajah Soliman* rolled and the bow moved to seaward. *Grasp's* anchors dragged again; her engines were going full ahead for maximum pull. The bow lift craft's wire parted on the deck edge. The attempt stopped.

For the fourth attempt, one lift craft lifted at each end of the *Rajah Soliman*, and the YD–127 lifted from outboard amidships. This attempt failed only because the chain on the bow lifting parted. The lift was rerigged. Salvors' spirits were high, because all were convinced that only an old crack in the chain had prevented the wreck from being righted. All other gear had held. The salvors were right; with much creaking and groaning the wreck rolled upright. The salvage ships slipped their beach gear and moored alongside the pier.

A combination of belly-lifting with two lift craft, cofferdamming, and pumping had brought the wreck to the surface. Cofferdams fabricated from 55-gallon drums were fitted throughout the ship. The YD–127 provided lateral control by lifting the stern.

The belly lift with heavy lift craft was new to the U.S. Navy. The process goes as follows:

- One craft, with her ballast tanks empty, is located along each side of the wreck.

- A wire rope, in this case of 9-inch circumference,[30] is passed down

---

[30] U.S. practice is to designate wire rope size by the diameter of the rope, but European wire rope is designated by circumference. The wire rope provided with the lift craft was of European origin and, therefore, correctly designated as 9-inch. In U.S. Navy practice, it quickly became known as 3-inch wire.

the inboard side of the first lift craft, under the wreck and the second lift craft, and up the outboard side of the second lift craft. A second wire is passed alongside the first the opposite way, starting down the inboard side of the second craft.

- The lift craft are ballasted down.

- The slack is hauled out of the wires and they are clamped together with a Bullivant clamp filled with unlaid manila line to absorb grease and prevent slippage.

- The craft are deballasted. The buoyancy of the craft and the rising tide lift the wreck.

After the lifting and pumping operation brought *Rajah Soliman* afloat, she was taken alongside the pier for discharge of ammunition, removal of silt, and preparation for tow. When ready, she left for Subic Bay and disposal.

Not only had *Rajah Soliman* been successfully salvaged, but all the objectives of the salvage operation had been accomplished. Probably the most important was the demonstration of the usefulness of specialized lift craft in clearance operations. The value of these craft as salvage tools would be proved on other kinds of jobs in the not-too-distant future. The U.S. Navy's involvement in Vietnam was growing. The instincts of those who were planning the expansion of the Navy's salvage capabilities turned out to be dead on target.

MEKONG DELTA

CHAPTER SEVEN

The Vietnam Era

For Navy salvors the Vietnam era from 1965 to 1973 was a time of intense activity and great change. Unlike the Korean War mobilization, salvage ships and tugs were not commissioned for the war in Vietnam and reserves were not called up. Indeed, naval Reserve salvage units had never been formed, and most World War II salvors and many Korean War salvors had completed their service. Salvage ships and tugs were all at least 20 years old; most had seen hard service.

The combat in Vietnam required a considerable amount of direct salvage support both offshore and in that country's harbors, rivers, and canals. Logistic support required operating close to shore, landing through the surf, and steaming through the reefs of the South China Sea. The increased shipping meant more casualties than normal throughout the Pacific, especially since many older ships, subject to frequent breakdown, had been mobilized from the National Defense Reserve Fleet. Operations within Vietnam were subject to casualties from direct combat and from sabotage and sapper operations. Responsibility for the salvage work fell primarily upon the Pacific Fleet.

On 1 May 1964 USNS *Card* (T–AKV 40)[1] arrived in Saigon with a load of helicopters and other materials and berthed in the commercial port district. All cargo had been discharged and some helicopters scheduled for return to the United States had been loaded when, in the early morning of 2 May, explosions on the starboard side rocked the ship. She began to take water, and power failed throughout the vessel. An immediate response by the ship's force and local military and civilian agencies stopped the progressive flooding and stabilized the ship. Further assistance from a number of sources came rapidly:

- Commander U.S. Naval Forces, Philippines, dispatched his salvage

---

[1] Originally *Card* (CVE 11), a conversion from a C3–S–A1 merchant ship hull.

officer, Lieutenant W.H. Smith,[2] and four divers to Saigon.

• The Seventh Fleet salvage officer, Lieutenant Commander Huntly Boyd, got under way from Sasebo, Japan, for Saigon.

• Commander Military Sealift Command sent his salvage officer, Commander R.E. Wurlitzer, and Mr. John Giberman, a naval architect, to the scene.

• *Reclaimer*, bound for Subic Bay, Philippines, from Hong Kong changed course and headed to Saigon at her best speed.

• Captain Scotty Marshall, a former Pacific Fleet salvage officer and Supervisor of Salvage, now commanding officer of the Ship Repair Facility, Guam, was ordered in.

• *Tawakoni* (ATF 114) in Subic Bay was placed on standby, then ordered to get under way for Saigon.

• Equipment from the Emergency Ship Salvage Material Pool in Subic was air shipped to Saigon.

Lieutenant Smith's divers, the first on the scene, found a rupture in *Card*'s hull 12 feet long and 3 feet high amidships on the starboard side. After thorough examination of the damage, orders were placed with the Vietnamese Naval Shipyard in Saigon for fabrication of a large cofferdam.

Diving conditions in the Saigon River are terrible. There is no visibility and the current limits diving to brief periods of slack water. These poor conditions prevented inspecting the damage from outside the ship; dislodged storage bins and shelves blocked access from inside. Diving conditions had made accurate surveys and measurement for the cofferdam difficult, and so on first fitting it did not cover a previously undiscovered dished section of the hull. The cofferdam was sent back to the shipyard for modification.

Initially, *Card*'s stability was thought to be critical. A complete analysis showed that no stability problem existed and that pumping could begin without undue concern. The obvious plan was to pump the ship as quickly as possible and get her out of Vietnam.

Reinstallation of the modified cofferdam was completed about noon on 7 May. Divers located additional indented plating that complicated making the cofferdam watertight. To expedite the operation, pumping began in the after end of the ship with leaks stopped as they were located.

---

[2] Lieutenant Smith, a capable salvor known to his shipmates as "Horrible," was one of many larger-than-life men who have blessed Navy salvage. "Horrible" Smith stories have become legends. Folklore says that the name originated when Smith was a young sailor. He was said to fill his tray to overflowing in the mess line, wolf his food down, then throw his utensils onto his empty tray and declare in stentorian tones, "Horrible, horrible, just . . . horrible!"

Water pours over the side as 6-inch submersible pumps discharge from USNS *Card* in Saigon.

Considerable progress was made. Free surface caused the list to increase to as much as 7 degrees, but pumping out pockets of loose water reduced it. The two 10-inch gasoline-driven pumps in the way of the cofferdam failed from vapor lock despite efforts to cool them with portable blowers and fans. Both the gasoline-driven 10-inch pumps and 6-inch electrical submersible pumps were failing in the miserable working conditions. More pumps were flown in; more pumps failed.

Installation of a heavy J-bolt between the cofferdam and hull succeeded in holding the cofferdam tightly enough to reduce flooding significantly. As the internal water level dropped, the pressure differential caused the cofferdam to seal more tightly, and pumping became more effective. With the interior of the ship reasonably dry, preparations for the ocean tow were made by strengthening the damaged area and placing concrete in way of hull ruptures.

Pumping was now easily able to control the remaining leakage. Six 6-inch submersible pumps, enough to provide a large margin of capacity, were put on board for this purpose. The priority was to get the ship out of Vietnam rather than to seal every leak. Discharging locked-in ballast and oil from the aft-bunker, tanks lightened the ship for the tow down the Saigon River. Arrangements were made for a riding crew of salvors and a load of generators and other emergency equipment to be put on board.

On 20 May, *Card*, towed by *Tawakoni* with *Reclaimer* as a drogue, started down the twisting, shallow Saigon River. On one right-angle bend *Card* ran aground, fortunately on a rising tide. The tugs had her under way again in less than two hours. Increased leakage as the hull worked in the seaway and continuing failure of the pumps marked the tow from Vung Tau to Subic. Pumps failed on an average of one per day, the last failing just six hours before *Card* entered Subic Bay.

The salvage of the USNS *Card*, a major patching and pumping job, had been successfully completed. But the operation raised two red flags for salvors. The first was the miserable performance of pumps from the salvage ships and from the Emergency Ship Salvage Material Pools. The pumps were hard to get running, harder still to keep running. If the salvage capability of the Navy was to be maintained, both the gasoline-driven pumps and the 6-inch electric submersible pumps would have to be replaced. Conversion of the Navy's salvage machinery to diesel drive was clearly indicated, and *Card* provided the impetus to get it going. The poor performance of the electric pumps was unexpected. A depot rehabilitation for these pumps was started and a search begun for better machines.

The second red flag raised by the *Card* involved strategic thinking about the Vietnam War. U.S. strategists believed that the Vietcong would not attempt to block approaches to Saigon and its port facilities because most of their own supplies also arrived through this port. The attack on *Card* showed this thinking to be fallacious. Saigon and its approaches in the Saigon River were vulnerable. The Navy's salvage organization had responded effectively, but if Saigon was to be kept open there would have to be an organization capable of immediate response with appropriate clearance equipment. Senior salvors set to work on the problem.

Pacific Fleet Salvage Posture

The heavy salvage requirements in the Pacific affected the Navy as a whole. Salvage in support of combat operations placed formidable demands on personnel and equipment resources. The Atlantic Fleet, although faced with its normal salvage demands, necessarily had lower priority; its resources were stretched to the limit. Because of the salvage workload in the fleet and an aggressive attitude on the part of the Supervisor of Salvage toward fulfilling the Navy's reponsibilities under the Salvage Act, contractor salvage became more significant during the Vietnam era. Work that could have been accomplished by fleet units in peacetime passed to Navy salvage contractors.

Eight salvage ships (ARS) and eighteen fleet tugs (ATF)—all ships of World War II construction—formed the primary Pacific Fleet salvage resources. Several auxiliary tugs (ATA) with very limited salvage capability were also in commission. The salvage ships had been modified considerably since their World War II days. Highly reliable Caterpillar diesel engines had been added, and the ships now carried eight legs of beach gear. The new diesel-powered, Power Pack salvage machinery had begun replacing the World War II vintage, gasoline-driven machinery. The ships' diving capability had been upgraded and each ship carried a complement of eighteen divers. Mustangs—officers who had come up through the ranks—commanded about half the ships; hard-charging young officers, well qualified for their jobs, commanded the remainder. Officers and crew had a high level of experience and equally high levels of training and enthusiasm for their work.

Stockpiles of equipment in emergency ship salvage material pools and bases directly supported the salvage ships. Five pools, each containing the equivalent of two ships' allowance of salvage equipment, and seven smaller bases were located throughout the Pacific. Submarine salvage equipment was positioned in Pearl Harbor and San Diego. The Supervisor of Salvage in the Bureau of Ships controlled the Emergency Ship Salvage Material System.

The Supervisor of Salvage had contracts with Merritt-Chapman and Scott and Luzon Stevedoring. The former operated *Gear* from her home port in San Pedro; the latter operated a fleet of tugs from its Manila base. The fleet had asked the Supervisor of Salvage to explore the possibility of obtaining additional agreements with commercial salvors to back up the fleet.

The equipment problem had not been totally solved, but a number of efforts were in the works to get better salvage equipment into the hands of the men who needed it.

• Diesel-driven machinery was being ordered to replace both the Power Pack machinery, which had proved less than totally successful, and the elderly gasoline machinery.

• The useful and reliable high-capacity, high-head, 6-inch electric submersible pumps were being completely refurbished by their manufacturer.

• A 4-inch electric submersible pump with the same capacity as the 6-inch was being evaluated.

• Divers' tools, workboats, and communications equipment were being improved and delivered to fleet salvage units.

• The design of the first new class of salvage ships since World War II

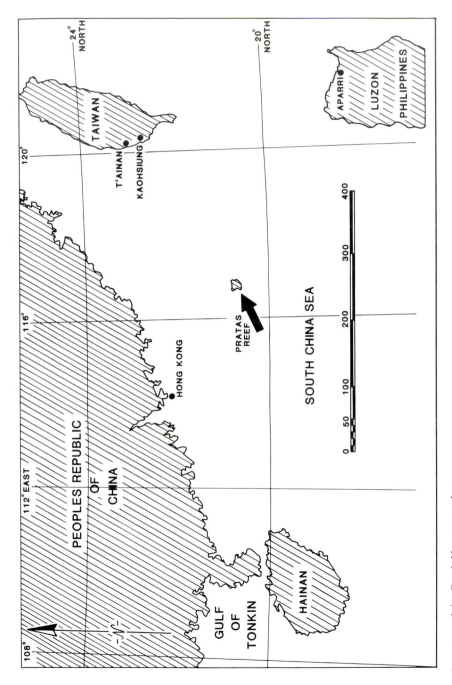

Location of the *Frank Knox* grounding.

was well advanced. These ships, the *Edenton* (ATS 1) class, would be built in the fiscal year 1966 and 1967 shipbuilding programs.[3]

The Supervisor of Salvage was now Commander Willard Searle, Jr. As Pacific Fleet salvage officer he had become familiar with the situation in the area and had been deeply involved in salvage planning for the coming hostilities. Searle had been relieved in the Pacific by Commander Eugene B. Mitchell. He and Mitchell made a powerful team. Both men were capable officers with global viewpoints. They differed markedly in their styles of operation, but both styles worked well. Just as Rear Admiral Sullivan, when a commander, had foreseen and made preparations for salvage in World War II, these two commanders anticipated the salvage needs in Vietnam and took action to meet them.

One important capability was missing from the Pacific salvage fleet. There was no mobile salvage unit that could provide rapid salvage assistance in the rivers, harbors, and canals of Vietnam. Mitchell and Searle worked together to solve this problem. A new unit would be formed and specially outfitted for this purpose. Formulating the requirement and obtaining authorization for such a unit would demand close coordination and skillful maneuvering both in Pearl Harbor and in Washington. But its formation and operating method turned out to be the most significant salvage event in the U.S. Navy since World War II.

Knox on the Rocks

While planning and preparation for salvage in and around Vietnam dominated the thinking of senior Navy salvors during 1965, a major warship casualty that summer demanded their immediate attention and hands-on experience. At 2:35 a.m. on 18 July 1965, *Frank Knox* (DDR 742) steaming at 16 knots in the South China Sea grounded on Pratas Reef. Within an hour and a half *Grapple*, *Munsee*, and *Cocopa* changed course for *Knox*, and the Seventh Fleet salvage officer, Lieutenant Commander J. Huntly Boyd, left Sasebo, Japan, for Pratas Reef. An immediate survey by Nationalist Chinese Underwater Demolition Team (UDT) divers showed the ship to be aground for about half her length, with some hull and propeller damage. The situation was serious and could easily

---

[3] The three ships of this class would be too late for the war in Vietnam. *Edenton*, the class leader, was commissioned 23 January 1971 and assigned to the Atlantic Fleet. *Beaufort* (ATS 2) and *Brunswick* (ATS 3) were commissioned in January and December 1972, respectively, and assigned to the Pacific. All three were built by Brooke Marine, Lowestoft, England. ATS-4 and ATS-5 were authorized for the fiscal year 1972 and 1973 shipbuilding programs. Their construction was deferred in 1973, then canceled. ATS originally indicated "salvage tug"; on 16 February 1971, just after the commissioning of the first ship, the designation was changed to "salvage and rescue ship."

worsen. The ship lay hard aground in an exposed position in typhoon season. Operations would be hampered by a strong lateral current and poor holding ground at the reef. Because of the ship's location, politics also entered the picture. The vessel was near the coast of the People's Republic of China, with whom the United States did not enjoy good relations. Leaving a warship hulk in this position was less than desirable.

Taking weight off, getting beach gear out, and pulling were the most urgent needs. The first task was to rig a beach gear leg aboard *Frank Knox* to prevent broaching. Then one of the Army barges that *Grapple* had had in tow when ordered to the scene was put alongside to receive ammunition from the stranded destroyer. *Grapple* prepared to lay and pull two legs of beach gear; *Munsee* would lay one leg if she had time, otherwise she would simply pull with her engines. *Frank Knox* pumped fuel aft to lighten the ship forward.

Munsee's crew rigged the hauling part of one leg of beach gear on board *Knox*. *Grapple* laid the ground leg for this set, but had difficulty with her own gear. When the tide was right for the pull at midday on 20 July, only the leg to *Knox* and one leg to *Grapple* were ready. The pull was made anyway, though it was nowhere near the 168 tons required. After three hours *Knox* had moved about 12 feet. Success seemed close. More beach gear would be ready for another refloating try at high water the following day. What happened next illustrates how critical time is in stranding salvage and how quickly a situation can deteriorate.

Typhoon Gilda, still well to the south, had been a concern on the first day of the operation, but was reported to have dissipated in passing over the island of Luzon. Gilda was stubborn and regenerated as she cleared land and moved into the South China Sea. Just after the first pulling effort, the winds, which had been westerly all day, shifted to southeast. As winds and seas built rapidly, *Frank Knox* took a beating. She began to roll and work; her head swung to starboard. *Grapple* hauled her beach gear and went ahead full to prevent the destroyer from broaching, but the beach gear anchor dragged. The weather continued to build. *Grapple* slipped her beach gear and cleared the area. It looked as though *Frank Knox* would have to be abandoned, but high seas made boating impossible. Commander Seventh Fleet ordered the carrier *Midway* (CVA 41) and an amphibious task force that included *Iwo Jima* (LPH 2) to the scene so that helicopters could assist with the abandonment.

By midnight the worst of the storm had passed. *Knox* would not have to be abandoned, but a simple stranding had turned into a major salvage operation in a few hours. The destroyer had moved laterally about 75 feet and was entrenched in the coral with the forward machinery spaces now flooded.

The basic salvage plan now called for increasing the pulling force and dewatering the flooded machinery spaces. Two salvage ships, each pulling two legs of beach gear, would be positioned astern of the destroyer with a fleet tug between them. *Conserver* (ARS 39), *Sioux* (ATF 75), and *Greenlet* (ASR 10) were ordered to the scene to provide maximum power for the high tides of 29 and 30 July. Additional 6-inch salvage pumps were flown in from the Emergency Ship Material Base at Subic Bay. Captain Scotty Marshall, Captain William A. Walker, Commander Service Squadron Five, the home unit for the salvage ships, and Lieutenant Commander Charles K. (Boom-Boom) Nayler, commanding officer of Explosive Ordnance Disposal Unit One and an expert in explosives, were ordered to the scene. While beach gear was being laid and the salvage ships were getting into harness, other ships with various capabilities arrived and departed.

Frank Knox continued to work up on her strand and to develop numerous leaks in the bottom. Patching attempts led only to frustration. Fuel oil tanks were sealed off and prepared for blowing. Pumps and compressors were brought on board. In the early morning hours of 25 July, another retraction attempt was made. Blowing of fuel tanks started late. The ancient, gasoline-driven 10-inch pumps gave the salvors fits. *Conserver*'s beach gear dragged. *Frank Knox* gave one shudder but did not move; the attempt was terminated.

Typhoon Harriet was approaching and seemed likely to pass close aboard within twenty-four hours. Orders were received to remove all hands from *Knox* and evade the typhoon if the destroyer was not refloated on 26 July. More pumps were brought aboard, tank and compartment blowing systems and procedures reviewed and improved, patching efforts continued, and more beach gear laid for *Cocopa* to pull from directly astern of *Frank Knox*.

The pull was made on rising seas. First *Grapple*'s tow wire, then *Cocopa*'s towing winch failed. With *Conserver* heaving and *Frank Knox* backing hard, the destroyer was swinging, but in the wrong direction; she was starting to broach. The pull terminated. The ship had moved about 30 feet but remained hard aground.

Although the wind and seas were building, the barometer held steady. Permission was received to stay with the ship. The salvors and destroyer crew had a rough ride, but held on until the storm had passed.

The summer looked endless for the salvors on Pratas Reef. *Frank Knox* clung hard to the reef. Only a series of pulls, each moving her a little, seemed likely to get her off. The damage in the machinery spaces was such that nothing but a long, slow program of sealing the leaks with cement from the inside seemed likely to work. The South China Sea in typhoon season is not a place where such a long-drawn-out salvage operation has a high probability of success.

Salvors, however are a bullheaded lot. There was no thought of quitting. More beach gear had been requested from the Emergency Ship Salvage Material Pool in Subic Bay. A pulling plan was laid out to maximize the pull. Most legs of beach gear would have two anchors. Plans were made to dewater the engine room with air, although a very real possibility existed that the structure could not tolerate the air pressure.[4] Collision mats were fabricated for hogging under the midships section. Chief Warrant Officer W.D. Thomas, salvage officer for Commander Naval Forces Philippines, arrived, bringing with him Chief Petty Officers R.M. McKenzie, R.J. Smeller, and T.J. (Doc) Bennett.[5]

Back in Washington, steps were being taken to try some new technology in this difficult salvage job. In 1964 Murphy-Pacific Corporation of Emeryville, California, had raised the barge *Lumberjack* in Humboldt Bay with cast-in-place polyurethane foam. The low-density, solid foam, formed with a mixing gun, displaced the water in a compartment and restored much of its buoyancy. The Supervisor of Salvage had become interested in the material and was sponsoring its development for deep depths. The foam might be the answer to the problem of the flooded machinery spaces on *Knox*. Preparations were made to bring foam chemicals, equipment, and technicians to Pratas Reef.

The next pulling attempt was made on 31 July. *Knox* had been aground for two weeks. *Grapple*, *Conserver*, and *Sioux*; *Greenlet*, in tandem with *Cocopa*, pulled with engines. Beach gear anchors dragged. *Knox* swung to port and moved 6 feet astern. Another attempt on 2 August had similar results. Again, beach gear anchors dragged; the destroyer moved 4 feet. The salvors began to suspect the ship was impaled on the coral bottom. Another new salvage plan was developed. The majority of the beach gear would be rerigged to be pulled directly from *Frank Knox*. The damage to the hull had become so severe by this time that there was a danger of it breaking in half. Steel was brought aboard to reinforce the hull; helicopters lowered welding machines; stiffeners were welded to the main deck.

The foaming materials and technicians arrived on 3 August, and the first foam was produced on 6 August. There was not enough material for the forward machinery spaces and all the other spaces that needed it; more was ordered. Foam went into the forward machinery spaces and into tankage and compartments forward; it drove out the water and

---

[4] Air pressure to exceed the hydrostatic head and drive the floodwater out of the bottom of the ship would also exceed the design limits of the destroyer's main deck structure and bulkheads. However, the question became academic when salvors were unable to seal the engine room tightly enough to contain more than $1/4$ psi of air pressure.

[5] After retirement Chief Warrant Officer Thomas and Chief Petty Officer McKenzie joined a major American salvage company. McKenzie was killed during a salvage operation on the California coast in 1982.

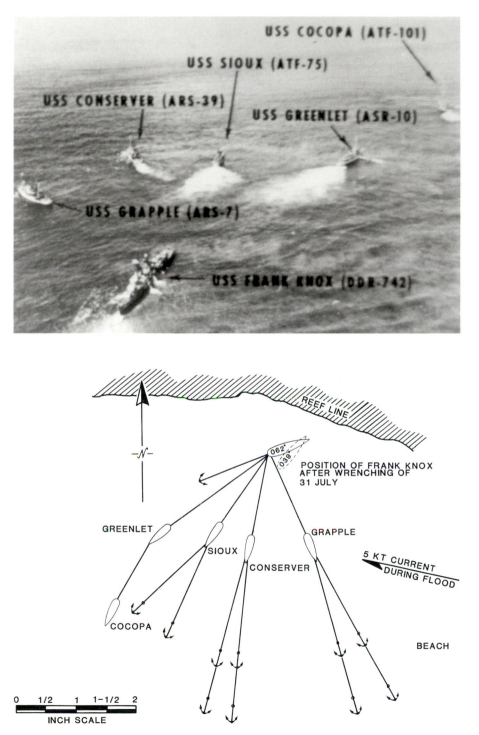

This pulling arrangement freed the *Frank Knox.*

restored buoyancy. The foam also made a contribution to the residual strength of the ship's hull girder.

Explosive charges set in holes drilled in the coral had some success in shattering coral and reducing the effect of the ground on the ship. Unfortunately, hose charges[6] laid in a trench to break down the coral trench wall did an unfortunate amount of damage to the ship. Additional foaming was necessary.

With the sea bottom broken by explosives, foam in the ship, six sets of beach gear ready, and as much weight as practical removed, another attempt to refloat the destroyer was made on 11 August. It was the same old story; *Frank Knox* moved 6 feet but remained hard aground. Efforts the following two days—*Grapple* pulling, *Mars* (AFS 1) making waves, and hose charges set off 15 feet from the hull—had no success at all.

More foam went in; beach gear was fine tuned; more weight came off; more charges were shot. But more storms threatened. On 22 August the time was ripe again; the ship moved another 8 feet aft. Pontoons were rigged forward and *Cogswell* (DD 651) came in to make waves as *Mahan* had done when *Omaha* was aground twenty-eight years before. Divers cut away structure that dragged in the bottom, and compartments aft were ballasted. The final pull started at 2:30 a.m. on 24 August. Every time one of *Cogswell's* waves hit *Frank Knox* she moved aft; she was ready to come off. She floated before breakfast.

Frank Knox and *Grapple* slipped out of their beach gear and *Grapple* towed the destroyer clear. While *Conserver* made up to tow *Frank Knox* to Kaohsiung, Taiwan,[7] *Grapple* and *Sioux* started picking up beach gear.

The forty-day, offshore salvage job in a remote, stormy area had coupled the latest in salvage technology with the most basic techniques. Many things had been tried; some worked, some didn't. Although the ship had been saved and would ultimately be returned to service, damage incurred during the salvage had been extensive. Much had been learned; much remained to be learned.[8] The effort gave Navy salvors a lot to think about.

The Floodgates Open

Constant salvage work began in Vietnam in the summer of 1965 and

---

[6] The hose charges used were 25-foot, flexible line charges filled with 50 pounds of high explosives.

[7] *Frank Knox* went to the Chinese Navy's Fourth Naval Shipyard for emergency repairs. *Munsee* then towed her to Ship Repair Facility, Yokosuka, where, after a thorough survey, she was repaired and returned to service in the fall of 1966.

[8] A practice first followed in World War II was resurrected in the *Frank Knox* salvage. At the instigation of the Supervisor of Salvage, five newly trained salvage officers were ordered to the scene for training on a real salvage job. The results were excellent. The officers made a real contribution to the work and learned a lot. The practice has become standard for major salvage operations.

continued for several years. Initially, there was no change in the Pacific Fleet salvage organization and operational approach. Salvage operations in Vietnam were handled on much the same basis as peacetime operations without special organizations or deployments.

The first operation following *Frank Knox* involved no salvage forces but was accomplished by *Krishna* (ARL 38) and USCGC *Point Young* (WPB 82303). The crews of these ships patched and raised two Viet Cong junks off An Thoi in September 1965. Salvage forces came into the picture in November, when *Terrell County* (LST 1157) broached at Tuy Hoa. *Molala* laid one leg of beach gear and, pulling in tandem with *Mahopac* (ATA 196), hauled the LST off the beach. After this the work started coming fast.

- *Hitchiti* pulled LCU–1494 from a beach near Danang and salvaged a Marine Corps LVT at Phu Thuin December 1965.

- On the same day that Hitchiti salvaged the LVT, *Safeguard* got the task of recovering special equipment from a crashed reconnaissance aircraft off the coast.

- *Reclaimer*, *Bolster*, and a contingent from the newly formed Harbor Clearance Unit One refloated *Sea Raven*, a Panamanian-registry T–1 tanker, at Chu Lai.

- Less than a month later, also at Chu Lai, *Hitchiti* towed *Summit County* (LST 1146) off the beach after patching her and pumping out the engine room. *Bolster* then took the LST to Sasebo.

- *Arikara*, facing heavy surf on a lee shore, refloated YFRN–412 just north of the mouth of the Perfume River.

- *Current* salvaged a broached LCM–8 at Qui Nhon.

- *Greenlet* recovered the bodies, personal effects, and weapons from an AC–141 aircraft that crashed off Camrahn Bay.

- When the British tanker *Amastra* was mined at Nha Trang, *Current*, *Greenlet*, and Commander John B. Orem, the Seventh Fleet salvage officer, were ordered to the scene. They patched her for tow by a commercial tug.

- *Hitchiti* picked up the mined *Coconino County* (LST 603) inside the mouth of the Cua Viet River and delivered her to Danang.

- *Abnaki*, assisted by the dredge *Davidson*, refloated the grounded transport *Geiger* (T–AP 197) at Danang.

The Paracel Islands lie almost astride the great circle route between Danang and Subic Bay. These low-lying coral islands and reefs are almost awash at high water and nearly invisible to radar at all times. During the

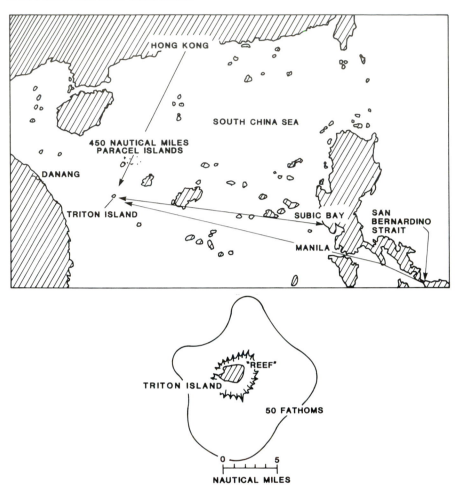

Location of Triton Island.

Vietnam War, they became the site of regular groundings. The first job presented itself when the U.S. Department of Commerce-owned ship *Excellency* grounded on Triton Island in April 1966. Lieutenant Commander Boyd and Chief Warrant Officer Thomas discharged hundreds of tons of ammunition, then used *Bolster*, *Reclaimer*, *Ute*, *Coucal*, and six sets of beach gear to refloat her.

Two years later *Minot Victory* grounded on North Reef and was refloated by *Current*, *Mahopac*, *Mataco*, *Tawakoni*, and *Hitchiti* under the direction of Lieutenant Commander James J. Goodwin. Goodwin came back to Triton Island in September 1969 when *Norwich Victory* grounded there. Under his direction, *Conserver*, *Grasp*, *Grapple*, *Chowanoc*, and a number of barges and small tugs successfully salvaged the ship. *Falcon*

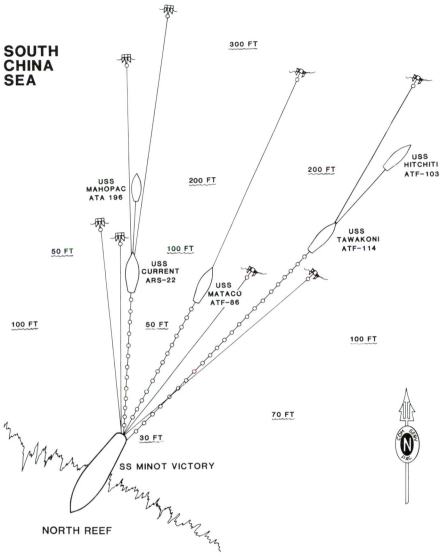

Pulling arrangements on *Minot Victory*.

Lady later fell victim to Triton Island and was refloated by Lieutenant Commander Billy B. Savage in *Reclaimer*. When American participation in the Vietnam War was over and major pieces of equipment were being returned to the United States, USNS *Sgt. Jack J. Pendelton* (T–AK 276) became the last ship to run aground on Triton Island. After a valiant try at refloating, described later in this chapter, and a series of typhoons that moved *Pendelton* across the reef and into the lagoon, she was abandoned. Triton Island is no longer invisible to radar.

Salvage ships were in great demand during the Vietnam War because of their varied capabilities. Repair of the single-point moorings for the transfer of petroleum products became a common task for salvage ships throughout the western Pacific. These moorings, then in the relatively early stages of operational service, proved invaluable in moving petroleum products ashore from tankers to storage facilities. The heavily used moorings were exposed to the ravages of the open-sea locations where the weather could be particularly foul. The buoy serving the Chang Chung Quang Air Base[9] in Taiwan had a nasty habit of sinking just before a tanker arrived. Before design faults could be corrected and the mooring made more reliable, the buoy had become known to the salvors who repeatedly refloated it as "The Beast of the Taiwan Straits." Salvage ships kept this and other buoys afloat and working.

The same salvage ships that had been assigned to flycatcher interdiction operations in Korea also had important nonsalvage tasks off the coast of Vietnam. Soviet intelligence collection ships stationed close to carrier task force operations attempted to disrupt flight operations and cause the carrier to maneuver radically. When not assigned to salvage work, tugs and salvage ships would act as blocking ships. In this role a salvage vessel interposed itself between the Soviet ship and the carrier in such a way as to become the "privileged ship" under the International Rules of the Road and to cause the Soviet ship to maneuver clear. These operations required the same cool nerve and high-quality seamanship as salvage operations.

Harbor Clearance Unit One

Following a series of closely coordinated recommendations and a great deal of behind-the-scenes maneuvering, the Secretary of the Navy authorized the establishment of a harbor clearance unit capable of clearing any waterway or port in Vietnam. Part of the work leading to this authorization had involved getting widespread recognition for the term "harbor clearance" and establishing the need for a highly mobile unit to do the work. The careful groundwork included using the term "harbor clearance" to describe the harbor salvage work in Guam following typhoon Karen and the British lift craft effort to salvage the *Rajah Soliman*. The term intentionally harkened back to the harbor clearance units of World War II and the spectacularly successful work they did. Although the new unit had little in common with its namesakes, its establishment was aided by pointing out that the new unit would be a direct heir of the

[9]This base was important to the Vietnam War because Air Force KC–135 tankers flew from here to support B–52 bombing raids.

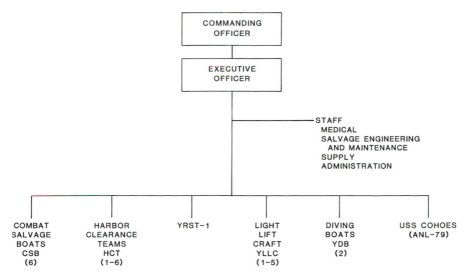

```
                    ┌─────────────────┐
                    │   COMMANDING    │
                    │    OFFICER      │
                    └─────────────────┘
                    ┌─────────────────┐
                    │   EXECUTIVE     │
                    │    OFFICER      │
                    └─────────────────┘

                                  STAFF
                                  MEDICAL
                                  SALVAGE ENGINEERING
                                    AND MAINTENANCE
                                  SUPPLY
                                  ADMINISTRATION

COMBAT      HARBOR        YRST-1     LIGHT     DIVING    USS COHOES
SALVAGE     CLEARANCE                LIFT      BOATS     (ANL-79)
BOATS       TEAMS                    CRAFT     YDB
CSB         HCT                      YLLC      (2)
(6)         (1-6)                    (1-5)
```

The organization of Harbor Clearance Unit One.

old ones. In reality, the new unit and its operational concept represented an elemental change in Navy salvage. The new concept, which matured over the next several years, called for committing a small and mobile team of well-qualified salvage specialists to a job rather than relying on salvage ships.

Harbor Clearance Unit One, or HCU-One, was established at Subic Bay on 1 February 1966 with a hand-picked cadre of five officers and sixty-five enlisted men. Homeporting the unit in Subic Bay allowed it to operate not only in Vietnam but throughout the Pacific. In addition, deployed units in Vietnam on temporary duty did not count as part of the total number of military personnel assigned there. This shell game with numbers later proved helpful in circumventing manning restrictions for the unit.

An unusual command and control system was also applied to the unit. As a western Pacific unit, HCU-One should have come under the total control of Commander Service Group Three.[10] Instead, the Service Force Commander retained operational control of the unit, except for teams deployed to Vietnam. This method of command and control insured the flexibility to operate both in Vietnam and throughout the Pacific. As with any new or unusual system, there were problems and misunderstandings that required tact and wisdom to resolve. All in all,

---

[10] Commander Service Group Three had an operational role as Commander Task Force Seventy-Three, the logistic arm of the Seventh Fleet.

though, command and control for HCU-One must have been satisfactory, because it worked.

Most of the people in the unit were attached to harbor clearance teams of two officers and about eighteen men. The rest operated and maintained the various craft. The men who were assembled from throughout the world for HCU-One were specialists. They were the Navy's best and most experienced salvors.[11]

The unit had its headquarters aboard a barge specially converted to a salvage tender, YRST-1.[12] A direct descendent of the World War II ARS(T)s, this barge was outfitted with all the shop facilities, storage, and accommodation necessary to support a major salvage operation. Although its original design did not include adequate medical, office, and armory facilities, HCU-One artificers rectifed this situation immediately after the craft arrived in Subic. YRST-1, when not deployed for major salvage operations, remained in Subic as the unit's headquarters and maintenance facility.

The main battery of the unit at its formation were four leased 750-ton British lifting craft of the type that had served well during the European harbor clearances of World War II and had been used on the *Rajah Soliman*. Two of these craft, informally designated YMLC, were deployed to Vietnam, where they were positioned at Vung Tau to serve as a base for deployed teams and to stand ready to go to salvage sites. The other two, held in readiness at Subic, were rotated at intervals with those in Vietnam. The craft, designed for the temperate European climate, required some modification to make them suitable for service in the tropics. For instance, the coal-fired galley below the main deck was replaced by a galley built atop the deckhouse, and showers were installed on the afterdeck.

Because LCTs fitted with shear legs had proven so useful during World War II, direct descendants were constructed for Vietnam. Five LCUs were converted into light lift craft (YLLC) at Sasebo by installing on each a 25-ton shear leg and additional machinery. These craft had permanently assigned crews that could be augmented by harbor clearance teams.[13] The weight of the additional machinery that was placed aft in

---

[11] As might be expected, the officers and men assembled for HCU-One were a colorful and confident lot. Typically, they took on self-deprecating nicknames. Lieutenant Edmond B. Bennett's Harbor Clearance Team Five became "Bennett's Bastards"; Lieutenant John C. (Dirty John) Naquin's Harbor Clearance Team One was called "Naquin's Nitwits."

[12] YRST-1 started its service as a covered lighter, YFNB-12. After several conversions, including service as a special projects barge for the Office of Naval Research, it was specifically converted for HCU-One, and designated a diving tender, YDT-11. Its designation was changed to the more accurate salvage craft tender (YRST) shortly after its arrival at HCU-One.

[13] YLLC-5, the last converted, benefited from the earlier conversions and was a more satisfactory craft. This boat was lengthened and carried a heavier shear leg.

Harbor Clearance Unit One in the early days of work in Vietnam (left to right): Lieutenants Moose Kohl and Sam Delanoy; Petty Officers Red Greer, Brady One, Goose Langdon, and Snipe Landstra. Good salvors, good sailors, good shipmates. Photo courtesy Commander Billie L. Delanoy.

the deckhouse and engine room gave the first four boats a severe trim by the stern and affected their speed. For this reason it was more efficient to tow the craft on river transits than to have them proceed on their own power. Once at the salvage site, however, the YLLC was an excellent salvage platform.

In the late spring of 1967, HCU-One received two heavy lift craft (YHLC) that had been purchased by the Navy from the West German salvage firm of Bugsier Reederei und Bergungs. These craft could lift 600 tons each with their stern gantries and 2,400 tons each on a side or belly lift. The craft, *Energie* and *Ausdauer*, had been built in the 1930s and had served throughout World War II and afterwards.[14] Following World War II, they had participated in the salvage of the British submarine *Truculent* in the Thames Estuary in 1950 and in the 1956 clearance of the Suez Canal. They were remarkable craft, unmatched at the time in their

---

[14] During World War II the Germans ballasted the two craft down in Hamburg harbor during the day so that they appeared to be sunk to Allied photo-reconnaissance aircraft. An alert photo-interpreter noticed that the craft weren't always "sunk" in the same place. They were targeted for a raid. *Energie* was sunk, but was raised after the war and returned to service.

capability. Like the British YMLCs, they were designed for European waters and were scarcely habitable in the tropics. On 15 October 1967 the craft were renamed *Crilley* (YHLC 1) and *Crandall* (YHLC 2) in honor of Medal of Honor winners Chief Petty Officers Frank Crilley and Orson Crandall.[15] A program to refurbish them to increase their habitability and replace their steam machinery with diesel-electric machinery was started soon after the ships arrived in Subic. So that maintenance of the craft did not unduly stretch the limited personnel of HCU-One, a crew of local civilian mechanics was hired for routine maintenance work.

The most numerous craft in HCU-One were its six combat salvage boats. These boats had been converted from LCM–6s by adding a 10-ton shear leg, pneumatic deck machinery, a diving system, compressors, and accommodation. When delivered to HCU-One in the fall of 1968, the boats needed more work before they could be sent into a combat zone, for they were completely without the armor they would need to support riverine combat operations. As much bar and plate armor as the boats could carry was added, and the haze-gray shipyard paint job was covered by the olive drab of the riverine forces. When the boats got to Vietnam, the more enthusiastic of the petty officer skippers managed to add a variety of armament as well.

HCU-One also had two 65-foot boats originally built to tend distribution boxes in electrically fired mine fields. These boats, now called diving boats (YDB), had been modified by installing diving air systems. They were versatile craft for light salvage in the river and canals of the Mekong Delta. *Cohoes* (ANL 78) was also modified as a harbor- and river-clearance craft by improving her bow lift capability, which gave her the ability to handle beach gear, and by installing a diver's air system. She served throughout Vietnam.

In addition to the craft described above, HCU-One operated a variety of work boats, LCMs, and other craft. Toward the end of HCU-One's activity in Vietnam, two of the LCM–8s were converted to salvage boats, LCM(S), by adding a 35-ton A-frame, machinery, armor, and armament. These boats were converted specifically for logistic operations in the U Minh Forest area of southwestern Vietnam.

A complement of salvage machinery and equipment was carried aboard the craft and stockpiled in a dedicated warehouse in Subic. Because money was readily available for the Vietnam War, a great deal of equipment, more than HCU-One could ever use, was purchased.[16] This

---

[15] Chief Petty Officers Crilley and Crandall both won their Medals of Honor for diving work on salvage jobs. Crilley's came after the salvage of the submarine F–4, Crandall's after the *Squalus* salvage.

[16] Excess equipment was later used to dieselize the obsolete gasoline-powered equipment in the Emergency Ship Salvage Material System.

equipment did not begin to arrive in the Philippines until some months after HCU-One was formed. In the interim, the unit was outfitted with what was available—obsolete and well-worn, gasoline-powered World War II-vintage equipment from the decommissioned salvage lifting ships and the Emergency Ship Salvage Material System.[17]

The most unusual item of equipment in HCU-One had nothing to do with harbor clearance, but it added another dimension to the versatile unit. It was a commercial deep-diving system called ADS-IV, which was leased from Ocean System, Inc. Harbor Clearance Team Two, led by Lieutenant Orlin A. (Moose) Kohl and Lieutenant (j.g.) Richard D. Jones, was designated as the deep-diving team and taken out of the deployment cycle. Divers throughout the salvage force were trained in the diving system so they could reinforce the HCU-One team during extended deep-diving operations. The compact system could take divers to depths of 450 feet and could be operated from a fleet tug or salvage ship.

HCU-One grew in men and equipment for the first years of its existence and amassed a record of success. Besides the many decorations earned by individual members of the unit, the unit itself was awarded two Navy Unit Commendations, a Meritorious Unit Commendation, and a Vietnamese Unit Cross of Gallantry covering the entire period of its existence in the Philippines. It was not all roses. There were deaths and injuries from combat and from the hazards that accompany all salvage operations. One salvage craft, YLLC-4, was a combat loss. HCU-One was involved in so many salvage operations that the Navy designed a special short-form salvage report that could be filled out in the field en route to the next job. Although there were a number of major jobs, the great value of the work done by the unit in Vietnam lay in the hundreds of small jobs undertaken by a hastily deployed crew or a single light lift craft, combat salvage boat, or diving boat. By removing countless minor obstacles and salvaging resources on these jobs, salvors enabled the war to go forward.

HCU-One Goes to Work

HCU-One's first operation came in April 1966 when a fallen bridge section was removed in Danang. After that, the work came fast and

---

[17] In the initial outfitting of HCU-One, there were some oversights and shortfalls. One of these was in material-handling equipment, specifically forklift trucks. None were assigned. Normal procedures to get one would take too long, and material needed to be moved. Unusual measures, the salvors' specialty, were called for. A sailor was sent to the forklift operator's school with instructions that when he learned to drive it, he should drive it home. He did. A quick paint job—and HCU-One had its first forklift. Other material was acquired by similar unconventional means.

furious. Harbor Clearance Team One and YLLC–1[18] started the first deployment cycle later that month. Their introduction to combat salvage came when they salvaged contraband cargo from a grounded Vietcong trawler in May.

The first use of the larger lift craft came in late May. A French steamer, *Paul Bert*, sunk years before, blocked the approach to the new river patrol boat base at My Tho. The two British lift craft that had been brought over earlier and moored in the roads at Vung Tau were brought up river for the job. Lieutenant Naquin's Harbor Clearance Team One and Lieutenant Richard H. Giebner's Harbor Clearance Team Three did the work. The operation went well. The wreck was lifted three times and carried across the river, where it was set down well clear of patrol operations. During the *Paul Bert* removal, several divers were diverted to search for limpet mines in the Saigon River. Others in the unit went to Phu Bai to retrieve weapons and intelligence material from a capsized patrol boat. Such interruptions of salvage work for higher priority jobs had been common in World War II and would be in Vietnam as well.

There was concern lest the lift craft in the open roadstead of Vung Tau made far too inviting a target for the Vietcong. Following the removal of *Paul Bert*, the lift craft were towed to Saigon and moored to a ramshackle pier in a backwater canal. Here a bitt on the pier carried away on a falling tide and struck Warrant Officer W.R. Savage, killing him. Shortly thereafter, the lift craft returned to Vung Tau, where they were based for the remainder of their time in Vietnam.

By late summer the tempo of operations began to increase. On 23 August a Vietcong sapper who had been waiting in a hideout along the Long Tau River got his chance. His command-detonated mine blew a hole in the side of the SS *Baton Rouge Victory* inbound for Saigon with a full load of government cargo. The ship continued ahead and grounded on the riverbank. *Baton Rouge Victory* provided a major test for HCU-One and became one of the few jobs that involved almost the entire unit.

Tugs from Saigon sailed to the scene and held the ship against the bank, pending the arrival of Lieutenant (j.g.) Anthony Greene with Harbor Clearance Team Four and YLLC–2. Under the direction of Lieutenant Greene, the light lift craft set a mooring to hold the ship in place. Lieutenant Billie L. (Sam) Delanoy, the executive officer of HCU-One, and Lieutenant J.J. Goodwin, the salvage engineer, arrived the following

---

[18] Harbor Clearance Team One and YLLC–1 had been scheduled to make the first deployment. When the time to go approached, it became apparent that YLLC–1 would not be ready in time, though YLLC–2 would. It would never do for the second boat to make the first deployment. A paint brush solved the problem. With a few strokes of the brush in the vicinity of the hull numbers, YLLC–2 became YLLC–1, and vice versa—forever.

Salvors work "head down, backside up" on deck of their British lift craft during the *Paul Bert* salvage. The heavy pieces on deck are Bullivant clamps used to clamp the lift wires together. Unlaid manila line in the clamps absorb grease squeezed from the wire and prevent slippage. The clamps are tightened by large pneumatic wrenches called "windy spanners." Photo courtesy Commander Billie L. Delanoy.

Lieutenants Dick Giebner (left) and John Naquin (center) stand with Warrant Officer Bill Savage on the side of the French steamer *Paul Bert*. Savage was killed in an accident a few days later. Photo courtesy Commander Billie L. Delanoy.

Tugs, barges, and other craft bustle around *Baton Rouge Victory*, lying mined and beached in the Long Tau River.

morning. After their survey of the damaged merchantman, they sent for the remainder of HCU-One.

The first task was to get the damaged ship out of the river and eliminate the chance that it might sink or capsize and block logistic traffic. The damage to *Baton Rouge Victory* was confined to the engine room and number three hold. Both spaces, nonetheless, were flooded, the double bottoms open, and the deck and side shell heavily buckled. For any attempted move of the ship, heavy lift craft would have to be placed alongside to prevent capsizing and excessive bending of the weakened hull. All four YMLCs would be needed to do the job right.

While Harbor Clearance Teams One and Two were preparing the lift craft in Saigon, the situation changed dramatically at the site. On 27 August, after all deck cargo had been removed, *Baton Rouge Victory* suddenly began moving downstream, taking her moor with her. Tugs took the ship in hand and brought her under control. Afterwards, only the highest priority cargo was removed; the two available lift craft were hurriedly brought down river from Saigon and put in position for rigging.

Baton Rouge Victory had no intention of settling down. Around midnight on 29 August, she got underway again in hard rain and strong winds. Tugs forced her ashore 1,200 yards upstream on the opposite side of the river, well clear of the Army's security perimeter. Anchors were scattered; the ship was not in a good position. She had to be moved quickly.

As soon as lift wires had been rove, a river pilot came aboard and the nest got underway for Vung Tau, where it was put aground by the tug *Patrick*. YRST-1 came alongside that evening and the next phase of the salvage operation began—a patch and pump job to secure the ship for tow to a repair yard. Pumps were rigged aboard, construction of a large wooden patch began, and reinforcing structure was welded on in way of the buckled shell.

The weather that had caused the ship to break loose up river continued to be a problem that occupied the salvors and disrupted the work. By 21 September the patch had been fitted and a test pumping made. The following day the water level dropped sharply as the pumps were started. Though their tired World War II pumps began to fail, the salvors were holding their own—until the patch failed.

Because the patch did not have sufficient strength for repair and replacement, it was discarded. A long delay followed while Ship Repair Facility, Subic, built a 62-ton steel patch complete with its own ballast and blow system. The installation of this new patch and subsequent pumping of the ship went smoothly. Cargo discharge was completed and the ship made ready for sea. On 8 December the tug *Osceola* took *Baton Rouge Victory* in tow for the Philippines.

The tow didn't get far. *Baton Rouge Victory*, irascible to the end, bumped the Chinese-flag vessel *Ever Fortune* and damaged the patch-securing mechanism. As the tow went to sea, the patch worked loose to the point that Warrant Officer Donnie E. Gable of HCU-One aboard the *Baton Rouge Victory* recommended returning to Vung Tau. The patch was removed and sent back to Subic Bay, where it became the roof of a Ship Repair Facility welding shop. *Baton Rouge Victory* was towed to Singapore without the patch and without incident. Expediency rather than careful seamanship had governed both moves of *Baton Rouge Victory*. Fortunately the ship was tough enough and other measures thorough enough that the moves could be made.[19]

While *Baton Rouge Victory* was showing herself to be what the British call "bloody minded," a sister ship, *Clarksburg Victory*, was much more docile and cooperative. On 12 October, *Clarksburg Victory*, under Military Sea Transportation Service charter and carrying government-owned cargo, struck a submerged object and holed herself in the engine room while entering Vung Tau. Over a five-day period a heavy wooden patch

---

[19] The success of the tow is best credited to good fortune, for without the patch the tow was very risky. A combination of factors—the complexity of the patch, the value of the ship, and other demands on HCU-One—forced the decision to take the risk.

was placed over the hole, the floodwater pumped down, an internal cement patch placed, and the ship sent on her way with none of the complications and frustrations of the job going on across the harbor.

HCU-One teams often joined other salvage units on jobs. This was the case on New Year's Eve 1966, when *Mahnomen County* (LST 912) parted her anchor chain, blew ashore, and broached at Chu Lai. Harbor Clearance Unit people, *Grapple*, *Sioux*, and the Seventh Fleet salvage officer, Commander Orem, went to the scene. They found the LST had grounded hard on a rocky shore with seas breaking over her. The northeast monsoon was blowing full; winds were up to 25 knots, the surf to 18 feet. All hands labored to get the ship off using a variety of salvage techniques. Foam like that used in *Frank Knox* was brought in and put into the hull;[20] explosives removed rocks on the seaward side. Nothing was enough. In mid-January, with her tanks open to the sea, *Mahnomen County* began to break up. There was no choice but to abandon her.

The mundane marine task of dredging had particular importance in Vietnam. The Mekong River and the many branches that form its estuary carry a huge amount of silt; therefore, deposits of silt constantly change the depth of the rivers and make navigation hazardous. As constant dredging was necessary to keep traffic moving and to keep open the ports and bases supplied by the river, dredges were operated in Vietnam by the United States and many other nations.

Dredges make interesting salvage work. They are poorly subdivided, existing subdivisions are often ineffective, they have very heavy components, and their structure is relatively light compared to seagoing ships. During the war, U.S. dredges were considered fair game for attack. Harbor Clearance Unit One worked on three large dredges, all sunk by enemy action and all near the Ninth Infantry Division base at Dong Tam in the My Tho River. Each job involved different problems, approaches, and solutions.

JAMAICA BAY

Vietcong swimmer-sappers kicked off the first job by placing charges

---

[20] The use of chemical foam unfortunately resulted in a casualty. Because toxic fumes and oxygen-displacing gases were present when the foam was being made, salvors wore lightweight diving equipment for breathing and followed diving procedures even when foaming above water. Petty Officer Clyde Gordon was foaming in *Mahnomen County*'s shaft alley when his air supply failed. He immediately removed his mask and headed for the exit. He didn't make it. His tender, Petty Officer Roy Wells, entered the compartment and moved Gordon closer to the exit before he too fell unconscious. At this point Petty Officer Joe Nestor donned the spare mask and rescued both Gordon and Wells. Conscious and objecting, Gordon and Wells were removed to *Sanctuary* (AH 17) for observation. Both men developed chemical pneumoconiosis. Wells died; Gordon had a long recovery and eventually returned to diving duty. Petty Officers Roy Wells and Joe Nestor were awarded the Navy-Marine Corps Medal.

on the suction-cutter dredge *Jamaica Bay* on 9 January 1967. The dredge sank in approximately three minutes, coming to rest on her starboard spud at about a 30-degree list, with the starboard side of her main deck above water. There were two large holes in her hull.

Jamaica Bay had been engaged in fill operations for the new base at Dong Tam, the first permanent U.S. thrust into the Mekong Delta. The dredge hulk, lying as it did, impeded progress in the construction of the base and blocked the approaches to the LST landing ramp that supplied the base. Since removal was urgent and would require a major salvage effort, a special organization was set up for the job. Commander Eugene B. Mitchell, the Pacific Fleet salvage officer, took charge at the scene. Lieutenant Delanoy was in charge of HCU-One assets. There was direct liaison between Mitchell and now-Captain Searle, the Supervisor of Salvage who would coordinate special efforts by contractors and the technical resources of the Naval Ship Systems Command. Searle arranged for the temporary assignment of three salvage engineers—Lieutenant Commanders John L. Ulrich and Oliver H. Porter, and Lieutenant William I. Milwee—to augment the salvage forces on the scene.

The dredge was badly holed and had no internal watertight integrity. Bodily lifting and removal was called for. The weight to be lifted was about 2,100 tons. Because the two YHLCs had not yet arrived, the only way this amount of lift could be attained with an adequate margin was by using all four of the YMLCs. Only once before had four lift craft been used, and then under far more favorable conditions.[21] These four had to be carefully positioned in order to obtain the maximum lift, let the load come on the lift wires evenly, and reduce the unsupported length of hull between lift wires.

As is usual in salvage operations, much margin was inserted in calculations to allow for the many unknown conditions that were sure to be present. Because of the fixed lifting capacity, additional weight would be removed from *Jamaica Bay*, including the pierced steel planking armor, and the hull would be patched and pumped to decrease the required lift as much as possible. Plans were also made to bring in foam if additional buoyancy was needed. To do the job expeditiously, four harbor clearance teams were assigned to it, and the YRST–1 was brought over as a salvage base.

The work went forward in a logical sequence:

- Patches were designed.
- A bow-to-bow lift craft arrangement was chosen.

---

[21] The previous use of four lift craft was in the removal of the wreck of the French destroyer *Maille Breze* at Greenock, Scotland, in 1953.

- Deballasting sequences were determined.

- Large wooden fenders were constructed and rigged to prevent the lift craft from moving in and damaging themselves and the dredge.

- Lift wires were passed.

- An analysis of bilge cutting by lift wires was made and reinforcing bolster plates were designed.[22]

- Construction of patches and bolster plates began.

- Spuds were shot away with explosives to reduce the list.

- Beach gear to move the lifted wreck was hauled ashore and additional legs were laid in the river by YLLC–2.[23]

The first lift came on 4 February 1967. An important function of this lift was to work out procedures and to use and stretch the wires. But most important, the first lift demonstrated that the lifting scheme worked and the dredge could be lifted. Lifts continued and the dredge gradually moved into shallower water. Following the fourth lift, one of the lift craft hung up on the wreck and sank on the rising tide by flooding through an open hatch. The lift craft was raised and returned to service in five days.

While the lift craft was being raised, foam was injected into *Jamaica Bay*'s two forward wing tanks. With the lift craft back in service, lifts continued. A total of eleven lifts were made in moving the wreck toward the riverbank and into shallow water. The lifts stopped when the lift craft rested on the river bottom with the gunwales awash during low tide.

With the *Jamaica Bay* in shallow water, the patches were installed and pumps placed on board. With no effective subdivision in the hull of the dredge, a large, stability-destroying free surface existed. To achieve stability during dewatering, two lift craft were held alongside. On the first pumping attempt, the dredge took an 8-degree list as soon as she came clear of the bottom, the list immersed one of the main deck doors, and the dredge went back down. On the next pumping attempt, the list increased to 21 degrees. To control it, loose gear and mud were removed, as much water as possible was pumped out, and the lift craft were positioned to maximize the lift on the low side.

---

[22] The original analysis of the bilge cutting was made on the scene with less than the most sophisticated methods. A check calculation made after the operation showed that although the method was not precise, the results were correct. After the job Lieutenant Commander Ulrich developed and published a more precise method of analysis.

[23] The Eells anchors for the shore legs of beach gear were buried ashore, well outside the security perimeter established by the Vietnamese Army. When the legs were hauled, the anchors did not hold in the swampy ground and dragged toward the perimeter, forcing mounds of earth ahead of them. They resembled nothing so much as giant moles. The Vietnamese troops, suspecting some insidious Vietcong secret weapon, abandoned their positions with haste.

Four lift craft, assisted by YDT–11, YLLC–2, and various other craft, raise the dredge *Jamaica Bay* near the Ninth Infantry Division base at Dong Tam, Vietnam.

The original plan had been to take the dredge to Saigon for repair. Patching and pumping was directed toward making the hull tight and secure enough for a safe tow there.

The repairs needed, however, were too extensive for the Saigon facilities. *Jamaica Bay* would have to be towed across the open sea to a shipyard. Because salvage repairs are seldom adequate to prepare a vessel for open-sea towing, the dredge was to be towed first to Saigon for drydocking and temporary repairs, then towed overseas for final repairs. She would go down river, across 15 miles of open sea to Vung Tau, then back up river to Saigon. The large patches were a major problem. Loss of one of them could cause the dredge to sink. To prevent possible flooding, salvors filled the stern compartments with foam after stacking as many 55-gallon drums as possible into them.

On 12 March *Jamaica Bay* floated free with no list, ready for tow, just over two months after she was attacked. She was picked up by the Alaska Barge and Transport tugs *Patrick* and *Pacific Mariner*. Twenty-seven men rode the dredge. The voyage would cross the My Tho River entrance bar at high water in daylight. Any other tide would have required a night transit or lying to overnight. Neither idea was attractive, for the Vietcong controlled both the riverbanks and the night.

At the bar the tow encountered short-crested waves changing to long sea swells, coupled with afternoon winds increasing in strength. After some deliberation the transit started. Almost immediately, waves began to break over the dredge; one sailor was washed overboard but was picked up by *Patrick*. The gasoline pumps were gradually flooded by the waves and stopped. Leakage through seams and discharges increased; salvors stripped off their clothes and stuffed them in the holes. It was a losing fight. The flooding increased, as did the list. A door cover ripped off; water poured in. The order to abandon was given. *Jamaica Bay* rolled over and sank.[24] *Patrick* and *Pacific Mariner* picked up the riding crew.

A long, hard salvage job had ended. The object of the salvage had been lost, but much had been gained and learned:

• A 2,100-ton wreck had been removed from a critical position under combat conditions.

• Four lift craft had successfully lifted a structurally flimsy hull under less than optimum conditions.

• Foam was again shown to be a promising salvage tool, but one that definitely was no panacea and required more development to be truly practical in the field.

• The gasoline-powered salvage machinery again proved to be obsolete, cantankerous, and deserving of immediate replacement.

SANDPUMPER

It was more than two and a half years after the work on *Jamaica Bay* that the Navy-owned dredge *Sandpumper* (YM 24) sucked a mine into her dredge pump on 22 September 1969. The mine exploded and *Sandpumper* sank in seven minutes. The dredge settled in 35 feet of water; the spuds jammed against the spud gates, holding the stern 6 feet proud of the bottom.

The salvors looked at their options on this job. For pumping to succeed, extensive patching and strengthening of the hull would be needed to get enough buoyancy to float the dredge. This would be a long operation under difficult conditions. Lifting was an attractive alternative, particularly because the heavy lift craft *Crilley* and *Crandall* were available. The lifting operation would be considerably easier than the four-craft operation on *Jamaica Bay*.[25]

---

[24] The wreck of *Jamaica Bay* was marked approximately 9 miles, 230 degrees true from Vung Tau, formerly Cap St. Jacques. Much of the wreck of the *Jamaica Bay* was removed by Navy salvage ships during the next several years. In 1970 a team from HCU-One blew the remaining wreckage below the surface.

[25] The YHLCs were considerably easier to work and less labor intensive than the YMLCs. The primary reason was that the larger craft carried far more deck machinery for handling heavy lift wires and materials. Also, rather than clamping the two wires of a lift pair together with Bullivant clamps, as required on the YMLCs, built-in deck-edge clamps were provided on the YHLCs, allowing wires to be handled individually.

Water pours out of *Jamaica Bay*, extracted by the recently acquired diesel-powered pumps, but she will sink while on tow to Saigon.

Salvors take a break during the *Jamaica Bay* salvage operation. Left to right: Lieutenant William Milwee, Commander Gene Mitchell, and Lieutenant Billie Delanoy during the *Jamaica Bay* salvage operation. Photo courtesy Commander W.I. Milwee, Jr.

Led by their commanding officer, Commander Joseph F. Madeo, and the salvage engineer, Lieutenant Herbert Tufts, HCU-One salvors laid out a four-part salvage plan using both the stern lift and side lift capabilities of the YHLCs. Before the lift craft arrived, the wreck would be secured against further sinking, lift craft moors laid, the dredge ladder disconnected, and messenger wires for the lift wires passed under the dredge. The first job for the lift craft would be to lift the dredge ladder clear and set it on a barge. Then the dredge itself would be lifted and moved to shallow water for patching and pumping, the final step before refloating.

The first phase of the operation came off without a hitch, but when the salvors tried to lift the dredge ladder with the stern gantry of *Crilley* they had a double portion of problems. Three attempts were made. The first failed when lifting straps parted and shackles bent. The second removed the ladder from its trunnion bearings; then the lifting winches stalled. The third lift removed the ladder but could not raise it high enough to be placed on the waiting barge. The ladder had to be set on the bottom and dragged clear by *Crandall*.

With the ladder out of the way, the lift craft were put alongside *Sandpumper*. Previously positioned messengers hauled twenty-four lift wires under the dredge. The spud gates were blown open with explosives, the starboard spud removed, and the port spud broken off. Six successful lifts

The heavy lift ships *Crilley* and *Crandall*, held apart by large spreader bars, lift the dredge *Sandpumper* in the My Tho River, Vietnam.

were made between 12 and 24 November. *Sandpumper* was grounded in 14 feet of water. Now came the hard part.

The hull and superstructure were patched, but a considerable amount of damage lay inaccessible in the mud. The salvors first attempted simply to outpump the flooding, but it didn't work. In fact, nothing seemed to go right. Blowing air into the pontoons on the bow caused a list that eventually forced removal of the pumps on the port side. Pumping had created additional problems arising from the fact that the Mekong River matches or exceeds Mark Twain's description of the Mississippi as "too thick to drink, too thin to plow." Pumping had drawn more silt-laden water into the hull, where the silt joined the viscous mud in the wreck, adding weight and clogging pumps. After a frustrating month of losing ground, salvage attempts were abandoned on 30 December, over three months after *Sandpumper* went down.

NEW JERSEY

On 22 November 1969 Vietcong sappers mined the dredge *New Jersey*, which was working just 1,200 yards from the *Sandpumper* salvage operations. The damage would not have been enough to sink *New Jersey* if the integrity of her watertight design had been intact. As it was, she flooded progressively while tugs pushed her toward the riverbank and finally sank in 20 feet of water and 4 feet of mud.

As with *Sandpumper*, the choice was between pumping and lifting. With the lift craft already present, lifting would have been convenient, but other considerations swung the decision toward patching and pumping. Lifting would have required two or three weeks of preparation and at best would have gained 7 feet, leaving the main deck below water.

Once the decision to patch and pump had been made, the work went forward systematically. Flooding boundaries were established, and a decision was made to isolate and bypass the damaged areas. Test pumping was carried out and holes sealed when located.

New Jersey showed an unfortunate tendency to take severe lists as she broke free of the bottom and had to be put back down. A blowdown system for the fuel tanks, isolation of flooded spaces until it was time to pump them dry, and a larger pumping capacity succeeded in controlling the free surface that caused the list. *New Jersey* refloated on 2 December. Bulldozers hauled her toward the beach for emergency repairs. After preparation for tow, she departed for repairs in Singapore on 13 December.

The three dredges had been major challenges for HCU-One. Each was met with different techniques, best suited for the work at hand. Although two of the dredges were lost, the principal objective of the work, clearing the wrecks, was accomplished.

Minding the Store

All three levels of salvage activity were carried out by HCU-One during the time it operated in Vietnam. At the top were the peaks of activity—the major jobs described above and others like them. These jobs involved several teams and a variety of salvage craft. At the second level were the routine operations, consisting of so-called little jobs that formed the bulk of the unit's work. Most of these jobs involved only one team, or part of a team, or one or two of the light salvage craft. There were hundreds of such jobs. *Sea Raven*, *Clark County*, *Robin Hood*, *Seatrain Texas*, *Transcolorado*, *Green Bay Victory*, and many other ships were aided by the salvors of HCU-One. Aircraft were salvaged, fires extinguished, weapons and special equipment recovered; a variety of objects, ranging from railway bridge spans to howitzers and garbage trucks, were raised, removed, or demolished. The unit was always busy.

The riverine force required regular support. Of all the sites of frequent salvage activity, none was busier or more dangerous than an area deep in the Mekong Delta that came to be called Solid Anchor or Sea Float. HCU-One maintained an active salvage station there. Although attacks occurred almost daily, because the Viet Cong controlled the banks of the tidal river, continuous salvage operations kept the backlog down to four or five sunken or stranded craft at any given time.

The third level of HCU-One activity was planning and management. This was done at the unit's headquarters in Subic and included:

• Maintaining and rehabilitating equipment and craft coming back from deployment.

• Resting men back from regular deployments.

• Training new men.

• Training all teams with the unit's varied equipment.

• Preparing craft and men for deployment.

• Fulfilling the unit's responsibilities for salvage throughout the Pacific.

HCU-One was a busy organization, and proud of it. Many of those who served with the unit in Vietnam consider their tour as the best of their Navy career.

Around the Pacific

While HCU-One was the principal salvage unit operating in the harbors and rivers of Vietnam, Pacific Fleet salvage forces were busy throughout the Pacific at all types of salvage operations:

- On 3 October 1965, *Conserver* and the small Army LT–43 tug assisted *Britain Victory* when the merchantman lost power in the South China Sea.

- *Tawakoni* took *Ekaterina G.* in tow[26] after the Greek-flag vessel lost a propeller 600 miles south of Adak, Alaska. During the tow, the ship's anchor chain, part of the tow rig, parted during foul weather and the ship was lost on Great Sitkin Island.

- In a similar incident *Mataco* picked up the Chinese freighter *Tai-Nam* and delivered her to the Canadian salvage ship *Sudbury II*.[27]

- On 13 January 1967 *Mataco* extinguished a fire on the fishing vessel *Mondego* off San Diego, and *Grasp* went to the aid of *Guam Bear* after she collided with *Esso Victory* off Apra Harbor, Guam. *Guam Bear* was towed into the harbor and beached alongside *Glass Breakwater*, where her cargo was salvaged.

- Rear Admiral Frederick E. Janney, Commander Service Group Three, and his salvage officer, Lieutenant Commander Huntly Boyd, flew to Okinawa when USNS *General Daniel I. Sultan* (T–AP 120) grounded on Rukon Shoal at the entrance to Naha. With indigenous resources, improvised beach gear, construction equipment, and Army tugs, they freed the ship.

- *Krishna* personnel, working under sniper fire, raised the mined PCF–4 in the Gulf of Siam.

- Harbor tugs at Pearl Harbor refloated the tanker *Casstot* at the harbor entrance.

- During the summer of 1969 the Navy provided technical assistance and equipment from the Emergency Ship Salvage Material System to assist the Mexican Navy in the salvage of the 600-ton pipeline dredge *Mazatlan*, sunk in Puerto Vallarta.

- *Sunnadin* (ATA 197), then *Wandank* (ATA 204), towed the SS *Old Westbury* to Guam after that ship had a boiler casualty 850 miles from Guam.

- *Takelma* towed *Waddell* (DDG 24) to Pearl Harbor after the destroyer touched bottom off Midway and damaged both propellers.

---

[26] From shortly after World War II until early in the 1970s, an ATF was regularly deployed to Adak to be available for rescue towing and salvage service in these waters. The ATFs were withdrawn toward the end of the Vietnam War when U.S. Government shipping interests declined and ATFs were required for higher priority work. These were much the same reasons that caused the withdrawal of ATFs from Alaskan waters in World War II.

[27] *Sudbury II* was originally *Caledonian Salvor* (BARS 1). She served throughout the war under the Australian flag for the Commonwealth Marine Salvage Board. She was transferred to the Royal Australian Navy in 1948 and subsequently sold to Island Tug and Barge of Victoria, B.C.

• *Grasp* refloated the Chinese Navy's Floating Drydock Number One in Tsoying Harbor, Taiwan.

• The ever-busy *Hitchiti* towed the *Diodon* (SS 349) to Yokosuka after the submarine suffered a fire and loss of propulsion.

• *Chowanoc* sailed from the northern Pacific salvage station at Adak to assist the disabled *Sea Flyer*. She was damaged while passing the tow line but towed the disabled merchantman toward Seattle until relieved by a commercial tug.

In addition to these "routine" salvage operations, there were some of particular note. The submarine *Tiru* (SS 416) grounded on Frederick Reef about 415 miles north of Brisbane, Queensland, Australia, on 19 November 1967. *Florikan* sailed from Kaohsiung, Taiwan, *Conserver* from Subic Bay, and *Taussig* (DD 746) from Melbourne. HMAS *Sydney* was first on the scene and made a comprehensive survey. HMAS *Vendetta* got underway from Brisbane with Commander Bruce Meader, a submarine officer assigned to HMAS *Albatross*. *Vendetta* divers carried out an underwater survey in preparation for the arrival of the Australian ocean-going tug *Carlock*. When *Carlock* arrived, she passed a towline and pulled on the first available tide. *Tiru* blew all forward ballast and went full astern when the tug pulled. The submarine floated.[28]

The wreck of the armored cruiser *Rochester* (ACR 2)[29] blocked the approaches to a fuel buoy in Subic Bay. Tankers approaching the buoy for discharge needed 55 feet of clearance over the wreck. HCU-One got the job of flattening the wreck. Because the ship lay on its side, the plan called for explosives to sever the armor belt and the side at the deck edge and pound it into the interior. The plan worked well and dropped the structure, with the exception of two frames, to a clear depth of 65 feet. Two small charges took care of these frames.[30]

Explosives were also used in September 1967 after the Standard Oil tanker *R.C. Stoner* ran aground while attempting to enter Wake Island to deliver a load of aviation gasoline. The cargo immediately began leaking into the harbor. Coast Guard cutter *Mallow* (WLB 396), *Noxubee* (AOG

---

[28] Because she was not secured on the reef with an anchor astern, concern about *Tiru*'s broaching led to some experimentation with air-droppable ground tackle with a hauling purchase. Tests of such a system were carried out in Hawaii in early 1968. The system was never placed in service.

[29] Originally *New York* (ACR 2), *Rochester* was considered the best armored cruiser in the world when built by William Cramp and Sons of Philadelphia in the early 1890s. The ship was renamed *Saratoga* on 16 February 1911 and renamed *Rochester* on 1 December 1917. She served until 1933, when she was decommissioned at Cavite and steamed to Subic Bay. In 1938 she was stricken from the Navy list as an "unclassified hulk." She was sunk by Japanese air attack early in World War II.

[30] There was one small problem on the *Rochester* job. The first shot went as scheduled, but the salvage officer had forgottom to remind the base commander about the large explosion. The admiral was somewhat surprised when his windows shook and his lights swayed. Shortly afterwards he asked Lieutenant Delanoy not to surprise him any more.

10), and *Mataco* were diverted to Wake; *Conserver* and *Grapple* got under-way from Pearl Harbor; *Wandank* came from Guam; Harbor Clearance Team Two flew in from Subic; and Commander Orem, who had relieved Commander Mitchell as Pacific Fleet salvage officer, flew in from Pearl Harbor. It was of little avail; the surf took its toll and the ship began breaking up before all the salvage forces could assemble. The pollution problem presented by the leaking cargo was solved when typhoon Sarah hit the island with 145-knot winds and dispersed the pollutant. Following the storm, the wreck was flattened by explosives in an operation compli-cated by high winds and seas and kibitzing sharks.

On Christmas Eve 1967 the submarine *Guardfish* (SSN 612) ran aground at 24 knots entering Pearl Harbor. The shallow gradient of the reef and the shape of the hull combined to slow the ship gradually so that she came to rest 8 feet out of her draft and some 500 yards from where she first took the ground. *Current*, with Captain T. Grabowski, Com-mander Service Squadron Five, and Commander Orem aboard was un-der way within half an hour. *Current* was soon joined by *Grapple*, *Arikara*, and several TYBs. There were two major problems: where to grab onto the smooth hull of *Guardfish*, and how to develop enough pull in the poor holding ground offered by the coral reef.

The first problem was solved by passing beach gear chain down through the after hatch, through the boat, and out the torpedo loading hatch, then shackling it back onto itself. Three chains were made up this way for three pulling lines. To get as strong a hold as possible on the ground, the pulling ships were rigged in tandem with beach gear anchors set in the coral with explosives. Little buoyancy could be expected from the tide; its range was only about 18 inches, but salvors have to take what they can get. Pulls were made on three consecutive days at high water; the submarine moved about 100 yards each time. On the third day, she floated.

On the night of 2 June 1969 the aircraft carrier HMAS *Melbourne* collided with the destroyer *Frank E. Evans* (DD 754), cutting her in two. The bow section sank in minutes; the stern wallowed in the open sea in imminent danger of flooding, capsizing, and sinking. The first ship on the scene was *Everett F. Larson* (DD 830), which took the stern section along-side and secured it. *Tawasa* arrived while this initial work was in progress and put trained salvage men on board. The *Tawasa* crew worked for sixteen hours and brought the destroyer's stern section almost to an even keel with adequate stability and reserve buoyancy.

To get the stern section ready for tow, weight was jettisoned, pumps and a flooding alarm installed, free water pumped out, and possible sources of flooding eliminated. *Tawasa* towed the section, stern first with a bight of towing wire around her aft 5-inch gun mount. The 825-mile tow to Subic Bay was made in six days. Unlike her sister, *Frank Knox*, *Evans* was not rebuilt.

When typhoon Rose struck Hong Kong in August 1971, twenty-six ships were driven aground in the harbor, among them *Regulus* (AF 57), which had tried to ride out the storm at anchor. Both anchors dragged in the storm and *Regulus* was blown onto the hard rock and sand of Kau Yi Chau Island. Salvage forces began to assemble. *Grasp*, *Safeguard*, and *Abnaki* were sent to Hong Kong. Rear Admiral Philip P. Cole, Commander Service Group Three; his salvage officer, Lieutenant Commander William N. Klorig; and the Pacific Fleet salvage officer, Lieutenant Commander Allan A. Ovrom, flew in.

Regulus was in dire straits. She was port side to the island, buckled amidships, three holds flooded, apparently impaled on the rock, and badly holed. The crew was taken off and removal of the salvageable cargo, material, and equipment began. The possibility that decaying organic cargo would generate hydrogen sulfide caused particular concern. The toxic gas was controlled by pumping the holds constantly to keep them flushed out. The ship was secured against movement, beach gear laid, and foam made ready for the holds.

Evaluation of the condition of the wreck showed that cutting the ship in half and removing the two halves separately was the only feasible method of salvage. In view of the age and condition of the ship, salvage in this somewhat drastic manner followed by lengthy and expensive repairs was not deemed sensible. The fleet operation terminated on 10 September and the ship was turned over to the Supervisor of Salvage, who would oversee the removal of the wreck by a Navy contractor. The removal is described later in this chapter when Navy contractor operations are discussed.

As previously mentioned, in the early morning of 25 September 1973, the USNS *Jack J. Pendelton* (T–AK 276), outbound from Southeast Asia with a cargo of old ammunition and generators, ran aground on Triton Island. *Beaufort* (ATS 2) was ordered to the scene for the first use of the new salvage ship in a classic stranding operation. It was soon apparent that the work would require more than one salvage ship. *Reclaimer* and *Hitchiti* were ordered in. Rear Admiral John D. Johnson, Jr., Commander Service Group Three, and his salvage officer, Lieutenant Commander Harley Oien, also headed for Triton Island.

Cargo discharge proceeded with painful slowness, hampered by cargo on the crucial number two hatch that was too heavy for the handling equipment. Moving liquids trimmed the ship down hard by the stern. Several retraction attempts were made with the ship trimmed and loads decreasing as cargo was removed. The chances of success were high when operations had to be suspended for typhoon evasion. Four typhoons

Regulus lies aground in Hong Kong harbor, showing the break in her hull caused by typhoon Rose. Cut apart, her bow and stern were floated to a junkyard and sold.

passed through the area in a period of fifteen days. Aerial photography from the carrier *Hancock* (CVA 19) showed *Pendelton* gradually being broached and driven 70 yards farther onto the reef by the storms. When the typhoons had finished their work, salvage was no longer feasible. Ships could not get alongside and the ship's machinery could not be operated. Still, before the ship could be abandoned, a large amount of critical or dangerous cargo had to be discharged. The foremast was blown off to accommodate two Marine Corps helicopters and an aerial shuttle was started to remove ammunition. Attempts to blast a channel in the coral in order to bring a crane alongside resulted in hull damage and an oil spill before being called off. Fuel was removed by beaching *Tioga County* (LST 1158) nearby and pumping fuel to her. After all dangerous materials and potential pollutants were removed, salvage efforts were terminated on 6 November and *Pendelton* was abandoned.

The Vietnam era wound down. In 1970 HCU-One began to pull out of Vietnam and to turn most of its boats and some equipment over to the Vietnamese. The leased lift craft went back to their British owners; *Crilley* and *Crandall* were laid up in Subic Bay. YRST–1 went back to Pearl Harbor, where it continued to serve as headquarters for a greatly reduced HCU-One. Salvage had undergone a fundamental change. The concept of fly-away salvage—flying a small team of minimally equipped salvors to the scene to live off the land and to make the most of local equipment and ships—was firmly established as a principal way of doing business.

The World War II-built salvage ships had given good service in the Vietnam era, but signs of wear were obvious. Although still capable, they were old and tired. Two of the new salvage and rescue ships (ATS) had joined the Pacific Fleet, but they were virtually untried.

Salvage forces in the Pacific had made a major contribution to the war effort by their work in Vietnam, their support of logistic shipping, and the myriad of other tasks they were called on to perform. At the same time, they had continued their regular support of fleet operations and provided salvage services to shipping throughout the Pacific where no commercial salvors operated.

At the end of the Vietnam War, the salvage capability in the Pacific Fleet was greater than at any time since the end of World War II. There had been fundamental changes, some quite subtle, in Navy salvage, but as at the end of that earlier war, the future was not clear. The effects would take time to sort out.

In the Atlantic

Combat salvage and the salvage work generated by increased shipping in the Pacific dominated Navy salvage during the Vietnam era, but salvage forces in the Atlantic were far from idle. Although Atlantic salvors were active at all three levels of salvage, there were few major operations. Most of the work focused on day-to-day planning and management and routine salvage tasks.

The Atlantic and Caribbean generally had been favored operating areas of commercial salvors, both American and foreign. *Cable* and *Curb*, under charter to Merritt-Chapman and Scott and later to the successor company, Murphy Pacific, were stationed on the East Coast of the United States. Merritt-Chapman and Scott's *Rescue*, under a Liberian flag, was on salvage station in Jamaica, and ships of European salvors were often on station in Caribbean ports. The ready availability of salvage services to commercial shipping created a far different climate from that in the Pacific, where U.S. Navy salvors were "the only game in town" over an area of thousands of square miles. Government-owned and -chartered ships and privately operated vessels carrying government cargo plied the Atlantic, and thus became automatic candidates for Navy salvage whether or not adequate commercial resources were available. Often, however, it was more cost-effective to use commercial salvage services for these ships than to salvage them with Navy resources. Yet, although there were few calls for Navy salvors to assist commercial ships in the Atlantic, a variety of Navy casualties kept them busy.

Kellar

Storms play a major role in salvage, both by creating work for salvors and by disrupting their work. When Hurricane Betsy came ashore in the Gulf of Mexico in September 1965 and struck New Orleans, much work was created. Among the ships sunk by the storm was the survey ship USNS *Kellar* (T–AGS 25). *Kellar*, which lay awaiting the award of a contract to complete her construction, was struck by one of many drifting merchantmen, tore loose from her mooring, and sank somewhere in the Mississippi. A hard-luck ship from the laying of her keel, *Keller* was found about 900 yards up river from her berth. She had rolled over about 120 degrees and sunk, her hull awash, in 30 feet of water some 150 feet from shore between two sewer outlets. The lift craft *Windlass* and *Salvager* undertook the salvage of *Kellar*, beginning on 27 September 1965.

Salvors made a parbuckling rig by rigging *Windlass* on the bow, *Salvager* on the stern, and eight legs of beach gear ashore. This rig rolled *Kellar* upright. Divers then patched the three holes *Kellar* had suffered during the storm and made the hull as watertight as feasible. After a 20-foot-high cofferdam had been built on the forecastle, pumps were placed throughout the ship and a methodical process of sealing all hull leaks began. Before the final raising, eductors were rigged to remove the mud that had collected in the sunken ship. The eductors, with a 3-inch rubber hose used like a vacuum cleaner, moved mud, water, and catfish effectively. The ship was brought to the surface on 10 November and turned over to the Eighth Naval District's industrial manager.

The salvage of *Kellar* was the last job for the ARSDs, the salvage lifting ships known as "junk boats" to their crews because there was a consistent shortage of funds for their outfitting and upkeep. Thus they were highly dependent on disposal sites (junkyards) and the ingenuity of their crews to keep them operating. Salvors being salvors, the ships generally had both necessities and luxuries, but not always in matched sets. The two West Coast ARSDs, *Gypsy* and *Mender*, had been decommissioned ten years before. *Salvager* and *Windlass* were decommissioned and turned over to Merritt Chapman and Scott on 23 November for husbanding. Most of the salvage equipment and many of the men from these two ships went to the Pacific as part of the initial outfit and complement of HCU-One. Less than a year later, on 1 October 1966, Harbor Clearance Unit Two (HCU-Two) was formed in Norfolk.

In contrast to its sister unit in the Pacific, HCU-Two was formed entirely from an existing salvage organization, Service Squadron Eight. However, its concept of operations did not differ. The unit was headquartered on what had been for many years the Service Force's salvage barge YFNB–17 (later redesignated YRST–2). From its founding, Harbor Clearance Unit Two demonstrated the value of small teams of salvors outfitted with the proper equipment deployed to a salvage job by air or other rapid means. In most salvage cases rapid response greatly increases the probability of successful salvage. The new concept of salvage response embodied in these Harbor Clearance Units had become a reality in both fleets.

Bache

A major salvage job reminiscent of *Frank Knox* seemed to be in the offing when *Bache* (DD 470) grounded in high winds and seas 150 yards outside Rhodes harbor, Greece, on 6 February 1968. The response was immediate. *Hoist* and the destroyers *Volgelgesang* (DD 862) and *Conyngham* (DDG 17) were ordered to Rhodes; *Franklin D. Roosevelt* (CVA 42) got under way from Souda Bay, Crete. Task Force 65, the special salvage task force, was activated with Rear Admiral Isaac C. Kidd as Task Force Commander. Commander Huntly Boyd, now Atlantic Fleet salvage officer, boarded a plane in Norfolk and Captain Bill Searle alerted the Murphy-Pacific Marine Salvage Company to stand by with foam. As sometimes happens in salvage, all the frantic action came to naught. In a familiar scenario, one of the violent storms of the eastern Mediterranean winter struck on 18 February. When the storm was over, the entire bottom of *Bache* was gone and with it all chance of salvage. Operations terminated. The wreck of *Bache* was subsequently removed by the Greek salvage company N.E. Vernicos Shipping Co., Ltd., of Piraeus under contract to the Supervisor of Salvage.

Ocean Eagle

In March 1968 the Greek-flag tanker *Ocean Eagle*, fully laden with Venezuelan crude oil, lost steerage in the breaker line, then grounded and broke into two pieces at the entrance to San Juan harbor in Puerto Rico. A major oil spill seemed imminent. Under a contingency plan that authorized him to serve the public welfare in an emergency, Rear Admiral Alfred R. Matter, Commander Caribbean Sea Frontier, placed cleanup equipment on standby. The Supervisor of Salvage arranged for a contractor salvage master to fly in. Commander Boyd also hopped a plane. *Preserver* and two fleet tugs participating in a major fleet exercise nearby, *Paiute* (ATF 159) and *Utina* (ATF 163), were ordered to San Juan.

After breaking free, the tanker's stern section had drifted so that it partially blocked the channel. Following futile attempts by the Navy and local tugs to refloat the two halves of the ship, the owner abandoned the vessel and its cargo. Removal of the wreck and control of the pollution became the responsibility of the Army Corps of Engineers, the agency

On the sloping deck of *Ocean Eagle*'s bow section, salvors discuss their work.

Fleet tugs *Mosopelea* and *Utina*, along with the salvage ship *Preserver*, tow the bow section of *Ocean Eagle* out of San Juan harbor.

charged with maintaining navigable waterways in the United States. The Corps requested the Navy to take charge of the operation. The primary Navy salvage contractor, now Murphy-Pacific Marine Salvage Company, was tasked to remove the stern section while Navy forces undertook removal of the bow.

Before either section could be removed, the pollution problem had to be controlled. A major spill had already occurred and serious ecological damage had been done; oil cargo continued to leak from both sections. Oil removal was accomplished by pumping the oil into barges when the weather permitted putting them alongside. In this operation the newly acquired Prosser 4-inch submersible pumps got their first hard use in the field. While the pumps ran well as designed, it was discovered that they could be accidently connected to run backwards with terminal results. Running backwards, they pumped sufficient liquid to mask the improper hookup, then would inevitably proceed to burn out. This problem, which could be avoided by reasonable care, was overshadowed by the discovery that the pumps would pump oil without the expected burnout or explosive problems when properly used.[31]

When all the oil had been discharged, the bow section was first rotated about 130 degrees and deballasted. *Preserver* then hauled it off the reef and took it to deep water, where it was sunk. Murphy-Pacific handled the stern section similarly.

Navy and Navy-contractor salvage forces had dealt with *Ocean Eagle* promptly and professionally, but not before a major oil spill had occurred. The *Ocean Eagle* incident raised serious questions about the effectiveness of oil-spill contingency plans, available equipment, funding, and required legislation.[32] The authority and resources available to the government to control pollution in salvage cases no longer sufficed. Pollution considerations would be a governing factor in future operations, and both salvors and regulatory bodies had to be prepared to give the problem the highest priority.

Reuben James

In the spring of 1970 a different kind of salvage job showed the flexibility of Harbor Clearance Unit Two. Because of its mobility, HCU-Two had developed an informal specialty in aircraft salvage. When *Reuben*

---

[31] Following the *Ocean Eagle* salvage, and as a direct result of the experience with the pumps, a program to improve the capability of the pumps for pumping oil was initiated. The program was highly successful and resulted in special impellers to pump oils of different viscosities.

[32] History repeated itself over twenty years later with the grounding in March 1989 of the *Exxon Valdez* in Prince William Sound, Alaska. All the environmental concerns stemming from the relatively puny *Ocean Eagle* oil spill were reopened.

James (DE 153), a hulk used for explosive ordnance testing, capsized in the Potomac River off Dahlgren, Virginia, HCU-Two got into the heaviest kind of ship salvage.

Reuben James rested on her starboard at an angle of 87 degrees on a mud bottom. She lay about 2,000 feet from the shore, with about half of her hull out of the water. The commanding officer of Harbor Clearance Unit Two, Lieutenant Jere W. Woodall, was assigned overall responsibility for the job. Lieutenant Commander Karl Keay, the Service Squadron Eight salvage officer, supported him as salvage engineer.

Under the salvage plan, the wreck would be parbuckled to an upright position, then made watertight and pumped. The salvage schedule called for completing the job in six weeks. To parbuckle the wreck, two deadmen were built 120 feet inland and 140 feet apart; each deadman consisted of two 5,000-pound mushroom anchors buried in a pit 12 feet square and 8 feet deep. These anchors were connected by chains to stockless anchors fitted with antiburial baseplates in similar holes closer to the river. From the stockless anchors, 2 1/4-inch chain led through a gradually rising trench to a plate shackle at the bank. These deadmen served as moorings for two flat-deck barges (YC) upon which parbuckling purchases were rigged.

Two standard beach gear purchases from each barge went to chain bridles around gun mounts and the pilot house. HCU-Two's seaplane wrecking derrick *Mary Ann* (YSD–53) was anchored on the opposite side of *Reuben James* from the barges, with rigging bridles around the mast and one gun mount to provide restraint control.

Pumps on gimballed platforms were set up on *Reuben James*, and the YRST–2 was moored stern to stern with the wreck to help keep it in line; all was ready to take a strain. The winches took a light strain on the parbuckling purchases while YSD–53 eased off. Pumps pumped. Everything worked as planned.

Pulling then began in earnest and continued for two days with only two interruptions. One of these came when a chain on one of the deadmen carried away, the other when pins in a plate shackle bent. With the wreck uprighted to 24 degrees, additional pumps were put on board and the holes cut in the starboard hull for drainage were patched. The wreck of the *Reuben James* continued to come upright and became more stable as water and mud were removed. The wreck was ballasted, tested for stability, refloated, and delivered to the commanding officer of the Naval Weapons Laboratory, Dahlgren, two weeks ahead of schedule.

The early completion of the job reflects the deliberate and thorough planning that went into the effort as well as excellent on-scene leadership and coordination. *Reuben James* was the kind of job salvors dream about— no weather crises, no time constraints, and few outside pressures.

The Dredge *Atlantic*

Prevention of pollution provided the motivation for another type of salvage by HCU-Two. Throughout the summer of 1972, the dredge *Atlantic* lay partially submerged in approximately 30 feet of water in a cove on the Elizabeth River in Norfolk. The dredge leaked badly enough to require daily pumping. One evening the pumpman failed to do his job; *Atlantic* filled, sank, and immediately began leaking Bunker C fuel oil into the river.

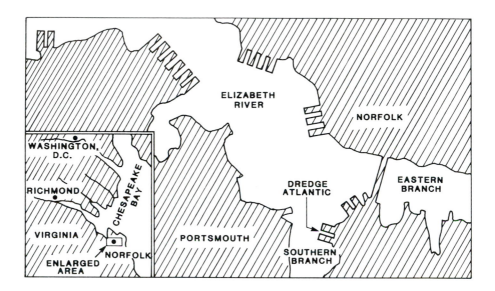

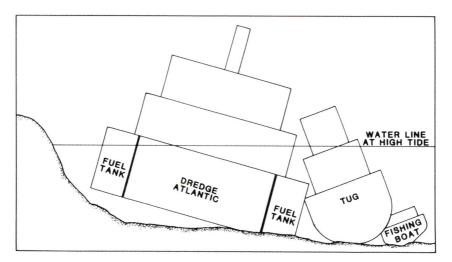

The dredge *Atlantic* presented this aspect to salvors.

292

On 11 August the Commandant of the Fifth Coast Guard District requested assistance from the Supervisor of Salvage in salvaging the dredge to prevent further pollution. The Supervisor of Salvage in turn arranged with the fleet salvage officer, Commander John M. Ringleberg, for the coordination of the efforts of fleet and contractor salvors.

Upon arrival at the salvage site, salvors found not one, but three wrecks. The dredge *Atlantic* was the largest of the three and the closest to shore; oil was leaking from the wing tanks on either side of the single center compartment. The tug *Marquette*, half the length of the dredge, was next outboard, leaning against the dredge. The tug, in turn, rested on a fishing boat half its length.

The first order of business was to contain the pollution and remove the oil from the sunken dredge. Then, the tug would be dragged clear and, finally, the dredge would be raised for disposal. After oil containment booms had been placed around the nest, a skimmer began picking up oil. Double diaphragm pumps pumped oil pocketed inside the dredge and in the tanks to a tank truck onshore. A low-density fibrous sorbent was spread over the water and the dredge collected the oil, which in turn, was loaded into 55-gallon drums for disposal.

Two legs of beach gear rigged from the dredge to concrete block deadmen ashore served as preventers if free surface in the large compartment caused the dredge to become unstable during pumping. Additional beach gear dragged the tug and fishing boat clear.

Atlantic proved no more amenable to salvage than the three dredges in Vietnam. After some patching, the first pumping attempt began with three 10-inch pumps. The attempt failed when a patch over the spoil-pipe opening collapsed. A stronger patch was installed, but the next pumping attempt failed because of leakage through two winch openings and throughout the entire wooden hull. For the third attempt the winches were removed, steel plates were placed over the openings, and the entire hull was wrapped in heavy plastic sheet nailed to the main deck. This attempt worked. The dredge was finally refloated and delivered to a shipbreaker.

Tucumcari

An unusual grounding in the fall of 1972 provided another opportunity for Navy and contract salvors to work together. The hydrofoil gunboat *Tucumcari* (PGH 2), while proceeding foilborne during night operations, struck Caballo Blanco Reef off Puerto Rico. She came to rest nose down in about 3 feet of water and began flooding forward. Salvage officers and divers from HCU-Two were quickly on the scene.

Survey results were summed up at a meeting on *Francis Marion* (LPA 249), as follows:

• *Tucumcari* lay hard aground in 3 feet of water, down by the bow approximately 25 degrees, listing 3 degrees to port with the aft end supported by its two stern struts.

• The hull had been punctured by the forward struts.

• There was no structural damage abaft the forward berthing compartment.

• The after struts appeared sound, but the port foil had been torn away.

• There were several coral heads astern of the gunboat.

After studying the survey results, salvors put together a four-element salvage plan: blast coral heads, using inflatable pontoons for buoyancy, pull with beach gear, and use tugs to guide the vessel off the reef.

The nearest salvage ship was *Rescue* in Kingston, Jamaica. Operated by Murphy-Pacific Marine Salvage Company, *Rescue* was dispatched to the scene under the Navy salvage contract. While she was on her way, Navy salvors on the scene rigged the attachment and pontoons, and underwater demolition team personnel blew the channel.

Rescue arrived and laid her beach gear. When the attachment to the bridle on the gunboat's struts was attempted, mismatching fittings caused some delay. A YTB's 8-inch, fiber towline was secured on *Tucumcari*'s port beam, and a YTM was made up to hold *Rescue*'s head. Initial pulls by the harbor tugs shifted *Tucumcari*'s head but did not free her.

In a bold change to the pulling strategy, a CH–53 helicopter was called in to lift the stern and free the port strut that was embedded in the coral. The YTM would also be rigged to lift the port strut. While waiting for the helicopter, *Rescue* and the YTM continued to pull and moved the gunboat 6 to 8 feet.

The helicopter arrived and made its connection to the boat's after lift pad. Pulling continued. *Tucumcari* came off the reef spectacularly. She heeled over hard to starboard, the aft lifting pad came away, and the foil on the starboard strut broke loose. She had moved some 30 feet aft but was not yet free. *Rescue* and the YTM finished the job and delivered her to *Fort Snelling* (LSD–30).

Throughout the Vietnam era Atlantic Fleet salvors used a broad spectrum of salvage techniques. Some of the operations continued the productive, close cooperation between fleet and contractor salvors that had started before World War II. The tasks undertaken by Harbor Clear-

The hydrofoil *Tucumcari*, while flying on her foils, grounded off Puerto Rico in about 3 feet of water and ripped off her forward strut.

ance Unit Two proved the universal value of rapid deployment of small expert teams of salvors.

Submarine Salvage

There had been no submarine salvage in World War II, and losses since the war had all been in water too deep for salvage with existing technology.[33] Thus the Navy's submarine salvage doctrine remained essentially the same as it had been for the spectacularly successful submarine salvage operations of the 1920s and 1930s. That doctrine had not been exercised, however, because the 1939 *Squalus* operation. Although the submarine salvage pontoons were still around and usable, all the faces

---

[33] In two of the four submarine losses since World War II—*Thresher* (SSM 593) and *Scorpion* (SSN 589)—elaborate deep-ocean operations were carried out to determine the cause of the casualty. In the loss of *Cochino* (SS 345) and *Stickleback* (SS 415), no such operations were necessary because the causes of the losses were known.

were new. No one in the Navy had any submarine salvage experience. Clearly, by 1969 it was time for an exercise under controlled conditions, dubbed Salvex '69, to train salvors in submarine salvage and to assure the continued viability of the Submarine Pontoon Salvage Method developed by Naval Constructor Furer more than half a century before.

Subsalvex '69

Hake (SS 256) had been acquired by the Atlantic Fleet Service Force as a submarine salvage hulk. A two-phase submarine salvage exercise was planned for the late spring of 1969 in the relatively protected waters of Chesapeake Bay.

In the first phase, *Hake* would be raised from about 100 feet with submarine salvage pontoons, rigged fore and aft in pairs. Each pair would consist of a lift pontoon just above the submarine and a control pontoon rigged at a depth of 40 feet. In the second-phase lift, an intentionally more complex operation, two internal compartments as well as ballast tanks would be flooded. The submarine would be raised by pontoons, combined with selected blowing of ballast tanks. The exercise would begin with a simulated rescue operation by *Petrel* (ASR 14) and her McCann chamber.

Captain B. Peters took command of the exercise; Lieutenant Commander Arnold F. Pyatt acted as salvage officer. *Hoist* and *Preserver* were to be the primary salvage ships with *Kiowa* and Harbor Clearance Unit Two providing support. Three flat-deck barges (YC) were assigned to carry air compressors and salvage equipment; YRST–2 would provide general support.

Norfolk Naval Shipyard carefully prepared *Hake*; *Hoist* towed her to the site and she sank as scheduled. *Petrel* moved in, laid her four-point moor, conducted her chamber runs, picked up her moor, and left the submarine to the salvors.

Hoist and *Preserver* positioned themselves in three-point moors over *Hake* and began salvage work. Not surprisingly, the submarine salvage pontoons proved no easier to handle and rig than they had thirty years earlier. When the pontoons were in place and blown, nothing happened. After several hours of blowing with no apparent result, an inspection revealed the pontoons to be a-cockbill and hoses either fouled or pinched. Once the hoses were sorted out, the pontoons were blown without further difficulty. When both control pontoons had surfaced, *Preserver* towed *Hake* to her new grounding site in 74 feet of water and sank her for the second phase of the exercise. Divers surveyed *Hake* and found her resting on an even keel about 2 feet in the mud. Pontoons were unrigged and the second phase of the exercise began. Everything went as planned and *Hake* surfaced with all internal compartments dry except the forward torpedo room bilges.

Subsalvex '69 had been a carefully planned and structured exercise using proven techniques under controlled conditions. It reaffirmed that submarine salvage using pontoons was a feasible method of salvage in water shallow enough for diving. No new technology or techniques were developed for this exercise but valuable training was obtained. Two years later in a similar exercise, Subsalvex '71, things would not go so smoothly.

Subsalvex '71

Subsalvex '71, conducted in the Plantation Flats of the Chesapeake Bay, was originally scheduled for April, but was delayed until late summer so that it would not interfere with the black drum game-fish season.

Some minor changes were made based on the Subsalvex '69 experience. This time pontoons would be towed to the site to prevent the damage that invariably occurred when pontoons were launched from barges. Only one salvage ship would work at any time in the moor over *Hake*, eliminating interference between ships.

Opportune picked up *Hake* and towed her to the site. While *Hake* was on the way, *Preserver* surveyed the site and found it unacceptably deep. A new site nearby was chosen and *Hake* was sunk. Neither the tow nor the sinking had gone particularly well; *Hake* had yawed badly during the tow, and air hoses kinked during the sinking. These minor problems were harbingers of things to come.

Sunbird (ASR 15) moved in to make simulated rescue runs. The submarine rescue ship could not lay a four-point moor because of shoal water near the sunken submarine. A two-point moor had to suffice. Chamber runs started, but the seat on the hatch was fouled and had to be cleared by divers. With the seat clear, the current set the chamber forward of the seat. After some time and some skillful seamanship, the chamber runs were made. During the runs, unplanned flooding in two compartments of the submarine was discovered. With the McCann chamber runs complete, *Sunbird* picked up her moor and departed.

Now salvage work began in earnest. *Preserver* laid a four-point moor, *Utina* (ATF 163) brought submarine salvage pontoons out, and HCU-Two's LCU–1490, acting as a compressor and air control platform, came to the scene. Numerous minor difficulties plagued the rigging of the pontoons; all were overcome. Preparations for the first lift were completed eleven days after the operation began.

The first lift attempt looked like a replay of the *Squalus*; the control pontoon, lift pontoon, and bow broke the surface in a great ebullition. The bow and control pontoon sank. The lift pontoon floated, wrapped in her rigging. An attempt to raise the submarine with the remaining pontoons failed.

Pontoons were rerigged and checked, but before another lift could be made, Mother Nature—who can't seem to leave a salvage job alone—gave a hand. A hurricane blew through. Salvage units buoyed off the submarine and sought shelter.

Mosopelea (ATF 158) was first on the scene after the storm. Her divers inspected the wreck and found *Hake* and the pontoons little affected. The remaining salvage units returned and took up where they had left off. *Opportune* and *Mosopelea* anchored off the bow and stern of *Hake* to control her as she rose. *Preserver* went into a two-point moor parallel to the wreck with LCU–1490 alongside in the Chinese naval tradition, that is, bow to stern. *Hake* and the pontoons were blown. The bow rose but was set back down. The following day *Hake* was lifted and moved to shallower water.

This final lift to surface required more buoyancy than could be obtained with the pontoons and ballast tanks. *Preserver* picked up twelve, 8.4-ton inflatable pontoons from the Norfolk Emergency Ship Salvage Material Pool for this purpose. These were rigged directly to the submarine salvage pontoons. For the lift *Opportune* took position on the bow, and *Preserver* with LCU–1490 alongside astern. Although some of the inflatable pontoons failed, the submarine surfaced and *Opportune* began towing her to shallow water. The boarding crew found considerable flooding in the submarine, but before pumps could be brought aboard, the current caught LCU–1490. Air hoses parted and the submarine began to sink. Hatches were quickly made tight and equipment removed. The submarine sank in 35 feet of water. The following day *Hake* was surfaced again and this time stayed on the surface. Except for picking up the pieces, the exercise had been completed.

Although it was a planned exercise, Subsalvex '71 bore a strong resemblance to a real salvage operation because of its many surprises and unexpected elements. The exercise showed, once again, that if salvors are to cope effectively with the unexpected incidents that are a part of every salvage operation, they must have as much realistic training at sea as possible. Furthermore, training exercises must be frequent and must include the full scope of salvage techniques and equipment.

Guittaro

Subsalvexes '69 and '71 were planned and scheduled exercises; *Guittaro* was not. The nuclear submarine *Guittaro* (SSN 665), under construction at the Mare Island Division of the San Francisco Bay Shipyard with all her nuclear equipment except the reactor aboard, sank at her berth on 15 May 1969.

Response was immediate. The shipyard's salvage officer, Lieutenant Commander James J. Coleman, was on the scene; the Pacific Fleet salvage officer, Commander John B. Orem, flew in from Pearl Harbor; the Supervisor of Salvage, Captain Mitchell, arrived from Washington.

There were many pluses for this salvage. The major one was that *Guittaro* had sunk in a naval shipyard—a large industrial facility with a variety of in-house or immediately accessible resources. On the negative side, a ship under construction posed some salvage problems. Most notably, all the hoses, piping, vent ducts, cables, and other things that passed through the hatches and doors compromised the watertight integrity of the hull.

The salvage plan was straightforward.

• Equipment would be removed from topside and from all doors and hatches.

   • All internal watertight fittings would be secured.

   • All hull openings would be patched or cofferdammed.

• Buoyancy would be restored by pumping and blowing. The two forward compartments would be dewatered first, then the engine room and the auxiliary machinery room. Main ballast tanks would be blown. The submarine should then rise to the surface. However, salvors always have an alternative plan ready. In this case, it called for reballasting, pumping the reactor room, and blowing ballast again.

• A floating crane would be positioned aft to provide additional stability.

Commander Orem took charge, and operations proceeded in accordance with the plan. Hatches and doors were cleared and closed. Cofferdams were designed, built, and fit to the reactor compartment and aft access hatch. With the hull secured and everything ready, blowing started in the forward compartments. Blowing continued for thirteen hours, then pumping started and the crane took a stabilizing strain on the stern. *Guittaro* surfaced as predicted, with enough buoyancy to permit her immediate drydocking. The ready availability of all the industrial resources that were required, coupled with superb individual performances, allowed salvage of *Guittaro* in only three days.

Navy Contract Salvage

There were two basic reasons for increased Navy contract salvage activity during the Vietnam era. First, fleet forces had their hands full with the war and were not available to conduct many of the salvage operations they would ordinarily undertake in peacetime. Second, the Supervisors of Salvage during this period, Captains Bill Searle and Gene Mitchell, took aggressive action to use salvage contractors to perform work for any government agency that needed it. Thus agencies outside the Department of the Navy were made aware that Navy contracts existed and could be effective and economical in satisfying their salvage requirements.

Such use of the Navy contractors helped to strengthen them and to provide a firm base for expansion in the event of wartime mobilization. This had, in fact, been the intent of the Congress when the Salvage Facilities Act was passed in 1948. Furthermore, existing salvage contracts strengthened by the Supervisor of Salvage's competent oversight were cheaper than a collection of individual contracts let by the several agencies with an interest in salvage.

A major change in the Navy's contract arrangements came about in 1967. Murphy-Pacific Corporation, a West Coast construction firm, acquired the marine salvage division of Merritt-Chapman and Scott, and as Murphy-Pacific Marine Salvage Company, became the primary Navy salvage contractor and the only major international salvor operating in the United States. Along with the Navy contract, Murphy-Pacific took over the charter of the salvage ships *Curb* and *Cable* and the operation of *Gear* on the West Coast.

The Drydock and Ol' Man River

One of the last large Navy contract operations undertaken by Merritt-Chapman and Scott was one of the most complex and spectacular salvage operations ever carried out in the United States. When hurricane Betsy, the storm that sank *Kellar*, hit New Orleans on 9 September 1965, the casualties were numerous. The most important to the Navy was the floating drydock AFDM-2 that had been leased to Todd Shipyards Corporation for their Algiers yard. When the storm was over, AFDM-2 was found capsized 3 miles upstream and across the river from her berth. The Mississippi River is not the ideal place for salvage. Divers have difficulty working effectively in the strong currents with zero visibility and large amounts of waterborne debris. On the other hand, New Orleans is located in a major industrial area where all types of support and material are readily available.

A survey and study of the results showed salvage to be technically feasible and economically sound, if a salvage plan could be worked out that would keep the costs within Todd Shipyards' insurance coverage. The alternative to salvage—piecemeal removal—would be an even longer, more expensive process.

Pending development of the full salvage plan, AFDM–2 had to be relocated, a most unusual operation. The wreck was moved three times: first to a site that removed her as a navigational hazard in the busy river, second to a suitable salvage work site, then a third time to return her to the work site after a river crest and surge of debris tore her from her moorings and deposited her across the river. Each time, the dock was moved by a combination of *Curb* or *Cable* and Navy ships *Salinan*, *Salvager*, or *Windlass*. Beach gear was laid upstream and, with a tug steaming into the current, the dock swung like a pendulum into its new position. Seldom do salvors have the opportunity to put a wreck in the most convenient place and orientation for salvage.

The salvage plan called for righting AFDM–2 by rolling her 180 degrees toward the levee in twelve carefully controlled steps. Each step would bring the wreck to a position of equilibrium by combining the pulling force of sixteen sets of beach gear with the buoyancy of inflatable pontoons and the judicious use of internal buoyancy and compressed air. Two former Navy salvage officers, Francis N. Oberle, now vice president of Merritt-Chapman and Scott, and "Bulldog" Thurmond, the company's

The floating drydock AFDM–2 set off a complex salvage job when it capsized and sank in the Mississippi at New Orleans. Here it is partially righted after 4,000 tons of mud had been removed.

project manager, had control of the project. Captain Henry A. Gerdes, Industrial Manager and Supervisor of Shipbuilding for the Eighth Naval District, oversaw the work for the Supervisor of Salvage through two salvage officers, Lieutenants "Horrible" Smith and Bill Klorig.

Careful control of the righting forces was essential throughout the operation. Tensiometers[34] in each beach gear leg helped balance the pull in the sixteen sets and avoid the possibility of structural damage to the dock or overstressing of the rigging and sequential failure. Sixty-eight pontoons were arranged at three levels so that a planned portion of the lift was lost with the dock's rotation, a measure further contributing to precise control.

Before rotation could begin, months of preparation were required to:

• Repair those sections of the hull that would be underwater during the parbuckling operation.

• Install valves, vents, padeyes, and other fittings that would be used during the operation.

• Build the deadmen,[35] set up the winches ashore, and reeve the purchases.

• Prepare a central control station.

Preparations for rotating the dock were completed in mid-July 1966, more than ten months after AFDM-2 had sunk. The initial ballasting and deballasting operation failed to move the wreck as planned because Ol' Man River had packed mud into the hull. Over 2,000 tons of mud was removed after high-pressure water jetting turned the mud into a pumpable slurry. With the mud removed and a pull of more than 550 tons on the beach gear, the dock moved but failed to reach the predicted position. After another 2,000 tons of mud had been removed, the dock began to rotate as the calculations indicated she should.

Only one other major problem interfered with the execution of the salvage plan. The plan called for an essentially level bearing area. Dredging had not been planned, in the belief that the erosive action of the river current, combined with compaction from the weight of the drydock, would sufficiently flatten the bottom. This had not happened and, despite the addition of more ballast, dredging along 360 feet of the drydock's 614-

---

[34] Because no suitable tensiometers were available, they were specially developed by the Navy's David Taylor Model Basin. The readouts at the central control station gave the engineer the ability to stress the beach gear to known levels in sequence, thus providing a greater degree of control than had previously been possible.

[35] Each deadman consisted of four 10-foot long, 12-by-12-inch timbers lashed together with a wire-rope bridle and laid horizontally parallel to the axis of the dock in a 6-foot-deep trench. The trench was faced with 6-foot long, 6-by-6-inch timbers buried vertically.

foot length was required. After dredging, salvage progressed in accordance with the salvage plan until the drydock floated and could be pumped out and stabilized.

The salvors returned the refloated dock to the Todd Shipyard on 25 August 1966, eleven and-a-half months after she had broken free in the hurricane. A job that had demonstrated the value careful and complete engineering to a complex salvage operation was finished, and an important dock would soon return to service.

Alamo Victory

When Betsy's sister Camille struck the Gulf Coast in the summer of 1969, the Supervisor of Salvage used his contract resources to fulfill a salvage requirement of the Military Sea Transportation Service. Three ships, *Alamo Victory*, *Hulda*, and *Silver Hawk*, had been driven ashore together in Gulfport, Mississippi. The operator of *Alamo Victory*, the Military Sea Transportation Service, immediately requested the Supervisor of Salvage to undertake the salvage. The Supervisor, in turn, tasked Murphy-Pacific, and *Curb* sailed from her salvage station in Key West.

Refloating *Alamo Victory* was a classic stranding salvage involving cargo discharge and beach gear, complicated by the need for extensive dredging and debris removal. Six sets of beach gear, all attached to the stern of the ship, were used to pivot *Alamo Victory* around her bow and haul her off the beach. The operation was completed within a month. Once again, the value of the Navy contractor for immediate response when no fleet salvage ships or units were available had been demonstrated.

Regulus

The 1971–72 removal of the Navy stores ship *Regulus* from Kau Yi Chau Island in Hong Kong harbor demonstrated an important use of Navy salvage contractors—releasing fleet resources with heavy commitments from lengthy operations that would stretch them too thin. Initial fleet response and the ultimate decision to turn the wreck over to the Supervisor of Salvage was described earlier in this chapter. The subsequent removal of *Regulus* required many months. The Marine Department of Hong Kong is responsible for that city's harbor and has extremely high standards for salvage operations, and so the conditions for wreck removal had been made clear in writing at the beginning of the operation.

Initially the Supervisor of Salvage proposed to use his long-standing contract with Luzon Stevedoring Corporation to remove the *Regulus*; however, the seldom-used contract had expired. Because of the administrative time required by the contracting office, a new contract could not be issued to Luzon Stevedoring in time for the *Regulus* removal. The Supervisor of Salvage then tasked Murphy-Pacific, whose contract called for "worldwide salvage services." With no resources in the western Pacific, Murphy-Pacific subcontracted to a Hong Kong marine contractor, Fuji Marden and Company, to carry out the work under the supervision of Murphy-Pacific salvage experts. They, in turn, would be under the technical supervision of a Supervisor of Salvage representative.

Captain Cyrus Alleman, one of Murphy-Pacific's more experienced salvage masters and a retired Navy lieutenant, was assigned to *Regulus*, as was Lieutenant Commander James C. Bladh from the Supervisor of Salvage's office. The plan called for cutting the wreck in half, cutting down the hull, taking out as much machinery as possible, then floating the remainder of the stern and bow sections across Hong Kong harbor to Fuji Marden's yard at Junk Bay. Fuji Marden agreed to purchase the scrap and apply the price against the charge for wreck removal.

A pumping system was set up to prevent further sinkage and settling of the wreck; barges came alongside and removals began with masts and the stack. A series of major work disruptions began with a fire started by a cutting torch and continued with other fires, a series of typhoons, and some unexpected holiday celebrations. By late November beach gear had been laid to hold the stern section, but attempts to float it did not succeed because the wreck was not light enough to float clear of impaling rocks. By mid-December the draft aft had been reduced 3 feet and the stern had been pulled clear of a major impalement.

Shortly after the new year began, the stern section pivoted around 75 degrees and floated free. Some of the beach gear was shifted to the forward section and lightening continued; by the end of the month, both sections floated free of the island. In late February, after careful preparation for tow across the busy harbor, the two sections were delivered to Fuji Marden's Junk Bay yard and final cleanup at the Kau Yi Chau Island was completed. No trace of *Regulus* remained.

The Supervisor of Salvage realized that, as a fallout of the *Regulus* operation, the inadvertent expiration of the Luzon Stevedoring contract had left the Navy without an important resource in the western Pacific. This loss was particularly significant because of the increased importance of the naval base at Subic Bay and the fact that Philippine cabotage laws, modeled on those of the United States, did not allow salvage by foreign-flag salvors in their waters. The Supervisor of Salvage took immediate steps to reestablish the contract with Luzon Stevedoring. Under the terms of the new contract, diesel-powered machinery replaced the gasoline-powered Emergency Ship Salvage Material Pool equipment that had been given to Luzon Stevedoring following World War II and had been well maintained. In addition, the MV *Virginia City*, originally the *Pakana* (ATF 108), which had been transferred to the Bureau of Mines after World War II but was now unneeded, passed to Luzon Stevedoring on a conditional sale agreement.[36]

A short time later and as part of a plan to increase contractor salvage support, United Salvage Pty., Ltd., of Melbourne, Australia, received a contract for standby salvage services in the South Pacific. Neither ships nor equipment were provided to United Salvage under this contract.

The Summer of '72

The summer of 1972 saw two major harbor clearance jobs in widely separated parts of the United States. The jobs were conducted concurrently by one Navy contractor, Murphy-Pacific, for one government agency, the Army Corps of Engineers. During the same summer in the far reaches of the Pacific, Luzon Stevedoring, operating under its new contract, undertook what was rapidly becoming a major part of any salvage operation, the removal of oil from a grounded ship.

The Last Days of the *Warrior*

The first of the two harbor clearance jobs involved the *Oriental Warrior*. The 535-foot passenger-cargo ship caught fire at sea off Jacksonville, Florida, on 27 May 1972. The ship was towed to the Jacksonville Port Authority container pier at Blount Island on the St. John's River, where it sank in 34 feet of water during fire-fighting efforts.

The most immediate problem was to prevent a major spill of bunker oil from *Oriental Warrior*. After the oil spill problem had been brought under control, the burned-out hulk had to be removed, because it blocked the container terminal. When the ship sank, the owner had abandoned it. Pollution control then became the responsibility of the Coast Guard; removal was the responsibility of the Corps of Engineers. Both agencies requested assistance from the Supervisor of Salvage, who assumed control of the operation on 10 June and tasked Murphy-Pacific to assist.

Because of the strong currents in the river and the wakes of passing ships, a triple boom was placed around the stern of *Oriental Warrior* to contain any oil spillage. Two skimmers, pumping directly to a recovery barge, and sorbents were put to work inside the boom. Vacuum trucks, pressurizing tanks through sounding tubes, bucket skimming, and hot

---

[36] Several years later, Luzon Stevedoring Corporation was effectively nationalized by the Philippine government. When this happened, the Philippine government unilaterally abrogated the contract and refused to return either the ship or the salvage equipment.

The burned-out hulk of *Oriental Warrior* sank alongside Jacksonville's new container port, blocking two important berths.

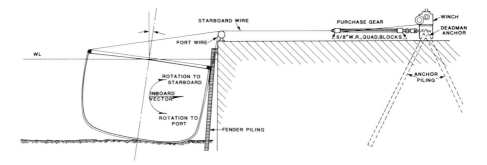

This rigging was used to keep *Oriental Warrior* upright.

tapping[37] recovered the oil that had spread throughout the ship. The oil recovery operation terminated on 15 July and salvage planning began.

Lieutenant Commander Bladh, recently returned from the *Regulus* disposal, was designated as Supervisor of Salvage representative. Murphy-Pacific assigned Captain Robert T. Belsher, a veteran of early HCU-One operations in Vietnam, as salvage master, and Captain Bruce B. McClosky as assistant salvage master. Mr. Alex Rynecki, also a former Navy salvage

---

[37] Hot tapping is an oil removal method adapted for salvage from an oil industry technique. It allows removal of oil from submerged and inaccessible tanks without spillage. Hot tapping consists of four basic steps: (1) a spool piece is attached to the tank boundary using a velocity actuated stud gun; (2) a gate valve is bolted onto the spool piece; (3) an extendable rotary cutter, fitted to the top of the gate valve, extends through the valve and spool piece and cuts the tank boundary; (4) when the cut is completed, the cutter is withdrawn, the valve closed, and the cutter replaced with a suction hose to discharge the tank. This method was first used in salvage during removal of oil from the sunken tanker *Arrow* at Chedabucto Bay, Nova Scotia, in the winter of 1970.

officer, was salvage engineer. Diving was subcontracted to Taylor Diving and Salvage of New Orleans; additional diving was done by Buck Steber Company.

The salvage operation was basically a patch-and-pump salvage complicated by two factors. First, the fire had severely damaged the structure of *Oriental Warrior*, causing, among other problems, buckling of the main deck. To avoid structural collapse and loss of ability to refloat the ship, the main deck had to be kept in tension. Second, the partial immersion of the main deck resulted in a significant loss of transverse stability. The removal of low weight in the form of bunker fuel carried in the double-bottom tanks and the consumption of an indeterminate amount of cargo by the fire also contributed to a critical problem of stability.

To refloat the ship, floodwater had to be removed from the engine room and the contiguous, and now common, number three hold. However with the weight of this water removed, the ship's center of gravity would rise, the other liquid weight in the ship would shift, there would be a large free surface with its consequent loss of stability, and the hull would be in a sagging condition on the verge of structural collapse. The addition of solid weight and water ballast at the ends of the ship would put the ship in a hogging condition and keep the main deck in tension— the condition where it had some residual strength—as well as keep the center of gravity low.

Three steps added weight in the needed places:

- Forepeak, after peak, and deep tanks under number one and five holds were pressed full with water.
- More than 400 cubic yards of concrete was placed in the shaft alley. The concrete also sealed the shaft alley against flooding.
- One-ton lead pigs on loan from the National Contingency Reserve in Louisiana were placed in number one and two holds. Following refloating the pigs were removed and returned to their normal storage.

To restrain the ship's rotation and to hold it against the pier, ten sets of parbuckling wires hauled the ship close to special fender pilings and restricted upsetting moments. As *Oriental Warrior* lay starboard side to with a starboard list, eight parbuckling wires were rove for rotating the hull to port. These wires attached to the starboard deck edge, ran across the ship, down the port side, under the ship, and up and over a fairlead on the pier edge. Two wires for rotating to starboard ran from the deck edge directly to the pier edge fairleads. From the pier edge fairleads, all the wires ran either to winch-hauled beach gear purchases or continuous-pull linear pullers.

The unstable soil conditions in the area required heavy construction for the deadmen. At each station three 14-inch steel pilings were driven and 4-by-4-by-5-foot reinforced concrete caps were placed on top of the pilings. Winches or pullers were then mounted on the caps.

With the parbuckling system under construction and weight going into the ship, the diving crew and a crew of carpenters worked to restore watertight integrity to the hull and to subdivide the ship for pumping. The divers encountered an unusual problem similar to the one faced on *Regulus*. A portion of the cargo in *Oriental Warrior* consisted of uncured animal hides. The decay of this organic material generated hydrogen sulfide, forming an acid when dissolved in water and bubbling off in dangerous quantities. The hydrogen sulfide generation could not be controlled, but its effect could be reduced by flushing water through the holds and ventilating them to reduce its concentration.

With all preparations complete, pumping finally began on 22 September. Initial pumping operations were plagued by numerous leaks that had to be chased down and stopped by divers. Once the leaks were under control and the parbuckling wires tensioned, pumping went forward and the ship refloated. With the ship afloat, as much floodwater as possible was stripped out, hull openings previously buried in the mud were patched, and the lead ballast was removed.

Consultation between the Supervisor of Salvage, the Corps of Engineers, the Coast Guard, the Environmental Protection Agency, and local groups resulted in the decision to tow the *Oriental Warrior* to sea and sink her in deep water as quickly as possible. The last days of the *Warrior* had been full ones; now they were over.

Sidney E. Smith

The second job for the Army Corps of Engineers in the summer of 1972 started near Port Huron, Michigan, in the early hours of 5 June 1972. The 9-knot current of the St. Clair River caught the bow of the Great Lakes freighter *Sidney E. Smith* and carried her into the path of *Parker Evans*. Following the collision, the 66-year-old *Smith* rolled on her starboard side and sank, partially blocking the busy waterway. The current of the St. Clair wasn't through with the old laker. It scoured the bottom that supported the sunken ship until the bow section broke away and began sinking into the scoured hole. By 8 June the bow section was completely submerged.

At the time of her sinking, *Smith* had an estimated 49,000 gallons of Bunker C oil on board. The danger of a major spill was compelling. The Coast Guard reacted quickly and effectively, setting up systems to remove the remaining oil from the ship and to control pollution should a spill

The Great Lakes ore carrier *Sidney E. Smith* lies capsized and sunk in the St. Clair River near Port Huron, Michigan. A bit later, the ship broke in two. Both sections settled into the bottom as the current, clearly visible here, scoured the bottom sand away.

occur. A cooperative effort using the ADAPTS oil pumping system[38] of the Coast Guard's National Strike Force commercial equipment removed the oil from the ship.

Immediately after the accident, it appeared that *Sidney E. Smith's* owners, Erie Sand Steamship Company, would take responsibility for the work. However this did not occur and the Corps of Engineers requested the Supervisor of Salvage to remove the wreck. As is typical of financial arrangements for wreck removal, the Corps of Engineers provided funding to the Supervisor of Salvage on a cost-reimbursable basis. The corps could then bring suit against the owner to recover the government's costs.

As with the *Oriental Warrior*, the Supervisor of Salvage immediately tasked Murphy-Pacific to do the work. A project team was formed with Commander Robert B. Moss, USNR, as the Supervisor of Salvage representative and Mr. Earl Lawrence, Lieutenant Craig Mullen, and Mr. Jerry Totten as his principal assistants. The Murphy-Pacific group was led by

---

[38] ADAPTS is an acronym for Air Deliverable Anti-Pollution Transfer System. The system consists of a submersible, 10-inch hydraulic pump and associated equipment including a diesel-driven hydraulic power source that may be parachuted for pickup on the surface. The system was developed to Coast Guard specifications to meet that agency's statutory responsibility in pollution control operations.

salvage master Robert McKenzie. The district engineer provided a derrick barge with a 60-ton crane and a variety of small craft.

The salvage plan gave priority attention to the stern section because the bow was completely submerged and going down further each day. Urethane foam in the cargo holds would lighten the section so it could be dragged ashore. Foam was chosen over the more conventional pumping and patching to eliminate the complex underwater work inherent in patching and to give salvors the flexibility to work around structural damage.

The strong currents in the river made underwater work outside the hull impossible and called for unusual methods for divers to gain access inside the hull. Tubes 60 feet long and 30 inches in diameter were designed and placed for diver access. Divers would descend inside the tube, protected from the current, and enter and exit the hull through a window in the tube. Preparations for foaming the holds would include removing residual coal cargo and river mud from the holds with airlifts and fitting hatch covers to contain the foam.

Initial plans called for moving the stern section to the beach on its starboard side. However bottom surveys showed a ridge only 23 feet deep, followed by a depression nearly 90 feet deep between the stern section and its destination. Attempting to drag the hulk over the ridge would increase the ground reaction to the point that the section could not be moved. Parbuckling the section upright would allow it to be dragged across the ridge without developing additional ground reaction. Attachment points were chosen so that the section could be first parbuckled and then dragged by a pull acting at the same points.

Pulling the *Sidney E. Smith* presented a problem not encountered in either the AFDM-2 work in New Orleans or the *Oriental Warrior* job in Jacksonville. In those jobs the shore was broad enough to lay out beach gear purchases and to design deadmen without worrying about the space they occupied. This situation did not exist in Port Huron. A railway line and an asphalt plant limited the space on the bank and dictated pulling with continuous-pull linear pullers that did not require long purchases and an anchoring system that occupied a minimum of space.

The pullers were manufactured for the job by Luker Manufacturing Company to a standard design. Deadmen were constructed by drilling into the soil at a 45-degree angle, placing multiple strands of wire rope in the holes, and pressure grouting the rope in place. The wire rope anchored concrete blocks to which the linear pullers were attached with wire rope bridles. The pullers rested on timber skids, where they could change their angle as the wreck moved.

Salvage of the stern section went forward with only minor problems; the most severe was the quality of the foam. Heating the chemicals to maintain the minimum temperature required for formation of good-quality foam solved this problem. On 21 July with all in readiness, a strain was taken. Nothing happened. Divers found the stern and bow sections still connected by shell plating and some longitudinal members. Explosives and oxy-arc torches cut the connections. Before the second pull attempt, additional foam was added and the pulling arrangement modified to increase the pull. On the second attempt the stern moved 31 feet toward the shore. Still more foam went in to insure that the stern dragged through the depression easily. Just after midnight on 6 August the final pull began; by 2:30 a.m. the stern section was secured alongside the bank and the salvors' attention turned to the bow.

The salvage plan for the bow, now at a maximum depth of 90 feet, had the same elements as the stern: foaming and pulling. However the depth of the bow section complicated its salvage. A mooring to hold the derrick barge in position over the bow was required; an improved foam delivery system with in-line heating of chemicals had to be used; and cofferdams reaching from the surface to the bottom of the wreck were needed for diver access.

In addition, uncertainty about the location of the conveyor boom and the amount of coal and river mud in the ship called for more pulling power. Two heavy winches with a combined pull of 500 tons were set up to complement the hydraulic linear pullers. A huge amount of work was required. The most serious problems came from handling the 100-foot-long diver access cofferdams in the current.

By 21 September *Smith*'s bow section had a negative buoyancy of between 400 and 600 tons, light enough for a pull. Pulling began at 7 o'clock that night. When rigging failures caused the pulling effort to be secured, the bow had moved 40 feet closer to the shore but still blocked the channel. After rigging repairs, pulling began again until the section moved within 100 feet of the shore, clear of the channel.

Scrapping and refloating of the stern section began while bow foaming and pulling operations were in progress. Weight was removed from the ship and piled ashore; watertight boundaries were established within the section and pumped dry. After the stern section was moved clear, the bow was dragged clear of the channel. With the bow section near the shore, the conveyor boom and cofferdams were cut off, critical hull openings sealed, and the section parbuckled to a nearly upright position. More foam went into the hull and topside structure came off until, on 29 October, the bow was heavy and listing but afloat.

Attempts by the Corps of Engineers to sell the two hull sections at auction were unsuccessful, and the sections were sunk in a dredged excavation as a dock and erosion bulkhead. *Sidney E. Smith* had found her final resting place.

The Green Sea Turtles of West Fayu

In December 1971 the Liberian-registry, break-bulk cargo vessel *Solar Trader* ran aground on a shallow reef at West Fayu Island, an atoll in the Trust Territories of the Pacific. No salvage attempt was made, and after some time the ship began slowly leaking oil into the sea. The leakage presented a hazard to the breeding grounds of the green sea turtle, a food staple for the people of neighboring islands. In June 1972 the Coast Guard requested assistance from the Supervisor of Salvage to remove the oil. The Supervisor of Salvage tasked Luzon Stevedoring with the work.

A survey made by Luzon Stevedoring on 16 June formed the basis for the oil removal plan, which was to moor a barge or hold it with a tug off the *Solar Trader*, tap into piping systems, and pump oil to the barge with positive displacement pumps. The remote location of the *Solar Trader* required a backup plan and the transport of everything necessary to the scene. The alternate plan called for installing prefabricated cofferdams around tank-top manholes and pumping the tanks with submersible pumps. Oil-containment and clean-up equipment would be on hand.

The tug *Stanford* with a 1,000-deadweight ton barge left Manila for West Fayu on 26 June and arrived at the site on 8 July. Mr. Denis E. Irons of the Supervisor of Salvage's office and Lieutenant William Key, the salvage officer at the Ship Repair Facility, Guam, were on board. Sea conditions caused by the passage of typhoons made it advisable to moor the receiving barge inside the lagoon rather than offshore and to run the discharge hose across the reef. The salvors found much of the starboard side of *Solar Trader* open to the sea and only a limited amount of oil in the ship.

Pumping began after sunrise on 14 July and continued until dusk, when it secured because of the difficulty of detecting oil spill in darkness. The pumping continued in this dawn-to-dusk manner through 17 July, when the compartments were washed down and the hose contents water-pushed through the hose to purge it. To leave the vessel as secure as possible against further spillage, salvors opened all tanks, including those with submerged manholes. This led to the discovery of additional oil and a small spill, which was cleaned up by a skimmer. The oil in the double bottoms and all remaining petroleum products were then removed from the ship. On 23 July *Stanford* and her barge got under way for Manila. The green sea turtles of West Fayu were safe from the destructive effects of the oil.

In the summer of 1972 the Supervisor of Salvage had used commercial contracts to assist the U.S. Government in advancing the maritime interests of the United States in the three important and very different operations just examined. The value of these contracts in serving the

nation's interest under the control of an agency with the technical expertise to supervise them properly had been demonstrated again.

Salvage Posture After Vietnam

The first new class of salvage ships built since the war, the *Edenton*-
class salvage and rescue ship, had joined the fleet during the Vietnam
era. The capability of these ships seemed great, but had not yet been
proven in the unforgiving venue of actual salvage operations. And there
were only three of these ships, one in the Atlantic and two in the Pacific,
certainly not enough to provide a force large enough to replace the aging
World War II-vintage salvage ships and fleet tugs.

In fact, the roles of the salvage ships and fleet tugs were not at all
clear. Difficulty in manning the salvage fleet had caused Navy planners
to look at the possibility of manning auxiliary types of ships with civilian
crews and operating them under the auspices of the Military Sealift
Command, much as the Royal Navy has traditionally done with their
auxiliaries. One of the ship types to be manned by civilians was the fleet
tug. With civilian manning, the World War II-vintage fleet tug and her
successor, the T–ATF–166 class, would be essentially point-to-point tugs—
a far cry from the rescue-towing and combat salvage roles for which the
older ships had been built. There was no serious consideration given to
civilian manning of the existing salvage ships at this time, but the ships
were nearing the end of their useful life.

The Harbor Clearance Units and the concept of quick response and
flyaway salvage that they represented had added a new dimension to
Navy salvage, one that would dominate the immediate future. The Harbor Clearance Units formalized and expanded the method of operation
demonstrated early in World War II in the Pacific, when men like Lebbeus
Curtis and Emile Genereaux flew off to salvage jobs to do the work with
whatever resources they could muster. These units and the concepts that
they represented were the most significant changes in Navy salvage since
the passage of the Salvage Act in 1948.

For the first time at the end of a war, steps were taken to develop a
salvage organization in the Naval Reserve. Reserve Harbor Clearance
Unit detachments were organized at ten locations around the United
States and divided so that there were equal numbers with HCU-One and
HCU-Two as parent units. These reserve units were manned by officers
and men who had gained experience in the field while assigned to Harbor
Clearance Units and salvage ships. As salvors they loved their trade and
took advantage of every opportunity to practice it, to keep their hands
in, and to hone skills that would otherwise grow dull through inaction.
The Naval Ships Systems Command strongly supported the units. The

Reserve Harbor Clearance Units and supporting units in the Naval Ship Systems Command headquarters were established largely through the efforts of the Deputy Supervisor of Salvage, Commander Robert B. Moss. A reserve officer himself, Moss undertook much of the laborious, unexciting, and vital work of justifying the units; the dividends of his valuable work may never be fully paid.

Just as William A. Sullivan dominated Navy salvage during World War II, two leaders among the many of the Vietnam era stand out. They are the successive Supervisors of Salvage who, between them, occupied the office for almost nine years, Captains Willard F. Searle and Eugene B. Mitchell. When Captain Searle became Supervisor of Salvage in the fall of 1964, the office was only a small technical office in the Bureau of Ships. But the forthcoming conflict and expanding ocean technology offered an opportunity for aggressive and imaginative leadership that would:

- Expand the technical function of the office.
- Broadly interpret the law and responsibilities of the Navy under the Salvage Act.
- Develop new sophisticated salvage techniques.
- Improve the equipment that fleet units were using, including wholesale dieselization of the aged gasoline-driven equipment.
- Institute a broadly based research program in ocean technology related to salvage and recovery.
- Establish the Navy's position in newly emerging salvage-related disciplines such as pollution control and abatement, deep submergence systems, and deep diving.
- Expand the Navy's capability by using salvage contractors, thereby gaining flexibility and ensuring the continued existence of salvage and salvage-related industrial capability.

When Captain Searle left office in 1969, each of these goals had begun to be realized, and the office of Supervisor of Salvage was becoming an important player not just in the Navy and the United States, but in the world salvage community. This growth continued under Captain Mitchell, who reaffirmed the key role of salvage in the Navy, the Navy's position as the government's agency for salvage, and the Navy's technical excellence among salvors of the world.

Two difficulties, however, would not clear quickly. First, despite efforts in Washington and in the fleets, no office in the Chief of Naval Operations organization had yet been designated as the sponsor for salvage.

This meant that salvage often lacked the advocacy it required in the annual budget battles and policy formulation processes.

A second negative factor was the low priority that the fleet staffs gave to the involvement of fleet forces in salvage operations that were not clearly their responsibility. Heavy demands on salvage units during the Vietnam war, the particular difficulties affecting the Navy in the early 1970s, the Supervisor of Salvage's ability and willingness to use contractors—all contributed to this attitude. The inevitable result was that the experience levels, and then the performance, of fleet units declined.

Thus although the record established by Navy salvors should have assured them of a clear place in the sun, this was not the case. The next few years would be interesting ones.

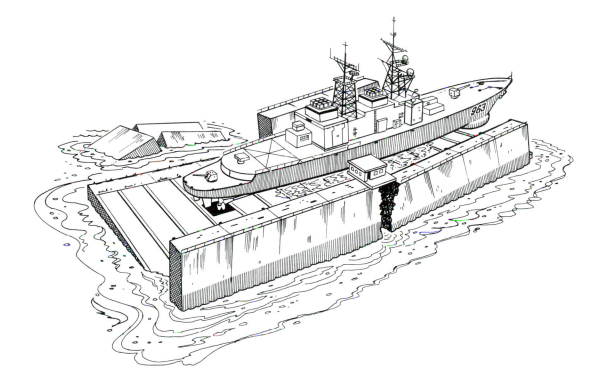

CLOSE CALL

CHAPTER EIGHT

Moving Toward the Nineties

The thirteen years from 1974 to 1987 were a time of relative peace for the United States although, as powerful nations have done throughout history, the nation found occasion to use its great military force in response to crises around the world. For the Navy's salvage forces, however, this period was a time of concern and great, if not always consistent and planned, change. In seeking a soundly based future for U.S. Navy salvage, many approaches were tried. Some worked better than others. All affected each element of the Navy's salvage ability: people, ships, equipment, and operational doctrine. During this period, the salvage ships were wearing out and many of the methods that had served well for years no longer seemed appropriate. By the early 1970s, the fleet's salvage capability was perceived by professionals to be declining. The reasons were clear: Although no salvage job goes perfectly, ineptness was becoming too general, and fundamental mistakes that should not be made were too common.

The Atlantic and Pacific Fleets and the Supervisor of Salvage worked hand in glove to identify the causes of the declining capability and to develop recommendations for the Chief of Naval Operations (CNO). Two events that took place in Washington were giant steps toward clarifying and continuing the Navy's salvage role.

The first event was scarcely noticed outside the capital. It involved the reassignment of salvage responsibility to the Surface Warfare and Logistics offices of the Chief of Naval Operations staff. For the first time since World War II, salvage had an advocate that could take its case to the highest levels. The fight for a fair share of budget dollars, for recognition of need, and even for continued existence would be far easier from now on. In the early stages of the shift, the split of sponsorship responsibilities between the offices of Surface Warfare and Logistics was ill defined, but would soon be clarified.

The second important event began with a series of presentations in which the Supervisor of Salvage, Captain Robert B. Moss, detailed the Navy's declining salvage position to his immediate superiors and new sponsors. Ultimately, on 30 April 1979, Captain Moss gave a highly refined version of this presentation to the Chief of Naval Operations Executive Board; it was to become a watershed in the history of Navy salvage.

There were several results, either direct or indirect. First, a five-ship building program was authorized to maintain a total Navy force of ten salvage ships. Second, the Emergency Ship Salvage Material funding base was revitalized. Third, the fragmented sponsorship issue was clarified, with primary sponsorship of the Navy salvage program assigned to the Surface Warfare office. With these moves the dragon of civilianization of the Navy's salvage program, which had been lurking in the background, was finally slain. In sum, the Navy had now adopted a structured and sensible salvage policy.

The Elements of Salvage

The new salvage policy eased considerably the struggle for direction that had affected each element of Navy salvage in the preceding years. The challenge now became one of building, or rebuilding, all aspects of the Navy salvage force to meet the demands of the future.

Much of the problem of declining Navy salvage capability lay in its human resources. Although Navy salvors remained as dedicated and resourceful as ever, experience levels were dropping in the officer wardrooms, chief petty officer quarters, and crew quarters. This decreasing experience began at the highest level with the commanding officers of the salvage ships. The so-called "mustangs" who had traditionally commanded salvage ships and tugs were no longer being assigned to those jobs. The mustangs had been seasoned officers, skilled in bridge and seamanship evolutions, and familiar with salvage prior to assuming command. They had the experience necessary to evaluate the performance of their crews and to take advantage of every opportunity to train them and hone their salvage skills. Instead of the mustangs, front-running unrestricted line officers were being assigned salvage commands. They were certainly men of great potential, but their training and experience lay far afield from salvage. They had neither the specialized seamanship skills nor the experience to recognize the salvage deficiencies of their crews.

Other officers were not encouraged to seek successive tours in salvage. Personnel managers saw concentration in the salvage specialty as detrimental to an officer's career in surface warfare. As a result, valuable men left the Navy to remain in salvage work as civilians. Some inappropriate assignments were made. In several cases, men who had been quartermasters on nuclear submarines received warrants as boatswain and assignments to salvage ships. They did not have the knowledge of specialized salvage rigging needed to lead their deck crews. Enlisted experience dropped as the frequency of salvage jobs diminished following the end of hostilities in Vietnam, and as the ability of officers to provide technically sound leadership for their crews declined.

Establishment of the Special Operations Officer designation in 1978 was a major step toward solving the problem of officers' inexperience. Officers were now permitted to specialize in salvage, and career patterns were developed to ensure that commands were held by men well qualified in the technical aspects of their jobs. The foundation was laid for the development of a cadre of well-trained senior Regular Navy salvors that could be expanded in wartime. This core of salvage specialists was supported by salvage-trained engineering duty officers. The combination gave a breadth and depth of professionalism to Navy salvage that had not been possible before.

Fortunately, Reserve Harbor Clearance Units had already been formed. Now, they began to pay off as the numbers of experienced, active-duty salvors dropped. Within a short time many of the Reserve units had a level of experience higher than active-duty units. To preserve the salvage skills of these Reserve units, training programs were set up for their annual two-week active duty with their parent Harbor Clearance Units. Reserve units were included in fleet operations whenever possible, and some operations were specifically assigned to the Reserves. The Reserve units quickly became proficient in locating work in their home ports for drill weekends. The Reserve headquarters unit worked with the Supervisor of Salvage's office not only to administer the Reserve program, but also to plan for mobilization and work on various headquarters projects.

To improve communications at all levels within the Reserves and with their active-duty counterparts, the Supervisor of Salvage sponsored a program of annual meetings. With strong support from the fleet commanders and the office of the Chief of Naval Reserves, the Reserve units were accorded high-priority status. The Reserve Harbor Clearance Unit program succeeded not only in providing a capability that had not previously existed in the Naval Reserve, but also in serving as a model of cooperation between the Regular Navy and the Naval Reserve.

Ships

Ships, or rather the lack of them, also contributed to the decline in salvage capability after the Vietnam era. By this time, the World War II-built salvage ships and fleet tugs were reaching the end of useful life. Ships were being retired and, in the case of the fleet tugs, being turned over to the Naval Reserve or to the Military Sealift Command, where they operated as point-to-point towing ships without salvage crews. The fleets expressed growing concern that the number of available ships were declining to the point where only minor salvage jobs could be supported.

Except for three salvage and rescue ships commissioned in 1972 and 1973, the building program begun in 1975 for *Powhatan* (T–ATF 166) class tugs was the first for oceangoing tugs since World War II. Seven of these ships were built in two groups: the first four in the fiscal year 1975 shipbuilding program and three more in the fiscal 1978 program. These ships were quite different from their predecessors. A primary difference stemmed from the economics of both construction and operation, which dictated that they be manned by civilians and operated by the Military Sealift Command.

The hull and overall configuration of these ships is similar to commercial, offshore supply boats and anchor-handling tugs. There is a large, open, low freeboard deck aft, and the superstructure is well forward. The ships were built with no automatic towing winch. They have no organic salvage capability other than a quick-reaction, high-holding-power anchor designed to hold a stranding casualty until a more capable salvage ship arrives. The ship serves as a platform for salvage equipment; Navy crews are provided on a case-by-case basis for specific salvage work.[1] There is little capability in these ships for the types of combat salvage and rescue towing that the *Navajo*-class fleet tugs provided so well in three wars and in the intervals of peace between them.

Following much official and unofficial discussion of their characteristics, and as a direct result of the Supervisor of Salvage's presentation to the CNO Executive Board, the *Safeguard* (ARS 50) class of salvage ships began construction in the early 1980s.[2] These are true salvage ships, fully equipped and capable of sustained salvage operations. They are a logical evolution of the previous salvage ships and have avoided many of the problems of the salvage and rescue ships (ATS) that resulted from detail designers' not fully understanding and appreciating how salvage ships do their work. They carry an automatic towing engine that suits them for rescue towing as well as for stranding salvage and assistance in harbor clearance. In compliance with Navy policy existing at the time of their

---

[1] The ships were built with quarters for Navy salvage crews and facilities to support them and the equipment they bring aboard. Neither people nor billets were specifically designated for salvage crews.

[2] The first ship was constructed in the fiscal year 1981 shipbuilding program, two more in the fiscal 1982 program, and the fourth ship in the fiscal 1983 program. All were constructed by Peterson Builders at Sturgeon Bay, Wisconsin. At this writing, funding for the fifth and final ship remains deferred.

design and construction, the ships were designed for 25 percent of their crew to be women. They were so crewed.

With the construction and commission of these ships and the decision to put Navy crews aboard, the concept of an organic salvage capability in the Navy was reaffirmed over the idea of manning the Navy's salvage organization with civilians.

Equipment

Unlike the wholesale introduction of diesel-driven equipment in the Vietnam era, the development of salvage equipment since then has been evolutionary. Improvements and modifications to existing systems have been the norm, along with a moderate infusion of improved equipment. An important initiative has brought about major changes in the Emergency Ship Salvage Material System.

As discussed earlier, the Emergency Ship Salvage Material bases located at the sites of various naval activities were not under the direct control of those who would use or be responsible for the use of the equipment. The stories are legion of poorly maintained and incomplete equipment being received on salvage jobs. In 1971, a committee of experienced salvors and administrators assembled to develop a more satisfactory Emergency Ship Salvage Material System. Sixteen bases with standard allowances and inventory control systems resulted. Wherever possible, these bases were located at sites of field activities of the Naval Ship Systems Command and were supported from two pools, one on each coast. The allowance of the pools, several times that of a base, contained material for deep-ocean recovery, oil-pollution control, submarine salvage, and a variety of ocean engineering work. The system had been vastly improved.

Within a few years, however, budgetary restraints forced a significant reduction in the number of salvage material bases. This caused great concern in the fleets, which felt that concentrating all emergency ship salvage material in two U.S. bases and two overseas bases would significantly decrease response time. Concern was particularly strong in the Pacific, where distances are great and the existence of an Emergency Ship Salvage Material base on Guam had recently allowed critical work to move ahead without delay. Fleet planners foresaw that in the event of a major incident or multiple casualties, other priorities for air transportation would delay shipment of urgently needed salvage equipment. Despite these objections, the reduction in bases and consolidation of the system went forward. Later analysis showed the correctness of the fleets' position.

Following the Supervisor of Salvage's 1979 presentation to the CNO Executive Board, the Emergency Ship Salvage Material funding base was increased. This permitted the opening of additional material bases in Pearl Harbor; Sasebo, Japan; and Aberdeen, Scotland. Another move placed the management of the Emergency Ship Salvage Material System in the hands of contractors directly responsible to the Supervisor of Salvage. This resulted in major improvements in the operation and readiness of the system. The problem of control of inventory and maintenance of equipment had been solved.

Unlike other aspects of salvage, emergency ship salvage material management is neither glamorous, nor fun, but it is one of the most important functions of the Supervisor of Salvage's organization. There are few things more frustrating and disheartening to a salvor than to have equipment arrive that is inoperable or missing vital pieces. To paraphrase Benjamin Franklin, for want of a pump fitting, the ship may be lost. The restructuring of the material maintenance and supply system, along with the continuing evolution of salvage equipment during the 1970s and 1980s, has contributed significantly to the overall strength of U.S. Navy salvage forces.

Operational Concepts and Doctrine

Operational concepts and doctrine may be considered the element of salvage that bonds the other three elements into a single entity. Without sound common sense and the lessons of experience formalized into operational concepts and doctrine, even the best salvors, ships, and equipment cannot function effectively. Concepts and doctrine must then be able to change to meet new kinds of casualties, the conditions under which they can be expected to occur, and the restraints that will govern possible responses.

If there is a single lesson to be learned from naval history, it is that operational doctrine must be continuously modified to suit the changing situation. Nowhere is this truer than in salvage. Salvage doctrine is extremely sensitive to new technologies, new ship types, new strategic and tactical concepts, and new weaponry. Salvage history is replete with examples of changing concepts and doctrine. For instance, early concepts in World War II reflected the expectation that salvage ships would be used primarily in harbor clearance. This changed at Casablanca, the first harbor to be cleared, when salvage ships proved impractical for the work. Initially during the war, salvage ships were held out of the immediate combat zone and tugs brought them their work. An appreciation of the ability of salvage ships to work effectively close in to casualties and the sheer quantity of work changed this practice. Salvage ships were soon in the thick of it. Salvage ships and tugs were used interchangeably during and after the Korean War. This doctrine resulted from the relative scarcity of ships. The concept of fly-away salvage became reality with the employment of Harbor Clearance Unit One in widely separated locations in Vietnam. It became refined in Harbor Clearance Unit Two and was further refined when Harbor Clearance Unit One returned to Pearl Harbor and maintained Pacific-wide responsibilities.[3]

For some time after their formation, naval planners had looked askance at the Harbor Clearance Units. There had never been a need for such units to conduct harbor clearances in peacetime. In reality, the term "Harbor Clearance Unit" fell well short of describing the capabilities of these versatile organizations. Thus the name that had been instrumental in establishing the units in the first place had served its purpose and had become a liability. The solution seemed simple—change the name. After much agonizing, the active units and the Reserve units they supported became Mobile Diving and Salvage Units on 1 February 1982, the sixteenth anniversary of the establishment of Harbor Clearance Unit One. The new name represented much more accurately what the units actually did and stressed their responsibilities in the fly-away salvage concept.

Concern for the environment began to have a profound effect on salvage doctrine and operations. Even before World War II, salvors had seen the undesirable effects of oil spills. With the increased tanker traffic that followed World War II came the inevitable casualties—*Mission San Francisco, Potomac, Ocean Eagle, Torrey Canyon, Pacific Glory, Amico Cadiz, Exxon Valdez.* More and more, the hazards of pollution from cargo and even bunkers were coming to the attention of both a public feeling increasing anxiety about damage to the environment and their legislators. The Navy accepted the responsibility for its own spills, and the Supervisor of Salvage took on the major responsibility within the Navy for pollution control. He began to work with the Long Beach Naval Shipyard and other organizations within and outside the Navy to develop pollution containment systems and cleanup equipment. At the same time, he formed an organization to respond to pollution incidents with appropriate equipment and expertise.

The passage of federal water-pollution-control legislation assigned major pollution control and abatement responsibilities to the Coast Guard. That agency now had the right and responsibility to assume control of any operation when it believed insufficient attention was being given to pollution aspects. Increased capability accompanied this new responsibil-

---

[3] The concept of flying men and material from central pools developed concurrently in commercial salvage. The increasing cost of ship operations that made it impractical to keep ships on salvage station and the increasingly specialized nature and cost of salvage equipment forced the change.

ity. The Coast Guard rapidly trained and equipped its National Strike Force for response to pollution incidents. The Navy took responsibility for pollution control in all operations involving naval vessels and installations, but the Coast Guard's position, authority, and responsibilities had to be considered and its capabilities used.

In executing his responsibilities for dealing with the pollution aspects of salvage, the Supervisor of Salvage purchased pollution control and cleanup equipment and positioned it in the Emergency Ship Salvage Material System. Open-ocean and incident-to-salvage pollution control became a major responsibility of the Supervisor of Salvage's office and oil-spill response equipment became major items in the inventory and operation of the Emergency Ship Salvage Material System. These changes signaled an important shift in operational emphasis. When a ship casualty occurred, the primary consideration had now become protecting the environment; saving the ship itself took second place.

The contractor situation also changed. During the period beginning after World War I, when Merritt-Chapman and Scott had been formed, until the mid–1970s, the Navy had only one American salvage contractor. This contractor had conducted salvage operations throughout the world. In the late 1970s, for complex corporate financial reasons, Murphy-Pacific Corporation, including Murphy-Pacific Marine Salvage, was forced into bankruptcy. The Supervisor of Salvage recognized that no other single salvage contractor could provide the same geographic coverage. To make the best of this situation and to encourage participation by and competition among smaller contractors, the United States was divided into zones and separate contracts were let for each zone. Eventually there were three zones: East, West, and Gulf Coasts.

The weakness of using an American-based salvage company throughout the world had come to light during the removal of *Regulus* in Hong Kong. Before the removal was complete, the Supervisor of Salvage renewed his contract with Luzon Stevedoring for salvage services in the western Pacific and the Indian Ocean. Good business practice and the nationalization of Luzon Stevedoring prompted competitive procurement after the initial contract expired. United Salvage of Melbourne, Australia, received a contract for Australian waters. Discussions with European salvors regarding contract salvage coverage in European and Mediterranean waters broke down when agreement on contract terms could not be reached.[4]

---

[4]European salvors prefer to work on open-form salvage contracts, whereby the financial aspects of the salvage are settled by arbitration. The Navy prefers predetermined rates for services. Open-form contracts are difficult for the Navy, because commanding officers of ships have no authority to contract for services or to bind the United States to settlement in foreign courts.

Salvage Operations

How the changes in salvage elements—salvors, ships, equipment, and operational concepts—along with pollution considerations and contractual arrangements affected Navy salvage can best be illustrated in the salvage operations conducted during this period.

In peacetime, as in the past, Navy salvage forces and their contractors have performed a variety of salvage services not only within the Navy but also for foreign governments, commercial interests, and a variety of other government agencies. The diversity of the customers for the Navy's salvage services clearly demonstrates the broad need for these services and their value to the maritime world and the nation as a whole.

International Customers

Salvage work for international customers may vary from salvaging a warship for a friendly nation that cannot do the work itself to major foreign affairs efforts. Salvage for international customers deserves, and usually gets, attention at the highest levels of government because the prestige of the United States is obviously on the line.

THE SUEZ CANAL CLEARANCE

Shortly after the end of the United States' military involvement in Vietnam, there came an unusual opportunity for the Navy salvage organization to play a highly visible role in global politics. The Suez Canal had been blocked since the Six Day War of 1967, but after the Yom Kippur War of 1973 and the disengagement of forces that followed in 1974, the possibility of reopening the canal could be considered. With the canal open, trade routes that had been blocked could be reestablished and Egypt would have a badly needed source of hard currency income.

The Suez Canal Authority originally intended to undertake the clearance as a purely commercial venture and had nearly completed negotiations with a major international salvor.

Murphy-Pacific Marine Salvage Company, fighting hard for the contract, advised the Suez Canal Authority that, as the principal U.S. Navy salvage contractor, it had access to the heavy lift ships *Crilley* and *Crandall*. The impressed Egyptians, who were familiar with the capabilities of these ships,[5] saw a possibility of the United States' paying for the clearance work as an adjunct to its involvement in the minesweeping and

---

[5] *Crilley* and *Crandall* under their original names, *Energie* and *Ausdauer*, had participated in the 1956 clearance of the Suez Canal under charter to the British Admiralty.

ordnance removals in and near the canal. Negotiations began immediately. On 11 June 1974 the United States and the Arab Republic of Egypt concluded a bilateral agreement for U.S. assistance in the removal of ten wrecks from the Suez. Under this agreement, the Navy would be the principal salvage agent and could use contractors other than Egyptian nationals.

The Navy declined to commit its own salvage forces to such a lengthy effort and instead used its standing contract with Murphy-Pacific. Mobilization of *Crilley* and *Crandall*, laid up at Subic Bay, began along with negotiations for the heavy lift cranes *Thor* and *Roland* belonging to Bugsier Reederei und Bergungs of Hamburg, West Germany, the former owners of *Crilley* and *Crandall*.[6] Captain J. Huntly Boyd, the Supervisor of Salvage, became Commander Task Group 65.7, the salvage force.

The salvage work was a part of a large-scale operation to reopen the canal. The overall effort consisted of French, British, American, and Egyptian forces working to sweep mines and clear unexploded ordnance, both ashore and in the water, as well as to clear wreckage from the canal. These job were all preparatory to the dredging necessary before the canal could be opened.[7]

Captain Boyd had support primarily from officers and specialists on his Washington-based staff. These men operated both on scene and in Washington to provide the extensive technical, logistical, and management support that the complex operation required. The Murphy-Pacific project manager was Commander Joseph F. Madeo, Jr., USN (Ret.), a former commanding officer of Harbor Clearance Unit One. Senior operational and technical people were almost all former Navy salvage men, many of them Harbor Clearance Unit veterans.

Ten wrecks—a passenger ship, a cargo ship, a tanker, two tugs, four dredges, and a concrete caisson—in various attitudes and depths blocked the 101-mile-long waterway. One of the dredges, *Dredge 23*, had been salvaged during the 1956 clearance and returned to service; she would be one of the nine wrecks scrapped this time. All nine wrecks were lifted, either intact or in sections, and transported to one of three designated dump areas along the canal. Four of the nine wrecks—the tug *Mogued*, the dredges *Kasser* and *Dredge 23*, and the concrete caisson, were lifted by *Crilley* and *Crandall*. *Thor* and *Roland* cleared the passenger ship

---

[6] *Thor* and *Roland* were heavy-lift, self-propelled shear leg cranes capable of lifting 500 tons 95 feet above water with a 36-foot horizontal clearance on the main hooks. The pontoon was equipped with two gin tackles that, when used with the hooks, were capable of a total lift of 1,000 tons. Bugsier built these craft after selling *Energie* and *Ausdauer* to the U.S. Navy.

[7] American forces in Task Force 65 under Rear Admiral Brian McCauley and later Rear Admiral Kent Carroll were divided into four categories: minesweeping operations (Nimbus Star), land ordnance clearance (Nimbus Moon–Land), underwater ordnance clearance (Nimbus Moon–Water), and salvage operations (Nimrod Spar).

The wreck of the passenger ship *Mecca* lies athwart the Suez Canal. *Mecca* was the largest and one of the most formidable obstacles to the 1974 clearance of the canal.

An artist's conception of *Crilley* and *Crandall* lifting the small tug *Mogued* in the Suez shows how the lift wires form a cradle to support the wreck.

Mecca, the cargo vessel *Ismailia*, the tanker *Magd*, the tug *Barreh*, and *Dredge 22*. The tenth wreck, the 30-inch suction cutter dredge *15 September*, had been scuttled with very little damage. This wreck was parbuckled and lifted to the surface by *Thor* and *Roland*, pumped out, and delivered to the Suez Canal Authority for refurbishment. The clearance work started on 29 May 1974 and ended almost seven months later on 20 December.[8]

As with other salvage operations of this size, the technical problems encountered were numerous and varied. Many of them, as is typical of heavy lift operations, were not predictable but were solved with ingenuity and hard work.

To facilitate the clearance, trim and rig teams moved ahead of the lift craft and prepared each wreck so that the expensive lift craft and cranes would be tied up for the minimum time. This technique proved effective. Each of the two types of lift craft demonstrated its limitations. Several times *Crilley* and *Crandall* were limited by the absence of gradually shelving water into which to lift the wreckage. The shortage of sufficient

---

[8] A detailed account of the operations in the Suez was published by the Supervisor of Salvage following the operation. That report discusses the operation, the problems encountered on each wreck, and their solution in detail. Supervisor of Salvage, *Suez Canal Salvage Operations in 1974*. (Washington: Naval Sea Systems Command) 1975.

dredges to create the necessary inclined planes compounded this problem. *Thor* and *Roland* were limited in quite different ways—in outreach and an inability to move sections being lifted without moving the pontoons. These problems are inherent in shear leg cranes and salvors can usually work around them.

Logistics and support operations during the clearance demanded the lion's share of management attention. The cities on the bank of the canal, along with all their support facilities, had been virtually destroyed by long years of war. The conditions compared with those encountered by harbor clearance units in North Africa and Europe in World War II with one important difference. In the Suez, no huge, well-equipped support force provided berthing, messing, transportation, communication, medical services, and the many other kinds of support that a large salvage operation requires. The Suez Canal Authority, Murphy-Pacific, and the Navy worked together on logistical problems. It was tough going.

The Suez Canal Authority supported the clearance operation to the limit of its abilities, but the breadth and standard of support required was greater than it could sustain. The situation became aggravated as the authority faced competing priorities for its resources during preparations for the canal's opening. The lesson was clear: Any operation of this sort should be as self-contained as possible.

Training of Navy salvage officers and senior enlisted people formed an important part of the operation. Excess Egyptian currency available to the project was used effectively by the Supervisor of Salvage to assure that almost all active-duty salvage officers and many senior enlisted people were ordered to Egypt to observe and participate in some stage of the work.

The salvage ship *Escape* and, later, *Opportune*, deployed with the Sixth Fleet in the Mediterranean, carried out additional salvage work up and down the canal. These ships worked constantly in the canal during their deployment, using every technique available, doing work of major importance to help reopen the canal, and providing unsurpassed training for their crews.

The heavy lift craft *Crilley* and *Crandall*, purchased for use in the Vietnam War but finding only modest employment there, provided their most important service to the United States in the Suez—though not in their salvage work, which could have been done by other means. Their importance lay in the influence they exerted on the Suez Canal Authority and the government of the Arab Republic of Egypt to choose Murphy-Pacific and the U.S. Navy to clear the Suez. After the operation, the craft were refurbished in Greece and returned to lay up in the James River.

These craft provide a useful lesson in salvage management. Just as the operators of a commercial enterprise must be concerned with their return on investment, so too must the planners and executors of naval salvage efforts. For the commercial operator the definition of return on investment is simple—money made relative to money spent. For the naval planner, the definition is not so simple. It includes factors such as the development of national assets, the pursuit of national interests, and the accomplishment of military objectives. Cost effectiveness is a consideration; the question, Does the result justify the cumulative expense? must be answered.

Crilley and *Crandall* did not provide much return on the investment required for their purchase and conversion. The liftships saw little salvage service in Vietnam and were expensive to prepare for Suez and refurbish afterwards. A strong argument could be made that their purchase was a mistake. However when they were being purchased, technical developments were changing the face of heavy lifting. Offshore oil and construction needs were forcing the development of heavier cranes than had ever been built before. As the work of the shear leg cranes *Thor* and *Roland* side by side with *Crilley* and *Crandall* in the Suez Canal showed, the cranes surpassed lift ships in effectiveness. *Crilley* and *Crandall*, once outstanding tools, had simply been overtaken by technology.

The importance of the reopening of the Suez Canal and its impact

Captain Huntly Boyd (left), Supervisor of Salvage, and Commander James J. Coleman confer during the Suez clearance.

on world shipping and world affairs are best left to historians knowledge-able in these fields, as is any discussion of the correctness of the U.S. involvement. That it was an excellent salvage operation under the most trying conditions is not open to question. The award of the Distinguished Service Medal to Captain Boyd, one of three awarded to salvors during and since World War II,[9] bears clear testimony to the priorities of the United States and the Navy at the time.

TWO KOREAN SHIPS

The Suez clearance demonstrates the role salvage played in a highly visible political arena. A double grounding some nine years later illus-trates the more usual cooperative salvage effort between nations.

On 13 March 1983, following a dress rehearsal for an amphibious landing at Tok Son Ri, Korea, the Korean LST *Suyong* (LST 677) broached in suddenly increasing wind and surf. In an incident reminiscent of the grounding of *Seize* at Clipperton Island, the Korean salvage ship *Gumi* (ARS 26)[10] grounded on nearby rocks while attempting to free the landing ship. The Korean Chief of Naval Operations requested U.S. assistance. USNS *Catawba* (T–ATF 168), under the command of Captain Wesley D. McKenzie, sailed from Pohang, Korea, and *Beaufort* (ATS 2), under the command of Commander Frederick B. Fisher, sailed from Sasebo, Japan. *Catawba* arrived early on the morning of 14 March. With no salvage gear or crew aboard, the T–ATF could do little. *Beaufort* steamed in the following day after having radioed ahead a recommendation to ballast both ships down until the situation could be defined by a complete survey. Several amphibious force ships were ordered in to provide logistics sup-port. The first days of the operation were confused because senior Korean officers at the scene were anxious about the possible loss of two ships and had priorities that were not exactly the same as the American salvors. After some discussion the decision was made to salvage the salvage ship first despite the more severe damage and more perilous position of the LST.

Two additional Korean salvage ships arrived, *Yong Mon* (ATA 31) and *Chang Won* (ARS 25). *Chang Won* laid two legs of beach gear and got into harness for pulling *Gumi*. *Beaufort* laid two legs of beach gear and rigged for a pull. The first pull terminated after almost three hours when the attachment point for *Beaufort*'s tow wire carried away. Weight was re-moved from *Gumi* before the next pull. This pull rotated the ship but did

---

[9] The two other medals were awarded to Captain Homer Wallin for his salvage work at Pearl Harbor following the Japanese attack, and to Commodore W.A. Sullivan for his work as Chief of Navy Salvage during World War II.

[10] Aficionados of coincidence will recall that the hull number of *Seize* at the time of her grounding was also 26, apparently an unlucky number for salvage ships.

not move it, confirming suspicions that rocks impaled the ship.

Catawba and *Yong Mon* shifted beach gear for the two salvage ships to improve the angle of pull, but no pull could be made until enough buoyancy had been gained to raise *Gumi* clear of impaling rocks. *Beaufort* sailors identified compartments that could be blown dry and turned to making fittings; *Yong Mon* laid one leg of beach gear and got into harness. The weather turned miserable with high winds and seas. On the morning of 25 March, the compartments were blown and and tension slowly built up on the beach gear. *Gumi* was lively; she came free in the early evening and was towed away by *Chang Won*.

Attention now turned to the badly damaged *Suyong*. Weight had been removed and numerous holes patched while salvage operations on *Gumi* were going on. *Chang Won* returned to the scene and laid one leg of beach gear; two small tugs made up alongside. A salvage party from *Beaufort* stayed aboard pumping, patching, and plugging. In the early evening of 29 March *Suyong* came free and was towed to Pohang by *Catawba*.

In Korean salvage as well as in the Suez clearance—salvage operations that had differed in almost every respect—the Navy had provided services that assisted friendly nations and brought credit to itself in highly visible situations.

Commercial Ship Salvage

When the Navy undertakes salvage of commercial ships, the operations are almost as visible as work for other governments. The Navy enters the world of commercial salvage, a world dominated by professional mariners of other nations and, as the accounts of the accounts of the *Andrea Lukenbach* and *Quartette* salvages have shown, one filled with legal and financial considerations not relevant to most Navy salvage.

There has been more Navy involvement in commercial salvage operations in the Pacific than in other areas because of the scarcity of commercial salvage services in that ocean, particularly in the mid-Pacific. However the salvage of commercial ships is not always undertaken as a service to shipping when no other salvage services are available. In fact, the types of operations, the reasons for them, and the results have been so varied as to defy easy categorization. The incidents described below are examples of some of the ways Navy salvors have become involved with commercial shipping in peacetime.

THE SAGA OF *CARIBIA*

Some ships that normally have great dignity behave badly when they are in an undignified situation. The British battleship *Warspite* did so during her wartime tow in the Mediterranean and beat the shipbreakers by going ashore during her final tow to their yard. The liner *Caribia*[11] had a similarly independent mind.

Caribia had been laid up in New York for some years when she was sold to breakers in Taiwan and taken in tow by the West German tug *Hamburg* in 1974. The tow was uneventful until it reached the coast of Baja California, and ran into a Pacific hurricane. *Caribia* saw her chance. *Hamburg* lost the tow in the rough weather, but recovered it some four days later. As the tow approached Hawaii, *Caribia* began taking on water and listing. *Hamburg*'s agents in Honolulu requested Navy help. *Takelma*, with a salvage crew from Harbor Clearance Unit One, was dispatched to rendezvous with the ship. Salvors boarded the liner at sea and found leakage into the shaft alley. *Takelma* carried no portable submersible pumps, so electric pumps and a generator were flown out and put aboard by a Marine Corps helicopter. The flooding was stopped and repairs made during a stop in Honolulu.

The old lady had been foiled twice, but she wasn't through. *Hamburg* and *Caribia* approached Guam in foul weather. Harbor tugs asked *Hamburg* to approach more closely than planned. Close inshore, *Hamburg* lost an engine. In the high wind, the tow took charge and began dragging the tug toward the rocky shore. *Hamburg* headed into the sea and slipped her tow. *Caribia* appeared to be holding course fair for the entrance to Apra harbor. Rather than enter the harbor, however, she yawed and grounded on the end of Glass Breakwater. Her bottom gone, she fell onto her side and began to slide off the breakwater. Within twenty-four hours she had sunk completely out of sight.

Caribia had beaten the shipbreakers, but she now posed a serious problem. Where was she? Did she block the only harbor entrance to ships bringing food and other supplies to the island? Could the ballistic missile submarines based at Guam safely make the passage into and out of their home port? The fleet salvage officer flew in. To define the position of *Caribia* and determine what danger she presented, a search team of a Supervisor of Salvage contractor was ordered in. The situation was so serious that Rear Admiral John D. Johnson, Commander Service Group Three, also flew in to Guam. *Bolster* (Lieutenant Commander John Siemer) sailed from Subic to augment *Grasp* (Lieutenant Commander Robert J. Hillis), which was home ported in Guam and already on the scene.

The high resolution side-scan sonar needed by the search contractor made a classic journey to Guam. The sonar had to come from the Gulf of Mexico, but a piece of Hughes Tool Company equipment bumped it

---

[11] Originally the Cunard Line liner *Caronia*.

off the airplane in Houston. It couldn't be found in the Los Angeles air cargo terminal until technicians entered the holding area, identified it, and carried it to its flight for San Francisco. In San Francisco someone phoned in a warning that the air cargo on the Guam-bound flight contained a bomb. All cargo came off the plane, destined to be left in San Francisco until it could be cleared. Only after a Fleet Ballistic Missile priority had been invoked were FBI sniffer dogs brought in and the sonar cleared. It arrived in Guam as the only piece of cargo on the flight. Salvage officers met the aircraft on the runway and, with the cooperation of U.S. Customs officials, loaded the equipment directly from the aircraft into a truck.

By the next afternoon, the position of the wreck had been defined, and precautions for ships passing through the harbor entrance had been determined. As far as the Navy was concerned, the saga of the *Caribia* was done. What had started off Hawaii as an assist to commercial interests had become a very different job in Guam, undertaken for very different reasons. *Caribia* was abandoned to the Corps of Engineers, which decided to contract her removal competitively. Nippon Salvage of Tokyo won the contract and removed the wreck by cutting it up and removing the pieces with a 1,500-ton shear leg crane. The operation was

Stormy seas break over *Caribia* after the liner, released from her tow, drifted onto the end of Glass Breakwater at the entrance to Apra harbor, Guam. The ship later broke forward of the bridge and sank, partially blocking the harbor entrance.

unprofitable. The location of the ship and unusually bad weather for prolonged periods raised costs beyond the limits of the fixed-price contract. Nevertheless Nippon Salvage stayed on the job and completed the work.

THE LOSS OF *LINDENBANK*

In late 1975 the fivefold, British-flag freighter *Lindenbank* grounded and broached, port side to, on Fanning Island, a small atoll some 1,000 miles south of Honolulu. The owners requested assistance from the Navy because the nearest commercial salvor was in the Caribbean, some eighteen days away. The fleet salvage officer, Commander Bill Milwee, flew to the scene in a chartered aircraft along with Captain John Hellendorn, a Salvage Association surveyor,[12] and Captain Alistair McNab, the owner's marine superintendent. *Brunswick* (ATS 3) and later *Bolster* sailed from Pearl Harbor.

The salvage plan called for beach gear to be laid to the stranded ship and to salvage ships in harness in a manner that would rotate the bow to starboard and take the ship off by her head. *Lindenbank* would have to be lightened, which presented a problem. She carried bulk copra, a cargo that, except at specially equipped ports, can only be discharged by hand because of its oiliness. Marshallese laborers hired from the island proved to be less-than-diligent workers. The work, however, was urgent because the ship lay on a lee shore where the swell, with a fetch that ran virtually unimpeded all the way to New Zealand, built into great mounds that pounded the ship toward the beach. As soon as the salvage ships arrived, preparations were made to lay beach gear and Navy crews turned to shoveling the oily, insect-infested cargo into cargo nets and dumping it over the side. It was slow, nasty going.

Three types of problems plagued the operation. The first factor, the inexperience of the salvage ships' commanding officers and crews, played a major part in this operation. There was an inordinate amount of difficulty with basic salvage seamanship like passing lines and rigging and laying beach gear, primarily because the crews had seldom laid beach gear before. Legs were laid in the wrong place or, even worse, in water so deep they may still be falling. Some of the commanding officers displayed timidity in ship-handling close alongside and in recovering beach gear—routine operations for seasoned salvage crews. The position of *Lindenbank*

---

[12] The Salvage Association, Ltd., sometimes called London Salvage, is composed of experienced salvage surveyors and other maritime professionals. Operating from offices throughout the world, they represent the interests of Lloyd's of London underwriters who hold hull insurance on ships. As was the case with *Lindenback*, Salvage Association surveyors are usually present at all casualties where the hull insurance is written on the London market.

and her fittings called for compromises in rigging. These compromises resulted in wire ropes being bent around too short radii and in sharp nips in them that reduced their capacity to carry loads, so that many of them failed. Numerous wire ropes failed. The second problem was caused by some unexpected equipment failures; the most spectacular was a bitt that split down the middle. Amazingly, despite the large number of rigging failures there were no injuries. The final problem was the ships. Many of the weaknesses in design that limited the effectiveness of the new salvage and rescue ship class showed up in the course of the *Lindenbank* operation.

• A bow thruster not designed for sustained operation made it hard to hold position for long periods.

• Salt water evaporators had been designed to use waste heat from the engines as a heat source, meaning that *Brunswick* had to break out of harness and steam offshore at night in order to produce fresh water.

• Very slow anchor windlass speeds made weighing anchor in confined waters a hazardous process.

• Bower anchors did not provide sufficient holding power.

• Engines and generators operated from a common fuel source, making loss of all propulsion and electrical power inevitable from a single casualty.

After numerous failures, *Brunswick* returned to Pearl Harbor. *Safeguard* replaced her.

Operations continued for five weeks, during which more than 6,000 tons of copra were removed by hand. *Lindenbank* had become very light and nearly ready to refloat when, on a night of howling winds punctuated by the snapping of the lines holding her to seaward, she was driven farther ashore, beyond salvage. The ship and the operation were abandoned. The lessons of the operation were clear and steps were taken to remedy the problems. Salvage training was bolstered to improve the readiness and salvage skills of the crews. A program of ship alterations began to eliminate as many as possible of the material deficiencies in the ships. Some conditions inherent in the design of the ships could not be modified. Salvors would have to learn to live with those limitations.

ANANGEL LIBERTY

In late April 1980 the four-year-old Greek freighter *Anangel Liberty* carrying 19,200 tons of bags of kaolin clay[13] grounded on French Frigate

---

[13] A fine-powdered, nontoxic, refined silica and alumina mix.

Shoals while making 15 knots. French Frigate Shoals in the Hawaiian archipelago is a national wildlife preserve inhabited by two endangered aquatic species. What followed, though it involved Navy salvors and a commercial shipping casualty, was not purely a case of the Navy providing salvage assistance to industry. It illustrates several of the factors that have entered modern salvage—particularly the importance of pollution and how far pollution considerations can extend.

Upon receiving news of the stranding, the owner's Honolulu agent hired the tug *Mana* and sailed her for French Frigate Shoals. Mr. Rod Sambrook of the Salvage Association's New York office headed to the scene. The Coast Guard, acting under its Federal Water Pollution Control Act authority, entered the picture because of the pollution danger from the ship's fuel oil and possibly from her cargo. Commander A.D. Utara, USCG, was appointed federal on-scene coordinator; the Regional Response Team was activated. An overflight was made by Commander Utara and Lieutenant Kenneth Harvey of Harbor Clearance Unit One to inspect the ship and her condition. The Coast Guard quickly determined that the owner had taken insufficient action to free the vessel and control pollution; it then exercised its legal prerogative and placed the operation under federal control. The Coast Guard asked for and got Navy assistance. *Reclaimer* (Lieutenant Commander Bruce Banks) got under way with a detachment from Harbor Clearance One; *Beaufort* (Lieutenant Commander Rob Wells) followed. Commander Robert Bornholdt, Pacific Fleet salvage officer, flew in, as did the Coast Guard's pollution control specialists, the Pacific Strike Team.[14]

Technically, *Anangel Liberty* was a straightforward salvage job. It only required getting some ground tackle out to prevent the ship from broaching or being driven farther ashore, jettisoning cargo to reduce the weight of the ship and the ground reaction, laying beach gear, and hauling the ship off.

That is the way the salvage would have been done at another time and place, but not at French Frigate Shoals in 1980. Here, the potential for pollution in jettisoning the cargo became a major factor in the salvage approach.

The Environmental Protection Agency confirmed that the kaolin clay was nontoxic and raised no objections to jettisoning the cargo to lighten the ship. The U.S. Fish and Wildlife people felt differently. They had no data on what the effects of reasonably large quantities of kaolin dumped into the area's fragile ecology would be. Throughout the operation, they

---

[14] The Pacific Strike Team, a part of the National Strike Force, is a Coast Guard group specially trained and equipped to deal with pollution and potential pollution incidents of all types.

continued to exert pressure to unload both the cargo and fuel from the ship by lighter.

Commander Utara evaluated the position of *Anangel Liberty* as a seaman and saw the impracticality of lightering the clay cargo as she lay. It would take several days to bring a lightering craft to French Frigate Shoals; even then, putting it alongside was simply too dangerous to consider. Leaving *Anangel Liberty* on her strand ran the risk of exacerbating the problem already presented by her stranding. As the pressure from outside continued, Commander Utara made the decision to dump the cargo.

Upon arrival, Commander Bornholdt and *Reclaimer* conducted a complete survey and laid one leg of beach gear to the freighter to hold her. Cargo jettisoning began. *Reclaimer* laid three more legs of beach gear, one to the ship and two for herself. The tug *Mana*, *Reclaimer*, and the four legs of beach gear pulled. *Anangel Liberty* didn't move. More cargo went over the side. *Beaufort* arrived and laid two legs of beach gear. With approximately 2,200 tons of cargo removed, the two salvage ships and the tug *Mana* pulling, the legs on *Anangel Liberty* pulling, and the ship backing full, she floated. *Anangel Liberty* continued her voyage to Japan after no measurable environmental damage.

The *Anangel Liberty* operation demonstrated that possible pollution hazards in sensitive areas can often be dealt with by a commonsense approach to the pollution problem and expeditious salvage of a ship to remove the source of the problem. Comparing this operation with the ill-fated *Lindenbank*, one striking difference appears—the effectiveness of the beach gear operations. One reason for the difference is obvious. In the *Anangel Liberty* operation the officers commanding the two salvage ships were both salvage professionals and special operations officers. Both had many years of salvage experience, knew what could be done, and knew how to do it. Their experience made the difference.

Work for Government Agencies

As the government's principal agent for salvage, the Navy undertakes work for many federal agencies. Not surprisingly, the Coast Guard and the Navy work closely in marine casualties and the Coast Guard often seeks early consultation from the Navy.

A minor case that clarified an important principle involving Navy salvage authority occurred in September 1976 when an ex-Navy rescue tug of uncertain ownership sank in Duwamish waterway in Seattle. The Coast Guard became involved because the tug spilled oil into the waterway. Navy assistance was requested. A crew from Harbor Clearance One led by Lieutenant (j.g.) Timothy B. Stark flew in and, with equipment

Reclaimer and *Beaufort* pull on *Anangel Liberty*, grounded hard on French Frigate Shoal.

from the Emergency Ship Salvage Material base at Puget Sound Naval Shipyard, refloated the tug long enough for the Coast Guard's Pacific Strike Team to remove the oil. The cost was modest. The ruckus came after the job when a Navy salvage contractor complained to the Naval Surface Force Commander,[15] Vice Admiral W.R. St. George, that the contractor should have been called on for the job and that the Navy had competed unfairly. After consultation with his legal staff and salvage officer, Vice Admiral St. George took the position that when salvage work became the responsibility of the government, the government was obligated to do the work as economically as possible. The Navy had no obligation to use contractors when Navy resources could do the work more cheaply and gain the extra benefit of training. The matter has not been raised again.

COAST GUARD

When the Coast Guard experiences casualties to its own vessels, it calls on the Navy because it has no salvage resources of its own. The losses following collisions of the Coast Guard cutters *Cuyahoga* (WIX 157) in 1978 and *Blackthorn* (WLB 391) in 1980 illustrate this aspect of interservice cooperation.

---

[15] The Cruiser-Destroyer Force, Amphibious Force, and Service Force had been combined in 1975 to form the Naval Surface Force.

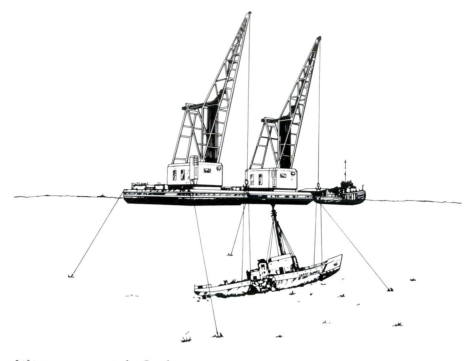

Lifting arrangements for *Cuyahoga.*

Cuyahoga

In October 1978 *Cuyahoga* at 51 was the oldest cutter in the Coast Guard as well as one of the smallest. She had, in effect, been put out to pasture, serving for training cruises. On one such cruise in the Chesapeake Bay she collided with the merchant ship *Santa Cruz II* and sank, taking eleven of her crew down. A Coast Guard search operation located and buoyed the sunken cutter, and Coast Guard divers determined that no survivors were trapped in the wreck. Harbor Clearance Unit Two (Lieutenant Commander Rob Wells) was mobilized and a diving team flew to the scene.

Immediate operations centered around recovering the bodies of the lost crewmen and determining the condition of the vessel so that a salvage plan could be prepared. Body recovery operations continued until all but one set of remains had been recovered. After careful consideration, the diving officer concluded that the risk involved in diving operations to the interior of the ship outweighed the desirabliity of recovering the final body—always a hard decision to make.[16] Attention turned to salvaging the cutter.

---

[16] The eleventh body was finally recovered about a half mile from the wreck.

340

The collision had so badly damaged the hull that the most feasible plan was to lift the 260-ton ship intact and place her on keel blocks on a barge. Two harbor tugs, YTB–801 and YTB–824, brought the floating cranes YD–200 and YD–229 from the naval amphibious base at Norfolk and placed them in a four-point moor. Diving operations to pass messenger lines beneath the wreck began. Twenty-four hours after the cranes arrived, rigging had been completed and a strain taken. The initial lift brought the *Cuyahoga* upright; weather delayed lifting to the surface until the following day. When the weather had moderated, the cutter was lifted to the surface, pumped out, and placed on the blocks as planned. The operation had gone well. The Navy had assisted its sister sea service and gained valuable diving experience at the same time.

Blackthorn

On a mild, clear, moonlit night in January 1980, in a casualty not unlike that of *Cuyahoga*, the tanker *Capricorn* struck and sank the Coast Guard buoy tender *Blackthorn* in Tampa Bay. At the request of the Commandant of the Coast Guard, divers from Harbor Clearance Unit Two (Lieutenant Commander Stephen W. Delaplane) and the Explosive Ordnance Disposal Group Two detachment in Fort Lauderdale (Lieutenant (j.g.) M.W. Carr) were soon on the way by air, and *Preserver* (Lieutenant Commander F. Douglas Meyer) sailed from Norfolk. As at the *Cuyahoga* site, the first item of business was to recover remains of the twenty-three Coast Guardsmen who had died and to survey *Blackthorn*. Divers under Lieutenant J.H. Gibson and Master Chief Petty Officer James Starcher started work. The attitude of the ship on the bottom and debris blocking access kept divers from entering the wreck and prevented recovery of most of the bodies.

The salvage plan, developed from information provided by the divers, consisted of the following steps:

- The buoy tender's mast would be removed.
- She would be parbuckled upright from her position on her port side.
- Three lift platforms would be used—the 650-ton shear leg crane *Cappy Bisso*, the 100-ton crane *Little David*, and a 150-ton crawler crane mounted on a barge.[17]

---

[17] Lifting assets were arranged by the Supervisor of Salvage, who was represented at the salvage site by Commander Charles S. Maclin.

341

The 650-ton shear leg crane *Cappy Bisso* lifts the buoy tender *Blackthorn* from the waters of Tampa Bay, Florida.

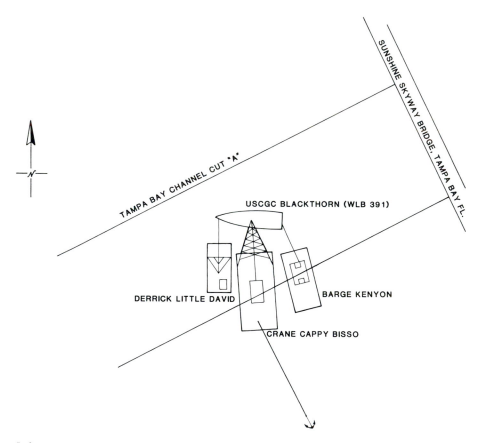

Lifting arrangements for *Blackthorn*.

• The buoy tender would be moved in the lifting slings until she cleared the channel.

• The wreck would be dewatered and refloated.

Following a practice that had often proved beneficial, the salvage team flew to Mobile, Alabama, to inspect another vessel of the same class, USCGC *Salvia* (WLB 400). Subsequently, the crane *Cappy Bisso* was positioned over the wreck, and wires for parbuckling were rigged on 9 February, when the operation halted for two days to allow divers working on *Capricorn* to inspect the wreck and survey the bottom nearby. When their work was completed, salvage operations continued. *Blackthorn* rolled upright and settled on her keel with a slight port list. For the final lift, the buoyancy of two water tanks was recovered by pumping and blowing. *Cappy Bisso* set amidships, *Kenyon* astern, and *Little David* forward. With all in readiness, an old story repeated itself—weather set in and delayed the operation for two more days.

On the morning of 19 February compressors and pumps were started and a strain taken on the lifting gear. As soon as the deck came awash, tugs moved the entire nest to shallow water and dewatering began. The bodies of the missing crewmen were located and removed. *Blackthorn* was delivered to drydock the following afternoon.

The *Blackthorn-Capricorn* collision generated a great deal of controversy, none of it centered about the salvage operation. Navy salvors had removed the wreck within two days of their original schedule, had provided the Coast Guard Marine Board of Investigation with necessary information, and had removed a blockage of one of the busiest harbors on the Gulf Coast. But this operation also had demonstrated that it is by no means enough for a salvage officer to be a capable technician. A salvage officer must be sensitive to the public interest, the legal ramifications of the work, and the interests of all involved parties. At Tampa Bay, for example, the salvors were still working at clean-up when the families of the recovered crew gathered on the beach and lawyers came in to protect their interests. The salvage officer therefore has to understand the economic interests involved, and represent the Navy in conferences and public appearances with tact, dignity, propriety, and technical accuracy. There is far more to the job of a salvor than refloating ships.

ARMY CORPS OF ENGINEERS

As the discussion of the *Oriental Warrior* and *Sidney E. Smith* salvages in the previous chapter indicated, the Army Corps of Engineers, responsibile for keeping inland waterways clear, is often a customer for Navy salvage. As was the case with the removal of *Caribia* from the harbor in Guam, the Corps has the right to hire outside contractors when this is deemed in its best interest. Often, however, there is a definite advantage in using the facilities and experience of the Navy, especially where expedience is an issue. Such was the case when the corps's dredge *A. Mackenzie* sank in a three-way collision in the Galveston Inner Bar Channel in April 1974.

Dredge A. Mackenzie

In the case of *Mackenzie*, the decision to use Navy contractors was made after an independent consultant reviewed the technical and business aspects of the removal. The consultant's reports were considered by the District Engineer's Office in his decision to use Navy resources and to do a cut-and-pick[18] operation. A task force was formed under Mr. J.D. Bissell, of the District Engineer's Office; Lieutenant Commander Charles A. (Black Bart) Bartholomew represented the Supervisor of Salvage, and Captain Cyrus Alleman, Murphy-Pacific's salvage master, was supported by Mr. Alex Rynecki, salvage engineer.

The salvage plan called for removing the top-hamper, offloading the dredge's bunker fuel, and cutting the wreck into eight transverse sections, mostly divided into upper and lower sections. Tidal currents of up to 5 knots ebbing and flooding in the channel complicated the work and limited diving outside the hull to times of slack water. When currents were running, divers worked inside the wreck, entering through the smokestacks that protruded above water. A large amount of topside gear came off to lighten the wreck and provide access. Both explosive and oxy-arc cutting techniques were used. Commercial divers using oxy-arc torches made most of the cuts because of the difficulty of placing shaped charges snugly against the hull plating and the unpredictable results from some types of charges. The cutting system that evolved during the job used oxy-arc cutting for the majority of the cuts while explosives assured complete separation.

Close liaison was established with federal and state environmental and wildlife-protection interests before the operation began and was maintained for the duration of the clearance work. This simple precautionary measure provided a process for settling problems regarding the use of explosives and a potential oil-spill in an amicable manner before they grew out of proportion.

---

[18] In a cut-and-pick salvage operation, the wreckage is cut in place into bits that can be picked up and removed by cranes. The size of the bits is determined by the lifting capacity of the cranes. The term "wrecking-in-place" is often used synonomously.

A 600-ton whirley crane lifts the stern section of the Corps of Engineers' dredge *Mackenzie* onto a waiting barge. The dredge's stacks still protrude from the water.

Sections of *Mackenzie* are lined up on a barge after having been lifted out. All of the cutting was performed by divers working underwater in near zero visibility.

Teledyne Movable No. II, an offshore construction whirley crane with a 600-ton capacity, did the lifting.[19] Lifts were made near the capacity of the crane in order to improve the efficiency, reduce the amount of under-water cutting, and keep time and cost down.

The plan and its implementation were successful. The dredge wreckage was removed from the channel in three series of lifts at reasonable cost in less time than was initially estimated. Professional salvors had done the job under the direct supervision of Navy salvage personnel. Some major changes had occured since 1911, when it was the Corps of Engineers that had removed the wreck of the battleship *Maine* in Havana harbor for the Navy.

Barges on the Arkansas

On the evening of 4 December 1982 heavy rains had increased the flow in the Arkansas River almost fourfold. As a result of the rapid rise thirty-eight barges broke their moors in a holding area and were carried downstream. Thirteen of the barges were carried into Dam No. 2, a gated spillway dam near Dumas, Arkansas, that controls water levels in the river. The thirteen barges fetched up on chisel-shaped ice-breaking piers between the spillway gates. The barges were sunk, jammed in the gates, or impaled on the piers. Obstruction of the gates by the barges could cause damage that might destroy the dam. It was a mess.

Conferences were held, surveys made, more conferences held, salvage plans and cost estimates prepared, more conferences held. On 17 December the Corps of Engineers gave the Supervisor of Salvage the go-ahead to remove the wrecks. The Supervisor of Salvage, in turn, called on his Gulf Coast salvage contractor, Tracor Marine, to do the work. Mr. Jerry Totten oversaw the job for the Supervisor of Salvage; Mr. Jim Jacobs was Tracor's project manager.

Two heavy lift cranes were brought upriver from New Orleans, and the tug *Mississippi* came over from the Corps of Engineers' Memphis district to serve as the quarters and hotel facility; the Little Rock district provided the tug *Shorty Baird*. While waiting for the cranes to come up river, Tracor built a pulling barge on site.

Salvage work started just before Christmas. Relatively simple lifts removed the first seven barges. Removal of the final six was not so easy.

---

[19] The existence of heavy lifting equipment designed to support the offshore oil industry has made radical changes in salvage work requiring heavy lifting. The use of such lifting equipment is very cost-effective when planned to minimize the waiting time of the expensive cranes. The technique is most useful near offshore oil fields where the equipment is readily available and long transit times are not necessary.

Four separate operations, each of them a major salvage job in its own right, were needed to remove the final six barges. These operations required coordinated pulling and lifting, precise cutting, and an I-beam made into a huge chisel to cut wreckage for removal. Some pieces were cut free and allowed to fall through the gates behind the dam. All did not go smoothly. A barge got away during a lift and slammed into one of the cranes, putting it out of action for ten days; wreckage tore away unexpectedly leaving a difficult situation. Other work went beautifully. After almost sixty days of continuous salvage effort, all the wreckage was free of the dam and the Corps of Engineers was again able to control water levels in the river.

Cargo Vessel Eaglescliffe

It seemed almost a case of *déjà vu* when the Corps of Engineers asked the Supervisor of Salvage to undertake the removal of the wreck of the small cargo vessel *Eaglescliffe* that had sunk off Galveston in early 1983. Some months after the vessel went down, hurricane Alicia had broken the wreck and moved it near the channel. The Corps of Engineers determined removal to be necessary. It contacted the Supervisor of Salvage, who again called on one of his contractors for the work. Since the *A. MacKenzie* job, Murphy-Pacific had been ordered into bankruptcy, and the Supervisor of Salvage had instituted the contracting practice that gave him regional contractors. Tracor Marine, the contractor for the Gulf of Mexico, was mobilized, and Chief Warrant Officer Leon Ryder, USN (Ret.) became salvage master. Jim Bladh represented the Supervisor of Salvage.

The location of the operation in the Gulf of Mexico, an area of major offshore industrial activity, affected all aspects of the job, including the approach taken and the equipment used. As with the *MacKenzie* salvage, a large offshore construction crane, *Foster Parker*, made the two lifts. In a first for Navy salvors, a small self-elevating work platform, *Walter Reetz*, used in offshore oil fields, became the salvage work platform. The little jackup was invaluable because it provided a stable and comfortable workspace that made surface tasks easier and faster. The removal of *Eaglescliffe* took only fifteen days.

OTHER AGENCIES

While the Coast Guard and the Army Corps of Engineers are the government agencies that most frequently call upon the Navy for salvage services, other agencies solicit these services at irregular intervals. This work is often unusual and interesting.

S.S. *Indiana*

The summer of 1975 saw the discovery of the historically significant wreck of S.S. *Indiana* in Lake Superior by Wisconsin SCUBA[20] diver John Steele. This find opened the door for Navy salvors to make a contribution to the marine heritage of the nation and to work out some operational procedures.

Indiana, a small screw steamer about the size of a modern oceangoing tug, was built in Ohio in 1848 and hauled miscellaneous freight throughout the Great Lakes until she sank just above Whitefish Point in 1858. Interest in the wreck of *Indiana* centered on her machinery. The steamer had an early example of screw propulsion and had machinery, little altered in her ten years of service, that predated by many years any other remaining examples of early Great Lakes marine propulsion machinery. Great Lakes marine historian Dr. Richard J. Wright of Bowling Green State University recognized the importance of the machinery. Dr. Wright contacted the Smithsonian Institution and started the chain that resulted in the tasking of Harbor Clearance Unit Two (Lieutenant Commander Rob Wells) to recover the machinery in the summer of 1979.

The recovery effort was a joint operation between Harbor Clearance Unit Two, Reserve Harbor Clearance Unit Two, Detachment 813 of Chicago (Lieutenant Commander Steve Chubb, USNR), and the Headquarters Group, Naval Sea Systems Command Detachment 1006 (Captain W.A. Cleary, USNR–R).[21] The most modern diving equipment in the Navy's inventory was brought in for the work. The operation started on 31 July 1979 from a barge and tug lent by the Corps of Engineers. When the operation was completed nine days later, over 100 dives had been made and all important pieces of the machinery were recovered with virtually no damage.

Navy salvors had aided the academic community in recovering a valuable marine artifact that increased our knowledge of the history of technology and provided important artifacts for the Smithsonian Institution's National Museum of American History. Of direct importance to the Navy, this job used new equipment in an operational environment and demonstrated the power of the Navy's combination of Regulars and Reserves, kept up to speed by operations like this one.

---

[20] SCUBA is the acronym for Self-Contained Underwater Breathing Apparatus. By common usage, a SCUBA diver is a diver using such an apparatus—usually an open-circuit device rather than the more sophisticated semiclosed- and closed-circuit types used almost exclusively by military divers.

[21] Captain Cleary, though not mentioned previously, was a maritime professional who was active in the Naval Reserve for many years and played a key role in the establishment of the Reserve Harbor Clearance Units. Before these units were established, Cleary undertook many projects for the Supervisor of Salvage and for the training of fleet salvage officers.

Air Florida Flight 90

Early 1982 saw the Navy performing a tough job for yet another government agency. It was one of the grim, unpleasant, but totally necessary jobs that salvors are sometimes called on to do. On a cold, snowy 13 January, Air Florida Flight 90 crashed into the Potomac River on takeoff from Washington's National Airport. The Metropolitan Police Department requested Department of Defense assistance, and by early the following afternoon a joint services recovery team had been assembled.[22]

It stayed cold. The river was frozen and a wind chill factor of –20 degrees Fahrenheit prevailed throughout the operation. Initial surveys showed that the aircraft had been demolished, but the wreckage was concentrated. First priority went to recovering remains. When found, they were brought to the surface and immediately turned over to the Medical Examiner's Office. Flight recorders were of interest to the National Transportation Safety Board; these units were located quickly but immediate access was blocked by wreckage.

Army engineers laid out a grid to establish the location of all the wreckage, and a topography unit scanned the area with high-resolution sensors in helicopters and boats to develop a detailed picture of the location of the wreckage. Harbor Clearance Unit Two divers, under the direct supervision of Master Diver Charlie Wetzel, continued the miserable work of recovery for twelve days. When the work was completed on January 25, all bodies and 95 percent of the aircraft—including all critical wreckage and the flight recorders—had been recovered.

The operation was unique because of the extreme weather, media pressure, and the high public and official visibility of the operation. Recently introduced diving equipment made it possible for the divers to operate effectively in the icy waters. The quality of the men made possible an operation requiring exceptional teamwork and the utmost professionalism, propriety, and sensitivity.

NAVY JOBS

Although Navy salvage forces work for a variety of customers, the majority of their work is carried out within the Department of the Navy. A 1975 grounding demonstrated the value of a capability that would soon disappear.

Hermitage (LSD 34) lost steering control and grounded while proceed-

---

[22]The joint services team included detachments from Harbor Clearance Unit Two, Naval Explosive Ordnance Disposal School and Technology Center, Coast Guard Atlantic Strike Team, and the 86th and 115th Army Engineering Detachments. Lieutenant Commander Steve Delaplane, Commanding Officer of Harbor Clearance Unit Two, was designated as on-scene commander.

ing into Morehead City, North Carolina. *Shakori* (ATF 162) left an air-craft recovery operation off Hatteras Inlet and steamed to the grounded ship. Working in concert with two commercial harbor tugs and the Coast Guard ship *Chilula* (WMEC 153),[23] *Shakori* freed the grounded ship in short order. In his endorsement to the salvage report, the Surface Force Commander noted:

> If the salvage extraction had been delayed for a few days, the *Hermitage* would have worked into the bottom more, making the salvage task more difficult. The importance of the quick reaction capability of the salvage Navy *and the ATF* [emphasis supplied] was demonstrated vividly in this salvage operation. In determining the complements and capabilities of the T–ATF soon to be constructed, this should be considered. If the ships are all manned with civilian crews without salvage equipment and crew on board, this quick reaction capability is reduced.[24]

Indeed, the quick reaction capability has been cut, as the performance of *Catawba* in dealing with the two stranded Korean Navy ships showed. The T–ATF–166 class ships, however, are far from useless in salvage situations. Two operations in the early 1980s, one in the Atlantic, the other in the Pacific, illustrated how these ships can be effective.

The first of these operations followed the grounding of two pontoon sections of the floating drydock *Los Alamos* (AFDB 7) at Ponta Delgada, Azores, in October 1981. The grounding itself resembled the *Caribia* grounding at Guam in that the towing ship *Recovery* (ARS 43), Lieutenant Commander H.A. Stephan commanding, had turned the tow over to commercial tugs while she refueled. Severe weather set in during *Recovery's* retrieval and the pontoons went ashore. Salvage response was immediate.

- Lieutenant Commander Delaplane, commanding officer of Harbor Clearance Unit Two, accompanied by salvage engineer Lieutenant L.M. (Bud) Sawyer, and an eight-man diving team left for the Azores by air.

- USNS *Powhatan* (T–ATF–166), commanded by Captain H. Pouttu, picked up a load of salvage equipment and a team from *Opportune* and sailed for the Azores.

- The Supervisor of Salvage put the 16,000 horsepower Bugsier tug

---

[23] *Chilula* was a former Navy fleet tug (ATF) transferred to the Coast Guard following World War II. She retained her original name and hull number. *Chilula's* ability to act as a salvage ship or rescue tug was significantly reduced by the removal of salvage equipment and her automatic towing winch. During the *Hermitage* salvage, she pulled with an 8-inch circumference nylon hawser borrowed from *Shakori* rather than a wire rope hawser.

[24] Ltr, Commander Naval Surface Force, U.S. Atlantic Fleet, 4740 serial N4A/6146, 24 July 1975.

Simpson under contract, and Jim Bladh headed east from Washington, D.C.

• Lieutenant Commander Gary Tettelbach, an experienced salvage engineer, traveled to the scene from Pearl Harbor Naval Shipyard.

• Preparations began to bring in a Marine Corps CH–53 helicopter[25] to put salvage equipment aboard the pontoons.

• *Recovery* remained on the scene.

The same basic salvage plan sufficed for both pontoons—compressed air would force water out through the badly damaged bottom. Work started immediately on the pontoon in the most hazardous position. The area's resources were thoroughly scoured for usable materials. Industrial materials are scarce in the Azores, but the salvors made do with what they could find. Putting material and equipment aboard the pontoon was difficult, but ingenuity overcame the difficulties, and by the eighth day the pontoon was ready for pulling. Because of the poor holding ground for *Recovery*'s beach gear, *Simpson* made the pull with her 16,000 horsepower. When the tug had made full power for only fifteen minutes, the pontoon floated free.

As work started on the second pontoon, *Powhatan* arrived with her load of salvage equipment and fresh men, and the helicopter was ready to fly. The helicopter proved effective in putting equipment on board the pontoon quickly. As the tanks filled with air, the pontoon became lively, seeming almost eager to be off the rocks. *Simpson* hooked up, and the pontoon came afloat after only three days of work.[26]

In this first participation by a T–ATF in a salvage operation, four problems were evident:

• Because of the high turnover of the crew, the level of expertise did not remain constant throughout the operation.

• Because of the ship's infrequent use for salvage, some items of salvage rigging were found either to be missing or couldn't be located in the ship.

• The open, low freeboard deck aft did not provide adequate protec-

---

[25] The helicopter had a lift capacity of 12,500 pounds.

[26] The pontoons were subsequently loaded aboard submersible barges and towed to the United States by *Powhatan* and the Crowley Maritime Corporation's tug *Bulwark*. The study accompanying the salvage report on this operation, "Comparative Study of the Stability of Salvaged AFDB-7 in Three Towing Methods," by Lieutenant Commander Tettelbach, is a classic of its type. (Enclosure to the salvage report: Ltr, Commanding Officer, Harbor Clearance Unit Two, serial 268, 24 April 1981.)

Lieutenant Commander James C. Bladh, USN (Ret.), seen here in the Azores, took an active part in many major salvage operations both as a naval officer and as a civilian member of the Supervisor of Salvage's staff.

tion for salvage gear stowed there during transit, and some items sustained damage.

• The personal relationship between the master of the T–ATF and the Navy salvage officer directly affects the operation. With the salvage officer aboard for only infrequent missions, the mutual confidence necessary in salvage operations often does not have time to develop.

These problems could properly be called growing pains and would be worked out with time and experience. The next opportunity to do so came in the Pacific a little over a year later, when *Sioux* (T–ATF 171), towing with a synthetic line, lost her tow—the mess-service and support barge YRBM–26—in the outer Strait of Juan de Fuca. The barge grounded near Pachena Point on the south end of Vancouver Island. Sixty-five knot winds and 20-foot swells drove the barge up the beach close to the tree line.

Salvors from Mobile Diving and Salvage Unit One, led by the commanding officer, Commander Gary Cassat, headed for the scene to augment *Sioux*; *Reclaimer* sailed; and equipment came in from Mobile Diving and Salvage Unit One and the Emergency Ship Salvage Material Pool in Stockton. Holes were patched, the barge dewatered, a channel blasted by Canadian Navy divers, and the barge hauled off by *Sioux* on her second attempt—before *Reclaimer* had an opportunity to rig her beach gear.

In this operation the T–ATF had proved excellent in all respects as a platform for the operation, but the operation itself took sixteen days and required that men and equipment for the salvage be flown in from relatively great distances. If the T–ATF had had an inherent salvage capability and carried salvage crew, salvage work could have begun immediately after the stranding, and the barge would not have been exposed in a dangerous position for ten days waiting for salvage to begin.

As is generally the case in peacetime, major salvage work came relatively infrequently. There were fairly frequent small jobs, numerous aircraft recoveries,[27] and the occasional major incident. The work covered the world and required varied types of responses. With the fly-away salvage concept becoming more firmly established with the passage of time, a greater variety of responses to salvage situations became available.

The salvage that followed the sinking in 1975 of a special launch platform at the Ingalls Division of Litton Industries in Pascagoula, Mississippi, demonstrated the Navy's ability to conduct complex salvage operations with a minimum of trained and experienced personnel in supervisory positions.

The launch platform, a structure similar to a floating drydock, had been specifically built to launch the thirty-five ships of the DD–963 and LHA–1 classes under construction at the Ingalls yard. During a routine undocking of the *Spruance* (DD–963), correct operating procedures were not followed, and the platform failed structurally amidships and sank in two pieces. Fortunately *Spruance*, in danger of actually falling off the blocks, sustained only minor damage as the platform sank beneath her. Because only ten of the thirty-five ships had reached the launch stage, the loss of the dock would be disruptive, if not catastrophic, to the building program. Technically it was a Litton Industries problem since

---

[27] Aircraft recoveries in the Atlantic Fleet became so numerous that some black humor began to emerge. An enterprising and anonymous sailor made some bumper stickers reading "Fly Navy-Our Divers Need the Work." Navy aviators were not amused.

The newly built destroyer *Spruance* lies askew in the broken Litton Launch Platform. The break in the platform appears about halfway along the wing wall.

none of the ships had been delivered to the Navy. However, the Navy had a strong interest in solving the problem. Admiral Isaac C. Kidd, the Chief of Naval Material, invited the Supervisor of Salvage, Captain Boyd, and Lieutenant Commander Bartholomew to go to Pascagoula to assess the situation with Ingalls management. After looking at the situation, and with the concurrence of Ingalls management, Admiral Kidd directed Captain Boyd and Lieutenant Commander Bartholomew to stay on the scene until the salvage was completed. These two officers provided the technical direction for the salvage operations.

The quickest means of refloating the platform would be to displace the floodwater with compressed air. This was tried, but did not succeed because of the extensive damage that included internal ruptures of boundaries. Pumping, the next choice, wouldn't work because the differential pressures across bulkheads would cause additional structural failures. What made sense and what was ultimately done was to pump sufficient air pressure in some compartments to keep differential pressures across bulkheads within acceptable limits.

Twenty-five 4-inch submersible pumps were brought in from the

Emergency Ship Salvage Material bases, and six more from commercial sources. With this battery of pumps pumping, and air pressure kept up in selected compartments, the two halves of the platform were independently surfaced. After repairs, the platform was returned to service in the destroyer-building program. The job had been successful in just fifteen days because two salvage officers had been present to add their special knowledge to that of the shipyard work force.

When typhoon Pamela went through Guam the following year (1976), leaving the harbor cluttered with wrecks, a minimum number of salvage officers were again flown in to do the clearance job. The fleet salvage officer, Commander Milwee, and the commanding officer of Harbor Clearance Unit One, Lieutenant Commander Paul W. Wolfgang, flew to the devastated island on the second aircraft to arrive after the storm. Their initial mission was to evaluate the damage and determine salvage requirements.

The two men found a number of wrecks scattered about the harbor—some sunk, some hard aground, some barely aground, some slightly damaged, some badly beaten up. The wrecks were quickly put into four categories:

1. Those needed immediately for operations.
2. Those that presented a potential pollution hazard.
3. Those that blocked a berth or were a hazard to navigation.
4. Those that fit none of the preceding categories and were not of immediate concern.

The preferred plan of action would be to fly in men and equipment from Harbor Clearance Unit One, or bring in salvage ships and get on with the salvage. In this case, there were several constraints that precluded this approach. First, use of Seventh Fleet assets had to be avoided if possible, so that they could continue to support fleet operations—a drastic change from typhoon Karen in 1962, when the salvage work in Guam was recognized as an excellent training opportunity. Second, introduction of additional people onto the island had to be minimized, because Guam was in no condition to feed and house them. Finally, only minimal demands, or preferably none at all, were to be placed on normal and emergency logistic channels into the island. Disaster relief efforts required all available sea and air space.

Working within these constraints and with the full cooperation of local commanding officers ashore and afloat, the two salvage officers formed a salvage group from divers assigned to *Proteus* (AS 19), *Jason*

Salvors working in Guam after typhoon Pamela undertake a variety of tasks. Top: Pumping out a sunken torpedo retriever. Center: Using a fire hose to wash away the bottom from under a stranded barge. Bottom: Rigging beach gear to refloat a grounded tug.

(AR 8), *Dixie* (AD 14),[28] and the Ship Repair Facility in Guam. Lieutenant (j.g.) Carl Albury and Chief Petty Officer Don Mackenzie, the diving officer and the master diver in *Proteus*, and Chief Petty Officer G.R. Cason, diving supervisor in *Jason*, became the principal assistants to the salvage officers and were invaluable. The groups were kept together and a spirited competition soon developed. To obviate the need for valuable aircraft cargo space, the Emergency Ship Salvage Material base administered by the Ship Repair Facility provided most of the salvage equipment; only a few urgently needed pieces that were unavailable on the island were flown in. Some emergency ship salvage material was used to convert a flat-deck barge into a pulling barge capable of hauling two legs of beach gear.

Within three weeks of the storm, the nine most critical wrecks had been salvaged for return to service. Two wrecks previously scheduled for disposal were left and sold as-is-where-is; two were later salvaged by Harbor Clearance Unit One; one was abandoned. The fly-away concept had worked well by supplying experienced leadership. It had not been fully implemented in the initial phases because of the constraints on facilities and transportation space, but the advantages accruing from the prepositioned Emergency Ship Salvage Material base and the experience gained by salvage-trained divers not in salvage units outweighed the variation from doctrine.

There were other Navy salvage jobs throughout the world during the period from 1974 to 1987.

• Acting in response to a request from the State Department, a team from Harbor Clearance Unit One conducted a radiological examination and prepared a salvage plan for the German cruiser *Prinz Eugen* that sank at Kwajalein following the Bikini nuclear weapons testing.

• *Edenton* (ATS–1), assisted by the Italian salvage ship *Proteo*, hauled the amphibious assault ship *Guadalcanal* (LPH 7) off her strand at Augusta Bay, Sicily.

• In an operation that demonstrated that small ships are often more difficult salvage jobs than large ones, Harbor Clearance Unit One cut through the rubble that formed an artificial reef and dragged a Coast Guard boat shoreward into a lagoon off Honolulu.

• *Moctobi* assisted her sister *Lipan*, now operated by the Military Sealift Command, when a tanker struck her near Port Angeles, Washington.

---

[28] All ships were not present in Guam throughout the entire operation. Divers from the ships were used when they were in port.

• A Harbor Clearance Unit One team cleared an LCU that was blocking a construction project at Tau Island in the Manua Islands near American Samoa.

• Using Navy hydraulic pullers modeled after those used on the *Sidney Smith* for the first time, *Edenton*, *Recovery*, *Shakori*, *Paiute*, and a detachment from Harbor Clearance Unit Two rigged ten legs of beach gear to twist *Ozark* (MCS 2), now an Air Force target ship, and haul her off Perdido Key near Pensacola, Florida.

• *Deliver* and *Moctobi* refloated the tanker *Austin* when she grounded entering Honolulu harbor.

• Harbor Clearance Unit Two, aided by two Reserve Units, raised a fireboat at Naval Weapons Station, Yorktown, Virginia.

• *Hoist* conducted an extensive video and X-ray survey of the German submarine U–352 and removed material hazardous to sport divers who wanted to explore the wreck.

• Harbor Clearance Unit Two refloated *Detroit* (AOE 4) after the fast combat support ship grounded on Thimble Shoals.

• Mobile Diving and Salvage Unit Two raised the sunken dredge *Leigh* in Big Foot Slough, North Carolina, and a barge sunk alongside *L.Y. Spear* (AS 36) at Norfolk.

• Many aircraft, anchors, stern gates, and other objects that supply the routine daily work of salvors in peacetime were also recovered.

Some jobs during this period stand out because they were especially difficult or unique. Among these was the removal in 1976 of the offshore tower structure called Argus Island, southwest of Bermuda. Since then, the removal of offshore structures has become relatively routine oilfield work.

The removal of Argus Island, however, was far from routine. The tower consisted of four major bearing legs driven into the hard coral bottom 192 feet below the surface and braced with horizontal members and diagonals, and supporting a platform some 65 feet above the surface. The removal plan called for cutting the legs while simultaneously pulling on the tower to topple it. Cutting would be done with shaped charges made especially for the operation by Jet Research, Inc., a company specializing in such charges and their use. To ensure that the charges, placed by divers, worked, cleaning charges would be used first to blast marine growth from the legs.

Escape and *Hoist* were to pull with two legs of beach gear each. Since the hard coral bottom militated against conventional beach gear anchors, Propellent Embedment Anchors developed by the Civil Engineering Laboratory in Port Hueneme were used.[29] Six anchors were placed, one for each leg of beach gear and one each to hold the salvage ships in working position next to the tower. *Escape* set each anchor separately. A precursor of future underwater operations was on the scene in the form of *Deep Drone*, a tethered, remotely operated underwater vehicle developed for the Supervisor of Salvage. *Deep Drone*, fitted with television cameras, still cameras, and search sonars would act as an inspection vehicle throughout the operation.

The work kicked off on 13 May 1976 and, except for the usual weather delays, went smoothly—until the first toppling attempt. With *Escape* and *Hoist* pulling, the cutting charges were fired. Nothing happened. *Deep Drone* and divers found three charges had produced partial cuts, and one had not fired. More charges were placed and another attempt was made. Again nothing happened. Satchel charges[30] were lowered inside one of the hollow legs and fired. That did it. The tower toppled and sank beneath the waves, as its platform broke away and settled upright on the bottom. To ensure adequate clearance over the structure, *Deep Drone* made a survey, and divers cut away high projections with explosives.

The operation was a total success. Explosive cutting worked reasonably well, the Propellent Embedment Anchors worked almost perfectly, and the remotely operated vehicle in conjunction with divers heralded an era of new methods in underwater work. Diving to 192 feet, deeper than normal for air diving, succeeded because the prototype of the recently developed Fly-Away Diving System was set up on *Hoist* and because the operation was carefully and competently supervised by master diver "Oakie" Sothers.

An equally successful but far different salvage operation took place six years later on the other side of the world. In mid-1982, USNS *Chauvenet* (T–AGS 29) grounded on Dauisan Reef in the Sulu Sea. *Brunswick* Commander John Drucker immediately got underway from Subic Bay; the Seventh Fleet salvage officer, Lieutenant Commander Kirk Boyd, and the Ship Repair Facility docking officer, Lieutenant Commander Mike Steading, went with them.

Upon arrival, they found *Chauvenet* hard aground at the bow, with the hull badly ripped, flooded, and in a condition of critical stability on the verge of deep water. As in the case of *Dona Ouriana*, beach gear would be useless because the water was too deep. Divers began patching

---

[29] Propellent Embedment Anchors develop their hold by using an explosive charge to drive the fluke into the sea bottom like a projectile. Flukes are tailored to the type of bottom into which the anchor is driven. A wire rope pendant toggled to the shank extends above the bottom for connection to the ground leg.

[30] These are haversacks filled with explosives, in this case the military plastic explosive C–4.

the hull, while two Eells anchors to hold the ship were floated ashore supported by *Brunswick's* mooring buoys. With the ship secured and patched, pumps were brought aboard and pumping started. The ship became more unstable as the tide fell and as the floodwater, weight low in the ship, was pumped out. As *Chauvenet* listed erratically to starboard, all but a skeleton crew of four officers left the ship. She seemed ready to capsize, but finally settled with a starboard list of nearly 30 degrees. More damage had occurred. A complete lack of internal watertight integrity, resulting from damaged transverse bulkheads as well as a shifting liquid load, had caused the unexpected behavior. This was no routine stranding.

Captain "Black Bart" Bartholomew came in from Commander in Chief, U.S. Pacific Fleet, Headquarters on short notice[31] to provide technical assistance. A detailed salvage plan, in which stability was a major consideration at every step, was laid out. The critical elements were

• Removing selected topside weight—ship's anchors and chain—and counterflooding to reduce ground reaction.

• Using selective pumping.

• Pressing up flooded spaces to prevent the development of free surface and concomitant loss of stabliity.

• Pulling with full power.

The plan was followed exactly. *Brunswick* wrenched the bow by varying the angle of her pull relative to *Chauvenet* and rotated the stranded ship's head through an angle of 10 degrees. In the early afternoon, *Chauvenet* started to move astern and came afloat. *Brunswick* towed her to Subic Bay by the stern.

Brunswick had performed competently as a salvage ship. She had operated in a difficult salvage operation in a remote location, laid a deep-water moor, rigged heavy ground tackle over a reef, manufactured and installed underwater patches, provided diving services, positioned and used salvage machinery and equipment, and generated sufficient bollard pull to retract a seriously stranded ship. *Chauvenet* was patched in Subic Bay, repaired in Sasebo Sadan, and returned to service.

The additional versatility of the salvage and rescue ship *Brunswick* was demonstrated in the salvage of the submarine *Bluegill* (SS 242) near

---

[31] When word of the near capsizing reached the Fleet Headquarters, Rear Admiral Bill Wyatt sent for Captain Bartholomew, who could not be found immediately because he was fifty miles away diving for lobster off the island of Molokai. But admirals as well as salvors are tenacious. When the captain surfaced from his first dive of the day, he found a Marine Corps helicopter overhead. Moments later he was plucked from the water. Twenty-three hours later another helicopter deposited him on *Chauvenet*.

Lahaina Harbor, Maui, in late 1983. In the fall of 1970, *Bluegill* had been placed on the bottom for training divers and submarine rescue chamber operators, with the understanding that the ship would be removed when it was no longer needed.[32] By 1983 the need for the submarine for training had passed, and the submarine presented a danger to sport divers; they had discovered that it made an interesting place to dive and were entering the hull—a dangerous practice. No definite provision had been made for future salvage when the submarine had been sunk, though a mooring had been provided as security against the current.

Since time was not critical to the operation, careful planning and engineering could be done. Commander Archibald G. Campbell, Commander of Service Squadron Five, was in charge of the operation. The initial plan called for dewatering the submarine and lifting by the bow lift gear of *Beaufort* (Lieutenant Commander Alan M. Nibbs) and *Brunswick* (Lieutenant Commander John Paul Speer). Lieutenant Commander James M. Evans, commanding officer of *Reclaimer*, would act as salvage master, and an engineering team led by Commander Gary Tettelbach and composed of Lieutenant Commander J.W. Bloomer and Lieutenants J.R. Wilkins and N. E. Hansen would support the operation. The engi-

---

[32] A submarine salvage exercise involving *Bluegill* was planned for 1974. On the first day of loading for the operation, it was canceled on the order of the Fleet Commander due to a higher-priority operation.

Chauvanet lies hard aground on Dauisan Reef.

neering team would develop lift plans and modify them using real-time input, with a microcomputer installed on *Brunswick*. Four master divers—W.H. Loudermilk, J.A. Ortiz, Scott Bradbury, and Donald H. Mac-Kenzie—all of them master chief petty officers—would supervise the diving and deck operations.

In early October equipment was staged on board the barge YC–1485, and moors were laid for the barge and the two salvage ships. It quickly became apparent to both seamen and engineers that the normal swell at the salvage site would cause unacceptably high dynamic stresses in the bow lift rigging. Rubber salvage pontoons from the Emergency Ship Salvage Material base would augment the buoyancy of the submarine. Using the microcomputer system, the engineering team prepared a detailed revised salvage plan that included predictions of the submarine's behavior throughout the dewatering sequence.

Even as the engineers revised the salvage plans, divers were busy on the bottom, sealing the submarine, rigging hoses, and fitting for the blow. After thirty days of around-the-clock work, over 700 dives, and the rigging of more than 2 miles of hose, all was ready for the lift. The pressure hull was dewatered and vented, and the pontoons and ballast tanks were blown. *Bluegill* didn't move. Blowing sequences were varied. Still nothing happened. *Bluegill* was flooding through unpatched openings more quickly than the air could blow the water out. Divers spent two more days locating and patching leaks. Engineers worked out a less conservative blowing sequence.

At midafternoon on 3 November blowing began again; by nightfall the computer indicated that the hull should be positively buoyant. As if on cue, the depth gauge needle began to flicker, then moved upward. *Bluegill* was on her way up. When the submarine surfaced, *Brunswick* took her to shallow water to be prepared for sinking in deep water. During the tow, a valve in the main ballast system blew and *Bluegill* began to settle. A salvage crew boarded and patched the valve, but it took compressors pumping constantly to keep the submarine afloat. *Brunswick* hooked up her tow and put to sea. All went well until the weather began to kick up. Just short of the designated sinking site, Lieutenant Commander Nibbs ordered an emergency breakaway. Air hoses were quickly disconnected and the tow broken. *Bluegill* went down by the stern. It was the end of a major salvage job. It would also be the last peak of Navy salvage activity for some time.

The operation had involved a lot of hard work but had gone smoothly. Two things had paid off: careful and complete planning, and use of a computer to develop, monitor, and modify the lift plan in real time. The computer had become a powerful tool for the salvage engineer, now allowing the engineer to examine more options and modify calculations and recommendations to suit what is actually happening.

Navy salvage, moving toward the 1990s, had performed well in a wide arena and demonstrated the value of trained and experienced salvors both to the Navy and to the nation. However the years from 1974 to 1987 had not been smooth sailing. Well-intentioned mistakes had been made but were ultimately corrected. The end result in the late 1980s was a Navy salvage organization that was small, professional, well managed, and well equipped.

Of the four elements of salvage—people, ships, equipment, and operational concepts and doctrine—people have always dominated. Navy salvors have imagination, ingenuity, perseverance, technical competence, and, most of all, guts. They revel in a challenge and in hard work. In the modern era, technology governs a part of this hard work—the part done underwater and in the deep ocean. The next chapter focuses on this aspect of salvage.

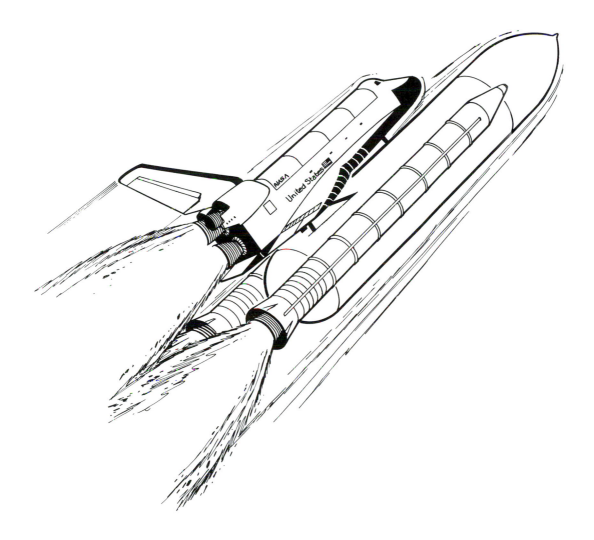

CHALLENGER

CHAPTER NINE

Navy Salvage in the Deep Ocean

The salvage work described in previous chapters was carried out on or near the surface of the sea. In this type of salvage the human element dominates; the work goes forward or fails primarily on the skills and abilities of the salvors. As the work moves further beneath the ocean's surface, however, difficulty increases and the importance of technology grows.

There is no more hostile environment than the deep ocean. It is dark, cold, treacherous, and unpredictable. Pressures are enormous. It is axiomatic that any two lines in the deep ocean will tangle, that things are never where they are supposed to be. Deep-ocean work has become possible only with the development of supporting technology and the determination and ability to turn that technology into action. Even so, recovering objects from the deep ocean is a challenge that few attempt.

The U.S. Navy has done some remarkable things in the deep ocean and has led the way in pushing the technology forward. Navy salvors in particular have spurred the development of the Navy's ability to work in the deep ocean; working there is natural for them. Ever since Naval Constructor Julius Furer recovered the submarine F–4, Navy salvors have faced the challenges of the depths with increasing frequency.

Because technology dominates deep-ocean operations, the contribution of the engineer almost exactly balances that of the seaman. Three of the most important roles of the engineer—selecting the tools for the work at hand, planning the operation in detail, and considering every contingency no matter how illogical—are played out long before going to sea. Planning and work-system selection are critical, for if they are done well, the difficulty of execution is eased; conversely, if they are poorly done, the operation will probably fail. Once at sea, the engineer is supported by the seaman who translates the planning into operational reality.

Most deep-ocean operations, and particularly deep-ocean salvage operations, consist of two phases. The first is the search phase. Objects below the surface of the ocean are very effectively hidden. No matter how large the object, it is minute in the huge volume of the sea. Obviously the object must be located and marked so that it may be found again if the operation is interrupted for any reason—such as the old bugaboo of ocean operations, weather. Integral to the search operation is positive identification and classification of the object. The survey to identify and gain information about the object may be a more extensive operation than the search itself, and requires quite a different set of tools. Even with the best of tools, however, searching for an object in the ocean is a tedious and frustrating process. With poor tools it is next to impossible.

Once the object has been located and identified, the second phase of the operation—recovery—can take place. Recovery techniques are totally dependent on the characteristics of the object to be recovered and the available tools. There never has been and, in all probability, never will be a cookbook for deep-ocean salvage. This will always be the province of human beings who can plan thoroughly, think on their feet, and maintain their flexibility and good humor when everything goes wrong at once.

There are three basic means for working underwater: divers, manned submersibles, and remotely operated vehicles. Each has its advantages and disadvantages; each is well suited for certain types of work. All three have been used in Navy deep-ocean salvage operations, often in combination to take advantage of the strong points of each.

Divers and Diving

Over the years, the definition of the deep ocean has changed. When divers were the only means of working under the ocean's surface, deep-ocean salvage was defined by the limits of their abilities. For this reason the changes in divers' abilities and the evolution of diving technology have been an important part of deep-ocean salvage. Even with the advent of other technologies, there have been few salvage jobs where divers have not played a part, and the art and science of diving is so closely related to salvage that almost all Navy salvors have been trained as divers.

The origins of diving in the U.S. Navy are dim. Generally, diving as a naval endeavor developed throughout the world in the nineteenth century. The ongoing development of human ability to work underwater, to build diving equipment that is both effective and efficient, and to discover and overcome the physiological limitations inherent in diving has been international. Although no one nation can claim dominance, the U.S. Navy has done notable work in developing diving technology. In the Navy diving has evolved from the casual work of shipboard gunners to a broadly based naval effort. In fact, a complete history of diving and the closely related disciplines of men underwater in the U.S. Navy would easily fill a companion volume. This chronicle, therefore, can only touch upon the high points of that history and the specific relationship that diving bears to deep-ocean salvage.

Early Development

Torpedoes, a weapon that revolutionized naval warfare, were also responsible for the formal organization of diving activity in the U.S. Navy. In 1882 the Navy established a school under retired Chief Gunner's Mate Jacob Anderson. Based at Newport, Rhode Island, the school trained divers to descend to 60 feet to recover exercise torpedoes. Training in simple diving had been part of the course at the Gunnery School for some time because gunner's mates were assigned as ships' divers, but Chief Anderson's two-week course was the first designed solely to train divers.

Diving is not an end in itself but a means of doing work. A good diver is much more than a "horse" underwater or someone who can descend to great depth. He or she must be able to work effectively and to act as the eyes of the nondiving technical people topside. One of the limitations of early generations of Navy divers became apparent when *Maine* sank in Havana harbor in 1898. Navy divers examining the wreck soon after the sinking had little knowledge of ship construction and were unable to report meaningfully what they saw. Thus their work did little or nothing to assist the Board of Inquiry in determining the causes of the sinking. This failure on the part of men who were undoubtedly fine mechanics illustrates one of the most important attributes of good divers—an ability to understand the work they are doing and an ability to report what they find in such a way that the information will be meaningful.

To customers of diving services, diving technology is of little interest. They do not care what kind of equipment the divers wear or what gas is breathed; they simply want the diver to do the job well. To the diver, however, technology is paramount for, if equipment and work are well matched, the diver can get the job done. If the match is wrong or restrictive, no diver can succeed.

The Navy's first *Diving Manual*, published in 1905, reflected the state of the art, but lacked sophistication. Soon after, diving technology began to evolve rapidly. That same year the British Admiralty appointed a committee under Captain F.T. Hamilton, RN, to consider proposals made by Professor John Scott Haldane to permit diving in depths up to 30 fathoms. Haldane's work focused on the effects of carbon dioxide and stage decompression rather than on the continuous-ascent decompression developed by the French physiologist Paul Bert[1] that was generally used around the world. Haldane's results were verified in experimental dives and published. The work of the Admiralty committee had a great effect on the development of diving in the U.S. Navy.

One American who read the Admiralty report was Warrant Gunner George D. Stillson, who, because of his knowledge and experience, had become the Navy's expert on diving. In December 1912, he wrote the Chief of the Bureau of Construction and Repair and described the methods of diving used in the Navy as obsolete. As a result of his well-founded criticism, Gunner Stillson was ordered to the New York Navy Yard where he, Assistant Surgeon George French, and four divers were given a free hand to improve diving techniques and equipment in the U.S. Navy. They reviewed technical material on diving from around the world, studied and tried all available diving apparatus, and conducted dives—first under controlled conditions, then in the open sea from the destroyer *Walke* (DD 34). As a result of their work and their December 1914 report, diving in the Navy took some major steps forward.

As described in chapter 2, when the submarine F–4 sank off Honolulu in March 1915, Stillson, French, and the four divers were sent to the scene and performed excellent work, diving to depths over 300 feet while breathing compressed air. The operation, although successful, plainly showed the limitations of divers who worked under such conditions. The divers were limited to observation only and did little physical work; all suffered from decompression sickness during the operation and Chief Loughman was permanently crippled by "the bends." Inert gas narcosis, a completely unknown phenomenon at the time, also seriously affected the divers. Given the equipment and techniques available and the imperfectly understood human physiology, the eight dives made to 304 feet were a magnificent achievement. Furthermore, the deployment of Gunner Stillson and his crew to the F–4 salvage established an important precedent— sending a small specialized crew of deep divers to augment fleet divers for unusual diving operations. The practice continues today.

New Air and Better Training

The closing of the Diving School at Newport in order to send students and staff to Europe in World War I brought diving development and training to a near standstill. The school was not reestablished immediately after the war, but interest in diving and in improving the

---

[1] One of the early jobs of Harbor Clearance Unit One in Vietnam was the removal of a steamer named in honor of this hyperbaric physiologist. The coincidence was not lost on the divers on that salvage job. Their work is described in chapter 7.

abilities of divers remained alive within a small community. The relative ineffectiveness of divers on the F–4 operation received much study. While the physiology that created the limitations remained unclear, many correctly believed that ordinary air was the wrong breathing gas for deep diving. The eminent American physicist and chemist Elihu Thompson suggested that the incidence of decompression sickness could be drastically reduced and decompression schedules could be shortened by breathing a mixture composed primarily of a very light inert gas. Helium seemed a logical choice. In 1924 the Navy joined with the Bureau of Mines in the latter's Experimental Station in Pittsburgh to conduct the first experimental hyperbaric tests with helium-oxygen breathing mixtures. As is customary in such testing, experiments were made first on animals and verified on human subjects. The test results were promising, but not totally in accordance with expectations.

Decompression times were shortened somewhat with the new mixtures, but the incidence of decompression sickness did not seem to be greatly reduced. The unexpected benefit was the elimination of the not-yet-understood inert gas narcosis caused by the nitrogen in regular air. Divers diving deep on air had been reported to exhibit behavior ranging from over-cheerfulness through stupidity to complete loss of memory and judgment. These symptoms were atrributed to increased oxygen pressures or high concentrations of carbon dioxide. Using helium as the inert constituent of the new breathing mixture eliminated these symptoms.[2]

Along with its significant advantages, helium also presented some drawbacks. Problems with storage, mixing, and supplying the gas required the development of a recirculating helmet that would remove carbon dioxide from the expired gas and permit rebreathing by replacing metabolically consumed oxygen. Helium's high thermal conductivity also required that additional heat be provided to avoid hypothermia in the diver. Finally, the gas made the diver's speech difficult to understand. With all of these problems, helium-oxygen diving was a long way from becoming a practical reality.

In 1928 the Navy Experimental Diving Unit was established at the Washington Navy Yard to develop equipment and procedures for deep diving with helium-oxygen mixtures. The unit was taking on double duty experimental work and diving. In addition to helium-oxygen experimentation, its mission included both the development of air-diving procedures and tools for divers, and the deployment of deep-diving teams to special jobs.

---

[2] In 1935 Dr. Albert Behnke, a Navy medical officer, advanced the correct theory that the mental disturbances in deep dives on air were caused by the increased pressure exerted by nitrogen, a gas that is more soluble in fatty organs than in water.

Meanwhile fleet diving capability had actually diminished. With no diving school other than limited training aboard *Widgeon* (AM 22),[3] and little attention devoted to deep diving, attrition took its inevitable toll, reducing the overall number of Navy divers. When the submarine S–51 sank in 1925 in 132 feet of water, only twenty Navy divers were qualified to dive below 90 feet. During the salvage of S–51 and the other submarine salvage operations of the 1920s, a major deficiency in the training of divers came to light. A surprisingly small number of divers could actually perform specific tasks. About half of those available could only assist the diver actually doing the work. The problem had a simple origin—training had been devoted totally to the mechanics of diving; student divers never had to perform tasks that required using tools underwater.

When the Diving School was reestablished at the Washington Navy Yard in 1927,[4] the curriculum specifically included training with hand and power tools, including underwater burning with oxygen-hydrogen and oxygen-arc torches. Divers became rated as first class or second class depending on their demonstrated proficiency with tools. The qualifying depth became 150 feet, and students were exposed to pressures of 300 feet in hyperbaric chambers.

No officers were trained as divers until World War II.[5] Until then the only officers with empathy for and understanding of diving that comes from personal experience were those who had spent time as enlisted divers and those such as Edward Ellsberg, who had become a diver in the winter between salvage efforts on S–51. The lack of senior divers and diving advocates militated against rapid technical development and the budgeting required to support a growing technology.

The dedicated group at the Navy Experimental Diving Unit in its wooden building on the Anacostia River in Washington, D.C., continued the work of making helium-oxygen diving a reality. A recirculating helmet had been developed from the standard spun-copper diving helmet. Electrically heated underwear alleviated the diver's heavy heat loss in the helium atmosphere. This underwear, although badly needed in cold water diving, never became popular with divers who feared electricity in sea

---

[3] Later ASR 1.

[4] The first officer-in-charge of the new school was Lieutenant Henry Hartley, who had received his diving training in the old Newport school as a young seaman early in the century. Hartley had been warranted as boatswain in 1915 and commissioned during World War I. In 1925 as commanding officer of *Falcon*, Hartley participated in the S–51 salvage and shortly afterwards in the S–4 salvage. In recognition of his work on these jobs he was awarded the Navy Cross and the Distinguished Service Medal. During the rescue of the *Squalus* survivors, then-Commander Hartley acted as technical advisor to Rear Admiral Cyrus Cole in his old ship, *Falcon*. This pioneer of Navy diving spent forty-seven years in the Navy, retiring in 1947 as rear admiral.

[5] The first officer formally trained as a diver in the U.S. Navy was Lieutenant (later Rear Admiral) C. Monroe Hart. Admiral Hart's work in Navy salvage is described in earlier chapters.

water and in high-oxygen atmospheres. New means of storing and distributing helium-oxygen mixtures were developed. Decompression schedules were calculated and tested. Successful dives were made to depths of 500 feet in hyperbaric chambers,[6] and, in the summer of 1938, to 400 feet in the open sea from *Falcon*. By the late 1930s the Navy Experimental Diving Unit had developed the hardware and procedures required for operational helium-oxygen diving.

The physical problems of decompression continued to exist. Although proper schedules had been worked out, the diver on a line or stage fully dressed in his diving dress was not in the ideal decompression environment. In Britain the Royal Navy had developed the Davis Submerged Decompression Chamber. As its name implies, this was a submerged chamber that the diver could enter at his first decompression stop and in which he could remove his helmet and decompress in the relative comfort of a dry chamber under the watchful eye of a tender. A similar chamber, built and tested at the Navy Experimental Diving Unit around 1938, was never adopted by the U.S. Navy. When the deep-diving team from the Navy Experimental Diving Unit deployed on its first operational helium-oxygen diving job, the chamber did not go with them. U.S. Navy divers would make their decompression stops on a stage.

The first operational, open-sea, helium-oxygen dives took place during the salvage of *Squalus*.[7] Twelve divers from the Navy Experimental Diving Unit were deployed to the accident site as soon as word of the disaster came in. Initial dives on the *Squalus*, including that of Petty Officer Martin C. Sibitzky who connected the downhaul wire for the rescue chamber, were made on air because the officer in charge of the rescue operation felt the job was too important to include the element of risk represented by a relatively untried diving technique.

Air diving at 240 feet proved remarkably inefficient. Air divers accomplished little work, and Petty Officer F.E. Smith and Master Diver Orson Crandall passed out on the bottom. The desirability of shifting to helium-oxygen mixtures became clearer with each dive.

On 27 May 1939, after Coxswain F.H. O'Keefe and Petty Officer R.M. Metzger made shallow dives to check out the system, Chief Petty Officer William F. Badders,[8] a master diver, made the U.S. Navy's first operational

---

[6] The diver making the 500-foot dive was not told his depth; when asked to estimate it, he replied that it "felt like a hundred feet." During decompression he was switched to air at 300 feet and immediately suffered from inert gas narcosis.

[7] Described in chapter 2.

[8] Just two days before, Chief Badders had participated in the most dangerous operation of the rescue and salvage work. Though it was virtually certain all survivors had been rescued from the forward part of the submarine, it would take a check of the after torpedo room to confirm that no living soul remained on board. The conditions in the room were unknown. The pressure in the

helium-oxygen dive. It was the first of 210 such dives made during the *Squalus* salvage operation. The efficiency of divers breathing helium-oxygen mixtures at these depths proved greater than that of air divers. As could be expected, the system had teething troubles in its first operation and field modifications were necessary. Because of the success of the diving on the *Squalus* salvage, however, the U.S. Navy subsequently adopted helium-oxygen techniques for deep diving and the first submarine rescue ships, the *Chanticleer* (ASR 7) class, were built with helium-oxygen diving systems. These ships, like the fleet tugs and salvage ships of the same vintage, were to be long lived. Some remain in commission at this writing some fifty years later.

There was a negative side to the *Squalus* success. Because they had worked so well, the procedures used during the *Squalus* operation became locked in as the correct way to do things without a thorough analysis to see why they worked or how they could be improved. Thus the evolution of diving procedures did not advance as rapidly as it might have if the *Squalus* operation had been less successful and if World War II had not come along to distract the attention of everyone, including divers.

Diving During World War II

During World War II a great deal of diving took place. Divers made invaluable contributions to hundreds of salvage and harbor clearance jobs. More divers were trained than ever before, but the state of the art remained almost stagnant. There simply were few resources to devote to the agonizingly slow development of decompression schedules, diving techniques, and diving equipment. All divers were in the field working on salvage, battle damage repair, and a host of other activities needed to support a rapidly growing Navy at war. For the duration of the hostilities there was no choice but to use available resources, make do with equipment and procedures on hand, and adopt hastily modified apparatus.

Amid the constant everyday work performed by Navy divers in support of the war effort, a few operations stand out. One unusual tasking of divers even became routine: Divers were used to obtain intelligence information—code books and the like—from sunken Japanese ships. Sub-

---

chamber had to be brought up to bottom pressure because, if the room was flooded or partially flooded, water would be blown into the bell. The danger of breathing compressed air at a depth of nearly 200 feet had been demonstrated when Crandall and Smith passed out on the bottom. Badders and the other bell operator, Petty Officer John Mihalowski, blew the bell down and slowly opened the hatch. The after room was filled with water; there were no survivors. Badders and Mihalowski vented the chamber and returned to the surface, their dangerous job done. It was time to get back to the routine work of what would be the first helium-oxygen diving operation. Badders and Mihalowski were awarded the Congressional Medal of Honor for their "bell run" to the after torpedo room.

marine rescue ships were often employed in this work because of their deep diving capability, and because their formally assigned mission did not include combat salvage.

One of the most unusual diving operations of the war took place in the Philippines where American prisoners of war, working under the supervision of their Japanese captors, recovered a portion of the Philippine Treasury that had been dumped into Manila Bay. In this operation the American divers demonstrated a marked inefficiency—or perhaps efficiency—in denying the silver to the Japanese. After the enemy had been driven out of Manila, however, other Navy divers worked much more efficiently from the net tenders *Teak* (AN 35) and *Elder* (AN 20) to recover the Philippine silver.

Most of the diving done during the war lacked this glamor. It was simply the backbreaking, cold, dirty, exhausting work of salvage diving.

By the end of World War II, the position of divers in the Navy had changed. Now there were diving officers who were not only trained but also experienced in the supervision of diving operations. As was the case with overall salvage operations, no single office on the staff of the Chief of Naval Operations represented divers and their interests. As the senior employer of divers in the Bureau of Ships, the Supervisor of Salvage inherited the technical responsibility for diving. However for several years following World War II, naval diving existed and progressed mainly because of the interest and initiative of a small number of people who understood its value and perhaps foresaw the explosion of technology and capability that still lay over the horizon.

New Diving Technologies

The introduction of SCUBA was a precursor of the technological explosion. A free diver carrying his own breathing gas supply obviously had great value for many diving missions and had been the subject of inventive thought for many years. The bits and pieces for the technology had been around for some time, but it remained for a French naval officer, Captain Jacques Yves Cousteau, and an engineer, Emile Gagnan, to put all the pieces together. Working in a Mediterranean village under the difficult and restrictive conditions of the German occupation to build a workable open-circuit air SCUBA, they developed and tested the equipment, dubbed "Aqua-Lung," to the point where it became a commercial success following the war. The U.S. Navy quickly acquired the technology.

Interest in deep diving continued. Experiments focused on deeper diving with helium-oxygen deep-sea equipment. The deepest open-sea dive reached with this equipment came in 1950 when Petty Officer Peter

Pritchett reached 500 feet off the Galapagos Islands. These extreme depths remained in the realm of experimental work. The helium-oxygen decompression tables published in the *Diving Manual*, the bible for working divers, extended only to 410 feet; in 1956 it retreated to 380 feet. But new factors that would have profound effects on deep diving were coming into play.

In conventional diving, decompression is the greatest consumer of time and generally the part of the dive when trouble is most likely to develop. For instance, a diver working for an hour at 200 feet requires more than two hours of nonproductive but necessary decompression to reach the surface. There is no way to avoid decompression, but there is a length of stay at any particular depth at which body tissues become saturated with gas and the duration of decompression becomes independent of the duration of the dive. With theory as their jumping-off place, three men—the U.S. Navy's Captain George F. Bond (MC), Jacques Cousteau, and Edwin A. Link, the builder of the famous Link Trainer aviation simulator—worked independently to turn saturation-diving theory into practice. The implications of saturation diving are tremendous. Theoretically, a diver provided with satisfactory living conditions at bottom pressure could live there indefinitely until completing his work, then slowly return to surface pressure, paying his decompression debt in one lump sum. Saturation diving held great potential for extending the depths at which operational diving could be undertaken practically.

Bond, Commander Robert D. Workman (MC), and Commander Walter F. Mazzone (MSC) began the initial animal tests in 1961, and, after sorting out problems caused by the density and high oxygen content of air, moved to human tests. The human tests, designated Genesis I and II, were conducted on Navy divers at the Submarine Medical Research Laboratory in New London, Connecticut. These tests culminated in a twelve-day exposure to a simulated depth of 200 feet. Before the work of the Genesis projects could be put to the test in the deep ocean, however, a tragedy triggered a major deep-ocean effort and provided the impetus for a wave of new developments.

Thresher

The nuclear attack submarine *Thresher* sank in 8,400 feet of water off the New England coast during trials following her postshakedown availability on 10 April 1963. At the time she went down, the Navy had no organization, no search techniques, and no specific procedures for mounting a deep-ocean search and identification operation. The response to the casualty, however, was immediate. Within a few hours, a full-scale search effort with thirteen ships had been laid on to seek any signs of life from *Thresher*. After some twenty hours, all hope of finding survivors had passed. The operation changed from a search and rescue operation to an *ad hoc* oceanographic effort under Captain Frank A. Andrews to locate the wreck of the submarine. The Navy had an intense interest in determining the cause of the loss for the same reasons it had had in the loss of F–4 nearly fifty years before. If the cause of the disaster could be identified, it could be eliminated in other submarines.

As with all deep-ocean operations, the first step was to find the lost object. Designated as the search area was a square, 10 miles on a side and centered on the position of *Thresher*'s escort, *Skylark* (ASR 20), when contact had been lost. The search team consisted of three elements:

The first part of the team was the sea element, designated Task Force 89.7. This element constantly changed in the number and types of ships depending on the specific task in progress. Captain Andrews commanded the sea element.

The second element was an eleven-man, shore-based brain trust, the CNO Technical Advisory Group, that provided technical guidance and a myriad of other services to support the at-sea effort. Dr. Arthur Maxwell, senior oceanographer from the Office of Naval Research, and Captain Charles B. Bishop chaired this group.

The third element was the *Thresher* Advisory Group set up at Wood's Hole Oceanographic Institution under Mr. Arthur Molloy of the Navy's Oceanographic Office in Suitland, Maryland. This group analyzed all data obtained at sea and prepared search charts. It also performed the necessary work of briefing senior naval officers and the officers of ships joining the search operation.

Just three days after the loss of the submarine, the initial plan for locating *Thresher* was formulated in a conference aboard the Wood's Hole oceanographic research ship *Atlantis II*. This conference included a lengthy radio telephone conversation with Dr. Brackett Hersey, chief physical oceanographer at Wood's Hole, who confirmed the basic plan's consistency with the thinking prevalent in the oceanographic community.

There were four phases to the plan. First, sonic depth-finding sweeps would cover the entire 100-square-mile area in sweeps 300 yards wide. Second, all contacts classified as "possible" would be investigated with deep-towed Geiger counters, side-scan sonars, or magnetometers. Third, all contacts remaining after the first two phases would be photographed with either a deep-sea television camera or a still camera. Finally, photographed wreckage would be examined visually from the bathyscaph *Trieste*.

This imaginative overall plan had a high degree of logic, but there were a few problems. No one knew for sure if the hull of *Thresher* would return an echo from the search fathometer. Some thought the hull would be buried; others suggested it had broken up. Nor did anyone know if navigation of the disaster area could be carried out accurately enough to ensure complete coverage. No one had any real experience at towing the various search sensors near the bottom at great depth or in placing a camera for precise deep photography. It looked like a tough job. It would be.

The search started in accordance with the plan. However, it soon became apparent that because of unpredictable surface currents that forced relatively imprecise navigation, the search would be coarse. Overcoming the problems called for the cluster technique. With this technique, all echoes reported by survey ships are plotted; then a second, third, and even a fourth ship goes into the same area and their echoes are plotted. When a cluster of contacts develop in a small area, it is considered worthy of further investigation.

Twelve positions were defined in this way. As the operation continued, search techniques were refined by better navigation. Unfortunately, with the improvements the twelve positions grew to ninety, many suspected to be bottom topography. Side-scan sonars, cameras, and magnetometers produced no beneficial results, because the towing surface ship had no idea of the position of the sensor on its 9,000-foot towline.

The break that made the difference came on 14 May. *Atlantis II*, working around a high-probability contact designated "Delta," obtained photographs of some very suspicious debris—paper, wire, and twisted metal. The search concentrated on a 2-by-2 mile square—one twenty-fifth of the original search area—centered on Delta. By 15 June debris that obviously came from *Thresher* had been identified. It was time to call in *Trieste*.

With *Fort Snelling* (LSD 30) as a support base and *Preserver* as an assist vessel, *Trieste* made ten dives under the command of Lieutenant Commander Don Keach with Lieutenant John B. (Brad) Mooney, Jr., as copilot. On 6 September the bathyscaph found a large portion of *Thresher*'s wreckage and a debris field that Keach characterized as a huge junkyard. *Thresher* had broken up; hope of determining the specific cause of the accident diminished sharply; the search was over.

Although debris recovered from *Thresher* underwent careful examination, the exact cause of her loss could not be determined. Evidence pointed to rapid flooding resulting from a hull piping failure. Steps were taken to ensure the integrity of hull piping and other submarine systems. In this case the lessons learned by those working in the deep ocean were as important as the modifications that made submarines safer. Locating the wreck of *Thresher* had been a marvelous achievement, but severe problems in search-and-navigation systems, organization, and doctrine remained to be solved. In time, they would be. The solutions would be evolutionary, for each new operation pushed the state of deep-ocean work forward.

The Deep Submergence Review Group

Ten days after the *Thresher*'s loss, Secretary of the Navy Fred H. Korth established a Deep Submergence Review Group chaired by Rear Admiral Edward C. Stephan, then the Oceanographer of the Navy. The dual mission of the Deep Submergence Review Group was to assess the Navy's capabilities in search, rescue, and recovery of objects and to evaluate the concept represented by saturation diving.

The Deep Submergence Review Group's charter called for the group to outline programs for immediate development, draft a five-year program to achieve the ultimate capability the Navy and the nation needed, and recommend an organization to carry out the program. The 2,000-page report of the group affirmed that the Navy lacked the means of operating successfully on rescue and recovery missions in the deep ocean.

Most of the recommendations of the Deep Submergence Review Group, as well as their implementation, are beyond the scope of this chronicle, which is devoted to salvage and the technologies that directly support it. However some of the recommendations did affect salvors. Among these were the group's recommendations to develop the capability to recover both large and small objects from the deep ocean, develop a more modern submarine rescue system and a surface platform to support it, and pursue an operational saturation-diving capability.

The pre-World War II submarine salvages that extended from F–4 to *Squalus* were remarkable deep-ocean operations for their time but, with the exception of helium-oxygen diving on *Squalus*, did little to advance the state of the art. In fact, deep-ocean technology did not progress significantly until well after World War II.

In the late 1950s and early 1960s commercial and research activity in the oceans surged, motivated by the exploration for offshore oil and the Navy's desire to work more effectively in the ocean depths. New tools were required for the development of geophysical and oceanographic information. Commercial submersibles began to appear and to proliferate. Meanwhile, the Navy's mine-warfare community had developed a series of prototype remotely operated vehicles called MERMUT[9] that could swim to underwater ordnance and work on it. The Naval Ordnance

---

[9] MERMUT is the acronym for Mobile Electronics Robot Manipulator and Underwater Television System.

Test Station at Pasadena, California, while working on the launch system for the *Polaris* missiles, borrowed MERMUT. In the course of this program MERMUT became CURV[10] and an ancestor to the successful series of remotely operated vehicles[11] of the CURV family.

Despite all the activity in industry and in the research community within the Navy, there had been relatively little change in real ability to work deep in the ocean until the loss of *Thresher* in 1963 and the impetus given by the recommendations of the Deep Submergence Review Group. A major move forward came on 28 May 1964 when Secretary of the Navy Paul H. Nitze announced the assignment of deep submergence responsibilities to the Chief of Naval Material and the formation of the Deep Submergence Systems Project within the Naval Material Command. At the same time, funding was made available for the necessary applied research and hardware development. Applications for deep-ocean technology could not and would not wait for the scientists and engineers to complete their work.

Major Search and Recovery Jobs

As if to reinforce the urgency of implementing the Deep Submergence Review Group's recommendations, several deep-ocean casualties occurred in the mid-to-late sixties. In each case the U.S. Navy was called on to undertake a major deep-ocean search and recovery operation. Each job challenged the skill and imagination of the Navy's salvage organization. The valuable lessons learned, in terms of both the management of such operations and the effective use of appropriate technologies, pushed forward the state of the art of deep-ocean salvage.

Palomares

A major incident with potentially serious international complications began on 17 January 1966 when two Air Force planes, a B–52 bomber and a KC–135 tanker, collided during a refueling operation 30,500 feet over Spain. The B–52 carried four unarmed nuclear weapons. Three of these were located within twenty-four hours in and about the coastal village of Palomares. The distribution of debris, the location of survivors, and the report of the master of a fishing vessel, Sr. Francisco Simo-Orts,[12] suggested a high probability that the fourth weapon had fallen into the

---

[10] CURV is the acronym for Cable-Controlled Underwater Recovery Vehicle.
[11] A remote-operated vehicle is generally known by the acronym ROV.
[12] The report of Sr. Simo-Orts garnered high credibility because of his ability to return without navigational aids to the spot where he was fishing on the day of the accident.

water, a situation that made the Navy responsible for its recovery.[13]

The Deep Submergence Review Group had identified object location and small-object recovery as one of the technical areas requiring development. A program to develop capabilities in the field had been initiated by the Deep Submergence Systems Project working under Technical Development Plan 46–16, but this had not resulted in any interim capability for deep-ocean search and recovery.[14] From start to finish, the entire Palomares search and recovery operation would have to be improvised and synthesized from diverse elements. It would be a mammoth operation. In fact, the search for the nuclear weapon off Palomares would exceed the *Thresher* search in numbers of persons involved, problems, and logistic requirements.

Even though no specific organization or procedures existed within the Navy for deep ocean search and recovery operations, much had been learned from the *Thresher* search and the emphasis given to deep submergence in the years immediately preceding the weapon loss at Palomares. When the Air Force requested Navy assistance on 22 January, two steps were taken. First, Commander Sixth Fleet ordered the formation of Task Force 65 under the command of Rear Admiral William S. Guest to conduct the surface and subsurface operations off Palomares. Guest reported to Major General Delmar E. Wilson, USAF, the Commander of the 16th Air Force and the overall commander of the recovery. Second, as in the case of *Thresher*, the Chief of Naval Operations formed a Technical Advisory Group in Washington, this time under Rear Admiral Leroy V. Swanson, to act for him and to provide equipment and technical people.

The time between the request for Navy assistance and the recovery of the weapon fell into three distinct periods. The first phase, 22 January through 17 February, was devoted to mobilization—designating, readying, and transporting the equipment—and, insofar as possible, identifying the problems. The search phase lasted from 17 February until 15 March, and the recovery phase extended from 15 March to 7 April.

During the build-up phase, Explosive Ordnance Disposal and Underwater Demolition Team divers searched the bottom from the high-water mark to a depth of 80 feet. Their work recovered a great deal of aircraft wreckage and provided assurance that the weapon did not lie in this inshore area. Simultaneously, sonar searches were made with the Ocean Bottom Search Sonar and mine-hunting sonars. The mine-hunting sonar

---

[13] Department of Defense policy, implemented by a Chief of Naval Operations directive, gave the Navy the responsibility of disposing of the explosive ordnance of all services when it lay to seaward of the high-water mark.

[14] Congressional testimony following the operation resulted in appropriation of a $2.5 million add-on to the fiscal year 1967 budget for deep-ocean search and recovery.

contacts were investigated by the small Perry submersible *Cubmarine* or by divers.

By 17 February two deep-diving submersibles—*Alvin*, operated by Wood's Hole Oceanographic Institution for the Office of Naval Research, and *Aluminaut*, owned and operated by Reynolds Aluminum—were ready to operate. Guest designated two high-priority search areas: Alfa I, a circular area of one-mile radius around the position reported by fisherman Simo-Orts, and Alfa II, an inshore area where most of the debris had been found. *Alvin* and *Aluminaut* were assigned to Alfa I because the rugged bottom topography made acoustic search virtually useless.

The submersibles conducted an effective visual search in Alfa I, although detection ranges rarely exceeded 15 feet. The weapon was ultimately found by a modified random search enhanced by good luck that balanced limited vision. *Alvin*'s pilots, Valentine Wilson and Marvin McCamas, elected to search along the contours of the steep bottom slopes, reasoning correctly that the weapon may have slid down a slope leaving a discernible track.

On 1 March during her tenth dive *Alvin* sighted a bottom furrow, but lost it while tracking it down the slope. On 15 March *Alvin* relocated the furrow. In an outstanding feat of seamanship, she backed down the slope, keeping the furrow in view through her bow ports until, at a depth of 2,550 feet, she was dramatically rewarded by the sight of a parachute enshrouding a cylindrical object of the right size and shape. *Aluminaut* immediately rendezvoused with *Alvin* and baby-sat the object for twenty-two hours while *Alvin* replenished and prepared to return. The oceanographic research ship USNS *Mizar* (T–AGOR 11), a veteran of the *Thresher* search, fixed the position so the submersibles could return without delay.

Wedged in a "vee" on a 70-degree slope, the object presented a difficult recovery problem. The first attempt on 24 March failed when the hoisting line parted, and the object, still enshrouded in the parachute, fell back to the bottom. The search began all over again. On 2 April *Alvin* again located the weapon, now 120 yards from its original position and 300 feet deeper. Again *Aluminaut* stood watch while *Alvin* surfaced to recharge, then marked the position.

When the first lift attempt failed, the Technical Advisory Group ordered CURV to be modified for operation at 3,000 feet and flown to the scene. *Petrel* (ASR 14) loaded CURV in Cartagena and took it to the site. On 5 April CURV, guided to the weapon by *Alvin*'s copilot Wilson, attached a line to the apex of the parachute. The following day she attached a line to a bundle of parachute shrouds. On 7 April, while attempting to attach a final line, CURV became entangled and could not be freed. Rear Admiral Guest made the decision to hoist the bundle with

CURV still entangled. Hoisting began from *Petrel*; *Alvin* stood by in the water tracking the weapon during the lift. An hour later the weapon came aboard *Petrel*.

The recovery of the nuclear weapon off Palomares was the first time all three types of underwater work systems—divers, submersibles, and remote-operated vehicles—complemented one another in a single operation. Each was properly employed and demonstrated its place in deep-ocean work.

The operation had been totally ad hoc in nature, assembling its resources from a wide variety of sources within the Navy and from industry. Navy elements were generally overstaffed in numbers but lacking in the required experience. Industry elements were the opposite—understaffed but expert in their capabilities. After the operation, the entire task force was disbanded, leaving only the residual expertise of individuals, an outcome inherent in task force operations. Edward Ellsberg had vociferously decried this practice following the submarine salvage operations of the 1920s, and the CNO Technical Advisory Group decried it following Palomares. Along with the President's Panel on Oceanography, the Technical Advisory Group saw a national need for small-object recovery from the deep ocean and deemed it the responsibility of the Navy to develop and maintain this capability.

A major factor driving the development of a ready-to-go, deep-ocean recovery capability was the degree of interest of other nations or commercial firms in gaining access to lost objects and their ability to do so. It

The early remote-operated vehicle CURV is hoisted aboard *Petrel* during the search for the nuclear weapon lost off Spain in 1966.

The nuclear weapon lost off Palomares, before and after recovery.

behooved the United States as a major world power and a major user of the world's oceans and airways to have an object-recovery capability that could be mobilized quickly anywhere in the world.

Both technology and economics militate against developing and maintaining an all-encompassing standby capability for deep-ocean recovery. The capability must be constantly updated—as must the hardware—or it will become obsolete sitting in a warehouse between jobs. And because work in the deep ocean is tremendously expensive—the Navy sent the Air Force a bill for more than $5 million for the Palomares bomb recovery—it is not economically feasible to maintain a seldom-used, deep-water contingency capability.

Although the Navy has developed the ability to recover a wide variety of objects at various depths, major and complex recoveries still require an ad hoc force assembled from both within and outside the Navy, wherever the best technology and experience exist.

Two Searches

By the late 1960s submersibles and remotely operated vehicles were working in the Navy's laboratories and test ranges recovering weapons and other objects from the bottom. Appropriately, these vehicles found their employment in the same type of work—recovering modern weaponry—that had formalized diving in the Navy in the preceding century. Within a short time after the recovery of the nuclear weapon at Palomares, nine experimental torpedoes were recovered from a depth of 3,000 feet off St. Croix, and a classified test shape was picked up near Vieques in Puerto Rico. As it had so many times before, improvisation played a major role in both cases. Making the best of the resources available, and changing plans to meet changing conditions, has always been the hallmark of the salvor, and especially in deep ocean recovery operations, it will always be necessary.

A major search operation in response to an emergency occurred when the Liberty ship *Robert Louis Stevenson*, loaded with 2,000 tons of explosives, was intentionally scuttled off the Aleutians. The ship, part of a program to dispose of deteriorated or defective ammunition and to assist the Advanced Research Project Agency's nuclear explosion detection program, failed to sink as planned. Libertys had always been tough; *Stevenson* proved no exception. She drifted for sixteen hours, hid in a fog bank, and finally sank in water too shallow to activate the water pressure detonators designed for 4,000 feet. A unique emergency resulted; it was feared that the pressure signature of a ship passing over the sunken hulk would be enough to explode *Stevenson*'s cargo.

To eliminate the danger, the Navy Oceanographic Office sent the

USNS *Silas Bent* (T–AGS 26) to locate the sunken ship, positively identify it, and either detonate the cargo or provide a high level of assurance that the cargo could not be detonated. Rear Admiral Donald M. White, Commander, Alaskan Sea Frontier, in his role as Commander Task Force 93, had overall responsibility for eliminating the emergency; Captain Alfred F. Betzel, Commander Service Squadron Seven, was on-scene commander as was Commander John Orem, the Pacific Fleet salvage officer.

Attempts to detonate *Stevenson* by dropping aircraft bombs on the best available datums proved unsuccessful. After a long delay for refurbishing equipment idle since the *Thresher* search, a deep-towed magnetometer search started on 5 September. On 11 September a contact with the expected characteristics was detected and confirmed, first by narrow beam echo sounder and then by additional runs with both sensors. Following location of the wreck the towed camera took photographs that supplied positive identification of the ship. Accurate bombing runs with explosions within the desired range failed to detonate the cargo. *Robert Louis Stevenson* could be declared not hazardous to shipping. The operation ended. A complex search operation had again been carried out by an ad hoc organization with equipment available off the shelf. The only significant delays were in putting together the people and equipment to do the job.

Another effective ad hoc organization reacted to an emergency more in the manner of the Palomares bomb recovery when the search was on for the submarine *Scorpion* (SSN 589). In May 1968, *Scorpion* disappeared crossing the Atlantic en route to her home port of Norfolk, Virginia. A mammoth search along her projected route, including intensive searches of numerous seamounts, failed to turn up any trace of the submarine. A prolonged search by *Mizar*'s deep-towed camera system finally located *Scorpion*'s hull some 400 miles southwest of the Azores in more than 10,000 feet of water. The winter season in the North Atlantic allowed no more than extensive photography of the hull, and so the Navy's Court of Inquiry had little information on which to base a determination of the possible cause of the loss.

Two means of investigating the hull were seriously considered. The first, simpler and less costly, would also provide less information about the cause of the casualty. It involved inspection of the wreck as she lay by submarine technical experts in the bathyscaph *Trieste*. The second approach, much more complex, involved a more detailed exterior survey, entry into the hull, and recovery of selected items. A paper study of the engineering and operational requirements for the second option and designs for some special tools for entering the hull showed the work at this depth would be horrendously expensive and would probably produce few significant results.

The first option was chosen. Captain Harry Jackson, a submarine design expert, inspected the hull from *Trieste* the following spring. The inspection was not conclusive, and the specific cause of the *Scorpion*'s loss remains unknown.

An accident to a small submersible a few months after the loss of *Scorpion* had a happier ending.

The Recovery of *Alvin*

On 16 October 1968, *Alvin*, the star of the Palomares weapon recovery and arguably the most successful small submersible ever built, was preparing for a routine dive to inspect some oceanographic buoy moorings 90 miles south southeast of Cape Cod. The dive turned out to be far from routine. Lifting lines aboard *Alvin*'s tender *Lulu* parted, and *Alvin* plunged 5,051 feet to the bottom with her hatch open.

Although no object of *Alvin*'s size and weight had ever been recovered from such a depth, an immediate operation to raise *Alvin* began under the sponsorship of the Supervisor of Salvage. Unfortunately time did not permit the careful planning and selection of work systems that can spell the difference between success and failure in deep-ocean operations. In the initial recovery operation, the submersible DOWB[15] attempted to place a lift device in *Alvin*'s open hatch; the submersible would then be lifted by a long line suspended from the Wood's Hole research ship, *Chain*.[16] Casualties and handling difficulties with DOWB plagued the operation, but the storms that swept the area were even more disruptive. It was obvious that the North Atlantic winter would be no more hospitable to the *Alvin* recovery than it had been to the recent *Scorpion* search. The operation terminated without success on 23 November 1968.

Alvin remained on the bottom throughout the winter, a powerful challenge to salvors and ocean engineers alike. In June 1969, *Mizar* photographed *Alvin* lying intact on the sea bottom, the only apparent damage being a broken tail shroud and propeller. Salvage planning now began in earnest. The Supervisor of Salvage, Captain Gene Mitchell, would be in overall charge; Lieutenant Commander Milwee of his office was assigned as on-scene commander, with Mr. Earl F. (Curly) Lawrence as his principal assistant. The work would be planned and executed as an ordinary salvage job rather than a complex ocean-engineering operation; there would be no Technical Advisory Group in Washington providing expertise. This would be the first major deep-ocean operation conducted in this manner.

The basic salvage plan followed the pattern of the previous autumn's

[15] DOWB is the acronym for Deep Ocean Work Boat.
[16] Formerly *Chain* (ARS 20).

operation. A submersible would insert a lift device in *Alvin*'s hatch, and a surface craft would make the lift. Three factors dominated the planning: the submersible and the platform to make the lift, and the weather. There weren't many options to choose from—only a few submersibles could operate below 5,000 feet, suitable lift platforms were limited, and suitable weather could be expected only in late summer. *Aluminaut*, *Alvin*'s old friend from Palomares, had the best qualities for the submerged operations. *Mizar*, in addition to being a sophisticated oceanographic platform, had the stability and space needed for a lift ship. Adequate room existed on her deck to install the traction winch for hauling the recovery line. The lift could be made through the ship's center well, eliminating many sources of excitation of the lift line, a major consideration in a lift line that was almost a mile long.

Salvage forces gathered in Boston for preparations and sailed for the lift site on 12 August. While *Aluminaut* rehearsed in Provincetown harbor, *Mizar* went to sea. Once she had located and marked the sunken submersible, the recovery operation began.

On her third dive *Aluminaut* approached *Alvin* and climbed her side, tearing away the fiberglass sail to reach the hatch more easily. After several trips pilot Bob Canary, a former Navy submariner, placed the lift

Aluminaut crew and support people work to rig the line reel on the submersible's bow early in the operation that recovered *Alvin*.

bar in *Alvin's* open hatch, tripped the toggle, and set it with a pull. The bitter end of the toggle line was hooked into the lift line and *Aluminaut* surfaced after a dive of almost eighteen hours.

Aluminaut surfaced in moderating seas and cleared the area while the lift line was transferred to *Mizar* and rigged to the traction winch. Hauling started. Tension in the line climbed to 9,000 pounds—near the in-water weight of *Alvin*—and held steady. When *Alvin* reached 90 feet, divers attached her regular lifting sling and secured all the loose equipment. At 30 feet they wrapped the submersible in a nylon net and transferred the load to three inflatable salvage pontoons that would support *Alvin* during the 96-mile tow to shallow water.

On 1 September 1969, Labor Day morning, a crane lifted *Alvin* from the waters of Menemsha Bight and set her aboard a barge; preservation and restoration began immediately. Another deep-ocean operation had ended successfully. The outstanding record of *Alvin* in subsequent oceanographic research and ocean-engineering operations testifies to the value of the recovery.

The recovery operation itself showed the value of simple, highly detailed, and flexible plans with carefully thought-out alternatives. Rehearsal time was well spent and led directly to time-saving changes. The most significant lesson of the *Alvin* recovery was that deep-ocean operations can be conducted on a routine basis using Navy and industry resources. Meanwhile, as such operations were being carried out with increasing frequency, a portion of the ocean community was devoting its attention to developing the technology of diving. The results were spectacular.

The Deep-Diving Technological Explosion

Well before the Deep Submergence Review Group completed its study and made its recommendations, the Chief of Naval Research brought together experts from a number of laboratories to build on the foundations laid during the Genesis saturation-diving during project. The next step, SeaLab I, was a bottom-habitat, saturation-diving experiment at a depth of 195 feet on the Plantagenet Bank off Bermuda. The purpose of the experiment was to evaluate human ability to work under the water at moderate depths for prolonged periods. Although the operation had to be curtailed ten days early because of an approaching storm, it achieved all its goals and, most importantly, it conclusively demonstrated the feasibility of open-sea saturation diving. The technological explosion that would last more than a decade was well under way.

SeaLab I had not been planned as an isolated trial but as the first in

SeaLab I and the men who operated it.

a series of bottom habitat experiments in a program of physiological research, scientific investigations, and work tests. With the establishment of the Deep Submergence Systems Project, responsibility for the SeaLab series moved to that organization under the auspices of the Man-in-the-Sea Program, and their technical office in San Diego did the field work.

In late 1965 the second SeaLab experiment was carried out in 205 feet of water 65 miles off La Jolla, California. An ambitious ocean-floor program occupied SeaLab II divers on the bottom. It consisted of scientific construction and salvage tasks; some went well, some not so well, some didn't go at all. Much, however, was learned about working in the ocean, and contributions were made to a number of undersea science and engineering disciplines. SeaLab II represented another significant step forward in enabling human beings to live and work in a hostile environment.

Immediately after SeaLab II planning began for the next experiment. SeaLab III would be a quantum leap downward, with habitat placement initially planned for 450 feet, then finalized at 600 feet. Highly specialized surface support technology would be needed to support life at the greater depth. This required a complex and capable diving system in which divers could live or decompress in pressurized chambers on deck and travel between the SeaLab and the support ship in a pressurized personnel transfer capsule. To fulfill this requirement, the prototype of the Mark II Deep Dive System that would be installed in the newly constructed ASR–21 class, catamaran-hulled, submarine-rescue ships was built and installed in *Elk River* (IX 501). *Elk River*, LSMR–501 before conversion to a surface-support ship for SeaLab II, would have a long career as the home of this diving system.

The order-of-magnitude increase in complexity when going from 205 to 600 feet caused delays while hardware was developed, tested, improved, and retested. When the habitat was put in place in February 1969, numerous helium leaks developed. During an attempt to repair the leakage and open the habitat for occupancy, one of the divers, Barry Cannon, an engineer from the Mine Defense Laboratory, died. The SeaLab series died with him. Shortly after, the program was cancelled and never taken up again. With the termination of the SeaLab Project, the need for the operational diving organization at the Deep Submergence Systems Project Technical Office in San Diego no longer existed. The organization and all its people and assets were transferred intact to the recently formed Submarine Development Group One, where they became the Navy's largest and most varied operational diving group.

In the sixties, under the impetus of offshore oil development, commercial operators were diving deeper than the Navy and had built a number of deep-dive systems. New helmets and suits seemed to spring forth daily. The first commercial saturation dive took place in 1966. But the Navy had not been idle, nor were all the Navy's diving eggs in the SeaLab basket. There was considerable interest in deep diving for salvage.

The Navy Experimental Diving Unit, for some time a joint command with the Deep Sea Divers School, separated into its own command with an engineering duty officer in charge.[17] The name of the diving school was changed to Naval School, Diving and Salvage, to emphasize the salvage portion of its mission. Just as salvage training in World War II had benefited from the lessons learned in the field, training at the renamed school included the lessons being learned in Vietnam.

Divers at the Navy Experimental Diving Unit had been working toward greater depths, but their accomplishments had not yet been translated into operational capability. In fact, as a result of an accident in which two divers diving from *Skylark* were killed, surface-supplied diving had been limited to a maximum depth of 300 feet. Two aircraft crashes off Vietnam in the mid–1960s drew attention to the need for modernizing the Navy's deep-diving capability. The crashes required salvage work at depths that commercial divers could reach but that were too deep for Navy divers.

Captain Bill Searle, now Supervisor of Salvage, looked to industry as a means of providing a quick solution to the Navy's deep-diving problem.

---

[17] Commander Eugene B. Mitchell was the first engineering duty officer in charge of the Navy Experimental Diving Unit.

Petty Officer P.A. Wells applies salvage foam to a sunken aircraft during SeaLab II.

Senior officers at the SeaLab II site. Left to right: Captain George Bond (MC); Captain Bill Searle, the Supervisor of Salvage, and Commander Tom Blockwick. Photo courtesy Captain Willard F. Searle, Jr.

The capabilities of the ADS–IV diving system—operated by Ocean Systems, Inc., in oil field service—seemed just what the doctor ordered. The system increased diving depth, improved safety, and added flexibility to diving operations.

Ocean Systems divers, including ex-Navy Master Diver Del Thomason, demonstrated the system and then, when leasing arrangements had been completed, trained an initial team from Harbor Clearance Unit One off Santa Barbara. The Navy and Ocean Systems team moved to Subic Bay via Hawaii. Commander Paul G. Linaweaver (MC), an experienced diving medical officer, had been specially assigned to Harbor Clearance Unit One to provide medical coverage for the ADS–IV. While in Hawaii the Master Diver assigned to the system, Chief Petty Officer Richard C. (Blackie) Villasenor, made a demonstration dive with this ADS–IV system to 450 feet for the Service Force Commander, Rear Admiral Edwin B. Hooper. The system then became a part of Harbor Clearance Unit One. The ADS–IV was regularly installed on salvage ships and tugs passing through Subic, and divers assigned to those ships

Personnel transfer capsule of the ADS–IV diving system backs up three diving officers. Left to right: Lieutenant (jg) Rick Jones, Lieutenant Art Erwin, and Commander Paul Linaweaver (MC).

as well as all divers assigned to HCU-One were trained in the system.

The system's first operation came in October 1967 when an A3B aircraft crashed in Subic Bay. After the wreckage had been located in 144 feet of water, *Safeguard* loaded the ADS–IV aboard and began recovery. Although the wreck did not lie particularly deep, the flexibility offered by the ADS–IV allowed the work to go quickly. Recovery of the aircraft was completed in only four days. A black incident in U.S. naval history, the capture of *Pueblo* (AGER 2), provided the opportunity to demonstrate the system's portability. The ADS–IV flew to Japan to stand by for operations at the capture site; it departed Subic Bay less than twenty-four hours after the word to go came in.

Nevertheless, in terms of its usefulness in Navy operations, the system had its ups and downs. For most of its service the ADS–IV was in a training and standby status, giving many Navy divers their first experience with deep-diving systems. However one unfortunate incident during an actual operation dampened the Navy's enthusiasm. A diver was killed while diving from the system during an aircraft recovery operation off the Korean coast. The investigation that followed ruled out mechanical malfunction or system failure, but the system had little use for some time afterwards. The ADS–IV was later purchased by the Navy, and after a period of inactivity and refurbishment, returned to Harbor Clearance Unit One redesignated as the SDS–450. It never returned to full operation, however, and was eventually cannibalized to build a fly-away, surface-supplied, mixed-gas diving system.

Despite its limited operational use, the ADS–IV was a necessary step in the evolution of deep diving in the U.S. Navy, serving as a direct ancestor of the Navy's first deep-diving system built for that purpose, the Mark I.

The designers and planners of the new ATS-type salvage and rescue ships realized that, to keep the size of the ship within reason, some of the equipment must be carried abroad only when needed. This applied particularly to larger, seldom-used items. Deep-diving equipment fell within this category. The ship had space and gas storage for an 850-foot diving system capability. Thus whenever the mission included deep diving, the new Mark I Deep System would be loaded into a salvage hold below the after deck. The system bore a family resemblance to the ADS–IV but had greater capability and thus greater size and complexity.

The Mark I system was completed before the first of the new ships. For its initial checkout in 1970 it went to Port Hueneme, California, where it was loaded aboard *Gear*[18] in 1970. Ocean System divers, and then Navy divers, operated the system. The Navy's crew consisted of carefully selected ADS–IV and Navy Experimental Diving Unit veterans led by Lieutenant Lawrence T. Bussey, Chief Warrant Officer Russell McEntire, and Master Diver Joe Bates. The initial checkout included a saturation dive to 850 feet by Chief Petty Officers Tyrone Goacher and Joseph E. (Goose) Langdon, and Petty Officers John T. Brady and Charles D. Wetzel. Immediately afterward a full-fledged operational evaluation of the system, heavily supported by Submarine Development Group One's

---

[18] *Gear* was operated by the Navy's principal salvage contractor, Murphy-Pacific Marine Salvage, on behalf of the Navy.

Diving Division, took place off *Gear* with additional open-sea dives to 850 feet.

Experience with the system showed that to ensure reliability, the complex mechanism must be exercised regularly. If the salvage and rescue ship were the only platform[19] available for it, the system could not be exercised frequently enough to ensure its operability. A covered lighter, YFNB–43, was redesignated YDT–16 and modified to receive the system. After installation and checkout of the barge-diving system, it joined Harbor Clearance Unit Two at Norfolk in late 1971, giving the Atlantic Fleet a first-class deep-diving capability.

The Mark I Deep Dive System operated in the Chesapeake Bay and off Panama City, Florida. Among the dives conducted were a dive to 500 feet in January 1974, a dive to 1,000 feet less than a month later, a dive to 1,148 feet by a combined team of U.S. Navy and Royal Navy divers,[20] and a dive to 300 meters by a Royal Navy dive team.

The future of the Mark I seemed bright, but electrical problems and high maintenance and operating costs plagued the system. It appeared that the Mark I represented an important deep-diving capability for which there was little demand. As a result of a management decision that weighed the costs of operation and maintenance against utility and competing priorities, the system went out of service in 1976. A civilian organization, the Institute of Diving, obtained custody of the Mark I Deep Dive System and put it on display at its museum in Panama City. The fate of the Mark I is representative of the problem of maintaining capabilities that are specialized but infrequently used—a problem faced by Navy salvage and diving planners from the beginning.

Another Navy deep-dive system met with considerably more success. Although contemporaneous with the development of the Mark I, the Mark II Deep Dive System was quite different. It was part of the submergence equipment slated for the new catamaran submarine-rescue ships *Pigeon* (ASR 21) and *Ortolan* (ASR 22). The construction of these ships resulted directly from the recommendations of the Deep Submergence Review Group. As previously noted, the Mark II prototype, the Mark II Mod 0, had been installed in *Elk River* to support the SeaLab III operation. That operation occupied the system only briefly but continued in service as the heart of the Navy's saturation diving school. The Mark II

---

[19] Experience on *Gear* showed that the system could be loaded aboard, and operated from, a narrow-hull ARS; however, modifications to the ship's boom, a special over-the-side handling system and additional generators and gas storage space would be required that were not truly practical for Fleet operations. The ARSs could not be considered a satisfactory platform of opportunity for the Mark I.

[20] One Royal Navy officer and one Chief Petty Officer were assigned to the Mark I Deep Dive System in exchange billets.

Mod I systems, built for the submarine-rescue ships, benefited from the elimination of many of the Mod 0 bugs identified during the SeaLab and subsequent operations.

The Mark II system has proved a valuable tool in a variety of jobs, ranging from the salvage of a Coast Guard boat off the mouth of the Columbia River to assisting scientific studies at great depth and providing standby capability for saturation-diver training. Perhaps most important, the system is available in a high state of readiness for dives to storage depths of 850 feet whenever and wherever they are required.

The Deep Dive Systems are the largest and most obvious manifestations of the deep-diving work done by the Navy, but many peripheral developments have been of equal importance. Deep diving pushed forward every aspect of diving technology. There were major advances in communications, materials, respiratory technology, use of electricity underwater, gas storage and mixing, decompression, excursions above and below saturation depths, chamber design, underwater tools, fire safety, and instrumentation for monitoring divers' physiological responses. With these advances came a new appreciation for the difference between practicality and pie-in-the-sky. Many paths were tried; many had dead ends. The deep ocean proved a very difficult environment that can be conquered only with painstaking care and engineering.

The complexity of deep diving changed the image of the diver. The stereotype of a diver as a sailor with a size 54 jumper and a size 3 hat, though never true, was now thoroughly outdated. The modern diver required not only a full measure of fitness, courage, and determination, but also had to be a skilled technician with a comprehensive understanding of life-support technology far more sophisticated than that used in space life support.

Besides providing general advances in technology and a deep-diving capability within the Navy, the deep-diving program of the 1960s and 1970s had another advantage for the nation. The Navy had the resources—both money and facilities—to do research far beyond the capability of industry. By carrying out expensive and lengthy diving research and making the results available to the public, the Navy originated and disseminated technology that gave American diving companies a competitive position in the international market of oil field diving. A combination of basic research by the government and the practical acumen of American business for translating technology into practice led to American dominance of commercial deep diving for many years. And the street ran both ways. Commercial field experience was fed back to Navy programs.

Overall management of diving within the Navy had not fared well during the period of rapid technological development. Although management had been improved as a result of the recommendations of the Deep Submergence Review Group, it remained fragmented and without a sponsor in the office of the Chief of Naval Operations. This situation changed on 26 May 1969 when the office of the Supervisor of Diving was established in the Naval Ship Systems Command with resources available in the Supervisor of Salvage's office and the Navy Experimental Diving Unit. Despite the fact that most people in it now wore two or even three hats, Navy diving began to take on form and structure.

Not long afterward, the structure became significantly sturdier. On 31 October 1969 the Chief of Naval Operations announced the establishment of a Deep Submergence Systems Program under the direction of Rear Admiral Maurice H. Rindskopf as Deep Submergence Systems Coordinator.[21] The office had specific responsibility for helium-oxygen and saturation diving systems. It determined requirements, selected work, and appraised the value and military worth of work in progress for these systems.

The paperwork that formed the foundation of any modern program in the Navy—general and specific operational requirements—was written, rewritten, staffed, and approved for all types of diving. Diving continued to acquire the legitimacy and direction necessary to obtain and hold on to a budget for development and acquisition. While Navy diving was benefiting from both the explosion of technology and more effective management, actual operations in the deep ocean, many well beyond diving depths, continued.

A Variety of Work

As the Navy's ability to undertake recovery under the oceans increased, so did the calls for this work. By the early 1970s it was obvious that subsea search and recovery operations would form a major part of the work of Navy salvors. Because industry and advanced technology organizations like naval laboratories can keep abreast of rapidly changing technology better than the uniformed services, it also became apparent that contractor- and laboratory-supported operations would be the most efficient and cost-effective approach for deep-ocean work.

The Supervisor of Salvage undertook the design and construction of the remotely operated vehicle *Deep Drone* to support his work in deep recoveries. This vehicle would be husbanded by a contractor, with its work at sea supervised by the Supervisor of Salvage. In addition to the customary contracts for salvage services, the Supervisor of Salvage now maintained a contract for search and recovery services with a company

---

[21] Originally OP–03U, later OP–23.

specializing in this technology. Search and recovery contractors would work with the fleet to provide expertise and technology just as salvage contractors had for many years. The variety of the work that would be undertaken was fantastic.

All of this had just begun to happen when *Alvin* surfaced again in September 1969. A deeper job that lacked the sophistication of the *Alvin* recovery occurred almost immediately.

A Job for the AEC

The Atomic Energy Commission placed an acoustical beacon, known as SNAP–7E, on the ocean floor off Bermuda in 1964. After several years of perfect behavior, the beacon suddenly stopped functioning. The commission wanted it back to determine the cause of the failure. Recovery would not be easy; the beacon lay 16,000 feet down. A submerged riser buoy held SNAP–7E proud of the bottom, while a mooring of two LWT anchors, one 6,000 pounds, the other 2,000 pounds, kept it in place. Each anchor was connected to the buoy by a short piece of chain and about 4 miles of grapnel line.

Grappling, the process of dragging a grapnel along the bottom until it snags the object being sought, is perhaps the oldest and simplest means of underwater search. Many sailors can recall long days of grappling for aircraft and other wreckage before the side-scan sonar brought science to underwater search. Grappling is still an effective technique when the object being sought is long and slender—like 4 miles of line—and when runs with the grapnel can be made perpendicular to the object. Cable-laying ships often grapple to locate and retrieve submerged cables for repair. The unsophisticated but often effective technique of grappling was the obvious choice for grabbing the SNAP–7E mooring line.

The concept of the recovery called for the cable-laying ship *Aeolus* (ARC 3) to make grappling runs perpendicular to the mooring legs in an attempt to pick up the leg attached to the 2,000-pound anchor. Runs would start near the anchor and move progressively closer to the beacon.

The first run started in the small hours of 23 November 1969, following six hours of paying out 3 miles of grappling line. When this run failed, *Aeolus* made a second run one mile closer to the beacon. This too failed. The grappling line was hauled up and the rig overhauled. *Aeolus* then moved to within one-half mile of SNAP–7E and steamed ahead at one knot. This run succeeded; tension rose in the line and lifting began, slowly at first, then more rapidly when it was ascertained that the grapnel had engaged firmly.

Unlike the *Alvin* operation where the weather favored the salvors, the weather for the SNAP–7E recovery was more normal for winter in the

North Atlantic. Playing the line tension as though they were fighting a fish in the rising seas and skillfully controlling the lift with the cable-laying machinery in *Aeolus*, the salvors brought the beacon to the surface, checked it for radiation leakage, and swung it on board. Another deep-recovery operation had been completed.

No Mere Snapshots

Work kept coming. On 7 March 1970 the National Aeronautics and Space Administration had launched a rocket carrying a Naval Research Laboratory camera package for photographing a solar eclipse. Following the eclipse the instrumentation package fell into 6,000 feet of water some 75 miles east of Norfolk, apparently lost. The film had tremendous importance to the scientific community, and NASA and the Naval Research Laboratory asked the Supervisor of Salvage to undertake its recovery.

In a format that would become routine, the operation combined naval operating forces, naval laboratories, and industry in a single coordinated effort to complete a deep-water recovery. Arrangements were made with Service Squadron Eight for the salvage ship *Opportune* to be the base for the remotely operated vehicle CURV and to be also the command and control ship for the operation. CURV was flown to Norfolk from the West Coast, installed in *Opportune*, and taken to sea.

One advantage of remotely operated vehicles is that they are tireless. Unlike a diver or a manned submersible, a remotely operated vehicle can remain on the bottom doing its job while topside people rotate in a work-rest cycle. When *Opportune* arrived at the position of the film package, CURV made the 5,800-foot dive and began to search near two possible impact points some 2 miles apart. It was like looking for a piece of buckshot on a football field at night with a flashlight.

CURV's first dive came late on the night of 17 March. After sixteen hours on the bottom, electrical problems forced the vehicle to surface. *Opportune* returned to port, where repairs were quickly made. Selecting the other impact point, CURV dived again in the late afternoon of 21 March. Early in the first watch on 22 March, just eight hours after starting to search, CURV found the package, grasped it with its manipulator, and started for the surface a mile above. Surfacing proceeded slowly. More than twenty-one hours since starting her dive, *Opportune* hoisted CURV aboard, the valuable film package safe.

The Large Object Salvage System

Among the recommendations of the Deep Submergence Review Group that became part of the charter of the Deep Submergence Systems

Project, was the development of a capability to lift objects as heavy as 3,000 tons from continental shelf depths. Specific Operational Requirements 46–17 described what was needed and became the foundation for the Large Object Salvage System (LOSS) program.

Initial study presented a number of development concepts. The one selected was a direct descendent of the submarine pontoon salvage method that had been so successful before World War II. Steel pontoons, each with a lift capacity of a hundred tons, would be positioned by a specially constructed, remotely operated vehicle on the object to be lifted. Development efforts under the Deep Submergence Systems Project concentrated on individual components of the LOSS system. When management of the work shifted to the Supervisor of Salvage in 1969, component development had progressed to the point where integration of the components into a system and preparation for trials at sea could begin.

A series of tests, first in model, then in full scale off Panama City, Florida, proved both the concept and the individual pieces of hardware, including attachment, gas generation, and positioning methods. The testing was methodical, with complete and careful documentation. Each component was tested individually, and management decisions were based on analyses of the tests. Complete specifications were prepared and two pontoons were built.

By the fall of 1976 the system was ready for a technical evaluation with the participation of the Operational Test and Evaluation Force and fleet units. That year, with *Recovery* as the primary platform and with divers from Harbor Clearance Unit Two participating, the pontoons were positioned by their special pontoon implantment vehicle on a 150-ton test object in 125 feet of water. One pontoon and its liquid nitrogen deballasting system performed flawlessly. The second pontoon had some problems. Before they could be solved, the weather degenerated and the operation terminated. Even though incomplete, the test was successful enough to give rise to the decision to conduct an operational demonstration the following summer using commercial salvors.

On 14 June 1977 the pontoons were towed to the test site by commercial tugs. Currents prevented placing the pontoons for two days, but by 17 June both had been placed by the pontoon implantment vehicle, and the object was ready for lifting. The lift operation began around 3:30 p.m.; less than three hours later the pontoons were on the surface, the object hanging beneath them. In another five hours the pontoons and object were ready for tow. Unfortunately, the test object fell free of the pontoons while under tow. Despite this loss, the demonstration of the Large Object Salvage System had been a success. The Navy had in hand the technology and methods for recovering large objects from the continental shelf.

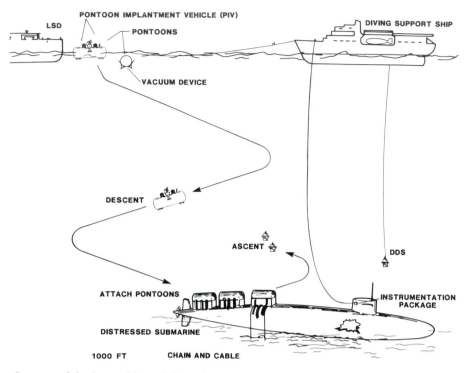

Concept of the Large Object Salvage System.

The decision to be made at this point reached beyond project management into salvage policy and posture. Should additional hardware be built and the system tested to its full depth capability, then stored ready to respond at the first need? Or should the technology be considered proven and placed on the shelf to serve as a basic building block when needed?

The fate of the old submarine-salvage pontoons provided a useful precedent. These pontoons, not used on an actual submarine salvage since *Squalus* in 1939, had sat in their storage yards for years. Despite periodic refurbishments they had gradually deteriorated until they were no longer useful. They were disposed of in the late 1970s. The Navy decided it would not encumber itself with an on-the-shelf capability for submarine salvage that would be infrequently, if ever, used. Instead, now that the technology was proven, the hardware would be placed in storage and the documentation placed in the custody of the Supervisor of Salvage. Should the requirement to salvage a large object from the ocean floor come up, additional components would be built and the system tailored to the job. This important salvage policy was formalized, then institutionalized by a Chief of Naval Operations directive. From now on, highly specialized and infrequently used systems, including submarine-salvage systems, would not be stockpiled and maintained.

A Very Long Piece of Pipe

Late in 1982 the National Oceanic and Atmospheric Administration (NOAA) requested Navy assistance for another far-from-routine operation. The Department of Energy had sponsored an Ocean Thermal Energy Conversion (OTEC) project off the island of Hawaii. In this project, cold water from the ocean floor came to the surface, where the difference in temperature between the cold bottom water and the surface water produced electrical energy. The project was quite successful, but had been abandoned following budget cuts. When the project was terminated, the suction pipe had been left in place. The pipe consisted of a bundle of three 4-foot diameter pipes 2,250 feet long, moored below the surface in 4,000 feet of water with the lower end of the pipe bundle on the bottom. NOAA asked the Navy for aid in retrieving the pipe because it was a potential navigation hazard and the state of Hawaii wanted the million-dollar pipe for an operational power plant.

The salvage plan called for the manned submersible *Turtle* (DSV 3)[22] (Lieutenant Commander Don Norris) to cut the anchor chain and release the pipe bundle so it could float to the surface. There it would be picked up by *Conserver* (Lieutenant Commander Robert J. Ventgen) and towed to port. YC-1525 from Mobile Diving and Salvage Unit One was converted to a lift barge to pick up the weighted end of the pipe.

The first task of any salvage job, the survey, turned out to be more difficult than expected. *Turtle* couldn't find the pipe bundle and was damaged during recovery in rough weather following its first dive. With the submersible laid up for repairs, *Conserver* hooked with a grapnel a 16-inch-circumference nylon line attached to a subsurface buoy and attached a surface buoy. Working from the buoy as a starting point, the repaired *Turtle* found and photographed the pipe bundle. The survey provided a firm basis for revising the salvage plans.

Turtle placed remotely fired cutters on the mooring and moved clear. The cutters were fired. *Conserver*, towing the lift barge YC-1525, grappled for the nylon line so the pipe could be pulled to the surface. Pull as she might, nothing came. *Turtle* went back down. The anchor chain had been partially cut and had become fouled on a seamount. The cables holding the pipe to the chain were severed. With the nylon line taken to the barge

---

[22] *Turtle* (DSV 3) and *Sea Cliff* (DSV 4) are Navy-owned and -operated deep-research submersibles based on the *Alvin* design. *Turtle* has an operating depth of 10,000 feet, *Sea Cliff* can work to 20,000 feet. Under the command of Lieutenant Commander Rick Williams, *Sea Cliff* dived to its maximum depth for the first time in the Middle America Trench off Central America on 10 March 1985.

lift wire, *Conserver* began to tow and the pipe bundle broke the surface. The tow was passed from the barge to *Conserver* and the ship began towing slowly to shallow water. She anchored in 40 feet of water with the deep end of the pipe bundle in 90 feet of water. Divers shackled the barge's lift wire into the deep end and the pipe surfaced. *Conserver* delivered the half-mile-long tow in Kawaihae harbor. Once again the Navy had completed an unusual deep-ocean job for another government agency.

The Navy's ability to work in the deep ocean had come a long way since the *Thresher* search. Like many advances in salvage this progress was a direct result of the recommendations that came from that disaster and from the work of the Deep Submergence Review Group. With access to the pool of talent and expertise of the naval laboratories, Submarine Development Group One, the Supervisor of Salvage staff, and industry, the Navy had an unparalleled capability to work in the deep ocean. A well-developed organization enhanced this capability. From the time the position was established, the Deep Submergence Coordinator on the Chief of Naval Operations staff had overseen deep submergence operations and used his influence to ensure that the tools best suited for the job were employed.

Fouled Submersibles

One of the great dangers to any work system in the ocean is fouling or entanglement with the lines in the water. When divers become fouled, standby divers are available to help free them. This is not the case with towed fish,[23] remotely operated vehicles, or manned submersibles. If the first two become fouled, they can be cut free. An expensive loss may result, but there is no danger to people. Submersibles are another story altogether. If a manned submersible is fouled while submerged, the highest priority is rescue of the crew. Because of the depths at which it operates, and the lack of any standardized rescue systems or fittings, rescue of a fouled submersible can best be accomplished by recovering the entire vehicle or freeing it so that it can surface on its own.

Off San Diego on 7 October 1969 the Lockheed submersible *Deep Quest*, diving to 432 feet to check out its newly built Large Object Recovery Module, tangled a polypropylene line in its port maneuvering screw. The submersible became fouled at three o'clock in the afternoon. At four o'clock Lockheed management asked the Navy for help. Responsibility for directing the Navy's assistance effort fell upon Captain Robert Gau-

---

[23] In the jargon of the deep ocean, sensors or other objects towed beneath the surface are referred to as "fish."

thier, Commander Submarine Development Group One. Response was immediate and broadly based. General Oceanics' submersible *Nekton*, available and ready to dive, started down by truck from Port Hueneme. *Gear*, with the Mark I Deep Dive System, sailed from Port Hueneme. North American's submersible *Beaver*, at sea aboard ship, sailed toward the site. International Hydrodynamic's submersible *Pisces* in Vancouver and CURV in Pasadena were placed on standby.

Nekton arrived first and dived shortly after midnight. On the bottom she operated just the way a standby diver works to free a fouled diver. She examined the line fouling *Deep Quest*, asked the fouled submersible to take up the slack, and, holding a knife in her manipulator, cut the line away. Free from the line, *Deep Quest* surfaced, none the worse for wear fifteen hours after starting her dive.

The rescue had been quick and efficient; the Navy's response to the emergency was impressive. The presence of a large number of deep-ocean assets nearby made the rapid response and its efficiency possible. This rapid and effective response to a commercial submersible working on a company project is particularly noteworthy because the Navy has no mission that includes such rescues.

Although the response to the next fouled submersible also came rapidly, the outcome was not so happy. On 17 June 1973 the Smithsonian Institution's *Johnson-Sea-Link*[24] became fouled while making a dive to 360 feet for ichthyological studies off Key West near the hulk of the scuttled World War II destroyer *Fred T. Berry* (DD 858). Four men occupied the two-compartment submersible, two in the pilot's compartment and two in the diver lock-out compartment.[25] An hour and a half into the dive, *Johnson-Sea-Link* was caught. An immediate request for Navy assistance went out. Rapid freeing of the submersible was vital. Her life-support capacity was severely reduced. The pilot had secured the carbon dioxide scrubbers because of a smell in the boat; low water temperatures, causing low internal ambient temperatures, further lowered the effectiveness of the scrubbing material.

Navy assets began to move. *Tringa* (ASR 16) recalled her crew and got underway from Key West; a diving team from Submarine Development Group in San Diego loaded their equipment and flew to Key West; Perry's submersible *Cubmarine* (PC 8) was trucked in from Riveria Beach; the deep-recovery ship *Alcoa Seaprobe*, then at sea, turned toward Key West; and the Tracor/MAS ship *A.B. Wood II* sailed from Fort Lauderdale. The

---

[24] *Johnson-Sea-Link* had been presented to the Smithsonian by its builders, Edwin A. Link and J. Seward Johnson, at its commissioning on 29 January 1971. Its purpose was to pursue scientific investigation of the continental shelf.

[25] On this dive no diving gear was carried by the men in the lock-out compartment.

latter was rigged to handle bottom installations over the bow. All the commercial assets were responding to Navy tasking.

Tringa arrived at the site, went into a moor and put hard-hat divers into the water. The depth of the dive, 360 feet, required a variation from standard procedures that normally limited Navy surface-supplied divers to 300 feet. With the lives of four men in danger, there was no choice. Two sets of two divers reached *Johnson-Sea-Link*, the first near midnight, the second at about 2:30 a.m. Neither could work in the clutter and three-knot current. The atmosphere in the submersible was becoming foul with carbon dioxide; the men in the lock-out compartment were hypothermic. Voice contact between the two compartments ended about 2:24 a.m.

By sunrise Sunday morning the diving team from San Diego had come aboard and prepared to dive. They had no more success than the hard-hat divers. In the early afternoon, the Perry *Cubmarine* arrived at the scene, deck loaded on *Amberjack* (SS 522). The boat dived, but a sonar casualty left it blind and forced it to surface. Though the *Johnson-Sea-Link* had been down only a little more than twenty-eight hours, the situation had become desperate.

A.B. Wood II, a very slow ship that had made only 6.5 knots enroute to the scene, arrived early Monday afternoon. She first looked over the situation with her underwater television, then began to grapple for the trapped submersible. At 3:00 p.m. she pulled it clear. Her tender, *Sea Diver*, took *Johnson-Sea-Link* aboard. The pilot and ichthyologist were saved; the two men in the lock-out compartment had died of carbon dioxide poisoning and hypothermia. A great many resources had been brought to bear in a brief period of total improvization. There were no resources anywhere in the world specifically designed to free a trapped submersible. There are none today, a cause for concern as tourist submersibles begin to proliferate.

In the discussions that followed the incident, it became apparent that no government had or should have the responsibility for maintaining a rescue system for commercial submersible operations. Furthermore, commercial operators and their underwriters had no interest in bearing the tremendous cost of a standby rescue capability. In the harsh, real world the most practical move seemed to be to minimize potential hazards by designing submersibles with few places where they could snag, and by providing them with sufficient life support capacity, duration, and redundancy to allow rescue assets adequate time to assemble if needed. An accident to *Pisces III* just two months later demonstrated the value of this approach.

On Wednesday, 29 August 1973, *Pisces III*, a two-compartment manned submersible owned and operated by Vickers Oceanics, Ltd., a British

Sweating out the recovery of *Pisces III*: Commander Bob Moss (left), Earl (Curly) Lawrence (center), and another salvor.

firm, operating in approximately 1,600 feet of water off the coast of Ireland, had surfaced from a five-hour dive. While *Vickers Voyager* towed *Pisces III* on a light line preparatory to picking her out of the water, a line fouled the hatch to the after compartment and jerked it open. The compartment flooded with seawater. *Pisces III* sank to the end of the line, hesitated there twelve minutes until the line broke, then plunged to the bottom.

The situation was serious but not critical. The two pilots on board were uninjured, the boat had suffered little impact damage, and the on-board life-support system had a duration of seventy-two hours. Vickers Oceanics moved quickly and professionally, taking the belt-and-suspenders approach that has so often proven successful in salvage operations. Two sister submersibles, *Pisces II and V*, were flown to Ireland and loaded aboard *Voyager*. Assistance from the U.S. Navy was requested. The request passed to the Supervisor of Salvage, who immediately began preparing CURV III and dispatched Commander Bob Moss and Curly Lawrence to the scene.[26]

---

[26] CURV III, completed in 1971, was the latest and most capable vehicle in the family of remotely operated vehicles that began with CURV (later called CURV I). Two CURV II vehicles were built in the late 1960s to support recoveries in weapon test ranges.

The salvage plan bore a great resemblance to the one that had worked so well for *Alvin*. Toggles with lift lines would be inserted into the open hatch and the boat lifted on these lines. *Pisces II* dived first, but damaged her manipulator and had to be hauled out for repair. Then *Pisces V* dived. Interference from trawlers in the area hampered tracking and underwater communications. *Pisces V* had a hard time finding *Pisces III*, but when she did she attached a light line by a snap hook to her sunken sister.[27] By this time, *Pisces V*'s battery was too slow to complete the work. She surfaced.

Meanwhile CURV III—air-shipped from San Diego to Cork, Ireland, and loaded on board the Canadian Coast Guard ship *John Cabot*—and arrived on the scene. CURV III made ready to dive, but a series of problems requiring repair arose. The situation could have been brighter: *Pisces II* and CURV III were down with mandatory repairs, *Pisces V*'s battery required a complete charge, and the life-support duration of *Pisces III* was being eaten up by passing time.[28] Finally, *Pisces II* and CURV III were ready to dive.

Pisces II went down first, inserted a toggle in the open hatch, and released a buoy allowing 2,000 feet of line to float to the surface. The line was too light for the primary lift line in the heavy weather that blew. CURV III went down and put another toggle in the hatch. At 10:50 on Saturday morning, when both lift lines had been taken aboard *John Cabot*, lifting began. Two and a half hours later, after more than over eighty-one hours submerged, almost seventy-six of them stranded, *Pisces III* surfaced. The pilots were soon on board *Voyager*, where they were declared fit.

The rescue of *Pisces III* was, like other civilian submersible rescue efforts, a strictly ad hoc operation. Appropriate action by the commercial operator and the good design of the submersible made the rescue-cum-salvage operation possible. The Navy's response with its specialized deep-ocean equipment and expertise provided the margin that ensured success. It also provided an excellent example of the Navy salvage and deep-ocean communities working together in the international workplace of the ocean.

Monitor

Another very different series of operations pointed up the breadth of the deep-ocean community and the cooperation that exists within it.

---

[27] As part of the belt-and-suspenders approach to this job, a lifting line would slide down the light line and shackle into the main lifting point.

[28] The *Pisces II* crew took measures to increase the duration of their life support system by decreasing pressure slightly to reduce oxygen consumption, sleeping as much as possible, and allowing carbon dioxide to build to higher levels than would be normally acceptable.

Monitor is one of the most famous ships ever to serve in the U.S. Navy. Every schoolchild knows how *Monitor* engaged the CSS *Virginia*[29] during the War Between the States. On New Year's Eve 1862, just nine months after the engagement with *Virginia*, *Monitor* was under tow by the paddlewheel steamer *Rhode Island*, bound for a new blockade station off Wilmington, North Carolina. She foundered during a heavy southeasterly gale. The ship that had been a milestone in the history of the U.S. Navy and of naval engineering and construction was lost forever, or so it seemed for more than a century.

In 1974 the Navy's interest in *Monitor* was rekindled. A historical research project by midshipmen at the Naval Academy had identified a 10-square-mile rectangle, an area one-tenth the size of the initial *Thresher* search area, as the probable location of *Monitor*. The midshipmen sought the advice of the Naval Ship Research and Development Center at Annapolis. The center, impressed with the depth and quality of the work, arranged an airborne magnetometer search. The search turned up eleven contacts judged to be wrecks. The large number of wrecks in such a small area was not surprising. The search area lay just south of Cape Hatteras, a location astride a major shipping lane that had been a favorite hunting ground for U-boats during World War II. The position of one of the wrecks coincided with that of a contact explored the previous summer by a group headed by Mr. John G. Newton of Duke University and Dr. Harold E. Egerton of Massachusetts Institute of Technology. That expedition had produced some well-resolved sonar pictures and closed-circuit television showing a capsized hull with *Monitor*'s unusual characteristics.

During a planning and coordinating conference at the Naval Research Laboratory, the Supervisor of Salvage undertook to provide the services of *Alcoa Seaprobe*, a unique, dynamically positioned, ocean-engineering ship that used a drill string to position sensing and recovery devices. The supervisor's motives were not totally altruistic; exploration of the probable *Monitor* wreck site would provide a needed opportunity to test *Seaprobe*'s capabilities. The combination of the need to test and a suitable test subject were right; although the test operation would be expensive, finding the wreck of *Monitor* would be a worthwhile return on the investment.

Alcoa Seaprobe, en route from her home port of Fort Lauderdale to Europe, called into Morehead City, North Carolina, where she embarked the *Monitor* expedition members—experts, scientists, and technicians from the Navy, Duke University, the state of North Carolina, and the National Geographic Society. On 31 March she got underway to investigate the

---

[29]*Virginia* was the former U.S. Navy steam frigate *Merrimack*, taken at the Norfolk Navy Yard early in the war.

wreck sites in a priority based on the likelihood of one of them being the *Monitor* wreck. Commander Colin M. Jones represented the Supervisor of Salvage at the site.

By breakfast time on April Fools' Day, *Alcoa Seaprobe* was over the first site and had begun the tedious and time-consuming work of a concentrated, side-scan sonar search. Results came quickly. A promising target was detected in early afternoon. *Seaprobe* lowered her special drill string with a television camera. *Monitor* appeared. She lay capsized on the bottom with a portion of her turret projecting beyond the armor belt. With the position established and *Monitor* identified, *Seaprobe*'s television guided a photographic survey.

Following the at-sea phase, the Naval Intelligence Support Activity assembled a complete photomosaic of the hull and turret of *Monitor*. Analysis of the photomosaic and comparison with specifications and original engineering drawings further confirmed the identity of the wreck. Navy salvage forces had made a valuable contribution to preserving the naval history and maritime heritage of the United States. The U.S. Congress made a more important contribution by declaring the *Monitor* wreck a marine sanctuary and passing legislation that protects it.

Interest in *Monitor* continues and periodic expeditions to investigate the wreck have been mounted. In 1987 a survey to gather data that would enable scientists and engineers to ascertain the condition of *Monitor* used technology that was very different from the 1974 expedition. The Supervisor of Salvage's remotely operated vehicle *Deep Drone*, operating from *Apache* (T-ATF 172), showed with its variety of sensors just how well remotely operated vehicles could do survey work.

Apache loaded *Deep Drone* at Little Creek, Virginia, and sailed for the *Monitor* Marine Sanctuary on 25 May 1987. Upon arrival she rendezvoused with *Hoist* (ARS 40), which carried additional precision navigational gear, assisted with *Apache*'s multipoint mooring, and provided manpower.

The survey had five distinct phases. During all phases a high frequency, long-baseline, underwater acoustic navigation system established a coordinate system for exact positioning of *Deep Drone*. A team from the Naval Civil Engineering Laboratory gathered data on hull corrosion with a specially designed corrosion probe mounted on *Deep Drone*. When their data were complete, the corrosion probe came off and video and 70mm still cameras went on for a variety of photographs that would be combined into a photomosaic of the entire hull. The whole operation with its state-of-the-art technology was completed on 10 June, two and a half weeks after its start. A wealth of information about this important national relic had been produced. It is particularly significant that the data-gathering process did not involve divers, even though the wreck lies in waters easily accessible to them. The deep-ocean technology of *Deep Drone* and similar vehicles offers the same advantages regardless of the depth of water.

In another interesting job in the spring of 1976, the CURV III vehicle conducted a video survey of the ore carrier *Edmond Fitzgerald*[30] that sank in a storm in Lake Superior. This ship was found broken in two, with the stern section upside down. Analysis of the wreckage permitted the Coast Guard to make a positive dermination of the cause of the sinking.

Aircraft Salvage

The technology of remotely operated vehicles and other deep-ocean technology has brought a new dimension to one of the most common salvage tasks, aircraft salvage. Ever since aircraft have been flying, there have been crashes into water. The recovery of these wrecks has become one of the most common salvage tasks undertaken by the Navy and one most affected by technology. Recoveries are undertaken for three reasons:

• To recover the aircraft itself or flight-recording instruments to assist in determining the cause of the accident. Recovery of aircraft parts for accident investigations is particularly important in the case of new aircraft or a rash of unexplained crashes.

• To recover important or classified material from the aircraft.

• To recover the remains of the occupants.

The Navy itself is the prime customer for Navy aircraft salvage services, but as in the case of ships, the Navy does aircraft salvage for the other military services and for other government agencies. Every modern Navy salvage ship has salvaged aircraft. Harbor Clearance Unit One salvaged many aircraft, recovered the bodies of many aviators, and recovered weapons and classified equipment from numerous crashed aircraft in Vietnam. Harbor Clearance Unit Two made a specialty of aircraft recovery ranging up and down the East Coast with special tools and equipment they developed for the task.

Aircraft salvage operations fall into the same pattern as deep-ocean operations: a search followed by a recovery operation. There is no record of the first aircraft recovery, but the techniques did not change for many years. Searches were made with grapnels, wire drags, and trawls, or by divers. The work was hard and slow, the probability of success low. The

---

[30] This is the same *Edmond Fitzgerald* made infamous by the popular ballad of Mr. Gordon Lightfoot.

development of sonars for mine location and shadowgraph sonars for object classification proved a boon to searches for downed aircraft. For this task, mine sweepers were often called into searches for aircraft wreckage. They did good work, but the development that made aircraft wreckage searches almost routine was the side-scan sonar.

Supported by a precision navigation system, side-scan sonar was a major leap forward, but operation of the sonar, particularly the interpretation of sonar traces, remained a black art requiring an experienced eye. Because of the experience and constant practice required, the operation of this technology remained with commercial firms, which made it available to the Navy when needed.

As previously described, the Supervisor of Salvage recognized that the rapidly developing search technology was the key to successful aircraft recovery operations. This recognition had led to Navy contracts with commercial firms for search and recovery similar in scope and intent to existing contracts for ship salvage. With these contracts the best available search technology and expertise could be brought to bear on any Navy aircraft salvage operation. Using the contracts became quite routine; the Supervisor of Salvage provided and maintained technical supervision of the services, and the agency or department that wanted an aircraft recovered paid the prices established in the contract. In time it became obvious that it was an advantage to the Navy for the Supervisor of

An ARS recovers a U.S. Navy aircraft.

Salvage to buy certain sophisticated hardware and place it in a contractor's hands for husbanding and operation.

Even with the most sophisticated search hardware, however, there is no guarantee a lost aircraft will be found. The probability of locating it is infinitely better than the old means of grappling and dragging, but much depends on the accuracy of the initial positioning. If this is off, the wreckage may not be located or expensive search time may exhaust the funds available for both the search and recovery, and the operation may be cut short.

Aircraft, particularly high-performance military aircraft, tend to break up when they hit the water at high speed. The resulting debris field has characteristic patterns that are identifiable to searchers, but the breakup is a problem for salvors trying to recover the aircraft. In the past the practice of recovering as much of the aircraft as possible prevailed. Small pieces were placed in baskets, larger pieces were recovered by surface lines, and very large pieces were lifted by specially devised lifting systems. When the pieces reached the surface, they were turned over to aircraft accident investigators to be sorted out. With the advent of underwater television systems, accident investigators have been able to determine whether or not specific pieces should be recovered while they are still undisturbed on the bottom. This simplifies recovery, and investigators get only the pieces in which they are interested.

Like all salvage operations, aircraft recovery requires a full ration of imagination and ingenuity to overcome the problems presented in the particular circumstances. Some operations are hallmarks.

One such operation in late 1970 was unusual in several aspects. The aircraft was a Cessna U–206 operated by the National Park Service. It was flying low over Lake Mead, Nevada, when a sudden downdraft forced it into the lake. As luck would have it, the plane crashed near the deepest part of the lake in almost 400 feet of water. Commissioner Theos J. Thompson of the Atomic Energy Commission was one of the occupants of the airplane. The AEC wanted to recover the commissioner's body; accordingly, Navy assistance was requested. The Supervisor of Salvage tasked his search contractor, Ocean Systems, Inc., with the job. The Ocean Systems operations manager, Mr. Robert E. Kutzleb, a retired Navy lieutenant commander and a world-renowned search and recovery expert, took charge at the scene.

It would be a tough job; the water's depth required bringing in one of the company's ADS–IV diving systems and constructing a work platform. The topography of the bottom would hide the wreckage and the steep sides of the canyon would reflect the sonar impulses. Conventional sonar towing techniques weren't going to work, and observation dives with the ADS–IV were useless in the poor underwater visibility.

411

The *Alcoa Seaprobe* recovery system.

Although towed sonar results were extremely poor, they did indicate an area of high probability. To refine the search, sonar transducers were strapped to the ADS–IV bell, and the bell was lowered. It was a tedious and time-consuming way to search. To move the bell, the support barge had to be repositioned in its moor. As tedious as it was, it worked. The barge gradually moved to within 11 feet of the wreckage. A diver locked out of the bell and attached a line. Additional lines were attached and the intact aircraft was lifted toward the surface. The bodies of Dr. Thompson and his aide were removed. Ingenuity and a thorough knowledge of the equipment and how to use it had made a difficult recovery possible.

Across the country some two and a half years later, the loss of a Navy patrol aircraft off Brunswick, Maine, set off another unique recovery. On 15 March 1973 a P3B aircraft, Bureau No. 152749, disappeared during a routine training flight. Within an hour, a sister aircraft spotted wreckage, providing a reasonable search datum. Nineteen of these aircraft had been lost, ten of them from unknown causes. It was important to determine the reason for this crash. The Commander Naval Air Force, U.S. Atlantic Fleet, asked for assistance from the Supervisor of Salvage. A search team went to the scene and began search operations on 20 March. Early the following morning a solid contact was registered. Subsequent runs confirmed that the debris pattern centered almost exactly on the initially reported position in 573 feet of water.

The depth and the scatter of the wreckage required a recovery vessel that could move freely in the debris area and also remain fixed in one position. The dynamically positioned *Alcoa Seaprobe* seemed ideal for this operation. After a weather delay, and accompanied by *Edenton*, *Seaprobe* sailed from Portsmouth Naval Shipyard on 6 April. Round-the-clock operations began upon arrival at the work site. *Seaprobe* first moved through the debris field, photographing and plotting the wreckage. Recovery started, first with a grapnel, then with a mechanical grabber. The first material came aboard *Seaprobe*, but when handling through the confined center well became too difficult, *Edenton* divers rigged lifting straps to the recovered material below the hull. The grab was then released, and the material was lifted aboard *Edenton*. In nine days, the aircraft wreckage had been identified, and all the pieces needed by the accident investigators had been recovered. The success of this mission, like so many others in the deep ocean, can be attributed to the expert application of the right technology.

The same techniques that work in the very deep ocean are often equally applicable in shallower waters. Searching in shallow water is not different in principle and only slightly less difficult from deep-ocean search. From the operators' viewpoint the major difference is the length of the cable between the ship on the surface and the sensors or vehicles on the bottom. With shorter cables in shallower depths, search rates are faster because the ships do not have to launch and recover long lengths of cable and are not impeded in their maneuvering by their long tails. A shallow-water job that occurred off the coast of Danang, Vietnam, in 1973 combined the sophistication of ocean search with the plain hard work of salvage.

With the end of American combat operations in Vietnam and the return of prisoners of war, the problem arose of establishing the fate of those listed as missing in action. A Joint Casualty Resolution Center was established at Nakhon Phanom, Thailand. Because a number of the missing were lost in aircraft accidents off Danang, that area became the focus of an intensive at-sea operation to recover remains for identification. The Supervisor of Salvage coordinated the at-sea operations because of his expertise and the resources available to him through his contracts with industry. Jim Bladh represented the Supervisor of Salvage at the scene.

A U.S.-flag, offshore-supply vessel, chartered in Singapore for the operation, arrived in Danang on 8 July and began loading the search team and equipment. The search employed what had become standard search techniques. The ship navigated with a shore-based precision navigation system, accurate to plus or minus 5 feet in the operating area, and carried a side-scan sonar to search the bottom with more than 100 percent coverage and a correspondingly high search effectiveness. Because the bottom off Danang is shallow, all promising contacts were investigated by divers.

Search operations began on 10 July and, with only minor interruptions, continued around the clock for the next eighty-two days, accomplishing little of real value. A great deal of wreckage was located and identified, most of little interest to the Joint Casualty Resolution Center, which knew the fate of the crews. Two aircraft reported to have crashed inland more than 15 miles away were identified as having actually crashed offshore. The recovery of human remains moved only two names from the missing-in-action to the killed-in-action list.

The search operation had been made more difficult by the variety of man-made and natural obstacles on the bottom, the imprecision of crash-site data, and the age of many of the crashes. Searching for human remains, many of which exist only as bone fragments, is always a grisly and unpleasant business. Although the results had been meager, Navy salvage had made a contribution to the important and emotional work of resolving the fate of at least two more servicemen.

A few months later the waters off the coast of Vietnam were the site of another important search and recovery operation conducted for a very different purpose. As the Air Force C5A transport #68218 flew outbound from Vietnam on 4 April 1975 with a load of refugees, mostly children, it suffered a rapid and complete decompression that carried away the after pressure door and a major portion of the after cargo ramp. The aircraft returned safely to Tan Son Nhut airport; the door and ramp fell into the South China Sea from 23,400 feet. Because passenger-carrying formed a major part of the mission of the C5A transport, the Air Force wanted the door and ramp back to determine the cause of the failure.

Seventh Fleet ships *Deliver*, *Abnaki*, and *Quapaw*, under the overall command of Commander Task Force 73, Rear Admiral John D. Johnson, proceeded to the scene at their best speed while the Supervisor of Salvage mobilized a contractor search team. The Air Force Accident Investigation Board undertook the task of determining the probable impact point from the inertial navigation position of the aircraft and a ballistic trajectory analogy.

Lieutenant Commander J.A. Mack, the Seventh Fleet salvage officer, was assigned to coordinate the overall operation, while Lieutenant Commander Gerald L. Anderson, commanding officer of *Deliver*, commanded the salvage force at the scene. While waiting for the search team to arrive from the United States, 230 dives were made to search the high probability impact area visually. Some pieces of debris located by the divers helped to refine the search areas.

The operation took on unusual urgency because North Vietnamese and Viet Cong forces were very close to delivering the *coup de grace* to the Republic of Vietnam. By the time the search team arrived, the Army of the Republic of Vietnam could not guarantee the security of shore-based precision navigation stations. Inability to place the navigation stations ashore resulted in an innovation. *Deliver* and *Abnaki* moored and became floating bases for the precision navigation equipment while *Quapaw* carried the side-scan sonar and navigation system receivers. The concept worked well.

Forty-eight hours of searching produced no contacts. Diving operations and refinement of the search position continued. Increasing pressure ashore began to affect the operation during the weekend of 26–27 April. Activity in the mountains north of Vung Tau increased and refugee boats began to appear in the search area. Around-the-clock search operations continued. On Sunday morning two substantial contacts were made and marked. Divers identified the cargo ramp and a major portion of the cargo door a few hundred yards away. *Quapaw* recovered the ramp first, then just at dark, the door. A search for the remaining section of the door began as soon as the first segment had been secured on board. By 10:30 on the night of Sunday, 27 April, only a few hours after the ramp and door segment had been recovered, Commander Seventh Fleet ordered the operation terminated and the area cleared. The situation ashore had deteriorated too much to continue.

Enough debris had been recovered to permit analysis of the failure.[31]

---

[31] The C5A aircraft was proscribed from carrying passengers for some time after the accident. Permission had to be obtained from an Air Force general in Washington for two salvage officers en route to Guam after typhoon Pamela in 1976 (chapter 8) to travel in a C5A, the only available transportation. The officers literally waited by the aircraft door while permission was sought.

The Navy's ability to recover objects from the ocean had taken on a new dimension with the recovery of free-falling debris from an altitude of several miles. Finding a needle in a haystack was easy compared to this kind of search. This operation and many similar ones were now demonstrating that objects lost in the ocean under almost any conditions could be located by combining the proper technology with the patience and determination to work thoroughly and methodically.

Another example of the challenging and vital role played by salvage teams in aircraft recovery was described in detail in chapter 8. The arduous recovery of the wreckage and human remains from Air Florida Flight 90, which crashed into the Potomac River in the winter of 1982, pointed up the importance of teamwork, appropriate equipment, and sheer determination for a successful operation.

While unique aircraft recovery operations provided highlights, several more routine recoveries each year continued using side-scan search techniques and plain old mud-diving to dig the wreckage out of the bottom in relatively shallow water. By the mid–1970s submersibles and remotely operated vehicles also began to play a broader role in the salvage of aircraft. These vehicles made recoveries possible at depths far lower than divers could reach. This technology was particularly worthwhile when the value of the aircraft was very high.

Remarkably intact, an F–14 from the carrier *John F. Kennedy* is hoisted aboard the support ship after being recovered from a depth of more than 1,800 feet in the North Sea.

One of the most significant of these operations took place in the fall of 1976 when an F–14 aircraft rolled off the flight deck of *John F. Kennedy* (CV 67) and sank in more than 1,890 feet of water in the North Sea. Recovery operations were initiated because of concern that the Soviet Union, smarting under the defection of a pilot with his MIG–25, would attempt a recovery of the relatively intact F–14. The recovery combined the fleet units *Shakori*, *Sunbird*, and the nuclear research submarine NR–1; remotely operated vehicle CURV III; several British and West German civilian offshore work ships; and the expertise of Commander W.N. Kloring, Lieutenant Bill Bacon, and Mr. Tom Salmon from the Supervisor of Salvage's office. The North Sea is seldom benign and certainly never so in the fall. The work went forward despite the foul weather and several failures of the lift line. The submarine NR–1 was effective in attaching lift lines to the limit of its capability. Less than two months after the aircraft was lost, the wreckage was lifted aboard the support ship and the operation was complete.

A number of other operations that involved submersibles and remotely operated vehicles in recovering aircraft were conducted between 1976 and 1980.

• *Sea Cliff* (DSV 4), her support ship *Maxine D.*, USNS *De Steiguer* (T-AGOR 12), and *Grapple* located and photographed an F–14 aircraft that had crashed into more than 500 fathoms of water off Ensenada, Mexico, in the summer of 1976, and recovered key pieces of the wreckage.

• *Chowanoc* (ATF 100); *Dolphin* (AGSS 555), a deep-diving research submarine; and *Sea Cliff* located, inspected, and photographed the wreckage of an F–14 aircraft in 6,000 feet of water off the coast of southern California in the summer of 1977.

• *Deep Drone*, operating from USCGC *Clover* (WMEC 292), located a component critical to the investigation of a helicopter crash in the rock ledges and canyons near Jamestown Bay north of Sitka, Alaska, in May 1978.

• In the summer of 1980 an SH3G helicopter crashed in 3,000 feet of water off St. Croix in the Virgin Islands. *Deep Drone* got the job. Operating from *Powhatan*, *Deep Drone* made thirty dives, first documenting the debris, then recovering the vital pieces of the wreckage.

Two aircraft salvage operations, both on foreign civilian aircraft in the first half of the 1980s, are worthy of note. Although they had very different results, these two operations confirmed the Navy's position as one of the world's eminent operators in the deep ocean.

In an effort to help an ally, *Deep Drone* and sophisticated search equipment were deployed to the probable impact area when Korean Airlines Flight 007, a Boeing 747 passenger flight, was shot down by the Soviets over the Sea of Japan in the fall of 1983. Along with the equipment went the best the Navy had to offer in expertise: Captain Charles S. Maclin, the Supervisor of Salvage; Commander Harley Oien, a former Seventh Fleet salvage officer; Commander Bill Clifford, the Pacific Fleet salvage officer; and Mr. Tom Salmon, a highly experienced specialist in remotely operated vehicles. The search, operating from USNS *Narragansett* (T–AFT 167), USCGC *Munro*, and *Conserver*, went on for almost two months. Weather was difficult, but that is the norm for any kind of salvage operation. Soviet ships in the area constantly harassed the search group, forcing them to maneuver and disrupt their search runs, attempting to snag lines and cables to sensor fish, picking up bottom-planted equipment, and interfering with the operation in any way they were able. Tiny Moneron Island, Soviet territory, limited the operations. Search forces were proscribed from entering the island's territorial waters, the area of highest probability. Soviet vessels made certain there were no violations of their territorial waters and strove to keep the searchers in international waters clear of high-probability areas.

Despite all the difficulties, numerous contacts were made; *Deep Drone* was often launched to investigate them. All were topography or junk; none were the aircraft. When the search ended on 8 November, over 250 square miles had been thoroughly searched with no positive result, primarily because the searchers were prevented from entering the area around Moneron Island.

A very different situation existed in 1985 when Air India Flight 182, another Boeing 747, disappeared from the screens of the tracking radar at Shannon, Ireland, on 23 June; the aircraft had crashed into the sea. The political situation in India, coupled with the sudden disappearance of the aircraft, gave rise to the suspicion that it might have been deliberately destroyed. Thus identification of the cause of the accident became a paramount consideration.

A number of nations were involved: India as the owner of the aircraft, Canada as the country of origin of the flight, the United States as the country where the aircraft was built, and Britain and Ireland because they had been first to provide a search and rescue effort. The U.S. and French governments aided in the recovery work at the request of Canada and India. The operation had two distinct phases, both involving the Supervisor of Salvage. The first phase, conducted immediately after the crash, consisted of locating and mapping the debris field with side-scan sonar and recovering the cockpit voice and flight data recorders with the deep-diving remotely operated vehicle, *Scarab*. Diving to almost 7,000 feet, *Scarab* also photographed wreckage on the bottom so that selected pieces could be recovered if the recorders did not give sufficient information about the cause of the crash.

Because the information from the recorders was not conclusive, Navy assistance in recovering wreckage was requested by the Canadian Aviation Safety Board. The offshore supply vessel *Kreuzturm* was hired as a support platform. The plan for the second phase of the operation called for *Scarab*, operating from the Canadian government-leased ship *John Cabot*, to attach lift lines to selected wreckage. The lift lines would be transferred to *Kreuzturm* and the wreckage brought to the surface. The operation, with Commander James R. Buckingham representing the Supervisor of Salvage on board *Kreuzturm*, went as planned, with only minor difficulties in handling lines and making attachments. Even the weather held. When the operation terminated in early November, almost 5,000 pounds of selected wreckage had been recovered. The operation was a complete success. Investigators were able to determine that an explosion had destroyed the aircraft. Most important, the ability of the Navy to work in the depths of the ocean had taken another step forward.[32]

---

[32] Deep-ocean operations took yet another quantum leap downward when the Navy located a 747 that had crashed off the island country of Mauritius in November 1987 in 14,600 feet of water. The cockpit flight recorder and substantial wreckage of the South African Airways aircraft were recovered by the remotely operated vehicle *Gemini* in the deepest such operation ever conducted.

A Soviet harasser crosses the bow of *Conserver*, disrupting search operations for the wreckage of KAL Flight 007.

A component of the earth-orbiter *Challenger* is hoisted aboard the venerable salvage ship *Preserver*.

With high technology systems to probe into and work in the deep ocean, and with a combination of high technology, hard work, and mud diving, aircraft salvage will continue to be a part of the Navy's salvage work. Undoubtedly, there will be successes, failures, and borderline cases. As in the past, success will lie in the appropriate choice of tools, the will to see the job through, and a measure of luck.

Challenger—The Biggest Challenge

At 11:30 a.m. Eastern Standard Time on 28 January 1986 a magnificent aircraft, the space shuttle *Challenger*, lifted off Launch Pad 39B at the John F. Kennedy Space Center. Seventy-three seconds later the spacecraft exploded over the Atlantic. The loss of *Challenger* set off the largest search and salvage operation the Navy has ever conducted. Several thousand people, sixteen surface ships, the nuclear-powered research submarine NR–1, and a host of manned submersibles and remotely operated vehicles participated. For nearly seven months Navy salvors systematically inspected and mapped almost 500 square miles of the ocean floor in depths ranging from 10 to more than 1,200 feet. Seven hundred and eleven sonar contacts were visually classified, one hundred and eighty-seven were confirmed as part of the spacecraft, one hundred and sixty-seven recovered.

Inevitably, the environment affected how salvage was conducted. Surface currents from the Gulf Stream ran as strong as 5 knots. Frequent fronts passed through the area bringing high winds and rough seas. Other factors also influenced the operation's structure and conduct:

• All the detritus found in a heavily used sealane had mixed with the debris of the spacecraft.

• The recovery organization, composed of several government departments and agencies, along with numerous contractors and subcontractors, was extremely complex.

• The level of interest of the public and the media remained high throughout the operation. Ensuring a flow of accurate information and controlling access to work sites required special attention.

• To satisfy the requirements of the National Aeronautics and Space Administration and the Presidential commission investigating the accident, pressure was high from the outset to locate and recover critical components of the solid rocket booster and of the orbiter and its payload.

Undertaking a major search and recovery operation was very different when *Challenger* exploded from what it was when *Thresher* went down or the bomb was lost off Palomares. Command and control organizations and procedures that had worked well in numerous other operations were not substantially altered, however. The search and recovery capability within the Navy or immediately available to it through existing contracts provided the way to bring all the needed resources and talent to bear. The experience and ability of the Supervisor of Salvage and his staff provided the means to manage and effectively employ these resources.

Navy salvage forces were in the picture almost from the time the spacecraft exploded. The Kennedy Space Center contacted the National Military Command Center within two minutes, and the Supervisor of Salvage was quickly brought in. Dr. Dale Uhler, the Deputy Supervisor of Salvage, outlined the Navy's preliminary plan at Cape Canaveral. Tasking followed. The Chief of Naval Operations directed the Commander Naval Sea Systems Command to carry out the search and recovery operation and the Commander in Chief, U.S. Atlantic Fleet, to provide whatever support was needed.

The search would use side-scan sonar search techniques with central evaluation and classification of contacts. Promising contacts would be investigated by divers, submersibles, or remotely operated vehicles, as the specific condition dictated. After contacts had been identified, recovery would be handled in conformance with a priority established by NASA.

The job got under way as men and equipment poured in from every corner of the nation. Navy and chartered commercial ships sailed for

Cape Canaveral. A command post ashore was established. Captain "Black Bart" Bartholomew, now Supervisor of Salvage, took charge at the scene. Air Force Colonel Ed O'Connor was assigned by NASA to head the overall accident reconstruction effort.

The search operation, with the NASA support ships *Freedom Star* and *Liberty Star* and the Supervisor of Salvage contract ships *Paul Langevin III* and *G. W. Pierce*, started on 8 February. The initial search area was 10 by 25 miles with depths of from 70 to 1,200 feet. It lay well within the Gulf Stream, where strong currents slowed operations. The search area gradually expanded as data became more refined and contacts were classified. The nuclear-powered research submarine NR–1 (Lieutenant Commander James Holloway), a ship with excellent search capabilities, entered the operation along with her escort ship *Sunbird* (ASR 15). The submarine conducted three search missions that provided invaluable intelligence. In all the search would last sixty days.

Search results went every day to the command post for analysis and evaluation. A sophisticated computer system with high-speed graphic printers had been set up to manage the burgeoning data base of contact information and to print up-to-date and meaningful geographic information. Each contact was assigned a priority number based on the strength of the return, the size of the contact, and its position in the search area.

What it's all about: Recovery of this section of *Challenger*'s right solid rocket booster with the burn hole allowed investigators to pin down the cause of the disaster.

From this evaluation decisions on further investigation and recovery could be made.

The primary object of the operation was to recover the section of the right solid rocket booster, which was thought to have failed. Debris from this booster had scattered widely and mixed with debris from the left rocket booster. The mixing was not suspected until the operation was well underway and initial results had been analyzed. Due to the mixing, a huge number of contacts had to be visually classified. The task was especially difficult because, even though the water in portions of the area where the solid rocket booster debris had landed was not deep, neither divers nor *Deep Drone* could work in the surface current. Thus visual classification of solid rocket booster components fell almost exclusively to the Harbor Branch Foundation submersibles *Sea-Link I* and *II*. The two submersibles could classify about five contacts each day. When the backlog of contacts to be classified began to govern the schedule, NR–1 returned and in two weeks classified two hundred and eighty-two contacts. The backlog was eliminated.

As debris from the solid rocket boosters was classified and identified, the nitty-gritty recovery work began in earnest. The contract vessel *Stena Workhorse*, a heavy offshore work vessel, became the primary recovery ship for this debris. *Stena Workhorse* had the remotely operated vehicle *Gemini*, capable of working in the strong currents, installed amidships. Following a practice that has proved invaluable since the earliest days of salvage, recovery and attachment procedures were rehearsed in shallow water before work began on the actual pieces. The very strong and hard materials of the solid rocket boosters made attachment difficult. Developing attachment procedures required a combination of engineering and seamanship, both seasoned with imagination. The procedure that developed called for one of the *Sea-Link* submersibles to attach a shackle or choker connecting a wire pendant to the piece of debris. Then the remotely operated vehicle *Gemini* would attach a weighted lift line, plumbed from *Stena Workhorse*, to the previously attached pendant. The work vessel would then haul the wreckage aboard. *Stena Workhorse* didn't do it all; *Sunbird* and *Kittiwake* (ASR 13) also recovered pieces of the solid rocket booster.

When the solid rocket booster operation wrapped up on 29 April, more than 50 percent of the two solid rocket boosters had been recovered from water depths ranging from 168 to 1,295 feet. Two of the pieces recovered allowed positive determination of the cause of the accident by disclosing a 30-inch circular burn hole in the right solid rocket booster casing.

While the solid rocket booster recovery featured sophisticated application of deep-ocean technology, recovery of the orbiter and its payload employed old-fashioned mud-diving. Radar and optical data from the launch indicated that the orbiter wreckage lay in the western part of the search area in nominal depths of 80 to 100 feet. The venerable and once battle-damaged veteran of World War II, *Preserver* (Lieutenant Commander John Devlin), arrived on site two days before the recovery operation started. When the operation kicked off, *Preserver*, along with an Air Force operated LCU (C115–1925), went to work in the orbiter impact area with divers searching for and recovering debris.

Almost a month into the operation, on 7 March, divers operating from the LCU classified a contact as the crew compartment debris. *Preserver* divers confirmed the classification the next day and increased the tempo of the recovery operation. As happens so often at critical points in salvage operations, the weather kicked up. Currents stirred the bottom silt, and variable eddy currents made working on the bottom nearly impossible. Recovery operations kept going when weather allowed. By 4 April all astronaut remains and visible crew compartment debris had been recovered. But the orbiter recovery operation was far from complete.

Recovery operations involving *Opportune*, divers from Mobile Diving and Salvage Unit Two, Explosive Ordnance Group Two, the Coast Guard Atlantic Strike Team, and the remotely operated vehicles *Deep Drone*, *Scorpi*, and ASD 620 continued until the end of August. When the operation was completed, parts from almost every *Challenger* system, subsystem, and payload had been recovered for analysis.

The *Challenger* salvage operation had been a success. The Navy's ability to synthesize a response to a unique and nationally important assignment in the ocean had once again been effective. A variety of technologies mobilized from military and industrial sources had been well employed. As important as the operation's success and the effectiveness of its management was its economics. The total Navy effort in the search and recovery cost approximately $13 million,[33] a paltry sum when weighed against the value of the lessons learned by NASA from analysis of the wreckage and the emotional benefit to the nation from recovery of the astronauts' remains. It was the largest and most complex and sophisticated salvage operation undertaken.

---

[33] Ironically, during the operation *Sunbird* recovered a floating duffle bag containing a quantity of cocaine. The street value of the drug was estimated to be $13 million, just enough to cover the cost of the Navy effort.

SAFEGUARD

CHAPTER TEN

In Retrospect

Six events stand out as watersheds in the history of Navy salvage. These events gave form and structure to Navy salvage by providing policy direction and the basis for operational and technical development.

The first significant event was the meeting shortly after World War I between Assistant Secretary of the Navy Franklin D. Roosevelt and the principals of the major American salvage companies. As a result of that meeting the importance of salvage to the nation was recognized, the course of the Navy was set, and the formation of a major marine salvage firm was initiated. All three outcomes had long-term effects on Navy salvage, the salvage industry in the United States, and the relationship between the two.

The most important result of the meeting was recognition that the U.S. Government had an interest in maintaining an American marine salvage industry and that it could do this best with a contract that made the services of the major American salvage company available to the Navy. The succession of Navy salvage contracts provided a de facto subsidy to contractors by giving them a business base that kept them operating far longer than their purely commercial operations would have permitted. It has been argued that these salvage contracts actually hastened the demise of the major American commercial salvors by artificially supporting them. As the argument goes, American salvage firms were not forced to be lean and innovative enough to compete in the international salvage marketplace. However the general decline of the entire maritime industry in the United States following World War II makes this argument pale. Marine salvage, never a tremendously lucrative business for American operators, became even less so following World War II until competition in the international marketplace was no longer economically feasible.

Whatever their impact on the commercial U.S. salvage industry, the salvage contracts themselves proved extremely valuable to the nation. They ensured that salvage services were available to the Navy, there was an effective basis for mobilization in World War II, and commercial shipping on the coasts of the United States was protected by professional salvors. The early contractors, operating in the traditional way with salvage ships on station along heavily traveled sea lanes, may be gone, but contracts and the close relationship between the Navy and salvage operators continue. These contracts are now more limited in geographical scope, and U.S. salvors operate as salvors of other nations now do: They provide their own expertise and highly specialized equipment, then hire any additional equipment and ships they need at the site. Though not a foundation for mobilization, this type of operation satisfies the Navy's current needs.

World War II was the second significant event in the history of Navy salvage. In that worldwide cataclysm the importance of salvage to broadly based naval operations was recognized, a permanent organization within the Navy for salvage was established, the first training program to make salvors out of farm boys was set up, and a construction program for some of the most successful salvage ships ever built was carried out. All these accomplishments had their roots in the necessities of the war.

In preparing for war and in mobilizing the American salvage industry, the foresight of the Navy was particularly noteworthy. Two tragic events, the capsizing of *Lafayette* in New York harbor and the warship damage at Pearl Harbor, provided the impetus to get a major naval salvage organization functioning quickly. The early work in North Africa, specifically the work supporting amphibious operations and harbor clearance, showed the breadth required of naval salvage forces. By the end of the war salvage was firmly established as an integral and vital part of the fleet's logistic forces. The Navy's organization for salvage had attained its basic form.

Unfortunately, during demobilization the billet for the Chief of Navy Salvage was deleted from the Chief of Naval Operations staff. For many years Navy salvage lacked an advocate at this level and existed almost hand-to-mouth, staying alive through the merit and the efforts of dedicated men. The Supervisor of Salvage in the Bureau of Ships, and the systems commands that followed it, remained and became the focus of salvage in the Navy, gaining responsibilities and becoming more influential with time.

The lessons of the war were still quite clear when the third watershed event, the 1948 passage of the Salvage Facilities Act, occurred. This legislation gave the Navy specific responsibilities for marine salvage in the United States and provided the legal authority for carrying out these responsibilities. Continuation of a salvage organization in the Navy to carry out statutory obligations was assured. Most important, forward-looking men had obtained a foundation upon which to erect future Navy salvage programs.

The loss of the submarine *Thresher* in 1963 and the recommendation of the Deep Submergence Review Group that followed constitute the fourth major event in Navy salvage history. They led Navy salvage into the deep ocean and opened the door to salvors' use and development of the technology that deep-ocean work requires. Salvors took readily to the depths with the same imagination and can-do attitude that had brought success to so many conventional salvage operations. Navy salvage has played an increasingly important role in the nation's ability to work in the deep ocean and to apply deep-ocean technology. The United States is stronger for it.

The fifth watershed event had neither the stature of an act of Congress nor the drama of a deep-ocean search. Nonetheless it represented a major change of course for Navy salvage. The idea of a highly mobile salvage force that could respond quickly with skills and a minimum of equipment did not spring up overnight. It originated in the Atlantic Fleet's salvage barge and developed into a practical possibility as air transport became a primary means of moving men and equipment. Fly-away salvage as a distinct policy with a means of implementation became a reality when Harbor Clearance Unit One was established on 1 February 1966. Since that date dependence on salvage ships has decreased and Navy salvors are able to respond promptly by air to a salvage requirement almost anywhere in the world. Driven by some of the same motivations and by some quite different ones, commercial salvors have also adopted this method of operation. A primary reason for the change has been the worldwide proliferation of large, extremely capable crane ships and barges. Built primarily to support the offshore oil and construction industries, the cranes have greater lift capacity and flexibility than any specialized salvage lift ships. They may be hired for a particular job to complement the salvor's assets and returned when the work is complete. In this way they are available to the salvor when needed, but require neither a large capital investment nor ongoing maintenance costs.

For all its virtues, fly-away salvage is no panacea. It is only one more important tool in the salvor's bag. Capable salvage ships and a broad spectrum of specialized and general-purpose equipment also have a place in that bag. British operations in the Falklands and recent U.S. Navy operations in the Arabian Gulf have shown clearly that in modern warfare salvage ships in proximity to combatants remain a requirement to facilitate and augment fly-away capability. The need for close support of combatants by afloat salvage forces is perhaps greater now than during World War II.

The sixth and final watershed event occurred as recently as 1979. That year saw the salvage presentation to the Chief of Naval Operations Executive Board that ensured the construction of the ARS–50-class salvage ships, resulted in a substantial funding base for the Emergency Ship

Salvage Material System and, most important, resolved the problem of sponsorship for salvage on the Chief of Naval Operations staff. With the assignment of salvage responsibilities to officers in the surface-warfare and logistics directorates, salvage acquired the advocacy and, to some degree, the organizational legitimacy it had lacked for nearly thirty-five years.

It is particularly noteworthy that the history of salvage has turned not so much on specific salvage operations but on the policy and organizational decisions that have made conducting these operations possible. None of the decisions were spontaneous. They were the result of careful and deliberate action by men who fully understood the potential of a strong salvage organization and the means of building it. They had the advantage of unusual foresight and the ability to translate that foresight into action. With few exceptions, Franklin Roosevelt being the most notable, they were men who had gained their understanding of salvage on wet, slippery decks where winches were groaning and wire ropes singing.

Throughout, ships, equipment, operational doctrine, and people remain the basic building blocks of the salvage organization. At any given time, operational doctrine has been the glue that binds the other three elements of salvage into a functioning whole. Not surprisingly, this doctrine has changed with the changing demands made on salvage forces. The operational doctrine for support of the combatant fleet developed in the hard venue of World War II. Following that war, operational doctrine was driven by the availability of resources and the threat of future war. More recent experience has demonstrated that rapidly delivered assistance to extend the inherent damage-control capabilities of combat casualties is, more than ever before, necessary to successful combat salvage. Providing this rapid assistance requires operational doctrine that will place salvage resources where they can be most effective and that will assign resources most appropriate to the tasks. The doctrine developed in World War II wherein fleet tugs and salvage ships operated in different roles that each was most suited to perform was a sound approach that may be applicable to modern naval warfare.

The tugs and salvage ships are the most visible manifestation of the salvage forces. Although fly-away salvage has provided a means of getting salvors and specialized equipment to remote casualties quickly, it does not provide the salvage support required for fleet operations. At sea there is no substitute for properly designed and equipped salvage ships. The tugs and salvage ships built by the Navy during World War II were very good— perhaps too good. They have lasted a long time. Because of their toughness, replacement programs have been sporadic rather than evolutionary. The few shipbuilding programs undertaken since World War II have not been guided by clearly established operational doctrine and a comprehensive understanding of the function of these ships in the fleet. Although these programs have produced good ships, we may never know whether they are the right ships.

Like the ships, the salvage equipment acquired for World War II was plentiful and good. It lasted a long time, but when the end of its useful life had been reached, it required wholesale replacement. Since the extensive replacement of salvage equipment in the late 1960s and early 1970s, Navy equipment development has been an evolutionary process. Through the Emergency Ship Salvage Material System, piles of equipment in the back of scattered warehouses have evolved into a well-organized and effective system for maintaining equipment and keeping it ready for use.

Over the years, the Navy's salvage posture has varied widely. This posture has a direct effect on the development of the individual elements that make up the salvage organization. Salvage posture has been and will continue to be affected by perceived threat, the overall funding climate, the appreciation of salvage by senior officers, and the effectiveness of senior salvors in putting forward the case for salvage. Whatever the fluctuations, a salvage posture that is matched to the threat is essential to naval readiness. Time is needed to build a salvage organization. And when salvage posture changes, the four basic elements cannot change or develop overnight. Just how long it can take became obvious in World War II. Even with the nation fully mobilized and salvage preparations predating mobilization, the first new-construction, steel-hulled salvage ship did not enter service until the second half of 1943.

Like equipment and ships, the fourth element of salvage—a competent salvage force—also requires time to develop. Even with the Navy's excellent salvage training, a cadre of experienced professionals is required as a foundation. In World War II this core was made up of a few naval officers, a larger number of warrant officers and senior petty officers, and professionals from the maritime industry. A corps of professional salvors has developed in the Navy and needs to be maintained. A professional officer-and-enlisted corps with knowledge of the specialized engineering and seamanship of salvage is necessary to an ongoing salvage organization and to rapid and effective mobilization. The heart of this corps, the regular Navy, must be supported by a strong Reserve organization. There is no substitute for training and experience in salvage. Attempting salvage with untrained or inexperienced officers and sailors is a sure road to disappointment.

Throughout the history of Navy salvage to date, men have been the dominant element. No work could have gone forward without them. Salvors have been and will always be determined, courageous, imaginative, and even tougher than the work they do. Navy salvage has been graced with strong and colorful personalities that have given it strength. Personal relationships have not always been smooth, but the controversies and differences have invigorated the organization and ensured that the best overall course was taken.

Navy salvage has served the interests of the Navy and the nation well. In great measure its contribution is due to those who have given their sweat and blood to the work, enjoyed the successes, been devastated by the defeats, and taken on the burdensome tasks that have moved the art and science of salvage forward. Navy salvage has been and is many things, but always the most important have been the salvors, who have toiled in the mud and strained their muscles to accomplish the miracles of Navy salvage.

APPENDIXES

A. Supervisors of Salvage, U.S. Navy

Commander W.A. Sullivan	December 1941–November 1942
Captain B.E. Manseau	November 1942–March 1946
Commodore W.A. Sullivan	March 1946–April 1948
Captain John Zabilsky	April 1948–August 1950
Captain J.E. Flynn	August 1950–January 1952
Commander W.M. Bjork	January 1952–July 1954
Commander J.W. Greely	July 1954–May 1957
Commander J.P. Lehan	May 1957–September 1959
Commander W.L. Marshall	September 1959–May 1961
Commander T.F. Bacheler	May 1961–October 1964
Captain W.F. Searle, Jr.	October 1964–May 1969
Captain E.B. Mitchell	May 1969–September 1973
Captain J.H. Boyd, Jr.	September 1973–May 1976
Captain R.B. Moss	May 1976–June 1979
Commander W.N. Klorig	June 1979–September 1979
Captain C.M. Jones	September 1979–April 1982
Captain C.S. Maclin	April 1982–August 1985
Captain C.A. Bartholomew	August 1985–Present

B. Federal Laws of the United States Affecting Navy Salvage

SALVAGE FACILITIES

10 USC 7361. Naval salvage facilities: contracts for commercial facilities

(a) The Secretary of the Navy may provide, by contract or otherwise, necessary salvage facilities for public and private vessels upon such terms as he determines to be in the best interest of the United States.

(b) The Secretary shall submit to the Secretary of Transportation for recommendation and comment each proposed contract for salvage facilities that affects the interests of the Department of Transportation.

(c) Term contracts for salvage facilities may be made under this section only if:

(1) The Secretary of the Navy determines that available commercial salvage facilities are inadequate to meet the requirements of national defense; and

(2) public notice of the intention to enter into the contracts has been given in a manner and for a period that will, in the Secretary's judgment, provide the maximum competition for such contracts among commercial salvage organizations.

10 USC 7362. Commercial use of naval facilities

The Secretary of the Navy may acquire or transfer, by charter or otherwise, for operation by private salvage companies, such vessels and equipment as he considers necessary.

10 USC 7363. Transfer of equipment: contract provisions

Before any salvage vessel or salvage gear is sold, chartered, leased, lent, or otherwise transferred by the Department of the Navy to any private party, the transferee must agree in writing with the Department that the vessel or gear will be used to support organized offshore salvage facilities for a period of as many years as the Secretary considers appropriate. The agreement shall contain such other provisions as the Secretary considers appropriate to assure the fulfillment of the undertaking.

FINANCIAL ARRANGEMENTS

10 USC 7364. Advancement of funds for salvage operations

The Secretary of the Navy may advance to private salvage companies such funds as he considers necessary to provide for the immediate financing of salvage operations. These advances shall be made on terms that the Secretary considers adequate for the protection of the United States.

10 USC 7365. Settlement of claims

The Secretary of the Navy, or his designee, may consider, ascertain, adjust, determine, compromise, or settle and receive payment of any claim by the United States for salvage services rendered by the Department of the Navy.

10 USC 7366. Limitation on appropriations

Not more than $3,000,000 may be appropriated annually for the administration of this chapter.

10 USC 7367. Disposition of receipts

Money received under this chapter shall be credited to appropriations for maintaining salvage facilities by the Department of the Navy. However, if the amount received in any year exceeds the cost incurred by the Navy during that year in giving and maintaining salvage services, the excess shall be covered into the Treasury.

OIL POLLUTION AND OTHER HAZARDS

33 USC 1472. Grave and imminent danger from oil pollution casualties to coastline or related interests of United States; Federal nonliability for Federal preventive measure on high seas

Whenever a ship collision, stranding, or other incident of navigation or other occurrence on board a ship or external to it resulting in material damage or imminent threat of material damage to the ship or her cargo creates, as determined by the Secretary [of Transportation], a grave and imminent danger to the coastline or related interests of the United States from pollution or threat of pollution of the sea by convention oil or of the sea or atmosphere by a substance other than convention oil which may reasonably be expected to result in major harmful consequences, the Secretary may, except as provided for in section 1479 of this title, without liability for any damage to the owners or operators of the ship, to her cargo or crew, to underwriters or other parties interested therein, take measures on the high seas, in accordance with the provision of the [International Convention relating to Intervention on the High Seas in Cases of Oil Pollution Casualties, 1969], the protocol and this chapter, to prevent, mitigate, or eliminate that danger.

FOREIGN VESSELS

46 USC 316. Use Of Foreign Vessels In United States Ports— Towing United States vessels; fines and penalties

(a) Towing vessels

It shall be unlawful for any vessel not wholly owned by a person who is a citizen of the United States within the meaning of the laws respecting the documentation of vessels and not having in force a certificate of documentation issued under section 12106 or 12107 of Title 46 to tow any vessel other than a vessel in distress, from any port or place in the United States, its Territories or possessions, embraced within the coastwise laws of the United States, to any other port or place within the same, either directly or by way of a foreign port or place, or to do any part of such towing, or to tow any such vessel, from point to point within the harbors of such places, or to tow any vessel transporting valueless material or any dredged material, regardless of whether it has commercial value, from a point or place in the United States. The owner and master of any vessel towing another vessel in violation of the provisions of this section shall each be liable to a fine of not less that $250 nor more than $1,000, which fines shall constitute liens upon the offending vessel enforceable through the district court of the United States for any district in which such vessel may be found, and clearance shall not be granted to such vessel until the fines have been paid. The towing vessel shall also be further liable to a penalty of $50 per ton on the measurement of every vessel towed in violation of this section, which sum may be recovered by way of libel or suit.

(b) Person defined

The term "person" as used in subsection (a) of this section, shall be held to include persons, firms, partnerships, associations, organizations, and corporations, doing business or existing under or by the authority of the laws of the United States, or of any State, Territory, district, or other subdivision thereof.

(c) Foreign railroad companies using ferries, tugboats, or towboats

Any foreign railroad company or corporation, whose road enters the United States by means of a ferry, tugboat, or towboat, may own such vessel and operate the same in connection with the water transportation of the passenger, freight, express, baggage, and mail cars used by such road, together with the passengers, freight, express matter, baggage, and mails transported in such cars, without being subject to any other or different restrictions that those imposed by law on any vessel of the United States entering ports of the United States from ports in the same foreign country: Provided, That except as authorized by section 883 of this title, such ferry, tugboat, or towboat shall not, under penalty of forfeiture, be used in connection with the transportation of any merchandise shipped from any port or place in the United States, its Territories or possessions, embraced within the coastwise laws of the United States, to any other port or place within the same.

(d) Salvaging operations by foreign vessels

No foreign vessel shall, under penalty of forfeiture, engage in salvaging operations on the Atlantic or Pacific coast of the United States, in any portion of the Great Lakes or their connecting or tributary waters, including any portion of the Saint Lawrence River through which the international boundary line extends, or in territorial waters of the United States on the Gulf of Mexico, except when authorized by a treaty or in accordance with the provisions of section 725 of this title: Provided, however, That if, on investigation, the Commissioner of Customs is satisfied that no suitable vessel wholly owned by a person who is a citizen of the United States and documented therein is available in any particular locality he may authorize the use of a foreign vessel or vessels in salvaging operations in that locality and no penalty shall be incurred for such authorized use.

CLEARANCE OF WATERWAYS

33 USC 414. Clearance of Waterways i.e.—Removal by Secretary of Army of Sunken Watercraft Generally

Whenever the navigation of any river, lake, harbor, sound, bay, canal, or other navigable waters of the United States shall be obstructed or endangered by any sunken vessel, boat, water craft, raft, or other similar obstruction, and such obstruction has existed for a longer period than thirty days, or whenever the abandonment of such obstruction can be legally established in a less space of time, the sunken vessel, boat, water craft, raft, or other obstruction shall be subject to be broken up, removed, sold, or otherwise disposed of by the Secretary of the Army at his discretion, without liability for any damage to the owners of the same: Provided, That in his discretion, the Secretary of the Army may cause reasonable notice of such obstruction of not less than thirty days, unless the legal abandonment of the obstruction can be established in a less time, to be given by publication, addressed "To whom it may concern," in a newspaper published nearest to the locality of the obstruction, requiring the removal thereof: And provided also, That the Secretary of the Army may, in his discretion, at or after the time of giving such notice, cause sealed proposals to be solicited by public advertisement, giving reasonable notice of not less than ten days, for the removal of such obstruction as soon as possible after the expiration of the above specified thirty days' notice, in case it has not in the meantime been so removed, these proposals and contracts, at his discretion, to be conditioned that such vessel, boat, water craft, raft, or other obstruction, and all cargo and property contained therein, shall become the property of the contractor, and the contract shall be awarded to the bidder making the proposition most advantageous to the United States: Provided, That such bidder shall give satisfactory security to execute the work: Provided further, That any money received from the sale of any such wreck, or from any contractor for the removal of wrecks, under this paragraph shall be covered into the Treasury of the United States.

33 USC 415. Summary removal of watercraft obstruction navigation

Under emergency, in the case of any vessel, boat, water craft, or raft, or other similar obstruction, sinking or grounding, or being unnecessarily delayed in any Government canal or lock, or in any navigable waters mentioned in section 414 of this title, in such manner as to stop, seriously interfere with, or specially endanger navigation, in the opinion of the Secretary of the Army, or any agent of the United States to whom the Secretary may delegate proper authority, the Secretary of the Army or any such agent shall have the right to take immediate possession of such boat, vessel, or other water craft, or raft, so far as to remove or to destroy it and to clear immediately the canal, lock, or navigable waters aforesaid of the obstruction thereby caused, using his best judgment to prevent any unnecessary injury; and no one shall interfere with or prevent such removal or destruction: Provided, That the officer or agent charged with the removal or destruction of an obstruction under this section may in his discretion give notice in writing to the owners of any such obstruction requiring them to remove it: And provided further, That the expense of removing any such obstruction as aforesaid shall be a charge against such craft and cargo; and if the owners thereof fail or refuse to reimburse the United States for such expense within thirty days after notification, then the officer or agent aforesaid may sell the craft or cargo, or any part thereof that may not have been destroyed in removal, and the proceeds of such sale shall be covered into the Treasury of the United States.

ADMIRALTY CLAIMS

10 USC 7622. Admiralty claims against the United States

(a) The Secretary of the Navy may settle, or compromise, and pay in an amount not more than $1,000,000 an admiralty claim against the United States for:

(1) damage caused by a vessel in the naval service or by other property under the jurisdiction of the Department of the Navy;

(2) compensation for towage and salvage service, including contract salvage, rendered to a vessel in the naval service or to other property under the jurisdiction of the Department of the Navy; or

(3) damage caused by a maritime tort committed by any agent or employee of the Department of the Navy or by property under the jurisdiction of the Department of the Navy.

(b) If a claim under this section is settled or compromised for more than $1,000,000, the Secretary shall certify it to Congress.

(c) In any case where the amount to be paid is not more than $10,000, the Secretary may delegate his authority under this section to any person designated by him.

(d) Upon acceptance of payment by the claimant, the settlement or compromise of a claim under this section is final and conclusive notwithstanding any other provision of law.

10 USC 7623. Admiralty claims by the United States

(a) The Secretary of the Navy may settle, or compromise, and receive payment of a claim by the United States for damage to property under the jurisdiction of the Department of the Navy or property for which the Department has assumed an obligation to respond for damage, if—

(1) the claim is—

(A) of a kind that is within the admiralty jurisdiction of district court of the United States; or

(B) for damage caused by a vessel or floating object; and

(2) the net amount to be received by the United States is not more than $1,000,000.

(b) In exchange for payment of an amount found to be due the United States under this section, the Secretary may execute a release of the claim on behalf of the United States. Amounts received under this section shall be covered into the Treasury.

(c) In any case where the amount to be received by the United States is not more than $10,000, the Secretary may delegate his authority under this section to any person designated by him.

(d) Upon acceptance of payment by the Secretary, the settlement or compromise of a claim under this section is final and conclusive notwithstanding any other provision of law.

(e) This section does not apply to any claim while there is pending as to that claim a suit filed by or against the United States.

C. Salvage Ships of the U.S. Navy

The Navy has operated tugs since before the beginning of the twentieth century and designated its first submarine rescue ships in 1926. Salvage ships as a distinct type have been in the fleet since the beginning of World War II. Salvage ships and tugs have traditionally fallen under the Service Force Commanders or, since 1975, the Naval Surface Force Commanders. The Submarine Force Commander has operated the submarine-rescue ships. Submarine rescue ships have customarily been commanded by an officer qualified in submarines. This brief appendix describes most of the major types of salvage-related ships that have served in the Navy.

Basic Salvage Ships—ARS

Salvage ships (ARS) have been continuously active since World War II. Five general types served in that war: conversions from Bird-class minesweepers (seven ships); wooden-hulled, 183-foot, purpose-built ships (nine ships): two classes of steel-hulled, 213-foot, purpose-built ships; the *Divers* (sixteen ships) and slightly beamier *Bolsters* (six ships); and four miscellaneous ships that were acquired for the war. Five of the ex-Bird-class and three of the miscellaneous ships were operated by the Navy Salvage Service in American waters; all the other ships were operated by the Navy worldwide. No new ARS type ships were acquired until the *Safeguard* (ARS 50) class of four ships was built in the early 1980s.

Bird-Class Minesweepers

Forty-nine, steel-hulled, steam-powered ships were built as minesweepers during and immediately after World War I in a high-priority shipbuilding program. The ships proved sound, rugged, and suited to a variety of tasks. Seven became salvage ships.

Two ships (*Warbler* and *Willet*) were acquired by Merritt-Chapman and Scott shortly after World War I and operated by the company as commercial salvage vessels between the wars. They were returned to the Navy immediately before World War II, designated ARS 11 and 12, then given back to Merritt-Chapman and Scott for operation by the Navy Salvage Service.

Another three ships (*Viking*, *Crusader*, and *Discoverer*) were operated by the Coast and Geodetic Survey (USC&GS) as survey vessels between the wars. Returned to the Navy and designated ARS 1, 2, and 3, all three were operated by the Navy Salvage Service during World War II.

The remaining two ships (*Redwing* and *Brant*) were designated ARS 4 and 32 early in World War II and operated by naval crews in the Atlantic and Mediterranean. They were not totally satisfactory in this role because space limitations precluded adequate accommodation for salvage crews. *Redwing* sank after striking a mine in the Mediterranean on 28 June 1943. *Brant* was damaged by friendly gunfire.

Warbler (ARS 11) was a Bird-class minesweeper operated as a salvage ship by Merritt-Chapman and Scott between the world wars and by the Navy Salvage Service during World War II.

Characteristics

Principal dimensions:	187'10" × 35'5" × 8'10"
Displacement:	Standard 1,190 tons; original displacement was increased 300–400 tons during conversion to salvage ships
Propulsion:	Steam, reciprocating, single screw
Horsepower:	1,400
Speed:	14.0 knots
Complement:	72
Years built:	1917–1919
Builders:	New Jersey Drydock and Transportation, Elizabethport, NJ (1)
	Gas Engine and Power Co., Morris Heights, NY (2)
	Todd Shipyard, New York (3)
	Baltimore Drydock & Shipbuilding Co., Baltimore, MD (4)
	Philadelphia Navy Yard, Philadelphia, PA (11, 12)
	Sun Shipbuilding, Chester, PA (32)

Ships in the Class

Viking (ARS 1)	Ex-*Flamingo* (AM 32), ex-USC&GS *Guide*; Navy Salvage Service
Crusader (ARS 2)	Ex-*Osprey* (AM 29), ex-USC&GS *Pioneer*; Navy Salvage Service
Discoverer (ARS 3)	Ex-*Auk* (AM 38); Navy Salvage Service
Redwing (ARS 4)	Ex-AM–48. Served with U.S. Coast Guard 1924–1941; war loss
Warbler (ARS 11)	Ex-AM–53; Navy Salvage Service
Willet (ARS 12)	Ex-AM–54; Navy Salvage Service
Brant (ARS 32)	Ex-AM–24, ex-AT–132

Anchor Class

Nine wooden-hulled salvage ships of World War II wartime construction served in the Atlantic and the Pacific. Two ships, *Swivel* (ARS 35) and *Weight* (ARS 36), were built as BARS under Lend-Lease for Great Britain but were retained in the U.S. Navy. Two ships were lost: *Extractor* (ARS 15) was torpedoed by a U.S. submarine in the Marianas on New Year's Day 1945, and *Extricate* was lost at Okinawa in a typhoon on 9 October 1945. All ships were operated by Navy crews, and were disposed of following World War II. An additional four ships were built as BARS and transferred to Great Britain.

Characteristics

Principal dimensions:	183'3" × 37' × 14'8"
Displacement:	1,089 tons
Propulsion:	Diesel-electric, twin screws
Horsepower:	1,200
Speed:	12 knots
Complement:	65
Years built:	1942–1944
Builders:	Colberg Boat Works, Stockton, CA (13, 14, 15)
	Snow Shipyards, Inc., Rockland, ME (16, 17)
	Bellingham Marine Railway, Bellingham, WA (28, 29)
	American Car and Foundry, Wilmington, DE (35, 36)

Brant (ARS 32) enters Argentia harbor early in World War II still wearing her AT hull number. She was one of two Bird-class minesweepers redesignated ARS and manned with Navy crews.

Anchor (ARS 13) was the class leader of a class of nine wooden-hulled salvage ships built during World War II. Note the absence of rollers for bow lifting.

Ships in the Class

Anchor (ARS 13)	Decommissioned in 1947
Protector (ARS 14)	Later *Pakistan Protector*
Extractor (ARS 15)	War loss
Extricate (ARS 16)	Lost in service
Restorer (ARS 17)	Later *Vitus Bering* Naval Vessel No. 6 (Denmark)
Valve (ARS 28)	Decommissioned in 1948
Vent (ARS 29)	Later *Western Pioneer*
Weight (ARS 35)	Ex-*Plymouth Salvor* (BARS 7)
Swivel (ARS 36)	Ex-*York Salvor* (BARS 8)
American Salvor (BARS 5)	*Lincoln Salvor* (BARS 9)
Boston Salvor (BARS 6)	*Southhampton Salvor* (BARS 10)

Diver Class

These steel-hulled, purpose-built, salvage ships of World War II construction served in the Atlantic and Pacific during World War II and with both fleets since then. Some of these extremely durable ships remain in commission in the late 1980s. The ships were originally planned without an automatic towing winch, and so winches were diverted from ocean-going tugs for them. None have been lost. Two ships, *Clamp* (ARS 33) and *Gear* (ARS 34), were retained BARS. Two additional ships built as BARS were transferred to Australia and operated under the auspices of the Commonwealth Salvage Board.

The BARS differ in detail from the standard *Diver* class, with the most obvious difference in the masts and weight-handling installation.

Characteristics

Principal dimensions:	213'6" × 39' × 13'
Displacement:	1,530 tons standard; 1,970 tons full load
Propulsion:	Diesel-electric, four engines, twin screw. Cooper-Bessemer engines replaced in surviving ships by Caterpillars in 1960s and 1970s
Horsepower:	3,000
Speed:	14.8 knots
Complement:	69
Years built:	1942–1945
Builder:	Basalt Rock Company, Napa, CA (all ships)

Ships in the Class

Diver (ARS 5)	Sold after World War II to Merritt-Chapman and Scott and renamed *Rescue*
Escape (ARS 6)	Transferred on loan to U.S. Coast Guard as WMEC–6 in 1980
Grapple (ARS 7)	Transferred to Republic of China in 1977
Preserver (ARS 8)	Seriously damaged in Japanese air attack but served through the 1980s
Shackle (ARS 9)	Transferred to U.S. Coast Guard and renamed *Acushnet* (WMEC 167) after World War II
Cable (ARS 19)	Bare boat charter to Merritt-Chapman and Scott following World War II; sunk as target (Sinkex)
Chain (ARS 20)	Converted to oceanographic research ship (AGOR 17); operated by Woods Hole Oceanographic Institute
Curb (ARS 21)	Bare boat charter to Merritt-Chapman and Scott following World War II; sunk as target (Sinkex)
Current (ARS 22)	Decommissioned in 1972
Deliver (ARS 23)	Transferred to Republic of China in 1979
Grasp (ARS 24)	Transferred to Republic of China in 1978
Safeguard (ARS 25)	Earned a Presidential Unit Citation during Korean War
Seize (ARS 26)	Grounded and refloated at Clipperton Island during World War II; transferred to U.S. Coast Guard and renamed *Yocona* (WMEC 168) after World War II
Snatch (ARS 27)	Converted to oceanographic research ship and renamed *Argo* (AGOR 18); operated by Scripps Institution
Clamp (ARS 33)	Ex-*Atlantic Salvor* (BARS 3); first steel-hulled salvage ship commissioned in the Navy
Gear (ARS 34)	Ex-*Pacific Salvor* (BARS 4). Later operated under charter by Merritt-Chapman and Scott as USNS *Gear*; sunk as target (Sinkex)
Caledonian Salvor (BARS 1)	Later *Sudbury II* (Canadian). Transferred to Australia
Cambrian Salvor (BARS 2)	Transferred to Australia

Signs of the sea show plainly on *Clamp* (ARS 33), the first steel-hulled salvage ship commissioned in the U.S. Navy. The twin kingpost aft is characteristic of ships that were originally BARS.

Diver (ARS 5), the class leader of the steel-hulled salvage ships, served for many years after World War II as the commercial salvage ship *Rescue*.

Bolster (ARS 38) Class

Near sisters of the *Divers*, the major difference is the slightly greater beam that gives better stability characteristics, more internal room, and a greater full-load displacement. Twelve ships were originally ordered, but six were canceled near the end of World War II. Evenly divided between the Atlantic and Pacific fleets, all remained on active Navy service into the 1980s.

Characteristics

Principal dimensions:	213'6" × 43' × 13'
Displacement:	1,530 tons standard; 2,045 tons full load
Propulsion:	Diesel-electric, four engines, twin screw. Cooper-Bessemer engines replaced by Caterpillars in 1960s and 1970s
Horsepower:	3,000
Speed:	16 knots
Complement:	69
Years built:	1944–1946
Builder:	Basalt Rock Company, Napa, CA (all ships)

Ships in the Class

Bolster (ARS 38)	
Conserver (ARS 39)	
Hoist (ARS 40)	
Opportune (ARS 41)	
Reclaimer (ARS 42)	
Recovery (ARS 43)	
Retriever (ARS 44)	Canceled
Skillful (ARS 45)	Canceled
Support (ARS 46)	Canceled
Toiler (ARS 47)	Canceled
Urgent (ARS 48)	Canceled
Willing (ARS 49)	Canceled

Miscellaneous Acquisitions

Four ships of varied backgrounds were acquired and designated ARS during World War II. Three were operated by the Navy Salvage Service; the fourth, *Tackle* (ARS 37), was used by naval forces in the Mediterranean. A fifth ship was not acquired. *Rescuer* (ARS 18) was lost; *Tackle* was seriously damaged by a mine in Marseilles harbor.

Characteristics

Varied.

Over a long life the configuration of a salvage ship changes considerably. *Reclaimer* (ARS 42) is shown here as she appeared during the Vietnam War.

Hoist (ARS 40) is shown here in the configuration common during the Korean War.

Harjurand (ARS 31) was requisitioned by the War Shipping Administration and placed in service as a Navy Salvage Service salvage ship.

Grapple (ARS 53).

Ships in the Class

Medric (ARS 10)	Not acquired
Rescuer (ARS 18)	Ex-*Caspar*; Navy Salvage Service. Wrecked during salvage operations at Seal Cape, Alaska
Accelerate (ARS 30)	Ex-*Toteco*, ex-*Walling*; Navy Salvage Service
Harjurand (ARS 31)	Built in Spain; sailed under the Spanish, Estonian, British, United States, and Panamanian flags. Ex-*Olesa*, ex-*Per Skogland*, ex-*Camberway*, ex-*Tento*, ex-*Margot*, later *Dodecanese*. Navy Salvage Service
Tackle (ARS 37)	Ex-*W.R. Chamberlain, Jr.*, later ARS(T)-4, IX–217

Safeguard (ARS 50) Class

These four ships were constructed in the shipbuilding programs of fiscal years 1981 through 1983. They are the first ARS-type salvage ships built since the end of World War II.

Characteristics

Principal dimensions:	254′11″ × 51′ × 15′5″
Displacement:	2,300 tons standard; 2,880 tons full load
Propulsion:	Geared diesel, four Caterpillar diesels, controllable pitch propellers in shrouds, 500 horsepower bow thruster.
Horsepower:	4,200
Speed:	13.5 knots
Complement:	90 (25% women)
Years built:	1982–1986
Builder:	Peterson Builders, Sturgeon Bay, WI

Ships in the Class

Safeguard (ARS 50)
Salvor (ARS 52)
Grasp (ARS 51)
Grapple (ARS 53)

Other Salvage Ships

Salvage Ships—ARS(D)

The four, self-propelled, salvage lifting ships (ARS(D)) were unique in the Navy. They were converted from LSM hulls in anticipation of the harbor clearance work following the invasion of Japan. The bow doors and ramps were removed, and the vehicle deck was converted to a salvage hold. Their construction was influenced by the usefulness of the British lift ships in the European harbor clearances. They were capable of lifting 300 tons by the bow, using sixfold purchases.

Characteristics (ex-LSMs)

Principal dimensions:	244′9″ × 34′11″ × 8′
Displacement:	816 tons
Propulsion:	Diesel-electric, two shafts
Horsepower:	2,800
Speed:	13 knots
Complement:	65
Years built:	1945–1946
Builder:	Brown Shipbuilding Company, Houston, TX (all ships)

Ships in the Class

Gypsy (ARS(D) 1)	Ex-LSM–549
Mender (ARS(D) 2)	Ex-LSM–550
Salvager (ARS(D) 3)	Ex-LSM–551
Windlass (ARS(D) 4)	Ex-LSM–552

Salvage Base Ships—ARS(T)

Three ships were LSTs converted to support the major harbor clearance operations that were expected to follow the invasion of Japan. Bow doors and ramps were retained, bridge and controls were moved forward, and a 25-ton

Salvager (ARS(D) 3) was one of four salvage lifting ships built near the end of World War II. These ships were to be used in the harbor clearances that would follow the planned invasion of Japan.

Palmyra (ARS(T) 3) was one of three LST hulls converted to salvage base ships in anticipation of large harbor clearance operations in Japan.

crane was installed amidships. These ships were designed to carry 330 tons of salvage equipment and a salvage crew of one hundred and twenty in addition to ship's company. The ships were commissioned too late for World War II. All were decommissioned in 1947. *Laysan Island* and *Palmyra* were retained in the Reserve Fleet until the early 1970s. *Okala* was sold to the Columbia River Packer's Association. *Palmyra* was reported acting in her design role during the clearance work in Bangladesh in the 1970s.

The ex-*W.R. Chamberlain, Jr.* as *Tackle* was briefly designated ARS(T)-4. She served in the European theater.

Characteristics (ex-LSTs)

Principal dimensions:	379′ × 50′1″ × 11′1″
Displacement:	4,500 tons
Propulsion:	Diesel, twin screw
Horsepower:	1,800
Speed:	10 knots
Complement:	168
Years built:	1944–1945
Builder:	Jeffersonville Boat & Machine Co., Jeffersonville, IN

Ships in the Class

Laysan Island (ARST(T) 1)	Ex-LST–1098
Okala (ARS(T) 2)	Ex-LST–1099
Palmyra (ARS(T) 3)	Ex-LST–1100
Tackle (ARS(T) 4)	Ex-*W.R. Chamberlain, Jr.*, ex-ARS-37, later IX–217

Submarine Rescue Ships—ASR

Bird-Class Minesweepers

As a result of the submarine disasters and salvages of the 1920s, six Bird-class minesweepers were fitted out with diving systems and recompression chambers and designated as submarine rescue ships in 1925. The ships were stationed in submarine operating areas. One ship, *Pigeon*, was a World War II loss.

Characteristics

Same as the Bird-class minesweepers converted to salvage ships (ARS).

Builders: Sun Shipbuilding, Chester, PA (1)
                Gas Engine and Power Co., Morris Heights, NY (2)
                Todd Shipyards, New York (3)
                Staten Island Shipbuilding, Staten Island, NY (4, 5)
                Baltimore Drydock and Shipbuilding, Baltimore, MD (6)

Falcon (ASR 2) was one of six Bird-class minesweepers designated as submarine rescue ships.

Ships in the Class

Widgeon (ASR 1)	Ex-AM–22
Falcon (ASR 2)	Ex-AM–28
Chewink (ASR 3)	Ex-AM–39
Mallard (ASR 4)	Ex-AM–44
Ortolan (ASR 5)	Ex-AM–45
Pigeon (ASR 6)	Ex-AM–47; war loss

Chanticleer (ASR 7) Class

Eleven ships were originally ordered for this class, but two were canceled. Three additional ships were conversions from fleet tug hulls, but were smaller and more crowded. Large tug-type ships of wartime construction, these ships were designed specifically for submarine rescue with the McCann Rescue Chamber. All ships have an installed helium-oxygen diving system and four-point moor capability. Some ships remained in Navy service into the late 1980s, others were transferred to foreign navies. One ship, *Macaw*, was wrecked during World War II.

Characteristics (except ATF conversions)

Principal dimensions:	251'4" × 42' × 14'10"
Displacement:	1,670 tons standard; 2,015 tons full load
Propulsion:	Diesel-electric, four engines
Horsepower:	3,000
Speed:	15 knots
Complement:	103
Years built:	1942–1947
Builders:	Moore Shipbuilding, Oakland, CA (7–11)
	Savannah Machine and Foundry, Savannah, GA (13–18)

Ships in the Class

Chanticleer (ASR 7)	
Coucal (ASR 8)	
Florikan (ASR 9)	
Greenlet (ASR 10)	
Macaw (ASR 11)	Wrecked at Midway during World War II
Penguin (ASR 12)	Ex-*Chetco* (ATF 99)
Kittiwake (ASR 13)	
Petrel (ASR 14)	
Sunbird (ASR 15)	
Tringa (ASR 16)	
Verdin (ASR 17)	Canceled
Windhover (ASR 18)	Canceled
Bluebird (ASR 19)	Ex-*Yurok* (ATF 164)
Skylark (ASR 20)	Ex-*Yustaga* (ATF 165)

The *Chanticleer* class were the first purpose-built submarine rescue ships. *Chanticleer* (ASR 7) appears here as she looked in the early 1960s.

Skylark (ASR 20) was one of three fleet tugs converted to submarine rescue ships. These ships were somewhat smaller and less capable than the *Chanticleer*s.

Pigeon (ASR 21) Class

These are catamaran ships built primarily to serve as platforms for the Deep Submergence Rescue Vehicle (DSRV) and to support deep saturation diving operations with the Mark II Deep Dive System. The ships also carry the McCann Submarine Rescue Chamber. A precision, three-dimensional tracking system is provided for DSRV operations. Ten ships were planned originally as replacements for the remaining *Chanticleer*-class ships. All but two were canceled.

Characteristics

Principal dimensions:	251′ × 86′ (each hull 26′ with 34′ separation) × 25′6″
Displacement:	3,411 tons standard; 4,570 tons full load
Propulsion:	Geared diesel, four engines, two screws, one bow thruster in each hull
Horsepower:	6,000
Speed:	15 knots
Complement:	195 plus 14 salvage staff and 24-person DSRV team
Years built:	1968–1973
Builder:	Alabama Dry Dock and Shipbuilding, Mobile, AL

Ships in the Class

Pigeon (ASR 21)
Ortolan (ASR 22)

Tugs—AT

The AT designation for oceangoing tugs existed from the early part of the twentieth century until 15 May 1944, when the designation was broken down to eliminate the confusion caused by ships with widely varying characteristics and capabilities having the same general mission. There were three new designations:

1. ATA: auxiliary tugs—small, steel-hulled, diesel oceangoing tugs. The series contained five ships started as net tenders, ANs. Fifty ships built as ATRs were redesignated ATA.

2. ATF: fleet tugs—large tugs of the *Navajo* class.

3. ATO: old tugs—a miscellany of seagoing tugs built for the Navy, a few ships acquired from private sources, and seventeen Bird-class minesweepers.

Auxiliary Tugs—ATA

These tugs were built in large numbers in the same numerical series as the large *Navajo*-class fleet tugs during World War II. They were equipped with constant-tension towing winches, but had very limited salvage or fire-fighting capability. They were designated ATR until 15 May 1944. One ship, ARA–171, ex-ATR–98, was a war loss. A number of ships were sold and worked in commercial service or with foreign navies following World War II. Only two ships originally had names, *Chetco* (ATA 166) and *Chatot* (ATA 167). Those remaining in the Navy were given the names of retired ATs in 1948. Some ships served through the Vietnam era.

Characteristics

Principal dimensions:	143′ × 33′ × 15′
Displacement:	600 tons standard, 835 tons full load
Propulsion:	Diesel-electric, single screw
Horsepower:	1,500
Speed:	12.5 knots
Complement:	45
Years built:	1943–1946
Builders:	Various, with most in Gulf of Mexico

Ships in the Class

ATA–121 through 125, 146, 166, 167, and 170 through 213 were formerly ATRs. ATA–214 through 218, originally ordered as wooden-hulled net tenders, were reordered as steel-hulled tugs; they retained the rounded AN stern. Other ships built as ATAs were ATA–219 through 240.

Pigeon (ASR 21).

Navajo- and *Abnaki-*Class Fleet Tugs—ATF

Large, powerful tugs, the first three ships were constructed as part of the 1938 shipbuilding program, the remainder during World War II. With their diesel-electric propulsion and constant-tension towing winches, the ships were considered innovative. All were extremely capable towing vessels and suitable for salvage. Some, especially fitted for salvage, carried nearly as much salvage equipment as the ARS. Three ships were lost during World War II, one immediately afterward, and a fifth in Korea. Some ships served into the late 1980s.

Characteristics

Principal dimensions:	205′ × 38′6″ × 15′4″
Displacement:	1,240 tons standard; 1,589 tons full load
Propulsion:	Diesel-electric, four engines, single screw
Horsepower:	3,000
Speed:	16.5 knots
Complement:	85
Years built:	1938–1946
Builders:	Bethlehem Shipbuilding, Staten Island, NY (64, 65, 66)
	Charleston Shipbuilding and Drydock, Charleston, SC (67 through 72, 81 and 82, 96 through 105, 148 through 165)
	United Engineering Co., Alameda, CA (83 through 86, 106 through 118)
	Cramp Shipbuilding Co., Philadelphia, PA (87 through 91)
	Commercial Iron Works, Portland, OR (92 through 95)

Ships in the Class

Navajo (ATF 64)	War loss
Seminole (ATF 65)	War loss
Cherokee (ATF 66)	Transferred to Coast Guard following World War II
Apache (ATF 67)	Ex-*Catawba*
Arapaho (ATF 68)	
Chippewa (ATF 69)	
Choctaw (ATF 70)	
Hopi (ATF 71)	
Kiowa (ATF 72)	
Menominee (ATF 73)	
Pawnee (ATF 74)	
Sioux (ATF 75)	
Ute (ATF 76)	Transferred to Military Sealift Command, later to Coast Guard on loan
Bannock (ATF 81)	
Carib (ATF 82)	
Chickasaw (ATF 83)	
Cree (ATF 84)	
Lipan (ATF 85)	Transferred to Military Sealift Command, later to Coast Guard on loan

Mahopac (ATA 196).

ATA–216, started as a steel-hulled net tender, was completed as a tug. She retains the rounded stern of the ATA.

458

Mataco (ATF 86)
Moreno (ATF 87)
Narragansett (ATF 88)
Nauset (ATF 89)   War loss
Pinto (ATF 90)
Seneca (ATF 91)
Tawasa (ATF 92)
Tekesta (ATF 93)
Yuma (ATF 94)
Zuni (ATF 95)   Grounded hard during Iwo Jima campaign; refloated and trans-
                                      ferred to Coast Guard; renamed *Tamora* (WMEC 166)

Abnaki (ATF 96)
Alsea (ATF 97)
Arikara (ATF 98)
Chetco (ATF 99)   Converted to *Penguin* (ASR 12) while building
Chowanoc (ATF 100)
Cocopa (ATF 101)
Hidatsa (ATF 102)
Hitchiti (ATF 103)
Jicarilla (ATF 104)
Moctobi (ATF 105)
Molala (ATF 106)
Munsee (ATF 107)
Pakana (ATF 108)   Transferred to Bureau of Mines; renamed *Virginia City*
Potowatomi (ATF 109)
Quapaw (ATF 110)
Sarsi (ATF 111)   War loss (Korea)
Serrano (ATF 112)
Takelma (ATF 113)
Tawakoni (ATF 114)
Tenino (ATF 115)
Tolowa (ATF 116)
Wateree (ATF 117)   Wrecked following World War II
Wematchee (ATF 118)
Achomawi (ATF 148)
Atakapa (ATF 149)
Avoyel (ATF 150)
Chawasa (ATF 151)
Cahuilla (ATF 152)
Chilulu (ATF 153)   Transferred to Coast Guard following World War II
Chimariko (ATF 154)
Cusabo (ATF 155)
Luiseno (ATF 156)
Nipmuc (ATF 157)
Mosopelea (ATF 158)
Paiute (ATF 159)
Papago (ATF 160)
Salinan (ATF 161)
Shakori (ATF 162)
Utina (ATF 163)
Yurok (ATF 164)   Converted to *Bluebird* (ASR 19) during building
Yustaga (ATF 165)   Converted to *Skylark* (ASR 20) during building

Luiseno (ATF 156).

Old Tugs—ATO

Ships designated ATO were a mixed bag of former ATs. Including tugs built before the turn of the century, a number were stricken between the world wars. Some of the oldest were small tugs that had been designated YT, then YTM or YTB, depending on their power, after May 1944. Of the old tugs only the *Bagaduce* class of World War I construction, seventeen Bird-class minesweepers, and seven of the older tugs received the ATO designation. Numbers 40 through 45, 78 through 80, and 128 through 130 were not acquired. Numbers 126 and 127 became ATR 48 and 49.

OLDER TUGS

There were a large group of tugs of varying sizes and characteristics that served from the Spanish-American war until World War II. Many were redesignated YT, then in 1944 either YTM or YTB depending on their power. Seven ships—*Sonoma, Ontario, Allegheny, Sagamore, Undaunted, Acushnet,* and *Esselen* were designated ATO with the same hull numbers. *Sonoma* was lost during World War II.

Characteristics
_____

Varied.

460

Ships in the Class

Wahmeta (AT 1)	Later YT–1; stricken 1922
Iwana (AT 2)	Later YT–2, later YTM–2
Narkeeta (AT 3)	Later YT–3; stricken 1923
Umadilla (AT 4)	Later YT–4, later YTM–4
Samoset (AT 5)	Later YT–5, later YTM–5
Penacook (AT 6)	Later YT–6, later YTM–6
Pawtucket (AT 7)	Later YT–7, later YTM–7
Pentucket (AT 8)	Later YT–8; stricken 1937
Sotoyomo (AT 9)	Later YT–9, later YTM–9
Patapsco (AT 10)	Stricken 1936
Patuxent (AT 11)	Stricken 1925
Sonoma (AT 12)	War loss, 1944
Ontario (AT 13)	
Arapaho (AT 14)	Stricken 1937
Mohave (AT 15)	Stricken 1936
Tillamook (AT 16)	Later YT–122, later YTM–122
Wando (AT 17)	Later YT–123, later YTB–123
Chemung (AT 18)	Later YT–124; stricken 1937
Allegheny (AT 19)	
Sagamore (AT 20)	
Iroquois (AT 46)	Acquired 1896; stricken 1927
Osceola (AT 47)	Acquired 1898; stricken 1922
Peoria (AT 48)	Ex-YT 109; stricken 1922
Piscataqua (AT 49)	Acquired 1898; stricken 1930
Potomac (AT 50)	Acquired 1898; stricken 1930
Uncas (AT 51)	Ex-YT–110; stricken 1922
Navajo (AT 52)	Acquired 1907; stricken 1937
Delaware (AT 53)	Acquired 1917, later YT–111
Conestoga (AT 54)	Acquired 1917; stricken 1921
Genesee (AT 55)	Acquired 1917; scuttled at Corregidor
Lykens (AT 56)	Acquired 1917; stricken 1933
Sea Rover (AT 57)	Acquired 1917; stricken 1922
Undaunted (AT 58)	Ex-YT–125
Challenge (AT 59)	Acquired 1918, later YT–126, YTM–126
Bay Spring (AT 60)	Acquired 1921, later YNg–19
Cahokia (AT 61)	Later YT–135, YTB–135
Tamaroa (AT 62)	Later YT–135, YTB–136
Acushnet (AT 63)	Acquired from U.S. Coast Guard
Tuscarora (AT 77)	Later YT–341, YTB–341

BAGADUCE CLASS

Nineteen ships of this class were built as seagoing tugs by the Navy during and immediately after World War I. They were primarily towing ships and had a minimum of salvage facilities. Three ships were stricken between the wars; one, *Napa*, was scuttled at Bataan. All surviving ships were designated ATO in 1944. They retained their original hull numbers.

Characteristics

Principal dimensions:	156'8" × 30' × 14'7"
Displacement:	1,000 tons
Propulsion:	Steam, reciprocating
Horsepower:	1,000
Speed:	13 knots
Complement:	44
Years built:	1917–1919
Builders:	Various

Ships in the Class

Bagaduce (AT 21)	
Tadousac (AT 22)	Stricken 1938
Kalmia (AT 23)	
Keywadin (AT 24)	
Umpqua (AT 25)	
Wandank (AT 26)	
Tatnuck (AT 27)	
Sunnadin (AT 28)	
Mahopac (AT 29)	
Sciota (AT 30)	
Koka (AT 31)	Stricken 1938
Napa (AT 32)	Scuttled at Bataan in 1942
Pinola (AT 33)	
Algorma (AT 34)	
Carrabasset (AT 35)	To Coast Guard
Contocook (AT 36)	Stricken 1933
Iuka (AT 37)	
Keosanqua (AT 38)	
Montcalm (AT 39)	

Tatnuck (AT 27), later ATO–27, seen here in Kodiak, was one of two units in the Aleutians before the arrival of new construction tugs and salvage ships.

CONVERTED BIRD-CLASS MINESWEEPERS

Seventeen Bird-class minesweeper ships were converted to tugs and designated ATs. Two were war losses. In 1944 all surviving ships—except *Brant*, which was already ARS–32—were designated ATO with their same hull numbers.

Characteristics

Same as the ships of the class converted to ARS except that the displacement was not increased.

Builders:
Baltimore Drydock and Shipbuilding, Baltimore, MD (131, 168)
Todd Shipbuilding, New York (133, 137, 140, 169)
Staten Island Shipbuilding, Staten Island, NY (134, 136)
Sun Shipbuilding and Drydock Company, Chester, PA (132)
Puget Sound Navy Yard, Bremerton, WA (135, 139)
Chester Shipbuilding, Chester, PA (138, 143, 145)
Chas. L. Seaburg with Gas Engine and Power, Morris Heights, NY (141, 142)
Philadelphia Navy Yard, Philadelphia, PA (144)

Ships in the Class

Bobolink (AT 131)	Ex-AM–20
Brant (AT 132)	Ex-AM–24, later ARS–32
Cormorant (AT 133)	Ex-AM–40
Grebe (AT 134)	Ex-AM–43; war loss
Kingfisher (AT 135)	Ex-AM–25
Oriole (AT 136)	Ex-AM–7
Owl (AT 137)	Ex-AM–2
Partridge (AT 138)	Ex-AM–16; war loss
Rail (AT 139)	Ex-AM–26
Robin (AT 140)	Ex-AM–3
Seagull (AT 141)	Ex-AM–30
Tern (AT 142)	Ex-AM–31
Turkey (AT 143)	Ex-AM–13
Vireo (AT 144)	Ex-AM–52
Woodcock (AT 145)	Ex-AM–14
Lark (AT 168)	Ex-AM–21
Whippoorwill (AT 169)	Ex-AM–35

Rescue Tugs—ATR

Originally wooden-hulled, steam-propelled tugs of World War II construction designed for support of convoys, these ships were well fitted for fire fighting and had reasonably good salvage facilities as well as accommodation for survivors. They were fitted with towing reels rather than constant tension towing winches. Fifty steel-hulled, diesel-driven ships were redesignated ATA in 1944. Fifteen ships

ATR–21.

were transferred under Lend-Lease as BATRs. One ship, ATR–15, was a war loss. The ships were not named.

Characteristics

Principal dimensions:	165′ × 33′4″ × 17′
Displacement:	852 tons
Propulsion:	Steam, reciprocating
Horsepower:	1,600
Speed:	12.5 knots
Complement:	35
Years built:	1942–1945
Builders:	Various

Ships in the Class

ATR–1 through 16	
ATR–22 through 40	
ATR–50 through 89	
ATR–90	Ex-AT–146, later ATA–146
ATR–43 through 47	Ex-AT–121 through 125, later ATA–121
ATR–97 through 140	Later ATA–170 through 213
ATR–17 through 21	Transferred to Great Britain as BATRs
ATR–41 and 42	Transferred to Great Britain as BATRs
ATR–48 and 49	Transferred to Great Britain as BATRs
ATR–91 through 96	Transferred to Great Britain as BATRs

Powhatan-Class Fleet Tugs—T-ATF-166

Seven tugs were built for Military Sealift Command manning with accommodations for transient salvage crews. The ships resemble offshore supply boats/

tugs with the superstructure well forward and an open deck aft for mission-loaded equipment and workspace.

Characteristics

Principal dimensions:	240'6" × 42' × 15'
Displacement:	2,000 tons standard, 2,260 tons full load
Propulsion:	Geared diesels, twin screws, 300-horsepower bow thruster
Horsepower:	7,200
Speed:	15 knots
Complement:	17 civilians, 4 Navy communications specialists, 20 salvage crew
Years built:	1977–1981
Builder:	Marinette Marine, Marinette, WI (all ships)

Ships in the Class

Powhatan (T-ATF 166)
Narragansett (T-ATF 167)
Catawba (T-ATF 168)
Navajo (T-ATF 169)
Mohawk (T-ATF 170)
Sioux (T-ATF 171)
Apache (T-ATF 172)

Navajo (T–ATF 169).

Beaufort (ATS 2).

Salvage and Rescue Ships—ATS

These were the first salvage ships built for the Navy following World War II. The three large ships were constructed in a British shipyard. They have hydraulic cranes, bow thrusters, four-point moor capability, and mixed-gas diving systems. Two follow-on ships scheduled for procurement in the 1972 and 1973 shipbuilding programs were canceled. The ships were named for cities in the United States that had been named for cities in England.

Characteristics

Principal dimensions:	282'8″ × 50' × 15'2″
Displacement:	2,650 tons standard; 3,200 tons full load
Propulsion:	Geared diesels, four engines, two controllable pitch propellers, 300-horsepower bow thruster
Horsepower:	6,000
Speed:	16 knots
Complement:	115
Years built:	1967–1972
Builder:	Brooke Marine, Lowestoft, England (all ships)

Ships in the Class

Edenton (ATS 1)
Beaufort (ATS 2)
Brunswick (ATS 3)

466

Bibliography

The detailed bibliography that follows delineates several hundred references used in the development of *Mud, Muscle, and Miracles*. Of greatest value were the articles in contemporary periodicals, a broad range of official publications, and unpublished manuscripts. The relative contribution of the three resources varied according to the period being chronicled.

Except for the brief period of World War I, for example, there was neither a formal Navy salvage organization nor full-time Navy salvors in the early days of salvage—and thus no body of official records and correspondence. Surprisingly however, salvage work during that time was well documented in periodicals. Of particular value in reconstructing the events of this era were articles appearing in the U.S. Naval Institute *Proceedings* and the *Journal of the American Society of Naval Engineers* (later the *Naval Engineers Journal*).

The dramatic and spectacularly successful major submarine salvages that the Navy undertook between the two world wars are well documented in official reports and in the writing of the participants. Notable among the latter are the popular works of Edward Ellsberg, which help balance the dryness of the official reports and capture the flavor and spirit of the operations. World War II itself produced enough documentation to occupy historians and researchers for at least a millennium. Unfortunately, little of it addresses salvage. Major and definitive naval histories of the war such as Samuel Eliot Morison's focus on strategic and tactical history and devote little space to logistics and even less to salvage. On the other hand, Worral Reed Carter's two excellent accounts of World War II naval logistics, *Beans, Bullets, and Black Oil* and *Ships, Salvage, and the Sinews of War*, help place salvage and harbor clearance in perspective.

In addition to being an outstanding salvor and organizer, William A. Sullivan was a prolific and analytical writer. His paper, "Marine Salvage," presented to the Society of Naval Architects and Marine Engineers (SNAME) in 1948 remains a classic. Of even more use to our chronicle were the numerous speeches, lectures, and presentations made by Sullivan after the war. These works are analytical and are generally directed to a professional audience. One regrets that Sullivan died before completing his autobiography. It would have been a fascinating read and no doubt would have provided many details that now can only be deduced from slim evidence.

Ellsberg's World War II trilogy, *Under the Red Sea Sun*, *No Banners, No Bugles*, and *The Far Shore*, are interesting on a different level. Ellsberg's accounts are highly personal; he shows a penchant for hyperbole. An experienced salvor reading between the lines finds much of value in Ellsberg's descriptions of the work in Mesewa and early work on the Mediterranean coast of Africa. There is little else extant on the salvage work in these areas.

The intensity of World War II and the necessity for getting on with the work often precluded preparation of detailed technical reports. The NAVSHIPS report on the salvage of the *Lafayette* is excellent, but virtually unique, and C. Monroe Hart's notes and recollections add color and depth to the official technical report. Homer N. Wallin's *Pearl Harbor: Why, How, Fleet Salvage and Final Appraisal* is a definitive description of the work at Pearl Harbor early in the war; F.H. Whitaker's 1944 article on the salvage of *Oklahoma* is a valuable supplement. The official history of the Navy Salvage Service, *A Short History of the Navy Salvage Service*, published by the Bureau of Ships, contains most of the available information on that service. There is no parallel document for the Navy Rescue Towing Service, but the videotape on "Salvage Posture of the United States" with E.J. Moran provides solid background on the towing service's organization and operation.

In general the salvors of the Pacific wrote less than those of the Atlantic. A search failed to turn up a reported book of war experiences by Lebbeus Curtis V. Emile C. Genereaux's autobiography, *The Captain Loved the Sea*, published serially by the tiny Humboldt County (California) Maritime Museum, contributes much of the fact and flavor of salvage in the Pacific. Genereaux's account, like Ellsberg's, is personal. He is matter-of-fact and makes no attempt to set salvage in a strategic context. The official reports of the Pacific war that did survive were useful in filling in the blanks left by personal accounts.

With the decrease in the intensity of salvage operations following World War II, technical and operational reporting improved. The Navy had a permanent salvage organization to produce the correspondence, messages, and myriad other records that accompany a military organization. Thus *Mud, Muscle, and Miracles* relies heavily upon official records for the period from the end of World War II to the present. The correspondence that flowed between the fleets, the Supervisor of Salvage, and the Chief of Naval Operations addressing policies, desires, and requirements proved especially useful in tracing the evolution of Navy salvage policy and posture.

Official records concerning salvage for the Korean War period are skimpy. We relied heavily on the records in the hands of individuals and their recollections of the period. Salvage reports following World War II generally fall into two distinct categories. The first, and far the most numerous, are the reports from the fleet forces that conducted the operations. Following a prescribed format that evolved with time, they provide a complete record of the operations they describe. Unfortunately it is these reports that have suffered the most from paperwork purges. Many, including a number from the Vietnam War, survive only in the files of the participants. The second group of reports are those prepared for or sponsored by the Supervisor of Salvage on large operations such as the *Missouri*, *Frank Knox*, and clearance of Guam following typhoons Karen and Olive, and work done by contractors or by a combination of contractor and fleet resources. Covering a range of salvage activities, from *Lafayette* to *Challenger*, they are a resource that reflects the growth of technology and sophistication in salvage and deep-ocean operations.

One group of publications deserves special mention. These are the annual summaries of salvage operations (SALVOPS) published by the Naval Sea Systems Command from 1969 to 1974. These volumes provide brief reports of major operations conducted during the title year. They are not in themselves detailed salvage reports. Their value lies in reflecting the types of operations in progress and in directing the researcher toward specific salvage jobs.

The number of articles on salvage operations in the general professional press decreased following World War II. Occasional articles from a small number of writers appear in the U.S. Naval Institute *Proceedings*, the *Naval Engineers Journal*, and similar periodicals. Just as in the pre-World War II press, these later articles are by officers who headed major operations. One periodical was particularly useful. From 1970 until the early 1980s the Supervisor of Salvage published a quarterly magazine, *Faceplate*. It provided a forum where many salvors could describe and discuss operations in which they participated. Virtually every salvage job conducted by the Navy or under Navy auspices during the period of the *Faceplate*'s existence is described.

Films and videotapes and unpublished primary sources and manuscripts cited in this bibliography are housed in the Operational Archives, Naval Historical Center. The library of the Supervisor of Salvage holds the published summaries of salvage operations as well as copies of *Faceplate*. Other periodicals and all books are in the Navy Department Library.

Primary Sources

Published Documents

Bureau of Ships. *Harbor Clearance Operations in Guam Following Typhoons Karen and Olive*. NAVSHIPS 250–638–5. Washington: Department of the Navy, January 1964.

———. *Refloating of the USS Missouri (BB–63)*. NAVSHIPS 250–694–3. Washington: Department of the Navy, 1 June 1950.

———. *Safety Manual for Ship Salvage Operations*. Prepared by Arthur D. Little, Inc. NAVSHIPS 250–880–2. Washington: Navy Department, December 1942.

———. *Salvage of the USS Lafayette*. NAVSHIPS 0994–001–3010. Washington: Navy Department, 1946.

———. *Ship Salvage*. Washington: Navy Department, 1 August 1944.

———. *Ship Salvage Operations, Miscellaneous Techniques*. BUSHIPS 0283–261–0000. Washington: Navy Department, February 1946.

———. *A Short History of the Navy Salvage Service*. NAVSHIPS 250–694–1. Washington, Navy Department, 1948.

Chief of Naval Operations. *Ocean Towing and Salvage Study*. Report prepared by Presearch, Inc. Washington, 30 April 1980.

Chief of Naval Operations Technical Advisory Group. *Aircraft Salvage Operations Mediterranean, Lessons and Implications for the Navy*. Washington: Department of the Navy, 7 April 1967.

Commander *Squalus* Salvage Unit. *Salvage Report USS Squalus (SS 192)*. Report to the Chief of Naval Operations. 1939.

BIBLIOGRAPHY

Director of Ocean Engineering. *USS Regulus Salvage and Disposal Operations*. Washington: Naval Sea Systems Command, 1972.

Headquarters, Commander in Chief, U.S. Fleet. *Navy Seagoing Tugs and Related Craft, General Characteristics and Considerations Governing Use Of*. COMINCH P–03. Washington, 21 June 1944.

Naval Oceanographic Office. *Chase VI Search Operations*. Special Publication SP–120. Washington, February 1968.

Naval Ship Research and Development Center. *Salvage of the Dredge Jamaica Bay, January to March 1967, My Tho, Vietnam*. NAVSHIPS 0994–002–0810. Washington, Department of the Navy, January 1968.

Navy Department. *Salvage Report of USS* Squalus *(SS–192)*. Washington, 1940.

Richey, Commander Thomas B. *Ship Salvage*. Technical Bulletin No. 2–25. Washington: Bureau of Construction and Repair, May 1925.

Supervisor of Salvage. A. Mackenzie *Salvage Operation*. NAVSHIPS 0994–016–7010. Washington: Naval Sea Systems Command, 1975.

———. *Arrow*. NAVSHIPS 0994–008–1010. Washington: Naval Sea Systems Command, 1970.

———. *Harbor Clearance Operations*. U.S. Navy Ship Salvage Manual, Vol. 2. NAVSHIPS 0994–000–3030. Washington, Naval Sea Systems Command, 1973.

———. *Monitor Survey May–June 1987*. Final Report. Washington, Naval Sea Systems Command, January 1988.

———. *M.V.* Oriental Warrior *Salvage, Jacksonville, Florida, 1972*. Washington: Naval Sea Systems Command, 1973.

———. *Recovery of Deep Research Vehicle ALVIN*. NAVSHIPS 0994–004–5010. Washington: Naval Sea Systems Command, December 1969.

———. *The Salvage of the Litton Launching Platform*. NAVSEA 0994–LP–017–5010. Washington: Naval Sea Systems Command, 1975.

———. *SALVOPS 69*. NAVSHIPS 0994–012–6010. Washington: Naval Sea Systems Command, 1969.

———. *SALVOPS 70*. NAVSHIPS 0994–012–6020. Washington: Naval Sea Systems Command, 1970.

———. *SALVOPS 71*. NAVSHIPS 0994–012–6030. Washington: Naval Sea Systems Command, 1971.

———. *SALVOPS 72*. NAVSHIPS 0994–012–6040. Washington: Naval Sea Systems Command, 1972.

———. *SALVOPS 73*. NAVSHIPS 0994–012–6050. Washington: Naval Sea Systems Command, 1973.

———. *SALVOPS 74*. NAVSHIPS 0994–012–6060. Washington: Naval Sea Systems Command, 1974.

———. *Space Shuttle* Challenger *Salvage Report*. Washington: Naval Sea Systems Command, 29 April 1988.

———. S.S. Sidney E. Smith, Jr. *Salvage Operation*. NAVSHIPS 0994–LP–017–4010. Washington: Naval Sea Systems Command, 1972.

———. *Submarine Salvage. U.S. Navy Ship Salvage Manual*, Vol. 2. NAVSHIPS 0994–000–3020. Washington: Naval Sea Systems Command, 1970.

———. *Suez Canal Salvage Operations in 1974*. Washington: Naval Sea Systems Command, 1975.

———. *Summary Report on Salvage Survey of* Prinz Eugen. SUPSALV Report No. 6–74. Washington: Naval Sea Systems Command, June 1974.

———. *Technical Report on Salvaging of AFDM–2*. NAVSHIPS 0994–001–4010. Washington: Naval Sea Systems Command, 1967.

———. *U.S. Navy Diving Manual*. NAVSEA 0994–LP–001–9010. Washington: Naval Sea Systems Command, 1985.

———. USNS Chauvenet *(T-AGS 29) Stranding Salvage Operations*. 82–01 SUPSALV Report. Washington: Naval Sea Systems Command, 1982.

———. USS Frank Knox *(DDR 742) Stranding Salvage*. NAVSHIPS 0994–002–6010. *Washington: Naval Sea Systems Command, 1968.*

Unpublished Documents

Assistant Supervisor of Salvage. "Legislative History of Salvage Related Statutes." Memorandum serial 00C–L–177 to Supervisor of Salvage, 1 August 1980.

Badders, Chief Machinist's Mate William C. USN, (Ret.). Interview by John T. Mason, Jr., U.S. Naval Institute, Oral History Collection. Annapolis, 14 September 1971.

Chief, Bureau of Ships. "Expansion of Navy Salvage Service in Time of War or National Emergency; BUDOCKS part in." Memorandum, serial 694–56 to Chief, Bureau of Yards and Docks. 5 March 1951.

———. "Salvage and Firefighting—Use of LCI(L) and LCT for." Letter, C–LCI(L)/S93(688–880), C–LCT/S93 to Commander Amphibious Training Command, Pacific Fleet. Washington, 12 August 1944.

———. "Ship Salvage, U.S. Navy—Expenditures and Returns (War Period)." BUSHIPS memorandum, code 882 CMH/mck. Washington, 19 December 1945.

———. "Ship Salvage Equipment." Letter, to Chief of Naval Operations 9940 serial 638C–1250. 21 October 1960.

———. "The Use of Lifting Devices in Harbor Clearance Operations." BUSHIPS Memorandum, code 880. Washington, 17 July 1945.

Chief of Naval Operations. "Deep Diving and Salvage Operations Mediterranean, Lessons and Implications for the Navy." Washington: Department of the Navy, 7 April 1967.

BIBLIOGRAPHY

————. "Diving and Salvage and/or Recovery Services for Non-DOD Purposes." Message 202318Z to RUEH/SECSTATE. March 1979.

————. "Ship Salvage." Letter, OP–09H1E/dag serial 102P09B1E to Commanders in Chief, U.S. Atlantic Fleet and U.S. Pacific Fleet. 27 May 1960.

————. "Ship Salvage." Letter, Op341C/pas serial 0142P34 to Commander in Chief, U.S. Pacific Fleet. 2 November 1960.

————. "Ship Salvage Equipment." Letter, serial 3537P41 to Chief, Bureau of Ships. 8 September 1960.

Commander in Chief, U.S. Pacific Fleet. "Diving, Salvage, Aircraft and Object Recovery." Letter, FF4–5/kd 4740 serial N44–7812 to a distribution list of Pacific Fleet Commands. 7 September 1978.

————. "Ship Salvage Operations, Pacific." CINCPACFLT Instruction 4740.1. 6 April 1953.

————. "Ship Salvage." Letter, FF1 4740 serial 73/OM37 to Chief of Naval Operations. 3 October 1960.

Commander Naval Surface Force, U.S. Atlantic Fleet. "Recommended Command Assignment Policies for ARS/ATS/ATF to Offset Declining Pacific/Atlantic Fleet Salvage Capability." Letter, 5000 serial N63/6909 to Chief of Naval Personnel. 3 June 1976.

————. "Salvage Operation to Refloat USS *Hermitage* (LSD 34); report of." Letter, 4740 serial N4/6146 to Chief of Naval Operations. 24 July 1975.

Commander Naval Surface Force, U.S. Pacific Fleet, and Commander Naval Surface Force, U.S. Atlantic Fleet. "Ship Salvage." Joint letter, FF4/3/436:jb 9940 serial N4–8894 of 5 October 1976 and 9940 serial N4/13165 of 29 October 1976 to Chief of Naval Operations.

Commander Salvage Force, Northwest African Waters. "Action Report of Amphibious Operations from 9 to 25 August 1944, of Salvage Ships in Western Task Force." Letter, to Commander in Chief, United States Fleet. 1 October 1944.

Commander Salvage Group, Northwest African Waters. "Resume of Salvage and Fire-fighting Activities Incident to Dragoon Operation." Letter to Naval Commander Western Task Force, 31 [sic] September 1944.

Commander Service Force, U.S. Atlantic Fleet. "Salvage of USS *Monssen* (DD 798), March-April 1962." Letter, FF4–16(741:gt) 4740 serial 70/5679 to Distribution List. 16 July 1962.

————. "Search, Recovery, and Rescue Operations." Message 031821Z to Commander in Chief, U.S. Atlantic Fleet. July 1973.

Commander Service Force, U.S. Pacific Fleet. "Fleet Salvage Organization and Ship Salvage Organization." COMSERVPAC Instruction 4740.2. 6 April 1953.

————. Joint Letter, COMSERVPAC FF4–15 9940 serial 70.4–9806 of 4 November 1959 and COMSERVLANT FF4–16/9940:(rnp) serial 40/8912 of 19 October 1959, with endorsements of Commander in Chief, U.S. Pacific Fleet, and Commander in Chief, U.S. Atlantic Fleet.

———. "Ship Salvage Capability; status of." Letter, serial 70.44 7447 to distribution 4740. 2 September 1960.

Commander Service Squadron Five. "Fleet Requirements in Diving, Salvage and Ocean Engineering." Letter, LC:N8:jlk 3960 serial 329 to Chief of Naval Operations. 1 November 1972

———. "Recommended Command Assignment Policies for ARS/ATS/ATF to Offset Declining Pacific Fleet Salvage Capability." Letter, FC:00:wlm 5000 serial 133 to Chief of Naval Personnel. 27 February 1976.

Commander Service Squadron Eight. "Bow Section of S/T *Ocean Eagle* Salvage Operation; report of." Letter, N–01 4740 serial 709 to Commander Naval Ship Systems Command. 18 June 1968.

———. "Salvage of USCGC *Cuyahoga*; report of." Letter N41 4740 serial 65 to Commander Naval Sea Systems Command. 19 January 1979.

———. "Salvage of USNS *Bluejacket*." Letter, N2 4740 serial 495 to Commander Service Force, U.S. Atlantic Fleet. 4 May 1965.

Commander Task Group 33.5. "Operation Order PACFLTSALVEX–83." 23 September 1983.

Commander Task Group 77.8. "Activities of Task Group 77.8 during MIKE ONE Operation; Report of." Letter to Commander Task Force 77. 17 January 1945.

Commander Task Unit 78.3.7. "CYCLOPS Operation—Report of." Letter, serial 27–45, 78.3.7/394/BSH:mm to Commander Task Group 78.3. 21 February 1945.

Commanding Officer, Harbor Clearance Unit One. "Ex-USS *Rochester*, Salvage Operations Report, submission of." Letter, HCU–1/BLD/cly 4740 serial 345 to Commander in Chief, U.S. Pacific Fleet. 6 September 1967.

———. "MSB–54 Salvage Operation; Report of." Letter, HCU–1/bld/glh 4740 serial 250 to Commander in Chief, U.S. Pacific Fleet. 7 July 1967.

———. "Post Salvage Report on Dredge *New Jersey*; submission of." Letter, HCU–1/HWT/ ldf 4740 serial 147 to Commander Naval Ship Systems Command. 19 March 1970.

———. "Radiological and Potential Salvage Survey of ex-German Cruiser *Prinz Eugen* (IX 300)." Letter, HCU–1/TFS/hl 4740 serial C–3–74 to Commander Naval Ship Systems Command. 2 June 1974.

———. "SS *Baton Rouge Victory* Salvage Operation; Report of." Letter, HCU–1/BLD/gth 4740 serial 182 to Commander in Chief, U.S. Pacific Fleet. 29 May 1967.

———. "SS *Clarksburg Victory* Salvage Report." Letter, HCU–1/BLD/gth 4740 serial 235 to Commander in Chief, U.S. Pacific Fleet. 26 June 1967.

Commanding Officer, Harbor Clearance Unit Two. "AFDB–7 Pontoon Salvage Operations in Ponta Delgada, Azores; report of." Letter, HCU–2/00 4740 serial 268 to Commander Naval Sea Systems Command. 24 April 1981.

———. "Fleet Requirements in Diving, Salvage and Ocean Engineering." Letter, HCU–2/ 20:gpa 4740 serial 214 to Chief of Naval Operations. 7 July 1973.

BIBLIOGRAPHY

Commanding Officer, Mobile Diving and Salvage Unit One. "Salvage Operation YRBM–26; report of." Letter, MDSU1/DS:bd 4700 serial 155 to Commander Naval Sea Systems Command. 18 February 1982.

Commanding Officer, Mobile Diving and Salvage Unit Two. "Salvage of Air Florida Airlines Boeing 737 Aircraft (Flight 90); report of." Letter, MDSU–2/00:ety 4740 serial 335 to Commander Naval Sea Systems Command. 10 May 1982.

Commanding Officer, USS *Beaufort* (ATS 2). "Post Salvage Report, ROKN ARS–26 *Gumi* and ROKN LST–677 *Suyong*, Tok Sok Ri, ROK; submission of." Letter, ATS–2:RSD:sr 4740 serial 197 to Commander Naval Sea Systems Command. 10 June 1983.

Commanding Officer, USS *Bolster* (ARS 38). "*Rajah Soliman* (RPS–66), Republic of the Philippines; salvage report of." Letter, ARS38:01:RJS/pk 4740 serial 018 to Commander in Chief, U.S. Pacific Fleet. 15 March 1965.

Commanding Officer, USS *Brunswick* (ATS 3). "Post Salvage Report ex-*Bluegill*; salvage operation." Letter, FC:N614, 4700 serial 133 to Commander Naval Sea Systems Command. 2 April 1984.

Commanding Officer, USS *Conserver* (ARS 39). "Salvage Operation OTEC–1 Cold Water Pipe (CWP); report of." Letter, ARS39/RJV:my 3000 serial 227 to Commander Naval Sea Systems Command. 15 December 1982.

Commanding Officer, USS *Grasp* (ARS 24). "ROK Navy LST M–370 Salvage Operation; report of 3 June to 28 June 1951." Letter, ARS24/S94/A4–3/egs, serial 014 to Commander Service Force, U.S. Pacific Fleet. 16 July 1951.

Commanding Officer, USS *Opportune* (ARS 41). "Post Salvage Report, Phase II Operations on ex-German Submarine U–352." Letter, ARS41 4740 serial 229 to Commander Naval Sea Systems Command. 3 September 1981.

Commanding Officer, USS *Preserver* (ARS 8). "Post Salvage Report, USCGC *Blackthorn* (WLB–391)." Letter, ARS8:FDM;mwa 4740 serial 55 to Commander Naval Sea Systems Command. 30 April 1980.

Commanding Officer, USS *Reclaimer* (ARS 42). "Salvage of Greek Freighter *Anangel Liberty*; report of." Letter, ARS42:BCB:lht 3051 serial 169 to Commander Naval Sea Systems Command. 23 June 1980.

———. "USNS *Card* Salvage Operations; report of." Draft letter, ARS 42:WEE:jn 4740. Undated.

Commanding Officer, USS *Safeguard* (ARS 25). "Post Salvage Report on Operations to Refloat the ex-USS *Ozark* (MCS–2)." Letter, 4740 serial 164 to Commander Naval Sea Systems Command. 30 April 1980.

———. "Salvage of Hulk of ex-USS *Reuben James* (DE–153); report of." Letter, HCU–2/11:jmb 4740 serial 155 to Commander Service Force, U.S. Atlantic Fleet. 15 June 1970.

———. "Salvage of S.S. *Indiana* Propulsion System off Crisp Point, Michigan, in Lake Superior; report of." Letter, HCU–2/20:tlm 4740 serial 135 to Commander Naval Sea Systems Command. 19 September 1979.

———. "Salvage of the U.S. Trust Territory vessel Y–101 at Tanapag Harbor, Saipan; report of." Letter ARS25:BLD:raw 4740 serial 280 to Commander in Chief, U.S. Pacific Fleet. 16 July 1963.

————. "Typhoon Olive Salvage Operations at Apra Harbor, Guam; report of." Letter, ARS25:BLD:raw 4740 serial 274 to Commander in Chief, U.S. Pacific Fleet. 15 July 1963.

————. "USS *Detroit* (AOE 4) Salvage Operation; report of." Letter, HCU–2/10:jl 4740 serial 459 to Commander Naval Sea Systems Command. 4 August 1981.

Ellsberg, Rear Admiral Edward, USNR (Ret.). Interview by Captain Bruce B. McCloskey, USNR (Ret.). Tape recording. Fort Lauderdale, Florida, 18 November 1972.

Force Salvage Officer, Naval Surface Force, U.S. Pacific Fleet. "Declining Salvage Capability in the Force." Memorandum to the Force Assistant Chief of Staff, Maintenance and Engineering. 18 February 1976.

————. "Future Navy Salvage Capabilities." Memorandum to the Force Assistant Chief of Staff, Maintenance and Engineering. 19 March 1976.

Force Salvage Officer, Service Force, U.S. Pacific Fleet. "Salvage Capability in the Event of Civilian Manning of ARS's." Memorandum 6255 to Service Force Commander. 31 August 1973.

Naval Ship Systems Command. "Rapidly Approaching Crisis in ARS and ATF Categories and Recommendations thereon." Memorandum 638–M48 from Code 630 to Code 400 638–M481. 10 March 1960.

Senior Salvage Officer, Task Force 81. "Operation Salvage Unit, 10 July 1943 to 8 August 1943, with DIME Attack Force." Letter to Commanders Task Force 81, 84, and 86. 15 August 1943.

Sherman, Lieutenant Commander Frederich C., USN, "Salvage of USS R–6." File no. 2–SS83–7. Washington, Bureau of Construction and Repair.

Stark, Admiral H.R., USN, and Admiral E.J. King, USN. "Organization and Operation of Rescue Land Salvage Services." Washington: Navy Department, 26 February 1942.

U.S. Naval School Deep Sea Diving. "Ship Salvage Notes." Washington, September 1960.

U.S. Naval Small Craft Training Center. "ARS Shakedown Schedule." Roosevelt Base, Terminal Island, San Pedro, California, 1 July 1945.

Letters

Boyd, Captain J. Huntly, USN (Ret.), to Commander W.I. Milwee, Jr., USN (Ret.), 20 January 1987.

Curtis, Lieutenant Commander Lebbeus, VII, to Commander W.I. Milwee, Jr., USN (Ret.), 19 March 1988.

Furer, Rear Admiral Julius A., USN (Ret.), to Mr. James Dugan, 30 August 1961.

Greely, Captain James W., USNR (Ret.), to Commander W.I. Milwee, Jr., USN (Ret.), 16 January 1987.

———— to Commander W.I. Milwee, Jr., USN (Ret.), 10 June 1987.

BIBLIOGRAPHY

Hart, Rear Admiral C. Monroe, USN (Ret.), to Commander W.I. Milwee, Jr., USN (Ret.), 18 January 1988.

Jackson, Rear Admiral D.H., USN, to Rear Admiral R.C. Gooding, USN, 15 June 1971.

Marshall, Captain Walter L., USN (Ret.), to Mr. Jerry Totten, 10 February 1986.

—— to Lieutenant Commander James C. Bladh, USN (Ret.), 18 December 1987.

Orem, Captain John B., USN (Ret.), to Commander W.I. Milwee, Jr., USN (Ret.), 8 June 1987.

Schultz, Rear Admiral Floyd, USN (Ret.), to Vice Admiral Earl Fowler, USN, 9 May 1982.

Sullivan, Commodore W.A., USN, to Captain B.E. Manseau, 20 June 1944.

—— to Captain B.E. Manseau, 5 July 1944.

—— to Captain B.E. Manseau, 8 August 1944.

—— to Miss Helen R. Bebout, 3 August 1982.

Secondary Sources

Books

Bunker, John Gorley. *Liberty Ships—The Ugly Ducklings of World War II*. Annapolis: Naval Institute Press, 1972.

Carter, Rear Admiral Worral Reed, USN (Ret.). *Beans, Bullets and Black Oil*. Washington: Department of the Navy, 1951.

Carter, Rear Admiral Worral Reed, USN, and Rear Admiral Elmer Ellsworth Duvall, USN (Ret.). *Ships, Salvage, and the Sinews of War*. Washington, Department of the Navy: 1954.

Chesneau, Roger, ed. *Conway's All the World's Fighting Ships 1922–1946*. London: Conway Maritime Press, 1980.

Chesneau, Roger, and Eugene M. Kolesnik, eds. *Conway's All the World's Fighting Ships 1860–1905*. New York: Mayflower Books, 1979.

Davis, Robert H. *Deep Diving and Submarine Operations*. 7th ed. Chessington, Surrey, England: Siebe, Gorman and Company, 1962.

Doust, Captain W.A., CBE. *The Ocean on a Plank*. London: Seely, Service & Co., 1976.

Earl and Wright, Consulting Engineers. *A Report on the Removal and Disposal of the Derelict Barge Lumberjack by the Cast-in-Place Urethane Process*. San Francisco, 1974.

Ellsberg, Edward. *The Far Shore*. New York: Dodd, Mead & Company, 1960.

——. *Men Under the Sea*. New York: Dodd, Mead & Company, 1956.

——. *No Banners, No Bugles*. New York: Dodd, Mead & Company, 1949.

——. *On the Bottom*. New York: Blue Ribbon Books, 1928.

——. *Under the Red Sea Sun*. New York: Dodd, Mead & Company, 1948.

Fahey, James C. *The Ships and Aircraft of the U.S. Fleet*. var. eds. Annapolis: Naval Institute Press.

Friedman, Norman. *U.S. Battleships*. Annapolis: Naval Institute Press, 1985.

Genereaux, Captain Emile C., USNR (Ret.). *The Captain Loved the Sea*. Ship's Log. Eureka, California: Humboldt County Maritime Museum, 1985–86.

Gray, Robert, ed. *Conway's All the World's Fighting Ships 1906–1921*. London: Conway Maritime Press, 1980.

Great Britain. Admiralty. *Manual of Seamanship*. 2 vols. London: His Majesty's Stationery Office, 1908–09.

Grundt, E., S.I. Lavroff, and K. Nechajew. *Schiffbergungs*. Berlin: Richard Carl Schmidt & Co., 1927.

Hancox, Captain David. *Reed's Commercial Salvage Practice*. New Malden, Surrey, England: Thomas Reed Publications, 1986.

Hooper, Vice Admiral Edwin B., USN. *Mobility, Support, Endurance*. Washington: U.S. Naval History Division, 1972.

Karneke, Joseph Sidney. *Navy Diver*. New York: G.P. Putnam's Sons, 1960.

King, Fleet Admiral Ernest J., USN. *A Naval Record*. New York: W.W. Norton, 1955.

Marine Technology Society. *Equipment for the Working Diver*. Symposium Proceedings. Washington: Marine Technology Society.

———. *Man's Extension into the Sea*. Transactions of a Joint Symposium. Washington, 1966.

———. *Progress into the Sea*. Transactions of the Symposium. Washington, 1969.

———. *The Working Diver—1972*. Symposium Proceedings. Washington, 1972.

———. *The Working Diver—1974*. Symposium Proceedings. Washington, 1974.

———. *The Working Diver—1976*. Symposium Proceedings. Washington, 1976.

———. *The Working Diver—1978*. Symposium Proceedings. Washington, 1978.

Morison, Samuel Eliot. *History of United States Naval Operations in World War II*. 15 vols. Boston: Little, Brown and Company, 1955.

———. *The Two Ocean War*. New York: Atlantic Monthly Book Press, 1963.

Polmar, Norman. *The Ships and Aircraft of the U.S. Fleet*. 14th ed. Annapolis: Naval Institute Press, 1987.

Potter, E.B., ed. *The United States and World Sea Power*. Edgewood Cliffs, NJ: Prentice-Hall, 1955.

Rickover, H.G. *How the Battleship Maine Was Destroyed*. Washington: U.S. Naval History Division, 1976.

U.S. Naval Historical Center. *Dictionary of American Fighting Ships*. 8 vols. Washington: Department of the Navy, 1959–81.

Wallin, Vice Admiral Homer N., USN (Ret.). *Pearl Harbor: Why, How, Fleet Salvage and Final Appraisal*. Washington: U.S. Naval History Division, 1968.

Webber, Bert. *Silent Siege*. Washington: Ye Galleon Press, 1984.

BIBLIOGRAPHY

Williams, Captain Sir John P. *So Ends This Day*. Fitzroy, Victoria, Australia: Globe Press, 1981.

Articles

Abshier, Lieutenant Roy, III, USN. "Apra Harbor Clearance . . . Continued." *Faceplate* (Winter 1980).

Andrews, Captain Frank A., USN. "Searching for the *Thresher*." U.S. Naval Institute *Proceedings*. (May 1964).

"Atlantic 'Probed' in Search and Recovery." *Faceplate* (Summer 1973).

Austin, Chief Metalsmith H.O., USN. "Deeper Diving with the Oxy-Helium Mixture for Breathing." U.S. Naval Institute *Proceedings* (April 1949).

———. "The Experimental Diving Unit: Pioneer in Pressure." U.S. Naval Institute *Proceedings* (March 1951).

———. "Salvaging the USS *Lafayette*." U.S. Naval Institute *Proceedings* (August 1951).

Bacon, Captain R.H., RN, DSO. "Submarine Boats and Their Salvage." *Naval Engineers Journal* (June 1905).

Baker, Earl. "ESSM Assets Relocated." *Faceplate* (Fall 1977).

———. "ESSM System Expands Capabilities." *Faceplate* (Summer 1973).

———. "ESSM System Upgraded." *Faceplate* (Spring 1979).

Barbante, Petty Officer Felimon, USN. "Sultana Shoals Grab USNS *Chauvenet*." *Faceplate* (Fall 1982).

Barracca, Peter S. "History of Marine Salvage in the United States." *Symposium on Marine Salvage* (30 April 1974).

Bartholomew, Lieutenant Commander Charles A., USN. "Litton Launching Platform Salvaged." *Faceplate* (Summer 1975).

———. "USNS *Chauvenet* on the Rocks." *Faceplate* (Winter 1982).

Biesemeier, Commander H.W., USN. "Salvage." U.S. Naval Institute *Proceedings* (April 1957).

Bladh, James C. "C5A Salvops 'Needle in a Haystack.'" *Faceplate* (Summer 1975).

———. "Salvage of the *Eaglescliffe*." *Faceplate* (Spring 1984).

Blockwick, Commander Thomas N., USN. "The Ocean Engineering Aspects of Sealab II." *Naval Engineers Journal* (April 1966).

———. "An Unusual Case of Ship Salvage." U.S. Naval Institute *Proceedings* (September 1966).

Brown, Lieutenant George T., USN. "Navy Salvors Raise the *Bluegill*." *Faceplate* (Summer 1984).

Bryant, W. Robert. "For Those in Peril . . ." U.S. Naval Institute *Proceedings*. (April 1976).

Bushey, Commander Arthur C., USN. "Salvage of the *M.H. DeYoung*." *Journal of the American Society of Naval Engineers* (May 1954).

Buttermore, Lieutenant (j.g.) J.R., USN. "*Edenton* Successful in Mediterranean Salvops." *Faceplate* (Summer 1976).

Cassat, Lieutenant Gary, USN. "A New Direction in Diving Organizations." *Faceplate* (Winter 1979).

Coulombe, Lieutenant M.A. "Mk 12 Mixed Gas OPEVAL Conducted." *Faceplate* (Spring 1980).

Crabtree, Lieutenant Commander Alan B., USN. "Diving on the Wreck of Texas Tower No. 4." U.S. Naval Institute *Proceedings* (March 1963).

"Deep Ocean Rescue Shows International Cooperation." *Faceplate* (Winter 1973).

Delaplane, Lieutenant Commander Stephen W., USN. "Aftermath of a Tragedy—HCU-Two Raises *Blackthorn*." *Faceplate* (Spring 1980).

———. "HCU-2 Raises Cutter *Cuyahoga* from Chesapeake Bay." *Faceplate* (Winter 1978).

———. "Ponta Delgada—A Nice Place to Visit . . . But No Place for Salvage." *Faceplate* (Fall 1981).

———. "Salvage of *Ozark*." *Faceplate* (Spring 1980).

Delaplane, Lieutenant Commander Stephen W., USN, and Petty Officer Mark Faram, USN. "Recovery of Air Florida Flight 90." *Faceplate* (Spring 1982).

Disney, Commander D.G., USN. "USN Mk 1 Mask Tested." *Faceplate* (Winter 1972).

Drabik, Anton. "Marine Salvage." A collection of articles written by author for *Compass*. Marine Office of America (MOAC) (1962–67).

"Dredge *Atlantic* salvaged from the Elizabeth River." *Faceplate* (Spring 1973).

"*Edenton*—New Ship on the Salvage Scene." *Faceplate* (Summer 1971).

Edgar, Lieutenant Ken, USN. "Argus Island in Retrospect." *Faceplate* (Fall 1976).

"ESSM to Streamline Salvage Operations." *Faceplate* (Fall 1971).

"F-14 Found at 5184 Foot Depth." *Faceplate* (Fall 1979).

"F-14 Salvaged from North Atlantic." *Faceplate* (Summer 1977).

Fenwick, Chief Warrant Officer J.J., USN. "Raising the 41332." *Faceplate* (Summer 1979).

Furer, Naval Constructor Julius A., USN. "Salvage of the F-4." *Journal of the American Society of Naval Engineers* (November 1915).

———. "Salvage Operations on Submarine F-4." U.S. Naval Institute *Proceedings* (November-December 1915).

"Giant Cofferdam Used to Raise *El Eestero*." *Black Horse News*. Merritt-Chapman & Scott Corporation (February 1954).

Giles, John Warren. "Greatest Salvage Project." *Black Horse News*. Merritt-Chapman & Scott Corporation (February 1955).

———. "The Role of the Salvor." U.S. Naval Institute *Proceedings* (February 1964).

Grenfell, Vice Admiral E.W., USN. "USS *Thresher* (SSN-593) 3 August 1961–10 April 1963." U.S. Naval Institute *Proceedings* (March 1964).

BIBLIOGRAPHY

Grigore, Captain Julius, USNR. "The 0–5 Is Down." U.S. Naval Institute *Proceedings* (February 1972).

Hall, Lieutenant William (CEC), USN. "Argus Island Demolition." *Faceplate* (Summer 1976).

———. "Mk 1 Diver's System." *Faceplate* (Spring 1976).

Hartley, Lieutenant Henry, USN. "Some Historical Facts on Diving." U.S. Naval Institute *Proceedings* (March 1931).

Hauser, Ernest O. "Commodore of Sunken Ships." *The Saturday Evening Post* (7 October 1944).

Hawkins, Lieutenant Thomas L., USN. "Model 1500 UBA Tested." *Faceplate* (Summer 1973).

Heywood, Lieutenant Commander William M., USNR, "In Wake of Invasion." U.S. Naval Institute *Proceedings* (April 1948).

Hilliard, Commander Robert B. (CC), USN. "The Salvage of S–19." U.S. Naval Institute *Proceedings* (August 1925).

Hurt, Captain David A., Jr., USN. "SADKAS: A New Concept in Salvage." U.S. Naval Institute *Proceedings* (May 1968).

". . . In Search of the *Monitor*." *Faceplate* (Summer 1974).

Irons, Denis E. "Salvors in the Far Pacific." *Faceplate* (Fall 1972).

Jaffee, Walter W. "Salvor of the South Pacific." *Sea Classics* (date unknown).

"Joint Effort Raises Tug in Qui Nhon." *Faceplate* (Winter 1971).

King, Captain Ernest J., USN. "Salvaging U.S.S. S–51." U.S. Naval Institute *Proceedings* (February 1927).

Little, Ensign H.H. "The Salvage of the USS *Princeton* at Pago Pago, Samoa." *Journal of the American Society of Naval Engineers* (November 1916).

"A Look at One of Diving's Forgotten Heros." *Faceplate* (Fall 1979).

Lusty, Lieutenant Robert, RN. "Mark 1: Part 2." *Faceplate* (Spring 1974).

McDonell, R.J.F. "Commonwealth Marine Salvage Board." *The Log*. Nautical Association of Australia, Inc. (23 February 1980).

McKee, Rear Admiral Andrew Irwin, USN (Ret.). "A Review of United States Navy Submarine Salvage: A Lecture." *Marine Technology Society Journal* (August-September 1979).

MacKinnon, Lieutenant Commander Malcolm C., USN. "The Design, Construction and Outfitting of SeaLab II." *Naval Engineers Journal* (April 1966).

Maclin, Commander Charles S., USN, and Commander Clarence M. Kunstmann, USN (Ret.). "Salvage and the Future." *Naval Engineers Journal* (April 1979).

Magaraci, Lieutenant (j.g.) Frank, USN. "HCU–2 'Unsinks' a Fireboat." *Faceplate* (Winter 1980).

———. "Sunken Dredge Removed from Channel." *Faceplate* (Fall 1983).

480

Manseau, Captain B.E., USN, and Lieutenant C.M. Hart, CC–V(S), USNR. "The Salvage of the USS *Lafayette*." *Journal of the American Society of Naval Engineers* (1943).

"Mark XII TECHEVAL update." *Faceplate* (Summer 1974).

"Mk 12 Era Officially Begins." *Faceplate* (Fall 1979).

"Mk 12 SSDS Completes OPEVAL." *Faceplate* (Winter 1976).

"MK XII SSDS: Quiet and Working." *Faceplate* (Spring 1975).

"Mk 12 Update." *Faceplate* (Summer 1976).

Marshall, Commander W.L., USN. "Japanese Treasure Hunt in Manila Bay." U.S. Naval Institute *Proceedings* (March 1958).

———. "Polyurethane Foam, a New Salvage Tool." U.S. Naval Institute *Proceedings* (January 1969).

———. "Ship Salvage in the Navy." U.S. Naval Institute *Proceedings* (February 1966).

———. "Unique Use of a Floating Drydock." U.S. Naval Institute *Proceedings* (October 1965).

Melson, Captain Lewis B., USN. "Contact 261." U.S. Naval Institute *Proceedings* (June 1967).

Milner, Lenny. "Swimmer Life Support System (SLSS) Mk 1." *Faceplate* (Winter 1976).

Milwee, Commander William I., Jr., USN. "Clearance of Apra Harbor, Guam, After Typhoon Pamela." *Naval Engineers Journal* (February 1979).

———. "Clearing Harbors Imaginatively." *The Military Engineer* (September-October 1980).

———. "Fly-away: A Salvage Concept for Today's Navy." U.S. Naval Institute *Proceedings* (September 1975).

———. "Guam Harbor Clearance, Phase 1." *Faceplate* (Fall 1976).

———. "Let's Salvage the Salvage Force." U.S. Naval Institute *Proceedings* (December 1979).

———. "The Saga of the *Caribia*." *Faceplate* (Winter 1974).

Milwee, Commander William I., Jr., USN, and Lieutenant Paul W. Wolfgang, USN. "The Last of the *Prinz*?" U.S. Naval Institute *Proceedings* (November 1974).

Mitchell, Captain Eugene B., USN, and Lieutenant Commander William I. Milwee, Jr., USN. "Recovery of *Alvin*—A Practical Ocean Engineering Operation." *Naval Engineers Journal* (December 1969).

Nelson, Lieutenant William B. (CC), USN. "Salvage of the USS *DeLong* (DD–129)." U.S. Naval Institute *Proceedings* (February 1922).

Nemeth, Lieutenant Commander Christopher, USNR. "Reserve Divers Sweep Hazards from Great Lakes Harbor." *Faceplate* (Fall 1983).

"New ATF Design Underway." *Faceplate* (Fall 1973).

"New Tools Tested at NCEL." *Faceplate* (Fall 1972).

Nisley, Lieutenant Commander R.E., USN. "YBC Salvops." *Faceplate* (Summer 1984).

BIBLIOGRAPHY

"Operations of Harbor Clearance Unit-One." *Faceplate* (Winter 1970).

"Our Underwater Sailors." *All Hands* (August 1947).

Powers, Commander Melville W. (CC), USN. "USS *Omaha* Salvage Operations." U.S. Naval Institute *Proceedings* (September 1939).

"Reserve HCU Formation Near." *Faceplate* (Fall 1973).

"Reserve HCU's Provide On-Call Salvage Expertise." *Faceplate* (Summer 1974).

St. John, Lieutenant (jg) John J. "Those Who Can . . . " U.S. Naval Institute Proceedings (October 1959).

Salmon, Thomas B. "*Deep Drone* Aids Coast Guard in Alaska." *Faceplate* (Summer 1978).

———. "*Deep Drone* is a Valuable Deep Ocean Vehicle." *Faceplate* (Fall 1976).

———. "*Deep Drone* Recovers Helo from 3,000 FSW." *Faceplate* (Fall 1980).

"The Salvage of *Reuben James*." *Faceplate* (Fall 1970).

"Salvage of the M/V *Anangel Liberty*." *Faceplate* (Summer 1980).

"Salvage of the SS *Indiana*." *Faceplate* (Spring 1980).

"Salvage Operations Show New Skills—*Sidney E. Smith, Oriental Warrior*." *Faceplate* (Winter 1972).

"Salvage Savvy." *All Hands* (February 1947).

"Salvaging the Submarine H–3." Professional Notes. U.S. Naval Institute *Proceedings* (October 1917).

Sea, Roy L. "Mark I Proves Mobility." *Faceplate* (Summer 1971).

Searle, Commander Willard F., Jr., USN. "A History of Man's Deep Submergence." U.S. Naval Institute *Proceedings* (March 1966).

———. "The History of the Development of Salvage Ships in the U.S. Navy." *Faceplate* (Spring 1984).

———. "Palomares—Exercise in Ocean Engineering." U.S. Naval Institute *Proceedings* (June 1967).

———. "USS *Bache*." *Naval Engineers Journal* (August 1968).

Searle, Captain Willard F., Jr., USN, and Alex Rynecki. "Salvage of the USS *Frank Knox*." *The Military Engineer* (March-April 1968).

Sheats, Master Chief Torpedoman (Master Diver) Robert C., USN. "Saturation Diving." U.S. Naval Institute *Proceedings* (September 1972) with comment by Commander W.I. Milwee (August 1973).

Slaughter, Lieutenant Commander Robert H., Jr., USN. "Learning Marine Salvage." *U.S. Naval Training Bulletin* (February 1952).

Smith, Rear Admiral Allan E., USN. "Refloating the USS *Missouri*." U.S. Naval Institute *Proceedings* (February 1951).

Smith, Lieutenant Commander Ken, Jr., USN. "ARS–50: New Workhorse of the Fleet." *Faceplate* (Winter 1982).

Spaulding, Mark McIntyre. "Early Salvage Work on the USS S–51." U.S. Naval Institute *Proceedings* (March 1936).

"S.S. *St. Paul* Salvaged by Rolling." *Black Horse News.* Merritt-Chapman & Scott Corporation. (May 1954).

Stark, Lieutenant Timothy B., USN. "HCU–1 Raises ex-Navy ATR." *Faceplate* (Summer 1977).

———. "*Hoist* Surveys U–352." *Faceplate* (Spring 1981).

Steinke, Commander Harris E., USN. "Navy Builds Catamaran Rescue Ship." U.S. Naval Institute *Proceedings* (January 1969).

Strother, Lieutenant Commander E.W., USN. "Diving and the Diving School." U.S. Naval Institute *Proceedings* (April 1918).

"SUBSALVEX 71 Successful Despite Interruptions." *Faceplate* (Winter 1971).

"Suez Canal Clearance Operations." *NAVSEA Journal* (April 1975).

"Suez: Central Zone." *Faceplate* (Summer 1975).

"Suez: Salvage Operations." *NAVSEA Journal* (April 1975).

Sullivan, Rear Admiral W.A., USN (Ret.). "The History of Naval Salvage." *Faceplate* (Spring 1984).

Sullivan, Commodore W.A. "Marine Salvage." In *Transactions of the Society of Naval Architects and Marine Engineers for 1948.* New York, 1949.

"T-ATF: A New Addition to the MSC Fleet." *Faceplate* (Winter 1980).

"Tau Island Harbor Clearance." *Faceplate* (Spring 1980).

Teague, Joel. "CURV III Recovers SH–2F Helo." *Faceplate* (Fall 1980).

Tettelbach, Lieutenant Commander Gary, USN, and Lieutenant Commander R.J. Ventgen, USN. "Record Recovery–2250 Feet of Cold Water Pipe." *Faceplate* (Winter 1982).

Thomas, Warren D., and Peter S. Barracca. "The Salvor and the Prevention of Water Pollution by Marine Transportation." *Fairplay International Shipping Journal* (29 March 1973).

Thurber, Frederick B. "The Great Freeze, 1917–18." U.S. Naval Institute *Proceedings* (March 1962).

Thurman, Commander R. "Bulldog," USN (Ret.). "Clearing Apra Harbor." *Faceplate* (Fall/ Winter 1985).

Totten, Jerry. "Salvage on the Arkansas River." *Faceplate* (Spring 1983).

"*Tucumcari.*" *Faceplate* (Spring 1973).

Tusler, Lieutenant Commander Floyd A. (CC), USN. "The Salvage of The USS *Squalus.*" *Journal of the American Society of Naval Engineers* (May 1940).

Uhler, Dale. "Large Object Salvage System." *Faceplate* (Fall 1972).

"Up From Oblivion." *Faceplate* (Summer 1979).

"The USS Beaufort," *Faceplate* (Summer 1972).

"USS *Regulus* Succumbs." *Faceplate* (Summer 1972).

"USS *Brunswick* (ATS 3)." *Faceplate* (Spring 1973).

Wadman, Rex W. "Three New Navy Fleet Tugs." *Journal of the American Society of Naval Engineers* (May 1940).

Wallin, Vice Admiral Homer N., USN (Ret.). "USS *Oglala*, A Proud and Cantankerous Old Lady." *Naval Engineers Journal* (April 1965).

Whitaker, Captain F.H., USN. "The Salvage of USS *Oklahoma*." *Transactions*. The Society of Naval Architects and Marine Engineers (1944).

Winer, A., and Captain W.F. Searle, USN. "Foam-in-Salvage." *Naval Engineers Journal* (June 1967).

———. "Plastic Foams for Marine Salvage." *Naval Engineers Journal* (August 1970).

Wolfgang, Lieutenant Commander Paul W., USN. "HCU–1 Salvages 41-Foot Coast Guard UTB." *Faceplate* (Summer 1976).

Wright, Ensign J.M.P., USN. "Harbor Clearance: Casablanca to Naples." *Journal of the American Society of Naval Engineers* (May 1957).

Young, Captain Sir Frederick W. "Salvage Operations." Section 4, chapter 15 in *Manual of Seamanship*, volume 2. London: His Majesty's Stationery Office, 1909.

Unpublished Manuscripts

Beatman, J.W. "The History of Ship Salvage in the U.S. Navy." Washington: Bureau of Ships, December 1951.

Brown, Buster J., and David Hancox. "Tugs and Salvage Craft of the Royal Navy." Singapore, circa 1986.

Hart, Rear Admiral C. Monroe, USN (Ret.). "Navy Ship Salvage During the Korean War." Provo, Utah, 1988.

———. "Some History of U.S. Navy Ship Salvage." Provo, Utah, 1987.

Milwee, Commander William I., Jr., USN. "The Marine Salvage Industry." San Diego, circa 1975.

Mitchell, Commander Eugene B., USN. "Ship Salvage in the Pacific." Presentation to Hawaii Section, Society of Naval Architects and Marine Engineers, Honolulu, 11 January 1966.

Momsen, Commander Charles B., USN. "Rescue and Salvage of USS *Squalus*." Delivered to the Harvard Engineering Society, Cambridge, 6 October 1939.

Moss, Commander Robert B., USNR. "Catching *Pisces*." Delivered to Society of Naval Architects and Marine Engineers, Hawaiian Section, August 1974.

Nelson, Stewart B. "Resurrection of the Surveying Ship USS *Kellar* (T–AGS25)." Delivered to Fourth Annual Technical Symposium, Association of Senior Engineers, Naval Ship Systems Command. Washington, 1967.

Rynecki, Alex and Helen Sliteri. "Salvage in the U.S. Navy, A History." Sausalito: Alex Rynecki, Inc., circa 1985.

Sullivan, Lieutenant Commander William A., USN. "The Navy Has a Salvage Problem." Photocopy. Washington, circa 1939.

———. "Harbor Clearance Problems During the War." Washington, 31 January 1946.

Sullivan, Commodore W.A., USN. "The Salvage Problem in the Event of Hostilities." Photocopy. Washington, 18 November 1941.

———. "Ship Salvage and Harbor Clearance." Lecture delivered at U.S. Naval War College, Washington, 4 December 1947.

Supervisor of Salvage, U.S. Navy. "Salvage Presentation." Before the Chief of Naval Operations Executive Board, Washington, 30 April 1979.

Ulrich, Midshipman J.L., USN. "Naval Salvage as a Facet of Logistics in the Mediterranean in World War II." Essay. U.S. Naval Academy, Annapolis, 1957.

Films and Videotapes

The Last Days of the Warrior. *An Historical Account of Salvage and Oil Spill Control as Conducted by U.S. Navy Supervisor of Salvage.* New York: Carl Ragsdale Associates, Ltd., 1973.

Nimbus Moon Water (Explosive Ordnance Water), Conducted by the United States Navy in the Suez Canal, Egypt by Task Force 65 in 1974. Washington: U.S. Naval Photographic Center, 1974.

Salvage of the Floating Drydock AFDM-2, Conducted by the Supervisor of Salvage, Naval Ship Systems Command. USN NAVSHIPS Technical Film IAD00601, New Orleans, LA, 1965.

Salvage of the Rajah Soliman. Bureau of Ships Technical Film Report. 1-A-PAA-05- 11. Washington: U.S. Naval Photographic Center, n.d.

Salvage of the Sidney Smith, *Conducted by the U.S. Navy Supervisor of Salvage, at Lake Huron-St. Claire River, Michigan.* Washington: U.S. Naval Photographic Center, June 1972.

Salvage of the Space Shuttle Challenger. 803424DN. Washington: Naval Sea Systems Command, 1988.

Salvage of the Submarine Squalus. Sea Power for Security Film MN10375. American Film Productions, Inc., 1968.

Salvage Operations on the Arkansas River at Dam No. 2. Lexington Park, MD: Tracor Inc., n.d.

Salvage Posture of the United States. Washington: Marine Board, National Research Council, National Academy of Engineering, 1981.

Suez Canal SALVOP, Conducted by the U.S. Navy Supervisor of Salvage, Naval Sea Systems Command in the Suez Canal, Egypt. Washington: U.S. Naval Photographic Center, May-December 1974.

U.S.S. Lafayette *Salvage, Conducted by the Bureau of Aeronautics for the Bureau of Ships in New York.* Washington: U.S. Naval Photographic Center, February 1942-November 1943.

Index